Charles Forster Smith

Thucydides

Book III

Charles Forster Smith

Thucydides
Book III

ISBN/EAN: 9783337179151

Printed in Europe, USA, Canada, Australia, Japan

Cover: Foto ©ninafisch / pixelio.de

More available books at **www.hansebooks.com**

COLLEGE SERIES OF GREEK AUTHORS

EDITED UNDER THE SUPERVISION OF

JOHN WILLIAMS WHITE AND THOMAS DAY SEYMOUR.

THUCYDIDES

BOOK III.

EDITED

ON THE BASIS OF THE CLASSEN-STEUP EDITION,

BY

CHARLES FORSTER SMITH

PROFESSOR OF GREEK IN VANDERBILT UNIVERSITY.

BOSTON, U.S.A., AND LONDON:
PUBLISHED BY GINN & COMPANY
1894.

PREFACE.

This edition of the Third Book of Thucydides is based upon Steup's revision of Classen's edition, Berlin, 1892. Professor Steup's studies in Thucydides had long ago pointed to him as the rightful successor of the aged Classen, and even before the latter's death (August 31, 1891), he had issued the fourth edition of Book II. (1889).

The variations from the text of the Steup-Classen edition — which, with few exceptions, are restorations of the Ms. reading — are explained in the notes and referred to in the Index. The exegetical notes of the German edition have generally been closely followed, but a more independent attitude has been maintained than was the case in the editor's edition of Book VII. As in that book, so in this, Stahl's edition and critical articles have proved of most assistance; but other editions also — those of Bloomfield, Arnold, Boehme, and especially that of Krüger — as well as Jowett's translation and notes, have been of great service, and helpful suggestions have been derived from many other sources. Except where matter might be regarded as common property, the editor's intention has been to acknowledge indebtedness, but this has not always been practicable. The recent appearance of Steup's revision has made it possible to bring citations of important Thucydidean literature more nearly up to date than might otherwise have been the case. The critical notes are mainly those of the Steup-Classen edition; but, full as they may still appear, they have been considerably compressed, yet it is believed without impairment of their value.

Acknowledgment of especial indebtedness is gratefully made to Professor Ferrell of the University of Mississippi, who has kindly read all the proofs, and to Professor Seymour, whose suggestions and criticisms have been found most helpful and stimulating.

VANDERBILT UNIVERSITY,
January, 1894.

INTRODUCTION.

For the convenience of the student, an outline is here given of the First and Second Books, which describe the causes of the war (I.), and the events of the first three years of the conflict (II.).

CONTENTS OF BOOK I. — In his famous introduction (1–23) Thucydides justifies his choice of a subject for historical treatment, showing by a comparison with earlier times and conditions that the Peloponnesian war exceeded in importance all preceding events of Greek history, and indicates the pains he had taken to secure accurate information, and to set forth a true account of what was said and done on both sides. Then follows a statement of the *ostensible* causes of the war : 1) the dispute between Corcyra and Corinth (24–55), in which Athens, after hearing both sides (32–36 ; 37–43), took the part of Corcyra ; 2) the hostilities between Athens and Corinth on account of Potidaea, which had revolted from Athens (56–66). A Lacedaemonian popular assembly, called to listen to complaints of the Corinthians and other allies against Athens (67–87), after hearing a speech from the Corinthians (68–71) and from some Athenian envoys who happened to be at Sparta (72–78), as well as from King Archidamus (80–85) and the ephor Sthenelaidas (86), voted that Athens had violated the thirty years' truce. Having thus stated the pretexts for the war and the decision of the Lacedaemonian assembly, the historian now gives as the *real* cause of the great conflict, — the apprehension felt by the Lacedaemonians at the growing power of Athens, which had been secured by the fortification of the city, the formation of a new alliance, and the subjugation of allies, as well as by expeditions in various quarters (88–118). Resuming the narrative as left off at c. 87, Thucydides next describes the last debates and negotiations at Sparta and at Athens before the outbreak of the war (119-146), including the episodes of the end of Pausanias and of Themistocles (128-138). The final demands of the Spartans having been rejected on the advice of Pericles (140-144), negotiations are broken off.

CONTENTS OF BOOK II. — *First year of the war*, 431-30 B.C. (2-46). At the opening of spring the Thebans make a daring attempt to get possession of Plataea (2-6). This was a glaring violation of the thirty years' truce, and both sides prepare for war (7 f.). The allies on either side are enumerated in c. 9. The Peloponnesian army assembles at the Isthmus of Corinth (10), and King Archidamus, after an address to his chief officers (11), sends once more an ambassador to the Athenians, who, however, refuse to admit him to their city (12). Pericles outlines the policy to be pursued by the Athenians, and encourages them with a statement of the great military resources of Athens (13). By his advice the inhabitants of the rural demes of Attica remove to the city (14-17), though reluctantly, for they had always loved a country life. Incidentally the historian describes the 'synoecismus' of Theseus (15). The Peloponnesians invade Attica, but do not remain long; meanwhile the Athenians send a fleet to ravage the coasts of Peloponnesus (18-25). Afterwards the latter make expeditions against Locris and Euboea, expel the Aeginetans, conclude an alliance with the Thracian king Sitalces, take the island of Cephallenia, as well as Sollium and Astacus on the coast of Acarnania, invade Megaris, and fortify Atalante (26-32). In the winter, the Corinthians send an expedition to recover Astacus (33), and the Athenians, in accordance with an old national custom, publicly bury the bones of those citizens that had fallen in the war, in whose honour Pericles pronounces his famous Funeral Oration (34-46).

Second year, 430-29 B.C. (47-70). With the return of summer, Attica is invaded a second time by the Peloponnesians, who remain about forty days (47, 55, 57), and is simultaneously attacked by the plague (47-54). The Athenians, however, despatch 100 ships against the coasts of Peloponnesus (56), and send reinforcements to Potidaea (58); but soon wearied with both war and pestilence, they make proposals of peace, and when these are rejected they turn against Pericles (59), who defends himself and encourages the faint-hearted (60-64). Chapter 65 contains the historian's remarkable estimate of the great statesman. The Peloponnesians make an expedition against Zacynthus (66), and send envoys to the king of Persia, who, however, are seized by Sitalces in Thrace, delivered to the Athenians, and put to death (67). Toward the close of summer the Ambraciots attack Amphilochian Argos (68); in the winter an Athenian fleet sails around Peloponnesus and against Caria and Lycia (69), and about the same time Potidaea capitulates (70).

Third year, 429-28 B.C. (71-103). The following summer the Peloponnesians lay siege to Plataea (71-78). An Athenian expedition into Thrace is defeated at Spartolus (79), as is a Lacedaemonian invasion of Acarnania at Stratus (80-82), and a Lacedaemonian fleet at Naupactus (83 f.). The naval battle is renewed, but without decisive issue (85-92). In the winter Brasidas makes a bold attempt to surprise the Peiraeus, which might have succeeded, had not the Peloponnesians become frightened at their own audacity and turned against Salamis (93 f.). On the Athenian side, Sitalces marches against Perdiccas of Macedon (95-101), and Phormio makes an expedition into Acarnania (102 f.).

CONTENTS OF BOOK III.—*Fourth year*, 428-27 B.C. (1-25). The Peloponnesians invade Attica a third time (1), and immediately thereafter the island of Lesbos, except Methymna, revolts from Athens. The Athenians send thither a fleet (2-6), and despatch another against Oeniadae and Leucas (7). The Mytileneans are admitted into the Peloponnesian alliance at a meeting held at Olympia, and a fresh invasion of Attica is ordered; which, however, is not made, owing to the slowness of the allies in assembling at the Isthmus (8-15). Meanwhile the Athenians send a fleet against Peloponnesus (16), and shortly afterwards despatch another armament against Mytilene under Paches, who invests the city (18). During the following winter the depletion of the treasury obliges the Athenians to impose for the first time a special war-tax (ἐσφορά), and Lysicles is sent out to collect money from the allies (19). About this time 212 of the beleaguered Plataeans escape from the town by night and reach Athens in safety (20-24). The Lacedaemonians send Salaethus to encourage the Mytileneans to hold out (25).

Fifth year, 427-26 B.C. (26-88). In the spring the Peloponnesians overrun Attica for the fourth time (26), and the Mytileneans capitulate (27 f.). Alcidas, the dilatory commander of the Peloponnesian fleet, having come too late to save Mytilene, sails along the coast of Ionia homeward (29-32), pursued by Paches as far as Patmos (33). Paches, returning to Mytilene after taking the Colophonian Notium by the way (34), sends Salaethus and 1000 Mytilenean captives to Athens (35), where the assembly at first decrees the death of the whole male population and the enslavement of the women and children, but on the following day reopens the question (36). Cleon urges the death-penalty for all alike (37-40), and Diodotus replies (41-48). Mercy prevails (49), and a boat, hastily despatched to overhaul the one which twenty-four hours before had sailed with the death-sentence, arrives in time to prevent the butchery of a whole people. The ringleaders of the Mytileneans are put to death and the land confiscated (50). The same summer, Nicias captures the island of Minoa (51), and the remnant of the Plataeans is forced by famine to surrender (52). Before five judges sent from Sparta to decide their fate the Plataeans plead their cause (53-59), and the Thebans reply (61-67). The court gives sentence against the Plataeans, who are all put to death, and the following year the city is razed to the ground and the lands rented to the Thebans (68). Corcyra being at this time in a state of civil commotion (69-81), Alcidas sails thither in the hope of winning the island over to the Peloponnesians (76), but flees at the approach of an Athenian fleet (81). The demoralization and excesses of both factions in Corcyra furnish occasion for a masterly digression on the moral effects of the civil war in general (81-84). The troubles in Corcyra continue (85), and before the summer ends the Athenians send a fleet to Sicily,—their first fateful interference in the quarrels of that island (86-88). The following winter the plague reappears at Athens and rages for a year (87).

Sixth year, 426-25 B.C. (89-116). The next summer the Peloponnesians prepare for their usual invasion of Attica, and get as far as the Isthmus, but turn back upon the occurrence of earthquakes. These earthquakes are attended by inundations at various points (89). During the same season the Athenians capture Mylae and Messene (90), and despatch one fleet around Peloponnesus, and another against Melos (91); the Peloponnesians re-found Trachinian Heraclea (92 f.); Demosthenes suffers defeat in an expedition against Leucas and the Aetolians (94-98); the Athenian fleet in Sicilian waters attacks Locris (99); the Aetolians, supported by the Lacedaemonians, make an unsuccessful expedition against Naupactus (100-102). During the following winter the Athenians in Sicilian waters attack the Sicilian Inessa and Italian Locris (103), and later invade Himeraea and renew the attack upon the Locrians (115); Delos is purified by the Athenians (104); in the conflicts in Acarnania between the Ambraciots and Peloponnesians on the one side, and the Acarnanians and Demosthenes on the other, Demosthenes is successful (105-113), and returns to Athens laden with spoils (114). The following spring there is an eruption of Aetna (116).

In addition to the value of Book III. simply as history, many parts of it are of unusual literary merit. At the very outset, the historian, in his account of the revolt and capture of Mytilene, describes in a masterly manner the new danger which, not less than foreign invasion, menaced the empire of Athens, showing how the most powerful of the allies, who by their own admission had no oppression to complain of, but simply found, as an aristocratically governed community and as an alien race, longer dependence on the Athenian democracy too galling to endure, had seized the first favourable moment to renounce their allegiance. Here, too, we see displayed, under the most trying circumstances, the same indomitable spirit and energy which had won for Athens such renown in the Persian wars, and which it required twenty-seven years of war and devastation and pestilence to wear out. By the debate in the Athenian Ecclesia on the proposal to butcher the whole male population of Mytilene, one is prepared in some measure for the enormities committed at Corcyra only a few months later. Cleon's speech, as reported by Thucydides, is worthy of the most serious attention as expressing the deliberate opinion of the gravest and most impartial of historians concerning the arch-demagogue Cleon, as a symptom of the demoralization of that brilliant democracy which had created the Athens of Pericles, but which already was in sore need of the strong hand of the great statesman. The humaner and wiser policy, which Pericles would certainly have advocated, and Nicias doubtless supported, finds voice in the splendid speech of Diodotus. In this case, as elsewhere in the history, 'without our own choice we find ourselves involved in the conflict of interests, and are put in a position to form a judgment for ourselves from the situation of affairs and the feeling of parties.'

Chapter 49, which describes the race of the second trireme with its message of mercy for the Mytileneans, is as graphic as life, and produces an effect not equalled perhaps in any other single chapter of the book except 113 — the short dialogue between the Ambracian herald and a soldier of the army of Demosthenes. But the most interesting episode is doubtless the thrilling account of the sortie of 220 of the beleaguered Plataeans, who on a rough and stormy night mastered a portion of the enemy's wall and killed the guards of the two adjacent towers, thus enabling the whole party to scale the wall and cross the outer ditch; so that, with the exception of seven who turned back and one who was captured, all these brave men reached Athens in safety at the very hour when their countrymen who remained in Plataea, supposing that they had perished, were sending heralds to King Agis asking for their bodies. The sentence about to be imposed upon the Plataeans, who were finally compelled to capitulate, gives occasion for a speech on their part perhaps the most pathetic of the whole history; and the Thebans make answer in a spirit that cannot hide the malignant hatred cherished toward the gallant little people of their own race who for nearly one hundred years had stood as faithful allies by the side of Thebes' most hated rival.

In the description of the party feuds in Corcyra the historian paints a wonderful picture of the demoralization already manifest in many parts of the Greek world as the outcome of civil war, and in the reflexions that follow he touches the high-water mark of his peculiar style. 'Such a drama,' says Grote, 'could not be acted, in an important city belonging to the Greek name, without producing a deep and extensive impression throughout all the other cities. And Thucydides has taken advantage of it to give a sort of general sketch of Grecian politics during the Peloponnesian war; violence of civil discord in each city, aggravated by foreign war, and by the contending efforts of Athens and Sparta,— the former espousing the democratical party everywhere, the latter the oligarchical. The Korkyraean sedition was the first case in which these two causes of political antipathy and exasperation were seen acting with full united force, and where the malignity of sentiment and demoralization flowing from such an union was seen without disguise. The picture drawn by Thucydides of moral and political feeling under these influences will ever remain memorable as the work of an analyst and a philosopher. . . . He has described, with fidelity not inferior to his sketch of the pestilence at Athens, the symptoms of a certain morbid political condition, wherein the vehemence of intestine conflict, instead of being kept within such limits as consists with the maintenance of one society among the contending parties, becomes for the time inflamed and poisoned with all the unscrupulous hostility of foreign war, chiefly from actual alliance between parties within the state and foreigners without.'

The final chapters of the book, with the exception of the purification of Delos in 104, and 113, do not admit of so high an order of literary treatment, but they enable one especially to form a fair estimate of the genius and energy of the ablest general whom Pericles left behind him, Demosthenes, who was in constant and conspicuous service from this time until he perished with the ill-fated Sicilian armament thirteen years later.

THUCYDIDES III.

* Ol. 87, 4 ; B.C. 428, May.

1   Τοῦ δ' ἐπιγιγνομένου θέρους Πελοποννήσιοι καὶ οἱ 1
    ξύμμαχοι * ἅμα τῷ σίτῳ ἀκμάζοντι ἐστράτευσαν ἐς τὴν
    Ἀττικήν (ἡγεῖτο δὲ αὐτῶν Ἀρχίδαμος ὁ Ζευξιδάμου, Λα-
    κεδαιμονίων βασιλεύς), καὶ ἐγκαθεζόμενοι ἐδῄουν τὴν γῆν.
5   καὶ προσβολαί, ὥσπερ εἰώθεσαν, ἐγίγνοντο τῶν Ἀθη-
    ναίων ἱππέων ὅπῃ παρείκοι, καὶ τὸν πλεῖστον ὅμιλον τῶν
    ψιλῶν εἶργον τὸ μὴ προεξιόντας τῶν ὅπλων τὰ ἐγγὺς τῆς

Book III., 428 B.C. to 425 B.C. See Grote, *History of Greece*, chaps. L. and LI. ; Curtius, *History of Greece*, Book IV., chap. II. *Cf.* Diodorus XII., 52–60.

FOURTH YEAR OF THE WAR.

Chaps. 1–25.

1. *Third Peloponnesian Invasion of Attica.*

1. Πελοποννήσιοι καὶ οἱ ξύμμαχοι : designation for the whole Peloponnesian alliance, as in c. 26. 1, 4 ; ii. 47. 4 ; 71. 1 ; iv. 2. 2. For Πελοποννήσιοι alone in this comprehensive sense, *cf.* c. 2. 1, and see on ii. 13. 1. — **2**. ἅμα τῷ σίτῳ ἀκμάζοντι : indicates more sharply than τοῦ σίτου ἀκμάζοντος (ii. 19. 5 ; 79. 4) the beginning of the ripening of the corn. For the pred. partic., see Kr. *Spr.* 50, 11, 13. See App. on ii. 4. 11 (Steup). — **3**. ἡγεῖτο ... βασιλεύς : parenthetical, as ii. 47.

6 ; iv. 2. 3 ; the relation of the other clauses also is the same as there. — **4**. ἐγκαθεζόμενοι : here, as in iv. 2. 4, indicates more clearly than καθεζόμενοι (ii. 47. 7) a definite place from which raids were made. — **5**. προσβολαὶ κτέ. : *cf.* ii. 22. 7. — ὥσπερ εἰώθεσαν : sc. γίγνεσθαι. *Cf.* i. 132. 26. — ἐγίγνοντο : pass. of ποιεῖν. II. 820. See on i. 73. 1. — **6**. ὅπῃ παρείκοι : *wherever opportunity offered*, as Arr. *Anab.* vi. 9. 2. The Schol. explains, ὅπου ἐνεδέχετο καὶ ἐνεχώρει. *Cf.* iv. 36. 7 κατὰ τὸ αἰεὶ παρεῖκον, Plato *Symp.* 187 e καθ' ὅσον παρείκει, *Rep.* 374 e ὅσον γ' ἂν δύναμις παρείκῃ, Soph. *Phil.* 1048 εἴ μοι παρείκοι. — τὸν πλεῖστον ὅμιλον : the main body, as opp. to the small predatory bands which kept up the devastation. ὅμιλος in this sense seems to be Ionic and poetic. See *Proc. Amer. Phil. Assoc.* vol. xxii. p. xix. — **7**. τὸ μὴ ... κακουργεῖν : for τὸ μή with inf. after verbs of hin-

πόλεως κακουργεῖν. ἐμμείναντες δὲ χρόνον οὗ εἶχον τὰ 2
σιτία ἀνεχώρησαν καὶ διελύθησαν κατὰ πόλεις.

2 Μετὰ δὲ τὴν ἐσβολὴν τῶν Πελοποννησίων εὐθὺς 1
Λέσβος πλὴν Μηθύμνης ἀπέστη ἀπ' Ἀθηναίων, βουληθέντες μὲν καὶ πρὸ τοῦ πολέμου (ἀλλ' οἱ Λακεδαιμόνιοι
οὐ προσεδέξαντο), ἀναγκασθέντες δὲ καὶ ταύτην τὴν ἀπό-
5 στασιν πρότερον ἢ διενοοῦντο ποιήσασθαι (τῶν τε γὰρ 2
λιμένων τὴν χῶσιν καὶ τειχῶν οἰκοδόμησιν καὶ νεῶν ποί-

dering, see GMT. 811; II. 963, 1029;
Kr. *Spr.* 67, 12, 4; Kühn. 479, 1 and
516, s. 9 l. — τῶν ὅπλων: *camping
places*, as in i. 111. 6; vi. 64. 20; vii.
28. 8.
8. ἐμμείναντες: aor. partic., as in
ii. 23. 10; viii. 31. 16. See App. on
ii. 19. 14. — οὗ: depends on τὰ σιτία.
Cf. ii. 23. 11 ὅσον εἶχον τὰ ἐπιτήδεια.
G. 1085, 5; II. 729 d. See on i. 48. 2.
— **9. ἀνεχώρησαν . . . κατὰ πόλεις**:
the same formula in c. 26. 17; ii. 78.
8; v. 83. 10.

2. *All Lesbos except Methymna immediately revolts from the Athenians,
who had been informed of the designs
of the Mytileneans.*

2. Λέσβος πλὴν Μηθύμνης ἀπέστη:
Mytilene, which was itself under oligarchical rule, had extended its authority over the three smaller places,
Antissa, Pyrrha, and Eresos (c. 18. 5);
only Methymna on the northern
coast retained its democratic constitution and connexion with Athens.
See W. Herbst, *Der Abfall Mytilenes*,
1861, and Leithäuser, *Der Abfall Mytilenes*, 1874. — **βουληθέντες**: agreeing κατὰ ξύνεσιν with Λέσβος. Kr. *Spr.*
58, 4, 2; Kühn. 359, 3 a. *Cf.* c. 79.
10; i. 24. 9. — **3. πρὸ τοῦ πολέμου**: *cf.*

c. 13. 5 καὶ πάλαι . . . ἔτι ἐν τῇ εἰρήνῃ.
It was doubtless after the conclusion
of the τριακοντούτεις σπονδαί, 445 B.C.,
as the Schol. says, οὐ προσεδέξαντο, ἵνα
μὴ λύσωσι τὰς τριακοντούτεις σπονδάς.
See W. Herbst, *ibid.* p. 10, 22. — **ἀλλ'
. . . οὐ προσεδέξαντο**: the full const.
would be ἀλλ' οὐκ ἀπέστησαν· οἱ γὰρ
Λακεδαιμόνιοι οὐ προσεδέξαντο. For similar brachylogy, *cf.* i. 26. 17. As the
clause refers only to βουληθέντες, it is
to be construed parenthetically. προσεδέξαντο, as c. 13. 6; i. 45. 2; ii. 70. 10,
without expressed obj., τοὺς λόγους,
or a similar word, being understood.
— **4. ἀναγκασθέντες**: the explanatory
partics. with μέν, δέ are placed after
the leading verb with effect similar to
the μέν and δέ clauses in ii. 93. 19, 22.
— **καὶ ταύτην**: *i.e.* τὴν τότε, even this
revolt, as opp. to that which they had
failed to make.

**5. τῶν τε γὰρ . . . μεταπεμπόμενοι
ἦσαν**: explanatory of πρότερον ἢ διενοοῦντο, as 9 ff. Τενέδιοι γάρ, . . . Λέσβου
is of ἀναγκασθέντες. τε is co-ord. with
καὶ before ὅσα. — **6. τὴν χῶσιν . . .
οἰκοδόμησιν . . . ποίησιν**: the art.
covers the three substs. with their
genitives. *Cf.* c. 56. 7, and see on i.
120. 10. χῶσις τῶν λιμένων means the

ησιν ἐπέμενον τελεσθῆναι καὶ ὅσα ἐκ τοῦ Πόντου ἔδει
ἀφικέσθαι, τοξότας τε καὶ σῖτον καὶ ἃ μεταπεμπόμενοι
ἦσαν). Τενέδιοι γάρ, ὄντες αὐτοῖς διάφοροι, καὶ Μηθυ-
10 μναῖοι καὶ αὐτῶν Μυτιληναίων ἰδίᾳ ἄνδρες κατὰ στάσιν,
πρόξενοι Ἀθηναίων, μηνυταὶ γίγνονται τοῖς Ἀθηναίοις
ὅτι ξυνοικίζουσί τε τὴν Λέσβον ἐς τὴν Μυτιλήνην βίᾳ

building of moles, by which the entrance to the harbours was narrowed and could at will be closed by a chain. 7. ἐπέμενον : takes two consts. : *a*) acc. with inf., τὴν ποίησιν τελεσθῆναι (*cf.* c. 26. 13 ; Soph. *Trach.* 1176) ; *b*) the acc. alone, ὅσα ἔδει ἀφικέσθαι. See Haase, *Lucubr. Thuc.* p. 110 f. So περιέμενε, vii. 20. 16. Thus most of the editt. explain. Cl. makes ὅσα ἔδει ἀφικέσθαι subj. of ἀφικέσθαι understood, on the ground that ἐπιμένειν does not take the acc. alone ; but *cf.* Eur. *Suppl.* 624 ; Plato *Rep.* 361 d. — 8. τοξότας : Scythian bowmen, hired by the ruling aristocracy, and always ready to serve as mercenaries. — ἃ μεταπεμπόμενοι ἦσαν : *whatever they were engaged in fetching*. *Cf.* ii. 67. 9 ἦν πολιορκοῦν, and see App. on i. 1. 5. Kr. *Spr.* 56, 3, 1 ; Kühn. 353, N. 3. Cobet's conjecture μεταπεπεμμένοι ἦσαν is unnecessary, as is shown by L. Herbst, *Gegen Cobet*, p. 37–39. On the subject of periphrases with εἶναι, see *Amer. J. of Ph.* iv. p. 297.

9. Τενέδιοι : members of the Attic symmachy (vii. 57. 22). They feared the influence of Mytilene on the Aeolic coast, as did Methymna on the island. See W. Herbst, *ibid.* p. 24. — 10. Μυτιληναίων : the earlier form, acc. to inscriptions and coins ; later, and therefore in many Mss., Μιτυληναίων. See Meisterhans, *Grammatik der Att. Inschriften*[2] p. 23. — ἰδίᾳ κατὰ στάσιν : *on account of factions. Cf.* κατὰ στάσιν ἰδίᾳ, c. 34. 3 ; κατὰ στάσιν, c. 62. 19 ; 68. 17 ; 82. 11 ; v. 33. 4 ; κατὰ τὴν στάσιν, viii. 106. 21. ἰδίᾳ also ii. 67. 4. The phrase gives the motive of μηνυταὶ γίγνονται, to which πρόξενοι Ἀθηναίων is added by way of explanation. Aristotle, *Polit.* v. 4, mentions Doxander as the Attic proxenus who, in revenge for the rejection of his proposal of marriage for his sons with the daughters of the aristocrat Timophanes, betrayed the plot to the Athenians. — 11. μηνυταὶ γίγνονται : the same periphrasis as in i. 132. 31 ; viii. 50. 15. *Cf.* also c. 58. 13 (εὐεργέτης) ; i. 4. 3 (οἰκιστής) ; i. 37. 12 (δικαστής) ; c. 59. 12 ; i. 136. 9 (ἱκέτης) ; c. 40. 31 (προδότης) ; ii. 43. 8 (ἐραστής) ; c. 23. 13 ; i. 35. 12 ; v. 9. 38 ; viii. 86. 23 (κωλυτής) ; c. 42. 7 ; v. 30. 2 ; viii. 45. 9 (διδάσκαλος) ; c. 105. 14 ; i. 95. 4 ; vi. 76. 13 ; vii. 56. 19 (ἡγεμών) ; viii. 51. 4 (ἐξάγγελος). See Dissen *ad Dem.* xviii. 72. — 12. ξυνοικίζουσί τε τὴν Λέσβον ἐς τὴν Μυτιλήνην : the Schol. explains, ἄκοντας τοὺς Λεσβίους ἀναγκάζουσιν ἐς τὴν Μυτιλήνην οἰκῆσαι. ἐβούλοντο γὰρ ἐκ μιᾶς πόλεως ὁρμώμενοι πολεμεῖν. *Cf.* i. 58. § 2. This view is held also by Goell., Bl., Kr. and

καὶ τὴν παρασκευὴν ἅπασαν μετὰ Λακεδαιμονίων καὶ Βοιωτῶν ξυγγενῶν ὄντων ἐπὶ ἀποστάσει ἐπείγονται· καὶ
15 εἰ μή τις προκαταλήψεται ἤδη, στερήσεσθαι αὐτοὺς
3 Λέσβου. οἱ δ' Ἀθηναῖοι (ἦσαν γὰρ τεταλαιπωρημένοι 1 ὑπό τε τῆς νόσου καὶ τοῦ πολέμου ἄρτι καθισταμένου καὶ

Jowett. But it is incompatible with c. 18. § 1; so that political concentration must be meant, as in the case of Athens under Theseus, ii. 15. § 2, the communal independence of the other places being abolished. The *purpose* (pres. ξυνοικίζουσι) is in part carried out in c. 18. § 1. So explain also Arn., St., and Böhme. See W. Herbst, *ibid.* p. 19.—13. **Λακεδαιμονίων**: *cf.* c. 5. 13.—14. **Βοιωτῶν**: esp. the Thebans. *Cf.* c. 5. 13; 13. 7.— **ξυγγενῶν ὄντων**: since Lesbos was considered a Boeotian colony. Strab. xiii. 1. 3. *Cf.* vii. 57. 24; viii. 100. 16. See Curtius, *Hist. of Greece*, i. p. 127 f. — **ἐπὶ ἀποστάσει**: *with a view to a revolt*. *Cf.* i. 3. 9; 37. 8; 73. 14.— **ἐπείγονται**: trans. also iv. 5. 9; vi. 100. 5; viii. 9. 2.—15. **εἰ μή τις**: with fut. indic. a common expression of warning. *Cf.* iv. 68. 28; viii. 53. 18; 83. 13; 91. 12. On εἰ with the fut. indic. in minatory and monitory conditions, see GMT. 447; Gildersleeve, *Trans. Amer. Philol. Assoc.* 1876, p. 5 ff., *Amer. J. of Ph.*, ix. p. 491 f., xiii. p. 123 f. — **προκαταλήψεται**: *shall prevent*, abs., as in c. 3. 9; 46. 25; v. 57. 4; vi. 18. 13. See on i. 57. 15. — **ἤδη**: *forthwith*, belongs to the prot., as ἤδη in viii. 91. 13, and ἐν τάχει in v. 57. 5; 64. 2. — **στερήσεσθαι**: pass. also in c. 39. 44. στερηθήσομαι seems to occur only in late

writers. See Veitch *s.v.* — **αὐτούς**: *i.e.* τοὺς Ἀθηναίους.

3. *After fruitless remonstrance against the preparations of the Mytileneans and the proposed 'synoecismus' of the island, the Athenians detain 10 Mytilenean ships with their crews, and send to surprise Mytilene 40 triremes, whose coming was, however, betrayed to the Mytileneans.*

1. **ἦσαν γὰρ κτέ.**: the causal sent. in parataxis before the main one, not rare in Thuc. See on i. 31. 7. — **τεταλαιπωρημένοι**: Cl. considers this a mid., as also in c. 78. 3; iv. 27. 2; 35. 12; vii. 28. 10, with the same force as the act. in i. 99. 5; 134. 9. But it seems better, with St., to regard it as pass. in all the passages cited. *Cf.* Plut. *Brut.* 37 τὸ σῶμα ταλαιπωρούμενον, and Isoc. viii. 19 (ὁ πόλεμος) τεταλαιπώρηκεν ἡμᾶς. The act. occurs with ὑπό in ii. 101. 19. — 2. **ἄρτι καθισταμένου καὶ ἀκμάζοντος**: pred., *being just fairly afoot and at its height*. **ἄρτι καθισταμένου** as in c. 68. 29. On ἄρτι see Lobeck *ad Phryn.* p. 20; Rutherford, *New Phryn.* p. 70 f. ἀκμάζειν also of pestilence, ii. 49. 27. Steup, comparing both this passsage and c. 68. 29 with καθεστηκυῖα ἡλικία in ii. 36. 9, understands the reference to be to the *middle period* of the war, in which case, of course,

ἀκμάζοντος) μέγα μὲν ἔργον ἡγοῦντο εἶναι Λέσβον προσπολεμώσασθαι, ναυτικὸν ἔχουσαν καὶ δύναμιν ἀκέραιον,
5 καὶ οὐκ ἀπεδέχοντο πρῶτον τὰς κατηγορίας, μεῖζον μέρος
νέμοντες τῷ μὴ βούλεσθαι ἀληθῆ εἶναι· ἐπειδὴ μέντοι
καὶ πέμψαντες πρέσβεις οὐκ ἔπειθον τοὺς Μυτιληναίους
τήν τε ξυνοίκισιν καὶ τὴν παρασκευὴν διαλύειν, δείσαντες
προκαταλαβεῖν ἐβούλοντο. καὶ πέμπουσιν ἐξαπιναίως 2
10 τεσσαράκοντα ναῦς, αἳ ἔτυχον περὶ Πελοπόννησον παρεσκευασμέναι πλεῖν (Κλεϊππίδης δὲ ὁ Δεινίου τρίτος αὐτὸς
ἐστρατήγει). ἐσηγγέλθη γὰρ αὐτοῖς ὡς εἴη Ἀπόλλωνος 3

the ten years', not the twenty-seven years', war would be meant. — 3. **μέγα**: *great*, i.e. difficult. *Cf.* ii. 45. 2; 89. 45; vi. 12. 16. — **προσπολεμώσασθαι**: obs. the force of the middle. The Schol. rightly explains, πρὸς τοῖς οὖσι πολεμίοις ... καὶ αὐτὴν πολεμίαν ποιῆσαι. *Cf.* v. 98. 6. — 5. **πρῶτον**: acc. to most and best Mss., without art. Both forms are about equally common. — **μεῖζον μέρος νέμοντες ... εἶναι**: *giving too much weight to the wish that it might not be true.* For the sentiment, *cf.* iv. 108. § 4 ; v. 113, and the evident imitation of the present passage in Philo *Leg. ad Caium* 10 πλεῖστον διδόντες μέρος τῷ μὴ βούλεσθαι ... δοκεῖν ὠμόν. Also Dio C. xxxvii. 11 τῇ βουλήσει πλέον ἢ τῇ δυνάμει νέμων, Dem. iii. 19 ὃ γὰρ βούλεται, τοῦθ' ἕκαστος καὶ οἴεται, Caes. *Bell. Gall.* iii. 18 f e r e libenter homines id, quod volunt, credunt. For the phrase μεῖζον μέρος νέμειν, *cf.* c. 48. 2 ; i. 71. 7 ; vi. 88. 10. Also Eur. *Suppl.* 241 νέμοντες τῷ φθόνῳ πλέον μέρος, *Hec.* 868 τῷ τ' ὄχλῳ πλέον νέμεις, *Antiope*

(frg. 183) νέμων τὸ πλεῖστον ἡμέρας τούτῳ μέρος. — 6. **ἀληθῆ εἶναι**: sc. τὰ κατηγορημένα from τὰς κατηγορίας. Cl. explains ' without reference to any definite noun,' comparing ὄντων ἀκρίτων, iv. 20. 5. — 8. **τὴν ξυνοίκισιν**: found only here in Thuc., and prob. not elsewhere unless in late writers. — 9. **προκαταλαβεῖν**: see on c. 2. 15.

ἐξαπιναίως: as in c. 34. 17 ; 70. 25 ; i. 117. 1 ; ii. 3. 2 ; 48. 4 ; 93. 15 ; iv. 25. 48 ; vi. 100. 14. This form, as well as ἐξαπίνης (c. 89. 20 ; i. 50. 21 ; iv. 36. 10 ; iii. 12 ; 115. 13 ; v. 10. 33, — *cf.* Plat. *Rep.* 621 b ; Ps.-Dem. lix. 99 ; Arist. *H. An.* 636 a 31), seems to be Ionic and poetic, being used by Xenophon only, of other Attic prose writers. The regular Attic forms, ἐξαίφνης and αἰφνιδίως, occur also in both Thuc. and Xenophon. See Diener, *de Serm. Thuc.* 1889, pp. 24-26.

12. **ἐσηγγέλθη γὰρ ... ἐπιπεσεῖν ἄφνω**: explanation of πέμπουσιν ἐξαπιναίως. Hence the preceding sent. must be considered parenthetical.

Μαλόεντος ἔξω τῆς πόλεως ἑορτή, ἐν ᾗ πανδημεὶ Μυτιληναῖοι ἑορτάζουσι, καὶ ἐλπίδα εἶναι ἐπειχθέντας ἐπιπεσεῖν
15 ἄφνω. καὶ ἦν μὲν ξυμβῇ ἡ πεῖρα, — εἰ δὲ μή, Μυτιληναίοις εἰπεῖν ναῦς τε παραδοῦναι καὶ τείχη καθελεῖν, μὴ πειθομένων δὲ πολεμεῖν. καὶ αἱ μὲν νῆες ᾤχοντο · τὰς
δὲ τῶν Μυτιληναίων δέκα τριήρεις, αἳ ἔτυχον βοηθοὶ παρὰ σφᾶς κατὰ τὸ ξυμμαχικὸν παροῦσαι, κατέσχον οἱ

The following dependent clause, however, ἢν μὲν ξυμβῇ ... πολεμεῖν, contains in the usual const., καὶ ... μὲν ... δέ (*cf.* i. 19. 1 ; 22. 1, etc.), the execution of the task implied in πέμπουσιν. — **13. Μαλόεντος**: this epithet of Apollo seems to occur only in Lesbos. *Cf.* Schol. Patm. (*Rev. de Philol.* N. S. i. p. 185 ; *cf.* Hellanicus ap. Steph. Byz. *s.v.* Μαλόεις) ὥς ... ἑορτή] Μαλόεις Ἀπόλλων · οὗτος παρὰ Μιτυληναίοις ἐτιμᾶτο, ἀπὸ τοιαύτης δέ τινος αἰτίας. Μαντὼ ἡ Τειρεσίου θυγάτηρ περὶ τοὺς τόπους χορεύουσα τούτους μῆλον χρυσοῦν ἀπὸ τοῦ περιδεραίου ἐκπεσὸν ἀπώλεσεν · εὔξατο οὖν, εἰ εὕροι, ἱερὸν ἱδρύσειν τῷ θεῷ. εὑροῦσα δὲ τὸ μῆλον τὸ ἱερὸν ἱδρύσατο. καὶ Μαλόεις Ἀπόλλων ἐντεῦθεν παρ' αὐτοῖς ἐτιμᾶτο. The explanation of Meister (*Gr. Dial.* i. p. 65) is most prob. correct: *god of Malea*. *Cf.* c. 4. 18. For other explanations, see Wilamowitz, *Isyllos*, p. 99 f. and Preller-Robert, *Gr. Myth.* I.⁴ p. 252. — **14. ἐπιπεσεῖν**: aor. without ἄν after ἐλπίς, as ii. 80. 11 ; iv. 70. 20 ; v. 9. 27 ; 102. 4 ; vi. 87. 18 ; viii. 40. 14 ; 86. 34 ; so after ἐλπίζω, iv. 13. 4 ; 24. 10 ; 80. 3 ; vii. 21. 6. G. 1286 ; H. 948 a, 952 ; Kühn. 389, x. 8. See App. on ii. 3. 8. —**15. ἢν μὲν ξυμβῇ ἡ πεῖρα**: the Schol. explains ξυμβῇ by κατορθωθῇ. There is an ellipsis of some apod. like εὖ ἔχειν or ταῦτα ἄριστα εἶναι (*cf.* i. 82. 12), which is easily supplied from the second member of the hypothetical sentence. Such an ellipsis occurs possibly also in iv. 13. 14. *Cf.* Hom. A 135 ; Hdt. viii. 62. 3, and see Sauppe-Towle on Plato *Prot.* 311 d. GMT. 482 ; H. 904 a ; Kr. *Spr.* 54, 12, 12 ; Kühn. 577, 3 c. — **εἰ δὲ μή**: *otherwise*, after ἢν μέν, GMT. 478 ; H. 906 ; Kr. *Spr.* 65, 5, 12. — **16. εἰπεῖν**: depends on κελεύουσιν implied in πέμπουσιν. — **ναῦς, τείχη**: without art. in formulae of conditions of peace, also i. 101. 12 ; 108. 14 ; 117. 14. — **παραδοῦναι**: after εἰπεῖν, *to command*, as in i. 131. 9 ; ii. 6. 7. GMT. 99 ; H. 946 b.
17. τὰς δὲ δέκα τριήρεις: the art. on account of the rel. clause following, as in c. 22. 33 ; viii. 15. 9. *Cf.* also viii. 26. 2. Kühn. 465, 13 ; Kr. *Spr.* 50, 2, 7. — **19. παρὰ σφᾶς**: the reflexive pron. in a dependent clause refers to the subj. of the primary clause. G. 987 ; H. 683 a. *Cf.* c. 108. 14 ; i. 20. 3 ; 115. 23 ; vi. 32. 9. — **κατὰ τὸ ξυμμαχικόν**: the word is rare except in Thucydides. *Cf.* c. 91. 7 ; i. 107. 27 ; ii. 22. 17 ; 101. 15 ; iv. 61. 15 ; v. 6. 6 ; vii. 20. 5 ; 33. 22.

20 Ἀθηναῖοι καὶ τοὺς ἄνδρας ἐξ αὐτῶν ἐς φυλακὴν ἐποιήσαντο. τοῖς δὲ Μυτιληναίοις ἀνὴρ ἐκ τῶν Ἀθηνῶν 5 διαβὰς ἐς Εὔβοιαν καὶ πεζῇ ἐπὶ Γεραιστὸν ἐλθών, ὁλκάδος ἀναγομένης ἐπιτυχών, πλῷ χρησάμενος καὶ τριταῖος ἐκ τῶν Ἀθηνῶν ἐς Μυτιλήνην ἀφικόμενος ἀγγέλλει τὸν
25 ἐπίπλουν. οἱ δὲ οὔτε ἐς τὸν Μαλόεντα ἐξῆλθον τά τε 6 ἄλλα τῶν τειχῶν καὶ λιμένων περὶ τὰ ἡμιτέλεστα φραξάμενοι ἐφύλασσον.

4   Καὶ οἱ Ἀθηναῖοι οὐ πολὺ ὕστερον καταπλεύσαντες 1

— παροῦσαι : = παραγενόμεναι, hence παρὰ σφᾶς. Cf. γυναῖκες πάρεισιν... ἐπὶ τὸν τάφον, ii. 34. 11. Also c. S. 3; vi. 62. 19; 88. 51; vii. 50. 1. — 20. ἐς φυλακὴν ἐποιήσαντο : as viii. 1. 25 ἐς ἀσφάλειαν ποιεῖσθαι. Cf. also ἐντὸς ποιεῖσθαι, ii. 83. 26; vi. 67. 9.
22. διαβὰς κτέ.: obs. the effect of the five participles, which involuntarily portray the haste of the messenger. — Γεραιστόν : Schol. Γεραιστὸς ἀκρωτήριον Εὐβοίας ἔχον λιμένα. Cf. Hom. γ 177; Hdt. viii. 7. 5; ix. 105.
6. Livy (xxxi. 45) calls the harbour nobilis Euboeae portus, and Strabo (x. 1. 7) mentions the adjacent town with the celebrated temple of Poseidon. It is now called Mantelo. See Leake, Northern Greece, ii. p. 423; Bursian, Geogr. v. Gr. ii. pp. 399, 434. — 23. ἀναγομένης : the pres. as in i. 117. 4; 137. 7; ii. 90. 13. — ἐπιτυχών : with gen. also vii. 25. 8. Cf. Xen. Oec. 2. 3; 12. 20; Plato Phil. 61 d; Ar. Plut. 245. With the dat. c. 75. 20; viii. 14. 1; 34. 3; Lys. xii. 12. Kr. Spr. 47, 14, 2. — πλῷ : the Schol. explains ἀντὶ τοῦ εὐπλοίᾳ. Cf. i. 137. 13; Hes. Op. 630; Ant. v. 24; Xen. Anab. v. 9. 33. So most editt.

explain. But Arn. takes πλῷ χρησάμενος as merely opp. to πεζῇ ἐπὶ Γεραιστὸν ἐλθών, comparing vi. 97. 8, οὔτε πλοῦν οὔτε ὁδὸν πολλὴν ἀπέχει, where πλοῦς is thus opp. to ὁδός. — τριταῖος : pred. adj. for adverb. G. 926; H. 619; Kr. Spr. 57, 5, 4.
25. οἱ δὲ κτέ : 'illi vero neque in Maloentem exierunt et praeterea etiam imperfecta murorum portuumque opera obstruxerunt et excubias apud eos egerunt.' Haacke. See App. — ἐς τὸν Μαλόεντα : Steph. Byz. Μαλόεις Ἀπόλλων ἐν Λέσβῳ· καὶ ὁ τόπος τοῦ ἱεροῦ Μαλόεις. Since the reference is to the temple there is no objection to the preposition. — 26. φραξάμενοι : having blocked up, the walls prob. by means of palisades and battlements, the harbours by means of ships that were sunk.
4. Beginning of hostilities. Conclusion of an armistice, during which the Mytileneans send an embassy to persuade the Athenians that their designs are harmless and to induce them to recall their fleet. At the same time they secretly appeal to Sparta for aid.
1. καὶ οἱ Ἀθηναῖοι ... ὡς ἑώρων :

ὡς ἑώρων, ἀπήγγειλαν μὲν οἱ στρατηγοὶ τὰ ἐπεσταλμένα, οὐκ ἐσακουόντων δὲ τῶν Μυτιληναίων ἐς πόλεμον καθίσταντο. ἀπαράσκευοι δὲ οἱ Μυτιληναῖοι καὶ ἐξαίφνης 2
5 ἀναγκασθέντες πολεμεῖν ἔκπλουν μέν τινα ἐποιήσαντο τῶν νεῶν ὡς ἐπὶ ναυμαχίᾳ ὀλίγον πρὸ τοῦ λιμένος, ἔπειτα καταδιωχθέντες ὑπὸ τῶν Ἀττικῶν νεῶν λόγους ἤδη προσέφερον τοῖς στρατηγοῖς, βουλόμενοι τὰς ναῦς τὸ παραυτίκα, εἰ δύναιντο, ὁμολογίᾳ τινὶ ἐπιεικεῖ ἀποπέμψασθαι.
10 καὶ οἱ στρατηγοὶ τῶν Ἀθηναίων ἀπεδέξαντο, καὶ αὐτοὶ 3 φοβούμενοι μὴ οὐχ ἱκανοὶ ὦσι Λέσβῳ πάσῃ πολεμεῖν.

one of the cases rare in Att. prose where the subj. placed before the conj. does not belong to the leading clause. Cf. c. 5. 1; iv. 78. 1; vii. 32. 1; Hdt. ix. 61. 1. Cobet (Mnem. N. S. viii. p. 123 sq.) would omit οἱ στρατηγοί. But Thuc. nowhere uses ἀπαγγέλλειν with so comprehensive a subj. as οἱ Ἀθηναῖοι. — 2. ὡς ἑώρων: sc. τὰ ὑπὸ τῶν Μυτιληναίων πρασσόμενα, the obj. being unexpressed, as often with αἰσθάνεσθαι (c. 22. 22; i. 95. 21, etc.). So ἰδόντες, iv. 25. 49. — τὰ ἐπεσταλμένα: cf. c. 3. 16. — 3. ἐσακουόντων: give heed, comply. See on i. 82. 11. — ἐς πόλεμον καθίσταντο: commenced hostilities (cf. c. 5. 2; i. 23. 28; 99. 14; ii. 9. 2), according to the instructions mentioned c. 3. 17.
4. ἀπαράσκευοι καὶ ἐξαίφνης: pred. to ἀναγκασθέντες πολεμεῖν. Cf. c. 2. 4. For similar combination of adj. (or partic.) and adv., cf. c. 13. 12; 34. 17; 42. 23; 82. 13; i. 39. 2; 63. 7; vii. 32. 11. Kr. Spr. 59, 2, 3. — 6. ὡς ἐπὶ ναυμαχίᾳ: with a view to a sea-fight, as in vi. 34. 34. Placed thus before the prep., ὡς implies the 'purpose' of the subject. For distinction between the dat. and the acc. in this const., see L. Herbst, Philol. xlii. p. 675. — πρὸ τοῦ λιμένος: 'as there were two ports of Mytilene, ὧν ὁ νότιος κλειστὸς τριηρικὸς ναυσὶ πεντήκοντα, ὁ δὲ βόρειος μέγας καὶ βαθὺς χώματι σκεπαζόμενος (Strab. xiii. 2. 2), it is evident that the τριηρικὸς λιμήν is meant here.' St. — 7. ἤδη: now, in their present strait, what before they had not been willing to do. ἤδη often thus indicates a change of conditions. Cf. i. 18. 28; 49. 27. — 8. τὸ παραυτίκα: for the present, i.e. until they should be better prepared. Cf. i. 27. 4; iv. 121. 7; vi. 83. 14. — 9. ἐπιεικεῖ: i.e. if not strictly in accordance with the right, still fair and acceptable; so also in c. 9. 10; i. 76. 20. Cf. Arist. Rhet. 1374 a ἔστιν ἐπιεικὲς τὸ παρὰ τὸν γεγραμμένον νόμον δίκαιον. — ἀποπέμψασθαι: get rid of; usually dismiss, as in Hdt. i. 33. 3; 120. 35; ii. 25. 13; vii. 105. 3; Xen. Cyrop. i. 4. 27.
10. ἀπεδέξαντο: sc. τοὺς λόγους. See on c. 2. 4. — 11. Λέσβῳ πάσῃ: i.e.

καὶ ἀνοκωχὴν ποιησάμενοι πέμπουσιν ἐς τὰς Ἀθήνας οἱ 4
Μυτιληναῖοι τῶν τε διαβαλλόντων ἕνα, ᾧ μετέμελεν ἤδη,
καὶ ἄλλους, εἴ πως πείσειαν τὰς ναῦς ἀπελθεῖν ὡς σφῶν
15 οὐδὲν νεωτεριούντων. ἐν τούτῳ δὲ ἀποστέλλουσι καὶ ἐς 5
τὴν Λακεδαίμονα πρέσβεις τριήρει, λαθόντες τὸ τῶν
Ἀθηναίων ναυτικόν, οἳ ὥρμουν ἐν τῇ Μαλέᾳ πρὸς βορέαν
τῆς πόλεως· οὐ γὰρ ἐπίστευον τοῖς ἀπὸ τῶν Ἀθηναίων
προχωρήσειν. καὶ οἱ μὲν ἐς τὴν Λακεδαίμονα ταλαι- 6
20 πώρως διὰ τοῦ πελάγους κομισθέντες αὐτοῖς ἔπρασσον

not merely against Mytilene. *Cf.*
ii. 80. 2 Ἀκαρνανίαν πᾶσαν, although
Oeniadae is excluded, as here Methymna.
12. ἀνοκωχήν: *cf.* i. 40. 16; 66. 9;
iv. 38. 4; 117. 7; v. 25. 13, in all
which passages St. (*Qu. Gr.*² p. 44)
has shown this to be the correct
form, not ἀνακωχή. — **13. τῶν διαβαλλόντων**: partic. pres. of an enduring relation, as οἱ ἐπαγόμενοι, ii. 2.
22; οἱ προδιδόντες, ii. 5. 32. Kühn.
382, 4 b. The πρόξενοι of c. 2. 11 are
meant. — **14. εἴ πως πείσειαν τὰς
ναῦς ἀπελθεῖν**: *sc.* τοὺς Ἀθηναίους as
obj. of πείσειαν. The const. of πείθειν
with inf. and subj. acc. is unusual.
For the const. of the opt., see
GMT. 489. — **ὡς σφῶν ... νεωτεριούντων**: *with the understanding that
they did not intend to make any innovation.* GMT. 864. *Cf.* vii. 15. 13.
The subj. of the gen. abs. is here the
same as that of the leading clause, as
in c. 13. 30; vii. 48. 12. GMT. 850;
Kr. *Spr.* 47, 4, 2; Kühn. 494 a.
15. ἐν τούτῳ: *i.e.* while they were
waiting for an answer from Athens.
— **ἀποστέλλουσι ... ἐν τῇ Μαλέᾳ
πρὸς βορέαν τῆς πόλεως**: see App. —

18. τοῖς ἀπὸ τῶν Ἀθηναίων: τοῖς is
neut. as in i. 127. 5. αὐτά is to be supplied as subj. of προχωρήσειν. *Cf.* iv.
92. 36 πιστεύσαντας τῷ θεῷ πρὸς ἡμῶν
ἔσεσθαι, where the subj. of ἔσεσθαι is
to be supplied from τῷ θεῷ. Kr. *Spr.*
61, 6, 8; Kühn. 476, 2. A comparison with i. 127. 5 and the passages
there cited shows that Bk.'s conjecture, Ἀθηνῶν, is unnecessary.
19. ταλαιπώρως: aegre, in Thuc.
only here, and elsewhere in Attic
seldom (Ar. *Eccles.* 54); freq. in late
writers. — **20. διὰ τοῦ πελάγους**: *i.e.*
not touching at the intervening islands, as was commonly done for the
sake of security and comfort; so also
c. 33. 4; 69. 2; vi. 13. 12, and, in the
same sense, πελάγιαι πλέουσαι, viii.
39. 16; 60. 12. *Cf.* Hom. γ 174 πέλαγος μέσον τέμνειν. — **αὐτοῖς ἔπρασσον,
ὅπως τις βοήθεια ἥξει**: Cl., who understands αὐτοῖς of the Lacedaemonians,
explains αὐτοῖς ἔπρασσον, *negotiated
with them*, comparing iv. 106. 11;
110. 8; v. 76. 15; viii. 5. 22. But it
seems better, with the other editors,
to understand αὐτοῖς of the Lesbians,
and, with Kr. and Bm., to render
here, and in all the passages cited,

5 ὅπως τις βοήθεια ἥξει· οἱ δ' ἐκ τῶν Ἀθηνῶν πρέσβεις 1
ὡς οὐδὲν ἦλθον πράξαντες, ἐς πόλεμον καθίσταντο οἱ
Μυτιληναῖοι καὶ ἡ ἄλλη Λέσβος πλὴν Μηθύμνης· οὗτοι
δὲ τοῖς Ἀθηναίοις ἐβεβοηθήκεσαν, καὶ Ἴμβριοι καὶ
5 Λήμνιοι καὶ τῶν ἄλλων ὀλίγοι τινὲς ξυμμάχων. καὶ 2
ἔξοδον μέν τινα πανδημεὶ ἐποιήσαντο οἱ Μυτιληναῖοι
ἐπὶ τὸ τῶν Ἀθηναίων στρατόπεδον, καὶ μάχη ἐγένετο, ἐν
ᾗ οὐκ ἔλασσον ἔχοντες οἱ Μυτιληναῖοι οὔτε ἐπηυλίσαντο οὔτε ἐπίστευσαν σφίσιν αὐτοῖς, ἀλλ' ἀνεχώρησαν. 3

negotiated (or worked) *for them*. Cf. Dem. ix. 59 ἔπραττε Φιλίππῳ, *worked for Philip*, Plut. *Alc.* 24 πραττόντων Βοιωτῶν Λεσβίοις. Moreover, in three passages where it is beyond doubt that Thuc. meant *negotiate with*, the phrase is πράσσειν πρός τινα, c. 28. 10; i. 131. 6; ii. 5. 32. St., though referring αὐτοῖς to the Lesbians, makes it depend on ἥξει. Cf. c. 5. 12, and for dat. with such verbs see on i. 13. 12.

5. *Hostilities are resumed, but after an unsuccessful sortie the Mytileneans retire and await help from the Peloponnesian alliance.*

1. οἱ ἐκ τῶν Ἀθηνῶν: prolepsis, as in i. 8. 8; iv. 16. 17, and frequently. (G. 1225, 1; H. 788a; Kr. *Spr.* 50, 8, 10; Kühn. 448 a. — 2. οὐδὲν πράξαντες: = ἄπρακτοι. Cf. iv. 97. 8; viii. 91. 2. — ἐς πόλεμον καθίσταντο: the expression is somewhat peculiar, since hostilities had already occurred between the Mytileneans and the Athenians (c. 4. 3). — 3. ἡ ἄλλη Λέσβος: see on c. 2. 2. — οὗτοι: refers κατὰ ξύνεσιν to Μηθύμνης. Cf. c. 2. 2 Λέσβος . . . βουληθέντες. — 4. Ἴμβριοι καὶ Λήμνιοι: Attic cleruchs, often mentioned together as tried allies,

iv. 28. 18; v. 8. 7. Lemnos had been occupied by Miltiades (Hdt. vi. 140); Imbros prob. about the same time. — 5. τινές: in Attic allowed between the art. and subst. of the dependent gen. only when another modifier follows the article. Kr. *Spr.* 47, 9, 20. The reference is prob. to the Tenedians. W. Herbst, p. 24.

7. ἐπὶ τὸ τῶν Ἀθηναίων στρατόπεδον: *i.e.* against the camp which the Athenians had established as a ναύσταθμον, *a station on land* (see on c. 6. 11), near their fleet. The ἔξοδος, which the Mytileneans made πανδημεί, as well as ἐπηυλίσαντο, is to be understood of an expedition by land, and the μάχη as a πεζομαχία. — 8. οὐκ ἔλασσον ἔχοντες: *not being worsted*. See on i. 105. 23. Cf. Xen. *Anab.* i. 10. 8 μεῖον ἔχων. The pres. partic., as with νικᾶν (i. 13. 31), of enduring results. — ἐπηυλίσαντο: "held the field," as in iv. 134. 9. Schol. πλησίον τῶν πολεμίων νυκτὸς αὐλίσασθαι. This single exhibition of confidence is co-ord. with the whole (οὔτε ἐπίστευσαν σφίσιν αὐτοῖς); or, perhaps better, the effect (ἐπηυλίσαντο) is co-ord. with the cause (οὔτε ἐπίστευσαν κτέ.).

10 ἔπειτα οἱ μὲν ἡσύχαζον, ἐκ Πελοποννήσου καὶ μετ' ἄλλης
παρασκευῆς βουλόμενοι εἰ προσγένοιτό τι κινδυνεύειν (καὶ 4
γὰρ αὐτοῖς Μελέας Λάκων ἀφικνεῖται καὶ Ἑρμαιώνδας
Θηβαῖος, οἳ προαπεστάλησαν μὲν τῆς ἀποστάσεως, φθάσαι
δὲ οὐ δυνάμενοι τὸν τῶν Ἀθηναίων ἐπίπλουν κρύφα μετὰ
15 τὴν μάχην ὕστερον ἐσπλέουσι τριήρει, καὶ παρῄνουν
πέμπειν τριήρη ἄλλην καὶ πρέσβεις μεθ' ἑαυτῶν, καὶ
6 ἐκπέμπουσιν)· οἱ δὲ Ἀθηναῖοι πολὺ ἐπιρρωσθέντες διὰ τὴν 1
τῶν Μυτιληναίων ἡσυχίαν ξυμμάχους τε προσεκάλουν,
οἳ πολὺ θᾶσσον παρῆσαν ὁρῶντες οὐδὲν ἰσχυρὸν ἀπὸ τῶν
Λεσβίων, καὶ περιορμισάμενοι τὸ πρὸς νότον τῆς πόλεως

10. ἔπειτα : *from this time on.* Placed emphatically at the beginning of the whole following narration, it includes the events of the next chapter, the explanatory sent. ll. 12-17, καὶ γὰρ ... ἐκπέμπουσιν, being parenthetical. — ἐκ Πελοποννήσου ... εἰ προσγένοιτό τι κινδυνεύειν: const. εἰ ἐκ Πελοποννήσου προσγένοιτό τι, καὶ μετ' ἄλλης παρασκευῆς, (εἰ προσγένοιτό τι,) βουλόμενοι κινδυνεύειν. Goeller. Thucydides's propensity to put pred. modifiers before the conj. leads to an irregularity in the construction. Cl. thinks from what follows that Theban help is meant in μετ' ἄλλης παρασκευῆς, but Steup objects that Boeotia was at that time only a land power (*cf.* i. 27. 14 ; ii. 9. 11).

12. αὐτοῖς ἀφικνεῖται : for the terminal dat., rare in prose after simple verbs, see on Σαμίοις ἦλθε, i. 13. 12. Kühn. 423, 5. — 14. ἐπίπλουν : *i.e.* the 40 ships mentioned c. 3. 10, 25 ; 4. 1. The whole passage clearly shows that Thucydides dates the revolt of the Mytileneans from their refusal of the demands of the Athenians (c. 4. § 1). — μετὰ τὴν μάχην ὕστερον : for the pleonasm, *cf.* i. 3. 2 πρὸ τῶν Τρωικῶν πρότερον, v. 24. 9 μετὰ τὰς σπονδὰς οὐ πολλῷ ὕστερον. — 15. τριήρη ἄλλην : *i.e.* besides the one dispatched c. 4. 16, doubtless in order to announce the increased danger. — 16. καὶ ἐκπέμπουσιν : *sc.* οἱ Μυτιληναῖοι, with change of subj. in paratactic narration. *Cf.* c. 50. 13.

6. *The Athenians prepare to invest the city.*

1. ἐπιρρωσθέντες : *cf.* iv. 36. 12 ; vi. 93. 4 ; vii. 2. 9 ; 7. 15 ; 17. 10 ; viii. 89. 8 ; 106. 21. — 3. παρῆσαν : = παρεγένοντο. See on c. 3. 19. — οὐδὲν ἰσχυρόν : the adj. with subst. force, "no energetic effort." *Cf.* οὐδὲν ἀληθές, v. 45. 12 ; βίαιον οὐδέν, vi. 54. 16 ; τι αἰσχρόν, iv. 27. 11 ; viii. 9. 14. — 4. περιορμισάμενοι τὸ πρὸς νότον τῆς πόλεως : *after they had come around to anchor south of the city.* But since a part of the fleet must have continued at anchor north of the city (*cf.* c. 4. 18), καί, *also*, was to be ex-

5 ἐτείχισαν στρατόπεδα δύο ἑκατέρωθεν τῆς πόλεως καὶ τοὺς ἐφόρμους ἐπ' ἀμφοτέροις τοῖς λιμέσιν ἐποιοῦντο. καὶ τῆς μὲν θαλάσσης εἶργον μὴ χρῆσθαι τοὺς Μυτιλη- 2 ναίους, τῆς δὲ γῆς τῆς μὲν ἄλλης ἐκράτουν οἱ Μυτιληναῖοι καὶ οἱ ἄλλοι Λέσβιοι προσβεβοηθηκότες ἤδη, τὸ δὲ περὶ
10 τὰ στρατόπεδα οὐ πολὺ κατεῖχον οἱ Ἀθηναῖοι, ναύσταθμον δὲ μᾶλλον ἦν αὐτοῖς πλοίων καὶ ἀγορᾶς ἡ Μαλέα.

7 Καὶ τὰ μὲν περὶ Μυτιλήνην οὕτως ἐπολεμεῖτο · κατὰ 1 δὲ τὸν αὐτὸν χρόνον τοῦ θέρους τούτου Ἀθηναῖοι καὶ περὶ Πελοπόννησον ναῦς ἀπέστειλαν τριάκοντα καὶ Ἀσώπιον τὸν Φορμίωνος στρατηγόν, κελευσάντων Ἀκαρνάνων τῶν

pected, after περιορμισάμενοι. See App.
— 5. ἑκατέρωθεν τῆς πόλεως : see App.
— 6. τοὺς ἐφόρμους ἐπ' ἀμφοτέροις τοῖς λιμέσιν ἐποιοῦντο : the two harbours which Strabo (xiii. 2. 2) describes, were formed, somewhat like the two Syracusan harbours, by an island lying in front of the city. ἐπί, which is wanting with ἐφορμεῖν in vii. 3. 21, is repeated, for the sake of clearness, with ἐφόρμους ἐποιοῦντο.
7. τῆς μὲν θαλάσσης εἶργον μὴ χρῆσθαι : unusual limiting inf. after τῆς θαλάσσης εἴργειν (see on i. 141. 16); or perhaps the natural obj. of the inf. is construed proleptically with εἶργον (Kr. Spr. 61, 6, 8 ; Kühn. 600, 3 β). For μή with inf. after verbs of hindering, see GMT. 807 ; H. 1029.
— 9. οἱ ἄλλοι Λέσβιοι : i.e. from the cities allied with Mytilene. Cf. c. 5. 3, and see on c. 2. 2. — 10. ναύσταθμον : here and vi. 49. 18, the base of operations, where material for the ships, as well as provisions for the crews, was kept. In this general sense of *station* it may properly take both gens., πλοίων καὶ ἀγορᾶς, after it.
— 11. μᾶλλον : sc. than the southern camp. The station first occupied at Malea was the more important of the two. See on c. 4. 15. — 12. τὰ μὲν περὶ Μυτιλήνην : most naturally construed as nom., as in iv. 23. 9. Cf. Xen. Anab. iv. 4. 1 ὅσα ἐπολεμήθη. This const. is rendered more prob. by the analogy of similar concluding formulae : c. 51. 1 ; 68. 39 ; 114. 24 ; ii. 54. 20 ; iv. 41. 17 ; vii. 30. 19 ; 87. 27. Kr. construes as acc., as in ii. 96. 17 ; iv. 108. 8 ; v. 52. 5.

7. *Asopius sent around Peloponnesus with 30 Attic ships, 12 of which go on to Naupactus. Unsuccessful attack upon Oeniadae and Leucas, and death of Asopius.*

2. καὶ περὶ Πελοπόννησον : as before to Lesbos. On the reading περί see App. — 4. τῶν Φορμίωνος : *of the kindred of Phormio*. Kr. Spr. 47, 5, 2. Cf. ii. 34. 5 τῷ αὐτοῦ. ἢ υἱὸν ἢ ξυγγενῆ is epexegetical apposition. Phormio himself, whose close relations with the Acarnanians dated from his

5 Φορμίωνός τινα σφίσι πέμψαι, ἢ υἱὸν ἢ ξυγγενῆ, ἄρχοντα.
καὶ παραπλέουσαι αἱ νῆες τῆς Λακωνικῆς τὰ ἐπιθαλάσσια 2
χωρία ἐπόρθησαν. ἔπειτα τὰς μὲν πλείους ἀποπέμπει 3
τῶν νεῶν πάλιν ἐπ' οἴκου ὁ Ἀσώπιος, αὐτὸς δ' ἔχων
δώδεκα ἀφικνεῖται ἐς Ναύπακτον. καὶ ὕστερον Ἀκαρνᾶ- 4
10 νας ἀναστήσας πανδημεὶ στρατεύει ἐπ' Οἰνιάδας, καὶ ταῖς
τε ναυσὶ κατὰ τὸν Ἀχελῷον ἔπλευσε καὶ ὁ κατὰ γῆν
στρατὸς ἐδῄου τὴν χώραν. ὡς δ' οὐ προσεχώρουν, τὸν 5
μὲν πεζὸν ἀφίησιν, αὐτὸς δὲ πλεύσας ἐς Λευκάδα καὶ
ἀπόβασιν ἐς Νήρικον ποιησάμενος ἀναχωρῶν διαφθείρεται
15 αὐτός τε καὶ τῆς στρατιᾶς τι μέρος ὑπὸ τῶν αὐτόθεν τε
ξυμβοηθησάντων καὶ φρουρῶν τινων ὀλίγων. καὶ ὕστερον 6
ὑποσπόνδους τοὺς νεκροὺς ἀποπλεύσαντες οἱ Ἀθηναῖοι
παρὰ τῶν Λευκαδίων ἐκομίσαντο.

8 Οἱ δὲ ἐπὶ τῆς πρώτης νεὼς ἐκπεμφθέντες Μυτιληναίων 1
πρέσβεις, ὡς αὐτοῖς οἱ Λακεδαιμόνιοι εἶπον Ὀλυμπίαζε

command in Naupactus (ii. 69. § 1 ;
81. § 1 ; 102. § 1), seems to have died
soon after his return to Athens (ii.
103). But see Müller-Strübing, *Aristoph. u. d. hist. Kritik*, p. 677 ff.
6. **παραπλέουσαι . . . ἐπόρθησαν**:
cf. c. 91. 20. **παραπλεῖν**, sail along the
coast, as in c. 32. 1 ; 33. 9 ; 34. 1 ;
95. 10 ; 112. 26.
10. **ἀναστήσας**: of levying troops,
as in ii. 68. 3 ; 96. 1 ; iv. 77. 11 ; 90.
2. — **ἐπ' Οἰνιάδας**: sc. to carry out
during the summer the undertaking
which his father had been unable to
accomplish the preceding winter. Cf.
ii. 102. § 2. — **11. κατὰ τὸν Ἀχελῷον**:
along the Achelous. κατά, on, along,
as in iv. 25. 29. — **ὁ κατὰ γῆν στρατός**: refers, as τὸν πεζόν (13), to the
Acarnanian troops.

14. **Νήρικον**: the same form also
in Hom. ω 377; in Strabo x. 2. 8
the Mss. vary between Νήρικος and
Νήριτος. — 15. **τῶν αὐτόθεν**: as in ii.
25. 18 ; iv. 29. 10 ; vi. 25. 13 ; vii. 34.
9. — 16. **φρουρῶν**: as opp. to τῶν αὐτόθεν ξυμβοηθησάντων these must be foreigners, possibly Corinthians, as in
iv. 42. 17. Cf. c. 94. 4.
καὶ ὕστερον κτέ.: i.e. they re-embarked and sailed off, then sent back
a herald to ask for their dead, as in
iv. 44. § 6. — 18. **ἐκομίσαντο**: used esp.
of the recovery of prisoners and the
corpses of the slain. See on i. 113. 14.
8. *Ambassadors of the Mytileneans
present their cause in an assembly of
the Peloponnesian allies at Olympia*.
1. **ἐπὶ τῆς πρώτης νεώς**: cf. c. 4. 16
and 5. 16. — 2. **εἶπον**: = ἐκέλευσαν,

παρεῖναι, ὅπως καὶ οἱ ἄλλοι ξύμμαχοι ἀκούσαντες βουλεύ-
σωνται, ἀφικνοῦνται ἐς τὴν Ὀλυμπίαν (ἦν δὲ Ὀλυμπιὰς
5 ᾗ Δωριεὺς Ῥόδιος τὸ δεύτερον ἐνίκα). καὶ ἐπειδὴ μετὰ τὴν
ἑορτὴν κατέστησαν ἐς λόγους, εἶπον τοιάδε·

9 "Τὸ μὲν καθεστὼς τοῖς Ἕλλησι νόμιμον, ὦ ἄνδρες 1
Λακεδαιμόνιοι καὶ ξύμμαχοι, ἴσμεν· τοὺς γὰρ ἀφισταμένους ἐν τοῖς πολέμοις καὶ ξυμμαχίαν τὴν πρὶν ἀπολεί-

as in c. 3. 16. See on i. 78. 10. —Ὀλυμπίαζε παρεῖναι : cf. ii. 34. 11; Xen. Anab. i. 2. 2 παρῆσαν εἰς Σάρδεις. Kühn. 447, x. 4. — 3. οἱ ἄλλοι ξύμμαχοι : i.e. the rest of the members of the Peloponnesian alliance. Cf. v. 62. 7, and see Steup on Thucydides's freq. use of ξύμμαχοι to indicate members of a confederation or coalition, Rh. Mus. xxxv. p. 323. — 4. ἦν δὲ ... ἐνίκα : explanatory clause inserted parenthetically. The date was Olympiad 88, B.C. 428. — 5. Δωριεύς : son of Diagoras, victor three times in succession at Olympia (Paus. vi. 7. 1), as well as in numerous other contests (Paus. vi. 7. 4). He fought in the Decelean war on the Spartan side (viii. 35. § 1 ; Xen. Hell. i. 1. 2 ; Diod. xiii. 38, 43), and was captured by the Athenians, but on account of his fame as an athlete was released without ransom (Xen. Hell. i. 5. 19 ; Paus. vi. 7. 4. 5). See Müller, Dorier, iii. 148 ff. — ἐνίκα : was victor, as in v. 49. 2. For the force of the pres. and impf. of this verb, see GMT. 27 ; Kr. Spr. 53, 1, 3-4. — μετὰ τὴν ἑορτήν : generally regarded as celebrated at the first full moon after the summer solstice. But Unger prob. rightly decides for the full moon in August, i.e. the 8th Elean month, Apollonios = Attic Metageitnion. See Philol. xxxiii. p. 227 ff. and Handbuch d. kl. Alterthumsw. i. p. 603 f.; also Nissen, Rh. Mus. xl. p. 349 ff.; and A. Mommsen, Über die Zeit der Olympien, 1891. — 6. κατέστησαν ἐς λόγους : met in council, sc. as subj. the Peloponnesians. Cf. c. 70. 8 ; iv. 58. 4.

9. The unfavourable opinion usually held of allies that revolt in time of war ought not to be applied to us.

1. τὸ μὲν καθεστὼς τοῖς Ἕλλησι νόμιμον: cf. c. 56. 5 κατὰ τὸν πᾶσι νόμον καθεστῶτα. The form καθεστώς, of the older editions, has been rightly restored by v. H., as also περιεστώς, iv. 10. 3. For acc. to the testimony of the ancient grammarians the shorter Attic form was -εστώς (from -αός), not -εστός. Hence the variation of the Mss. between -ώς and -ός cannot be urged in favor of -ός in the classical period. See O. Riemann, Bulletin de corr. hellén. iii. p. 440 ff., St. Qu. Gr.² p. 64. Thucydides uses elsewhere the fuller form (i. 98. 9 ; iv. 97. 11 ; vii. 67. 10 ; viii. 66. 7, 12). — νόμιμον: custom, found only here in the sing., though common in the plur. (c. 58. 17 ; i. 71. 11 ; 77. 24, etc.). — 3. ξυμμαχίαν τὴν πρίν: this order, by which stress is thrown on

πόντας οἱ δεξάμενοι, καθ' ὅσον μὲν ὠφελοῦνται, ἐν ἡδονῇ
5 ἔχουσι, νομίζοντες δὲ εἶναι προδότας τῶν πρὸ τοῦ φίλων
χείρους ἡγοῦνται. καὶ οὐκ ἄδικος αὕτη ἡ ἀξίωσίς ἐστιν, 2
εἰ τύχοιεν πρὸς ἀλλήλους οἵ τε ἀφιστάμενοι καὶ ἀφ' ὧν
διακρίνοιντο ἴσοι μὲν τῇ γνώμῃ ὄντες καὶ εὐνοίᾳ, ἀντίπαλοι δὲ τῇ παρασκευῇ καὶ δυνάμει, πρόφασίς τε ἐπιεικὴς
10 μηδεμία ὑπάρχοι τῆς ἀποστάσεως· ὃ ἡμῖν καὶ Ἀθηναίοις
οὐκ ἦν, μηδέ τῳ χείρους δόξωμεν εἶναι, εἰ ἐν τῇ εἰρήνῃ
τιμώμενοι ὑπ' αὐτῶν ἐν τοῖς δεινοῖς ἀφιστάμεθα.

the attribute, is common in Thuc. See on i. 1. 6. On the adv. with art. as adj., see Kühn. 461, 6. — **4. ἐν ἡδονῇ ἔχουσι**: *are pleased with*, the periphrastic expression denoting enduring relation. *Cf. ἐν θεραπείᾳ*, i. 55. 7; *ἐν ὀργῇ*, ii. 21. 22; *ἐν ὀρρωδίᾳ*, ii. 89. 3. — **6. χείρους ἡγοῦνται**: *consider them worse* (sc. than they otherwise would), as in iv. 114. 13. For the omission of the second member of the comparison, see Kühn. 542, N. 7; Matth. 457; and *cf.* Lys. xxxii. 1. With the sentiment of the passage, *cf.* Liv. xxvii. 17 transfugae nomen execrabile veteribus sociis, novis suspectum. Also Tac. *Ann.* i. 58; Dem. xviii. 47.
καὶ οὐκ ... ἐστιν, εἰ τύχοιεν: the apod., vividly introduced by καί (*and indeed*), has the indic., while the prot., as if stating a purely hypothetical case (*provided etc.*), takes the opt. GMT. 501; Matth. 524, N. 3. — **αὕτη ἡ ἀξίωσις**: *this estimate.* ἡ δόξα, ἡ κρίσις, ὁ λογισμός, Schol. *Cf.* Plut. *Per.* 28 οὐκ ἦν ἄδικος ἡ ἀξίωσις. — **7. ἀφ' ὧν διακρίνοιντο**: for rel. clause with omitted antec. standing for subst., see Kr. *Spr.* 51, 13, 5. For the opt. by

assimilation, see GMT. 558; H. 919 a.
— **8. ἴσοι μὲν τῇ γνώμῃ ὄντες καὶ εὐνοίᾳ**: *i.e.* having the same political views and being equally well-disposed toward each other. On Thuc.'s use of γνώμη, see Introd. to Book l. p. 32.
— **ἀντίπαλοι**: ἰσοσθενεῖς, ἴσοι, Schol. In this sense common in Thuc. and Dio C., rare in other authors. (Bl.) *Cf.* Eur. *I. T.* 446 ποινὰς δοῦσ' ἀντιπάλους, *Alc.* 922 ὑμεναίων γόος ἀντίπαλος. — **9. πρόφασις**: *excuse.* See on i. 23. 23. — **τε**: the 'postscript τε' introduces the third member, as in i. 2. 6 and freq. — **ἐπιεικής**: *reasonable, equitable. Cf.* c. 4. 9. Bl. compares Dion. H. *Antiq.* 595. 28 ἐπιεικεῖς αἰτίας, Polyb. iii. 91. 7 ἐπιεικῇ ἀπόφασιν. — **10. ὅ**: refers to the three preceding clauses (ἴσοι μὲν... ἀποστάσεως). See on i. 35. 15. Its influence extends to the following clause, μηδέ τῳ ... ἀφιστάμεθα. — **11. εἰ ... ἀφιστάμεθα**: the actual case is put in cond. form, as in c. 32. 6; 43. 19. μηδέ τῳ χείρους δόξωμεν εἶναι is about=μηδέ τις μεμφθῇ ἡμῖν (*cf.* iv. 85. 7), and so εἰ has the force of ὅτι. GMT. 494, 496; H. 926.
— **12. τιμώμενοι**: *treated with honour*, favoured, esp. in point of autonomy.

10 "Περὶ γὰρ τοῦ δικαίου καὶ ἀρετῆς πρῶτον, ἄλλως τε 1 καὶ ξυμμαχίας δεόμενοι, τοὺς λόγους ποιησόμεθα, εἰδότες οὔτε φιλίαν ἰδιώταις βέβαιον γιγνομένην οὔτε κοινωνίαν πόλεσιν ἐς οὐδέν, εἰ μὴ μετ᾽ ἀρετῆς δοκούσης ἐς ἀλλήλους 5 γίγνοιντο καὶ τἆλλα ὁμοιότροποι εἶεν· ἐν γὰρ τῷ διαλ-

Cf. c. 39. 9, 28; 56. 21. — **ἐν τοῖς δεινοῖς**: *in the hour of danger. Cf.* i. 70. 10; 84. 8. and see on ii. 87. 18.

10. *For our alliance with Athens, which rested on the common defence against the Medes, long ago lost the necessary basis of confidence, seeing that the Athenians have reduced the allied cities one after another to subjection.*

1. **περὶ γὰρ τοῦ δικαίου καὶ ἀρετῆς**: "concerning the justice of our cause and the honesty of our intentions." περὶ τοῦ δικαίως αὐτῶν ἀφίστασθαι, καὶ μὴ διὰ κακίαν τε καὶ πανουργίαν, Schol. 'τὸ δίκαιον corresponds to πρόφασις ἐπιεικής above, ἀρετῆς refers to χείρους.' St. The force of the art. extends to ἀρετῆς. Kühn. 451, 1; 463, 2. The whole phrase includes everything that is demanded not only by the strict letter of the law, but also by considerations of equity and morality. (On ἀρετή, *magnanimity*, fair or generous dealing, see Introd. to Book I. p. 36.) The reference is, however, not merely to the present revolt of the Mytileneans from the Athenians, but to their whole mutual relation, which is to be the basis of the judgment concerning the Mytileneans for the future. They base their request for admission to the Peloponnesian alliance on grounds, first, of worthiness, showing that for the best reasons and as soon as possible they had revolted from the Athenians (c. 10 to c. 13. §2), second, of expediency and advantage to the Lacedaemonians (c. 13. § 3-6). The two main ideas are summed up c. 13. 14 ἵνα φαίνησθε ... βλάπτοντες. — 2. **εἰδότες οὔτε ... γίγνοιντο καὶ τἆλλα ὁμοιότροποι εἶεν**: Cl. and Steup understand ἰδιῶται καὶ πόλεις as subj. of γίγνοιντο, which is taken to mean, *bear themselves* ('sich benehmen, verhalten'; see on i. 37. 12). The sense would then be: "Friendship between individuals and alliance between states cannot last, unless they bear themselves toward one another with a mutual recognition of honesty of purpose and are in other respects like in character." But see App. — 4. **ἐς οὐδέν**: *in any respect. Cf.* vii. 59. 10; 87. 23. — **μετ᾽ ἀρετῆς δοκούσης**: = μετὰ δοκήσεως τῆς ἀρετῆς, and δοκούσης signifies not appearance, but well grounded belief. οὐ γὰρ δὴ τὴν προσποιητὴν λέγει, Schol. — 5. **ὁμοιότροποι**: nearly equiv. to ἴσοι τῇ γνώμῃ. Also · i. 6. 24; vii. 55. 6; viii. 96. 27. The adv. occurs vi. 20. 12. *Cf.* Hdt. viii. 144. 16 ἤθεα ὁμότροπα. — **ἐν γὰρ τῷ διαλλάσσοντι τῆς γνώμης ... καθίστανται**: *for on divergence of sentiment rests diversity of action.* Bl. cites an imitation of the passage in Procop. *Bell. Vand.* 145, 32 τῷ διαλλάσσοντι τῆς γνώμης. διαλλάσσειν is

λάσσοντι τῆς γνώμης καὶ αἱ διαφοραὶ τῶν ἔργων καθίστανται. ἡμῖν δὲ καὶ Ἀθηναίοις ξυμμαχία ἐγένετο πρῶτον
ἀπολιπόντων μὲν ὑμῶν ἐκ τοῦ Μηδικοῦ πολέμου, παραμεινάντων δὲ ἐκείνων πρὸς τὰ ὑπόλοιπα τῶν ἔργων.
10 ξύμμαχοι μέντοι ἐγενόμεθα οὐκ ἐπὶ καταδουλώσει τῶν
Ἑλλήνων Ἀθηναίοις, ἀλλ' ἐπ' ἐλευθερώσει ἀπὸ τοῦ Μήδου
τοῖς Ἕλλησι. καὶ μέχρι μὲν ἀπὸ τοῦ ἴσου ἡγοῦντο, προ-

intr., as in Hdt. vii. 70. 4. The use of neut. partic. or adj. for abstract noun is a favourite one with Thucydides. It presents to the mind the abstract quality in operation. GMT. 829 a; II. 966 b; Kühn. 403 a, γ.

7. δέ: *now*, effects the transition to the special case. *Cf.* i. 32. 7; 121. 1; ii. 64. 28. — **Ἀθηναίοις ξυμμαχία ἐγένετο πρῶτον**: from what follows it is clear that the reference is to the beginning of the closer connexion of the Lesbians with Athens, *i.e.* the rise of the Delian confederation (i. 95). The orator represents Sparta's withdrawal from the Median war as preceding, not following, the formation of that alliance, in order not only to put the conduct of his state toward Sparta in a favourable light, but also to avoid touching the latter in a sensitive spot. *Cf.* i. 75. § 2, and see Steup, *Rh. Mus.* xxxv. p. 330 f. — **8. ἀπολιπόντων ἐκ**: this rare const. occurs also v. 4. 11 ἀπολιπόντες ἐκ τῶν Συρακουσῶν. Kühn. 447 c.; Matth. 495, 1. — **9. τὰ ὑπόλοιπα**: *what yet remained*, with τῶν ἔργων, as i. 75. 5, with τοῦ βαρβάρου.

10. ξύμμαχοι μέντοι κτέ.: *we became allies, not to the Athenians for the enslavement of the Greeks, but to the Greeks for their emancipation from the Mede*. The dats. Ἀθηναίοις (11) and τοῖς Ἕλλησι (12) belong grammatically to ξύμμαχοι ἐγενόμεθα, though the influence of the verbal nouns καταδουλώσει and ἐλευθερώσει on these dats., as in vi. 76. 20, is not excluded. This view, which is generally adopted, is supported by the const. in c. 13. 9, 10. But Kr. and Wilkins construe Ἀθηναίοις and τοῖς Ἕλλησι as **dativi commodi** with the verbal nouns alone. By οἱ Ἕλληνες are meant, both here and c. 13. 9 (*cf.* i. 139. 16; 140. 21), the states of the Delian confederation, whose treasurers were called Ἑλληνοταμίαι (i. 96. 6). — **καταδουλώσει**: occurs also vii. 66. 6; Plato *Legg.* 776 d; elsewhere prob. only in late writers. — **11. ἐλευθερώσει**: in this sense, c. 39. 39; Hdt. ix. 45. 18; *freedom* to slaves, i. 132. 22; Arist. *Pol.* v. 11. 19; *license*, Plato *Rep.* 561 a. — **ἀπὸ τοῦ Μήδου**: const. after the verbal noun as after the verb in i. 95. 3; ii. 71. 10; viii. 46. 21.

12. μέχρι: *while*, as in c. 98. 1. Kühn. 567, 1. — **ἀπὸ τοῦ ἴσου**: *on terms of equality*. κατὰ τὴν ἰσονομίαν, Schol. On ἀπό in this sense, see Kühn. 430, 1, 3 h. See on i. 77. 8. — **ἡγοῦντο**: abs., *maintained their hegemony*, as in i. 19. 2; 77. 23. *Cf.* ἐξηγεῖσθαι, i. 76. 3; 95. 26. —

θύμως εἰπόμεθα· ἐπειδὴ δὲ ἑωρῶμεν αὐτοὺς τὴν μὲν τοῦ
Μήδου ἔχθραν ἀνιέντας, τὴν δὲ τῶν ξυμμάχων δούλωσιν
15 ἐπειγομένους, οὐκ ἀδεεῖς ἔτι ἦμεν. ἀδύνατοι δὲ ὄντες καθ᾽ 5
ἓν γενόμενοι διὰ πολυψηφίαν ἀμύνεσθαι οἱ ξύμμαχοι ἐδου-
λώθησαν πλὴν ἡμῶν καὶ Χίων· ἡμεῖς δὲ αὐτόνομοι δὴ 6
ὄντες καὶ ἐλεύθεροι τῷ ὀνόματι ξυνεστρατεύσαμεν. καὶ
πιστοὺς οὐκέτι εἴχομεν ἡγεμόνας Ἀθηναίους, παραδείγ-
20 μασι τοῖς προγεγενημένοις χρώμενοι· οὐ γὰρ εἰκὸς ἦν

14. δούλωσιν : a Thucydidean noun, found also i. 141. 6 ; Plato *Legg.* 791 d.
— 15. ἐπειγομένους : *urging on*, Ross's and Bk.'s conjecture, for the vulgate ἐπαγομένους, seems to be required to contrast with ἀνιέντας, and has been adopted by St. and Cl. *Cf.* Va. tendentes ad. It is trans. also in c. 2. 14 ; iv. 5. 9 ; vi. 100. 5 ; viii. 9. 2 ; 82. 9. See App.

ἀδύνατοι δὲ ὄντες . . . ἀμύνεσθαι : *and disabled by diversity of opinion from combining and defending themselves.* Although in the development of the thought the subj. is divided into ξύμμαχοι πλὴν ἡμῶν καὶ Χίων and ἡμεῖς, the undivided subj. is to be understood with ἀδύνατοι ὄντες at the beginning. διὰ πολυψηφίαν belongs to ἀδύνατοι ὄντες, καθ᾽ ἓν γενόμενοι to ἀμύνεσθαι. πολυψηφία is *diversity of opinion* naturally arising from the fact that so many had the right to vote. The disadvantages of the ἰσοψηφία of the Peloponnesian alliance, which resulted in πολυψηφία, are set forth in i. 141. § 6, 7. The word is not found elsewhere.

17. δή : *scilicet*, intimates what is expressed in τῷ ὀνόματι. The ironical force occurs as early as Homer (A 110). *Cf.* iv. 46. 18, 20 ; 67. 17 ; vi. 10. 23 ; 54. 18 ; and δῆθεν, i. 92. 3 ; 127. 2. Kr. *Spr.* 69, 17, 2 ; Kühn. 500, 3. — 19. πιστούς : *to be trusted. Cf.* c. 92. 7. — παραδείγμασι τοῖς προγεγενημένοις χρώμενοι : since the παραδείγματα must have been facts already accomplished, Weidner's conjecture of the pf. for the pres. (προγεγενημένοις for προγιγνομένοις) is necessary here, as well as in i. 23. 25. See *Parerga Dinarch. et Thuc.*, 1875, p. 22. *Cf.* Procop. B. V. i. 10 παραδείγμασι δὲ τῶν προγεγενημένων χρωμένους — 20. οὐ γὰρ κτέ. : *for it was not likely that they after subduing those whom they had made sharers in the treaty with us would not have done the same to us who were left, if ever they had been able.* So Bm. correctly explains. δρᾶσαι, as well as καταστρέψασθαι, refers to the past ; hence Dobree's conjecture δυνηθεῖεν, Kr.'s δυνηθείησαν, are unnecessary. The arrangement is paratactic, though the first clause is in sense subord., as in i. 28. 15 ; 35. 4. On this form of apod. in unreal cond. (οὐ γὰρ εἰκὸς ἦν αὐτοὺς μὴ δρᾶσαι τοῦτο), see GMT. 420, 421 ; Kr. *Spr.* 53, 2, 7 ; Kühn. 392 b, 4. *Cf.* c. 40. 26 ; 74. 11 ; vi. 78. 22.

αὐτοὺς οὓς μὲν μεθ' ἡμῶν ἐνσπόνδους ἐποιήσαντο καταστρέψασθαι, τοὺς δὲ ὑπολοίπους, εἴ ποτε ἄρα ἐδυνήθησαν, μὴ δρᾶσαι τοῦτο.

11 "Καὶ εἰ μὲν αὐτόνομοι ἔτι ἦμεν ἅπαντες, βεβαιότεροι 1 ἂν ἡμῖν ἦσαν μηδὲν νεωτεριεῖν· ὑποχειρίους δὲ ἔχοντες τοὺς πλείους, ἡμῖν δὲ ἀπὸ τοῦ ἴσου ὁμιλοῦντες, χαλεπώτερον εἰκότως ἔμελλον οἴσειν καὶ πρὸς τὸ πλεῖον ἤδη 5 εἶκον τοῦ ἡμετέρου ἔτι μόνου ἀντισουμένου, ἄλλως τε καὶ ὅσῳ δυνατώτεροι αὐτοὶ αὐτῶν ἐγίγνοντο καὶ ἡμεῖς ἐρημότεροι· τὸ δὲ ἀντίπαλον δέος μόνον πιστὸν ἐς ξυμ-

11. And that our autonomy has hitherto been spared by their lust for power we owe alone to a regard for their own interests, which would, however, not have protected us much longer.
1. καὶ εἰ μὲν ... ἂν ἐπελθεῖν ἀποτρέπεται: the second ground of the untenableness of the federal relation: the growing strength of the Athenians and the increasing isolation of the Mytileneans. — βεβαιότεροι : pers. const., like δίκαιος in i. 40. 13. GMT. 762; II. 944; Kühn. 477 d. — 2. νεωτεριεῖν: used to express any innovation in established order, esp. harsh and violent changes. Cf. Lat. res novae. Cf. c. 4. 15; i. 58. 3; ii. 3. 6; iv. 51. 3. — 3. ἀπὸ τοῦ ἴσου : see on c. 10. 12. — 4. ἔμελλον οἴσειν : Thuc. uses the fut. inf. with μέλλειν far oftener than the present. See on i. 107. 13. The obj. of οἴσειν is to be supplied from ἡμῖν ... ὁμιλοῦντες. — καὶ πρὸς ... ἀντισουμένου : these words, which are closely connected, give the explanation of χαλεπώτερον ἔμελλον οἴσειν. While ὑποχειρίους ... ὁμιλοῦντες states the actual relation from the side of the Athenians, what follows expresses this from the side of the Mytileneans, but from the standpoint of the Athenians. Render : "because our state alone, even though the majority had already yielded, still maintained its equality." See App. καί, which belongs esp. to πρὸς τὸ πλεῖον ἤδη εἶκον, emphasizes the audacity of the Lesbians in the eyes of the Athenians. πρός, as against, as in i. 6. 15 ; ii. 91. 18. τοῦ ἡμετέρου is neuter. ἀντισόομαι is not found elsewhere except in late writers. See Steph. Thes. s. v. — 6. δυνατώτεροι αὐτοὶ αὐτῶν : more powerful than they were before. The comp. with gen. of reflex. pron. measures progress by change in the subj. itself. Cf. i. 8. 13; vi. 72. 22; vii. 66. 14. The const. is freq. in Hdt. II. 644; Kühn. 543, 6. — 7. τὸ δὲ ἀντίπαλον δέος μόνον πιστὸν ἐς ξυμμαχίαν: this clause, containing the second ground of the untenableness of the alliance, is closely connected with the preceding (δέ = γάρ), "for fear based on equal power is alone to be relied on

μαχίαν· ὁ γὰρ παραβαίνειν τι βουλόμενος τῷ μὴ προέχων ἂν ἐπελθεῖν ἀποτρέπεται. αὐτόνομοί τε ἐλείφθημεν 2
οὐ δι᾽ ἄλλο τι ἢ ὅσον αὐτοῖς ἐς τὴν ἀρχὴν εὐπρεπείᾳ τε
λόγου καὶ γνώμης μᾶλλον ἐφόδῳ ἢ ἰσχύος τὰ πράγματα
ἐφαίνετο καταληπτά. ἅμα μὲν γὰρ μαρτυρίῳ ἐχρῶντο μὴ 3
ἂν τούς γε ἰσοψήφους ἄκοντας, εἰ μή τι ἠδίκουν οἷς ἐπή-

in the case of an alliance." *Cf.* iv.
92. 14 πρός τε γὰρ τοὺς ἀστυγείτονας
πᾶσι τὸ ἀντίπαλον καὶ ἐλεύθερον καθί-
σταται, Tac. *Germ.* 1 Germania
a Sarmatis Dacisque mutuo
metu separatur. But Steup
gives strong reasons for bracketing
δέος. See App. — **8.** τῷ μὴ ... ἀποτρέπεται: the chief stress is on προέχων,
"is deterred only by the consideration that he would make the attack
not with superior force," *i.e.* not
with prospect of success.
9. τε: introducing *third* reason
(see on c. 9. 10), which covers the
remainder of the chapter; viz. that
only regard for appearances and for
present advantage kept the Athenians
from being more aggressive. — **10.**
ὅσον: quatenus, equiv. to καθ᾽
ὅσον, c. 9. 4; vi. 54. 25; 82. 11. ὅσον
instead of ὅτι, in order to restrict
the motive to the narrowest limits,
to concede as little as possible to
good intentions. — ἐς τὴν ἀρχήν ...
καταληπτά: "it was clear to them
that to extend their dominion they
could get control of affairs by fair
words and by an assault of policy
rather than by force." The main
object of the Athenians, ἐς τὴν ἀρχήν,
ad imperium quaerendum, is
emphasized by its position, separated
as it is from τὰ πράγματα ἐφαίνετο

καταληπτά (*cf.* c. 30. 11), of which it
expresses the motive. But see App.
εὐπρεπείᾳ λόγου is explained by the
following ἅμα μὲν ... ξυστρατεύειν,
and γνώμης μᾶλλον ἐφόδῳ ἢ ἰσχύος first
and esp. by ἐν τῷ αὐτῷ δὲ ... ἐχειρώσαντο, to which then two further reasons are added (19 and 21). — **11.** τὰ
πράγματα ... καταληπτά: here of
securing predominance (*cf.* Hdt. vi.
39. 4); c. 30. 11, of conquering in
battle. *Cf.* iv. 2. 13 κατασχήσειν ῥᾳδίως
τὰ πράγματα, c. 62. 11; 72. 3 ἔχειν τὰ
πράγματα, c. 28. 1 οἱ ἐν τοῖς πράγμασι,
i. 89. 2 ἦλθον ἐπὶ τὰ πράγματα, vii.
49. 3 τὸ βουλόμενον τοῖς Ἀθηναίοις
γίγνεσθαι τὰ πράγματα.
12. ἅμα μέν: the correlative is ἐν
τῷ αὐτῷ δέ (14), as in iv. 73. 10. —
μαρτυρίῳ ἐχρῶντο μὴ ἂν ... ξυστρατεύειν: the inf. clause is the obj. of
ἐχρῶντο, "they used as a proof (of
the propriety of their course) that
those at least who had equal votes
with them would be unwilling to
join in their expeditions, unless
those whom they went against were
guilty of some wrong." The condensed statement is about equiv. to
ἅμα μὲν γὰρ μαρτυρίῳ ἐχρῶντο, μὴ ἂν
τούς γε ἰσοψήφους, εἰ μή τι ἠδίκουν οἷς
ἐπῇεσαν, ξυστρατεύειν, οὐ γὰρ ἂν ἄκον-
τάς γε ξυστρατεύειν, ἰσοψήφους ὄντας.
(Goeller.) See App. — **13.** ἰσοψήφους:

εσαν, ξυστρατεύειν· ἐν τῷ αὐτῷ δὲ καὶ τὰ κράτιστα ἐπί τε
15 τοὺς ὑποδεεστέρους πρώτους ξυνεπῆγον καὶ τὰ τελευταῖα
λιπόντες τοῦ ἄλλου περιῃρημένου ἀσθενέστερα ἔμελλον
ἕξειν· εἰ δὲ ἀφ' ἡμῶν ἤρξαντο, ἐχόντων ἔτι τῶν πάντων
αὐτῶν τε ἰσχὺν καὶ πρὸς ὅ τι χρὴ στῆναι, οὐκ ἂν ὁμοίως
ἐχειρώσαντο. τό τε ναυτικὸν ἡμῶν παρεῖχέ τινα φόβον
20 μή ποτε καθ' ἓν γενόμενον ἢ ὑμῖν ἢ ἄλλῳ τῳ προσθέμενον

'It seems to be rhetorical exaggeration that the Lesbians, αὐτόνομοι and (though after the revolt only the Methymneans) ναυσὶ καὶ οὐ φόρῳ ὑπήκοοι (vii. 57. 22), call themselves ἰσόψηφους, mindful to be sure of the right and of the ancient statute, long ago abolished by the Athenians, acc. to which the allies consulted ἀπὸ κοινῶν ξυνόδων. Cf. i. 97. §1.' St. — 14. ἐν τῷ αὐτῷ δέ: on the position of δέ, to emphasize τῷ αὐτῷ, see Kühn. 528, 1. — καὶ τὰ κράτιστα : καὶ τοὺς κρατίστους ἡμᾶς, Schol. The neut. pl. of the adj. expresses a concrete idea. Kühn. 403, n. 2. — 15. τὰ τελευταῖα: as the last, pred. to τὰ κράτιστα, as the position of τε, καί shows. The art., which Kr., St., and Steup strike out, L. Herbst (Philol., 1860, p. 342 f.) explains as intended to sharpen the contrast with what precedes, 'as the last in the series, as it were the capstone of their work.' Cf. c. 85. 2; possibly c. 23. 15. — 16. τοῦ ἄλλου περιῃρημένου: "when all else was stripped from around them," like a tree lopped of its branches. Cf. ii. 13. 38; Plato Gorg. 502 c; Dem. xxi. 138. τοῦ ἄλλου collective, as in c. 107. 25; i. 48. 6; iv. 96. 8; viii. 42. 7. — ἀσθενέστερα ἕξειν: a favourite turn of Thuc., often used in expressions of change. See on i. 120. 9. — 18. αὐτῶν: themselves, intens., not possessive. — πρὸς ὅ τι χρὴ στῆναι: something to rally to. Cf. iv. 56. 17 πρὸς τὴν ἐκείνων γνώμην αἰεὶ ἕστασαν. The usual form is μετά τινος στῆναι, as in c. 39. 12; i. 33. 22; vii. 57. 4; 61. 12. χρή with inf. is a common periphrasis for the delib. subj. in dependent clauses. Cf. c. 53. 9; i. 40. 20; 91. 4; ii. 4. 10; iv. 34. 25; vii. 44. 15. Kr. Spr. 54, 7, 2; Kühn. 394, n. 3. — οὐκ ἂν ὁμοίως: sc. as they did with the course adopted. Cf. i. 2. 22; ii. 60. 21.

19. τό τε ναυτικὸν κτέ.: third cause of the ἔφοδος γνώμης μᾶλλον ἢ ἰσχύος, namely, that the Mytileneans might not become prematurely frightened and make an alliance dangerous to Athens. — 20. μή ποτε καθ' ἓν γενόμενον ... παρασχῇ: lest perchance a union might be effected, either by joining you or some one else, which would bring danger to themselves. καθ' ἓν γενόμενον, as in c. 10. 16. προσθέμενον, as in viii. 48. 29; 87. 25. Steup, who claims that, as the passage stands, καθ' ἓν γενόμενον can only be subord. to προσθέμενον, is inclined to bracket προσθέμενον, and explain καθ' ἓν ... ἄλλῳ τῳ after the analogy of δι' ἀνοκωχῆς γίγνεσθαί τινι, i. 40. 16.

κίνδυνον σφίσι παράσχῃ. τὰ δὲ καὶ ἀπὸ θεραπείας τοῦ 5
τε κοινοῦ αὐτῶν καὶ τῶν αἰεὶ προεστώτων περιεγιγνόμεθα.
οὐ μέντοι ἐπὶ πολύ γ' ἂν ἐδοκοῦμεν δυνηθῆναι, εἰ μὴ ὁ 6
πόλεμος ὅδε κατέστη, παραδείγμασι χρώμενοι τοῖς ἐς
25 τοὺς ἄλλους.

12   "Τίς οὖν αὕτη ἡ φιλία ἐγίγνετο ἢ ἐλευθερία πιστή; 1
ἐν ᾗ παρὰ γνώμην ἀλλήλους ὑπεδεχόμεθα, καὶ οἱ μὲν

21. τὰ δὲ καί: *partly also*, similar to τὸ δέ τι καί of i. 107. 19; 118. 12; vii. 48. 7. Kr. *Spr.* 50, 1, 15; Kühn. 459, 1 c. This introduces the last reason, though only as a subord. one, why the Lesbians were not deprived of their liberty. — ἀπὸ θεραπείας: *in consequence of our paying court.* ἀπό, as in i. 12. 5; 17. 4; 23. 27; 24. 10. Müller-Strübing (*Aristoph. u. d. hist. Kritik*, p. 366 ff.) rightly sees here, with the Schol., an allusion to bribery of Athenian statesmen, more clearly stated in Ar. *Vesp.* 675 ff. — 22. περιεγιγνόμεθα: *i.e.* αὐτόνομοι ἐλείφθημεν (?).

23. ἂν ἐδοκοῦμεν δυνηθῆναι: *sc.* περιγίγνεσθαι. Kr. *Spr.* 55, 4, 11. ἐδοκοῦμεν, *we thought*, as in i. 126. 20; 128. 30; iv. 14. 14; vii. 41. 14. ἂν belongs to δυνηθῆναι. Kr. writes δοκοῦμεν on the ground that only with the pres. can δυνηθῆναι ἄν stand for ἐδυνήθημεν ἄν. But Steup cites viii. 2. 3 ἐπηρμένοι ἦσαν ... νομίσαντες κἂν ἐπὶ σφᾶς ἕκαστοι ἐλθεῖν αὐτούς, εἰ τὰ ἐν τῇ Σικελίᾳ κατώρθωσαν. For Steup's objections to the impf., see App. — 24. τοῖς ἐς τοὺς ἄλλους: *their conduct toward the rest.* Schol. τεκμήρια ἦν ἡμῖν τὰ πρὸς τοὺς ἄλλους ὑπ' Ἀθηναίων γενόμενα.

12. *The question was simply, which should anticipate hostile action on the part of the other. Considering the circumstances, we have done no wrong in revolting before the Athenians attacked us.*

1. τίς οὖν αὕτη ... πιστή: "was this then a friendship or a freedom on which one could rely?" For the position of the subj. αὕτη after the interr. (G. 1602; H. 1012 a), after the analogy of consts. with the sup., see on i. 1. 8. ἐγίγνετο, not ἦν, to indicate the growing mistrust. πιστή belongs to φιλία as well as ἐλευθερία. Dindorf's conjecture ἢ φιλία for vulg. ἡ φιλία has the support of the Cod. Clarend., and has been generally adopted. Bl., however, thinks the vulg. makes good sense, 'supposing that the words φιλία and ἐλευθερία, though written *once*, are to be taken *twice*, thus: "What sort of friendship, then, was this friendship of ours? What assured or secure liberty was this liberty of ours?"' — 2. ἐν ᾗ ... ἔμελλον: description of the form their relation to Athens had at last taken. — παρὰ γνώμην ἀλλήλους ὑπεδεχόμεθα: *we received one another contrary to our real feelings.* παρὰ γνώμην, praeter animi

ἡμᾶς ἐν τῷ πολέμῳ δεδιότες ἐθεράπευον, ἡμεῖς δὲ ἐκείνους
ἐν τῇ ἡσυχίᾳ τὸ αὐτὸ ἐποιοῦμεν· ὅ τε τοῖς ἄλλοις μά-
5 λιστα εὔνοια [πίστιν] βεβαιοῖ, ἡμῖν τοῦτο ὁ φόβος ἐχυρὸν
παρεῖχε, δέει τε τὸ πλέον ἢ φιλίᾳ κατεχόμενοι ξύμμαχοι
ἦμεν· καὶ ὁποτέροις θᾶσσον παράσχοι ἀσφάλεια θάρσος,
οὗτοι πρότεροί τι καὶ παραβήσεσθαι ἔμελλον. ὥστε εἴ 2
τῳ δοκοῦμεν ἀδικεῖν προαποστάντες διὰ τὴν ἐκείνων μέλ-

sententiam, not in the usual sense of conviction or expectation (c. 42. 29; 60.4; iv. 40.1; v. 14.12; vi. 9.12). ὑποδέχεσθαι has been from the earliest period of the language the regular expression for every kindly, esp. hospitable, reception. *Cf.* Hom. Z 136, ξ 52, π 70; Pind. *Pyth.* ix. 9; Hdt. i. 41. 5; Ar. *Acharn.* 979; Xen. *Mem.* iii. 11. 10; Plato *Legg.* 952 e. From that is derived the more general signification of friendly courtesies, esp. between strangers. St. rightly observes that ὑποδέχεσθαι, which in Plato *Legg.* 952 e is connected with ἀγοραῖς καὶ λιμέσι, is the opp. of λιμένων καὶ ἀγορᾶς εἴργεσθαι (ψήφισμα περὶ Μεγαρέων, i. 67. 14), and therefore about = ἐπιμείγνυσθαι παρ' ἀλλήλους (ii. 1. 3). *Cf.* Liv. xxx. 14 benigno vultu excepisset. Plato *Meno* 91 a similarly connects ὑποδέχεσθαι and θεραπεύειν. — **3. ἐθεράπευον**: *cf.* c. 11. 22. — **ἡμεῖς δὲ ... ἐποιοῦμεν**: not contradictory to c. 9. § 2 ἐν τῇ εἰρήνῃ ... ἀφιστάμεθα, for there the reference is only to the outward position of the Mytileneans, which continued to be an honourable one, even though they had assiduously to court the favour of the Athenians. — **4. ὅ τε τοῖς ἄλ-**

λοις ... ἐχυρὸν παρεῖχε: Cl., St., and Steup strike out πίστιν. If the traditional reading be retained. Kr.'s explanation seems best : 'The sent., if complete, would read ὅ τε τοῖς ἄλλοις μάλιστα εὔνοια ποιεῖ (or παρέχει), πίστιν βεβαιοῖ, κτέ.' See App. — **6. κατεχόμενοι**: *overmastered, constrained*, as in c. 45. 18. *Cf.* Eur. *Hipp.* 27 καρδίαν κατέσχετο ἔρωτι δεινῷ. In Arr. *Anab.* ii. 17. 2 τῆς δὲ Ἀθηναίων πόλεως φόβῳ μᾶλλόν τι ἢ εὐνοίᾳ τῇ πρὸς ἡμᾶς πρὸς τὸ παρὸν κατεχομένης, which is an evident imitation of the present passage, the meaning is *restrained*. *Cf.* c. 107. 9. — **8. οὗτοι πρότεροί τι καὶ ... ἔμελλον**: *these were sure to be the first also to transgress*. καὶ introduces the immediate accomplishment of the anticipation of the prot., as in ii. 93. 18; viii. 1. 31. With πρότεροί τι παραβήσεσθαι, *cf.* c. 11. 8 ; also c. 54. 11 τὴν εἰρήνην οὐ λύσαντες πρότεροι, i. 123. 11 σπονδὰς οὐ λύσετε πρότεροι, vii. 18. 10 τὰς σπονδὰς προτέρους λελυκέναι.

ὥστε εἴ τῳ ... δεινῶν: *so that if, on account of their postponement of the evils intended for us, we seem to anyone to do wrong in revolting beforehand*. μέλλησις seems not to occur elsewhere in trans. significa-

10 λῆσιν τῶν ἐς ἡμᾶς δεινῶν, αὐτοὶ οὐκ ἀνταναμείναντες
σαφῶς εἰδέναι εἴ τι αὐτῶν ἔσται, οὐκ ὀρθῶς σκοπεῖ. εἰ 3
γὰρ δυνατοὶ ἦμεν ἐκ τοῦ ἴσου καὶ ἀντεπιβουλεῦσαι, καὶ
ἀντιμελλῆσαί τι ἔδει ἡμᾶς ἐκ τοῦ ὁμοίου ἐπ' ἐκείνους
ἰέναι· ἐπ' ἐκείνοις δὲ ὄντος αἰεὶ τοῦ ἐπιχειρεῖν καὶ ἐφ'
15 ἡμῖν εἶναι δεῖ τὸ προαμύνασθαι.

13 " Τοιαύτας ἔχοντες προφάσεις καὶ αἰτίας, ὦ Λακεδαι- 1

tion. τῶν δεινῶν, violent measures, as in ii. 77. 3; iv. 98. 1. For the position of μέλλησιν between the subj. and obj. gen., see on i. 25. 21. — 10. αὐτοὶ οὐκ ἀνταναμείναντες: *without ourselves having waited in turn*. ἀνταναμένειν, which seems to be found only here, takes a limiting inf., as ἀναμένειν, iv. 120. 19; 135. 8. *Cf.* also ἐπιμένειν, c. 2. 7; 26. 13; περιμένειν, vii. 20. 16. — 11. αὐτῶν : sc. τῶν δεινῶν. εἰ γὰρ δυνατοὶ ... ἰέναι : so Cl. reads, putting, with Heilmann, ἀντεπιβουλεῦσαι, καὶ ἀντιμελλῆσαί τι ἔδει ἡμᾶς for ἀντεπιβουλεῦσαι καὶ ἀντιμελλῆσαι, τί ἔδει ἡμᾶς, and, with Kr., ἐπ' ἐκείνους ἰέναι for ἐπ' ἐκείνοις εἶναι, "were we able equally with them to counterplot, so ought we then also in like manner to have delayed to proceed against them." The proleptic καὶ inserted in the prot., as often in rel. clauses, and repeated in the apodosis. See on i. 83. 7. ἀντιμελλῆσαι (so Bk., with the Schol. and T ; most Mss. ἀντεπιμελλῆσαι) is chosen with reference to the boasted μέλλησις of the Athenians. *Cf.* ἀνταναμείναντες above. The sense of the vulg., which all the English commentators retain, is probably: "if we were able on equal terms with them to counter-

plot and counter-delay, what need was there for us, being on equal terms, to be at their beck and call?" *Cf.* Schol. εἰ γὰρ ἴσοι αὐτοῖς ὑπήρχομεν ... τί ἔδει ἡμᾶς ἐπ' ἐκείνοις ταχθῆναι ἢ ὑπακούειν αὐτοῖς. See App. — 14. ἐπ' ἐκείνοις : *in their power*. *Cf.* ii. 84. 11; iv. 29. 18.

13. *Intending to revolt even before the present war, we were hindered by you. Now, invited by the Boeotians, we have promptly taken this step not only in our own interest, but in that of the Hellenes wh*) *are enslaved by the Athenians. But as our revolt has been made too hastily and without the necessary preparations, you are the more bound to assist us, in order that your readiness to help in such cases may be known. All the circumstances are favourable. The power of the Athenians, already weakened and divided, will lose by our defection one of its strongest supports, while your fleet will receive a considerable addition.*

1. τοιαύτας ἔχοντες : in close connexion with the preceding without connecting particle, as in ii. 74. 1; iv. 93. 1, and freq. — προφάσεις, αἰτίας : not essentially different, except that the former is more the immediate occasion for action, as in i. 23. 23;

μόνιοι καὶ ξύμμαχοι, ἀπέστημεν, σαφεῖς μὲν τοῖς ἀκούουσι γνῶναι ὡς εἰκότως ἐδράσαμεν, ἱκανὰς δὲ ἡμᾶς ἐκφοβῆσαι καὶ πρὸς ἀσφάλειάν τινα τρέψαι, βουλομένους μὲν καὶ
5 πάλαι, ὅτε ἔτι ἐν τῇ εἰρήνῃ ἐπέμψαμεν ὡς ὑμᾶς περὶ ἀποστάσεως, ὑμῶν δὲ οὐ προσδεξαμένων κωλυθέντας· νῦν δὲ ἐπειδὴ Βοιωτοὶ προυκαλέσαντο, εὐθὺς ὑπηκούσαμεν, καὶ ἐνομίζομεν ἀποστήσεσθαι διπλῆν ἀπόστασιν, ἀπό τε τῶν Ἑλλήνων μὴ ξὺν κακῶς ποιεῖν αὐτοὺς μετ' Ἀθηναίων,

118. 3; Dem. xviii. 156. See on c. 9. 10. — 2. **σαφεῖς γνῶναι, ἱκανὰς ἐκφοβῆσαι**: for inf. limiting adj., see GMT. 758; II. 952. *Cf.* i. 50. 25; ii. 61. 12; vii. 14. 6. — 4. **πρὸς ἀσφάλειάν τινα τρέψαι**: *to cause us to turn to some means of safety, i.e.* to an alliance with Sparta. *Cf.* vi. 59. 7. — **βουλομένους μέν, κωλυθέντας δέ**: *sc.* ἀφίστασθαι. The parties., though joined to a subord. clause, by their position at the end of the period come to have the force of the leading clause, so that the following *νῦν δὲ κτέ.* refers only to them. *Cf.* c. 2. § 1. — 5. **ἔτι ἐν τῇ εἰρήνῃ**: closely connected, as in ii. 2. 19. See on i. 30. 20. — 6. **ὑμῶν δὲ οὐ προσδεξαμένων**: *cf.* c. 2. 3. — 7. **Βοιωτοὶ προυκαλέσαντο**: this influence is not definitely mentioned above. But *cf.* c. 2. 14; 5. 13. — 8. **ἐνομίζομεν ἀποστήσεσθαι διπλῆν ἀπόστασιν ... προποιῆσαι**: *we thought to effect a twofold withdrawal: from the Hellenes, so as not to become partners with the Athenians in doing them harm, but to aid in freeing them, and from the Athenians, so as not to be destroyed ourselves by them afterwards, but rather to destroy them first* (προποιῆσαι, *i.e.* προδιαφθεῖραι). For

examples similar to ἀφίστασθαι ἀπόστασιν, see Lobeck, *Paralip.* ii. 516 f. See also on i. 37. 11. **ἐνομίζομεν** here, as freq., expresses a certain self-confidence. *Cf.* i. 84. 17; 105. 23; ii. 3. 7. As to τε, τε, for which καί, καί is more usual in prose, see on i. 8. 14; ii. 84. 14. In the const. of the sent. Thuc. evidently had in mind c. 10. § 3. Nominally the Mytileneans revolted not only from the Athenians, but also from the rest of the Hellenes of the Delian alliance, for whose enslavement they had, as they alleged, been obliged to aid the Athenians. But most editt. hold that ἀπόστασις is used here in a double sense, first, as regards the Greeks, of a b s i s t e n d i (*cf.* iv. 118. 40; vii. 7. 9), second, as regards the Athenians, of revolt. The object of the entrance into the alliance is expressed in c. 10. § 3 by ἐπί with the dat., while here the object of its renunciation is expressed by infs., the pres. (ξὺν κακῶς ποιεῖν, ξυνελευθεροῦν) in reference to the unlimited future, the aor. (διαφθαρῆναι, προποιῆσαι) to the case in hand. — 9. **ξὺν κακῶς ποιεῖν**: like ἀντ' εὖ ποιεῖν, Ar. *Plut.* 1029; Xen. *Anab.* v. 5. 21; Plato *Gorg.* 520 c; Dem. xx. 64, 124, 141;

10 ἀλλὰ ξυνελευθεροῦν, ἀπό τε Ἀθηναίων μὴ αὐτοὶ διαφθαρῆναι ὑπ' ἐκείνων ἐν ὑστέρῳ, ἀλλὰ προποιῆσαι. ἡ μέν- 2 τοι ἀπόστασις ἡμῶν θᾶσσον γεγένηται καὶ ἀπαράσκευος· ᾗ καὶ μᾶλλον χρὴ ξυμμάχους δεξαμένους ἡμᾶς διὰ ταχέων βοήθειαν ἀποστέλλειν, ἵνα φαίνησθε ἀμύνοντές
15 τε οἷς δεῖ καὶ ἐν τῷ αὐτῷ τοὺς πολεμίους βλάπτοντες. καιρὸς δὲ ὡς οὔπω πρότερον. νόσῳ τε γὰρ ἐφθάραται 3 Ἀθηναῖοι καὶ χρημάτων δαπάνῃ. νῆές τε αὐτοῖς αἱ μὲν περὶ τὴν ὑμετέραν εἰσίν, αἱ δ' ἐφ' ἡμῖν τετάχαται· ὥστε οὐκ εἰκὸς αὐτοὺς περιουσίαν νεῶν ἔχειν, ἣν ὑμεῖς ἐν τῷ 4

σὺν εὖ πάσχειν, Dem. viii. 65. *Cf.* Soph. *Ant.* 523 οὗτοι συνέχθειν, ἀλλὰ συμφιλεῖν ἔφυν. For ξύν as adv., see Matth. 594, 2.

12. θᾶσσον: *sc.* ἢ ἠβουλόμεθα. For the omission of the second member of the comparison, see Kühn. 542, N. 7. The adv. co-ord. with adj., as in c. 4. 4. As to the facts, *cf.* c. 2. § 1, 2; 4. § 2. — 13. ᾗ καὶ: used before a comp. adv. emphasizes an inference. *Cf.* i. 11. 8; 25. 22; ii. 2. 21; iv. 1. 14. — ξυμμάχους . . . ἀποστέλλειν: see App. ξυμμάχους is pred. to δεξαμένους ἡμᾶς, as i. 43. 7. — διὰ ταχέων: = ταχέως, as in i. 80. 8; iv. 8. 18; 96. 4; vi. 66. 10; viii. 101. 4. — 14. ἵνα φαίνησθε ἀμύνοντές τε κτέ.: summary of the two chief points on which the Mytileneans base their request. See on c. 10. 1. The grounds for the last clause (τοὺς πολεμίους βλάπτοντες) are given in what follows.

16. ὡς οὔπω πρότερον: *cf.* ii. 20. 5; v. 63. 4. — ἐφθάραται, τετάχαται: such Ion. forms of the pf. and plpf. occur also in iv. 31. 7; v. 6. 23; vii. 4. 34. G. 701; 777, 3; H. 464 a; Kühn.³ 214,

8; Kr. *Spr.* 30, 2, 7. — 17. χρημάτων δαπάνῃ: 'a plena locutio, which has, however, an intensive force.' Bl. It occurs also in [Dem.] lx. 13. — νῆες, αἱ μέν, αἱ δέ: part. appos. See on ii. 95. 5; vii. 71. 4. G. 914; H. 624 d; Kühn. 406, 7. — 18. αἱ μὲν . . . εἰσίν: *i.e.* the 30 ships sent under Asopius. *Cf.* c. 7. 3. περὶ τὴν ὑμετέραν = περὶ τὴν Λακωνικήν, as often in this speech the Lacedaemonians only are to be understood as addressed (*e.g.* ll. 6, 34). The territory of the Peloponnesian alliance was not such a unity that the orators could properly speak of a fleet as *about* this territory. See also on c. 16. 4, 12. — ἐφ' ἡμῖν: in hostile sense, rare instead of the accusative. *Cf.* c. 16. 4; 63. 8; i. 102. 19; ii. 70. 8.

19. οὐκ εἰκὸς αὐτοὺς περιουσίαν νεῶν ἔχειν: considering the statement above, l. 16, νόσῳ . . . δαπάνῃ, and that there could hardly have been a prospect of an actual lack of ships (*cf.* ii. 13. 55), the reference seems to be to the manning and maintenance of more ships. The inf. pres.

20 θέρει τῷδε ναυσί τε καὶ πεζῷ ἅμα ἐπεσβάλητε τὸ δεύτερον,
ἀλλ' ἢ ὑμᾶς οὐκ ἀμυνοῦνται ἐπιπλέοντας ἢ ἀπ' ἀμφοτέρων
ἀποχωρήσονται. νομίσῃ τε μηδεὶς ἀλλοτρίας γῆς πέρι 5
οἰκεῖον κίνδυνον ἕξειν. ᾧ γὰρ δοκεῖ μακρὰν ἀπεῖναι ἡ
Λέσβος, τὴν ὠφελίαν αὐτῷ ἐγγύθεν παρέξει. οὐ γὰρ ἐν
25 τῇ Ἀττικῇ ἔσται ὁ πόλεμος, ὥς τις οἴεται, ἀλλὰ δι' ἣν ἡ
Ἀττικὴ ὠφελεῖται. ἔστι δὲ τῶν χρημάτων ἀπὸ τῶν ξυμ- 6
μάχων ἡ πρόσοδος, καὶ ἔτι μείζων ἔσται, εἰ ἡμᾶς κατα-
στρέψονται· οὔτε γὰρ ἀποστήσεται ἄλλος τά τε ἡμέτερα
προσγενήσεται, πάθοιμέν τ' ἂν δεινότερα ἢ οἱ πρὶν δου-

with εἰκός on account of the notion
of duration. *Cf.* iv. 20. 16, and see
on i. 81. 13. — **20. ἐπεσβάλητε τὸ
δεύτερον**: ἐπι- is further defined by τὸ
δεύτερον. ἐπεισβαλεῖν, meaning *attack*,
is found elsewhere only in a fragment
of Palaephatus; in Eur. *El.* 498 it
means insuper inicere. The
first invasion was described in c. 1. —
21. ἀπ' ἀμφοτέρων: *sc.* ἡμῶν τε καὶ
ὑμῶν.
22. νομίσῃ τε μηδείς: order as in
iv. 95. 3; vi. 84. 1. Kühn. 512, N. 1.
— **ἀλλοτρίας ... ἕξειν**: *cf.* i. 78. 2. —
23. μακρὰν ἀπεῖναι: procul abesse.
Cf. μακρὰν ἀποικεῖν, c. 55. 5. Kr. *Spr.*
43, 3, 8. — **24. τὴν ὠφελίαν αὐτῷ**:
when an oblique case of αὐτός thus
follows its rel., it is equiv. to a weak
dem. and cannot stand first in its
clause. Kühn. 468, N. 4. *Cf.* iv. 92.
42; 126. 19; 128. 3. — **οὐ γὰρ ἐν τῇ
Ἀττικῇ ἔσται ὁ πόλεμος**: *for not
upon Attica will the war depend, i.e.
it will not draw its strength thence.*
For ἐν, not in local sense, *cf.* i. 74. 2
ἐν ταῖς ναυσὶ τὰ πράγματα ἐγένετο, ii.
35. 7 ἐν ἑνὶ ἀνδρὶ ... κινδυνεύεσθαι,

ii. 64. 11 μὴ ἐν ὑμῖν κωλυθῇ. Kr. *Spr.*
68, 12, 6. — **25. δι' ἥν**: *i.e.* ἐν ταύτῃ
δι' ἥν, nearly = δι' ἧς. *Cf.* i. 83. 4
δαπάνης, δι' ἣν τὰ ὅπλα ὠφελεῖ. Also
c. 39. 43; vii. 68. 18; Dem. i. 12.
26. ἔστι δὲ ... ἡ πρόσοδος: *cf.* ii. 13.
20 λέγων τὴν ἰσχὺν αὐτοῖς ἀπὸ τούτων
εἶναι τῶν χρημάτων τῆς προσόδου. —
27. καὶ ἔτι ... καταστρέψονται: the
proof of the claim made l. 24, τὴν
ὠφελίαν ... παρέξει. If the subjugation of the Mytileneans will increase
the revenues of the Athenians, it is
clearly to the interest of the Peloponnesians to prevent this. — **28. τά τε
ἡμέτερα**: nostrae opes. τε correl.
to οὔτε. — **29. πάθοιμέν τ' ἂν δεινότερα**:
esp. through an increase of taxes, as
it would seem from the context. τε
introduces a *third* circumstance. For
the opt. with ἄν exchanging with fut.
indic., see Kühn. 396, N. 1. — **ἢ οἱ
πρὶν δουλεύοντες**: *than those enslaved
before (us), i.e.* the ξύμμαχοι ὑποτελεῖς
(i. 80. 14; 99. 11). *Cf.* c. 10. § 4. 5.
Arnold explains: '*Worse than they
who were slaves before they revolted;*
because the Mytileneans would seem

30 λεύοντες. βοηθησάντων δὲ ὑμῶν προθύμως, πόλιν τε 7
προσλήψεσθε ναυτικὸν ἔχουσαν μέγα, οὗπερ ὑμῖν μάλιστα
προσδεῖ, καὶ Ἀθηναίους ῥᾷον καθαιρήσετε ὑφαιροῦντες
αὐτῶν τοὺς ξυμμάχους (θρασύτερον γὰρ πᾶς τις προσχω-
ρήσεται), τήν τε αἰτίαν ἀποφεύξεσθε ἣν εἴχετε μὴ βοηθεῖν
35 τοῖς ἀφισταμένοις. ἢν δ' ἐλευθεροῦντες φαίνησθε, τὸ
κράτος τοῦ πολέμου βεβαιότερον ἕξετε.

to have revolted on much less provocation. See Cleon's speech c. 39. § 5, where he calls for an exemplary vengeance upon Mytilene on this very ground.'

30. βοηθησάντων δὲ ὑμῶν: this alternative, which contains the main point of the thought, or rather of the whole speech, is expressed in gen. abs., although the verbs of the apod. have the same subject. GMT. 850; Kr. Spr. 47, 4, 2; Kühn. 494 a. See on c. 112. 21; ii. 83. 15; viii. 76. 12. — **32. προσδεῖ**: sc. besides what you already have. — **καθαιρήσετε**: of violent overthrow of an existing order of things, or a predominant person. See on i. 4. 6; 77. 20. — **ὑφαιροῦντες**: of gradual drawing out. Cf. c. 31. 8; 82. 17. Bl. calls this an architectural metaphor, namely to pull down (καθαιρεῖν) by undermining or pulling out stones from the foundation (ὑφαιρεῖν). — **33. πᾶς τις**: everyone, as comprehensive as possible. Kr. Spr. 51, 16, 11. Cf. c. 93. 10; ii. 41. 21; vi. 68. 7; vii. 60. 13. — **34. τὴν αἰτίαν**: the reproach, as in ii. 18. 9; 60. 25; vi. 60. 3. With ἔχειν also i. 83. 8; vi. 46. 27. — **ἀποφεύξεσθε**: cf. ii. 42. 23 τὸ αἰσχρὸν τοῦ λόγου ἔφυγον. — **ἣν εἴχετε**: refers to the period before the Peloponnesian war.

Cf. i. 69. § 5. The reading of Vat., ἔχετε — with which ἀποφεύξεσθε would mean *get rid of*, not *avoid* — would ill accord with the relation of the Mytileneans to the Lacedaemonians, and would hardly answer to the actual circumstances, since the Lacedaemonians had indeed, as they had promised and not far otherwise than the Mytileneans now demanded for themselves (c. 13. § 4; 15. § 1), sought to bring aid to the Potidaeans (cf. i. 58. § 1; 71. § 4; ii. 70. § 1, and, as an example of the opposite course in earlier times, i. 101. § 1 f.). — **35. ἢν δ' ἐλευθεροῦντες φαίνησθε**: *if you openly appear as liberators* (of the oppressed). Thus φανῆτε, which would be the more usual form before ἕξετε, is not necessary. There is an allusion to the boast made by the Lacedaemonians at the opening of the war, ὅτι τὴν Ἑλλάδα ἐλευθεροῦσιν (ii. 8. 15; iv. 85. 4). Cf. c. 32. 5. — **τὸ κράτος τοῦ πολέμου**: τὸ δύνασθαι περιγενέσθαι τῷ πολέμῳ, Schol. Cf. ii. 87. 27; Plato Legg. 962 a. Also Dem. xix. 130 κράτος πολέμου καὶ νίκην ... διδόναι, Dio C. (fragm.) 35. 4 τὸ κράτος τοῦ πολέμου ὑποχείριον ἔσχε. κράτος in this sense (*mastery, victory*) seems to be Ion. and poetic. — **βεβαιότερον ἕξετε**: see on c. 11. 16.

14   "Αἰσχυνθέντες οὖν τάς τε τῶν Ἑλλήνων ἐς ὑμᾶς ἐλπίδας καὶ Δία τὸν Ὀλύμπιον, ἐν οὗ τῷ ἱερῷ ἴσα καὶ ἱκέται ἐσμέν, ἐπαμύνατε Μυτιληναίοις ξύμμαχοι γενόμενοι, καὶ μὴ προῆσθε ἡμᾶς, ἴδιον μὲν τὸν κίνδυνον τῶν
5 σωμάτων παραβαλλομένους, κοινὴν δὲ τὴν ἐκ τοῦ κατορθῶσαι ὠφελίαν ἅπασι δώσοντας, ἔτι δὲ κοινοτέραν τὴν βλάβην, εἰ, μὴ πεισθέντων ὑμῶν, σφαλησόμεθα. γίγνεσθε δὲ ἄνδρες οἷοσπερ ὑμᾶς οἵ τε Ἕλληνες ἀξιοῦσι καὶ τὸ ἡμέτερον δέος βούλεται."

15   Τοιαῦτα μὲν οἱ Μυτιληναῖοι εἶπον. οἱ δὲ Λακεδαιμόνιοι καὶ οἱ ξύμμαχοι, ἐπειδὴ ἤκουσαν, προσδεξάμενοι τοὺς λόγους ξυμμάχους τε τοὺς Λεσβίους ἐποιήσαντο, καὶ

14. *Honour and advantage, therefore, alike bid you to assist us.*

1. ἐς ὑμᾶς: free use of the prep., as in i. 41. 8. Kühn. 432. 1. 3 a. *Cf.* Dio C. li. 13 μεταγιγνώσκειν ἐπλάσατο, ὡς καὶ ἐλπίδα πολλὴν μὲν ἐς ἐκεῖνον, πολλὴν δὲ καὶ ἐς τὴν Λιουΐαν ἔχουσα. — **2.** Δία τὸν Ὀλύμπιον: an exception to the rule that the art. stands with both the name and appellation of a god, or is omitted with both. Kr. *Spr.* 50, 7, 10. — ἐν οὗ τῷ ἱερῷ: this position of the gen. between the prep. and its noun is esp. common in Thuc., and is the usual one with οὗ. *Cf.* c. 70. 16; 81. 26; 96. 1; v. 47. 66. Kr. *Spr.* 47, 9, 19. — ἴσα καί: II. 1042 a; Kühn. 423, n. 18. *Cf.* ἐν ἴσῳ καί, ii. 60. 20; ἐν τῷ ὁμοίῳ καί, vi. 11. 15; παραπλησίαις καί, v. 112. 3; vii. 70. 2; ὁμοίως καί, vii. 28. 30; viii. 76. 13; Hdt. viii. 60. 25; ὡσαύτως καί, Hdt. vii. 86. 7; ὅτῳ γε νοῦς ἴσος καὶ σοὶ πάρα, Soph. *O. C.* 810; σεβίζω σ' ἴσα καὶ μάκαρας, Eur. *El.* 994. ἴσα is adv., as ὁμοῖα. i. 25.

18. ἴσα καί occurs also in late writers, e.g. Aristid. *Panath.* i. p. 285 ἴσα καὶ ἀήττητος. — **4.** ἴδιον... κοινὴν ... κοινοτέραν: "we alone make the sacrifice; the results, whether good or bad (the latter in still greater measure, κοινοτέραν), will fall upon all," — ἴδιον μὲν... παραβαλλομένους: unusual for μετ' ἰδίου κινδύνου τὰ σώματα παραβαλλομένους. σώματα means *life and limb*, as in i. 70. 19; 141. 18; ii. 42. 24. παραβάλλεσθαι, *to risk* (as at play), also c. 65. 12; ii. 44. 16; Hdt. vii. 10. θ 3; Hom. ι 322. But here the obj. is the danger instead of the thing endangered. — **5.** κατορθῶσαι, σφαλησόμεθα: usual antithesis, as in c. 39. 39; ii. 65. 28. — **7.** μή: belongs to the partic. only. *Cf.* i. 32. 24; 37. 6. — **8.** οἱ Ἕλληνες ἀξιοῦσι: cf. i. 69. 7. Supply εἶναι with ἀξιοῦσι and βούλεται.

15. *The Mytileneans are received into the Peloponnesian alliance and the Lacedaemonians prepare to invade Attica.*

τὴν ἐς τὴν Ἀττικὴν ἐσβολὴν τοῖς τε ξυμμάχοις παροῦσι
5 κατὰ τάχος ἔφραζον ἰέναι ἐς τὸν Ἰσθμὸν τοῖς δύο μέρεσιν
ὡς ποιησόμενοι. καὶ αὐτοὶ πρῶτοι ἀφίκοντο, καὶ ὁλκοὺς
παρεσκεύαζον τῶν νεῶν ἐν τῷ Ἰσθμῷ ὡς ὑπεροίσοντες ἐκ
τῆς Κορίνθου ἐς τὴν πρὸς Ἀθήνας θάλασσαν καὶ ναυσὶ
καὶ πεζῷ ἅμα ἐπιόντες. καὶ οἱ μὲν προθύμως ταῦτα
10 ἔπρασσον, οἱ δὲ ἄλλοι ξύμμαχοι βραδέως τε ξυνελέγοντο
καὶ ἐν καρποῦ ξυγκομιδῇ ἦσαν καὶ ἀρρωστίᾳ τοῦ στρατεύειν.

4. **τὴν ἐς τὴν Ἀττικὴν ἐσβολήν**:
cf. c. 13. § 4. The acc. placed first,
though grammatically dependent on
ὡς ποιησόμενοι, is almost abs., *and as
to the invasion of Attica. Cf.* ii. 62.
1; Soph. *El.* 1364. See on i. 32. 17.
— **παροῦσι κατὰ τάχος ... μέρεσιν**:
παροῦσι is to be connected with ἰέναι
and is dependent on ἔφραζον (= ἐκέλευον), *gave orders to present themselves speedily and march to the isthmus with a contingent of two thirds.*
So Lupus explains, *N. Jahrbb.* cxi.
p. 166. Stemp brackets παροῦσι. See
App. — 5. **ἔφραζον**: with dependent
inf., also vi. 58. 7. Kühn. 473, 2. The
impf. does not differ here essentially
from the aorist. GMT. 57; Kr. *Spr.*
53, 2, 1. The original subj. οἱ Λακεδαιμόνιοι καὶ οἱ ξύμμαχοι is here limited
to οἱ Λακεδαιμόνιοι alone. See on c. 10.
16; i. 18. 21. — **τοῖς δύο μέρεσι**: *i.e.*
with two thirds of their whole force
capable of bearing arms. This was
the regular contingent furnished by
the Peloponnesian states for expeditions beyond their own borders. *Cf.*
ii. 10. 6; 47. 2. — 6. **ὁλκούς**: ὄργανα οἷς
αἱ νῆες ἕλκονται. Schol. — 7. **ὡς ὑπεροίσοντες**: *sc.* τὰς ναῦς. (*Cf.* c. 81. 3;

iv. 8. 8; viii. 7. 7; Dio C. lxviii. 28
ὑπερενεγκὼν τὰ πλοῖα ὅλκοις, Liv. xlii.
16 per Isthmi iugum navibus
traductis Aeginam traiciunt.
See Wachsmuth, *Ant. Gr.* ii. p. 336.
Acc. to Strabo viii. 6. 22, the place
where the transfer was made was
called διολκος. — 9. **ἐπιόντες**: as fut.
partic. co-ord. with ὑπεροίσοντες and
dependent on ὡς.
10. **οἱ ἄλλοι ξύμμαχοι**: since just
above (ll. 4, 6) τοῖς ξυμμάχοις and αὐτοί
are opposed, ἄλλοι means here doubtless *besides*. See on i. 2. 12. G. 966,
2; H. 705. — 11. **καρποῦ**: collective
sing., like Eng. *fruit*, as in iv. 84. 5;
88. 4; Hom. A 156. *Cf.* κάλαμος, ii.
76. 2; ἄμπελος, iv. 90. 9; multa
fruge, Hor. *Ep.* i. 16. 10. Kr. *Spr.*
44, 1, 1; Kühn. 347, 1. The art. is
omitted on acc. of the close connexion
with ξυγκομιδῇ. Since the summer
was already advanced (see on date
of the Olympia, c. 8. 5), καρπός prob.
refers here, as in iv. 84. 5, esp. to
grapes. See A. Mommsen, *Über d.
Zeit der Olympien*, p. 57 ff. — **ἐν** . . .
ἦσαν: belongs to both the essentially
different expressions. ξυγκομιδῇ (of
action) and ἀρρωστίᾳ (of disposition

16   Αἰσθόμενοι δὲ αὐτοὺς οἱ Ἀθηναῖοι διὰ κατάγνωσιν 1
ἀσθενείας σφῶν παρασκευαζομένους, δηλῶσαι βουλόμενοι
ὅτι οὐκ ὀρθῶς ἐγνώκασιν, ἀλλ' οἷοί τέ εἰσι μὴ κινοῦντες
τὸ ἐπὶ Λέσβῳ ναυτικὸν καὶ τὸ ἀπὸ Πελοποννήσου ἐπιὸν
5 ῥᾳδίως ἀμύνεσθαι, ἐπλήρωσαν ναῦς ἑκατὸν ἐσβάντες αὐτοί
τε πλὴν ἱππέων καὶ πεντακοσιομεδίμνων καὶ οἱ μέτοικοι,
καὶ παρὰ τὸν Ἰσθμὸν ἀναγαγόντες ἐπίδειξίν τε ἐποιοῦντο

of mind); with the former after the analogy of ἐν παρασκευῇ εἶναι, ii. 101. 10; with the latter after that of ἐν ταραχῇ καὶ φόβῳ εἶναι, c. 79. 9. — ἀρρωστίᾳ: i.e. ἀπροθυμίᾳ, despondency, as in vii. 47. 3. Cf. viii. 83. 7 ἀρρωστότερον.

16. *But seeing the counter preparations made by the Athenians they give up this plan and fit out a fleet for the protection of Lesbos.*

1. διὰ κατάγνωσιν ἀσθενείας σφῶν: *because they imputed weakness to them.*   κατάγνωσις of unfavourable judgment, as καταγιγνώσκειν (c. 45. 4; vi. 34. 51; vii. 51. 3; Hdt. vi. 97. 7, and freq.) = καταφρονεῖν (viii. 8. 19 καταφρονήσαντες τῶν Ἀθηναίων ἀδυναμίαν). σφῶν, too, stands under the influence of κατα-, as in c. 45. 4. The Lacedaemonians had adopted the view of Athenian affairs expressed by the Mytileneans c. 13. § 3, 4. —
3. μὴ κινοῦντες τὸ ἐπὶ Λέσβῳ ναυτικόν: see on c. 13. 18. That here, in spite of the evident reference to c. 13. § 3, 4, Thuc. does not include under μὴ κινοῦντες also the fleet sent around Peloponnesus, is to be explained on the ground that 18 of the 30 ships of Asopius had meanwhile returned (c. 7. § 3). See Steup, *Rh. Mus.* xxiv. p. 356. As the Mytileneans had said, c. 13. 21 ἢ ὑμᾶς οὐκ

ἀμυνοῦνται ἐπιπλέοντας ἢ ἀπ' ἀμφοτέρων ἀποχωρήσονται, the words οὐκ ὀρθῶς ἐγνώκασιν were already justified when the Athenians could, without recalling a ship from Lesbos, easily repel the Peloponnesian fleet. — 5. αὐτοί τε . . . καὶ οἱ μέτοικοι: *cf.* i. 143. 4. Of citizens usually only the θῆτες, who were ψιλοί on land, served in the fleet (vi. 43. 10); in critical times members of the three upper classes, whose regular duty was hoplite service, might be pressed into service in the fleet (viii. 24. 12). See Bauer in *Handbuch der klass. Alterthumsw.* iv.[1] p. 282; Schoemann, *Gr. Ant.* i. p. 448. The use of αὐτοί where the πεντακοσιομέδιμνοι and ἱππεῖς are excepted shows how much more numerous were the two lower classes, ζευγῖται and θῆτες. Regarding the census-classes, see Boeckh *P. E.*[3] p. 579 ff.; Hermann *Gr. Ant.*[6] i. § 68. —
7. παρὰ τὸν Ἰσθμόν: *along the coast of the isthmus.* Const. with ἐπίδειξιν ἐποιοῦντο. They proposed by the mere display (ἐπίδειξιν) of a large fleet to show the enemy how hopeless was the execution of their plans.
— ἀναγαγόντες: the unusual act. for ἀναγαγόμενοι occurs also in the comp. ἀντανάγειν, vii. 37. 18; 52. 4; viii. 38. 19; 83. 5. For the intr. use,

καὶ ἀποβάσεις τῆς Πελοποννήσου ᾗ δοκοίη αὐτοῖς. οἱ δὲ 2
Λακεδαιμόνιοι ὁρῶντες πολὺν τὸν παράλογον τά τε ὑπὸ
10 τῶν Λεσβίων ῥηθέντα ἡγοῦντο οὐκ ἀληθῆ, καὶ ἄπορα
νομίζοντες, ὡς αὐτοῖς καὶ οἱ ξύμμαχοι ἅμα οὐ παρῆσαν
καὶ ἠγγέλλοντο καὶ αἱ περὶ τὴν Πελοπόννησον [τριάκοντα]
νῆες τῶν Ἀθηναίων τὴν περιοικίδα αὐτῶν πορθοῦσαι,
ἀνεχώρησαν ἐπ' οἴκου. ὕστερον δὲ ναυτικὸν παρεσκεύαζον 3
15 ὅ τι πέμψουσιν ἐς τὴν Λέσβον καὶ κατὰ πόλεις ἐπήγγελλον

cf. ἀπολιπεῖν, c. 10. 8. Kühn. 373, 2 a.
— 8. τῆς Πελοποννήσου: part. gen. depending on ᾗ, as i. 46. 17; ii. 4. 22.
— δοκοίη: for the form here, as in ii. 79. 26; 100. 22; iv. 105. 9, instead of δοκοῖ of the Mss., see St. *Qu. Gr.*[2] p. 62. G. 737; H. 374 a.
9. ὁρῶντες πολὺν τὸν παράλογον: *seeing that their miscalculation was great*. See on i. 65. 3. παράλογος with πολύς also ii. 61. 14; 85. 6; μέγας, vii. 55. 4; ὅσος, i. 78. 3; τοσοῦτος, vii. 28. 17. — τὰ ὑπὸ τῶν Λεσβίων ῥηθέντα: *cf.* c. 13. § 3, 4. The form ῥηθῆναι is about as common in Thuc. as λεχθῆναι. Both together in c. 53. 14, 15. — 10. ἄπορα νομίζοντες: *regarding it as impracticable*. For Thuc.'s freq. use of the neut. pl. of the adj., see on i. 7. 2. Kühn. 366. — 11. οὐ παρῆσαν: *cf.* c. 15. 10. — 12. καὶ ἠγγέλλοντο καί: the first καί is correl. of καί in l. 11, the second means *also*. *Cf.* c. 21. 10; 31. 8. ἠγγέλλοντο in pers. const. with the partic., as in viii. 79. 21. GMT. 904; Kr. *Spr.* 56, 7, 3; Kühn. 482, 2. With inf., iv. 25. 23; viii. 94. 4. Oftener impers., as c. 110. 1; i. 114. 3; iv. 93. 7; 125. 2; v. 10. 7; vi. 45. 2. — αἱ περὶ τὴν Πελοπόννησον [τριάκοντα] νῆες: the 100

ships just mentioned, not the fleet under Asopius (c. 7. § 1), as clearly proved by Steup (*Rh. Mus.* xxiv. p. 355 ff.), who rightly strikes out τριάκοντα. See App. — 13. τὴν περιοικίδα αὐτῶν: *i.e.* the district of the Lacedaemonian Perioeci in Laconia and Messenia.
14. ὕστερον δὲ ... ἐπιπλεύσεσθαι: Thuc. mentions here, at the close of his account of the first unsuccessful attempt of the Lacedaemonians to aid the Lesbians, the preparations for the second expedition, made in the following summer (c. 25. § 1; 26. § 1). The regular course of the narrative is resumed at ἀνεχώρησαν δὲ κτέ., l. 17. ὕστερον is common where such an anticipation in the narrative occurs. *Cf.* c. 7. 10; 34. 21; i. 64. 8; 87. 16; ii. 9. 7; 31. 15; 70. 20; 100. 4.
— 15. ὅ τι πέμψουσιν: rel. with fut. indic. to express purpose, as in iv. 22. 2; viii. 1. 28. GMT. 565; Kr. *Spr.* 53, 7, 8; Kühn. 387, 4. — ἐπήγγελλον: *imperabant*. *Cf.* v. 47. 13; vii. 17. 2; viii. 108. 21. So περιήγγελλον, ii. 85. 11; vii. 18. 27. The impfs. παρεσκεύαζον and ἐπήγγελλον indicate gradual accomplishment, the aor. προσέταξαν an ordinance which

τεσσαράκοντα νεῶν πλῆθος καὶ ναύαρχον προσέταξαν
Ἀλκίδαν, ὃς ἔμελλεν ἐπιπλεύσεσθαι. ἀνεχώρησαν δὲ
καὶ οἱ Ἀθηναῖοι ταῖς ἑκατὸν ναυσίν, ἐπειδὴ καὶ ἐκείνους
εἶδον.

17   [Καὶ κατὰ τὸν χρόνον τοῦτον ὃν αἱ νῆες ἔπλεον ἐν 1

took effect immediately. — **16. ναύαρχον**: the commander of the Lacedaemonian navy was elected for a definite period, prob. a year, and had unlimited power. *Cf.* Arist. *Pol.* ii. 6. (9) 22 ἡ ναυαρχία σχεδὸν ἑτέρα βασιλεία καθέστηκε. *Cf.* ii. 66. 6; 80. 12.
— **17. ὃς ἔμελλεν ἐπιπλεύσεσθαι**: *i.e.* to sail on them as commander. *Cf.* c. 76. 6; ii. 66. 4; iv. 11. 6; viii. 39. 5.
18. ἐπειδὴ καὶ ἐκείνους εἶδον: sc. διακεχωρηκότας. Kr. *Spr.* 56, 16; Kühn. 599, 2. *Cf.* i. 78. 10; 80. 2; ii. 11. 34; 86. 14; v. 80. 11; vii. 69. 3.
17. *Reflections evoked by the number of Attic ships then at sea, and remarks upon the exhaustion of the Attic treasury.*
This chapter is seen upon close examination to be clearly the work of a glossator, as Steup first argued in *Rh. Mus.* xxiv. p. 350. See App.
1. ὅν: κατά is omitted with the rel. after the prepositional phrase, as usual in Attic writers. G. 1025; H. 1007; Kühn. 451, 4; Kr. *Spr.* 51, 11, 1. — **ἔπλεον**: *were afloat*. This pregnant force seems not to occur elsewhere. πλεῖν is never without pred. modification: whether *local*, as ἐς Αἴγυπτον, i. 110. 11; ἐκ τῆς Μιλήτου ἐς τὸν Ἑλλήσποντον, viii. 108. 12; or *qualitative*, as ἄριστα, i. 48. 12; vii. 31. 22; viii. 104. 11; ἄμεινον, ii. 84. 12; οὐ σπουδῇ, iii. 49. 14; εὖ, vii. 23.

11. — ἐν τοῖς πλεῖσται: the purely formulaic ἐν τοῖς with the sup. is explained by some as *intensive* (H. 652 a; Kr. *Spr.* 49, 10, 6 and on i. 6. 6; Kühn. 349b, 7 i; Madv. *Syntax*² 96, 2, and others); by others as *restrictive* (Arn. here and vii. 19. 19; L. Herbst, *Philol.* xvi. p. 345 ff.; C. Spormann, *de ellipsis apud Hdt. et Thuc. usu*, 1888, p. 29 sqq., and others). Acc. to the latter view, not absolute pre-eminence, but prominence among competitors is indicated, so that ἐν τοῖς πλεῖσται would mean, *among the most*. At any rate, that ἐν τοῖς πλεῖσται (fem. with ἐν τοῖς also c. 82. 2) should be followed by παραπλήσιαι δὲ καὶ ἔτι πλείους, is very peculiar. With the first view, it must be assumed that the author corrected himself; with the second, it still seems strange that to a number thus emphasized another still greater should be immediately opposed. Steup thinks no absolutely certain case of the *restrictive* ἐν τοῖς with sup. has been found. Of the cases cited by Herbst, ἐν τοῖς is not formulaic in viii. 68. 4, καὶ Θηραμένης ἐν τοῖς ξυγκαταλύουσι τὸν δῆμον πρῶτος ἦν, while in viii. 90. 4, Ἀρίσταρχος, ἀνὴρ ἐν τοῖς μάλιστα καὶ ἐκ πλείστου ἐναντίος τῷ δήμῳ, the phrase ἐν τοῖς μάλιστα might well mean *most of all*. On the other hand, in i. 6. 6 and iii.

τοῖς πλεῖσται δὴ νῆες ἅμ' αὐτοῖς ἐνεργοὶ † κάλλει ἐγένοντο,
παραπλήσιαι δὲ καὶ ἔτι πλείους ἀρχομένου τοῦ πολέμου.
τήν τε γὰρ Ἀττικὴν καὶ Εὔβοιαν καὶ Σαλαμῖνα ἑκατὸν 2
5 ἐφύλασσον καὶ περὶ Πελοπόννησον ἕτεραι ἑκατὸν ἦσαν,
χωρὶς δὲ αἱ περὶ Ποτείδαιαν καὶ ἐν τοῖς ἄλλοις χωρίοις,

82. 2 the thought, he claims, suits the context far better with ἐν τοῖς intensive; and in vii. 19. 19 only the intensive meaning is admissible, since Thuc. could hardly have meant to compare the departure of the ὁλκάδες carrying hoplites to Sicily (vii. 19. 19) with that of the 25 Corinthian triremes (vii. 17. 14) sent to engage the attention of the Athenian fleet at Naupactus, esp. as the triremes were despatched in the winter, the ὁλκάδες the following summer. But Steup's objection to rendering ἐν τοῖς πρῶτοι (vii. 19. 19) 'among the first' does not seem conclusive, and certainly Aristarchus (viii. 90. 4) was, as Herbst and Jow. say, not the 'very' foremost among the subverters of democracy. If all the cases of ἐν τοῖς with the sup. be compared, it is hard to escape Jow.'s conclusion, that the formula is sometimes *restrictive*, as in vii. 24. 12; viii. 90. 4; sometimes *intensive*, as in c. 81. 2 (*cf.* c. 85. 2); Plato *Symp.* 178 b. — 2. ἐνεργοὶ κάλλει: ἐνεργός is not elsewhere used of ships, and both words occur only here in Thucydides. Goell., Arn., and Jow. explain, 'effective by their fine condition'; Bl., 'effective and handsome' (*by their handsomeness*); Sheppard, 'on active service in handsome trim.' Peile takes κάλλει as dat. consilii, *for display*. Of the emendations proposed — by Herbst κάλως, St. καὶ ἄλλῃ, v. II. ἄλλαι ἄλλῃ — none is satisfactory. — 3. παραπλήσιαι δὲ καὶ ἔτι πλείους: for similar expressions, see on vii. 19. 8. See App.

4. τήν τε γὰρ ... διακόσιοι καὶ πεντήκοντα: describes the disposition of the Attic fleet ἀρχομένου τοῦ πολέμου, which strangely alone of the two armaments here compared is more fully discussed. This follows necessarily from 1. 15, καὶ νῆες τοσαῦται δὴ πλεῖσται ἐπληρώθησαν, which can only refer to the 250 ships of 1. 7. For if 250 was the highest number reached, this, acc. to 1. 3, παραπλήσιαι δὲ καὶ ἔτι πλείους ἀρχομένου τοῦ πολέμου, must refer to the first year of the war. Besides, the reader would be more likely to reckon for himself the number of ships of the summer under consideration (428) than that of 431 B.C. Further the words in 1. 6 περὶ Ποτείδαιαν καὶ ἐν τοῖς ἄλλοις χωρίοις are unintelligible, if § 2 refers to the year 428. — 5. ἕτεραι ἑκατόν: *cf.* ii. 23. § 2; 25; 30; 31. § 1. — 6. χωρὶς δέ: *besides*, abs., without expressed or easily supplied predicate. In the passages cited by St. as parallel (Plato *Euthyd.* 289 c.; Soph. O. C. 808). χωρίς means of a *different kind*, not *besides*. In Thuc. χωρὶς δέ either has its own verb (ii. 31. 11),

ὥστε αἱ πᾶσαι ἅμα ἐγίγνοντο ἐν ἑνὶ θέρει διακόσιαι καὶ πεντήκοντα. καὶ τὰ χρήματα τοῦτο μάλιστα ὑπανήλωσε 8 μετὰ Ποτειδαίας· τήν τε γὰρ Ποτείδαιαν δίδραχμοι ὁπλῖται
10 ἐφρούρουν (αὐτῷ γὰρ καὶ ὑπηρέτῃ δραχμὴν ἐλάμβανε τῆς

or the pred. of the preceding clause belongs also to it (i. 61. 15; ii. 97. 16; vi. 31. 29), or is to be supplied with it (ii. 13. 29; 31. 13). Here ἦσαν cannot be supplied from the preceding clause, since there it means 'chanced to be.' — αἱ περὶ ... χωρίοις: see App. — **7. αἱ πᾶσαι**: *in all*. II. 672 a; Kr. *Spr.* 50, 11, 13. *Cf.* c. 85. 12; i. 60. 6; vii. 1. 31.

8. τοῦτο: must refer grammatically to the number of ships either of 431 or 428 B.C. But as ὑπαναλίσκειν, *gradually consume* (ll. 8, 14), suits neither of these cases, the author of the chapter must have meant to indicate by τοῦτο "this fitting out of such large armaments," — a loose form of expression without parallel in Thuc. Besides, there seem to have been in the summer of 429 B.C., if one excepts the ships which may have remained on the Thracian coast after the capture of Potidaea, as well as the few at stations like Salamis and Atalante, only 40 Attic ships at sea at one time (ii. 80. 21; 85. 17). — **ὑπανήλωσε**: *gradually consumed*. The word is found in Thuc. only here and l. 14 below. With neut. subj., as ἀπαναλίσκειν, vii. 11. 13. *Cf.* c. 13. 33 ὑφαιροῦντες, i. 77. 23 ὑπεδείξατε. On the augment see St. *Qu. Gr.*[2] p. 60; Meisterhans,[2] p. 137.
— **9. μετὰ Ποτειδαίας**: Potidaea had been already for a year and a half again in the possession of the Athenians (ii. 70). But still more strange is the manner in which Potidaea is here set over against the fitting out of large naval armaments, since Potidaea itself had been besieged by a fleet (i. 64. § 3). The costs of this siege had been 2000 talents (ii. 70. § 2). Besides, the building of ships had doubtless entailed considerable expense. — **δίδραχμοι**: *i.e.* one drachma each for the hoplite and for his attendant, — more than usual, since the average daily pay of a hoplite was 4 obols. *Cf.* vii. 27. 7. See Boeckh *P. E.* p. 373; Herm. *Gr. Ant.* i.[6] § 112. The word is found here only in Thuc., and seldom elsewhere. — **10. ἐφρούρουν**: obsidebant, as περιεφρουροῦντο, c. 21. 15. *Cf.* Arr. *Anab.* i. 7. 10; ii. 1. 4; iv. 3. 4; 5. 2; and Eur. *Or.* 760 φυλασσόμεσθα φρουρίοισι πανταχῇ. Elsewhere in Thuc., to *garrison* or *guard*, as i. 103. 15; 107. 16; iv. 1. 16; v. 33. 6, 10; 35. 28; 64. 12; vii. 60. 11. In the passage cited by Pp. and others, i. 64. 2, 4, there is no reason why both ἐφρούρουν and φρουρεῖν may not be intr., *keep watch* (*cf.* c. 90. 11; ii. 80. 22; 83. 7; iv. 24. 2; 66. 20). — **αὐτῷ**: for sing. after preceding plur., *cf.* i. 120. 20 ἀνδρῶν σωφρόνων ... ἡδόμενον. Otherwise such a const. is without parallel in Thuc., though common in Hdt. *Cf.* Plato *Prot.* 324 a οὐδεὶς κολάζει τοὺς ἀδικοῦντας ... τούτου ἕνεκα, ὅτι ἠδίκησεν. Kr. *Spr.*

ἡμέρας), τρισχίλιοι μὲν οἱ πρῶτοι, ὧν οὐκ ἐλάσσους διεπολιόρκησαν, ἑξακόσιοι δὲ καὶ χίλιοι μετὰ Φορμίωνος, οἳ προαπῆλθον, νῆές τε αἱ πᾶσαι τὸν αὐτὸν μισθὸν ἔφερον. τὰ μὲν οὖν χρήματα οὕτως ὑπανηλώθη τὸ πρῶτον, καὶ 4
15 νῆες τοσαῦται δὴ πλεῖσται ἐπληρώθησαν.]
18   Μυτιληναῖοι δὲ κατὰ τὸν αὐτὸν χρόνον, ὃν οἱ Λακε- 1
δαιμόνιοι περὶ τὸν Ἰσθμὸν ἦσαν, ἐπὶ Μήθυμναν ὡς προδιδομένην ἐστράτευσαν κατὰ γῆν αὐτοί τε καὶ οἱ ἐπίκουροι·
καὶ προσβαλόντες τῇ πόλει, ἐπειδὴ οὐ προυχώρει ᾗ
5 προσεδέχοντο, ἀπῆλθον ἐπ' Ἀντίσσης καὶ Πύρρας καὶ

61, 4, 1. — ὑπηρέτῃ : as in vi. 102. 10. Each Athenian hoplite was accompanied by an attendant, θεράπων, just as each Spartan by a Helot. *Cf.* iv. 16. 9. — ἐλάμβανε : sc. ὁπλίτης ἕκαστος, to be supplied from δίδραχμοι ὁπλῖται. ἕκαστος ἐλάμβανον was to be expected (*cf.* vii. 27. 8). The omission of ἕκαστος is without parallel in Thuc., or even in Hdt. — 11. τρισχίλιοι κτέ. : see App. — 12. διεπολιόρκησαν : ἅπαξ εἰρημένον. Schol. ἔμειναν ἕως ἁλώσεως τῆς πόλεως πολιορκοῦντες. — ἑξακόσιοι δὲ καὶ χίλιοι κτέ. : *cf.* i. 64. 8; 65. 13, and see on ii. 31. 11. — 13. τὸν αὐτὸν μισθόν : *i.e.* a drachma per man, since the seamen had no θεράποντες. This was double the usual pay of seamen. *Cf.* vi. 31. 19; viii. 45. 11, and see Boeckh, *P. E.* p. 377. — ἔφερον : Schol. ἐλάμβανον, as vi. 24. 13; viii. 97. 7.
15. δή : as l. 2 with the sup., so here with the emphatic τοσαῦται. *Cf.* i. 33. 13; ii. 17. 17; 77. 7. — πλεῖσται : pred., *as the largest number. i.c.* 250.
18. *After the Mytileneans fail in the attack on Methymna, and the*

Methymneans, on the other hand, are repulsed with loss from Antissa, the Athenians send reinforcements under Paches to Lesbos and invest Mytilene with a wall. Beginning of the winter 428-427 B.C.
1. Μυτιληναῖοι δέ : opp. to οἱ δὲ Λακεδαιμόνιοι, c. 16. 9, as well as to οἱ Ἀθηναῖοι, c. 16. 18, and resumes the narrative interrupted at c. 6 fin. — ὄν : see on c. 17. 1. — 2. περὶ τὸν Ἰσθμόν : *cf.* c. 15. 5 to 16. 14. — ἐπὶ Μήθυμναν : *cf.* c. 2. 2, 9. — ὡς προδιδομένην : pres. partic. because the betrayal was, as they thought, then being agitated or prepared for. Kühn. 382, 6 b. — 3. οἱ ἐπίκουροι : prob. mercenaries, mention of whom is made c. 2. 8. The term, which meant originally *allies*, was chiefly applied, prob. euphemistically, to hired soldiers in the service of despots or oligarchical factions. See on i. 115. 18. — 4. οὐ προυχώρει : impers., as in i. 109. 7; ii. 56. 12; iv. 59. 16. See on i. 109. 7. — 5. ἐπ' Ἀντίσσης καὶ Πύρρας καὶ Ἐρέσου : which, though already siding with

Ἐρέσου· καὶ καταστησάμενοι τὰ ἐν ταῖς πόλεσι ταύταις βεβαιότερα καὶ τείχη κρατύναντες διὰ τάχους ἀπῆλθον ἐπ' οἴκου. ἐστράτευσαν δὲ καὶ οἱ Μηθυμναῖοι ἀναχωρη- 2 σάντων αὐτῶν ἐπ' Ἄντισσαν· καὶ ἐκβοηθείας τινὸς γενομέ-
10 νης πληγέντες ὑπό τε τῶν Ἀντισσαίων καὶ τῶν ἐπικούρων ἀπέθανόν τε πολλοὶ καὶ ἀνεχώρησαν οἱ λοιποὶ κατὰ τάχος. οἱ δὲ Ἀθηναῖοι πυνθανόμενοι ταῦτα, τούς τε Μυτιληναίους 3 τῆς γῆς κρατοῦντας καὶ τοὺς σφετέρους στρατιώτας οὐχ ἱκανοὺς ὄντας εἴργειν, πέμπουσι περὶ τὸ φθινόπωρον ἤδη
15 ἀρχόμενον Πάχητα τὸν Ἐπικούρου στρατηγὸν καὶ χιλίους ὁπλίτας ἑαυτῶν. οἱ δὲ αὐτερέται πλεύσαντες τῶν νεῶν 4 ἀφικνοῦνται καὶ περιτειχίζουσι Μυτιλήνην ἐν κύκλῳ ἁπλῷ

the Mytileneans, were to be secured against overtures of the democratic party. — 6. **καταστησάμενοι**: with pred. adj. (βεβαιότερα), as i. 118. 8. — 7. **κρατύναντες**: a poetic word; act., also i. 69. 2; mid., c. 82. 40; iv. 52. 13; 114. 10. In tragedy it = κρατεῖν. — **τείχη**: without article, see on c. 3. 16.

8. **ἐστράτευσαν δέ**: emphatic repetition of the verb, l. 3 (ἐπαναφορά). See on i. 28. 8. A favourite usage of Hdt. — 9. **ἐκβοηθείας**: *a sortie*, found only here; corresponding to ἐκβοηθεῖν, i. 105. 29; Hdt. ix. 26. 11, and freq. in late writers. — 10. **πληγέντες**: μεγάλως νικηθέντες, Schol. Used only in aor. or pf. pass. and always in sense of a severe defeat. *Cf.* iv. 108. 25; v. 14. 5; viii. 38. 7; Hdt. v. 120. 7; viii. 130. 10; Soph. *O. C.* 605; Eur. *Rhes.* 867. — **τῶν ἐπικούρων**: *i.e.* those whom the Mytileneans had left there as a garrison, as indicated in καταστησάμενοι ... βεβαιότερα above. — 11. **πολλοί, οἱ λοιποί**: const. as in c. 13. 17.

12. **ταῦτα**: explained by the two following partic. clauses, which are construed with πυνθανόμενοι, as if ταῦτα had not preceded. Kühn. 469, 3 c. *Cf.* Soph. *Phil.* 1355 πῶς ταῦτ' ἐξανασχήσεσθε, τοῖσιν Ἀτρέως ἐμὲ ξυνόντα παισίν, Ar. *Nub.* 380 τουτί μ' ἐλελήθειν, ὁ Ζεὺς οὐκ ὤν. — 13. **τῆς γῆς κρατοῦντας**: *cf.* c. 6. 8. — 14. **εἴργειν**: *to shut in* the Mytileneans. *Cf.* l. 21. — **περὶ τὸ φθινόπωρον ἤδη ἀρχόμενον**: *cf.* c. 100. 6, and see on ii. 31. 1. μετόπωρον, in vii. 79. 10; viii. 108. 9, seems to be synonymous with φθινόπωρον. — 15. **χιλίους ὁπλίτας**: *cf.* Diod. xii. 85. The number of the fleet is not given here, because the object of the expedition is to strengthen the land force, not the fleet.

16. **αὐτερέται**: pred. The unusual fact that hoplites here served at the oar, evidently for economical reasons (*cf.* c. 19. § 1), is esp. emphasized. *Cf.* i. 10. 26; vi. 91. 15. — 17. **ἀφικνοῦνται καὶ περιτειχίζουσι** ... ἐγκατῳκοδόμη-

τείχει· φρούρια δὲ ἔστιν οἷ ἐπὶ τῶν καρτερῶν ἐγκατῳκο-
δόμηται. καὶ ἡ μὲν Μυτιλήνη κατὰ κράτος ἤδη ἀμφοτέ- 5
20 ρωθεν καὶ ἐκ γῆς καὶ ἐκ θαλάσσης εἴργετο, καὶ ὁ χειμὼν
ἤρχετο γίγνεσθαι.
19   Προσδεόμενοι δὲ οἱ Ἀθηναῖοι χρημάτων ἐς τὴν πολι- 1
ορκίαν, καὶ αὐτοὶ ἐσενεγκόντες τότε πρῶτον ἐσφορὰν
διακόσια τάλαντα, ἐξέπεμψαν καὶ ἐπὶ τοὺς ξυμμάχους

ται: Cl. explains 'to the historical presents corresponds the pf. ἐγκατῳκο-δόμηται, which seems to be used with reference to the forts (φρούρια) first built at suitable points (ἐπὶ καρτερῶν), in which the troops found safety while resting, as well as at night: "they proceed to invest the city with a single wall, and already at strong points in the circuit of the wall forts have been built in." Hence the changes proposed, ἐγκατῳκοδόμητο (Haase), ἐγκατοικοδομεῖται (Bl.), ἐγ-κατῳκοδομήθη (Bk.), ἐγκατῳκοδόμησαν (Kr.) are unnecessary.' Arn. compares Caes. *Bell. Civ.* iii. 37 erant enim circum castra Pompeii permulti editi atque asperi colles; hos primum praesidiis tenuit, castellaque ibi communiit; inde ut loci cuiusque natura ferebat, ex castello in castellum producta munitione, circumvallare Pompeium instituit. But Steup, who contends that the φρούρια were constructed *at the same time with the wall* and built in after the manner of the πύργοι in the double wall around Plataea (c. 21. 8), insists that the pf. is out of place here, since a mere statement of an occurrence was to be made, and that the aor. or impf. is required (*cf.* c. 7. 11; 70. 28, 74. 3). — ἐν κύκλῳ: also c. 74. 8; elsewhere without ἐν, i. 106. 6; ii. 78. 4; 84. 3, *etc.* — 18. ἔστιν οἵ: so most editt. read; Bk. and Bl., ἔστιν ᾗ with five Mss. — ἐπὶ τῶν καρτερῶν: cf. c. 110. 7; ii. 100. 3.

19. καὶ ... εἴργετο: *cf.* the conclusion of the account of the siege of Potidaea, i. 64. § 3. — κατὰ κράτος: applied to any energetic use of force, as in i. 64. 14, and freq. — 20. καὶ ἐκ γῆς καὶ ἐκ θαλάσσης εἴργετο: what had been already in part effected (c. 6. 7) is now completed. *Cf.* viii. 40. 6.

19. *At Athens an extraordinary war tax is levied for the first time. Lysicles, sent out to Caria to collect taxes, is killed there.*

2. καὶ αὐτοί: et ipsi, proleptic, referring to the demands made also upon the allies, καὶ ἐπὶ τοὺς ξυμμάχους. — ἐσφοράν: *i.e.* the extraordinary war tax often levied in later times. See Boeckh, *P. E.* p. 612, who says, doubtless correctly, that τότε πρῶτον (*cf.* i. 96. 6; ii. 56. 6) 'does not mean merely the first property tax levied in the Peloponnesian war, but the first absolutely.' — 3. διακόσια τά-

ἀργυρολόγους ναῦς δώδεκα καὶ Λυσικλέα πέμπτον αὐτὸν
5 στρατηγόν. ὁ δὲ ἄλλα τε ἠργυρολόγει καὶ περιέπλει, 2
καὶ τῆς Καρίας ἐκ Μυοῦντος ἀναβὰς διὰ τοῦ Μαιάνδρου
πεδίου μέχρι τοῦ Σανδίου λόφου, ἐπιθεμένων τῶν Καρῶν
καὶ Ἀναιιτῶν, αὐτός τε διαφθείρεται καὶ τῆς ἄλλης στρατιᾶς πολλοί.
20   Τοῦ δ' αὐτοῦ χειμῶνος οἱ Πλαταιῆς (ἔτι γὰρ ἐπο- 1
λιορκοῦντο ὑπὸ τῶν Πελοποννησίων καὶ Βοιωτῶν), ἐπειδὴ
τῷ τε σίτῳ ἐπιλιπόντι ἐπιέζοντο καὶ ἀπὸ τῶν Ἀθηνῶν

λαντα : appos. to ἐσφοράν. *Cf.* i. 96.
6; ii. 15. 17. — 4. ἀργυρολόγους ναῦς :
ef. iv. 50. 2; 75. 3. Cl. thinks that
the ships were sent out to collect
back tribute (see Köhler, *Abh. der
Berl. Akad.* 1869, p. 132 f.), and that
the unusual number of στρατηγοί (5
with 12 ships) was due to the fact
that this duty would have to be performed at different points. But St.
justly insists that καὶ αὐτοὶ ἐσενεγκόντες
indicates that the same kind of extraordinary tax (ἐσφορά) was levied
on both citizens and allies. — Λυσικλέα : doubtless the demagogue
ridiculed in Ar. *Eq.* 132 as προβατο-
πώλης, who married Aspasia after
Pericles's death. See Plut. *Per.* 24 ;
also Curtius, *Hist. of Gr.* iii. p. 90,
and Ad. Schmidt, *das Perikl. Zeital-
ter* i. p. 178 ff.
5. ἄλλα ἠργυρολόγει : *laid other regions under contribution*. The accus.
as in ii. 69. 7 ; viii. 3. 2. The like
issue of an expedition sent to the
neighbouring coast, as described in
ii. 69, shows with what bitterness the
half barbarian inhabitants of these
regions resisted the collection of the

Athenian tribute. — 6. τῆς Καρίας
ἐκ Μυοῦντος : order as in c. 89. 7 ;
105. 9; i. 100. 15. — 7. τοῦ Σανδίου
λόφου : Meineke (*Herm.* iii. p. 363)
conjectures Σάνδιος (nom. Σάνδις, — see
on i. 64. 10). — 8. Ἀναιιτῶν : without doubt those mentioned c. 32. 4 as
Σαμίων τῶν ἐξ Ἀναίων, namely those
of the oligarchical party, who after
the subjugation of Samos (i. 117. § 3)
settled on the opposite coast. *Cf.* iv.
75. 7 τὰ Ἄναια ἐπὶ τῇ Σάμῳ, and viii.
19. 3. These were always with the
enemies of Athens. — ἄλλης : *besides.
Cf.* c. 112. 7 Δημοσθένης . . . καὶ τὸ ἄλλο
στράτευμα. See on i. 2. 12 ; 128. 21. G.
966, 2 ; H. 705 ; Kr. *Spr.* 50, 4, 11. *Cf.*
Xen. *Cyrop.* vi. 4. 1 ; Tac. *Hist.* iv. 56
legatis . . . interfectis ceterum
vulgus facile accessurum.
    20. *The beleaguered Plataeans de-
termine upon a sortie and make preparations to that end.*
    The events of this and the follow-
ing chapters are briefly narrated also
by Pseudo-Dem. lix. 103; Polyaen.
vi. 19. § 2, 3 ; Diod. xii. 56.
    1. ἔτι . . . Βοιωτῶν : *cf.* ii. 78. § 2 ff.
— 3. σίτῳ ἐπιλιπόντι : partic. in pred.

οὐδεμία ἐλπὶς ἦν τιμωρίας οὐδὲ ἄλλη σωτηρία ἐφαίνετο,
5 ἐπιβουλεύουσιν αὐτοί τε καὶ Ἀθηναίων οἱ ξυμπολιορκού-
μενοι πρῶτον μὲν πάντες ἐξελθεῖν καὶ ὑπερβῆναι τὰ τείχη
τῶν πολεμίων, ἢν δύνωνται βιάσασθαι, ἐσηγησαμένου
τὴν πεῖραν αὐτοῖς Θεαινέτου τε τοῦ Τολμίδου, ἀνδρὸς
μάντεως, καὶ Εὐπομπίδου τοῦ Δαϊμάχου, ὃς καὶ ἐστρα-
10 τήγει· ἔπειτα οἱ μὲν ἡμίσεις ἀπώκνησάν πως τὸν κίνδυ- 2

position in the sense of the verbal subst., = τῇ ἐπιλείψει τοῦ σίτου. *Cf. c.* 29. 9. — **4. τιμωρίας** : = βοηθείας in Thuc. (i. 25. 2, 11; 38. 15; 58. 5; 69. 30, *etc.*) and Hdt. (iii. 148. 14; vii. 169. 11); later, 'vengeance.' — **5. ἐπιβουλεύουσιν** : in this signification only here in Thuc. with inf. (ἐξελθεῖν), freq. with verbal subst. (ἀποχώρησιν, c. 109. 21; κατάλυσιν τῇ τυραννίδι, vi. 54. 15; τὸν ἔκπλουν, vii. 51. 5). For other examples with the inf., *cf.* Hdt. i. 24. 8; Plato *Symp.* 203 b; and see Herbst on Xen. *Sympos.* 4. 52, and Stallbaum on Plato *Prot.* 343 c. —**Ἀθηναίων οἱ ξυμπο-λιορκούμενοι:** *cf.* ii. 6. § 4; 78. § 3. —**7. βιάσασθαι**: 'to force their way through,' abs. in const., as in vii. 67. 24; 79. 8. — **ἐσηγησαμένου τὴν πεῖραν**: *having suggested the attempt.* ἐσηγεῖσθαι = auctorem esse, also iv. 76. 8; vi. 90. 3; 99. 7; vii. 73. 5. —**8. ἀνδρὸς μάντεως**: for the subst. indicating vocation used as adj., see on i. 115. 9; Kr. *Spr.* 57. 1, 1; Kühn. 405, 1. Soothsayers in the army are mentioned also Hdt. ix. 37; Xen. *Hell.* ii. 4. 19. — **9. Εὐπομπί-δου**: so with Bk. (after Palat.) in preference to the clearly incorrect Εὐπολπίδου (of the remaining better

Mss.), as also to Εὐμολπίδου (of inferior Mss.), which Pp. prefers. The name occurs nowhere else, but its very rareness made it more likely to be miscopied. — **ὃς καὶ ἐστρατήγει**: *who was also strategus*, seems to indicate that the attitude of Eupompidas was of esp. importance to the plan of the Plataeans. A similar plan of the strategus Aristeus during the siege of Potidaea (i. 65. § 1) was unsuccessful. *Cf.* also viii. 51. 8; 98. 4. Cl.'s explanation, 'who also directed the execution' of the plan, will not do, since, acc. to c. 22. 1, Eupompidas was not alone in the direction of the scheme. Besides, such an anticipation in the narrative would require the aor. (*cf.* i. 14. 15).

10. ἀπώκνησαν: as in c. 30. 12 (*cf.* vi. 92. 23; viii. 12. 2), with κίνδυνον as obj., which belongs also with μέγαν ἡγησάμενοι. Bl. compares Dem. xviii. 197 οὐδένα κίνδυνον ὀκνήσας ἴδιον, and the imitation of Procopius *B. G.* i., p. 180, 11 τῶν δὲ ἰόντων οἱ ὑπὲρ ἥμισυ, κατωρρωδηκότες τὸν κίνδυνον, ὀπίσω ἀπεκομίζοντο. St. takes ἀπώκνησαν as abs., as in c. 55. 10; iv. 11. 16; vii. 21. 23, supplying from above ἐξελθεῖν καὶ ὑπερβῆναι τὰ τείχη. — **πως**: with omission

νον, μέγαν ἡγησάμενοι, ἐς δὲ ἄνδρας διακοσίους καὶ
εἴκοσι μάλιστα ἐνέμειναν τῇ ἐξόδῳ ἐθελονταὶ τρόπῳ τοιῷδε.
κλίμακας ἐποιήσαντο ἴσας τῷ τείχει τῶν πολεμίων· ξυνε- 3
μετρήσαντο δὲ ταῖς ἐπιβολαῖς τῶν πλίνθων, ᾗ ἔτυχε πρὸς
15 σφᾶς οὐκ ἐξαληλιμμένον τὸ τεῖχος αὐτῶν· ἠριθμοῦντο δὲ
πολλοὶ ἅμα τὰς ἐπιβολὰς καὶ ἔμελλον οἱ μέν τινες ἁμαρτήσεσθαι, οἱ δὲ πλείους τεύξεσθαι τοῦ ἀληθοῦς λογισμοῦ,
ἄλλως τε καὶ πολλάκις ἀριθμοῦντες καὶ ἅμα οὐ πολὺ
ἀπέχοντες, ἀλλὰ ῥᾳδίως καθορωμένου ἐς ὃ ἐβούλοντο

of unnecessary details. — 11. ἐς ἄν-δρας διακοσίους καὶ εἴκοσι μάλιστα: *about two hundred and twenty*, the prepositional phrase representing the subject, as in c. 85. 5; the object. in c. 111. 17; 114. 22; iv. 80. 17; v. 6. 22; vii. 30. 16. Kühn. 432, 1; Kr. *Spr.* 60, 8, 1. Though Arn. be right in saying that in the examples collected by Matth., *Gr. Gr.* 298, 1, ἐς = *up to*, μάλιστα certainly gives here the signification *about*. See on c. 21. 4. — 12. ἐνέμειναν: with dat. in figurative sense also viii. 23. 24. — ἐθελονταί: the resolution adopted by the whole had therefore been annulled.
13. ἐποιήσαντο: the mid., as with ναῦς, i. 14. 14; viii. 56. 21; σταυρώματα, vi. 74. 12. — ἴσας: *sc.* τὸ μῆκος. *Cf.* vii. 42. 10; viii. 10. 8, and freq., where the term denoting number is omitted. — ξυνεμετρήσαντο: *sc.* τὰς κλίμακας, with Heilm. (*cf.* l. 20), rather than τὸ τεῖχος (Pp.). ξυν- indicates the combination of particulars toward a result, as ξυντεκμηράμενοι, ii. 76. 5. *Cf.* Hdt. iv. 158. 6 ξυμμετρησάμενοι τὴν ὥρην τῆς ἡμέρας. As further instances of the same expedient adopted under similar circum- stances, Bl. cites Procop. *B. G.* i. 21; Polyaen. vii. 10. 5; Liv. xxv. 23. — 14. ταῖς ἐπιβολαῖς: *by the layers*, instrum. dative. G. 1181; H. 776; Kühn. 425, 6. — 15. οὐκ ἐξαληλιμμένον: '*not whitewashed*, a term found in Procop. *de Aedif.* p. 4, 22 and 27, 31; *Levit.* xiv. 42, 43, and 48. Thus Pollux vii. 124 τιτάνῳ χρίειν, ἀλείφειν, ἐπαλείφειν, καταλείφειν, ἐξαλείφειν. And so Eustathius explains ἀλείφειν τοῖχον by τὸ κονίᾳ χρίειν. Hence it appears that the translators have here wrongly rendered ἐξαληλιμμένον, "plastered over."' Bl. — ἠριθμοῦντο δὲ πολλοὶ . . . καὶ ἔμελλον: paratactic connexion, in effect = ἐπεὶ πολλοὶ ἠριθμοῦντο, ἔμελλον κτέ.; while, on the other hand, ἔμελλον οἱ μέν τινες ἁμαρτήσεσθαι, οἱ δὲ πλείους τεύξεσθαι = καὶ εἰ οἱ μέν τινες ἡμάρτανον, ὅμως οἱ πλείους τεύξεσθαι ἔμελλον. The rare mid. ἠριθμοῦντο does not differ in meaning from the act., as in Plato *Phaedr.* 270 d. For other examples, see Steph. *Thes. s.v.* Kr. *Spr.* 52, 8, 4; Kühn. 375, 4. — 16. ἔμελλον: see on c. 11. 4; i. 107. 13. — 19. ῥᾳδίως καθορωμένου ἐς ὃ ἐβούλοντο τοῦ τείχους: *sc.* καθορᾶν. *Cf.* Hdt. v. 35. 17 κατιδέσθαι ἐς τὴν

20 τοῦ τείχους. τὴν μὲν οὖν ξυμμέτρησιν τῶν κλιμάκων 4 οὕτως ἔλαβον, ἐκ τοῦ πάχους τῆς πλίνθου εἰκάσαντες τὸ 21 μέτρον. τὸ δὲ τεῖχος ἦν τῶν Πελοποννησίων τοιόνδε τῇ 1 οἰκοδομήσει. εἶχε μὲν δύο τοὺς περιβόλους, πρός τε Πλαταιῶν καὶ εἴ τις ἔξωθεν ἀπ' Ἀθηνῶν ἐπίοι, διεῖχον δὲ οἱ περίβολοι ἑκκαίδεκα πόδας μάλιστα ἀπ' ἀλλήλων. τὸ 2
5 οὖν μεταξὺ τοῦτο, οἱ ἑκκαίδεκα πόδες, τοῖς φύλαξιν οἰκή-

κεφαλήν. καθορωμένου is grammatically construed with τοῦ τείχους, though logically the subj. is ἐς ὃ ἐβούλοντο τοῦ τείχους. The sense of the passage (ἅμα οὐ πολὺ ἀπέχοντες . . . τοῦ τείχους) seems to be: "as they were not far off, but easily looked down upon the part of the wall which they wished to see." It is admissible to supply ὁρᾶν from καθορωμένου. Cf. Eur. Alc. 1065 δοκῶ γὰρ αὐτὴν εἰσορῶν γυναῖχ' ὁρᾶν. For the const. ὁρᾶν ἔς τι, cf. Dem. xi. 10 εἰς τὰ παρόντα ὁρῶν, Aesch. Suppl. 110 ἰδέσθω εἰς ὕβριν, Eur. Peliad. frg. 7 ὁρῶσι δ' οἱ διδόντες εἰς τὰ χρήματα, Paus. i. 24. 2 ἐς αὐτοὺς καιομένους ὁρᾷ. The part of the wall referred to is, of course, ᾗ ἔτυχε πρὸς σφᾶς οὐκ ἐξαληλιμμένον (l. 15). See App.
20. τὴν ξυμμέτρησιν . . . ἔλαβον : periphrasis, as in Plut. Aem. Paul. 15 μεθόδῳ καὶ δι' ὀργάνων εἰληφέναι δοκεῖ τὴν μέτρησιν. For similar periphrases, cf. Soph. Aj. 345; Phil. 536.
— 21. τῆς πλίνθου : the sing. used collectively, as τὸν ἀριστερὸν πόδα, c. 22. 11 ; τῆς κεφαλῆς, ii. 49. 5; τῆς νεώς, vii. 62. 14 ; 65. 7. One might infer from this passage that one thickness of bricks prevailed at that time in Greece, at any rate, in Boeotia. — εἰκάσαντες : aor. partic., synchronous

with ἔλαβον. Cf. ii. 68. 10. Kr. Spr. 53, 6, 8.
21. Description of the wall of circumvallation and of the manner of guarding it.
2. δύο τοὺς περιβόλους : the pred. position of δύο perhaps emphasizes the special precaution against an attack also from without. — πρὸς Πλαταιῶν : on the side toward Plataea. Kr. Spr. 68, 37, 1. Cf. iv. 31. 5; 100. 15 ; 130. 2. — 4. μάλιστα : as used with statements of quantity implies approximation, though the reality may be more or less. Cf. c. 109. 9; 113. 10 ; i. 13. 11.
5. τὸ οὖν μεταξὺ τοῦτο, οἱ ἑκκαίδεκα πόδες . . . ᾠκοδόμητο : this interval, the 16 feet, had been built up as dwelling-places assigned severally to the guards. οἰκήματα is pred., though Thuc. seems, by a sort of anacoluthon, to have construed ᾠκοδόμητο rather with it than with τὸ μεταξὺ τοῦτο, as the following ξυνεχῆ shows. Cl., who thinks the irregularity is caused by the insertion of οἱ ἑκκαίδεκα πόδες, explains οἰκήματα as the real subj. of both members, with τὸ μεταξὺ τοῦτο as adv. modifier. St. strikes out, with v. H. and Widmann, οἱ ἑκκαίδεκα πόδες, and explains οἰκήματα διανενημένα as accus., after the analogy

ματα διανενεμημένα ᾠκοδόμητο, καὶ ἦν ξυνεχῆ ὥστε ἐν
φαίνεσθαι τεῖχος παχὺ ἐπάλξεις ἔχον ἀμφοτέρωθεν. διὰ 3
δέκα δὲ ἐπάλξεων πύργοι ἦσαν μεγάλοι καὶ ἰσοπλατεῖς
τῷ τείχει, διήκοντες ἔς τε τὸ ἔσω μέτωπον αὐτοῦ καὶ οἱ
10 αὐτοὶ καὶ τὸ ἔξω, ὥστε πάροδον μὴ εἶναι παρὰ πύργον,
ἀλλὰ δι᾽ αὐτῶν μέσων διῇσαν. τὰς οὖν νύκτας, ὁπότε 4
χειμὼν εἴη νοτερός, τὰς μὲν ἐπάλξεις ἀπέλειπον, ἐκ δὲ τῶν
πύργων, ὄντων δι᾽ ὀλίγου καὶ ἄνωθεν στεγανῶν, τὴν

of ὄνομα ὀνομάζεσθαι, i. 122. 25. Bl. cites a. case of appos. similar to οἱ ἑκκαίδεκα πόδες from App. Bell. Civ. iv. 106 τὸ δὲ μέσον τῶν λόφων, τὰ ὀκτὼ στάδια, δίοδος ἦν. — 6. διανενημένα: cf. ii. 17. 18, where the more unusual κατανείμασθαι is used. — καὶ ἦν ξυνεχῆ: sc. τὰ οἰκήματα, though Steup thinks this incompatible with the rest of the sent., and renders, it was continuous (i.e. the περίβολοι were connected), the neut. pl. being indef., as in i. 7. 2; S. 8; 102. 6.

7. διὰ δέκα ἐπάλξεων: at intervals of ten battlements, i.e. there were ten battlements or turrets between each two of the greater towers. See Steph. Thes. s.v. διά. G. 1206, 1 c; H. 795, 1 e; Kühn. 434, i. 1 b; Kr. Spr. 68, 22, 3. Cf. δι᾽ ὀλίγου, l. 13; διέχοντες, c. 22. 8. — 8. ἰσοπλατεῖς: rare word for ἴσοι τὸ πλάτος. Thuc. is fond of compounds in ἰσο- (ἰσοδίαιτος, ἰσοκίνδυνος, ἰσόνομος, ἰσοπαλής, ἰσοπληθής, ἰσόρροπος, ἰσόψηφος). Cf. Aesch. Agam. 1444, 1471. — 9. διήκοντες ἔς τε τὸ ἔσω ... καὶ τὸ ἔξω: i.e. the towers united the two walls as if by a bridge. The first καί means and, the second also. See on c. 16. 12; 31. 8. ἐς is omitted before τὸ ἔξω

with nearly all the Mss. Kühn. 451, 2. See on i. 6. 20; vi. 78. 4. οἱ αὐτοί, which is pred., stands in the second clause, as in i. 23. 13, not in the first, as in c. 47. 18; ii. 40. 12; iv. 17. 3. It seems unnecessary to omit either the first καί with L. Herbst (Philol. xxiv. p. 681), or καὶ οἱ αὐτοί with Cobet. — 10. ὥστε πάροδον μὴ εἶναι παρὰ πύργον: so that it was impossible to pass by a tower, i.e. either on the inner or on the outer side. εἶναι in pregnant sense. = ὑπάρχειν, as often, particularly after a neg. See on i. 2. 5. παρὰ πύργον is bracketed by St., following Naber (in v. H.'s Stud. Thuc. p. 39). But it makes the sense clearer, and the sing. before δι᾽ αὐτῶν is used collectively. — 11. διῇσαν: sc. οἱ φύλακες, i.e. in going from one μεταπύργιον to another. For change from inf. to finite verb after ὥστε, see GMT. 603.

12. χειμὼν νοτερός: the adj. is not pred., but forms with χειμών a single conception, rain-storm. Schol. δίυγρος καὶ ὑετὸν ἔχων. The same idea is expressed in c. 22. 2 by χειμέριον ὕδατι καὶ ἀνέμῳ. χειμών is so used iv. 6. 6; 103. 5. — 13. ὄντων: as usual in supplementary causal clauses, placed

φυλακὴν ἐποιοῦντο. τὸ μὲν οὖν τεῖχος ᾧ περιεφρουροῦντο
15 οἱ Πλαταιῆς τοιοῦτον ἦν.

22 Οἱ δ', ἐπειδὴ παρεσκεύαστο αὐτοῖς, τηρήσαντες νύκτα 1
χειμέριον ὕδατι καὶ ἀνέμῳ καὶ ἅμ' ἀσέληνον ἐξῇσαν·
ἡγοῦντο δὲ οἵπερ καὶ τῆς πείρας αἴτιοι ἦσαν. καὶ πρῶτον
μὲν τὴν τάφρον διέβησαν ἣ περιεῖχεν αὐτούς, ἔπειτα προσ-
5 έμειξαν τῷ τείχει τῶν πολεμίων λαθόντες τοὺς φύλακας,
ἀνὰ τὸ σκοτεινὸν μὲν οὐ προϊδόντων αὐτῶν, ψόφῳ δὲ τῷ
ἐκ τοῦ προσιέναι αὐτοὺς ἀντιπαταγοῦντος τοῦ ἀνέμου οὐ

first. *Cf.* c. 2. 9; i. 124. 4. — **δι' ὀλίγου**: *at a little distance*, as c. 43. 14; ii. 89. 41; vii. 71. 9. — **14. περιεφρουροῦντο**: found only here in Thuc., and elsewhere only in late writers, *e.g.* Dio C. xl. 36. See on c. 17. 10.

22. *The 220 Plataeans, who persist in their purpose, scale on a rainy night the encompassing wall.*

1. παρεσκεύαστο: the impers. pass., rarer in Greek than in Latin. See on i. 46. 1. G. 1240, 2; H. 602; Kr. *Spr.* 61, 5, 6; Kühn. 378, N. 2. — **τηρήσαντες . . . ἀσέληνον**: τηρήσαντες also i. 65. 4; iv. 27. 10; vi. 2. 21; as φυλάξαντες, ii. 3. 17; vii. 83. 15. *Cf.* Dion. H. *Ant.* iii. 65. 2 φυλάξαντες νύκτα χειμέριον ὕδασι καὶ ἀνέμῳ, Dio C. lxxxi. 12 ἐτήρησε νύκτα ἀσέληνον καὶ ὑετῷ λάβρῳ βρονταῖς τε χειμέριον. For other imitations see Bl.'s translation (note). The rain was mixed with snow, as shown by ἀνέμῳ ὑπονειφομένῃ, c. 23. 25. — **2. ἐξῇσαν**: impf. of the act in progress, as i. 26. 23; 49. 2, the details of the execution being expressed by aors. διέβησαν (3), προσέμειξαν (4). — **3. οἵπερ καὶ τῆς πείρας αἴτιοι ἦσαν**: see on c. 20. 7, 9. — **4. ἣ περιεῖχεν αὐτούς**: *i.e.* the inner ditch next to the besieged. — **προσέμειξαν τῷ τείχει**: *they reached the foot of the wall.* προσέμειξαν of approach also c. 31. 12; i. 46. 8; vi. 104. 19. On the form see St. *Qu. Gr.*² p. 39; Meisterhans, p. 144. — **6. ἀνὰ τὸ σκοτεινὸν μέν**: *in the darkness.* ἀνά of local extension also iv. 72. 11 (Kühn. 433, 1, 2); not found elsewhere in Thucydides. For position of μέν, see Kühn. 528, 1. — **οὐ προϊδόντων, οὐ κατακουσάντων**: without obj., in the general sense of *see* and *hear*. The gens. abs. after preceding accus. (τοὺς φύλακας), on account of the independent importance of the causes expressed. GMT. 850; H. 972 d; Kr. *Spr.* 47, 4, 2; Kühn. 494 b. *Cf.* c. 13. 30; i. 114. 2. — **αὐτῶν**: *sc.* τῶν φυλάκων. — **ψόφῳ τῷ**: this order, by which stress is thrown on the attribute, is freq. in Thuc. See on i. 1. 6. The dat. depends on ἀντιπαταγοῦντος, which is found only here in Thuc.; elsewhere only in late writers, *e.g.* Arr. *Anab.* v. 12. 3; Dio C. xlviii. 48; Plut. *Mor.* 1000 b.

κατακουσάντων· ἅμα δὲ καὶ διέχοντες πολὺ ἦσαν, ὅπως 2
τὰ ὅπλα μὴ κρουόμενα πρὸς ἄλληλα αἴσθησιν παρέχοι.
10 ἦσαν δὲ εὐσταλεῖς τε τῇ ὁπλίσει καὶ τὸν ἀριστερὸν πόδα
μόνον ὑποδεδεμένοι ἀσφαλείας ἕνεκα τῆς πρὸς τὸν πηλόν.
κατὰ οὖν μεταπύργιον προσέμισγον πρὸς τὰς ἐπάλξεις 3
εἰδότες ὅτι ἐρῆμοί εἰσι, πρῶτον μὲν οἱ τὰς κλίμακας
φέροντες, καὶ προσέθεσαν· ἔπειτα ψιλοὶ δώδεκα ξὺν
15 ξιφιδίῳ καὶ θώρακι ἀνέβαινον, ὧν ἡγεῖτο Ἀμμέας ὁ

8. **διέχοντες πολύ**: *cf.* ii. 81. 14. The measure of πολύ here of course must not be supposed greater than necessity demanded. — 9. **τὰ ὅπλα**: placed for emphasis between ὅπως and μή. *Cf.* viii. 45. 15. — 10. **εὐσταλεῖς τῇ ὁπλίσει**: = ψιλοί, 14, 17. κούφην ὅπλισιν περιβεβλημένοι, Schol. *Cf.* Aesch. *Pers.* 797 εὐσταλῆ στόλον. The armour was of various sorts, acc. to § 3. — **τὸν ἀριστερὸν πόδα μόνον . . . πρὸς τὸν πηλόν**: the emphasis seems to be on μόνον, *i.e.* only the left foot was shod, the right being bare to prevent slipping in the mud. *Cf.* Sall. *Jug.* 94, Ceterum illi, qui escensuri erant, praedocti ab duce, arma ornatumque mutaverant, capite atque pedibus nudis, uti prospectus nisusque per saxa facilius foret. Arnold quotes from Scott's *Lay of Last Minstrel* iv. 8,

" Each better knee was bared to aid
The warrior in the escalade."

But many edd. think the meaning is, that the left foot was shod for security against slipping, the right unshod διὰ κουφότητα, as the Schol. explains. See App.

12. **κατὰ . . . προσέμισγον πρὸς τὰς ἐπάλξεις**: what is summarily stated at l. 5 in the aor. is here repeated, with somewhat more exact designation of the point of attack, in the impf., which tense prevails as far as ἔμελλον, l. 20. With προσέμισγον πρὸς τὰς ἐπάλξεις, *cf.* vii. 22. 8 πρὸς τὰς ἐντὸς προσμεῖξαι. But see App. — 13. **εἰδότες ὅτι ἐρῆμοί εἰσι**: *sc.* on account of the νὺξ χειμέριος, as explained c. 21. § 4. — **πρῶτον μὲν . . .** (19) **ἔφερον**: see App. — 14. **προσέθεσαν**, (16) **ἀνέβη**: these two particular facts alone of the whole account are expressed by the aorist. Arn. says, 'The transition from painting a scene to stating a fact is marked by the variation of tense from ἀνέβαινον to ἀνέβη; the first represents the party in the very act of mounting the wall, the second records the fact that their commander was the first man who did mount it.' — **ἔπειτα**, (17) **ἔπειτα**: after πρῶτον μέν, *cf.* Xen. *Cyrop.* i. 3. 14. — **ξὺν ξιφιδίῳ καὶ θώρακι**: for the collective sing., see Kr. *Spr.* 44, 1, 7. *Cf.* ii. 70. 14. For the use of ξύν, which is chiefly poetic, seldom occurring in Attic prose except in Xen., see G.

Κοροίβου, καὶ πρῶτος ἀνέβη (μετὰ δὲ αὐτὸν οἱ ἑπόμενοι ἐξ ἐφ' ἑκάτερον τῶν πύργων ἀνέβαινον)· ἔπειτα ψιλοὶ ἄλλοι μετὰ τούτους ξὺν δορατίοις ἐχώρουν, οἷς ἕτεροι κατόπιν τὰς ἀσπίδας ἔφερον, ὅπως ἐκεῖνοι ῥᾷον προσβαί- 20 νοιεν, καὶ ἔμελλον δώσειν ὁπότε πρὸς τοῖς πολεμίοις εἶεν. ὡς δὲ ἄνω πλείους ἐγένοντο, ᾔσθοντο οἱ ἐκ τῶν πύργων 4 φύλακες· κατέβαλε γάρ τις τῶν Πλαταιῶν ἀντιλαμβανόμενος ἀπὸ τῶν ἐπάλξεων κεραμίδα, ἣ πεσοῦσα δοῦπον ἐποίησε. καὶ αὐτίκα βοὴ ἦν· τὸ δὲ στρατόπεδον ἐπὶ τὸ 5 25 τεῖχος ὥρμησεν· οὐ γὰρ ᾔδει ὅ τι ἦν τὸ δεινὸν σκοτεινῆς νυκτὸς καὶ χειμῶνος ὄντος, καὶ ἅμα οἱ ἐν τῇ πόλει τῶν Πλαταιῶν ὑπολελειμμένοι ἐξελθόντες προσέβαλλον τῷ τείχει τῶν Πελοποννησίων ἐκ τοὔμπαλιν ἢ οἱ ἄνδρες αὐτῶν

1217; Kühn. 431, 2. — 16. μετὰ δὲ αὐτὸν οἱ ἑπόμενοι: i.e. Ammeas and his eleven companions, who were to attack in two squads of six each the two nearest towers. — 20. εἶεν: for the form. see on c. 42. 22. St. Qu. Gr.² p. 62.
21. ᾔσθοντο: without expressed obj. as i. 95. 21; 118. 9, etc. — οἱ ἐκ τῶν πύργων φύλακες: for the attraction of the prep., see on c. 5. 1 and i. 8. 9. — 23. δοῦπον: Cl. has adopted this reading of one Ms. (A), instead of the vulg. ψόφον, with Bk., Goell., and St., on the ground that it is not only the more appropriate, but also the rarer word, and hence rather to be attributed to Thuc. than to the copyist. It is used chiefly in poetry, but occurs in Xen. Anab. ii. 2. 19. But the vulg. seems to be supported by the imitations which Bl. cites from Dio C. (xliii. 11 and xliv. 17), where ψόφον is read.

24. τὸ δὲ στρατόπεδον ἐπὶ τὸ τεῖχος ὥρμησεν: i.e. the garrison, which had gone into shelter from the rain, now hastened each to his own station on the wall. στρατόπεδον, troops, without reference to any fixed array, as in ii. 25. 9. and freq. — 25. τὸ δεινόν: the danger. Cf. i. 70. 11; 84. 8; 120. 13. — σκοτεινῆς νυκτὸς . . . ὄντος: the partic. belongs to both substs., σκοτεινῆς νυκτός being treated as a single word. — 26. τῶν Πλαταιῶν: the part. gen. in the very unusual position between the art. and partic., as in c. 36. 19; 65. 14; i. 126. 33; vi. 102. 1. See Merriam, Trans. Am. Philol. Assoc. 1882, p. 45. Kr. Spr. 47, 9, 11. — 27. προσέβαλλον: so Stcup reads (for the vulg. προσέβαλον), with two Mss. (C and f), as being more natural in describing an event that was not momentary, and in accordance with the following impfs. Cf. esp. παρανίσχον, l. 35. — 28. ἐκ τοὔμπαλιν ἤ: from

ὑπερέβαινον, ὅπως ἥκιστα πρὸς αὐτοὺς τὸν νοῦν ἔχοιεν.
30 ἐθορυβοῦντο μὲν οὖν κατὰ χώραν μένοντες, βοηθεῖν δὲ 6
οὐδεὶς ἐτόλμα ἐκ τῆς αὐτῶν φυλακῆς, ἀλλ' ἐν ἀπόρῳ
ἦσαν εἰκάσαι τὸ γιγνόμενον. καὶ οἱ τριακόσιοι αὐτῶν, 7
οἷς ἐτέτακτο παραβοηθεῖν εἴ τι δέοι, ἐχώρουν ἔξω τοῦ
τείχους πρὸς τὴν βοήν, φρυκτοί τε ᾔροντο ἐς τὰς
35 Θήβας πολέμιοι. παρανῖσχον δὲ καὶ οἱ ἐκ τῆς πόλεως 8

the opposite side. ἔμπαλιν ἤ also in Hdt. i. 207. 13; ix. 56. 8. ἤ as in τοὐναντίον ἤ, vi. 68. 14; vii. 80. 6; Plato *Gorg.* 481 c. — 29. ὑπερέβαινον: with the corresponding οἱ ὑπερβαίνοντες (c. 23. 1), of what was at that time going on. — πρὸς αὐτοὺς τὸν νοῦν ἔχοιεν: *give attention to them.* Cf. vii. 19. 32; viii. 8. 16.
30. ἐθορυβοῦντο: *were in great excitement.* Cf. v. 65. 28. — **κατὰ χώραν**: *at their post.* Cf. i. 28. 18.
— **31. ἐκ τῆς αὐτῶν φυλακῆς**: *from the post assigned to each.* αὐτῶν, or ἑαυτῶν, is both by position and emphasis preferable to αὐτῶν of most of the Mss.; for as the οὐδείς clause is only the complement of κατὰ χώραν μένοντες, the pl. αὐτῶν refers back to the subj. of ἐθορυβοῦντο. G. 960; H. 673 b. Cf. c. 91. 6; viii. 48. 28. St. reads αὑτῶν (intensive). Kr. *Spr.* 47, 9, 12. — **ἐν ἀπόρῳ ἦσαν εἰκάσαι τὸ γιγνόμενον**: *they were at a loss to conjecture what was going on.* Cf. i. 25. 2 ἐν ἀπόρῳ εἴχοντο θέσθαι τὸ παρόν.
32. οἱ τριακόσιοι: for the art., see on c. 3. 18. The number is a favourite one for a corps of picked men, esp. among the Lacedaemonians. See Trieber, *N. Jahrbb.* ciii. p. 443 ff.

Cf. ii. 25. 17; iv. 70. 14; 125. 19. — **33. ἐτέτακτο**: impers., as in c. 61. 12, and with dat. and inf., as i. 19. 6; v. 31. 10 (Kr., ἐπετέτακτο; Cobet, προσετέτακτο). — **ἐχώρουν ἔξω τοῦ τείχους πρὸς τὴν βοήν**: since the towers from which the cry of alarm came were, as all the rest, ἰσοπλατεῖς τῷ τείχει (c. 21. 9), one could not know whether the danger was from the city or from without; but under the circumstances it was natural to think first of danger from without, *i.e.* from Athens. And so the 300, as well as the guards of the remaining towers, left the Plataeans, who were crossing, for the time unmolested. ἐχώρουν πρὸς τὴν βοήν, *i.e.* to the place whence the cry came, in the proper sense of βοηθεῖν. The φρυκτοὶ πολέμιοι were signals to indicate danger from the enemy. Cf. ii. 94. 1. From this place and c. 80. 7, Arn. infers (against the Schol. and Polyb. x. 40) considerable proficiency in the art of signalling. See Merriam, *Telegraphing among the Ancients*, Arch. Inst. Am., Classical Series iii.
— **35. παρανῖσχον**: lit. *raised by the side of*, *i.e.* so as to counteract the others. The compound not found elsewhere in Thuc.; intr. in Plut.

Πλαταιῆς ἀπὸ τοῦ τείχους φρυκτοὺς πολλοὺς πρότερον παρεσκευασμένους ἐς αὐτὸ τοῦτο, ὅπως ἀσαφῆ τὰ σημεῖα τῆς φρυκτωρίας τοῖς πολεμίοις ᾖ καὶ μὴ βοηθοῖεν, ἄλλο τι νομίσαντες τὸ γιγνόμενον εἶναι ἢ 40 τὸ ὄν, πρὶν σφῶν οἱ ἄνδρες οἱ ἐξιόντες διαφύγοιεν 23 καὶ τοῦ ἀσφαλοῦς ἀντιλάβοιντο. οἱ δ' ὑπερβαίνοντες 1 τῶν Πλαταιῶν ἐν τούτῳ, ὡς οἱ πρῶτοι αὐτῶν ἀνεβεβήκεσαν καὶ τοῦ πύργου ἑκατέρου τοὺς φύλακας διαφθείραντες ἐκεκρατήκεσαν τάς τε διόδους τῶν πύργων 5 ἐνστάντες αὐτοὶ ἐφύλασσον μηδένα δι' αὐτῶν ἐπιβοηθεῖν,

Aemil. Paul. 32. — 37. ὅπως ... ᾖ καὶ μὴ βοηθοῖεν : the same change of mood as in vi. 96. 18, 19 ; vii. 17. 15, 17 ; viii. 87. 14, 17. GMT. 321 ; Kr. *Spr.* 54, 8, 2 ; Kühn. 553, 6. — 38. τῆς φρυκτωρίας : as Ar. *Aves* 1161 ; Aesch. *Agam.* 33, 490. *Cf.* φρυκτωροί, viii. 102. 2 ; φρυκτωρεῖν, c. 80. 7. — 40. οἱ ἐξιόντες : *cf.* c. 20. 6 ; 22. 2. — πρὶν διαφύγοιεν : opt. by assimilation after μὴ βοηθοῖεν. GMT. 643 ; Kühn. 399, 6 b. — 41. τοῦ ἀσφαλοῦς ἀντιλάβοιντο: *reach safety. Cf.* iv. 128. 12 ; vii. 60. 17 ; 77. 29. For the gen., see G. 1099 ; H. 738 ; Kühn. 416, 2.

23. *They succeed in crossing the wall and the outer ditch.*

1. οἱ ὑπερβαίνοντες τῶν Πλαταιῶν : these words are the general subj. of the whole sent., which is afterwards distributed into οἱ μέν (7), οἱ δέ (9). The expression stands, as σφῶν οἱ ἄνδρες οἱ ἐξιόντες, c. 22. 40, opp. to οἱ ἐν τῇ πόλει τῶν Πλαταιῶν ὑπολελειμμένοι, c. 22. 27, or οἱ ἐκ τῆς πόλεως Πλαταιῆς, c. 22. 36 ; 24. 15, and answers to the const. ἐκ τοὔμπαλιν ἢ οἱ ἄνδρες αὐτῶν ὑπερέβαινον, c. 22. 29.

The pres. partic. is used to designate all the participants so long as the undertaking lasts. See on c. 4. 13. — **2.** ὡς οἱ πρῶτοι αὐτῶν ... ἐπιβοηθεῖν : parenthetical subord. clause. See Steup, following Pp., *Rh. Mus.* xxxiii. p. 253 f. Most commentators end the parenthetical clause at ἐκεκρατήκεσαν, and make τε, in l. 4, correl. to καί in l. 6. But, with this const., ἀπὸ τῶν πύργων ... βάλλοντες would be a mere repetition of τάς τε διόδους ... ἐπιβοηθεῖν. The first part of the parenthetical clause is not resumptive, but progressive, since above (c. 22. 21) only a number of the detachment of Ammeas was said to have ascended the wall, while here οἱ πρῶτοι αὐτῶν includes not only the whole twelve, but also those armed with spears. — **3.** τοῦ πύργου ἑκατέρου: *cf.* c. 22. 17. — **4.** τὰς διόδους τῶν πύργων : i.e. the passages through the lower part of the towers. *Cf.* c. 21. 11. — **5.** αὐτοί : opp. to the former guards. See on i. 100. 14. — ἐφύλασσον μηδένα ... ἐπιβοηθεῖν : *cf.* vii. 17. 5 ; also ii. 69. 4 φυλακὴν εἶχε μήτ' ἐκπλεῖν.

καὶ κλίμακας προσθέντες ἀπὸ τοῦ τείχους τοῖς πύργοις καὶ ἐπαναβιβάσαντες ἄνδρας πλείους οἱ μὲν ἀπὸ τῶν πύργων τοὺς ἐπιβοηθοῦντας καὶ κάτωθεν καὶ ἄνωθεν εἶργον βάλλοντες, οἱ δ' ἐν τούτῳ οἱ πλείους πολλὰς προσθέντες
10 κλίμακας ἅμα καὶ τὰς ἐπάλξεις ἀπώσαντες διὰ τοῦ μεταπυργίου ὑπερέβαινον. ὁ δὲ διακομιζόμενος αἰεὶ ἵστατο ἐπὶ 2 τοῦ χείλους τῆς τάφρου καὶ ἐντεῦθεν ἐτόξευόν τε καὶ ἠκόντιζον, εἴ τις παραβοηθῶν παρὰ τὸ τεῖχος κωλυτὴς γίγνοιτο τῆς διαβάσεως. ἐπεὶ δὲ πάντες διεπεπεραίωντο, οἱ ἀπὸ 3
15 τῶν πύργων, χαλεπῶς οἱ τελευταῖοι καταβαίνοντες, ἐχώρουν

The const., μή with inf., is the same as with κωλύειν. — **6. καί**: *also*. It was not deemed sufficient simply to guard the passages of the towers. — **7. πλείους**: *several, a number*, as in c. 22. 21, or possibly, *more, sc.* than those that guarded the passages below. — **8. καὶ κάτωθεν καὶ ἄνωθεν**: belongs to εἶργον, not to ἐπιβοηθοῦντας, and, with a reference to τὰς διόδους φυλάσσοντες, as well as to ἐπαναβιβάσαντες, more fully explains ἀπὸ τῶν πύργων. Kr. explains, '*they kept back from the towers* the advancing foe, shooting at them from below and from above.' — **9. οἱ δέ**: *i.e.* those still at the foot of the wall; οἱ πλείους being appos., as in viii. 80. 13, but not restrictive, as in ii. 4. 19. — προσθέντες: *sc.* τῷ τείχει. — **10. ἅμα**: connects προσθέντες closely with ἀπώσαντες. — **11. ὑπερέβαινον**: includes, acc. to what follows, also the crossing of the outer ditch.

ὁ δὲ διακομιζόμενος αἰεὶ ἵστατο: *always as one came over he halted*. αἰεί belongs not only to the iterative partic. ὁ διακομιζόμενος (= ὁπότε τις διακομίζοιτο), but also to ἵστατο, — hence its position. Kr. *Spr.* 50, 10, 5. See on i. 2. 4. The pl. idea implied in this clause finds expression in the verbs that follow. — **ἐπὶ τοῦ χείλους τῆς τάφρου**: *i.e.* the outer ditch (c. 24. 13), to be distinguished from the inner mentioned c. 22. 4. With χεῖλος, *bank, cf.* labrum fossae, Liv. xxxvii. 37. — **13. παρὰ τὸ τεῖχος**: *by the side of the wall*. — **κωλυτὴς γίγνοιτο τῆς διαβάσεως**: = κωλύοι τὴν διάβασιν. See on c. 2. 11.

14. πάντες: *sc.* except those still on the two towers. — **15. χαλεπῶς οἱ τελευταῖοι καταβαίνοντες**: parenthetical, *the last descending with difficulty*. οἱ τελευταῖοι is in part. appos. to οἱ ἀπὸ τῶν πύργων, as i. 119. 5; ii. 54. 4. Of the smaller detachment (= οἱ ἀπὸ τῶν πύργων = οἱ μέν, l. 7 above), under whose protection the larger division crossed the wall, those who descended last got down with difficulty, being hard pressed doubtless by the enemy, who must have pushed after them through the towers. See Steup, *Rh. Mus.* xxxiii. p. 255. Arn., Bl., and

ἐπὶ τὴν τάφρον, καὶ ἐν τούτῳ οἱ τριακόσιοι αὐτοῖς ἐπεφέροντο λαμπάδας ἔχοντες. οἱ μὲν οὖν Πλαταιῆς ἐκείνους 4
ἑώρων μᾶλλον ἐκ τοῦ σκότους ἑστῶτες ἐπὶ τοῦ χείλους τῆς
τάφρου, καὶ ἐτόξευόν τε καὶ ἐσηκόντιζον ἐς τὰ γυμνά, αὐτοὶ
20 δὲ ἐν τῷ ἀφανεῖ ὄντες ἧσσον διὰ τὰς λαμπάδας καθεωρῶντο. ὥστε φθάνουσι τῶν Πλαταιῶν καὶ οἱ ὕστατοι διαβάντες τὴν τάφρον, χαλεπῶς δὲ καὶ βιαίως · κρύσταλλός 5
τε γὰρ ἐπεπήγει οὐ βέβαιος ἐν αὐτῇ ὥστ' ἐπελθεῖν, ἀλλ'
οἷος ἀπηλιώτου † ἢ βορέου ὑδατώδης μᾶλλον, καὶ ἡ νὺξ
25 τοιούτῳ ἀνέμῳ ὑπονειφομένη πολὺ τὸ ὕδωρ ἐν αὐτῇ ἐπεποιήκει, ὃ μόλις ὑπερέχοντες ἐπεραιώθησαν. ἐγένετο δὲ

Jow. take only χαλεπῶς οἱ τελευταῖοι as parenthetical. — 16. οἱ τριακόσιοι: cf. c. 22. 33.
18. μᾶλλον: *more*, i.e. better. Cf. ἧσσον, l. 20. — ἐκ τοῦ σκότους: cf. Xen. *Anab.* vii. 4. 18 ἠκόντιζον εἰς τὸ φῶς ἐκ τοῦ σκότους. — 19. τὰ γυμνά: i.e. the unprotected parts of the body, as in v. 10. 17; 71. 6. Cf. Liv. xxii. 50 in latus dextrum quod patebat Numidae iacularentur.
— 20. διὰ τὰς λαμπάδας: i.e. the enemy's torches, which lighted only the space just around the bearers. —
22. βιαίως: *hard pressed.* Kühn. 497, 5. Cf. ii. 33. 14 βιαιότερον ἀναγόμενοι, iv. 31. 15 ἀναχώρησις βιαιοτέρα, v. 73. 22 ἀποχώρησις οὐ βίαιος.
κρύσταλλος ἐπεπήγει : cf. Aesch. *Pers.* 501 περᾷ κρυσταλλοπῆγα διὰ πόρον, Eur. *Rhes.* 441 φυσήματα κρυσταλλόπηκτα. — 23. ἐπελθεῖν: διαδραμεῖν, Schol. — 24. οἷος ἀπηλιώτου ἢ βορέου ὑδατώδης μᾶλλον: *such as (is formed) when the wind is east instead of north, rather watery.* This interpretation, given by the Schol. and

Va., and adopted by Arn., Bl., and Jow., is doubtless the best that can be made out of the text as it stands. For the omission of μᾶλλον before ἤ, which Jow. thinks is softened by its occurrence after ὑδατώδης, Arn. cites Soph. *Ajax* 966 ἐμοὶ πικρὸς τέθνηκεν ἢ κείνοις γλυκύς. Dobree brackets ἢ βορέου. Pp. would transpose ὑδατώδης μᾶλλον, or bracket ὑδατώδης. For the temporal gens., see G. 1136; H. 759; Kühn. 418, 8 b; Kr. *Spr.* 47, 2, 1. On the form ἀπηλιώτης, see Lobeck on Soph. *Aj.* 805. ὑδατώδης occurs only here in Thuc. — καὶ ἡ νὺξ . . . ὑπονειφομένη: *and the night with such a wind somewhat snowy* (lit. *besnowed*). A bold and rather poetic use of ὑπονειφομένη that seems not to be found elsewhere. Cf. ὑπένειφεν, iv. 103. 5. On the form ὑπονειφομένη, which most of the best Mss. have, see J. Schmidt, *zur Gesch. d. indogerm. Vokalismus* i. p. 134; Stahl *Qu. Gr.*² p. 39. Cobet, *ad Hyper.* p. 57, prefers ὑπονιφομένη.
— 26. ὃ μόλις ὑπερέχοντες ἐπεραιώθησαν: *which they crossed scarcely keep-*

καὶ ἡ διάφευξις αὐτοῖς μᾶλλον διὰ τοῦ χειμῶνος τὸ μέ-
24 γεθος. ὁρμήσαντες δὲ ἀπὸ τῆς τάφρου οἱ Πλαταιῆς ἐχώ- 1
ρουν ἁθρόοι τὴν ἐς Θήβας φέρουσαν ὁδόν, ἐν δεξιᾷ ἔχοντες τὸ τοῦ Ἀνδροκράτους ἡρῷον, νομίζοντες ἥκιστα
σφᾶς ταύτην αὐτοὺς ὑποτοπῆσαι τραπέσθαι τὴν ἐς τοὺς
5 πολεμίους· καὶ ἅμα ἑώρων τοὺς Πελοποννησίους τὴν
πρὸς Κιθαιρῶνα καὶ Δρυὸς κεφαλὰς τὴν ἐπ' Ἀθηνῶν
φέρουσαν μετὰ λαμπάδων διώκοντας. καὶ ἐπὶ μὲν ἓξ ἢ 2

ing (their heads) *above*. ὅ belongs to both partic. and verb. For ὑπερέχειν with acc. in fig. sense, *cf.* Eur. *Hipp.* 1365. — ἐγένετο ... μᾶλλον : Cl. explains that ἐγένετο is not merely passive of ποιεῖσθαι, but has the stronger meaning of successful accomplishment, as in v. 55. 15; vi. 74. 3; viii. 57. 8. "And their escape was accomplished more, etc." But *cf.* vii. 41. 3 τὴν κατάφευξιν ἐποιοῦντο. The idea of successful accomplishment is inseparable from the expression ἐγένετο ἡ διάφευξις. διάφευξις, which occurs elsewhere only in late writers, for διαφυγή, acc. to Thuc.'s preference for forms in -σις, which appears esp. in connexion with the pass. γίγνεσθαι. *Cf.* c. 92. 16; i. 73. 1; 75. 14; ii. 11. 17; 14. 7; 94. 2; iv. 74. 18; 85. 1; 113.1; 116. 10; v. 82. 18; vi. 103. 17; vii. 42. 7; viii. 21. 2; 66. 9; 89. 26; 97. 13. On Thuc.'s use of verbal nouns in -σις, see Introd. to Book I. p. 49, and Sihler, *Trans. Amer. Philol. Assoc.* xii. p. 96 ff. — **27. διὰ τοῦ χειμῶνος τὸ μέγεθος**: for the order, see on i. 32. 8.

24. *212 men, having eluded their pursuers, reach Athens.*

3. τὸ τοῦ Ἀνδροκράτους ἡρῷον: the temenos of the Platacan hero Androcrates, who is mentioned by Plut. *Arist.* 11, is referred to also by Hdt. ix. 25. 18, and Plut. *ibid.* — **νομίζοντες ... ἐς τοὺς πολεμίους**: *thinking those would least suspect that they had taken this road, which led to the enemy*. The irregularity in the order of words arose from emphasizing σφᾶς ταύτην. For the rare verb ὑποτοπῆσαι, used by Thuc. elsewhere only in aor. partic., see on i. 20. 9, and for aor. inf. after νομίζειν referring to the future, see note and App. on ii. 3. 9. St. inserts ἂν after ἥκιστα. GMT. 127; Kühn. 389, N. 8. — **5. τὴν πρὸς Κιθαιρῶνα καὶ Δρυὸς κεφαλάς**: through this pass, called by the Athenians, from the wood-covered peaks, Δρυὸς κεφαλαί, by the Boeotians, from the three easily distinguishable summits, Τρεῖς κεφαλαί (Hdt. ix. 39. 5), ran one of the three main roads between Boeotia and Attica in a southeasterly direction by Eleutherae. See Vischer, *Erinnerungen aus Griechenland*, p. 533; Bursian i. p. 249. — **7. μετὰ λαμπάδων**: *cf.* c. 23. 17. — **διώκοντας**: abs., *hastening forward*. For the acc. connected with διώκοντας, as well as those with ἐχώ-

ἑπτὰ σταδίους οἱ Πλαταιῆς τὴν ἐπὶ τῶν Θηβῶν ἐχώρησαν, ἔπειθ᾽ ὑποστρέψαντες ἦσαν τὴν πρὸς τὸ ὄρος φέρουσαν ὁδὸν ἐς Ἐρύθρας καὶ Ὑσιάς, καὶ λαβόμενοι τῶν ὀρῶν διαφεύγουσιν ἐς τὰς Ἀθήνας, ἄνδρες δώδεκα καὶ διακόσιοι ἀπὸ πλειόνων· εἰσὶ γάρ τινες αὐτῶν οἳ ἀπετράποντο ἐς τὴν πόλιν πρὶν ὑπερβαίνειν, εἷς δ᾽ ἐπὶ τῇ ἔξω τάφρῳ τοξότης ἐλήφθη. οἱ μὲν οὖν Πελοποννήσιοι κατὰ χώραν ἐγένοντο τῆς βοηθείας παυσάμενοι· οἱ δ᾽ ἐκ τῆς πόλεως Πλαταιῆς τῶν μὲν γεγενημένων εἰδότες οὐδέν, τῶν δὲ ἀποτραπομένων σφίσιν ἀπαγγειλάντων ὡς οὐδεὶς περίεστι, κήρυκα ἐκπέμψαντες, ἐπεὶ ἡμέρα ἐγένετο, ἐσπένδοντο ἀναίρεσιν τοῖς νεκροῖς, μαθόντες δὲ τὸ ἀληθὲς ἐπαύσαντο.

Οἱ μὲν δὴ τῶν Πλαταιῶν ἄνδρες οὕτως ὑπερβάντες

ρησαν and ἦσαν below, see G. 1057; Kühn. 409, 1, 7.

9. τὴν πρὸς τὸ ὄρος ... Ὑσιάς: this road, which branched off eastward not far from Plataea, is to be distinguished from that which led directly from Thebes to Hysiae, mentioned by Paus. ix. 1. 6 οὗ τὴν εὐθεῖαν ἀπὸ τῶν Θηβῶν τὴν πεδιάδα, τὴν δὲ ἐπὶ Ὑσιὰς πρὸς Ἐλευθερῶν τε καὶ τῆς Ἀττικῆς. — **10. ἐς Ἐρύθρας καὶ Ὑσιάς:** the remoter point is mentioned first, for Erythrae was east of Hysiae. Cf. c. 29. 6, and see on ii. 7. 16. For the accent of Ἐρύθρας, see Eustathius on Hom. B 499 Ἐρύθραι μὲν βαρυτόνως αἱ τῆς Βοιωτίας, Ἐρυθραὶ δὲ ὀξυτόνως αἱ τῆς Ἰωνίας. — **λαβόμενοι:** having reached, with gen., as in c. 106. 10; viii. 80. 13. G. 1099; H. 739; Kühn. 416, 2. Cf. ἀντιλαβέσθαι in the same sense c. 22. **1. — 12. ἀπὸ πλειόνων:** i.e. the 220 mentioned in c. 20. 11. ἀπό as in c. 112. 30; i. 49. 25; 110. 2; vii. 87. 26. Kühn. 414, N. 4. — **εἰσί τινες οἵ:** treated as a single subst., some, hence the pres. is retained. G. 1029; H. 998.

14. κατὰ χώραν ἐγένοντο: returned to their post. Cf. κατὰ ξυλλόγους γίγνεσθαι, c. 27. 7; κατὰ ξυστάσεις γίγνεσθαι, ii. 21. 15; ἐν ταῖς χώραις ἕκαστοι ἐγένοντο, Xen. Anab. iv. 8. 15. κατὰ χώραν is found elsewhere only with μένειν (c. 22. 30; i. 28. 18; ii. 58. 17; iv. 14. 28; 26. 3; 76. 26; vii. 49. 24; viii. 71. 21; 86. 16). — **15. τῆς βοηθείας:** see on c. 22. 34. — **οἱ ἐκ τῆς πόλεως:** the proleptic use of ἐκ caused by the following κήρυκα ἐκπέμψαντες. See on c. 22. 22. — **18. ἐσπένδοντο ἀναίρεσιν τοῖς νεκροῖς:** conative impf. Schol. σπονδὰς ἐζήτουν ποιῆσαι. GMT. 36; Kühn. 382, 6 b. With acc. of thing and dat. of person also c. 109. 10; 114. 11. Kühn. 424, N. 1 b. — **21. οἱ μὲν δὴ ... οὕτως ὑπερβάντες**

25 ἐσώθησαν. ἐκ δὲ τῆς Λακεδαίμονος τοῦ αὐτοῦ χειμῶνος τελευτῶντος ἐκπέμπεται Σάλαιθος ὁ Λακεδαιμόνιος ἐς Μυτιλήνην τριήρει. καὶ πλεύσας ἐς Πύρραν καὶ ἐξ αὐτῆς πεζῇ κατὰ χαράδραν τινά, ᾗ ὑπερβατὸν ἦν τὸ περι-
5 τείχισμα, διαλαθὼν ἐσέρχεται ἐς τὴν Μυτιλήνην, καὶ ἔλεγε τοῖς προέδροις ὅτι ἐσβολή τε ἅμα ἐς τὴν Ἀττικὴν ἔσται καὶ αἱ τεσσαράκοντα νῆες παρέσονται ἃς ἔδει βοηθῆσαι αὐτοῖς, προαποπεμφθῆναί τε αὐτὸς τούτων ἕνεκα καὶ ἅμα τῶν ἄλλων ἐπιμελησόμενος. καὶ οἱ μὲν Μυτιλη- 2

ἐσώθησαν: *cf.* c. 20. 12 ἐνέμειναν τῇ ἐξόδῳ ἐθελονταὶ τρόπῳ τοιῷδε. The fate of the city and of those who remained in it is narrated in c. 52–68.

25. *The beleaguered Mytileneans are encouraged to hold out by the Lacedaemonian Salaethus, who steals into the city.*

2. ὁ Λακεδαιμόνιος: the art., suspected by Kr., is protected by c. 100. 11; v. 52. 3; viii. 26. 8; 35. 2. The use of the art. is nowhere more variable than with names of peoples. — **ἐς Μυτιλήνην**: which was in the condition described c. 18. § 5. — **3. ἐς Πύρραν**: on the inmost recess of the bay which extends from the west coast deep into the island, whence the distance to Mitylene was shortest. — **4. κατὰ χαράδραν τινά**: *i.e.* along the dry bed of a torrent. *Cf.* c. 98. 7; 107. 14; 112. 22. — **ᾗ ὑπερβατὸν ἦν**: if the text be sound, either, as Bl., because the wall of the Athenians had not been completed across the ravine, or, as St., because it was lower there and less carefully guarded. Steup, who assumes that the wall must have been everywhere of the same height — measured from base to top — and hence not easier to *cross* in the ravine than elsewhere, favors Cl.'s suggestion of an outlet for the water left open in the bed of the torrent, in which case v. Herw.'s conjecture ὑποβατόν, for ὑπερβατόν, would be probable. — **5. διαλαθών**: *i.e.* λάθρᾳ διελθών or ὑπερβάς. Contrary to the usual const., λανθάνω takes here the form of the limiting participle. GMT. 893; Kühn. 482, s. 14. — **6. τοῖς προέδροις**: prob. the official title of the ruling board under the oligarchical constitution of Mytilene. *Cf.* viii. 67. 15. where the first five men to be chosen under the constitution proposed by Pisander are called πρόεδροι. See Plehn, *Lesbos*, p. 93. — **7. αἱ τεσσαράκοντα νῆες**: *cf.* c. 16. § 3. — **8. προαποπεμφθῆναί τε**: the particle introduces the *third* member. For the change from const. with ὅτι to inf., *cf.* c. 2. 12, 15; 3. 12, 14, and see on i. 87. 11. Kühn. 550, s. 3. — **9. καὶ ἅμα . . . ἐπιμελησόμενος**: for partic. co-ord. with prepositional phrase, *cf.* c. 34. 17; 42. 23; i. 39. 2; 80. 3; ii. 89. 22.

10 ναῖοι ἐθάρσουν τε καὶ πρὸς τοὺς Ἀθηναίους ἧσσον εἶχον τὴν γνώμην ὥστε ξυμβαίνειν. ὅ τε χειμὼν ἐτελεύτα οὗτος, καὶ τέταρτον ἔτος τῷ πολέμῳ ἐτελεύτα τῷδε ὃν Θουκυδίδης ξυνέγραψεν.

26 *Τοῦ δ' ἐπιγιγνομένου θέρους οἱ Πελοποννήσιοι, 1 ἐπειδὴ τὰς ἐς τὴν Μυτιλήνην [δύο καὶ τεσσαράκοντα] ναῦς ἀπέστειλαν, ἄρχοντα Ἀλκίδαν. ὃς ἦν αὐτοῖς ναύαρχος, προστάξαντες, αὐτοὶ ἐς τὴν Ἀττικὴν καὶ οἱ ξύμμαχοι 5 ἐσέβαλον, ὅπως οἱ Ἀθηναῖοι ἀμφοτέρωθεν θορυβούμε-

10. πρὸς τοὺς Ἀθηναίους: Cl. construes with ἧσσον εἶχον τὴν γνώμην, as v. 44. 7; 48. 10; Xen. Anab. ii 5. 29 (cf. also Thuc. v. 13. 8; 14. 4), they had their mind less turned (were less inclined) to the Athenians, ὥστε ξυμβαίνειν being an explanatory addition. But Steup connects πρὸς τοὺς Ἀθηναίους with ξυμβαίνειν, comparing c. 27. 3, in which case the order of words would be as in vii. 86. 12 τοὺς γὰρ ἐκ τῆς νήσου ἄνδρας τῶν Λακεδαιμονίων ὁ Νικίας προυθυμήθη ... ὥστε ἀφεθῆναι, and ὥστε pleonastic after εἶχον τὴν γνώμην, as often after πείθειν (see on c. 31. 10), παρασκευάζειν (c. 36. 20), δεῖσθαι (i. 119. 7), ψηφίζεσθαι (v. 17. 20; vi. 88. 47), δόξαν (viii. 79. 2). ξυγχωρεῖσθαι (v. 17. 12). Kühn. 473, n. 6. This certainly brings out more clearly the evident sense of the passage. — 11. ὅ τε χειμὼν κτέ.: only here is this formula for the conclusion of the year introduced by τε, and so this winter ended. Generally the connexion is looser: with καί, as c. 88. 13; ii. 47. 2; 103. 5; iv. 51. 5; 116. 14; 135. 8; v. 39. 18; 51. 10; 56. 19; 81. 10; 83. 20; vi. 7. 24; 93. 20;

vii. 18. 32; viii. 6. 32; 60. 16; or with μέν (in résumé), as c. 116. 7; ii. 70. 21.

FIFTH YEAR OF THE WAR.

cc. 26-88.

26. The next spring the Peloponnesians send a fleet to succour Mytilene, and make at the same time a fourth invasion of Attica.

1. οἱ Πελοποννήσιοι ... (4) αὐτοὶ καὶ οἱ ξύμμαχοι: see on c. 1. 1. — 2. [δύο καὶ τεσσαράκοντα]: Cl. explains that here, where the actual sending of the expedition is described, the exact number is given instead of the round number forty used elsewhere in the account (c. 16. 16; 25. 7; 29. 1; 69. 1). Arn. thinks the two additional ships may have been the Spartan contingent, which in such expeditions was always small. Cf. viii. 6. 31. Steup brackets the words. See App. — 3. ἄρχοντα: for ἔχοντα of the Mss. See App. — ὃς ἦν αὐτοῖς ναύαρχος: cf. c. 16. 17. Here, as ii. 66. 6; 80. 12, the nauarchy extends from the summer of one year to the next. — 5. ὅπως ... ἐπιβοηθήσουσιν:

νοι ἧσσον ταῖς ναυσὶν ἐς τὴν Μυτιλήνην καταπλεούσαις
ἐπιβοηθήσουσιν. ἡγεῖτο δὲ τῆς ἐσβολῆς ταύτης Κλεομέ- 2

the reason why the invasion was made exactly then, not earlier nor later. *Cf.* § 4 and c. 25. 6 ὅτι ἐσβολή τε... παρέσονται.—ἀμφοτέρωθεν θορυβούμενοι: *i.e.* not only threatened by the fleet sailing to Lesbos, but actually attacked by a land force in Attica. — 6. ἧσσον: *i.e.* less than they could but for the invasion then made into Attica, against which part of the Athenian forces would be engaged. The Spartan government did not anticipate, of course, that in consequence of the slowness and cowardice of Alcidas the Athenians would hear of the fall of Mytilene soon after they heard of the sailing of Alcidas, and so would not need to send thither any more ships. *Cf.* c. 29. § 1. — ταῖς ναυσὶν ἐς τὴν Μυτιλήνην καταπλεούσαις ἐπιβοηθήσουσιν: the sense of the whole final clause seems to be, "that the Athenians embarrassed both by sea and land might the less with their ships sail to Mytilene and bring aid " (lit. *with their ships sailing to Mytilene bring aid*). So St. explains (*G*:ett. *Gel. Anz.* 1882, p. 97), taking the dat. as instrumental. The text is generally interpreted, "that the Athenians might the less advance against the ships sailing to Mytilene." But ἐπιβοηθεῖν τινι means always, if the dat. is not instrumental, *hasten to the aid of* (cf. i. 73. 24; iv. 1. 11; 29. 23; 43. 15; Hdt. vii. 207. 9; viii. 1. 12; 14. 5); besides, to make καταπλεούσαις attrib. would require either that ναυσὶν follow ἐς

τὴν Μυτιλήνην, or that the article be repeated after ναυσίν. Steup brackets καταπλεούσαις. See App. καταπλεῖν does not differ essentially from the simple verb, as also in i. 51. 13; ii. 103. 3; iv. 26. 20; viii. 35. 4; 108. 1. ἐπιβοηθήσουσιν, with the best Mss., instead of ἐπιβοηθήσωσιν. GMT. 324; II. 881 c.

7. ἡγεῖτο τῆς ἐσβολῆς ταύτης: *cf.* ii. 10. 9. — Κλεομένης ὑπὲρ Παυσανίου: οὗτος ὁ Κλεομένης καὶ ὁ Πλειστοάναξ παῖδές εἰσι Παυσανίου τοῦ ἐν Πλαταιᾶσιν ἀριστεύσαντος ἐπὶ τῶν Μήδων, Schol. See on i. 94. 1; 114. 11. Archidamus, who had led the previous invasions, was prob. still alive, but hindered by illness. His death must have occurred soon after, for his son Agis, as king, leads the expedition of the following year, c. 89. 3. See Kr. *Hist.-phil. Stud.* i. p. 151. Elsewhere, in narrating Peloponnesian invasions of Attica, Thuc. always adds the father's name to that of the leader (c. 1. 3; i. 114. 11; ii. 19. 6; 47. 6; iv. 2. 3; vii. 19. 3 — *cf.* also c. 89. 3; ii. 71. 3). But everywhere else a Spartan king is the leader. The present passage differs, it is true, also from i. 107. 6, where in the account of the expedition into central Greece, which led to the battle of Tanagra, it is said, Νικομήδους τοῦ Κλεομβρότου ὑπὲρ Πλειστοάνακτος τοῦ Παυσανίου βασιλέως, νέον ὄντος ἔτι, ἡγουμένου. Still one is less inclined to accept, with G. Osberger (*Festgruss f. Heerwagen*, p. 89 f.), the loss

νης ὑπὲρ Παυσανίου τοῦ Πλειστοάνακτος υἱέος βασιλέως ὄντος καὶ νεωτέρου ἔτι, πατρὸς δὲ ἀδελφὸς ὤν. ἐδῄωσαν 3
10 δὲ τῆς Ἀττικῆς τά τε πρότερον τετμημένα [καὶ] εἴ τι ἐβεβλαστήκει καὶ ὅσα ἐν ταῖς πρὶν ἐσβολαῖς παρελέλειπτο· καὶ ἡ ἐσβολὴ αὕτη χαλεπωτάτη ἐγένετο τοῖς Ἀθηναίοις μετὰ τὴν δευτέραν. ἐπιμένοντες γὰρ αἰεὶ ἀπὸ τῆς Λέ- 4 σβου τι πεύσεσθαι τῶν νεῶν ἔργον ὡς ἤδη πεπεραιω-
15 μένων ἐπεξῆλθον τὰ πολλὰ τέμνοντες. ὡς δ' οὐδὲν ἀπέβαινεν αὐτοῖς ὧν προσεδέχοντο καὶ ἐπελελοίπει ὁ σῖτος, ἀνεχώρησαν καὶ διελύθησαν κατὰ πόλεις.

27 Οἱ δὲ Μυτιληναῖοι ἐν τούτῳ, ὡς αἵ τε νῆες αὐτοῖς 1 οὐχ ἧκον ἀπὸ τῆς Πελοποννήσου, ἀλλὰ ἐνεχρόνιζον, καὶ ὁ σῖτος ἐπελελοίπει, ἀναγκάζονται ξυμβαίνειν πρὸς τοὺς

of ὁ Παυσανίου before ὑπὲρ Παυσανίου, since the absence of Λακεδαιμονίων with βασιλέως is also unusual. In i. 107. 6, οἱ Λακεδαιμόνιοι occurs as subj.
8. ὑπέρ: *in place of.* Kühn. 435, i. 2 a.
— **υἱέος**: this form of gen. also i. 13. 26; 137. 2; ii. 100. 14; υἱοῦ, v. 16. 24. See on i. 13. 26. — **9. νεωτέρου ἔτι**: *yet too young, sc.* to rule. *Cf.* vi. 12.
10 νεώτερος ἔτι ὢν ἐς τὸ ἄρχειν. — **πατρὸς δέ**: see App.
10. [καί]: see App. — **11. ὅσα . . . παρελέλειπτο**: *cf.* ii. 57. 8, where, in the account of the second invasion, τὴν γῆν πᾶσαν ἔτεμον must mean, ravaged *all parts* of the land, not *every point. παραλείπειν, spare*, as in ii. 13. 7.
— **13. μετὰ τὴν δευτέραν**: *cf.* ii. 57. § 2.
— **ἐπιμένοντες . . . τι πεύσεσθαι**: for the const. with inf., see on c. 2. 7; 12.
11. — 14. ὡς ἤδη πεπεραιωμένων: as was natural to assume, since the fleet was expected to make all haste (c. 29. 2), instead of proceeding with the utmost slowness, as it did (c. 27. 2; 29. 3). For const. of the partic., see on c. 4. 15. — **15. ἐπεξῆλθον**: abs., *they went forward*, as i. 62. 24. *Cf.* Plato *Gorg.* 492 d. Bm. takes τὰ πολλὰ with ἐπεξῆλθον, comparing c. 67. 1 ταῦτα ἐπεξήλθομεν (used fig.), and ii. 94. 13 καταδραμόντες τῆς Σαλαμῖνος τὰ πολλά. — **16. ἐπελελοίπει ὁ σῖτος**: *i.e.* the corn brought with them. *Cf.* c. 1. 8; ii. 10. 4; 23. 11. — **17. ἀνεχώρησαν καὶ διελύθησαν κατὰ πόλεις**: for the formula, see on c. 1. 9.
27. 28. *In Mytilene the democratic party comes into power, whereupon the authorities surrender the city to Paches, on condition that the fate of the Mytileneans should be decided by the Athenians.*
1. ὡς . . . ἀπὸ τῆς Πελοποννήσου: as Salaethus had promised, c. 25. 7.
— **2. ἐνεχρόνιζον**: only here in Thuc., as ἐνδιατρίβειν, c. 29. 3; v. 12. 6; vii. 81. 20. — **3. ἐπελελοίπει**: not entirely,

Ἀθηναίους διὰ τάδε. ὁ Σάλαιθος καὶ αὐτὸς οὐ προσδε- 2
χόμενος ἔτι τὰς ναῦς ὁπλίζει τὸν δῆμον πρότερον ψιλὸν
ὄντα ὡς ἐπεξιὼν τοῖς Ἀθηναίοις· οἱ δέ, ἐπειδὴ ἔλαβον 3
ὅπλα, οὔτε ἠκροῶντο ἔτι τῶν ἀρχόντων, κατὰ ξυλλόγους
τε γιγνόμενοι ἢ τὸν σῖτον ἐκέλευον τοὺς δυνατοὺς φέρειν ἐς τὸ φανερὸν καὶ διανέμειν ἅπασιν, ἢ αὐτοὶ ξυγχωρήσαντες πρὸς Ἀθηναίους ἔφασαν παραδώσειν τὴν
πόλιν. γνόντες δὲ οἱ ἐν τοῖς πράγμασιν οὔτ' ἀποκωλύ- 1
σειν δυνατοὶ ὄντες, εἴ τ' ἀπομονωθήσονται τῆς ξυμβάσεως κινδυνεύσοντες, ποιοῦνται κοινῇ ὁμολογίαν πρός

as may be inferred from l. 8 below.
— **ξυμβαίνειν πρὸς τοὺς Ἀθηναίους**: for the const., see Kühn. 441, iii. 1 b. See on c. 25. 10.
5. **ὁπλίζει**: *i.e.* he gives them full hoplite armour (viii. 25. 4), which hitherto the δυνατοί had reserved to themselves, the lower classes of citizens serving as ψιλοί, with spear or bow, without breastplate and shield.
7. **τῶν ἀρχόντων**: = τῶν ἐν τοῖς πράγμασι (c. 28. 1). — **κατὰ ξυλλόγους γιγνόμενοι**: *i.e.* coming together in secret party meetings. So Xen. *Anab.* v. 7. 1 καὶ ξύλλογοι ἐγίγνοντο καὶ κύκλοι ξυνίσταντο, and Arr. *Anab.* v. 25. 2. *Cf.* κατὰ ξυστάσεις γιγνόμενοι, ii. 21. 15; and see on c. 24. 14.
— 8. **τὸν σῖτον**: the δυνατοί seem to have anticipated the lack of provisions, either by retaining for themselves the corn, which before the revolt had been ordered from the Pontus (*cf.* c. 2. 7, and see W. Herbst, *Der Abfall Mytilenes*, p. 11), or, if we suppose, with Steup. that this never arrived, by taking other precautions.
— **τοὺς δυνατούς**: *i.e.* the optimates or ὀλίγοι, as i. 24. 13; ii. 65. 8; v. 4. 8; viii. 21. 4. — 9. **αὐτοί**: *for themselves alone*, as i. 139. 15; v. 60. 4; vi. 37. 3. *Cf.* c. 28. 2 εἰ ἀπομονωθήσονται τῆς ξυμβάσεως. αὐτοί belongs with ξυγχωρήσαντες παραδώσειν. — **ξυγχωρήσαντες πρὸς Ἀθηναίους**: as ii. 59. 6. *Cf.* c. 28. 3; v. 29. 21; vii. 82. 7. See on l. 3; 25. 10.
28. 1. **οἱ ἐν τοῖς πράγμασιν**: as in Dem. ix. 56; Arist. *Polit.* v. 7. 12, = οἱ ἄρχοντες, οἱ δυνατοί, c. 27. 7, 8, whose executive committee perhaps were the πρόεδροι of c. 25. 6. *Cf.* οἱ ἐπὶ τοῖς πράγμασι, Dem. ix, 2, and οἱ ἔχοντες τὰ πράγματα, c. 62. 11; 72. 3. See on c. 11. 11, and W. Herbst *l.c.*
— **οὔτε, τε**: on the correlation see Kühn. 536, 3 a. — **ἀποκωλύσειν**: for fut. inf. limiting δυνατοὶ ὄντες, see on i. 27. 9; ii. 29. 26; vi. 6. 4. GMT. 113; Kühn. 389, x. 8. St. writes ἀποκωλύειν. See *Qu. Gr.*[2] p. 18 sqq.—
2. **δυνατοὶ ὄντες**: depends on γνόντες. GMT. 904. — **εἰ ἀπομονωθήσονται**: in accordance with the threat contained in αὐτοί, c. 27. 9. — 3. **κινδυνεύσοντες**: still dependent on γνόντες. The pres.,

τε Πάχητα καὶ τὸ στρατόπεδον, ὥστε Ἀθηναίοις μὲν
5 ἐξεῖναι βουλεῦσαι περὶ Μυτιληναίων ὁποῖον ἄν τι βού-
λωνται καὶ τὴν στρατιὰν ἐς τὴν πόλιν δέχεσθαι αὐτούς,
πρεσβείαν δὲ ἀποστέλλειν ἐς τὰς Ἀθήνας Μυτιληναίους
περὶ ἑαυτῶν· ἐν ὅσῳ δ' ἂν πάλιν ἔλθωσι, Πάχητα μήτε
δῆσαι Μυτιληναίων μηδένα μήτε ἀνδραποδίσαι μήτε
10 ἀποκτεῖναι. ἡ μὲν ξύμβασις αὕτη ἐγένετο, οἱ δὲ πράξαν- 2
τες πρὸς τοὺς Λακεδαιμονίους μάλιστα τῶν Μυτιληναίων
περιδεεῖς ὄντες, ὡς ἡ στρατιὰ ἐσῆλθεν, οὐκ ἠνέσχοντο,
ἀλλ' ἐπὶ τοὺς βωμοὺς ὅμως καθίζουσι· Πάχης δ' ἀναστήσας αὐτοὺς ὥστε μὴ ἀδικῆσαι, κατατίθεται ἐς Τένεδον
15 μέχρι οὗ τοῖς Ἀθηναίοις τι δόξῃ. πέμψας δὲ καὶ ἐς τὴν 3

κινδυνεύοντες, which several good Mss. have, is doubtless only a slip of the copyist due to the preceding ὄντες. — κοινῇ : *i.e.* together with the democratic party. *Cf.* v. 32. 16 ; 35. 11 ; 42. 19. — πρός τε Πάχητα καὶ τὸ στρατόπεδον : for the const., see on c. 25. 10; 27. 3, 9. Paches doubtless conferred with the most prominent of his officers. The Athenian army could settle only the preliminaries, the final decision belonging to the demos at Athens. τὸ στρατόπεδον is tacitly opp. to πόλις. as in viii. 72. 2 ; 76. 3. — 4. ὥστε : on condition that, as in l. 14. See on i. 28. 18. GMT. 587. 2 ; H. 953 b. — 5. βουλεῦσαι: aor., *to decide*, as in i. 85. 5 ; 132. 28 ; ii. 6. 10; iv. 41. 1 ; vi. 39. 5; pres., *to deliberate* (i. 97. 2 ; iv. 15. 3), except in c. 42. 25, *give advice*. — 7. πρεσβείαν δὲ... Μυτιληναίους : the natural const. would be Μυτιληναίους δὲ πρεσβείαν ἀποστέλλειν, but the interposition of καὶ τὴν στρατιὰν ... αὐτούς led to a change of const. ἀποστέλ-

λειν depends on ἐξεῖναι in spite of the intervening clause. — 8. ἐν ὅσῳ ἂν πάλιν ἔλθωσι : this concise expression is really a mixture of ἐν ὅσῳ ἂν ἀπῶσι (*cf.* viii. 87. 8) and πρὶν ἂν (or ἕως ἄν, i. 90. 20) πάλιν ἔλθωσιν (*cf.* i. 91. 10). See also i. 14. 12 for similar σύγχυσις. ἐν ὅσῳ, *until*, also c. 52. 16.

10. οἱ πράξαντες πρὸς τοὺς Λακεδαιμονίους : for the const. (πρός, *with*), see on c. 4. 20; i. 131. 7 ; ii. 5. 32. — 12. οὐκ ἠνέσχοντο : abs., *could not keep quiet*, as v. 45. 17. On the augments, see G. 544 ; H. 361 a. — 13. ὅμως : *i.e.* notwithstanding safety had been guaranteed them until the return of their embassy. For similar *breviloquentia*, *cf.* c. 49. 3 ; 80. 4 ; i. 105. 24 ; ii. 51. 24; iv. 96. 35. — καθίζουσι : sc. ἱκέται, which is expressed c. 70. 18 ; 75. 22 ; i. 24. 19 ; 126. 32. ἱκέται is omitted also c. 75. 15. — 14. κατατίθεται : *places for safe-keeping*. The mid. always in this sense. See on i. 115. 13. — 15. μέχρι οὗ : with subjv. with-

Ἄντισσαν τριήρεις προσεκτήσατο καὶ τἆλλα τὰ περὶ τὸ στρατόπεδον καθίστατο ᾗ αὐτῷ ἐδόκει.

29 Οἱ δ' ἐν ταῖς τεσσαράκοντα ναυσὶ Πελοποννήσιοι, 1 οὓς ἔδει ἐν τάχει παραγενέσθαι, πλέοντες περί τε αὐτὴν τὴν Πελοπόννησον ἐνδιέτριψαν καὶ κατὰ τὸν ἄλλον πλοῦν σχολαῖοι κομισθέντες τοὺς μὲν ἐκ τῆς πόλεως
5 Ἀθηναίους λανθάνουσι, πρὶν δὴ τῇ Δήλῳ ἔσχον, προσ-

ont ἄν also iv. 16. 16; 41. 2; 46. 12. GMT. 620; Kühn. 398, N. 2. See on i. 137. 13, and St. *Qu. Gr.*² p. 26. — **16. προσεκτήσατο :** *sc.* αὐτήν. Antissa had resisted the Methymneans, as described in c. 18. § 2. — **καὶ τἆλλα ... ᾗ αὐτῷ ἐδόκει :** *and arranged the other matters pertaining to the army as he deemed best.* Cf. c. 35. 7 ; i. 95. 8; ii. 6. 3.

29. *Seven days later the Peloponnesian fleet arrives in that region.*
2. ἔδει ἐν τάχει παραγενέσθαι : contrasted with πλέοντες ... κομισθέντες, not without irony, a trace of which is observable also elsewhere, when allusion is made to naval operations of the Peloponnesians. See on c. 31. 11 ; 81. 1; ii. 7. 9; 93. 20. — **3. ἐνδιέτριψαν :** see App. — **4. σχολαῖοι κομισθέντες :** *cf.* χρόνιοι ξυνιόντες, i. 141. 30. For other cases of the pred. adj. used adv., see on i. 12. 3. G. 926; H. 619; Kr. *Spr.* 57, 5, 4. — **τοὺς ἐκ τῆς πόλεως Ἀθηναίους :** understood by Cl., St., and Bm., with L. Herbst (*Philol.* xvi. p. 312 f. — *cf.* xlii. p. 696 ff.), to be the crew of the 100 ships mentioned c. 16. 5, made up from the *citizen* classes (and metics). Cf. c. 91. 11; i. 105. 19; ii. 31. 6; iv. 28. 18; 77. 2. But Steup is prob. right in understanding here, with

Müller-Strübing (*Thuk. Forsch.* p. 117 ff.), those in Athens and Attica, as opp. to those that had been sent to Lesbos. For the fleet of Alcidas was not despatched till the summer of 427 B.C.; otherwise Thuc. could not have delayed mention of it till c. 26. § 1, and Salaethus, who departed from Sparta τοῦ αὐτοῦ χειμῶνος τελευτῶντος (c. 25. 1), could not have said προαποπεμφθῆναι αὐτός (c. 25. 8). Besides, the return of the 100 Attic ships, which is mentioned c. 16. 18, certainly occurred before Paches was despatched to Mytilene (c. 18. 15). See Müller-Strübing *ibid.* p. 120, and Jow. *ad loc.* Further, in three at least of the passages cited by Herbst (c. 91. 11; i. 105. 19; ii. 31. 6). οἱ ἐκ τῆς πόλεως seems to mean, as here, simply those left in Athens and Attica, as opp. to those sent abroad. — **5. πρὶν δὴ τῇ Δήλῳ ἔσχον :** *until they reached Delos,* having thus accomplished the part of the voyage in which there was most danger of being sighted by Athenian ships. For πρίν with indic., see on i. 51. 5; 118. 13; 132. 28; and Gildersleeve, *Am. J. of Ph.* ii. p. 469. GMT. 635; H. 924. σχεῖν with dat. also c. 33. 5; vii. 1. 14; elsewhere with ἐς or κατά with acc. Kr. *Spr.* 48, 1, 2; Kühn. 423, 5. See

μείξαντες δ' ἀπ' αὐτῆς τῇ Ἰκάρῳ καὶ Μυκόνῳ πυνθάνονται πρῶτον ὅτι ἡ Μυτιλήνη ἑάλωκε. βουλόμενοι δὲ τὸ 2 σαφὲς εἰδέναι κατέπλευσαν ἐς Ἔμβατον τῆς Ἐρυθραίας· ἡμέραι δὲ μάλιστα ἦσαν τῇ Μυτιλήνῃ ἑαλωκυίᾳ ἑπτὰ ὅτ' ἐς τὸ Ἔμβατον κατέπλευσαν. πυθόμενοι δὲ τὸ σαφὲς ἐβουλεύοντο ἐκ τῶν παρόντων, καὶ ἔλεξεν αὐτοῖς Τευτίαπλος ἀνὴρ Ἠλεῖος τάδε·

30 " Ἀλκίδα καὶ Πελοποννησίων ὅσοι πάρεσμεν ἄρ- 1 χοντες τῆς στρατιᾶς, ἐμοὶ δοκεῖ πλεῖν ἡμᾶς ἐπὶ Μυτιλήνην πρὶν ἐκπύστους γενέσθαι, ὥσπερ ἔχομεν. κατὰ γὰρ 2 τὸ εἰκὸς ἀνδρῶν νεωστὶ πόλιν ἐχόντων πολὺ τὸ ἀφύ-

on vii. 1. 14. — 6. τῇ Ἰκάρῳ καὶ Μυκόνῳ: the reverse of the geographical order, as in c. 102. 4; ii. 7. 16; 77. 10; 93. 1; viii. 88. 10; 108. 3. The place where they first received the news of the fall of Mytilene is named first, and πυνθάνεσθαι πρῶτον belongs with this; hence Haase's conjecture (Luenbr. Thuc. p. 23), Πάρῳ, is unnecessary.

7. τὸ σαφές: the exact situation. Cf. l. 10; i. 22. 16; vi. 60. 12, 20. — 8. Ἔμβατον: τὸ στενὸν τὸ μεταξὺ Χίου καὶ Ἐρυθρᾶς [for Ἐρυθρῶν], Schol. More correctly Steph. Thes. s.v. τόπος τῆς Ἐρυθραίας.— 9. τῇ Μυτιλήνῃ ἑαλωκυίᾳ: the dat. to express the terminus a quo, as ταύτῃ in i. 13. 14. It was about seven days after the fall of Mytilene when etc. Kühn. 423, 25 f. Kr. Spr. 48, 5, 3. The pred. partic. has the same force as in ἐπιλιπόντι, c. 20. 3. — 11. ἐκ τῶν παρόντων: under present circumstances. ἐκ as in iv. 17. 4; v. 40. 19; 87. 2; vi. 70. 18; 93. 10; vii. 62. 4; 77. 1. Kr. Spr. 68, 17, 10; Kühn. 430, 2, 3 g.

Different is βουλεύεσθαι περὶ τῶν παρόντων, i. 79. 4.

30. But Teutiaplus the Elean advises to make without delay a night attack on Mytilene.

2. ἐμοὶ δοκεῖν πλεῖν ἡμᾶς: unusual change of subj., as in iv. 118. 2; vi. 22. 1. For the usual const., cf. i. 31. 9; iv. 15. 2; 71. 6; v. 53. 5; vii. 4. 15; 74. 3. — 3. πρὶν ἐκπύστους γενέσθαι: as in iv. 70. 14; viii. 42. 2. This expression is used of persons also by Dio C. xli. 44; xlviii. 39; elsewhere of things. Cf. καταγγέλτους γίγνεσθαι, vii. 48. 6; ἐξάγγελτοι γενέσθαι, viii. 14. 2; ἐπάϊστος ἐγένετο, Hdt. ii. 119. 10. — ὥσπερ ἔχομεν: just as we are, i.e. without delay. See on i. 134. 14.

4. ἀνδρῶν: grammatically dependent on τὸ ἀφύλακτον, in the loose connexion which is close akin to the gen. abs., on the part of men who ——. — πολὺ τὸ ἀφύλακτον εὑρήσομεν: for similar const., cf. viii. 66. 18 ἢ γὰρ ἀγνῶτα ἂν εὗρεν ᾧ ἐρεῖ ἢ γνώριμον ἄπιστον. πολύ is pred. with the

5 λακτὸν εὑρήσομεν, κατὰ μὲν θάλασσαν καὶ πάνυ, ᾗ ἐκεῖνοί τε ἀνέλπιστοι ἐπιγενέσθαι ἄν τινα σφίσι πολέμιον καὶ ἡμῶν ἡ ἀλκὴ τυγχάνει μάλιστα οὖσα· εἰκὸς δὲ καὶ τὸ πεζὸν αὐτῶν κατ' οἰκίας ἀμελέστερον ὡς κεκρατηκότων διεσπάρθαι. εἰ οὖν προσπέσοιμεν ἄφνω τε καὶ 3
10 νυκτός, ἐλπίζω μετὰ τῶν ἔνδον, εἴ τις ἄρα ἡμῖν ἐστιν ὑπόλοιπος εὔνους, καταληφθῆναι ἂν τὰ πράγματα. καὶ 4 μὴ ἀποκνήσωμεν τὸν κίνδυνον, νομίσαντες οὐκ ἄλλο τι

same position and effect as ἐλαχίστας, i. 34. 10; ἄμικτα, i. 77. 24. The use of a neut. partic. or adj. for an abstract noun is common in Thuc. It presents to the mind the abstract quality in operation. See on i. 36. 3. GMT. 829 a; H. 966 b; Kühn. 403 γ. —5. καὶ πάνυ: vel maxime, as c. 93. 10; i. 3. 5; ii. 11. 26; 51. 6; 65. 61; vi. 17. 32. —6. ἀνέλπιστοι: active, as also vi. 17. 31; viii. 1. 15; and τὸ ἀνέλπιστον, ii. 51. 13; elsewhere in Thuc. with passive force, iv. 55. 8; vi. 33. 24. — ἐπιγενέσθαι: of unexpected attack, as c. 108. 3; iv. 25. 52; 93. 12; vii. 32. 12. —7. ἡμῶν ἡ ἀλκὴ τυγχάνει μάλιστα οὖσα: "and where defence happens to be chiefly our role." This interpretation of Junghahn's (N. Jahrbb. cxix. p. 358) is adopted by Stenp. See also Amer. J. of Phil. x. p. 210, where the same explanation is given by C. F. Smith, independently of Junghahn. Cl. follows Herbst (Philol. xvi. p. 305), "where our strength at present chiefly lies." ἀλκή as in c. 108. 5; ii. 84. 24; Hdt. ii. 45. 7; iii. 78. 5; iv. 125. 21; ix. 102. 18. On Thuc.'s use of ἀλκή, see Diener, De Sermone Thuc. p. 12, and C. F. Smith, Proc. Amer. Philol.

Assoc. vol. xxii. p. xvii. — εἰκὸς δὲ καὶ τὸ πεζόν: opp. to κατὰ μὲν θάλασσαν καὶ πάνυ. —8. ὡς κεκρατηκότων: "in the confidence of victory."
10. ἐλπίζω: with inf. (pres. or aor.) and ἄν = think or expect. Cf. i. 127. 5; ii. 20. 4; v. 39. 5; vii. 61. 12, and ἀνέλπιστοι ἐπιγενέσθαι ἄν above. Cf. Chaucer, Reeve's Tale, 1. 109, 'I hope he wil be deed.' — μετὰ τῶν ἔνδον: in agreement with those within (cf. v. 44. 2; vi. 28. 11), as if an act. inf. clause were to follow; but the interposition of the εἰ clause has caused a slight anacoluthon. For καταλαμβάνειν τὰ πράγματα, see on c. 11. 10. — εἴ τις ἄρα ... εὔνους: intended not to express doubt, but to be as comprehensive as possible, whoever is left well-disposed toward us. For ἄρα, see on c. 56. 15.
12. ἀποκνήσωμεν τὸν κίνδυνον: see on c. 20. 10. — νομίσαντες οὐκ ἄλλο τι εἶναι: this const. with νομίζειν or ἡγεῖσθαι gives to an ambiguous expression a definite, and, in the view of the speaker, correct sense. This is the case with ἑορτή, i. 70. 29; τὸ ξυμφέρον, c. 56. 25; and here with the proverbial or formulary expression, τὸ κοινὸν τοῦ πολέμου. See App.

εἶναι τὸ κοινὸν τοῦ πολέμου ἢ τὸ τοιοῦτον, ὃ εἴ τις στρατηγὸς ἔν τε αὑτῷ φυλάσσοιτο καὶ τοῖς πολεμίοις ἐνορῶν
15 ἐπιχειροίη, πλεῖστ' ἂν ὀρθοῖτο."
31   Ὁ μὲν τοσαῦτα εἰπὼν οὐκ ἔπειθε τὸν Ἀλκίδαν. 1 ἄλλοι δέ τινες, τῶν ἀπ' Ἰωνίας φυγάδων καὶ οἱ Λέσβιοι οἱ ξυμπλέοντες, παρῄνουν, ἐπειδὴ τοῦτον τὸν κίνδυνον φοβεῖται, τῶν ἐν Ἰωνίᾳ πόλεων καταλαβεῖν τινα ἢ Κύμην
5 τὴν Αἰολίδα, ὅπως ἐκ πόλεως ὁρμώμενοι τὴν Ἰωνίαν ἀποστήσωσιν (ἐλπίδα δ' εἶναι· οὐδενὶ γὰρ ἀκουσίως ἀφῖχθαι), καὶ τὴν πρόσοδον ταύτην μεγίστην οὖσαν Ἀθη-

—13. τὸ τοιοῦτον: *i.e.* lack of precaution. — ὃ εἴ τις στρατηγὸς ... πλεῖστ' ἂν ὀρθοῖτο: *which, if a general both guard against in himself, and when he sees it in the enemy attacks, he would be most likely to succeed.* Cf. v. 9. § 4. — 14. τοῖς πολεμίοις: belongs both to ἐνορῶν and ἐπιχειροίη, but ὅ. which is obj. of φυλάσσοιτο in the first clause, belongs only to ἐνορῶν in the second. — 15. πλεῖστ' ἂν ὀρθοῖτο: cf. c. 37. 26; 42. 20; v. 9. 14.

31. *But Alcidas decides, in spite of the remonstrances of the Ionian fugitives and of those Lesbians who are present, to return to Peloponnesus.*

1. τοσαῦτα: occurs esp. after short speeches, "so much and no more." Cf. c. 52. 13; ii. 12. 1; 72. 1, 13; iv. 11. 1; vii. 49. 1; also c. 62. 25, and Plato *Prot.* 318 a τοσοῦτος ὁ ἡμέτερος λόγος. —2. ἄλλοι τινές: epexegetically explained by τῶν ἀπ' Ἰωνίας ... ξυμπλέοντες. For the part. gen., τῶν ... φυγάδων, cf. iv. 78. 17. These fugitives are mentioned only here. — 3. οἱ ξυμπλέοντες: οἱ rightly added

by Madvig (*Adv.* i. p. 315); for the Lesbians on the fleet, not the Lesbians in general, must be meant. Herbst (*Philol.* xlii. p. 704) justifies the vulgate by assuming οἱ Λέσβιοι to be the ambassadors at Olympia, c. 8 ff. But οἱ Λέσβιοι, though a sufficiently explicit designation for this embassy in c. 16. 10, by no means suffices here, after the narration of so many different events, among them the fall of Mytilene, esp. as the sending of a second *later* embassy is mentioned, c. 5. 16. Prob. the majority of both embassies were with Alcidas; but some representatives of Mytilenean interests must have remained at Sparta. — 5. ὅπως ... ἀποστήσωσιν: aor. subjv. after ὅπως, as c. 49. 6; 81. 4; v. 85. 3. GMT. 318. — ὁρμώμενοι: ὁρμητήριον ἔχοντες. Schol. Cf. c. 85. 7; i. 64. 10; 90. 12; iv. 8. 36; 52. 16. — 6. οὐδενί: sc. τῶν κατὰ ταύτην τὴν θάλασσαν Ἑλλήνων. — ἀκουσίως: *unwelcome, unwished for;* the passive force, which the adj. ἀκούσιος also has. — 7. καὶ τὴν πρόσοδον ... γίγνηται: καί connects ἀποστή-

ναίων ἦν ὑφέλωσι, καὶ ἅμα, ἦν ἐφορμῶσι σφίσιν, αὐτοῖς
δαπάνη γίγνηται · πείσειν τε οἴεσθαι καὶ Πισσούθνην
10 ὥστε ξυμπολεμεῖν. ὁ δὲ οὐδὲ ταῦτα ἐνεδέχετο, ἀλλὰ 2
τὸ πλεῖστον τῆς γνώμης εἶχεν, ἐπειδὴ τῆς Μυτιλήνης
ὑστερήκει, ὅτι τάχιστα τῇ Πελοποννήσῳ πάλιν προσμεῖξαι.
32 ἄρας δὲ ἐκ τοῦ Ἐμβάτου παρέπλει · καὶ προσσχὼν Μυον- 1
νήσῳ τῇ Τηίων τοὺς αἰχμαλώτους οὓς κατὰ πλοῦν εἰλή-
φει ἀπέσφαξε τοὺς πολλούς. καὶ ἐς τὴν Ἔφεσον καθ- 2

σωσιν and γίγνηται. On the text, see App. — 8. ὑφέλωσι : (so with Laur. and other Mss., not ἀφέλωσι, which Vat. and others have) of gradual withdrawal, as c. 13. 33; 82. 17. — καὶ ἅμα : also at the same time. See on c. 16. 12; 21. 10. — ἦν ἐφορμῶσι σφίσιν : second condition depending on καὶ (ὅπως) αὐτοῖς (i.e. τοῖς Ἀθηναίοις, δαπάνη γίγνηται. The subj. of ἐφορμῶσι is the Athenians; σφίσιν refers to the Peloponnesians. ἐφορμεῖν with dat. as in vii. 3. 21; 12. 18; the pass. in i. 142. 19; viii. 20. 3. — 9. Πισσούθνην : satrap of Lydia. Cf. i. 115. 17. — 10. ὥστε : pleonastic after πείσειν, as in c. 66. 9; 70. 21; 75. 4; 100. 4; 102. 22; ii. 2. 23; v. 16. 23; 35. 31; viii. 45. 21. GMT. 588; Kühn. 473, N. 6.

ἐνεδέχετο : impf. corresponding to παρῄνουν (l. 3). ἐνδέχεσθαι in this sense also viii. 50. 2. — 11. τὸ πλεῖστον τῆς γνώμης εἶχεν : he was for the most part of the opinion. There is a touch of irony in the expression. See on c. 29. 2. Cf. iv. 34. 5 τοῦ θαρσεῖν τὸ πλεῖστον εἰληφότες, Hdt. i. 120. 19 ταύτῃ πλεῖστος γνώμην εἰμί, v. 126. 2 αὐτῷ δὲ Ἀρισταγόρῃ ἡ πλείστη γνώμη ἦν, vii. 220. 5 ταύτῃ καὶ μᾶλλον τῇ

γνώμῃ πλεῖστός εἰμι. — τῆς Μυτιλήνης : short for τῆς ἁλώσεως τῆς Μυτιλήνης. — 12. ὑστερήκει : with gen., as in Xen. Anab. i. 7. 12; Ages. 2. 1; Hdt. vi. 89. 12. Cf. Dem. iv. 32, 35. G. 1120; H. 749.

32. Alcidas sails along the coast of Asia Minor as far as Ephesus. His barbarous treatment of captives.

1. παρέπλει : i.e. southward. — προσσχών : see App. on i. 15. 3. — 2. Μυοννήσῳ : Myonnesus promunturium inter Teum Samumque est, Liv. xxxvii. 27. Cf. Strabo, p. 643 (end), ἡ Μυόννησος ἐφ᾽ ὕψους χερρονησίζοντος κατοικεῖται. — κατὰ πλοῦν : without art., as in vii. 31. 14, corresponding to καθ᾽ ὁδόν, ii. 5. 3; v. 3. 14; 37. 6. Cf. ἐν πλῷ. vi. 34. 61. — 3. ἀπέσφαξε : as, acc. to ii. 67. § 4, the custom of the Lacedaemonians was. — τοὺς πολλούς : part. apposition. G. 914; H. 624 d; Kr. Spr. 57, 8, N. Cf. i. 18. 2.

ἐς τὴν Ἔφεσον καθορμισαμένου : cf. iv. 45. 3; vi. 97. 5; viii. 34. 11; 42. 20. Müller-Strübing (Thuk. Forsch. p. 128 ff.) denies the possibility of Alcidas having anchored at Ephesus, a city belonging to the Athenian alliance, and holds both Ἔφεσον here

ὁρμισαμένου αὐτοῦ Σαμίων τῶν ἐξ Ἀναίων ἀφικόμενοι
πρέσβεις ἔλεγον οὐ καλῶς τὴν Ἑλλάδα ἐλευθεροῦν αὐτόν, εἰ ἄνδρας διέφθειρεν οὔτε χεῖρας ἀνταιρομένους
οὔτε πολεμίους, Ἀθηναίων δὲ ὑπ' ἀνάγκης ξυμμάχους·
εἴ τε μὴ παύσεται, ὀλίγους μὲν αὐτὸν τῶν ἐχθρῶν ἐς
φιλίαν προσάξεσθαι, πολὺ δὲ πλείους τῶν φίλων πολεμίους ἕξειν. καὶ ὁ μὲν ἐπείσθη τε καὶ Χίων ἄνδρας
ὅσους εἶχεν ἔτι ἀφῆκε καὶ τῶν ἄλλων τινάς· ὁρῶντες
γὰρ τὰς ναῦς οἱ ἄνθρωποι οὐκ ἔφευγον, ἀλλὰ προσεχώρουν μᾶλλον ὡς Ἀττικαῖς, καὶ ἐλπίδα οὐδὲ τὴν ἐλαχίστην εἶχον μή ποτε Ἀθηναίων τῆς θαλάσσης κρα-
τούντων ναῦς Πελοποννησίων ἐς Ἰωνίαν παραβαλεῖν.

and Ἐφέσου in c. 33. 1 to be corrupt. But it seems, acc. to Strabo, p. 641 c, that at that time the harbour of Ephesus could not be closed, and so it was improbable that Alcidas could be kept out. See St. *Gött. Gel. Anz.* 1882, p. 98. — **4. Σαμίων τῶν ἐξ Ἀναίων**: see on c. 19. 8. — **5. τὴν Ἑλλάδα ἐλευθεροῦν**: this claim of Sparta occurs often. See on c. 13. 35; i. 69. 8. — **6. εἰ ... διέφθειρεν**: the fact expressed in hypothetical form, in tone of reproach. *Cf.* c. 43. 19; 55. 7; i. 33. 8; 76. 8; 86. 4; iv. 85. 4. — **χεῖρας ἀνταιρομένους**: *cf.* Hdt. vii. 209. 19. — **7. ὑπ' ἀνάγκης**: only here in Thuc. (but freq. in the poets; see Steph. *Thes. s.v.*), = ἐξ ἀνάγκης, c. 40. 9; vi. 44. 5; vii. 27. 17. *Cf.* ὑπὸ σπουδῆς, c. 33. 12. — **9. προσάξεσθαι**: *will bring over*, as in c. 91. 7; i. 99. 8; ii. 30. 7; iv. 86. 3; vi. 22. 4; vii. 7. 8.
11. ὁρῶντες ... παραβαλεῖν: on the relation and position of these words, see App. — **13. ἐλπίδα οὐδὲ τὴν ἐλαχίστην εἶχον μή ποτε ... παραβαλεῖν**: ἐλπίδα, *expectation*, as in ii. 64. 6; 85. 16; 102. 21; vi. 87. 18; vii. 61. 8. For μή with inf., as after a verb of denial, see GMT. 807; H. 1029; Kühn. 516, 3 a. So after ἀπιστεῖν, i. 10. 3; ii. 101. 3; vi. 49. 13; ἀπιστία, c. 75. 18; ἀπορία, ii 49. 25. *Cf.* also ii. 93. 14. See on vii. 6. 19. — **15. ἐς Ἰωνίαν παραβαλεῖν**: *cross over to Ionia*. παραβαλεῖν intr., as in Hdt. vii. 179. 3; Dem. xii. 16. So διαβάλλειν, ii. 83. 16. Kühn. 373, 2 a. Cl. rather favours Heilmann's explanation, *risk themselves thither*, like ἐς Ἰωνίαν παρακινδυνεύειν, c. 36. 11, and παραβάλλεσθαι, *risk* (as at play), i. 133. 11; ii. 44. 16; Hom. ι 322; τὸν κίνδυνον παραβάλλεσθαι, c. 14. 4; πλείω παραβάλλεσθαι, c. 65. 12; πρόθυμος ἦν παραβάλλεσθαι καὶ παρακινδυνεύειν, Polyb. iii. 90. 6; παραβόλως περαιωθείς, Polyb. i. 11. 9. *Cf.* παρατίθεσθαι, Hom. β 237; γ 74; ι 255. Though the uni-

THUCYDIDES III. 33. 65

33 ἀπὸ δὲ τῆς Ἐφέσου ὁ Ἀλκίδας ἔπλει κατὰ τάχος καὶ 1
φυγὴν ἐποιεῖτο· ὤφθη γὰρ ὑπὸ τῆς Σαλαμινίας καὶ
Παράλου ἔτι περὶ Κλάρον ὁρμῶν, αἳ δ' ἀπ' Ἀθηνῶν
ἔτυχον πλέουσαι. καὶ δεδιὼς τὴν δίωξιν ἔπλει διὰ τοῦ
5 πελάγους ὡς γῇ ἑκούσιος οὐ σχήσων ἄλλῃ ἢ Πελοποννήσῳ.
Τῷ δὲ Πάχητι καὶ τοῖς Ἀθηναίοις ἦλθε μὲν καὶ 2
ἀπὸ τῆς Ἐρυθραίας ἀγγελία, ἀφικνεῖτο δὲ καὶ πανταχόθεν
(ἀτειχίστου γὰρ οὔσης τῆς Ἰωνίας μέγα τὸ δέος

versality of the thought implied in μή ποτε makes it likely that παραβαλεῖν is fut., the aor. after ἐλπίς is not uncommon, c. 3. 14; ii. 80. 10; v. 9. 27; vi. 87. 18.

33. *Alcidas flees through the open sea back toward Peloponnesus, pursued in vain as far as Patmos by Paches.*

2. φυγὴν ἐποιεῖτο: *cf.* ἐποιεῖτο τὴν δίωξιν, l. 13; Lat. fugam facere. For this favourite form of periphrasis in Thuc., see on i. 50. 8. — **ὤφθη**: *had been seen, sc.* in the voyage from Embaton to Ephesus, as ἔτι shows; with which agrees the position of Clarus on the coast of Colophon, a few miles northwest of Ephesus. *Cf.* Strabo, p. 642 τὸ πρὸ Κολοφῶνος ἄλσος τοῦ Κλαρίου Ἀπόλλωνος. After leaving Ephesus he crossed the open sea, touching nowhere. For the further account of his voyage, *cf.* c. 69. § 1.
— **τῆς Σαλαμινίας καὶ Παράλου**: the two swift Athenian state triremes kept always manned ready for extraordinary occasions and purposes. *Cf.* c. 77. 12; vi. 53. 1; 61. 20; viii. 73. 25; 74. 1. See *Dict. Ant.*; Boeckh, *P. E.* pp. 235, 394, 702. — **3. αἳ δ' ἀπ' Ἀθηνῶν πλέουσαι**: they were

prob. sent out after news of Alcidas's expedition was received at Athens, to reconnoitre and take orders to Paches. — **4. τὴν δίωξιν**: *sc.* of the Attic fleet after it should have heard of the Peloponnesian fleet. — **ἔπλει διὰ τοῦ πελάγους**: see on c. 4. 20. This is a strengthened repetition of ἔπλει κατὰ τάχος, after the parenthetical clause (ὤφθη . . . πλέουσαι) stating the cause of the haste. — **5. ὡς γῇ ἑκούσιος οὐ σχήσων**: *determined not of his accord to put to land*. For σχεῖν with dat., see on c. 29. 5.

6. τῷ Πάχητι καὶ τοῖς Ἀθηναίοις: with these dats. the three clauses, that follow in inverse order of importance, are to be closely connected. The clause ἀτειχίστου γὰρ . . . τὰς πόλεις, which gives the ground of πανταχόθεν, being set off from the main sent., the increasing importance of the news that comes to Paches is apparent: ἦλθε μέν, the first fleeting rumour; ἀφικνεῖτο δὲ καὶ πανταχόθεν, of repeated urgent messages; αὐτάγγελοι ἔφρασαν, report based upon personal observation and giving exact details (ἔφρασαν as in i. 145. 4). The reference of αὐτόν to

ἐγένετο μὴ παραπλέοντες οἱ Πελοποννήσιοι, εἰ καὶ ὡς
10 μὴ διενοοῦντο μένειν, πορθῶσιν ἅμα προσπίπτοντες τὰς
πόλεις), αὐτάγγελοι δ' αὐτὸν ἰδοῦσαι ἐν τῇ Κλάρῳ ἥ τε
Πάραλος καὶ ἡ Σαλαμινία ἔφρασαν. ὁ δὲ ὑπὸ σπουδῆς 3
ἐποιεῖτο τὴν δίωξιν· καὶ μέχρι μὲν Πάτμου τῆς νήσου
ἐπεδίωξεν, ὡς δ' οὐκέτι ἐν καταλήψει ἐφαίνετο, ἐπανε-
15 χώρει. κέρδος δὲ ἐνόμισεν, ἐπειδὴ οὐ μετεώροις περιέ-

Alcidas becomes easier now through this closer connexion of the last clause with the two first. — **9. καὶ ὣς**: *even thus*, i.e. although the condition of Ionia (ἀτειχίστου κτέ.) was a temptation. καὶ ὣς also i. 44. 11; vii. 74. 2; 81. 30; viii. 51. 10; 56. 10; 87. 18. Jow. suggests "in any case," as in i. 44. 10 ἐδόκει γὰρ ὁ πρὸς Πελοποννησίους πόλεμος καὶ ὣς ἔσεσθαι αὐτοῖς, viii. 51. 9 καὶ οἱ μὲν τειχισμόν τε παρεσκευάζοντο, καὶ ἐκ τοῦ τοιούτου, καὶ ὣς μέλλουσα, Σάμος θᾶσσον ἐτειχίσθη. — **10. ἅμα**: connects πορθῶσιν προσπίπτοντες with παραπλέοντες. "They might in passing take advantage of the opportunity to plunder the cities." — **11. αὐτάγγελοι**: as in Plut. *Ant.* 71; *Cat. Maj.* 14; Arr. *Anab.* iv. 2. § 6; in the sense, *bringing one's own message*, Soph. *O. C.* 333; *Phil.* 568 (*cf.* αὐτὸς ἄγγελος, *Phil.* 500). — **12. ὑπὸ σπουδῆς**: as in v. 66. 9; viii. 107. 1; elsewhere σπουδῇ, κατὰ σπουδήν, or διὰ σπουδῆς. Kühn. 442, 1 d. — **13. Πάτμου**: the correct form, though against most of the Mss., which have Λάτμου. Latmus is a mountain in Caria, not an island. — **14. ἐπεδίωξεν**: of eager pursuit, also ii. 79. 27; iv. 43. 17; vii. 23. 11;

41. 5; Hdt. iv. 1. 8; 160. 11. — **ὡς δ' οὐκέτι ἐν καταλήψει ἐφαίνετο**: *when he appeared no longer within reach* (lit. *catching*). As Alcidas is to be understood as the obj. of ἐπεδίωξεν, so here he is subj. of ἐφαίνετο. That Dio C. so understood is clear from his close imitation (li. 1.), ἐπεδίωξαν μὲν αὐτούς, ἐπεὶ δ' οὐκ ἐν καταλήψει ἐφαίνοντο, ἀνεχώρησαν. Pp. takes ἐφαίνετο impers., as vi. 60. 7 οὐκ ἐν παύλῃ ἐφαίνετο. See also Pp. on i. 137. 25. — **ἐπανεχώρει**: *turned back again*, as in c. 96. 9; 108. 12; i. 63. 14; 131. 5; v. 41. 22; 55. 15; vi. 70. 16; 97. 24. — **15. κέρδος δὲ ἐνόμισεν κτέ.**: the emphasis is on ἐγκαταληφθεῖσαι. The result of the ships being overtaken at some place is expressed personally by ἠναγκάσθησαν and the infs. dependent on it. *He thought it fortunate, since he had not come up with them in the open sea, that they had not been hemmed in somewhere and compelled to encamp, and thus give themselves the trouble of watching and blockading them.* Such a blockade would have been expensive. See App. on c. 31. 7. Besides, Lesbos was not yet completely subdued (c. 35. § 1). — **μετεώροις**: Schol. ταῖς Ἀλκίδου ναυσίν. μετέωρος, in the

τυχεν, ὅτι οὐδαμοῦ ἐγκαταληφθεῖσαι ἠναγκάσθησαν στρατόπεδον ποιεῖσθαι καὶ φυλακὴν σφίσι καὶ ἐφόρμησιν
34 παρασχεῖν. παραπλέων δὲ πάλιν ἔσχε καὶ ἐς Νότιον τὸ 1
Κολοφωνίων, οὗ κατῴκηντο Κολοφώνιοι τῆς ἄνω πόλεως
ἑαλωκυίας ὑπὸ Ἰταμάνους καὶ τῶν βαρβάρων κατὰ στάσιν ἰδίᾳ ἐπαχθέντων (ἑάλω δὲ μάλιστα αὕτη, ὅτε ἡ δευ-
5 τέρα Πελοποννησίων ἐσβολὴ ἐς τὴν Ἀττικὴν ἐγίγνετο).

sense *out at sea*, freq. in Thuc. (i. 48. 4; ii. 91. 12; iv. 14. 3, etc.), not in Hdt. or Xenophon. — **17. σφίσι**: sc. τοῖς Ἀθηναίοις, since Paches is to be understood as subj. of ἐνόμισεν. Kr. Spr. 58, 4, 3. — **ἐφόρμησιν**: *blockade*, as ii. 89. 42; viii. 15. 14.

. 34. *On his return voyage Paches treacherously brings Notium, the port of Colophon, again into subjection to Athens.*

1. πάλιν: with παραπλέων, *on the way back*. — **Νότιον**: the port of Colophon, about two miles from the latter, or ἄνω πόλις (l. 2), acc. to Liv. xxxvii. 26. 5; acc. to Schuchhardt (*Mitt. d. deutsch. arch. Inst., Ath. Abth.* xi. p. 410) about nine miles. On the events of this chapter, see Ullrich, *Beitr.* p. 114, Λ. 130, Boeckh, *Staatsh.* ii.² p. 699, Wilamowitz, *Philol. Unters.* i. p. 86 f. The relation of the Νοτιῆς of the Attic tribute-lists to the Colophonian Notium is doubtful, for Hdt. mentions (i. 149. 3) an Aeolian Notium. See Boeckh *ibid.* p. 712. — **2. κατῴκηντο**: with adv. designation of place, as ii. 96. 6; 99. 20; v. 83. 13; with acc., i. 120. 8. Thuc. uses the pf. and plpf. always in the mid. (as in the passages just cited); the pres. and aor., only in the active (l. 6; viii. 6. 4; 108. 19). — **3. Ἰταμάνους**: not otherwise known. He seems to have been the leader of a Persian band who acted without orders from Pissuthnes. — **τῶν βαρβάρων κατὰ στάσιν ἰδίᾳ ἐπαχθέντων**: here, as often in Thuc., the attrib. partic. is placed after a noun which is attended by other modifiers. See on i. 11. 19; vii. 23. 14; and Merriam, *Trans. Amer. Philol. Assoc.* xiii. p. 39. ἰδίᾳ for ἰδίαν of the Mss. is doubtless correctly restored by Kr. As in c. 2. 10, it is to be taken with κατὰ στάσιν, "on account of party-discord by one of the factions."
— **4. μάλιστα**: used with statements of measure, numbers, dates, to imply that the account given is the best possible approximation, though the reality may be more or less. Cf. i. 13. 11; ii. 36. 9. — **ὅτε ἡ δευτέρα Πελοποννησίων ἐσβολή ... ἐγίγνετο**: sc. in the spring of 430 B.C. Cf. ii. 47. § 1, 2. The impf. of contemporaneous action. Thus is explained why the anti-Athenian party in Colophon ventured at this time to revolt; just as the Lesbians made the attempt when the Athenians ἦσαν τεταλαιπωρημένοι ὑπό τε τῆς νόσου καὶ τοῦ πολέμου, c. 3. 1.

ἐν οὖν τῷ Νοτίῳ οἱ καταφυγόντες καὶ κατοικήσαντες 2
αὐτόθι αὖθις στασιάσαντες οἱ μὲν παρὰ Πισσούθνου
ἐπικούρους Ἀρκάδων τε καὶ τῶν βαρβάρων ἐπαγαγόμενοι
ἐν διατειχίσματι εἶχον (καὶ τῶν ἐκ τῆς ἄνω πόλεως Κο-
10 λοφωνίων οἱ μηδίσαντες ξυνεσελθόντες ἐπολίτευον), οἱ δὲ
ὑπεξελθόντες τούτους καὶ ὄντες φυγάδες τὸν Πάχητα
ἐπάγονται. ὁ δὲ προκαλεσάμενος ἐς λόγους Ἱππίαν τῶν 3
ἐν τῷ διατειχίσματι Ἀρκάδων ἄρχοντα, ὥστε, ἢν μηδὲν
ἀρέσκον λέγῃ, πάλιν αὐτὸν καταστήσειν ἐς τὸ τεῖχος σῶν
15 καὶ ὑγιᾶ, ὁ μὲν ἐξῆλθε παρ' αὐτόν, ὁ δὲ ἐκεῖνον μὲν ἐν

6. οἱ καταφυγόντες καὶ κατοικήσαντες αὐτόθι : *those who had fled for refuge and settled there.* For the nom. in part. appos. (οἱ μέν, οἱ δέ, 10), see G. 914; H. 624 d; Kr. *Spr.* 56, 9, 1. — 7. Πισσούθνου : see on c. 31. 9. — 8. Ἀρκάδων : the Arcadians appear as mercenaries even in the Persian wars. *Cf.* Hdt. viii. 26. 2 βίου τε δεόμενοι καὶ ἐνεργοὶ βουλόμενοι εἶναι. *Cf.* vii. 57. 59. — ἐπαγόμενοι : on the form, see App. — 9. ἐν διατειχίσματι : here and vii. 60. 9, "a space cut off from the rest of the city by an enclosing wall." *Cf.* Polyb. viii. 36. 9; xvi. 31. 5, 8; 33. 1; Liv. xxxvii. 11. 10, 11. — καὶ τῶν . . . ἐπολίτευον: supplementary explanation, by which the regular const. (οἱ μέν . . . εἶχον, οἱ δὲ . . . ἐπάγονται) is interrupted, as in c. 33. 8–11. Among the Colophonians who had left the upper city at the time of the Persian occupation and settled in Notium, a pro-Persian party was again developed, and this, having declared itself by a combination with Pissuthnes, was joined by the original Medizing party in Colophon (ξυνεσελθόντες ἐπολίτευον). Colophon being thus in the power of the barbarians, the pro-Athenian party had to leave Notium also, but now by treachery and violence on the part of Paches again got the upper hand. Their enemies, οἱ μηδίσαντες, had to leave Notium, which for security was made an Attic colony. — 11. ὑπεξελθόντες : with acc. only here, as ὑποχωρεῖν, ii. 88. 11; ὑπεκφεύγειν, ii. 90. 21; 91. 4; ἐξανεχώρει τὰ εἰρημένα, iv. 28. 13. It is intr. iv. 74. 7; vi. 51. 9; viii. 70. 2; 98. 3. Kr. *Spr.* 46, 6, 8.
12. τῶν : for τόν of the Mss., since the art. is abs. necessary with Ἀρκάδων, while it is not indispensable with ἄρχοντα (*cf.* v. 51. 8; viii. 92. 32). — 13. ὥστε: see on c. 28. 4. — 14. ἀρέσκον : for the use of the partic. expressing an adj. notion always in readiness to exert itself, see on i. 38. 8; v. 41. 23; *Am. J. of Ph.* iv. p. 297. — καταστήσειν : *to put back,* as in c. 59. 24. For the fut. inf., see GMT. 591, 2. — σῶν καὶ ὑγιᾶ : *safe and sound.* Similar formulas are salvus et incolumis, salvus et sospes, sain et sauf. — 15. ὁ μὲν ἐξῆλθε . . . ὁ δ' ἐκεῖνον . . . εἶχεν : a very striking

φυλακῇ ἀδέσμῳ εἶχεν, αὐτὸς δὲ προσβαλὼν τῷ τειχίσματι ἐξαπιναίως καὶ οὐ προσδεχομένων αἱρεῖ, τούς τε Ἀρκάδας καὶ τῶν βαρβάρων ὅσοι ἐνῆσαν διαφθείρει· καὶ τὸν Ἱππίαν ὕστερον ἐσαγαγὼν ὥσπερ ἐσπείσατο, ἐπειδὴ ἔν-
20 δον ἦν, ξυλλαμβάνει καὶ κατατοξεύει. Κολοφωνίοις δὲ 4 Νότιον παραδίδωσι πλὴν τῶν μηδισάντων. καὶ ὕστερον Ἀθηναῖοι οἰκιστὰς πέμψαντες κατὰ τοὺς ἑαυτῶν νόμους κατῴκισαν τὸ Νότιον, ξυναγαγόντες πάντας ἐκ τῶν πόλεων, εἴ πού τις ἦν Κολοφωνίων.
35 Ὁ δὲ Πάχης ἀφικόμενος ἐς τὴν Μυτιλήνην τήν τε 1 Πύρραν καὶ Ἔρεσον παρεστήσατο καὶ Σάλαιθον λαβὼν

anacoluthon. The author instead of continuing with ἐξελθόντα αὐτὸν ἐν φυλακῇ ἀδέσμῳ εἶχεν, proceeds after the interposed clause, ὥστε ... ὑγιᾶ, by a transition in parataxis to const. with finite verb. See on i. 26. 16. Similar anacoluthon iv. 80. 16. Kr. *Spr.* 56, 9, 3. — **ἐν φυλακῇ ἀδέσμῳ**: in custodia liberâ. *Cf.* Dio C. xxxvi. 36 ἐκεῖνον ἐν φυλακῇ ἀδέσμῳ εἶχεν, Diod. iv. 46 ἐλευθέρα φυλακή. — 16. **τῷ τειχίσματι**: the διατείχισμα of l. 9, 13. — 17. **οὐ προσδεχομένων**: sc. τῶν ἐντός. Gen. abs. without expressed subj., as often in Thuc., when it can easily be supplied from the context. GMT. 848; II. 972 a. See on i. 2. 8. — 19. **ὥσπερ ἐσπείσατο**: *cf.* l. 13. Concerning this horrible perfidy, Grote expresses surprise that 'Thucydides recounts it plainly and calmly, without a single word of comment.' Cl.'s explanation, that the historian's indignation can be felt in the short, sharp way in which the occurrences are set one over against the other, ἐσαγαγὼν... ἐπειδὴ ἔνδον ἦν ... ξυλλαμβάνει, is, to say the least, not very convincing. *Cf.* Polyaen. iii. 2.

21. **πλὴν τῶν μηδισάντων**: *i.e.* those mentioned in l. 16, who now either returned, or in their turn φυγάδες ἐγένοντο. — 22. **οἰκιστάς**: as always in Thuc., not the colonists themselves, but those sent out to arrange the government and laws of the colony to be founded. *Cf.* c. 92. 22; i. 24. 4; 25. 8; iv. 102. 11; vi. 3. 2; 4. 23; 5. 11. The new Notium, whither were recalled all the Colophonians who had become fugitives during the disturbances, received now under Attic 'oecists' an Attic constitution, κατὰ τοὺς ἑαυτῶν νόμους. — 23. **κατῴκισαν**: *re-settled*, as vi. 5. 16; 48. 13; 76. 7, 9; 84. 6. — **ἐκ τῶν πόλεων**: *i.e.* from the neighbouring Ionic cities, whither the adherents of the Attic party had fled at the time of the Persian occupation.

35. *After subduing Pyrrha and Eresus, Paches sends the instigators of the revolt of Mytilene as prisoners to Athens.*

2. **Πύρραν καὶ Ἔρεσον**: which had

ἐν τῇ πόλει τὸν Λακεδαιμόνιον κεκρυμμένον ἀποπέμπει ἐς τὰς Ἀθήνας καὶ τοὺς ἐκ τῆς Τενέδου Μυτιληναίων ἄνδρας ἅμα οὓς κατέθετο καὶ εἴ τις ἄλλος αὐτῷ αἴτιος ἐδόκει εἶναι τῆς ἀποστάσεως (ἀποπέμπει δὲ καὶ τῆς 2 στρατιᾶς τὸ πλέον, τοῖς δὲ λοιποῖς ὑπομένων καθίστατο τὰ περὶ τὴν Μυτιλήνην καὶ τὴν ἄλλην Λέσβον ᾗ αὐτῷ ἐδόκει). ἀφικομένων δὲ τῶν ἀνδρῶν καὶ τοῦ Σαλαίθου οἱ 1 Ἀθηναῖοι τὸν μὲν Σάλαιθον εὐθὺς ἀπέκτειναν, ἔστιν ἃ παρεχόμενον τά τ' ἄλλα καὶ ἀπὸ Πλαταιῶν (ἔτι γὰρ ἐπολιορκοῦντο) ἀπάξειν Πελοποννησίους· περὶ δὲ τῶν 2 ἀνδρῶν γνώμας ἐποιοῦντο, καὶ ὑπὸ ὀργῆς ἔδοξεν αὐτοῖς

sided with Mytilene, c. 18. 5. Antissa had already been reduced (c. 28. 15). — παρεστήσατο: *reduced*, in Thuc. only in aor., serving as causative to προσχωρεῖν τινι, to *submit*. See on i. 29. 22. — Σάλαιθον: *cf.* c. 25. § 1; 27. § 2. — 4. τοὺς ἐκ τῆς Τενέδου: for the proleptic const., see on c. 5. 1. — 5. οὓς κατέθετο: acc. to c. 28. 15 this was done μέχρι οὗ τοῖς Ἀθηναίοις τι δόξῃ. In sending the instigators of the revolt to Athens, Paches doubtless obeyed a command received thence. — καὶ εἴ τις κτέ.: for the conditional clause co-ord. with a case, see Kr. *Spr.* 59, 2, 4; 60, 10, 1.

6. τῆς στρατιᾶς τὸ πλέον: as in c. 36. 22; i. 73. 27; 118. 10. — 7. τοῖς λοιποῖς: as τοῖς λειπομένοις, ii. 12. 19. It is construed with ὑπομένων alone, and is the usual dat. of accompaniment, used chiefly in reference to military forces. G. 1189, 1190; II. 774. — καθίστατο: see on c. 28. 17.

36. *The Athenians in the first impulse of their anger adopt the severest measures in regard to the Lesbian prisoners, as well as to all the inhabitants of Mytilene, but the matter is reconsidered in the ecclesia on the following day.*

2. ἔστιν ἅ: as in ii. 67. 26. G. 1029; H. 998. — 3. παρεχόμενον: Schol. πρᾶξαι ὑπισχνούμενον. *Cf.* i. 39. 7; iv. 108. 15. — τά τ' ἄλλα: before καί, which introduces a definite circumstance, only to emphasize the latter, in which case the use of the art. is regular. "He made various offers and especially ——." *Cf.* i. 129. 9; 132. 8; iv. 108. 11; v. 46. 21; 52. 12; vi. 8. 7; vii. 65. 6. — ἔτι γὰρ ἐπολιορκοῦντο: cf. c. 20-24; 52. 1. — 4. ἀπάξειν: *i.e.* to effect their withdrawal, as in i. 109. 6; vi. 73. 9.

5. γνώμας ἐποιοῦντο: only here in the sense of *deliberated*, lit. *offered their several views*, = γνώμας σφίσιν αὐτοῖς προυτίθεσαν, i. 139. 18. In ii. 2. 24, γνώμην ποιεῖσθαι means *form a plan*; in i. 128. 28; vii. 72. 8, *offer a plan*. — ἐποιοῦντο, καὶ . . . ἔδοξεν: paratactic const., as i. 48. 3; 61. 2.

οὐ τοὺς παρόντας μόνον ἀποκτεῖναι, ἀλλὰ καὶ τοὺς ἅπαντας Μυτιληναίους ὅσοι ἡβῶσι, παῖδας δὲ καὶ γυναῖκας ἀνδραποδίσαι, ἐπικαλοῦντες τήν τε ἄλλην ἀπόστασιν καὶ ὅτι οὐκ ἀρχόμενοι ὥσπερ οἱ ἄλλοι ἐποιήσαντο, καὶ
10 προσξυνεβάλετο οὐκ ἐλάχιστον τῆς ὁρμῆς αἱ Πελοποννησίων νῆες ἐς Ἰωνίαν ἐκείνοις βοηθοὶ τολμῆσαι παρακινδυνεῦσαι· οὐ γὰρ ἀπὸ βραχείας διανοίας ἐδόκουν

Concerning the decree, cf. Ael. Var. Hist. ii. 9; Diod. xii. 55.—7. ὅσοι ἡβῶσι: the orig. mood of the decree is retained in indir. discourse. GMT. 689, 2; H. 933; Kühn. 399, 3.—8. ἐπικαλοῦντες: construed loosely with ἔδοξεν αὐτοῖς, as if ἐβουλεύσαντο had preceded. H. 1003; Kr. Spr. 56, 9, 4; Kühn. 493, 1 a. For similar cases of anacoluthon, see on ii. 53. 13.— τήν τε ... καὶ ὅτι οὐκ ἀρχόμενοι: Cl. inserts καί before ὅτι. St. explains that τε is used as if the author had continued, as he seems to have intended, with καὶ ὅτι κτέ., or καὶ τὸ τὰς Πελοποννησίων ναῦς τολμῆσαι κτέ., but after the ὅτι clause the const. is changed to finite verb. For similar changes in const., see on i. 16. 2. Cf. Hdt. i. 85. 5; 129. 4; ii. 44. 5. See App. —10. προσξυνεβάλετο: this reading of almost all the better Mss. is protected by Thuc.'s usage. The sing. verb before a pl. subj. occasions no difficulty, since αἱ νῆες τολμῆσαι = τὸ τὰς ναῦς τολμῆσαι. Cf. iv. 26. 14; viii. 9. 11. προσξυμβάλλεσθαι, which is used also by Hippocr. 797 c; 807 c, is further protected by the similar use of ξυμβάλλεσθαι c. 45. 24; Plato Apol. 36 a.; Legg. 791 c; Xen. Cyrop.

i. 2. 8; Hell. vii. 1. 35. In apparent imitation of the present passage, Arist. says, 'Αθ. Πολ. 19, συνεβάλλετο δὲ οὐκ ἐλάττω μοῖραν τῆς ὁρμῆς τοῖς Λάκωσιν ἡ πρὸς τοὺς Ἀργείους τοῖς Πεισιστρατίδαις ὑπάρχουσα φιλία. Bl. and Kr. read προσξυνελάβοντο (with Laur. and some inferior Mss.), the former citing iv. 47. 3 ξυνελάβοντο δὲ τοῦ τοιούτου οὐχ ἥκιστα, κτέ., and Dio C.'s imitation, xliii. 47. 4 προσσυνελάβετο γὰρ τοῦ λόγου τούτου, ὅτι κτέ. — οὐκ ἐλάχιστον τῆς ὁρμῆς : = οὐκ ἐλαχίστην μοῖραν τῆς ὁρμῆς. Cf. ii. 21. 19, and Arist. l.c. The phrase is to be taken as obj. of προσξυνεβάλετο. Cf. Lys. xxx. 16; Dem. xli. 11. Cf. τὸ πλεῖστον τῆς γνώμης, c. 31. 11; τοῦ θαρσεῖν τὸ πλεῖστον, iv. 34. 5. See on i. 5. 10. Kühn. 416, N. 4. ὁρμή, excitement, impulse. Cf. iv. 4. 4; vii. 71. 32. — 11. ἐς Ἰωνίαν παρακινδυνεῦσαι : venture over to Ionia. See on c. 32. 15. παρακινδυνεύειν also iv. 26. 18. Cf. ἐς τὰς Ἐπιπολὰς διεκινδύνευσεν, vii. 47. 11. See on i. 63. 3. — 12. οὐκ ἀπὸ βραχείας διανοίας : after no slight consideration, i.e. after long premeditation ; or, with St. and others, non parvo consilio = ὀλίγον οὐδὲν ἐπινοοῦντες (ii. 8. 1). Kr. compares Liban. Basil. 117 d οὐκ ἀπὸ βραχείας γνώμης εἰς τὸν πόλεμον κατέ-

τὴν ἀπόστασιν ποιήσασθαι. πέμπουσιν οὖν τριήρη ὡς 3
Πάχητα ἄγγελον τῶν δεδογμένων, κατὰ τάχος κελεύοντες
διαχρήσασθαι Μυτιληναίους. καὶ τῇ ὑστεραίᾳ μετάνοιά 4
τις εὐθὺς ἦν αὐτοῖς καὶ ἀναλογισμὸς ὠμὸν τὸ βούλευμα
καὶ μέγα ἐγνῶσθαι, πόλιν ὅλην διαφθεῖραι μᾶλλον ἢ οὐ
τοὺς αἰτίους. ὡς δ' ᾔσθοντο τοῦτο τῶν Μυτιληναίων οἱ 5
παρόντες πρέσβεις καὶ οἱ αὐτοῖς τῶν Ἀθηναίων ξυμπράσσοντες, παρεσκεύασαν τοὺς ἐν τέλει ὥστε αὖθις
γνώμας προθεῖναι (καὶ ἔπεισαν ῥᾷον, διότι καὶ ἐκείνοις
ἔνδηλον ἦν βουλόμενον τὸ πλέον τῶν πολιτῶν αὖθίς

στησαν. For ἀπό in this sense, see on i. 91. 28; for βραχεία, see on i. 14. 11.

14. ἄγγελον: pred. to τριήρη, as viii. 106. 18 ἀπέστειλαν ἐς τὰς Ἀθήνας τριήρη ἄγγελον τῆς νίκης. — **15. διαχρήσασθαι**: *to destroy*, as i. 126. 37; vi. 61. 17; Hdt. i. 24. 12; 110. 18; Antiph. i. 23; Aeschin. iii. 244; Xen. *Mem.* iv. 2. 17.

16. ἀναλογισμός: not re-consideration, but *reflection*, as viii. 84. 1. So ἀναλογίζεσθαι, v. 7. 3; viii. 83. 10. — **ὠμὸν τὸ βούλευμα καὶ μέγα**: the pred. position of the adjs. throws the chief stress on them. μέγα pregnant = δεινόν. See on c. 3. 3. μᾶλλον ἢ οὐ, as in ii. 62. 18, and often in Hdt. and Dion. H. The neg. implied in μᾶλλον ἤ sometimes induces a pleonastic neg. in the following clause. Kühn. 516, 6; Kr. *Spr.* 49, 2, 4. — **18. τῶν Μυτιληναίων οἱ παρόντες πρέσβεις**: Steup thinks this cannot be the same embassy as that mentioned in c. 28. 7, because Paches could not have executed the decree of the Athenians without violating the agreement (c. 28. 8, 9). But it seems more natural, since Thuc. mentions neither the return of the embassy of c. 28. 7, nor the sending of another, to suppose that the πρέσβεις remained at Athens in the hope of persuading the Athenians to milder measures. The spirit of the agreement was fulfilled when orders came from Athens, whether the ambassadors returned or remained. — **19. οἱ . . . ξυμπράσσοντες**: *cf.* c. 101. 4. For the position of the gen. τῶν Ἀθηναίων, see on c. 22. 27. — **20. παρεσκεύασαν**: *induced*, as in iv. 132. 11; viii. 52. 1; and passive in vii. 35. 2. Kühn. 473, 2. — **τοὺς ἐν τέλει**: *i.e.* the prytanes, or the ten στρατηγοί, the former of whom ordinarily summoned assemblies, though the latter had this right in war and under extraordinary circumstances. See on ii. 22. 4; 59. 11; iv. 118. 53. See Schoemann, *Gr. Ant.* i.³ p. 404. — **21. αὖθις γνώμας προθεῖναι**: *to bring the subject again under consideration*, also c. 42. 1; vi. 14. 3; and in c. 38. 2, λέγειν προτιθέναι. See on i. 139. 18. — **22. ἔνδηλον ἦν**: with partic., as in ii. 64. 31.

τινας σφίσιν ἀποδοῦναι βουλεύσασθαι). καταστάσης δ' 6
εὐθὺς ἐκκλησίας ἄλλαι τε γνῶμαι ἀφ' ἑκάστων ἐλέγοντο
25 καὶ Κλέων ὁ Κλεαινέτου. ὅσπερ καὶ τὴν προτέραν ἐνενικήκει ὥστε ἀποκτεῖναι, ὧν καὶ ἐς τὰ ἄλλα βιαιότατος
τῶν πολιτῶν τῷ τε δήμῳ παρὰ πολὺ ἐν τῷ τότε πιθανώτατος, παρελθὼν αὖθις ἔλεγε τοιάδε ·

37 "Πολλάκις μὲν ἤδη ἔγωγε καὶ ἄλλοτε ἔγνων δημο- 1
κρατίαν ὅτι ἀδύνατόν ἐστιν ἑτέρων ἄρχειν, μάλιστα δ'
ἐν τῇ νῦν ὑμετέρᾳ περὶ Μυτιληναίων μεταμελείᾳ. διὰ 2
γὰρ τὸ καθ' ἡμέραν ἀδεὲς καὶ ἀνεπιβούλευτον πρὸς ἀλ-

G. 1589; II. 981. *Cf.* iv. 41. 14;
vi. 36. 6. — τὸ πλέον τῶν πολιτῶν:
see on c. 35. 6. — 23. τινας: indef.,
it is true, as in iv. 69. 4; vi. 41. 4;
vii. 29. 14, but referring to τοὺς ἐν
τέλει, 1. 20. — ἀποδοῦναι: with inf.
as i. 144. 12; ii. 71. 14.
23. καταστάσης ἐκκλησίας: as in
i. 31. 15, of an assembly convoked
for a special purpose. *i.e.* σύγκλητος.
See Schoemann *Gr. Antiq.* i.³ p. 403.
— 24. ἀφ' ἑκάστων ἐλέγοντο: ἀπό, on
the part of, as in c. 82. 41; v. 82. 16;
vi. 32. 18; with μηνύεσθαι, vi. 28. 1;
ἀγγέλλεσθαι, vi. 45. 2. See on i. 17. 4,
and Herbst, *Gegen Cobet*, p. 50. —
25. τὴν προτέραν ἐνενικήκει : here of
the person, as ii. 12. 6; 54. 7 of the
view that prevails. For the cognate
acc. τὴν προτέραν sc. γνώμην, see G.
1052; II. 716 a; Kr. *Spr.* 46, 6. *Cf.*
Plato *Gorg.* 456 a οἱ νικῶντες τὰς γνώμας, Ar. *Nub.* 432. See App. —
26. βιαιότατος : most arbitrary and
arrogant, as in i. 95. 1. — 27. παρὰ
πολύ : by far. Kühn. 349ᵇ, 7 b. *Cf.*
i. 29. 19; ii. 8. 13; 89. 16; viii. 6. 16.—
πιθανώτατος : *cf.* iv. 21. 10; vi. 35. 9;

and see Introd. to Book I., p. 45, 46.
Aristotle says of Cleon, 'Αθ. Πολιτ.
28, δοκεῖ μάλιστα διαφθεῖραι τὸν δῆμον
ταῖς ὁρμαῖς, καὶ πρῶτος ἐπὶ τοῦ βήματος
ἀνέκραγε καὶ ἐλοιδορήσατο καὶ περιζωσά-
μενος ἐδημηγόρησε, τῶν ἄλλων ἐν κόσμῳ
λεγόντων.

Speech of Cleon. cc. 37-40.

37. *The demos is too prone to mild
treatment of subject states; it incurs
thereby great harm, but will incur
greater still, if it does not enforce
decrees once adopted, and recognize
that for the welfare of the state, sober
judgment* (σωφροσύνη) *on the part of
citizens is above all things requisite.*
1. πολλάκις μὲν... καὶ ἄλλοτε...
μάλιστα δέ: *cf.* vii. 8. 5. — 2. ἀδύνατον : incompetent. See Ullrich, *Beitr.*
1862, p. 20 ff. For the neut. pred.
adj. with fem. subj., see G. 925; II.
617. *Cf.* 1. 16; vi. 39. 1; Hdt. i. 62.
6; Ar. *Eccl.* 236. — ἑτέρων : in the
general and comprehensive sense of
any others, as i. 85. 6; ii. 35. 14.
3. διὰ γὰρ τὸ... ἔχετε : *cf.* similar
thought in i. 68. § 1. — 4. τὸ καθ' ἡμέ-

5 δήλους καὶ ἐς τοὺς ξυμμάχους τὸ αὐτὸ ἔχετε, καὶ ὅ τι ἂν ἢ λόγῳ πεισθέντες ὑπ' αὐτῶν ἁμάρτητε ἢ οἴκτῳ ἐνδῶτε, οὐκ ἐπικινδύνως ἡγεῖσθε ἐς ὑμᾶς καὶ οὐκ ἐς τὴν τῶν ξυμμάχων χάριν μαλακίζεσθαι, οὐ σκοποῦντες ὅτι τυραννίδα ἔχετε τὴν ἀρχὴν καὶ πρὸς ἐπιβουλεύοντας αὐ-
10 τοὺς καὶ ἄκοντας ἀρχομένους· οὐκ ἐξ ὧν ἂν χαρίζησθε βλαπτόμενοι αὐτοί, ἀκροῶνται ὑμῶν, ἀλλ' ἐξ ὧν ἂν ἰσχύι μᾶλλον ἢ τῇ ἐκείνων εὐνοίᾳ περιγένησθε. πάντων δὲ 3

ραν... πρὸς ἀλλήλους: more fully expressed by Pericles in ii. 37. § 2. πρός and ἐς denoting general relations without difference of meaning here, as l. 7. 9 below; also c. 54. 2; i. 32. 10; 38. 1. — 5. τὸ αὐτό: sc. τὸ ἀδεὲς καὶ ἀνεπιβούλευτον. — καὶ ὅ τι ἂν... μαλακίζεσθαι: *and whatever false step you make through being misled by their words, or whatever you yield through pity, you do not consider that your yielding brings danger to yourselves and does not win favour from your allies.* — 6. ἢ λόγῳ πεισθέντες... ἢ οἴκτῳ ἐνδῶτε: i.e. the two chief sources from which Cleon has reason to fear opposition to his advice, to which is added in c. 40 ἡ ἐπιείκεια. Instead of ἐνδόντες, as was to be expected, ἐνδῶτε is made coord. with ἁμάρτητε. — οἴκτῳ: cf. c. 40. 7; 48. 1. — 7. ἐπικινδύνως ἐς ὑμᾶς: cf. i. 91. 26 ἐς τοὺς πάντας ὠφελιμώτερον. — καὶ οὐκ: and not, differing from οὐδέ as et non from neque. — οὐκ ἐς τὴν χάριν: lit. *not for the gratitude of.* Cf. c. 40. 19; ii. 40. 22. — 8. μαλακίζεσθαι: as in c. 40. 34; vi. 29. 11. — ὅτι τυραννίδα ἔχετε τὴν ἀρχήν: exactly as Pericles had expressed himself in ii. 63. 8. Thuc. prob. purposely puts into the mouth of Cleon turns of thought and expression which are clearly echoes of the speeches of Pericles. Cf. c. 38. § 1; 40. § 4. Far as Cleon was removed from him in mind and mode of thinking, he had yet learned from him what was effective in a speech. — 9. καὶ πρὸς ἐπιβουλεύοντας αὐτοὺς καὶ ἄκοντας ἀρχομένους: emphatically opp. to ἀνεπιβούλευτον πρὸς ἀλλήλους. *And indeed as against those who are themselves plotting against you and bear your rule unwillingly.* — 10. οὐκ ἐξ ὧν... περιγένησθε: this explanation of ἄκοντας ἀρχομένους is added without connecting word, as c. 63. 8 ἣν αὐτοὶ μάλιστα προβάλλεσθε· ἱκανή γε ἦν κτέ., iv. 10. 10 τὸ δυσέμβατον ἡμέτερον νομίζω· μενόντων ἡμῶν ξύμμαχον γίγνεται. In all three cases a rel. pron. (here οἵ) is read in only a few and inferior Mss. They obey you not in consequence of the kindnesses you do them to your own hurt, but in consequence of the superiority you have acquired by strength rather than by their good will. So Cl. and Bm. explain, but see App. ἐξ ὧν, for the assimilation, see G. 1032; H. 996 a. μᾶλλον ἢ completely subordinates the second member. Cf. l. 26; c. 63. 20; 64. 9.

δεινότατον εἰ βέβαιον ἡμῖν μηδὲν καθεστήξει ὧν ἂν δόξῃ
πέρι, μηδὲ γνωσόμεθα ὅτι χείροσι νόμοις ἀκινήτοις
15 χρωμένη πόλις κρείσσων ἐστὶν ἢ καλῶς ἔχουσιν ἀκύροις,
ἀμαθία τε μετὰ σωφροσύνης ὠφελιμώτερον ἢ δεξιότης
μετὰ ἀκολασίας, οἵ τε φαυλότεροι τῶν ἀνθρώπων πρὸς
τοὺς ξυνετωτέρους ὡς ἐπὶ τὸ πλεῖον ἄμεινον οἰκοῦσι τὰς

13. βέβαιον: the adj. is pred. to καθεστηκέναι, as c. 102. 25; i. 70. 2; 102.6; ii. 59.8; iv. 26.24; 78.12; vi. 15.17; vii. 28.31. Pred. adjs. occur with the pres. καθίστασθαι, iv. 92.15; with the aor. καταστῆναι, i. 6. 16; 23. 11; vi. 59. 4. — **ὧν ἂν δόξῃ πέρι:** *i.e.* περὶ τούτων, περὶ ὧν ἂν δόξῃ, or, with Ullrich (*Beitr.* p. 23), = περὶ τούτων ἃ ἂν δόξῃ, in which case it would be an instance of the rare attraction of the nom., as in vii. 67. 19. G. 1033; Kühn. 555, N. 4.— **15. κρείσσων ἐστίν:** *is stronger, i.e.* can use its strength more effectually, as also c. 48. 8. — **ἀκύροις:** *without authority, i.e.* not enforced. The antithesis to ἀκίνητοι is not logically exact, but suits the case. Alcibiades uses a similar paradox, vi. 18. § 7; but in neither case is the argument fair, because the question is not one of abolishing a fundamental law of the state (κινεῖν νόμον), but of rescinding a decree of the demos (καθαιρεῖν ψήφισμα), which could be set aside by another ψήφισμα. Cleon's wish seems to be 'to confound ψηφίσματα and νόμοι together, and to excite against the repeal of one of the former the same strong feeling which was entertained in Greece against any alteration of the latter.' Arn. On the relation of νόμος, which, acc. to Aristotle, was

a law of general application, to ψήφισμα, a decree for an individual case (*Eth.* v. 14; *Pol.* iv. 4), see Tarbell, *Am. J. of Ph.* x. p. 79 ff. See also Hermann. *Gr. Ant.* i.[6] § 91. *Cf.* Dio C.'s imitation of the passage (liii. 10), τὰ γὰρ ἐν ταὐτῷ μένοντα, κἂν χείρω ᾖ, συμφορώτερα τῶν ἀεὶ καινοτομουμένων, κἂν βελτίω εἶναι δοκῇ, ἐστίν. Junge, zur *Rede d. Kleon,* 1879, p. 2 ff., thinks that the words μηδὲ . . . ἀκύροις, and in § 4, οἱ μὲν φαίνεσθαι and οἱ δὲ . . . εἶναι, refer to a law against reconsidering, within a certain period, things concerning which there was already a ψήφισμα. A comparison with vi. 14 makes this argument seem plausible; but surely in that case Cleon would have made the charge of παρανόμων. — **16. ἀμαθία:** *ignorance, i.e.* lack of training and experience. *Cf.* i. 68. 4; ii. 40. 14. The whole sentiment is like that of Archidamus in i. 84. § 3 (*cf.* Arist. *Rhet.* i. 15. 12), and is more in accord with Spartan ideas than with Athenian, as expressed by Pericles in ii. 40. — **δεξιότης:** *cleverness,* = ξύνεσις, l. 23; c. 82. 50. — **17. οἱ φαυλότεροι:** *the simpler, i.e.* humbler, inferior, as c. 83. 8. *Cf.* also vii. 77. 9. — **πρός:** *in comparison with,* as in c. 56. 16; i. 6. 15; 10. 8; ii. 35. 11. Kühn. 441, iii, 3 c; Kr. *Spr.* 49, 2, 8. — **18. ὡς**

πόλεις. οἱ μὲν γὰρ τῶν τε νόμων σοφώτεροι βούλονται 4
20 φαίνεσθαι τῶν τε αἰεὶ λεγομένων ἐς τὸ κοινὸν περιγίγνεσθαι, ὡς ἐν ἄλλοις μείζοσιν οὐκ ἂν δηλώσαντες τὴν γνώμην, καὶ ἐκ τοῦ τοιούτου τὰ πολλὰ σφάλλουσι τὰς πόλεις·
οἱ δ᾽ ἀπιστοῦντες τῇ ἐξ ἑαυτῶν ξυνέσει ἀμαθέστεροι μὲν
τῶν νόμων ἀξιοῦσιν εἶναι, ἀδυνατώτεροι δὲ τοῦ καλῶς
25 εἰπόντος μέμψασθαι λόγον, κριταὶ δὲ ὄντες ἀπὸ τοῦ ἴσου
μᾶλλον ἢ ἀγωνισταὶ ὀρθοῦνται τὰ πλείω. ὡς οὖν χρὴ 5

ἐπὶ τὸ πλεῖον : *for the most part.* only here, like ὡς τὰ πλείω, c. 83. 8, for the usual ὡς ἐπὶ τὸ πολύ, ii. 13. 23; v. 107. 3. See App. on i. 12. 4. — ἄμεινον οἰκοῦσι τὰς πόλεις : *administer their states better.* The passive occurs viii. 67. 6 ἄριστα ἡ πόλις οἰκήσεται. *Cf.* also i. 17. 4; vi. 18. 44. For the sentiment, *cf.* Eur. *El.* 386 οἱ γὰρ τοιοῦτοι τὰς πόλεις οἰκοῦσιν εὖ καὶ δώματα.
19. οἱ μέν : *sc.* οἱ ξυνετώτεροι. —
20. τῶν τε αἰεί ... περιγίγνεσθαι : *and to surpass whatever is on every occasion said for the public good.* λέγεσθαι ἐς τὸ κοινόν = ἐς τὸ κοινὸν βουλεύεσθαι, i. 91. 29. *Cf.* in commune consulere, Ter. *Andria* iii. 3. 16; in commune consultare, Plin. *Epist.* vi. 15. 16. With the general sentiment Arn. compares Tac. *Hist.* i. 26 consilii quamvis egregii, quod non ipse adferret, inimicus, et adversus peritos pervicax. — **21. ὡς ἐν ἄλλοις ...**
τὴν γνώμην : *as if in no other affairs of greater importance could they display their opinion.* i.e. *show their insight.* *Cf.* Dio C. xlvii. 1 ὡς οὐκ ἂν ἄλλως τὴν ἑαυτοῦ δεινότητα διαδείξας. For partic. with ἄν representing aor. opt.,

see GMT. 215; II. 987 a; Kr. *Spr.* 69, 7, 1. See on vii. 67. 26. — **22. σφάλλουσι τὰς πόλεις :** *cf.* vi. 15. 20. —
23. οἱ δέ : *sc.* οἱ φαυλότεροι. — **τῇ ἐξ ἑαυτῶν ξυνέσει :** *their own cleverness.* *Cf.* τὸ ἀφ᾽ ἡμῶν αὐτῶν εὔψυχον, ii. 39. 6. — **ἀμαθέστεροι τῶν νόμων :** *cf.* the expression of Archidamus, i. 84. 13, ἀμαθέστερον τῶν νόμων τῆς ὑπεροψίας παιδευόμενοι. — **24. ἀδυνατώτεροι ... λόγον :** *less able to criticise the speech of a good speaker.* It is only in the order of the words that the clause is like the preceding. See on i. 69. 32. **ἀδυνατώτεροι,** *sc.* ἢ ξυνετώτεροι, limited by μέμψασθαι, τοῦ καλῶς εἰπόντος depending on λόγον. — **25. κριταὶ δὲ ὄντες ... ἀγωνισταί :** *being impartial judges rather than contending disputants.* For ἀπὸ τοῦ ἴσου, see on c. 10. 12; i. 77. 8. ἀγωνισταί has also the secondary meaning of partisans striving for personal pre-eminence and advantage. *Cf.* l. 27 ξυνέσεως ἀγῶνι, and c. 82. 50 ξυνέσεως ἀγώνισμα. — **26. ὀρθοῦνται τὰ πλείω :** *they are generally in prosperity,* and with them the state, which, as the antithesis to σφάλλουσι τὰς πόλεις shows, is esp. had in mind. ὀρθοῦνται as in c. 30. 15; 42. 20; ii. 60. 5; v.

καὶ ἡμᾶς ποιοῦντας μὴ δεινότητι καὶ ξυνέσεως ἀγῶνι
ἐπαιρομένους παρὰ δόξαν τῷ ὑμετέρῳ πλήθει παραινεῖν.

38 "Ἐγὼ μὲν οὖν ὁ αὐτός εἰμι τῇ γνώμῃ καὶ 1
θαυμάζω μὲν τῶν προθέντων αὖθις περὶ Μυτιληναίων

9. 14; 111. 24; vi. 9. 11; viii. 64. 18;
Hdt. i. 208. 8. τὰ πλείω is a little
stronger than τὰ πολλά in l. 22. Bl.
and Jow. render ὀρθοῦνται here *judge
rightly*, or *are in the right.*
ὥς: for καὶ οὕτως only here in
Thuc. and rare also elsewhere in
Attic prose. It occurs in Plato,
Prot. 338 a (as here with οὖν); *Rep.*
530 d. *Cf.* Hdt. ix. 18. 11. It is
common in Homer and other poets,
rare in the Attic poets. See Kr.
Dial. 77, 1. *Cf.* Soph. *O. C.* 1242;
Eur. *Bacch.* 1068. Kr. *Spr.* 25, 10,
11; Kühn. 561, N. 4. — **27**. ἡμᾶς: *we,
who come forward as orators, as
opp.* to ὑμέτερον πλῆθος. *Cf.* c. 43. 13.
— δεινότητι καὶ ξυνέσεως ἀγῶνι: *with
eloquence and the exercise of cleverness.*
Strictly the gen. δεινότητος was to be
expected, but instead of this, one
quality (δεινότης) and the ambitious
exercise of the other (ξυνέσεως ἀγών)
are loosely connected. δεινότητι, Schol.
τῇ ῥητορικῇ δυνάμει. *Cf.* viii. 68. 9.
— **28**. παρὰ δόξαν: "contrary to our
own judgment," as in Plato *Crit.* 49 c;
Prot. 337 b. So Steup explains, citing in support of his view c. 38. § 2,
and c. 42. 29 παρὰ γνώμην τι καὶ πρὸς
χάριν λέγοι. See also Junge, *ibid.* p.
7 f. But Cl. adopts, with St. and
Bm., Reiske's conjecture (see also
Ullrich, *Beitr.* 1862, p. 48) παρὰ τὸ
δόξαν (*contrary to the decree* of the
majority), because παρὰ δόξαν means
everywhere else in Thuc. *contrary to*

expectation, which is, of course, inadmissible here. *Cf.* c. 39. 25; 93.
4; i. 141. 21; ii. 49. 28; iv. 106. 10;
viii. 42. 13. With this view, τὸ δόξαν
is as τὸ δοκοῦν, c. 38. 11; i. 84. 8, and
παραινεῖν, absolute, as in ii. 13. 15;
vi. 24. 7; viii. 46. 29; 71. 25.
38. *That our magistrates should
suffer a reconsideration of our decision
concerning Mytilene is surprising, and
attempts to persuade you to a different conclusion can proceed only from
dishonest motives. But it is no wonder that attempts are made to mislead
you by fine-sounding words, since you
are wont to devote yourselves to the
enjoyment of brilliant speeches rather
than to forming a judgment from
actual circumstances.*

1. ἐγὼ μὲν ὁ αὐτός εἰμι: the very
words of Pericles, ii. 61. 5. *Cf.* Soph.
O. R. 557 καὶ νῦν ἔθ' αὐτός εἰμι τῷ βου-
λεύματι. Dio C. imitates the passage,
xxxviii. 44 ἐγὼ μὲν γὰρ καὶ τότε καὶ
νῦν τὴν αὐτὴν γνώμην ἔχω καὶ οὐ μετα-
βάλλομαι. *Cf.* also Soph. *Phil.* 521;
Eur. *Phoen.* 920. — **2**. θαυμάζω τῶν
προθέντων ... λέγειν: τῶν προθέντων is
short for τῶν προθέντων ὅτι προύθεσαν.
Cf. ὑμῶν θαυμάζω, εἰ μὴ βοηθήσετε,
Xen. *Hell.* ii. 3. 53; also Lys. xii.
86; Lycurg. *in Leocr.* 135. For the
gen., see G. 1126; H. 744; Kr.
Spr. 47, 10, 9; Kühn. 417, N. 9.
προθεῖναι λέγειν for the more usual
προθεῖναι λόγον, or προθεῖναι γνώμας
(c. 36. 21; *cf.* c. 42. 1) = ἀποδοῦναι

λέγειν καὶ χρόνου διατριβὴν ἐμποιησάντων, ὅ ἐστι πρὸς
τῶν ἠδικηκότων μᾶλλον (ὁ γὰρ παθὼν τῷ δράσαντι ἀμ-
5 βλυτέρᾳ τῇ ὀργῇ ἐπεξέρχεται, ἀμύνασθαι δὲ τῷ παθεῖν
ὅτι ἐγγυτάτω κείμενον ἀντίπαλον μάλιστα τὴν τιμωρίαν ἀναλαμβάνει), θαυμάζω δὲ καὶ ὅστις ἔσται ὁ ἀντε-

βουλεύσασθαι (c. 36. 23). *Cf.* Hdt. viii. 49. 2 προθεῖναι γνώμην ἀποφαίνεσθαι. See Schoemann, *de Comit. Athen.*, p. 104. — 3. ἐμποιησάντων: *causing.* as in i. 2. 17; ii. 51. 16. — πρὸς τῶν ἠδικηκότων: *in the interest of those who have done wrong.* For πρός with gen., see G. 1216 a; II. 805, 1 b; Kr. *Spr.* 68, 37, 1; Matth. 590, 6. *Cf.* c. 59. 1; ii. 86. 19; iv. 10. 8; 29. 11; 92. 36; vii. 36. 18; 81. 27; viii. 36. 9. — 4. ἀμβλυτέρᾳ τῇ ὀργῇ: *with duller anger, i.e.* anger that has already cooled off. The thought must be completed by supplying the words χρόνου διατριβῆς ἐμποιηθείσης. *Cf.* ii. 40. 21. — 5. ἐπεξέρχεται: with the dat. (τῷ δράσαντι), in the sense of *revenge* (v. 89. 3; vi. 38. 10), as in that of *attack* (c. 27. 6; ii. 23. 1; v. 9. 8). of *pursuit* (iv. 14. 20). — ἀμύνασθαι: without art. as subject. Kr. *Spr.* 50, 6, 3. *Cf.* ii. 35. 7; 39. 22; 54. 8; 63. 14; Xen. *Resp. Laced.* 9. 2 ἕπεται τῇ ἀρετῇ σῴζεσθαι εἰς τὸν πλείω χρόνον μᾶλλον ἢ τῇ κακίᾳ. — τῷ παθεῖν: the dat. depends not upon ἐγγυτάτω alone, which always takes the gen. in Thuc., but upon ἐγγυτάτω κείμενον, the partic. being pf. pass. of τιθέναι. Schol. εἰ τὸ ἀμύνεσθαι τῷ παθεῖν ἐγγὺς τεθείη. *Cf.* ἐγγυτέρω καταστῆσαι Ἀθηναίοις, ii. 89. 47. Kr. *Di.* 48, 9, 2; Matth. 542, N. 1. In Plut. *de Sera* 2, this passage is cited, and the sentiment approved by the speaker, — not by Plutarch. — 6. ἀντίπαλον μάλιστα τὴν τιμωρίαν ἀναλαμβάνει: *takes the punishment that is most adequate.* On the omission of ὅν, see App. ἀναλαμβάνει τιμωρίαν is not found elsewhere, but is to be compared with such expressions as ἔχθραν, ἀπέχθειαν, κίνδυνον ἀναλαμβάνειν. Reiske and Cl. conjecture λαμβάνει, considering the ἀνα- simply a repetition of the preceding -αν, and so St. writes. Kr. suggests ἀντιλαμβάνει. — 7. θαυμάζω δὲ καὶ ὅστις ἔσται ὁ ἀντερῶν κτέ.: as the first clause contains a defiant threat, so by ἀξιώσων ἀποφαίνειν τὰς μὲν Μυτιληναίων κτέ. the presumptive opponent is, with intentional perversion, forced into a false alternative. "Whoever does not vote for the severest punishment of the Mytileneans must show (*I wonder who will presume to show*) that the revolt of the Mytileneans is helpful to us, while our misfortunes are hurtful to our allies," *i.e.* that they, by their revolt, which was certainly detrimental to Athens (ἡμετέρας ξυμφοράς), did us good, but themselves harm. From the impossibility of proving this is to be deduced the necessity of extreme severity. That the guilt of revolting and the necessity of its punishment do not, however, neces-

ρῶν καὶ ἀξιώσων ἀποφαίνειν τὰς μὲν Μυτιληναίων ἀδικίας ἡμῖν ὠφελίμους οὔσας, τὰς δ' ἡμετέρας ξυμφορὰς τοῖς
10 ξυμμάχοις βλάβας καθισταμένας. καὶ δῆλον ὅτι ἢ τῷ 2
λέγειν πιστεύσας τὸ πάνυ δοκοῦν ἀνταποφῆναι ὡς οὐκ
ἔγνωσται ἀγωνίσαιτ' ἄν, ἢ κέρδει ἐπαιρόμενος τὸ εὐπρεπὲς τοῦ λόγου ἐκπονήσας παράγειν πειράσεται. ἡ δὲ πό- 3
λις ἐκ τῶν τοιῶνδε ἀγώνων τὰ μὲν ἆθλα ἑτέροις δίδω-
15 σιν, αὐτὴ δὲ τοὺς κινδύνους ἀναφέρει. αἴτιοι δ' ὑμεῖς 4

sarily imply the destruction of the guilty, Cleon purposely does not say. A correct conception of the connexion shows that every change proposed is unnecessary. See Junge, *ibid.* p. 9 f.

10. καὶ δῆλον ὅτι ... ἀγωνίσαιτ' ἄν: *and it is plain that either he has such confidence in his powers of speech as to contend that what is universally acknowledged is not established* (clearly known), or, to use St.'s words, id quod omnibus probatum est non constat. τὸ δοκοῦν is here used in the philosophical sense found in Xen. *Mem.* iv. 6. 15 διὰ τῶν δοκούντων τοῖς ἀνθρώποις ἄγειν τοὺς λόγους. For the force of ἔγνωσται, *cf.* Dem. xxi. 41 ἂν γὰρ ταῦθ' οὕτως ἐγνωσμένα ὑπάρχῃ παρ' ὑμῖν. For the inf., ἀνταποφῆναι, dependent on ἀγωνίσαιτ' ἄν, *cf.* c. 82. 59; iv. 87. 23; viii. 89. 30, and see Kr. *Spr.* 55, 3, 16. The term ἀγωνίζεσθαι is chosen as if the reference were to the delivery of a *show-piece* (ἀγώνισμα, i. 22. 19), and the figure of an oratorical competition is kept up in what follows (ἀγώνων l. 14, ἀγωνοθετοῦντες and θεαταί l. 16, ἀνταγωνιζόμενοι l. 25). The interpretation above is essentially that also of Heilmann, Arn., Kr., and Bm. Others (Portus, Duker, Kistemacher, Bredow, Haacke, Goell., and Bl.), understanding τὸ δοκοῦν to refer to the decree passed the day before, explain, "What was most certainly your resolution has really not been adopted." But this, it is objected, would require τὸ δόξαν. — **12. ἢ κέρδει ἐπαιρόμενος ... πειράσεται**: *or incited by gain* (i.e. bribed), *elaborating what is plausible in words he will try to mislead you.* Thus an insinuation of bribery is made in advance against any reply. It is the course which is aptly characterized in c. 42. 12 ἐκπλῆξαι ἂν τούς τε ἀντεροῦντας καὶ τοὺς ἀκουσομένους. For κέρδει ἐπαιρόμενος, see on ἀγῶνι ἐπαιρομένους, c. 37. 27. In c. 40. § 1 also, Cleon makes a distinction between those of his opponents who would display their oratorical skill and those who are bribed. παράγειν as in i. 34. 9; 91. 6; ii. 64. 1. For τὸ εὐπρεπὲς τοῦ λόγου, *cf.* c. 11. 10. For the neut. adj. in place of abstract noun, see on c. 30. 4; i. 36. 3.

14. ἑτέροις: Schol. τοῖς ῥήτορσι. —
15. ἀναφέρει: Schol. ἀναφέρει, ἀναδέχεται. It seems not to occur else-

κακῶς ἀγωνοθετοῦντες, οἵτινες εἰώθατε θεαταὶ μὲν τῶν
λόγων γίγνεσθαι, ἀκροαταὶ δὲ τῶν ἔργων, τὰ μὲν μέλλοντα ἔργα ἀπὸ τῶν 'εὖ εἰπόντων σκοποῦντες ὡς δυνατὰ
γίγνεσθαι, τὰ δὲ πεπραγμένα ἤδη, οὐ τὸ δρασθὲν πιστό-
20 τερον ὄψει λαβόντες ἢ τὸ ἀκουσθέν, ἀπὸ τῶν λόγῳ καλῶς ἐπιτιμησάντων· καὶ μετὰ καινότητος μὲν λόγου ἀπα- 5

where with κίνδυνον, but cf. ἀναφέρειν
φθόνους καὶ διαβολάς, Polyb. i. 36. 3;
ἀναφέρειν φθόνους καὶ τὸν πόλεμον, Polyb.
iv. 59. 10; ἀναφέρειν τὸν πόνον, Dion.
II. x. 24.

αἴτιοι δ' ὑμεῖς: just as unworthy
motives are imputed by Cleon to his
presumptive opponent, so the hearer
who would show himself favourable
to the former is charged with per-
verse conduct throughout, and this is
expressed in a series of partics. and
pred. adjs., continuing to the end of
the chapter. The charges made are
threefold : 1) that in the deliberation
more value is placed upon words
than facts (κακῶς ἀγωνοθετοῦντες ...
ἀπὸ τῶν λόγῳ καλῶς ἐπιτιμησάντων) ;
2) that in speeches what is new and
unusual is more applauded than what
is tried and in the long run wholesome (καὶ μετὰ καινότητος ... ἀποβησόμενα); 3) that in the hankering
after an ideal state actual conditions
are neglected (ζητοῦντές τε ... ἱκανῶς);
and finally all these errors are traced
to the mania for rhetorical and so-
phistical performances (ἁπλῶς τε ...
βουλευομένοις). — 16. ἀγωνοθετοῦντες:
cf. Aeschin. c. Ctes. 180 ὑπολάβετε
τοίνυν ὑμᾶς αὐτοὺς εἶναι ἀγωνοθέτας πολιτικῆς ἀρετῆς, Xen. Anab. iii. 1. 21
ἀγωνοθέται οἱ θεοί εἰσιν. — θεαταὶ μὲν
... τῶν ἔργων: "instead of seeing

facts as they are and listening to
speeches with judgment, you are on
the contrary *hearers of facts and
seers of speeches*, in that you view
facts past and future in the light of
what the orators say (ἀπὸ τῶν εὖ εἰπόντων) and attend upon the speeches as
spectators of a contest of sophists, in
which the prize is awarded for technical adroitness, not for the truth."
Bm. — 17. τὰ μὲν ... ἐπιτιμησάντων:
not in the facts, but in the discussion of them (τῶν εὖ εἰπόντων, τῶν
λόγῳ καλῶς ἐπιτιμησάντων), is found
the rule or measure by which is
determined (ἀπὸ ... σκοποῦντες) both
the practicability of the μέλλοντα
ἔργα, and the truth about the πεπραγμένα (though these ought to be ex-
perienced, not heard about). σκοπεῖν
ἀπό as in i. 21. 11; ii. 48. 14.—
19. τὰ δὲ πεπραγμένα ἤδη : sc. σκοποῦντες. — οὐ τὸ δρασθὲν πιστότερον
ὄψει λαβόντες ἢ τὸ ἀκουσθέν: *not
taking what is done as more to be
trusted, because you have seen it, than
what is heard*. λαβεῖν = ὑπολαβεῖν,
as in ii. 42. 17; iv. 106. 6. With the
sentiment of the whole passage, cf.
vii. 48. 20 ff. τὸ δρασθέν as in vi.
53. 8.

21. καὶ μετὰ καινότητος μὲν λόγου
... ἐθέλειν : *the best to be deceived
with novelty of words and to be un-*

τᾶσθαι ἄριστοι, μετὰ δεδοκιμασμένου δὲ μὴ ξυνέπεσθαι
ἐθέλειν, δοῦλοι ὄντες τῶν αἰεὶ ἀτόπων, ὑπερόπται δὲ τῶν
εἰωθότων, καὶ μάλιστα μὲν αὐτὸς εἰπεῖν ἕκαστος βουλό- 6
25 μενος δύνασθαι, εἰ δὲ μή, ἀνταγωνιζόμενοι τοῖς τοιαῦτα
λέγουσι μὴ ὕστεροι ἀκολουθῆσαι δοκεῖν τῇ γνώμῃ, ὀξέως
δέ τι λέγοντος προεπαινέσαι, καὶ προαισθέσθαι τε πρόθυμοι εἶναι τὰ λεγόμενα καὶ προνοῆσαι βραδεῖς τὰ ἐξ
αὐτῶν ἀποβησόμενα· ζητοῦντές τε ἄλλο τι, ὡς εἰπεῖν, ἢ 7

willing to follow with the rest in case of approved advice, i.e. where a proposition (λόγου) has been tested and approved. With μετὰ καινότητος λόγου, cf. Isoc. x. 2 ἐπὶ τῇ καινότητι τῶν εὑρημένων. ἄριστοι, sc. ὄντες, ironical, *adepts*. It is equiv. to ἐπιτήδειοι, as the Schol. says, just as in Hdt. i. 193. 13 ἀρίστη... Δήμητρος κάρπον ἐκφέρειν, iii. 80. 21 διαβολὰς ἄριστος ἐνδέκεσθαι. Cf. also Hdt. i. 136. 2 μάχεσθαι εἶναι ἀγαθόν, and Hes. *Op.* 763, 779, 813; Soph. *O. T.* 440; Ar. *Nub.* 430; Xen. *Cyrop.* v. 4. 44. G. 1526; H. 952. — 23. δοῦλοι ὄντες τῶν αἰεὶ ἀτόπων: *slaves of every new extravagance*. δοῦλοι ὄντες, i.e. χαίροντες καὶ πιστεύοντες, Schol. ἀτόπων as in ii. 49. 8; Schol. παραδόξων. Cf. Greg. Naz. i. p. 53 δοῦλοι ὄντες τῶν ἀεὶ παρόντων, Aristid. ii. 150 a τῆς χρείας ἀεὶ δούλους εἶναι. — ὑπερόπται δὲ τῶν εἰωθότων: *scorners of what is established*. ὑπερόπται not found elsewhere in Attic; Schol. καταφρονοῦντες. Both δοῦλοι and ὑπερόπται are explanatory of ἄριστοι, while τῶν αἰεὶ ἀτόπων represents καινότητος λόγου, as τῶν εἰωθότων does δεδοκιμασμένου. In illustration of the whole passage, Bl. compares Ar. *Eccles.* 581–588.

24. μάλιστα μέν, εἰ δὲ μή: as in i. 32. 4; ii. 72. 8; iv. 104. 20; v. 21. 15; viii. 91. 15. — αὐτὸς ἕκαστος βουλόμενος: the distrib. pron. after pl. subj. (ὑμεῖς), as in i. 141. 27; ii. 16. 11. — 25. ἀνταγωνιζόμενοι κτέ.: the pl. is resumed. On the partic. depends not only δοκεῖν, but also εἶναι with its preds. πρόθυμοι and βραδεῖς. On δοκεῖν depend both ἀκολουθῆσαι and προεπαινέσαι. *Vying with those that say such things, in seeming not to follow after them in insight, but when any one says anything clever to applaud it beforehand.* Cf. Dio C. lii. 8 ἀνταγωνιζόμενοι μὴ δοκεῖν ὀργίζεσθαι. — τοιαῦτα: sc. καινὰ and ἄτοπα. So generally explained, but Stenp brackets τοῖς τοιαῦτα λέγουσι. See App. — 27. προεπαινέσαι: found only here. Cf. ἐπαινέσαι, *approve*, iv. 65. 8; v. 37. 24. — καὶ προαισθέσθαι τε... ἀποβησόμενα: *and* (vying) *in being both eager to perceive beforehand what is said and slow to anticipate what will come of it.* The first καὶ connects εἶναι with δοκεῖν; while τε, καὶ connect προαισθέσθαι πρόθυμοι and προνοῆσαι βραδεῖς, the emphasis being on the former, as in ii. 39. 24. See App.

29. ἄλλο τι... ζῶμεν: *an entirely*

30 ἐν οἷς ζῶμεν, φρονοῦντες δὲ οὐδὲ περὶ τῶν παρόντων ἱκανῶς· ἁπλῶς τε ἀκοῆς ἡδονῇ ἡσσώμενοι καὶ σοφιστῶν θεαταῖς ἐοικότες καθημένοις μᾶλλον ἢ περὶ πόλεως βουλευομένοις.

39 "Ὧν ἐγὼ πειρώμενος ἀποτρέπειν ὑμᾶς ἀποφαίνω 1 Μυτιληναίους μάλιστα δὴ μίαν πόλιν ἠδικηκότας ὑμᾶς.

different world, so to speak, from that in which we live. ὡς εἰπεῖν as always in Thuc., not ὡς ἔπος εἰπεῖν, as in Plato and the orators. GMT. 777, 1; II. 956. *Cf.* i. 1.9. For the pl. οἷς after ἄλλο, see Kr. *Spr.* 58, 4, 5. — 31. ἁπλῶς τε: *and in a word*, as in c. 45. 29; 82. 34. τε inferential, *and so*, as que in Lat. See on i. 4. 5. — ἀκοῆς ἡδονῇ: *cf.* c. 40. 7 ἡδονῇ λόγων. —ἡσσώμενοι: with dat. as vii. 25. 41 οὐ τῇ τῶν πολεμίων ἰσχύι . . . ἡσσηθεῖεν. Elsewhere in figurative sense with the gen., as iv. 37. 6; v. 111. 15. In connexion with Cleon's placing the source of all evil in the prevailing enjoyment of fine speeches, is to be remembered the fact that about the end of this summer (see on c. 86. 12) Gorgias came to Athens for the first time, as ambassador from Leontini, and though Cleon could not have had him in mind in his real speech, Thuc. doubtless did, as he wrote the speech. — σοφιστῶν: only here in Thuc., in Cleon's mouth, in the same unfavourable sense as often in Aristophanes (*Nub.* 331, 1111), Xenophon (*Mem.* i. 6. 13), and Plato (*Phaedr.* 257 d ; *Prot.* 312 a, *etc.*). — 32. θεαταῖς ἐοικότες καθημένοις: the perversity of the practice of the sophists, whose object was not instruction, but vainglorious display, is characterized by θεαταὶ

(*cf.* θεαταὶ τῶν λόγων, l. 16). καθημένοις is usually taken as explanatory of θεαταῖς, *sitting idly*, as in Dem. ii. 23, 24; iv. 9, 44; viii. 77 — similarly iv. 124. 24. But Kr. objects that no activity is required of spectators, and Steup seems clearly right in considering (with Hude, p. 98) θεαταῖς as pred. *Like men sitting as spectators of sophists rather than like men deliberating about the welfare of the state.*

39. *Do not allow yourselves to be deceived in this case, but recognize that the Mytileneans have been guilty of an unpardonable crime, in that they have taken advantage of our embarrassment, in order to revolt, although they were far more favoured than other allies.* § 1–5.

All are alike guilty, the demos as well as the aristocrats, and untimely forbearance would only occasion further revolts, and bring upon you greater and greater losses. § 6–8.

1. ὧν : *sc.* ἐπιτηδευμάτων ὧν εἶπεν ἄρτι, Schol. It covers the whole course of the Athenians as described in c. 38. § 4–7. The rel. is emphatic, as in c. 43. 1; 46. 20; i. 9. 19, *etc*. — ἀποφαίνω : *I declare*, as in ii. 62. 10. *Cf.* c. 67. 10. v. H.'s conjecture, ἀποφανῶ, is unnecessary. — 2. δή: with the sup. as in c. 113. 22; i. 1. 8; vii. 87. 23, and freq. — μίαν πόλιν :

ἐγὼ γάρ, οἵτινες μὲν μὴ δυνατοὶ φέρειν τὴν ὑμετέ- 2
ραν ἀρχὴν ἢ οἵτινες ὑπὸ τῶν πολεμίων ἀναγκασθέντες
5 ἀπέστησαν, ξυγγνώμην ἔχω· νῆσον δὲ οἵτινες ἔχοντες
μετὰ τειχῶν καὶ κατὰ θάλασσάν μόνον φοβούμενοι τοὺς
ἡμετέρους πολεμίους, ἐν ᾧ καὶ αὐτοὶ τριήρων παρασκευῇ
οὐκ ἄφρακτοι ἦσαν πρὸς αὐτούς, αὐτόνομοί τε οἰκοῦν-
τες καὶ τιμώμενοι ἐς τὰ πρῶτα ὑφ᾽ ἡμῶν τοιαῦτα εἰργά-
10 σαντο, τί ἄλλο οὗτοι ἢ ἐπεβούλευσάν τε καὶ ἐπανέστησαν μᾶλλον ἢ ἀπέστησαν (ἀπόστασις μέν γε τῶν βίαιόν
τι πασχόντων ἐστίν), ἐζήτησάν τε μετὰ τῶν πολεμιωτάτων ἡμᾶς στάντες διαφθεῖραι; καίτοι δεινότερόν ἐστιν

appos. to Μυτιληναίους, as viii. 40. 7 τοῖς Χίοις ... μιᾷ γε πόλει ... πλεῖστοι γενόμενοι. For similar expressions, cf. c. 113. 21; i. 80. 13; vi. 20. 8; viii. 68. 5. Kr. Spr. 49, 10, 5.

3. οἵτινες: without τούτοις, as in v. 16. 10, about equiv. to εἴ τινες. Kr. Spr. 51, 13, 3. — δυνατοί: without ὄντες, co-ord. with the partic. ἀναγκασθέντες, as in c. 38. 22 ἄριστοι is with βουλόμενος and ἀνταγωνιζόμενοι.

— 5. νῆσον δὲ οἵτινες: νῆσον, as strongest security for an αὐτάρκης θέσις (i. 37. 11) and for immunity from attack (ἀληπτόν, i. 37. 20), placed before the rel. Cf. vi. 36. 1. Kr. Spr. 54, 17, 7; Kühn. 606, 6. Cf. δίκας δὲ ὅτι ἐθέλομεν, i. 144. 14. οἵτινες, though hypothetical, has so manifest a reference to the Mytileneans that in l. 8 the neg. is οὐ not μή. — 7. ἐν ᾧ καὶ αὐτοί: not entirely dependent, therefore, on Attic protection. ἐν ᾧ, in which case. See on i. 39. 11. — παρασκευῇ: force, as in vi. 31. 6; vii. 36. 3. Lesbian triremes are men-

tioned c. 4. 6; i. 116. 11; ii. 9. 20; 56. 7. — 9. τιμώμενοι: see on c. 9. 12. —ἐς τὰ πρῶτα: imprimis, as c. 56. 22. — 10. τί ἄλλο ἢ: as in c. 58. 24; v. 98. 8, with following finite verb. The same elliptical const. as οὐδὲν ἄλλο ἤ, ii. 16. 10. H. 612; Kr. Spr. 62, 3, 7; Kühn. 587, 18. — ἐπανέστησαν μᾶλλον ἢ ἀπέστησαν: rose up against rather than revolted from. For the paronomasia, freq. in Thuc., cf. c. 82. 31, and see on i. 33. 26. Cf. Dion. H. Ant. iii. 8. 2 οὐ μόνον ἀπόστασιν ἐβούλευσαν ἀφ᾽ ὑμῶν, ἀλλὰ καὶ ἐπανάστασιν, Dio C. lxxi. 24 δημοσία τε ἀπόστασις, μᾶλλον δὲ ἐπανάστασις. — 11. μέν γε: as if the explanation of the ἐπανάστασις also were to follow; but this is omitted since it is clear enough from the context. For the combination μέν γε, see on i. 40. 15. — 12. μετὰ τῶν πολεμιωτάτων στάντες: combining with our worst enemies. Cf. i. 33. 22; vii. 57. 4; 61. 12, and see on c. 11. 18. — 13. ἡμᾶς: emphatic position, as in i. 68. 1; 70.

ἢ εἰ καθ' αὑτοὺς δύναμιν κτώμενοι ἀντεπολέμησαν. παρά- 3
15 δειγμα δὲ αὑτοῖς οὔτε αἱ τῶν πέλας ξυμφοραὶ ἐγένοντο,
ὅσοι ἀποστάντες ἤδη ἡμῶν ἐχειρώθησαν, οὔτε ἡ παροῦσα εὐδαιμονία παρέσχεν ὄκνον μὴ ἐλθεῖν ἐς τὰ δεινά·
γενόμενοι δὲ πρὸς τὸ μέλλον θρασεῖς καὶ ἐλπίσαντες μακρότερα μὲν τῆς δυνάμεως, ἐλάσσω δὲ τῆς βουλήσεως,
20 πόλεμον ἤραντο, ἰσχὺν ἀξιώσαντες τοῦ δικαίου προθεῖναι· ἐν ᾧ γὰρ ᾠήθησαν περιέσεσθαι, ἐπέθεντο ἡμῖν οὐκ
ἀδικούμενοι. εἴωθε δέ, τῶν πόλεων αἷς ἂν μάλιστα καὶ 4

5; v. 82. 23; vii. 78. 26. — **14. καθ' αὑτούς**: *of themselves*, as in iv. 64. 14, 21, and freq. — **κτώμενοι**: *seeking to acquire*, as in ii. 62. 26. *Cf.* ἐπικτᾶσθαι, i. 144. 2; ii. 65. 24.
παράδειγμα: *warning example*. The sing. as in iv. 92. 18, but the plur. c. 10. 20; 11. 24; vi. 77. 4. It is placed first, as if to be pred. to both οὔτε clauses; but as εὐδαιμονία of course cannot be a warning, an anacoluthon arises. For similar const., *cf.* c. 96. 11. — **16. ὅσοι ... ἐχειρώθησαν**: *cf.* c. 10. § 4 ff.; i. 98. § 4; 99. — **17. παρέσχεν ὄκνον μὴ ἐλθεῖν**: for the neg., see on c. 32. 14. — **τὰ δεινά**: *dangers*. See on c. 22. 26. — **18. ἐλπίσαντες μακρότερα μὲν τῆς δυνάμεως, ἐλάσσω δὲ τῆς βουλήσεως**: the antithesis is well chosen, in order to rouse both contempt and bitterness. "Their hopes went indeed far beyond their strength, but not far enough to satisfy their hate." *Cf.* Schol. ἤλπισαν, φησίν, ἀποστῆναι ἡμῶν, ὅπερ μεῖζον μέν ἐστι τῆς δυνάμεως αὐτῶν, ἔλαττον δὲ τῆς βουλήσεως αὐτῶν. ἐβούλοντο γὰρ οὐ μόνον ἀποστῆναι ἡμῶν ἀλλὰ δὴ καὶ καθελεῖν τὴν δύναμιν τῆς πόλεως, διὰ τὸ λοιπὸν ἀδεῶς ζῆν. Herbst (Zu *Thuk. Erkl.*

u.s.w. 1892, p. 82) thinks that a contrast is intended between the Mytilenean view of their own power and that of the Athenians, *i.e.* they expected for themselves more than they could accomplish and from the Athenians less than they (the Mytileneans) could wish, so greatly did they underestimate the strength of the Athenians. — **20. ἰσχὺν ἀξιώσαντες ... προθεῖναι**: "having once determined to put might before right." The clause is all the more effective since a good word (ἀξιώσαντες) is made to serve in a bad cause. ἰσχύς, as i. 76. 15, of brute force. προθεῖναι with acc. and gen. also c. 84. 14; i. 76. 15; Hdt. iii. 53. 16; Soph. *O. C.* 419. — **21. ἐν ᾧ**: emphasizes here more sharply than usual the *moment*, when in the hope of getting the better of the Athenians, now hard pressed by war and pestilence (*cf.* c. 3. § 1; 13. § 3), they made an unprovoked attack. See on l. 7.
22. εἴωθε δέ ... ἐς ὕβριν τρέπειν: *unexpected good fortune is wont to make insolent those cities upon which it has come in the highest degree and in the shortest time.* With the sentiment, *cf.* Liv. xxx. 42. 15 raro

δι' ἐλαχίστου ἀπροσδόκητος εὐπραξία ἔλθῃ, ἐς ὕβριν τρέπειν (τὰ δὲ πολλὰ κατὰ λόγον τοῖς ἀνθρώποις εὐτυχοῦντα
25 ἀσφαλέστερα ἢ παρὰ δόξαν, καὶ κακοπραγίαν, ὡς εἰπεῖν, ῥᾷον ἀπωθοῦνται ἢ εὐδαιμονίαν διασῴζονται). χρῆν δὲ 5 Μυτιληναίους καὶ πάλαι μηδὲν διαφέροντας τῶν ἄλλων ὑφ' ἡμῶν τετιμῆσθαι, καὶ οὐκ ἂν ἐς τόδε ἐξύβρισαν· πέφυκε γὰρ καὶ ἄλλως ἄνθρωπος τὸ μὲν θεραπεῦον
30 ὑπερφρονεῖν, τὸ δὲ μὴ ὑπεῖκον θαυμάζειν.

"Κολασθέντων δὲ καὶ νῦν ἀξίως τῆς ἀδικίας, καὶ 6

simul hominibus bonam fortunam bonamque mentem dari; also Thuc. iv. 17. § 4; Dem. i. 23; Aristid. ii. 57. ἀπροσδόκητος εὐπραξία is subj. of both clauses. For the Mytileneans it consisted in the straits of the Athenians, indicated by ἐν ᾧ ... περιέσεσθαι. αἷς = ταύτας αἷς, the terminal dat. with ἐλθεῖν, as in c. 70. 2 and often. See on c. 5. 12; i. 13. 12. μάλιστα and δι' ἐλαχίστου are adv. with ἔλθῃ. Cf. δι' ὀλίγου, iv. 95. 1; v. 69. 19; vi. 47. 10; vii. 15. 13, and see on ii. 42. 24. ἐς ὕβριν τρέπειν has ταύτας understood as object. Cf. c. 13. 4. See App. — 24. τὰ πολλὰ κτέ.: the Schol. correctly explains = ὡς ἐπὶ τὸ πολύ. The subj. is εὐτυχοῦντα with its modifiers. "And for the most part success that comes to men in accordance with reasonable calculations is safer than that which surpasses expectation, and mankind apparently find it easier to repel adversity, than to maintain prosperity." εὐτυχοῦντα as in iv. 62. 17; 79. 4. For omission of art., cf. c. 48. 8. GMT. 827. διασῴζεσθαι as in v. 16. 11; 46. 9.
26. χρῆν δὲ ... τετιμῆσθαι: for the

const., see GMT. 415, 419; II. 834, 897. — καὶ πάλαι: iam pridem. Cf. c. 13. 5; 104. 14. — 27. μηδὲν διαφέροντας τῶν ἄλλων: pred. to τετιμῆσθαι, without any advantage over others. οὕτω τετιμῆσθαι ὑφ' ἡμῶν ὡς οὐδὲν διαφέροντας τῶν ἄλλων, Schol. διαφερόντως, which St. has adopted, is the reading of some of the Mss., and is supported by Thuc.'s usage (i. 38. 10; 138. 11; ii. 40. 11; 51. 2; viii. 68. 17), as well as by the imitation of Dio C. xxxviii. 39. 3 ἢ οὖν ἀπὸ πρώτης ἐχρῆν μηδὲν διαφερόντως ἡμᾶς τῶν ἄλλων ἀνθρώπων ηὐξῆσθαι. — 28. καὶ οὐκ: introduces in parataxis the result of the cond. implied in the preceding clause. — ἐς τόδε: adeo, as in i. 75. 8. — ἐξύβρισαν: also i. 84. 6. — 29. πέφυκε γὰρ καὶ ἄλλως κτέ.: passes from the present case to a general remark, as in i. 99. 6; viii. 45. 6; Plut. Tim. 52 a. With the sentiment, cf. iv. 61. 19. — τὸ θεραπεῦον, τὸ μὴ ὑπεῖκον: collective neuters with personal force, as ii. 45. 5; iv. 61. 20. Kr. Spr. 43, 4, 17. — 30. ὑπερφρονεῖν: with acc. also vi. 68. 10. Kr. Spr. 47, 23, 1.
31. κολασθέντων: on the form, see

μὴ τοῖς μὲν ὀλίγοις ἡ αἰτία προστεθῇ, τὸν δὲ δῆμον ἀπολύσητε. πάντες γὰρ ἡμῖν γε ὁμοίως ἐπέθεντο, οἷς γ' ἐξῆν ὡς ἡμᾶς τραπομένοις νῦν πάλιν ἐν τῇ πόλει εἶναι· ἀλλὰ
35 τὸν μετὰ τῶν ὀλίγων κίνδυνον ἡγησάμενοι βεβαιότερον ξυναπέστησαν. τῶν τε ξυμμάχων σκέψασθε εἰ τοῖς τε ἀναγ- 7
κασθεῖσιν ὑπὸ τῶν πολεμίων καὶ τοῖς ἑκοῦσιν ἀποστᾶσι τὰς αὐτὰς ζημίας προσθήσετε, τίνα οἴεσθε ὅντινα οὐ βραχείᾳ προφάσει ἀποστήσεσθαι, ὅταν ἢ κατορθώσαντι ἐλευ-
40 θέρωσις ᾖ ἢ σφαλέντι μηδὲν παθεῖν ἀνήκεστον; ἡμῖν δὲ 8
πρὸς ἑκάστην πόλιν ἀποκεκινδυνεύσεται τά τε χρήματα

App. — καὶ νῦν : *even now*, opp. to καὶ πάλαι, l. 27. — καὶ μή : covers both the following clauses. — 32. ἡ αἰτία προστεθῇ : for the act. with acc., cf. l. 38; 42. 25; iv. 20. 12. — ἀπολύσητε : for aor. subjv. in prohibition, see GMT. 259; H. 874; Kühn. 397, 3. — 33. ἡμῖν γε : i.e. against us at least they were united, even if they were at variance among themselves. — οἷς γ' ἐξῆν : grammatically construed with πάντες, though really only the δῆμος is had in mind here, as well as in the next clause. For const., see on l. 26 above. — 34. τραπομένοις : this reading of a few good Mss., is more appropriate with ἐν τῇ πόλει εἶναι than the vulg. τρεπομένοις. "Who might have turned to us and been now reinstated in their city." As to this rendering, which is essentially that of Va., see also L. Herbst, *Philol.* xlii. p. 711. — ἀλλὰ ... ξυναπέστησαν : *but considering the danger with the oligarchs safer* (than that with us), *they joined them in revolt.* Cf. c. 47. 3. Const. βεβαιότερον with κίνδυνον, as v. 108. 2.

36. τῶν τε ξυμμάχων : introduces the new consideration with emphasis. The part. gen. covers not only τοῖς τε ἀναγκασθεῖσιν ... ἀποστᾶσι, but also τίνα οἴεσθε ὅντινα οὐ. Both ἀναγκασθεῖσιν and ἑκοῦσιν are pred. to ἀποστᾶσι. — 38. τίνα ... ὅντινα οὐ : as in c. 46. 8, this becomes by attraction one word, as it were, in force and const. like οὐδεὶς ὅστις οὐ, c. 81. 24; vii. 87. 14. Cf. Xen. *Cyrop.* i. 4. 25 οὐδένα ἔφασαν ὅντιν' οὐ δακρύοντ' ἀποστρέφεσθαι. Kr. *Spr.* 51, 10, 11; Kühn. 555, 5. After the long protasis, οἴεσθε repeats σκέψασθε of l. 36. — βραχείᾳ προφάσει : *on a trifling pretext,* as in i. 141. 4. For the force of βραχεῖα, see on c. 36. 12; i. 14. 11. — 39. κατορθώσαντι, σφαλέντι : cf. c. 14. 5, 7; ii. 65. 28, 29; vi. 12. 7, 8. — ἐλευθέρωσις ἢ παθεῖν : for the noun and inf. co-ordinated as subj. of ᾖ, see Kr. *Spr.* 59, 2, 3.
40. ἡμῖν δέ : what follows, though logically dependent on σκέψασθε, is grammatically independent. — 41. ἀποκεκινδυνεύσεται : pass. prob. only here; in vii. 81. 26 intr. Kr. *Spr.* 52, 3, 4. Cf. ii. 43. 26 ἡ ἐναντία μετα-

καὶ αἱ ψυχαί, καὶ τυχόντες μὲν πόλιν ἐφθαρμένην παραλαβόντες τῆς ἔπειτα προσόδου, δι' ἣν ἰσχύομεν, τὸ λοιπὸν στερήσεσθε, σφαλέντες δὲ πολεμίους πρὸς τοῖς ὑπ-
45 άρχουσιν ἕξομεν, καὶ ὃν χρόνον τοῖς νῦν καθεστηκόσι δεῖ ἐχθροῖς ἀνθίστασθαι, τοῖς οἰκείοις ξυμμάχοις πολεμήσομεν.

40 "Οὐκ οὖν δεῖ προθεῖναι ἐλπίδα οὔτε λόγῳ πιστὴν οὔτε χρήμασιν ὠνητήν, ὡς ξυγγνώμην ἁμαρτεῖν ἀνθρωπίνως λήψονται. ἄκοντες μὲν γὰρ οὐκ ἔβλαψαν, εἰδότες

βολὴ ... ἔτι κινδυνεύεται, Dem. xviii. 278 τῶν ὅλων τι κινδυνεύεται τῇ πόλει, xxxiv. 28 τὰ χρήματα ἤδη κινδυνεύεται τῷ δανείσαντι, xix. 285 τὰ μέγιστα κινδυνεύεται τῇ πόλει. For fut. pf. expressing certainty that an action will immediately take place, see GMT. 79; Kr. *Spr.* 53, 9, 3. — **42. τυχόντες**: = κατορθώσαντες, as in c. 42. 18; 82. 31; iv. 63. 13; v. 111. 27. — **43. τῆς ἔπειτα προσόδου**: *the future revenue*, i.e. that which would have accrued if the state had not been destroyed. *Cf.* i. 123. 2. τὸ λοιπόν is pleonastic, it is true, but after the inserted rel. clause it is not without force. But see App. — **δι' ἥν**: elsewhere ᾗπερ (ᾗ) with ἰσχύειν, as i. 142. 12; ii. 13. 18. It is connected κατὰ ξύνεσιν with τῆς προσόδου without ἔπειτα. — **44. στερήσεσθε, ἕξομεν**: change of pers., as in v. 9. § 1. Kühn. 371, N. 5. — **45. δεῖ**: Cobet's conjecture, ἔδει, is unnecessary, since Cleon could hardly mean, either here or c. 40. 39, that their enemies would have to be entirely neglected, but only that conflicts with their ξύμμαχοι would cripple opposition to the νῦν καθεστηκότες ἐχθροί.

40. *As their guilt has been wilfully incurred, do not weakly allow yourselves to be moved by pity, charm of words, or a spirit of fairness to change your decree. They have merited the severest punishment, and this will secure the permanence of your rule; whereas by revoking your decree you would condemn yourselves.*

1. προθεῖναι: proponere, not προσθεῖναι (although in Vat. and other good Mss.); alone appropriate with ἐλπίδα. *Cf.* c. 52. 18 κατηγορία οὐδεμία προετέθη. — **οὔτε λόγῳ πιστὴν οὔτε χρήμασιν ὠνητήν**: neither relying on eloquence, nor to be bought with money. Both here and c. 38. § 2, those who would merely show their cleverness are set over against those who are bribed. πιστός in this sense also in Plato *Legg.* 824 b, and freq. in the poets. — **2. ὡς ξυγγνώμην ἁμαρτεῖν ἀνθρωπίνως λήψονται**: *that they will be excused as having erred humanly*, i.e. pardonably. *Cf.* Dem. xix. 238 ξυγγνώμη ἀδελφῷ βοηθεῖν. ξυγγνώμην λήψεσθαι = ξυγγνωσθήσεσθαι, hence the inf. clause, ἁμαρτεῖν ἀνθρωπίνως, giving the ground of the pardon. *Cf.* Hdt. i. 89. 14 ξυγγνόντες ποιέειν σε δίκαια.

δὲ ἐπεβούλευσαν· ξύγγνωμον δ' ἐστὶ τὸ ἀκούσιον. ἐγὼ 2
μὲν οὖν καὶ τότε πρῶτον καὶ νῦν διαμάχομαι μὴ μεταγνῶναι ὑμᾶς τὰ προδεδογμένα, μηδὲ τρισὶ τοῖς ἀξυμφορωτάτοις τῇ ἀρχῇ, οἴκτῳ καὶ ἡδονῇ λόγων καὶ ἐπιεικείᾳ,
ἁμαρτάνειν. ἔλεός τε γὰρ πρὸς τοὺς ὁμοίους δίκαιος ἀντι- 3

Kr. Spr. 61, 7, 5; Kühn. 473, 5. ξυγγνώμη as in c. 44. 6. For its const. with inf., cf. iv. 61. 17; v. 88. 1; Hdt. i. 39. l. With the sentiment of the passage, cf. c. 45. 7; Xen. Cyrop. vi. i. 37 ξυγγνώμων τῶν ἀνθρωπίνων ἁμαρτημάτων, Dio C. p. 24 τοῖς ἁμαρτάνουσι ξυγγνώμην κατὰ τὸ ἀνθρώπινον. — 4. ξύγγνωμον: = ξυγγνώμης ἄξιον (Schol.), as in iv. 98. 19. Cf. Dem. xviii. 274 ἐξήμαρτέ τις ἄκων; ξυγγνώμη ἀντὶ τῆς τιμωρίας τούτῳ, Dion. II. Ant. i. 58 ἅπαν δὲ ξυγγνώμης ἄξιον τὸ ἀκούσιον. On the accent of ξύγγνωμον (not ξυγγνῶμον) after the analogy of κακόδαιμον, see Göttling, Accentlehre, p. 329 f.
5. καὶ τότε: sc. διεμαχεσάμην. Cf. i. 86. 7; vi. 60. 13. — διαμάχομαι: with μή and inf. as in c. 42. 7; Xen. Anab. v. 8. 23; Eur. Alc. 694. Cf. also i. 143. 25; v. 41. 14; vii. 63. 1. Kühn. 597, 2 k. τότε refers to what happened in the assembly the day before. Cf. c. 69. 2; i. 101. 8. — μὴ μεταγνῶναι ὑμᾶς τὰ προδεδογμένα: depends only on νῦν διαμάχομαι, having no reference to the τότε πρῶτον clause. Kr. Spr. 55, 3, 16. μεταγνῶναι means rather unvote than repent. Cf. i. 44. 4. The view of Müller-Strübing (Thuk. Forsch. p. 187 ff.) and others, that τὰ προδεδογμένα refers to a decree adopted before the assembly of the previous day,

is inconsistent with τότε πρῶτον, whether the assumed decree were a general measure that was of importance for the question of the treatment of the Mytileneans, or a specific decree referring thereto. For Cleon would hardly have made so covert a reference to such a measure, and such an anticipatory decree would be wholly at variance with c. 35 f. — 6. τρισὶ τοῖς ἀξυμφορωτάτοις: the order as in i. 74. 3. — 7. ἡδονῇ λόγων: cf. ἀκοῆς ἡδονῇ, c. 38. 31; also i. 84. 9; ii. 37. 12. — ἐπιεικείᾳ: fairness (Matthew Arnold's 'sweet reasonableness'), esp. the benevolent treatment by the ἄρχουσα πόλις of her allies, which does not allow her superiority to be felt. Cf. l. 14; 48. 2; also i. 76. 20, τὸ ἐπιεικές and its result.
8. ἔλεός τε: the first of the τρία τὰ ἀξυμφορώτατα, the other two being οἵ τε τέρποντες (10), καὶ ἡ ἐπιείκεια (13). Note the different connexion in i. 74. 4 (τε, καί, καί). — τοὺς ὁμοίους: Cl., St. and Bl. interpret, those who are like-minded, as in i. 71. 7; but Steup rightly follows Kr. in understanding, those who are placed in like circumstances, i.e. only toward equals, and not subject-allies, is mercy in order. Only this view is compatible with ἐξ ἀνάγκης καθεστῶτας αἰεὶ πολεμίους. — δίκαιος ἀντιδίδοσθαι: for the pers.

δίδοσθαι καὶ μὴ πρὸς τοὺς οὔτ' ἀντοικτιοῦντας ἐξ ἀνάγ-
10 κης τε καθεστῶτας αἰεὶ πολεμίους· οἵ τε τέρποντες λόγῳ
ῥήτορες ἕξουσι καὶ ἐν ἄλλοις ἐλάσσοσιν ἀγῶνα, καὶ μὴ ἐν
ᾧ ἡ μὲν πόλις βραχέα ἡσθεῖσα μεγάλα ζημιώσεται, αὐτοὶ
δὲ ἐκ τοῦ εὖ εἰπεῖν τὸ παθεῖν εὖ ἀντιλήψονται· καὶ ἡ
ἐπιείκεια πρὸς τοὺς μέλλοντας ἐπιτηδείους καὶ τὸ λοι-
15 πὸν ἔσεσθαι μᾶλλον δίδοται ἢ πρὸς τοὺς ὁμοίως τε καὶ
οὐδὲν ἧσσον πολεμίους ὑπολειπομένους. ἕν τε ξυνελὼν 4
λέγω· πειθόμενοι μὲν ἐμοὶ τά τε δίκαια ἐς Μυτιληναίους
καὶ τὰ ξύμφορα ἅμα ποιήσετε, ἄλλως δὲ γνόντες τοῖς μὲν

const. with inf., see GMT. 762; II. 944 a. The unusual inf. pass., as in c. 94. 22; Xen. *Cyneg.* 3. 3; Plato *Legg.* 751 b. GMT. 763; II. 952 a. —
9. ἀντοικτιοῦντας: found only here. — **ἐξ ἀνάγκης**: *necessarily*, as in vi. 44. 5; vii. 27. 17. — **11. ῥήτορες**: here, in Cleon's mouth, as well as in the two other passages in Thuc. (vi. 29. 14; viii. 1. 5), used already in its unfavourable secondary meaning to characterize those who make a profession of oratory (cf. τέρποντες λόγῳ) and use it for personal or party purposes. — **ἕξουσι καὶ ἐν ἄλλοις ἐλάσσοσιν ἀγῶνα**: i.e. the orators who consider political deliberations as an ἀγών (c. 38. § 4) will have an opportunity to display their cleverness in other matters of less importance, which will be no hardship to those who treat every matter ὡς ἐν ἄλλοις μείζοσιν οὐκ ἂν δηλώσαντες τὴν γνώμην (c. 37. 21). —
12. βραχέα: combines the ideas of *short* duration and *slight* enjoyment. For the neut. adj. as cognate acc., see G. 1054; H. 716 b; Kr. *Spr.* 46, 5, 4. — **13. τὸ παθεῖν εὖ**: τὸ χρηματίσασθαι

ὑπὸ τῶν Μυτιληναίων, Schol. The same insinuation of bribery as in l. 2 above and c. 38. 12. The phrase is strengthened by its chiastic relation to the preceding. — **14. ἐπιτηδείους**: = πιστούς, *faithful* as allies, as in vi. 46. 8. — **15. ὁμοίως τε καὶ οὐδὲν ἧσσον**: on Thiersch's conjecture ὁμοίως for ὁμοίους, see App. With the expression, cf. μέγιστον δὲ καὶ οὐχ ἥκιστα, vii. 44. 32; πλεῖστος φόνος καὶ οὐδενὸς ἐλάσσων, vii. 85. 17. — **16. ὑπολειπομένους**: *who always remain*, chiastically opposed to μέλλοντας.
ἕν τε: the reading of one Ms. (C. acc. to Hude), adopted by St. and Cl. for ἐν δέ of the other Mss., acc. to Thuc.'s constant usage in a *resumé*. So ξυνελὼν τε, ii. 41. 1; vi. 80. 14; ἁπλῶς τε, c. 38. 31; 45. 29; 82. 34; τό τε ξύμπαν, c. 92. 17; iv. 63. 9; vii. 77. 33; τό τε ξύμπαν εἰπεῖν, vii. 49. 18; παράπαν τε, vi. 18. 41; παντί τε τρόπῳ, ii. 21. 21; iv. 4. 11. See Haase, *Lucubr.* p. 75. — **18. τὰ ξύμφορα**: sc. ὑμῖν αὐτοῖς. Cf. i. 42. 3. — **τοῖς μὲν οὐ χαριεῖσθε**: *you will not win their gratitude.* Cf. c. 37. 7 οὐκ ἐς τὴν

οὐ χαριεῖσθε, ὑμᾶς δὲ αὐτοὺς μᾶλλον δικαιώσεσθε· εἰ
20 γὰρ οὗτοι ὀρθῶς ἀπέστησαν, ὑμεῖς ἂν οὐ χρεὼν ἄρχοιτε.
εἰ δὲ δὴ καὶ οὐ προσῆκον ὅμως ἀξιοῦτε τοῦτο δρᾶν, παρὰ
τὸ εἰκός τοι καὶ τούσδε ξυμφόρως δεῖ κολάζεσθαι, ἢ παύεσθαι τῆς ἀρχῆς καὶ ἐκ τοῦ ἀκινδύνου ἀνδραγαθίζεσθαι.
τῇ τε αὐτῇ ζημίᾳ ἀξιώσατε ἀμύνασθαι καὶ μὴ ἀναλγη- 5

τῶν ξυμμάχων χάριν. — 19. δικαιώσεσθε: not found elsewhere in Thuc.,
who uses only δικαιοῦν = δίκαιον ἡγεῖσθαι. It is chosen here with reference
to τὰ δίκαια ἐς Μυτιληναίους ποιήσετε
above, *do justice to*, *i.e.* punish. It
seems to be an Ionic usage. *Cf.* Hdt.
i. 100. 8; iii. 29. 12; v. 92. β 14;
Plato *Legg.* 934 b. See Diener, *de
Serm. Thuc.* p. 30 f. For the mid.,
cf. κολάζεσθαι, l. 22; σφᾶς αὐτοὺς βε-
βαιώσασθαι, i. 33. 23. — εἰ γὰρ οὗτοι
ὀρθῶς ἀπέστησαν ... ἄρχοιτε: *for if
these had a right to secede, it would
follow that your dominion is unjust,
i.e.* a revocation of the former decree
(γνόντες ἄλλως) would be a confession
that the Mytilenean revolt was just,
and consequently the Athenian rule
unjust. For the mixture of the prot.
of the simple (not unreal) cond. with
an apod. of the ideal, to soften the
assertion, see GMT. 503; H. 901 b.
Cf. c. 9. 6; i. 121. 16. — 20. οὐ χρεών,
οὐ προσῆκον: acc. abs. GMT. 851;
H. 973; Kr. *Spr.* 56, 9, 5. οὐ προσῆκον also iv. 95. 4; vi. 82. 10; 84. 1.
— 21. εἰ δὲ δὴ ... ἀνδραγαθίζεσθαι:
not meant, as εἰ γὰρ ... ἄρχοιτε, to
substantiate ὑμᾶς ... δικαιώσεσθε, but
carrying out some such thought, to
be supplied, as "which you will certainly not acknowledge." See App.
— ἀξιοῦτε: *are resolved*. *Cf.* ii. 11.

33; 64. 24. — τοῦτο δρᾶν: *sc.* ἄρχειν.
For this expression referring to some
action just described, see on i. 5. 11.
— 22. τοι: occurs isolated only twice
more in Thuc. (ii. 41. 11; vii. 77. 5),
always introducing an emphatic assertion. — ξυμφόρως: τοῦ ξυμφέροντος
ἕνεκα τῇ ἀρχῇ, Schol. *Cf.* τὰ ξύμφορα,
l. 18. — κολάζεσθαι: not pass., but
as the whole context, esp. παύεσθαι,
shows, mid., as δικαιώσεσθε above.
Cf. vi. 78. 8; Ar. *Vesp.* 406, and
Steph. *Thes. s.v.* — ἤ: = εἰ δὲ μή, as
in ii. 63. 3, which passage is imitated
here both in thought and expression
(ἀνδραγαθίζεται). — 23. ἐκ τοῦ ἀκινδύνου: adv. periphrasis, as ἐκ τοῦ εὐθέος,
i. 34. 10; ἐκ τοῦ ἀσφαλοῦς, i. 39. 2;
ἀπὸ τοῦ προφανοῦς, i. 35. 17; ἀπὸ τοῦ
εὐθέος, c. 43. 5.

24. τῇ τε αὐτῇ ζημίᾳ ἀξιώσατε ἀμύνασθαι: the sentence would properly
read ᾗ εἰκὸς ἦν αὐτοὺς ὑμᾶς ἀμύνασθαι
κρατήσαντας ὑμῶν, but the natural
order having been interrupted by
καὶ μὴ ... φανῆναι, expressing the
neg. side of the thought, the force of
τῇ αὐτῇ is left to be inferred from
what follows. Schol. ᾗ ἂν ἐτιμωρή-
σαντο καὶ αὐτοὶ ὑμᾶς, περιγενόμενοι ὑμῶν.
But Steup would understand, "as
on the day before," objecting that
the above interpretation is strained,
and that one cannot see how Cleon

25 πότεροι οἱ διαφεύγοντες τῶν ἐπιβουλευσάντων φανῆναι,
ἐνθυμηθέντες ἃ εἰκὸς ἦν αὐτοὺς ποιῆσαι κρατήσαντας
ὑμῶν, ἄλλως τε καὶ προϋπάρξαντας ἀδικίας. μάλιστα δὲ 6
οἱ μὴ ξὺν προφάσει τινὰ κακῶς ποιοῦντες ἐπεξέρχονται
καὶ διολλύναι, τὸν κίνδυνον ὑφορώμενοι τοῦ ὑπολειπο-
30 μένου ἐχθροῦ· ὁ γὰρ μὴ ξὺν ἀνάγκῃ τι παθὼν χαλεπώ-

could have represented the course of the victorious Mytileneans toward the Athenians as a ζημία. — ἀναλγητότεροι: elsewhere in prose only in late writers. It means here, like δυσάλγητος, Soph. O. R. 12, *without feeling, not sensitive*; *unfeeling, cruel*, in Soph. *Aj*. 946; *Trach*. 126; Eur. *Hipp*. 1386. *Cf.* ἀναλγήτως, *unfeelingly*, Soph. *Aj*. 1333. — 25. οἱ διαφεύγοντες : the pres. partic. here expresses continued action, as in c. 4. 13; ii. 2. 22. It is appos. to ὑμεῖς understood. Kr. *Spr*. 50, 7, 14. — 26. εἰκὸς ἦν : as c. 10. 20. Without ἄν (as ἐξῆν, i. 37. 21; καλὸν ἦν, i. 38. 10) as apod. to κρατήσαντας (*i.e.* ἐκράτησαν). See on c. 10. 20. GMT. 420, 421; II. 897. — κρατήσαντας ὑμῶν : Cleon uses everywhere in c. 40 the second person in speaking of the Athenians. *Cf*. c. 39. 2, 44. ἡμῶν, which many editions have, seems to be unsupported by any good Ms. — 27. προϋπάρξαντας : *cf*. πρῶτοι τοῦ τοιούτου ὑπάρξαντες, i. 76. 11; τοῖς ὑπάρχουσι προτέροις, ii. 74. 17. The same force as the simple verb ὑπῆρξαν, ii. 67. 29.

μάλιστα δὲ κτέ. : *whoever without cause have wronged another, follow him up to destroy him utterly, apprehending always danger from the surviving (i.e. not yet completely destroyed) enemy.* The thought agrees in the main with the famous words of Tacitus, *Agr*. 42 proprium humani ingenii est odisse quem laeseris. *Cf*. Dryden:

Forgiveness to the injured does belong,
But they ne'er pardon who have done the wrong;

and Gladstone, *Nineteenth Century*, xxv. p. 151, 'The hatred which nations . . . are apt to feel towards those whom they have injured.' — 28. μὴ ξὺν προφάσει : as is charged against the Mytileneans c. 39. § 1, 2. — ἐπεξέρχονται καὶ διολλύναι : so with St. for the unintelligible διόλλυνται of the Mss. See *Rh. Mus*. xv. p. 475. The inf. of purpose as in i. 50. 3; ii. 65. 44. GMT. 770; II. 951. — 29. τὸν κίνδυνον . . . ἐχθροῦ : the gen. with κίνδυνος, as in ii. 63. 5. — 30. ὁ γὰρ μὴ ξὺν ἀνάγκῃ . . . ἐχθροῦ : contains at once the ground for the extreme fear and therefore extreme hostility of the Mytileneans, and the justification of the severest punishment by the Athenians. '*For he who has suffered evil without needful cause is more dangerous, if he shall have escaped, than one who was an enemy on equal terms, i.e. than one who has not suffered more than he has inflicted.*' (Arn.) ἀπὸ τῆς ἴσης as in i. 15. 11.

τερος διαφυγὼν τοῦ ἀπὸ τῆς ἴσης ἐχθροῦ. μὴ οὖν προ- 7
δόται γένησθε ὑμῶν αὐτῶν, γενόμενοι δ' ὅτι ἐγγύτατα
τῇ γνώμῃ τοῦ πάσχειν καὶ ὡς πρὸ παντὸς ἂν ἐτιμήσασθε
αὐτοὺς χειρώσασθαι, νῦν ἀνταπόδοτε μὴ μαλακισθέντες
35 πρὸς τὸ παρὸν αὐτίκα μηδὲ τοῦ ἐπικρεμασθέντος ποτὲ
δεινοῦ ἀμνημονοῦντες. κολάσατε δὲ ἀξίως τούτους τε καὶ 8
τοῖς ἄλλοις ξυμμάχοις παράδειγμα σαφὲς καταστήσατε,
ὃς ἂν ἀφιστῆται θανάτῳ ζημιωσόμενον. τόδε γὰρ ἦν

31. **προδόται γένησθε**: see on c. 2. 11. — 32. **γενόμενοι ὅτι ἐγγύτατα τῇ γνώμῃ**: = ὅτι ἐγγύτατα διανοηθέντες (i. 143. 22); from which ἐνθυμηθέντες must be supplied with ὡς πρὸ παντὸς ... χειρώσασθαι. *Recalling as nearly as possible the feelings* (of the moment) *of suffering, and how you would then have prized above everything to crush them.* Schol. εἰς εὔνοιαν ἐλθόντες ὧν ἐμέλλετε πάσχειν ὑπὸ Λεσβίων. Cf. Aesch. iii. 153 γένεσθε δή μοι μικρὸν χρόνον τὴν διάνοιαν μὴ ἐν τῷ δικαστηρίῳ. **πρὸ παντός** stronger than πρὸ πολλῶν with the similar expression in i. 33. 8; vi. 10. 16. — 34. **ἀνταπόδοτε**: here abs., in the same signification as with τὰ ὁμοῖα, c. 66. 8; τὸ ἴσον, i. 43. 5. — **μαλακισθέντες**: as in c. 37. 8; vi. 29. 11. — 35. **πρὸς τὸ παρὸν αὐτίκα**: the pleonasm is not greater than in ἐν τῷ τότε παρόντι, i. 95. 26; τῶν ἔπειτα μελλόντων, i. 123. 2; ἐν τῷ νῦν παρόντι, Plato *Phaedo* 67 c. See also on c. 39. 43. For the position, cf. πάλιν ἡ ἀποκομιδή, i. 137. 26. **πρὸς τὸ παρόν**, as in ii. 22. 1. Cf. πρὸς τὰ παρόντα, ii. 3. 15; 6. 3; 59. 10; iv. 80. 8; ἐπὶ τῷ παρόντι, ii. 36. 18; vi. 20. 3. — **τοῦ ἐπικρεμασθέντος ποτὲ δεινοῦ**: *the danger once hanging over you*. Cl. and Kr. conjecture τότε, as antithesis to αὐτίκα. See on i. 101. 8.
36. **τούτους τε καὶ τοῖς ἄλλοις**: τε καί on account of the antithesis of the pronouns. See on ii. 46. 1. Observe the chiastic order of the sentence. — 37. **τοῖς ἄλλοις ... ζημιωσόμενον**: *give to the rest of the allies plain warning that whoever revolts shall be punished with death.* 'The const. of the partic., depending on the phrase σαφὲς παράδειγμα καταστήσατε, seems to be protected by the similar examples, c. 67. 28 ποιήσατε ... παράδειγμα οὐ λόγων τοὺς ἀγῶνας προθήσοντες, ἀλλ' ἔργων, c. 64. 1 δῆλον ἐποιήσατε ... οὐ μηδίσαντες, Lycurg. 50 φανερὸν πᾶσιν ἐποίησαν οὐκ ἰδίᾳ πολεμοῦντες, where the partic. clauses take the place of the objects.' St. Cf. also Hdt. vi. 21. 8 Ἀθηναῖοι δῆλον ἐποίησαν ὑπεραχθεσθέντες τῇ Μιλήτου ἁλώσι. The const. is the same as with the simple verb δηλοῦν. GMT. 904, 907; H. 981; Kühn. 482, 2. The dat. with ζημιωσόμενον as in ii. 65. 12. Elsewhere with παράδειγμα, that which is to be proved, or of which an example is to be given, is expressed (if it be not clear from the context, as in c.

THUCYDIDES III. 40, 41, 42.

γνῶσιν, ἧσσον τῶν πολεμίων ἀμελήσαντες τοῖς ὑμετέροις
40 αὐτῶν μαχεῖσθε ξυμμάχοις."
41 Τοιαῦτα μὲν ὁ Κλέων εἶπε· μετὰ δ' αὐτὸν Διόδοτος 1
ὁ Εὐκράτους, ὅσπερ καὶ ἐν τῇ προτέρᾳ ἐκκλησίᾳ ἀντέλεγε μάλιστα μὴ ἀποκτεῖναι Μυτιληναίους, παρελθὼν καὶ
τότε ἔλεγε τοιάδε·
42 "Οὔτε τοὺς προθέντας τὴν διαγνώμην αὖθις περὶ
Μυτιληναίων αἰτιῶμαι οὔτε τοὺς μεμφομένους μὴ πολλάκις περὶ τῶν μεγίστων βουλεύεσθαι ἐπαινῶ, νομίζω

10. 20; 11. 24; 39. 14; ii. 37. 2; iv. 92. 18; v. 90. 7; vi. 77. 4) in the gen., as c. 57. 1; i. 2. 20; v. 95. 3. — 39. ἧσσον... ξυμμάχοις: cf. c. 39. 45 καὶ ὃν χρόνον τοῖς νῦν καθεστηκόσι δεῖ ἐχθροῖς ἀνθίστασθαι. — τοῖς ὑμετέροις ... ξυμμάχοις: the speech concludes with a trimeter, as shown by Meineke, Hermes iii. p. 347. Cf. i. 80. 6; iv. 17. 6, and the hexameters ii. 49. 18; vi. 36. 1.

41. *Diodotus replies to Cleon.*

1. **Διόδοτος**: of Diodotus, to whom Thucydides has raised in the following speech a splendid monument, nothing is known historically, not even whether his father Eucrates was the στυππειοπώλης among the successors of Pericles (Ar. *Eq.* 129; cf. CIA. iv. 179 a), or the brother of Nicias. See Roscher, *Leben etc. des Thuk.* p. 411. — 2. **ὅσπερ καὶ... Μυτιληναίους**: cf. c. 36. 25. — **ἀντέλεγε... μὴ ἀποκτεῖναι Μυτιληναίους**: *spoke most against putting the Mytileneans to death.* Cf. v. 49. 11 ἀντέλεγον μὴ δικαίως σφῶν καταδεδικάσθαι, Xen. *Anab.* ii. 3. 25; *Cyrop.* ii. 2. 20. For the inf. with μή after verbs of denial, see GMT. 807; H. 1029; Kr. *Spr.* 67, 12, 3.

SPEECH OF DIODOTUS. c. 42-48.

42. *Reconsideration of the question can be only helpful. The worst enemies of safe conclusions are haste and passion, and whoever disputes the utility of speeches is either a fool, or has a personal interest in the matter. The latter is the case with those who, in order to support a bad cause, resort to slander and intimidation. Orators should renounce such means, and the state should treat with consideration not only those counsellors that usually give good advice, but even those that are not so fortunate.*

1. **τὴν διαγνώμην**: used by Thuc. alone of Attic writers. Cf. c. 67. 33; i. 87. 17; and διεγνωσμένην, c. 53. 22; διέγνωστο, i. 118. 18. The reference is to c. 38. § 1. — 2. **μεμφομένους**: referring to the future, not, as usual, to the past, *reproachfully warning.* The reference is to c. 37. § 3. — 3. **περὶ τῶν μεγίστων**: not from the point of view of the μεμφόμενοι, but of the speaker; the former would demand περὶ μηδενὸς πολλάκις βουλεύεσθαι, the latter finds fault that this is not to be done even περὶ τῶν μεγίστων.

τε δύο τὰ ἐναντιώτατα εὐβουλίᾳ εἶναι τάχος τε καὶ ὀρ-
5 γήν, ὧν τὸ μὲν μετὰ ἀνοίας φιλεῖ γίγνεσθαι, τὸ δὲ μετὰ
ἀπαιδευσίας καὶ βραχύτητος γνώμης. τούς τε λόγους 2
ὅστις διαμάχεται μὴ διδασκάλους τῶν πραγμάτων γίγνεσθαι, ἢ ἀξύνετός ἐστιν ἢ ἰδίᾳ τι αὐτῷ διαφέρει· ἀξύνε-
τος μέν, εἰ ἄλλῳ τινὶ ἡγεῖται περὶ τοῦ μέλλοντος δυνα-
10 τὸν εἶναι καὶ μὴ ἐμφανοῦς φράσαι, διαφέρει δ' αὐτῷ, εἰ
βουλόμενός τι αἰσχρὸν πεῖσαι εὖ μὲν εἰπεῖν οὐκ ἂν ἡγεῖται περὶ τοῦ μὴ καλοῦ δύνασθαι, εὖ δὲ διαβαλὼν ἐκπλή-

— **4. τε**: with the best Mss. instead of δέ. It is not correlative to οὔτε, οὔτε, but introduces the *third* member. Steup follows Bk., with a few Mss., in writing δέ, on the ground that the clause νομίζω ... ὀργήν is antithetic to the preceding. — **δύο τὰ ἐναντιώτατα**: acc. to the analogy of c. 40. 6; 57. 15; 75. 5; i. 74. 3; 122. 22, these words are not to be construed as subj. and pred., but are equiv. to τὰ δύο ἐναντιώτατα, so that the subj. is τάχος τε καὶ ὀργήν, "that the two worst foes of correct conclusions are haste and passion." — **εὐβουλίᾳ**: cf. 44. 4; and εὖ βουλεύεσθαι, c. 48. 7. — **τάχος**: cf. c. 38. 3 ff. — **ὀργήν**: cf. c. 36. 5; 44. 15. — **5. τὸ μέν, τὸ δέ**: the former refers to τάχος, the latter to ὀργή. "Overhaste generally indicates lack of sense; passion, lack of self-control and shallowness of judgment." — **φιλεῖ**: is *wont*, in Thuc. in this sense only; and in Hdt., except in v. 5. 5. See on i. 78. 5. — **γίγνεσθαι**: *appear*, often used of natural phenomena. See on i. 54. 6. — **μετὰ ἀπαιδευσίας**: cf. c. 84. 7 ἀπαιδευσίᾳ ὀργῆς ἐκφερόμενοι, and the Tragic frag. quoted by Stob. *Flor*. 20.

12 (Nauck, *Trag. Gr.*², Adespota 523) πόλλ' ἔστιν ὀργῆς ἐξ ἀπαιδεύτου κακά. — — **6. καὶ βραχύτητος γνώμης**: cf. Dio C. frg. p. 64 ταχὺ μὲν ὑπὸ βραχύτητος γνώμης ὀργιζομένην. βραχύτης, *shallowness*, acc. to the usual sense of βραχύς in Thuc. See on i. 14. 11. **τούς τε λόγους κτέ.**: the order as in c. 39. 5. The clause is directed against c. 38. § 4 ff. Cf. ii. 40. 9 ff. — **7. διαμάχεται**: see on c. 40. 5. — **διδασκάλους ... γίγνεσθαι**: see on c. 2. 11. — **8. ἢ ἰδίᾳ τι αὐτῷ διαφέρει**: *or he has some private interest*. Cf. τῶν αὐτοῖς ἰδίᾳ διαφόρων, i. 68. 8; τὰ ἴδια διάφορα, ii. 37. 5; ἴδιά τινα διάφορα, v. 115. 8. Cf. also iv. 86. 23. — 10. **φράσαι**: *to throw light on*. See on i. 145. 4. — 11. **εὖ εἰπεῖν**: sneered at by Cleon, c. 38. 18; 40. 13; here assigned its true value. — **οὐκ ἂν ἡγεῖται**: ἄν, which belongs to δύνασθαι, separates the closely connected οὐχ ἡγεῖται. Cf. c. 37. 7 οὐκ ἐπικινδύνως ἡγεῖσθε κτέ. On the partiality of ἄν for the neg., see GMT. 219; II. 862. οὐ in prot. because it negatives a single word. GMT. 384; II. 1028; Kr. *Spr.* 67, 4, 1. — 12. **εὖ δὲ διαβαλὼν ... ἀκουσομένους**:

ξαι ἂν τούς τε ἀντεροῦντας καὶ τοὺς ἀκουσομένους.
χαλεπώτατοι δὲ καὶ οἱ ἐπὶ χρήμασι προκατηγοροῦντες ἐπί- 3
15 δειξίν τινα. εἰ μὲν γὰρ ἀμαθίαν κατῃτιῶντο, ὁ μὴ
πείσας ἀξυνετώτερος ἂν δόξας εἶναι ἢ ἀδικώτερος ἀπεχώ-
ρει· ἀδικίας δ' ἐπιφερομένης πείσας τε ὕποπτος γίγνεται καὶ μὴ τυχὼν μετὰ ἀξυνεσίας καὶ ἄδικος. ἥ τε πόλις 4
οὐκ ὠφελεῖται ἐν τῷ τοιῷδε· φόβῳ γὰρ ἀποστερεῖται τῶν
20 ξυμβούλων. καὶ πλεῖστ' ἂν ὀρθοῖτο ἀδυνάτους λέγειν
ἔχουσα τοὺς τοιούτους τῶν πολιτῶν· ἐλάχιστα γὰρ ἂν

excellent characterization of Cleon's whole speech, esp. of c. 38. εὖ is bitterly ironical.

14. χαλεπώτατοι . . . τινα: *most dangerous, however, are just those who charge beforehand rhetorical display for the sake of money*. χαλεπώτατοι as in iv. 24. 21; vii. 21. 14. καί, *just* (*erst*), as in Hdt. i. 71. 6, and freq.— ἐπὶ χρήμασι: placed for emphasis after οἱ, limits ἐπίδειξιν, the prep. having the same force (*for the sake of*) as in i. 3. 9; 38. 15; 73. 14; ii. 29. 17; 64. 25. v. II. conjectured ἐπιδείξειν τινά, the obj. to be supplied, *that one will display his art for money*. Cf. Ar. Acharn. 765. — προκατηγοροῦντες: this reading of Laur., adopted by St. and v. II. instead of προσκατηγοροῦντες of most Mss., is in place after the fut. partic. τοὺς ἀντεροῦντας (l. 13). The charge of venality (cf. c. 38. 12; 40. 2, 13) might well be treated as the worst form of εὖ διαβάλλειν (l. 12), but not as something *additional* to this. — **16.** ἀξυνετώτερος ἢ ἀδικώτερος: the double comp., as in Lat., implies that of two qualities in the same obj. one predominates. II.

645; Kühn. 543, 5. See on i. 21. 5. — ἀπεχώρει: *withdraw*. The verb is used in the same unfavourable sense as the Lat. discedere. Cf. Dem. xxxvii. 21. — **17.** ἀδικίας ἐπιφερομένης: *when corruption is charged*. The ἀδικία is τὸ ἐπὶ χρήμασι λέγειν. ἐπιφέρειν as in c. 46. 26; 81. 20; v. 75. 9. — **18.** τυχών: see on c. 39. 42. Cf. ἐπιτυχών, l. 29. — μετὰ ἀξυνεσίας: μετά, *besides*, as in i. 32. 8; ii. 15. 9. — ἄδικος: sc. γίγνεται, in the judgment of the many.

19. ἐν τῷ τοιῷδε: as in c. 43. 12; ii. 36. 2; v. 88. 1, the art. refers to what is known or just described. The prep. has the same force as in ἐν ᾧ, ἐν τούτῳ. See on i. 39. 11. — τῶν ξυμβούλων: only here in the general sense of "advising statesmen," as in Dem. xviii. 66. Elsewhere Thuc. uses it of Spartan officials with specific duties. Cf. c. 69. 7; ii. 85. 1; v. 63. 15; viii. 39. 7; 41. 3. — **20.** πλεῖστ' ἂν ὀρθοῖτο: see on c. 30. 15; 37. 26. For the sentiment of the passage, cf. Eur. Bacch. 270; Or. 907. — **21.** τοὺς τοιούτους τῶν πολιτῶν: referring to those described in l. 11 ff., esp. οἱ ἐπὶ χρήμασι προσκατηγοροῦντες, l. 14.

πεισθεῖεν ἁμαρτάνειν. χρὴ δὲ τὸν μὲν ἀγαθὸν πολίτην 5
μὴ ἐκφοβοῦντα τοὺς ἀντεροῦντας, ἀλλ' ἀπὸ τοῦ ἴσου
φαίνεσθαι ἄμεινον λέγοντα, τὴν δὲ σώφρονα πόλιν τῷ
τε πλεῖστα εὖ βουλεύοντι μὴ προστιθέναι τιμήν (ἀλλὰ
μηδ' ἐλασσοῦν τῆς ὑπαρχούσης), καὶ τὸν μὴ τυχόντα γνώμης οὐχ ὅπως ζημιοῦν, ἀλλὰ μηδ' ἀτιμάζειν· οὕτω γὰρ ὅ 6
τε κατορθῶν ἥκιστα ἂν ἐπὶ τῷ ἔτι μειζόνων ἀξιοῦσθαι
παρὰ γνώμην τι καὶ πρὸς χάριν λέγοι, ὅ τε μὴ ἐπιτυχὼν

ἐλάχιστα: opp. to πλεῖστα above. It is cognate acc. with ἁμαρτάνειν. *Cf.* c. 40. 12. — 22. πεισθεῖεν: the transition to the plur. is induced by τῶν πολιτῶν in the line above. Kr. *Spr.* 58, 4, 2. *Cf.* c. 72. 8; viii. 72. 13. On the shorter form πεισθεῖεν for πεισθείησαν of the Mss., see St. *Qu. Gr.*[2] p. 62, who cites Heracleides Milesius (Eustath. on Hom. ψ 195), ἡ ἀρχαία Ἀτθὶς τὰ εὐκτικὰ ξυγκόπτει κατ' ἐξαίρεσιν μιᾶς ξυλλαβῆς. — 23. μὴ ἐκφοβοῦντα... λέγοντα: the const. is φαίνεσθαι ἄμεινον λέγοντα, μὴ ἐκφοβοῦντα... ἀλλ' ἀπὸ τοῦ ἴσου. *The good citizen must show himself the better speaker, not by intimidation of his opponents, but by meeting them on equal terms.* ἀπὸ τοῦ ἴσου, as in c. 10. 12 = ἀπὸ τῆς ἴσης, c. 40. 31. — 24. τὴν δὲ σώφρονα πόλιν... ὑπαρχούσης: *the wise city should not indeed confer additional honour on him whose counsels are generally sound, but also not lessen that which he already has.* βουλεύειν, *give advice,* as in vi. 39. 5; viii. 76. 33. προστιθέναι τιμήν as in Xen. *Cyrop.* ii. 2. 18. *Cf.* c. 39. 32. ἀλλὰ μηδ' ἐλασσοῦν τῆς ὑπαρχούσης seems, as Arn. says, to refer to πείσας τε ὕποπτος γίγνεται

(l. 17). *Cf.* (concerning Antiphon) viii. 68. 8 ὑπόπτως τῷ πλήθει διὰ δόξαν δεινότητος διακείμενος. — 26. τὸν μὴ τυχόντα γνώμης: *the one who is not fortunate in his view, i.e.* whose advice is not so good. *Cf.* γνώμης ἁμαρτάνειν, i. 33. 17; vi. 92. 3; σφάλλεσθαι τῆς δόξης, iv. 85. 5. Or, perhaps, *the one whose advice is rejected,* as μὴ τυχών, l. 18. This rendering seems to be sustained by l. 28 f. *Cf.* τῆς ἑκάστου δόξης τυχεῖν, ii. 35. 19. *Cf.* Dio C. lii. 33. 7 τοὺς μὲν τυχόντας τῆς γνώμης καὶ ἐπαινεῖ καὶ τιμᾷ, ... τοὺς δ' ἁμαρτόντας μήτ' ἀτιμάσῃς ποτὲ μήτ' αἰτιάσῃ. Also xliv. 36. 3. See on c. 39. 42. — 27. οὐχ ὅπως, ἀλλὰ μηδέ: non modo non, sed ne... quidem. When the οὐχ ὅπως clause precedes, it always contains the weaker of the two contrasted notions. See on i. 35. 12. GMT. 707; Kühn. 525, 3 b.

28. ἥκιστα ἄν: belongs to both following clauses. — ἐπὶ τῷ ἔτι μειζόνων ἀξιοῦσθαι: *i.e.* if τιμὴν προστιθέναι were the sure reward of every successful speech. — 29. παρὰ γνώμην τι λέγοι: *cf.* vi. 9. 12, and see on c. 37. 28. — πρὸς χάριν: "to please the people." *Cf.* ii. 65. 35 πρὸς ἡδονήν

30 ὀρέγοιτο τῷ αὐτῷ, χαριζόμενός τι καὶ αὐτός, προσάγεσθαι
43 τὸ πλῆθος. ὧν ἡμεῖς τἀναντία δρῶμεν, καὶ προσέτι ἤν
τις καὶ ὑποπτεύηται κέρδους μὲν ἕνεκα τὰ βέλτιστα δ'
ὅμως λέγειν, φθονήσαντες τῆς οὐ βεβαίου δοκήσεως τῶν
κερδῶν τὴν φανερὰν ὠφελίαν τῆς πόλεως ἀφαιρούμεθα.
5 καθέστηκε δὲ τἀγαθὰ ἀπὸ τοῦ εὐθέος λεγόμενα μηδὲν
ἀνυποπτότερα εἶναι τῶν κακῶν, ὥστε δεῖν ὁμοίως τόν τε
τὰ δεινότατα βουλόμενον πεῖσαι ἀπάτῃ προσάγεσθαι τὸ

τι λέγειν, Dem. iii. 3 πρὸς χάριν δημηγορεῖν, iv. 38 πρὸς ἡδονὴν δημηγορεῖν.
In l. 30 the expression takes the form
χαρίζεσθαι, the clause χαριζόμενός τι
καὶ αὐτός, seeking applause also himself, being explanatory of τῷ αὐτῷ.
— **30. προσάγεσθαι**: win over, as in
c. 43. 7; 91. 7, etc.
43. But, unfortunately, this is not
the case with us. Besides, your inor-
dinate propensity to reject proposals,
through suspicion of self-interest on
the part of the orators that urge them,
makes it difficult to put through good
measures. Still, in such important
matters, we orators must look further
into the future than you, especially
since we alone are held responsible.
1. ὧν: see on c. 39. 1. For gen.
after τἀναντία, see G. 1146; H. 754 f;
Kr. Spr. 48, 13, 4. The reference is
to c. 42. 24 τῷ τε πλεῖστα ... ἀτιμά-
ζειν. — **ἤν τις καὶ ... λέγειν**: ὑποπτεύηται belongs strictly only to κέρδους
ἕνεκα, some such word as δοκῇ being
understood with τὰ βέλτιστα λέγειν.
The reverse would be the natural
order of the clauses in English.
"Even though one seem to say what
is best, if he be suspected of speaking
for money." On the correlation, see

Kr. Spr. 69, 16, 1. — **3. τῆς οὐ βεβαίου δοκήσεως τῶν κερδῶν**: because
of the unproved suspicion of gain,
i.e. begrudging him the gain which
we suspect he has got, although the
suspicion is unproved. Cf. ii. 35. 9
ἐν ᾧ μόλις καὶ ἡ δόκησις τῆς ἀληθείας
βεβαιοῦται. δόκησις, as in c. 45. 6;
ii. 35. 9; 84. 4; iv. 18. 21; 55. 16;
87. 2; 126. 17; vi. 64. 15; vii. 67. 3;
Hdt. vii. 185. 3. 'Often in Tragedy
and late writers, but avoided in simple Attic prose.' (Kr.) Cf. Soph.
Trach. 426, 427; O. T. 681; Ant. 324;
Eur. Hel. 36, 121; Heracl. 395. —
**4. τὴν φανερὰν ὠφελίαν τῆς πόλεως
ἀφαιρούμεθα**: antithesis to the foregoing. We deprive the city of an
undeniable advantage. ἀφαιρεῖσθαί τι
τινος as in c. 58. 29; vii. 13. 18; viii.
46. 33. G. 1118; H. 748 a.
καθέστηκε: it has come to pass,
with dependent inf., as i. 76. 11;
iv. 97. 11. — **5. ἀπὸ τοῦ εὐθέος λεγόμενα**: said right out. Cf. ἐκ τοῦ προφανοῦς, l. 10. See on ἐκ τοῦ εὐθέος,
i. 34. 10. — **7. τὰ δεινότατα**: the worst
measures. Cf. c. 59. 17; 82. 59; 93.
5. — **ἀπάτῃ**, (8) ψευσάμενον, (10) μὴ
ἐξαπατήσαντα**: cf. Cleon's words, c.
38. 12 κέρδει ἐπαιρόμενος τὸ εὐπρεπὲς

πλῆθος καὶ τὸν τὰ ἀμείνω λέγοντα ψευσάμενον πιστὸν γενέσθαι. μόνην τε πόλιν διὰ τὰς περινοίας εὖ ποιῆσαι 3 ἐκ τοῦ προφανοῦς μὴ ἐξαπατήσαντα ἀδύνατον· ὁ γὰρ διδοὺς φανερῶς τι ἀγαθὸν ἀνθυποπτεύεται ἀφανῶς πῃ πλέον ἕξειν. χρὴ δὲ πρὸς τὰ μέγιστα καὶ ἐν τῷ τοιῷδε 4 ἀξιοῦν τι ἡμᾶς περαιτέρω προνοοῦντας λέγειν ὑμῶν τῶν

τοῦ λόγου ἐκπονήσας παράγειν πειράσεται. —8. ψευσάμενον πιστὸν γενέσθαι: obtain credence by false representations. 9. μόνην τε πόλιν... ἀδύνατον: the conclusion drawn from the foregoing. And ours is the only city which it is impossible, on account of this overshrewdness, to benefit openly without deceiving it. μόνην πόλιν is pred. to ἡμᾶς, or τὴν ἡμετέραν πόλιν, understood. Kr., Cl., and St. take μόνην alone as pred. to πόλιν, which would make πόλιν, a state, the antithesis to individuals. But, as Jow. says, Diodotus cannot mean to say this of every state, nor is there any reason for, or hint in the context of, any greater liability to such suspicions on the part of the state than on the part of the individual. περίνοια, in this sense, is not found elsewhere, but acc. to analogy of περιουσία, περιεργία, περιτέχνησις (c. 82. 22), means an excess of cleverness which will not be content with a simple view of things. Cf. Ar. Ran. 958 ἅπαντα περινοεῖν. The pl. because of its manifestations everywhere apparent. The positive and negative modifiers, ἐκ τοῦ προφανοῦς and μὴ ἐξαπατήσαντα, without connective, as in c. 59. 4. — 11. ἀνθυποπτεύεται: coined for the occasion, as is freq. the case with Thuc.'s compounds. Cf. c. 12. 12, 13 ἀντεπιβουλεῦσαι, ἀντιμελλῆσαι, c. 40. 9 ἀντοικτιοῦντας, c. 44. 11 ἀντισχυριζόμενος, c. 61. 16 ἀντιπάσχειν. For forty such ἅπαξ εἰρημένα compounds with ἀντι-, see App. on iv. 80. 4. — ἀφανῶς πῃ πλέον ἕξειν: that in some underhand manner he will reap some advantage. Arn. compares Arist. Rhet. iii. 16. 9 ἀπιστοῦσι γὰρ ἄλλο τι πράττειν ἑκόντα πλὴν τὸ ξυμφέρον. 12. χρὴ δὲ...σκοπούντων: "still, with reference to the highest interests and under such circumstances as the present, we must deem it our duty to base our counsels on a somewhat wider forecast than your offhand deliberations allow." — πρὸς τὰ μέγιστα: cf. πρὸς τὸ παρὸν αὐτίκα, c. 40. 35. — καί: = atque. Steup follows Haase (Lucubr. p. 42) in taking it as = etiam. — ἐν τῷ τοιῷδε: as in c. 42. 19; ii. 36. 2; v. 88. 1. Cf. ἐν τῷ τοιούτῳ, c. 81. 23; iv. 56. 4. — 13. ἀξιοῦν τι: Reiske's conjecture (in Abresch, Dilucc. Thuc. p. 319) for ἀξιοῦντι of the Mss. See Haase, Lucubr. p. 36 sqq., who rightly remarks that an adj. cannot be joined to such a partic. The emendation has been adopted also by Kr., St., and Bm. The subj. is ἡμᾶς, we orators. Cf. c. 37. 27. But Steup follows Bm., who understands ὑμᾶς as

δι' ὀλίγου σκοπούντων, ἄλλως τε καὶ ὑπεύθυνον τὴν
παραίνεσιν ἔχοντας πρὸς ἀνεύθυνον τὴν ὑμετέραν ἀκρόασιν. εἰ γὰρ ὅ τε πείσας καὶ ὁ ἐπισπόμενος ὁμοίως ἐβλά-
πτοντο, σωφρονέστερον ἂν ἐκρίνετε· νῦν δὲ πρὸς ὀργὴν
ἥντινα τύχητε ἔστιν ὅτε σφαλέντες τὴν τοῦ πείσαντος
μίαν γνώμην ζημιοῦτε καὶ οὐ τὰς ὑμετέρας αὐτῶν, εἰ
πολλαὶ οὖσαι ξυνεξήμαρτον.

44 "Ἐγὼ δὲ παρῆλθον οὔτε ἀντερῶν περὶ Μυτιληναίων οὔτε κατηγορήσων. οὐ γὰρ περὶ τῆς ἐκείνων ἀδικίας ἡμῖν ὁ ἀγών, εἰ σωφρονοῦμεν, ἀλλὰ περὶ τῆς ἡμετέρας εὐβουλίας. ἤν τε γὰρ ἀποφήνω πάνυ ἀδικοῦντας

subj. and renders ἀξιοῦν, *grant* (*an-nehmen*). τι belongs to περαιτέρω. — **προνοοῦντας**: cf. c. 38. 28. — **14. δι' ὀλίγου**: temporal, as in i. 77. 22; ii. 85. 9. — **ὑπεύθυνον τὴν παραίνεσιν**: they were liable to the γραφὴ παρανόμων. For παραίνεσιν, cf. παραινεῖν, c. 37. 28. — **15. πρός**: *as against*, as in c. 56. 16; 112. 21; ii. 87. 23; 91. 18; 100. 21; v. 80. 15. — **ἀνεύθυνον**: as in Hdt. iii. 80. 11; Arist. *Polit.* ii. 9. Hence v. H.'s conjecture ἀνυπεύθυνον is unnecessary. — **ἀκρόασιν**: not simply *hearing*, but *hearkening to*, as the context shows. Cf. ii. 37. 16.

17. σωφρονέστερον: i.e. with greater circumspection and moderation. — **πρὸς ὀργὴν ἥντινα τύχητε**: "according to the passion of the moment." πρὸς ὀργήν, as in ii. 65. 36; Soph. *El.* 369. Cf. c. 44. 14. ἥντινα without prep. repeated, as in c. 17. 1; 18. 1; and with subjv. without ἄν, as in iv. 17. 6; 18. 13. GMT. 540; Kr. *Spr.* 54, 15, 3. St. writes ἥντιν' ἄν. As to the elliptical use of τύχητε, cf. viii. 48. 37, and see on i. 142. 25. A

grammatical supplement is doubtless to be assumed as original, but is not present to the mind of the speaker. Kr., Jow., Bm., and others supply ζημιοῦντες with τύχητε, while Arn. construes it with σφαλέντες. — **18. ἔστιν ὅτε**: belongs to σφαλέντες, as well as to ζημιοῦτε. — **19. εἰ ... ξυνεξήμαρτον**: a fact expressed in hypothetical form. See on c. 32. 6.

44. *The affair of the Mytileneans must be treated not as a question of right, but solely of our interest, which certainly cannot be subserved by Cleon's proposed death-penalty for all Mytileneans.*

1. οὔτε ἀντερῶν: sc. τῷ Κλέωνι. Cf. c. 38. 7; 41. 2; 42. 13, 23. — **2. οὔτε κατηγορήσων**: sc. τῶν Μυτιληναίων. — **οὐ γάρ ... εὐβουλίας**: "for, if we consider wisely, we shall find that for us it is a question not of their wrong-doing, but of our right counsel." The same brachylogy in i. 40. § 2; vi. 11. § 7. See Steup, *Thuk. Stud.* ii. p. 18. — **ἀδικίας**: cf. c. 38. 8; 39. 2, 31. — **4. εὐβουλίας**: c. 42. 4.

5 αὐτούς. οὐ διὰ τοῦτο καὶ ἀποκτεῖναι κελεύσω, εἰ μὴ ξυμ-
φέρον· ἤν τε καὶ ἔχοντάς τι ξυγγνώμης, ἐᾶν, εἰ τῇ πόλει μὴ ἀγαθὸν φαίνοιτο. νομίζω δὲ περὶ τοῦ μέλλοντος 3
ἡμᾶς μᾶλλον βουλεύεσθαι ἢ τοῦ παρόντος. καὶ τούτου ὃ
μάλιστα Κλέων ἰσχυρίζεται, ἐς τὸ λοιπὸν ξυμφέρον ἔσε-
10 σθαι πρὸς τὸ ἧσσον ἀφίστασθαι θάνατον ζημίαν προθεῖσι,

— πάνυ: common in cond. sents.
with conjs. or partics., vel maxime,
ever so. Cf. ii. 13. 35; 51. 6; vi. 17.
32; viii. 50. 22; 71. 5. — 5. ξυμφέρον:
without ἐστί also vi. 85. 2, as ἄξιον,
δεινόν, δίκαιον, αἰσχρόν, and similar
neuters. Cf. c. 59. 9, 23. Kr. Spr.
62. 1, 4; 65, 5, 11. — 6. ἥν τε καὶ
ἔχοντάς τι ξυγγνώμης: sc. ἀποφήνω.
So Cl., St., and Bm. explain, adopting
ἔχοντας, the reading of the Clarend.
Ms., instead of the vulg. ἔχοντες.
Against Cleon's brutal demand (c.
40. 1 οὐκ οὖν δεῖ προθεῖναι ἐλπίδα ... ὡς
ξυγγνώμην ... λήψονται) Diodotus offers his own view as modestly as possible; hence ἔχοντας τι ξυγγνώμης (cf.
ii. 49. 30; 51. 29). ξυγγνώμη, excuse,
as in c. 40. 2. — ἐᾶν: Lindau's and
Burgess's conjecture for εἶεν, adopted
by Dind., St., Bm., and Bl. It depends on οὐ διὰ τοῦτο κελεύσω, and
means to let go unpunished. For
the const., cf. Plato Euthyphr. 4 b
εἰ μὲν ἐν δίκῃ, ἐᾶν, εἰ δὲ μή, ἐπεξιέναι.
"And if I show that they have some
claim to forgiveness, I will not on
that account advise you to let them
go unpunished, if this should appear
disadvantageous to the state." See
App.
8. ἢ τοῦ παρόντος: without περί
repeated. Kr. Spr. 68, 9; Kühn.
451, 6. See on c. 43. 17; vii. 47. 16.

— καὶ τούτου ὃ μάλιστα κτέ.: τούτου,
which is Steup's emendation for τοῦτο
of the Mss., depends on τἀναντία, l.
12. If τοῦτο be retained, there would
seem to be, as Bm. says, a slight
anacoluthon, τοῦτο being repeated,
in part of its idea, in περὶ τοῦ ἐς τὸ
μέλλον καλῶς ἔχοντος. Cl., who with
Pp. and Kr., connects τοῦτο grammatically with ἀντισχυριζόμενος, explains that it is not really the obj.
of the partic., but is placed first with
almost the force of an abs. acc., as to
that which. See on c. 15. 4; i. 32. 17.
So also St. But Steup objects that
τοῦτο ὃ is nowhere else so used, though
ὃ alone, in this sense, occurs in other
writers (cf. Xen. Anab. v. 5. 20; vi.
1. 29, and see Kr. 51, 13, 13). —
9. ἰσχυρίζεται: maintains, as in v.
26. 19; vi. 55. 2; vii. 49. 1, 23. — ἐς
τὸ λοιπὸν κτέ.: cf. c. 39. § 7, 8; 40.
§ 8. The clause is epexegetical to
τούτου ὅ. ἐς τὸ λοιπόν also iv. 128. 21;
vi. 75. 16. — 10. πρὸς τὸ ἧσσον ἀφίστασθαι: sc. τοὺς ξυμμάχους. Cf. viii.
76. 25 πρὸς τὸ περιγίγνεσθαι τῶν πολεμίων ἡ πόλις σφίσι χρήσιμος ἦν. — θάνατον ζημίαν: also ii. 24. 9. — προθεῖσι: cf. c. 82. 61; ii. 46. 5, and
πρόκειται, c. 45. 1. The partic. agrees
with ὑμῖν understood after ξυμφέρον
ἔσεσθαι. Cf. i. 118. 20 εἰ πολεμοῦσιν
ἄμεινον ἔσται, Lys. xxv. 27 οὐκ ἀξιόν

καὶ αὐτὸς περὶ τοῦ ἐς τὸ μέλλον καλῶς ἔχοντος ἀντισχυριζόμενος τἀναντία γιγνώσκω. καὶ οὐκ ἀξιῶ ὑμᾶς τῷ εὐπρεπεῖ τοῦ ἐκείνου λόγου τὸ χρήσιμον τοῦ ἐμοῦ ἀπώσασθαι. δικαιότερος γὰρ ὢν αὐτοῦ ὁ λόγος πρὸς τὴν νῦν ὑμετέραν ὀργὴν ἐς Μυτιληναίους τάχα ἂν ἐπισπάσαιτο· ἡμεῖς δὲ οὐ δικαζόμεθα πρὸς αὐτούς, ὥστε τῶν δικαίων δεῖν, ἀλλὰ βουλευόμεθα περὶ αὐτῶν, ὅπως χρησίμως ἕξουσιν.

45 " Ἐν οὖν ταῖς πόλεσι πολλῶν θανάτου ζημία πρό-

ἐστι τούτοις χρῆσθαι πολλάκις ξυμβούλοις οἷς οὐδὲ ἅπαξ ἐλυσιτέλησε πειθομένοις.
— 11. **ἀντισχυριζόμενος τἀναντία γιγνώσκω**: *I emphatically assert the contrary.*
12. **καὶ οὐκ ἀξιῶ ὑμᾶς . . . ἀπώσασθαι**: *and I demand that you reject not*, etc. See on i. 102. 17. — **τῷ εὐπρεπεῖ**: *on account of the seeming fairness*, as in c. 38. 12. Schol. πιθανολογίᾳ. Cf. εὐπρέπεια, c. 11. 10. — 14. **δικαιότερος**: *i.e.* based more on strict justice, as τῷ δικαίῳ λόγῳ νῦν χρῆσθε, i. 76. 14. — **πρὸς τὴν νῦν ὑμετέραν ὀργήν**: *in your present anger*, belongs to ἐπισπάσαιτο. See on c. 43. 17. Cf. c. 36. 5; 42. 4. — 15. **ἐς Μυτιληναίους**: for position after ὀργήν, freq. in Thuc., see on c. 54. 18; i. 11. 19. G. 968; Kühn. 464, 1; Kr. Spr. 50, 9, 9. — **τάχα ἂν ἐπισπάσαιτο**: *may perhaps attract you*. Cf. v. 111. 15. — 16. **ἡμεῖς δὲ οὐ δικαζόμεθα πρὸς αὐτούς**: *but we are not at law with them*. δικάζεσθαι, as in i. 77. 7; Xen. Cyrop. i. 2. 7. Arn. compares, for the sentiment, Arist. Rhet. i. 3 τέλος τῷ μὲν συμβουλεύοντι τὸ συμφέρον καὶ βλαβερόν, τοῖς δὲ δικαζομένοις τὸ δίκαιον καὶ τὸ ἄδικον. — **τῶν δικαίων**: strict justice, as in c. 54. 1; Dem. xviii. 7. —
17. **ὅπως χρησίμως ἔξουσιν**: sc. ἡμῖν, *how they shall be useful to us*, *i.e.* how best to effect this, whether by severe punishment, or mild treatment.

45. *Mankind are so constituted that not even the danger of the death-penalty will keep either individuals or states from transgressions.*

1. **ἐν οὖν ταῖς πόλεσι κτέ.**: the discussion announced above (c. 44. § 3 f.), as to whether the interests of Athens will be subserved by inflicting the death-penalty on the Mytileneans, is introduced with a general remark on the inadequacy of punishments, even of the death-penalty, to suppress crime. At the beginning of the next chapter the transition to the present case, for which Cleon had maintained (c. 44. 9 f.), ἐς τὸ λοιπὸν ξυμφέρον ἔσεσθαι πρὸς τὸ ἧσσον ἀφίστασθαι θάνατον ζημίαν προθεῖσι, is made with οὐκ οὖν χρή. Kühn. 508, N. 2. This chapter represents the earliest attempt to combat the theory that men are deterred from crime by fear of punishment. See M. Büdinger, *Sitzungsberichte d. phil.-hist. Kl. d. Wiener Akad.* xcvi. p. 384. — **πολλῶν**: be-

κεῖται καὶ οὐκ ἴσων τῷδε, ἀλλ' ἐλασσόνων ἁμαρτημάτων· ὅμως δὲ τῇ ἐλπίδι ἐπαιρόμενοι κινδυνεύουσι, καὶ οὐδείς πω καταγνοὺς ἑαυτοῦ μὴ περιέσεσθαι τῷ ἐπιβου-
5 λεύματι ἦλθεν ἐς τὸ δεινόν. πόλις τε ἀφισταμένη τίς 2 πω ἥσσω τῇ δοκήσει ἔχουσα τὴν παρασκευήν, ἢ οἰκείαν ἢ ἄλλων ξυμμαχίᾳ, τούτῳ ἐπεχείρησε; πεφύκασι δὲ ἅπαν- 3 τες καὶ ἰδίᾳ καὶ δημοσίᾳ ἁμαρτάνειν, καὶ οὐκ ἔστι νόμος ὅστις ἀπείρξει τούτου, ἐπεὶ διεξεληλύθασί γε διὰ πασῶν
10 τῶν ζημιῶν οἱ ἄνθρωποι προστιθέντες, εἴ πως ἧσσον ἀδι-

longs with ἁμαρτημάτων, from which it is only locally separated by the almost parenthetical οὐκ ἴσων... ἐλασσόνων. — θανάτου ζημία: although, acc. to the analogy of c. 44. 10 and ii. 24. 9, θάνατος might have been expected (as Cobet suggests, *Nov. Lect.* p. 771), still the gen. is sufficiently protected by c. 46. 1 τοῦ θανάτου τῇ ζημίᾳ. Also in Isocr. viii. 50 θανάτου τῆς ζημίας ἐπικειμένης, θανάτου must be considered a limiting genitive. — πρόκειται: pass. of προθεῖναι, c. 44. 10. — 3. τῇ ἐλπίδι ἐπαιρόμενοι: as i. 81. 11. See on c. 37. 28; 38. 12. — 4. καταγνοὺς ἑαυτοῦ μὴ περιέσεσθαι: *passing sentence of failure on himself*, lit. *deciding against himself that he will not succeed.* καταγιγνώσκειν of unfavourable judgment, as in vi. 34. 51; vii. 51. 3; Xen. *Cyrop.* vi. 1. 36 αὐτὸς ἐμαυτοῦ κατέγνων μὴ ἂν καρτερῆσαι. See on c. 16. 1. Kühn. 476, 2. — 5. ἦλθεν ἐς τὸ δεινόν: as in c. 39. 17.
πόλις τε: *and so a state.* The subj. placed first before the interr. pron. has almost the same character of generality as before the dem., having nearly the effect of the part. genitive. See on i. 1. 8. — τίς πω: no exception to the general rule that πω is used in neg. sents., since the interr. sent. is here equiv. to a negative. — 6. ἥσσω τῇ δοκήσει: *in its view insufficient.* See on c. 43. 3. — 7. ἢ ἄλλων ξυμμαχίᾳ: co-ordinated with οἰκείαν the phrase has almost the force of an adjective. — τούτῳ: sc. τῷ ἀφίστασθαι.
πεφύκασι δὲ... ἁμαρτάνειν: cf. c. 84. 10, and Dio C.'s imitation, lii. 34. 6 πολλὰ γὰρ ἡ φύσις καὶ παρὰ τὸν νόμον πολλοὺς ἁμαρτάνειν ἐξάγει, Soph. *Ant.* 1023 ἀνθρώποισι γὰρ τοῖς πᾶσι κοινόν ἐστι τοὐξαμαρτάνειν, Eur. *Hipp.* 1433 ἀνθρώποισι θεῶν διδόντων εἰκὸς ἁμαρτάνειν. Cl. writes δέ, for τε of the Mss., making the clause epexegetical. *Cf.* i. 55. 9; v. 10. 21. — 9. διεξεληλύθασι διὰ πασῶν: *cf.* Dem. ii. 5 πάντα διεξεληλύθαμεν, and Xen. *Cyrop.* i. 2. 15 οἱ γεραίτεροι διὰ πάντων τῶν καλῶν ἐληλυθότες. — 10. προστιθέντες: *always adding to*, aggravating the punishments. *Cf.* Dem. iv. 20. — εἴ πως: *if haply.* The real apod. is distinctly implied, but not formally expressed. GMT. 489; H. 907; Kr. *Spr.* 65, 1, 10. *Cf.* i. 58. 2; ii. 67. 5; iv. 11. 12. —

κοῖντο ὑπὸ τῶν κακούργων. καὶ εἰκὸς τὸ πάλαι τῶν μεγίστων ἀδικημάτων μαλακωτέρας κεῖσθαι αὐτάς, παραβαινομένων δὲ τῷ χρόνῳ ἐς τὸν θάνατον αἱ πολλαὶ ἀνήκουσι· κἂν τούτῳ ὅμως παραβαίνεται. ἢ τοίνυν δεινό- 4
15 τερόν τι τούτου δέος εὑρετέον ἐστὶν ἢ τόδε γε οὐδὲν ἐπίσχει, ἀλλ' ἡ μὲν πενία ἀνάγκῃ τὴν τόλμαν παρέχουσα, ἡ

—11. καὶ εἰκός : not introducing a new consideration, but confirming the foregoing general remark (διεξεληλύθασί γε ... κακουργῶν). —12. κεῖσθαι : here and c. 47. 13 (ἐπικεῖσθαι, c. 70. 17; viii. 15. 6) of punishments, as ii. 46. 6 of rewards, ii. 37. 17 of laws, always as pf. pass. of τιθέναι.
—παραβαινομένων : as transgressions occurred. So with Bm., who compares, for the gen. abs. without expressed subject, i. 7. 2 πλοϊμωτέρων, i. 116. 15 ἐσαγγελθέντων. GMT. 848; II. 972 a. But St. understands τῶν ζημιῶν as subj., and gives παραβαινομένων the more general sense of disregarding, citing Aeschin. iii. 204 οὐ τοὺς νόμους μόνον παραβέβηκεν, ἀλλὰ καὶ τὸν καιρὸν τῆς ἀναρρήσεως καὶ τὸν τόπον, Dem. xxiv. 32 παραβὰς τὸν χρόνον τὸν ἐκ τῶν νόμων. Cf. also Din. i. 36 παραβεβηκὼς ἅπαντας τοὺς παρεληλυθότας καιρούς. —13. τῷ χρόνῳ . . . ἀνήκουσι : cf. Lycurg. in Leocr. 65 (οἱ ἀρχαῖοι νομοθέται) ὁμοίως ἐπὶ πᾶσι καὶ τοῖς ἐλαχίστοις παρανομήμασι θάνατον ὥρισαν εἶναι τὴν ζημίαν. The phrase ἀνήκειν ἐς, to express highest intensity, occurs only here in Thuc., and is elsewhere unusual in Attic (Soph. Trach. 1018), but common in Hdt. (ii. 104. 8; v. 49. 16; vii. 9. γ 4; 13. 6; 134. 13; viii. 111. 12). —14. κἂν τούτῳ ὅμως παραβαίνεται : and under these

circumstances transgressions occur all the same. κἂν τούτῳ is Kr.'s conjecture for καὶ τοῦτο of the Mss. Cf. i. 37. 15; 81. 9; ii. 89. 37. If the reading of the Mss. be retained, St.'s explanation is best, namely τοῦτο = τὸ ἐς τὸν θάνατον τὰς πολλὰς ἀνήκειν, and παραβαίνεται, is disregarded, as in l. 12. - Jow. explains : 'τοῦτο refers to θάνατος, but παραβαίνεται is said inaccurately, not of death, but of the law which is sanctioned by the penalty of death. So παραβαινομένων really refers to the idea of a law contained in ζημιῶν just above.' See App.

15. δέος : terror; fear, for the thing feared, as metus for periculum.
—τόδε : used perhaps to avoid repetition of the same pronoun (τούτου). Cf. Soph. Ant. 296 τοῦτο καὶ πόλεις πορθεῖ, τόδ' ἄνδρας ἐξανίστησιν δόμων.
—ἐπίσχει : Schol., κωλύει. —16. ἀλλ' ἡ μὲν . . . κινδύνους : but poverty, making men bold from necessity, and wealth, making them ambitious from insolence and pride, and the other relations of life, through passion, as each relation is enslaved by some mighty and invincible impulse, lure mankind to destruction. ἀνάγκῃ and ὕβρει καὶ φρονήματι belong to παρέχουσα, while ὀργῇ belongs to ἐξάγουσιν and answers to the παρέχουσα clauses above. Cl. changes τῶν ἀνθρώπων of

δ' ἐξουσία ὕβρει τὴν πλεονεξίαν καὶ φρονήματι. αἱ δ'
ἄλλαι ξυντυχίαι ὀργῇ τὸν ἄνθρωπον, ὡς ἑκάστη τις κατέχεται ὑπ' ἀνηκέστου τινὸς κρείσσονος, ἐξάγουσιν ἐς τοὺς
20 κινδύνους. ἥ τε ἐλπὶς καὶ ὁ ἔρως ἐπὶ παντί, ὁ μὲν ἡγού- 5
μενος, ἡ δ' ἐφεπομένη, καὶ ὁ μὲν τὴν ἐπιβουλὴν ἐκφροντίζων, ἡ δὲ τὴν εὐπορίαν τῆς τύχης ὑποτιθεῖσα πλεῖστα
βλάπτουσι, καὶ ὄντα ἀφανῆ κρείσσω ἐστὶ τῶν ὁρωμένων
δεινῶν. καὶ ἡ τύχη ἐπ' αὐτοῖς οὐδὲν ἔλασσον ξυμβάλλε- 6

the Mss. into τὸν ἄνθρωπον. St. re-
jects these words and writes ὀργήν
(libidinem) for ὀργῇ, on the ground
that it is demanded by the corre-
spondence to τόλμαν and πλεονεξίαν.
See App. With the sentiment, cf.
Eur. El. 375 πενία ἔχει νόσον, διδάσκει
ἄνδρα τῇ χρείᾳ κακόν. Arist. Rhet. i. 12
ἀδικοῦσι, ὅσοι ἂν ἐνδεεῖς ὦσι· διχῶς δέ
εἰσιν ἐνδεεῖς· ἢ γὰρ ὡς ἀναγκαίου, ὥσπερ
οἱ πένητες· ἢ ὡς ὑπερβολῆς, ὥσπερ οἱ
πλούσιοι, Dion. II. i. 25 ἡ ἀνάγκη ἱκανή
ἐστι τοῖς ἀπορουμένοις βίου τόλμαν παρασχεῖν.—17. ἐξουσία: opes, Va. Cf.
i. 38. 13; 123. 6; vi. 31. 33.—φρονήματι: in Thuc. always self-confidence,
spirit. See on i. 81. 14. —18. ξυντυχίαι: conditions of life, as in c. 82. 14.
Cf. c. 112. 26; i. 33. 1; v. 11. 17;
vi. 54. 2; vii. 57. 5. —19. ὑπ' ἀνηκέστου τινὸς κρείσσονος: it is possible
to supply simply ὀργῆς, but better
perhaps to take κρείσσονος as neut.,
as most of the editt. seem to do,
and render, by some mighty and invincible impulse. ἀνήκεστος has the
meaning insatiable, unappeasable,
acc. to the const. ἀκεῖσθαι παθήματα.
Cf. also Hom. N 115 ἀκεστί τοι
φρένες ἐσθλῶν. — ἐξάγουσιν: as in vi.
89. 22 = παράγειν. Cf. Eur. Alc. 1080

ἔρως τίς μ' ἐξάγει, Herc. Fur. 775 ἅ τ'
εὐτυχία φρονεῖν βροτοὺς ἐξάγεται, ibid.
1212; Ion. 361; Suppl. 79; Dio C.
lii. 23. 2; 34. 6.
20. τε: introduces a new consideration, besides; not correl. to καί. —
ὁ ἔρως: passionate desire. Schol. πρῶ-
τόν τις ἐρᾷ, εἶτα ἐλπίζει, εἶτα ἐγχειρεῖ.
— ἐπὶ παντί: comprehends all the
above definite and indefinite cases.
Cf. i. 20. 2; iv. 11. 13; v. 100. 4. —
21. τὴν ἐπιβουλήν: the plot. So Cl.
and Steup. with three Mss., for ἐπιβολήν, undertaking, which most Mss.
have. Hude calls attention to the
fact that ἐπιβούλευμα is used in the
same sense in l. 4. Cf. i. 93. 23;
iv. 77. 1; 86. 22; viii. 24. 38. But
see App.—ἐκφροντίζων: thinking out,
a rare word found also in Ar. Nub.
695, 697. — 22. ὑποτιθεῖσα: of the
delusive suggestions of hope, similarly in i. 138. 8; iv. 65. 18. For the
thought, cf. iv. 18. § 3; vii. 61. § 3.—
23. καὶ ὄντα . . . δεινῶν: and being
unseen they outweigh the dangers that
are seen. ὄντα neut., with the two
nouns of different gender. G. 924 a;
H. 617 a. ὁρώμενα opp. to ἀφανῆ, as
in ii. 42. 21; v. 113. 4.
24. καὶ ἡ τύχη κτέ.: as hope had

25 ται ἐς τὸ ἐπαίρειν· ἀδοκήτως γὰρ ἔστιν ὅτε παρισταμένη
καὶ ἐκ τῶν ὑποδεεστέρων κινδυνεύειν· τινὰ προάγει, καὶ
οὐκ ἧσσον τὰς πόλεις, ὅσῳ περὶ τῶν μεγίστων, ἐλευθερίας ἢ ἄλλων ἀρχῆς, καὶ μετὰ πάντων ἕκαστος ἀλογί-
στως ἐπὶ πλέον τι αὐτὸν ἐδόξασεν. ἁπλῶς τε ἀδύνατον, 7
30 καὶ πολλῆς εὐηθείας ὅστις οἴεται, τῆς ἀνθρωπείας φύ-

suggested that fortune would lend its support, so the latter too contributes toward leading men astray. τύχη is here almost personified, now unexpectedly favouring, but again by that very means luring into danger. — ἐπ' αὐτοῖς: besides these. Schol. μετὰ τὸν ἔρωτα καὶ τὴν ἐλπίδα. — ξυμβάλλεται: see on προσξυνεβάλετο, c. 36. 10. — 26. ἐκ τῶν ὑποδεεστέρων: even with inadequate resources. Schol. ἀπὸ μικροτέρων ἀφορμῶν. Cf. ii. 89. 22. — προάγει: leads on, even against their will, as in c. 59. 9. — 27. οὐχ ἧσσον: i.e. μάλιστα, as in i. 8. 1, and freq. — ὅσῳ: in so far as, because, even without comparative. See on i. 68. 11. Kr. Spr. 51, 10, 5. κινδυνεύουσιν, or, perhaps better, ὁ ἀγών ἐστι is to be supplied. See on iv. 63. 12. — ἐλευθερίας ἢ ἄλλων ἀρχῆς: Cl. explains that ἢ offers not a choice, but an alternative, and ἄλλων is subj. gen. But it would seem more natural to render, with Goell. and Jow., freedom or empire. So Valla. — 28. καὶ μετὰ πάντων ... ἐδόξασεν: the force of ὅσῳ continues. The causes by which states are drawn into dangerous undertakings are two: 1) for the whole, greater advantages may be won; 2) the individual, in company with many, easily overestimates his own strength. This overestimate on the part of individuals, however, has a hurtful influence on the decisions of the many. — μετὰ πάντων: Schol. τοῦ κοινοῦ. — 29. ἐπὶ πλέον τι: the indef. pron. added to the comp. πλέον, as in ii. 11. 32. Cf. ἧσσόν τι, c. 75. 11; ἀμελέστερόν τι, ii. 11. 14; μᾶλλόν τι, i. 49. 9; τι μᾶλλον, ii. 22. 4; iv. 21. 16; vii. 57. 4; τι ἀνεπιεικέστερον, c. 66. 7. — αὐτὸν: for the unintelligible αὐτῶν of most good Mss. — ἐδόξασεν: esp. used of erroneous estimate. Cf. i. 120. 28; Dio C. lxxv. 9 ἐπὶ πλεῖον ἐδοξάσθη. The aor. is gnomic. GMT. 155; H. 840; Kühn. 386, 7. See on i. 69. 31.

ἁπλῶς: see on c. 38. 31. — ἀδύνατον: const. with ἀποτροπήν τινα ἔχειν ... δεινῷ. — 30. πολλῆς εὐηθείας: sc. ἐστίν. Cf. i. 83. 4; 142. 24. G. 1094, 1; H. 732 d. This elliptical gen. is much less freq. than in Lat. — ὅστις: so very hypothetical in force that it is loosely connected, almost like εἴ τις, with the leading clause. On this free connexion of the pers. rel. pron. with a neut. adj. or pred. gen., see Kr. Spr. 51, 13, 11; Kühn. 563, 3 d. Cf. the similar const. with ὃς ἄν, ii. 44. 4; vi. 14. 7; vii. 68. 4. So the const. is usually explained, but Stemp thinks, if ὅστις οἴεται were so intended, Thuc. would have written πολλὴ εὐήθεια. He pre-

σεως ὁρμωμένης προθύμως τι πρᾶξαι ἀποτροπήν τινα ἔχειν ἢ νόμων ἰσχύι ἢ ἄλλῳ τῳ δεινῷ.

46 "Οὐκ οὖν χρὴ οὔτε τοῦ θανάτου τῇ ζημίᾳ ὡς ἐχεγ- 1 γύῳ πιστεύσαντας χεῖρον βουλεύσασθαι, οὔτε ἀνέλπιστον καταστῆσαι τοῖς ἀποστᾶσιν ὡς οὐκ ἔσται μεταγνῶναι καὶ ὅτι ἐν βραχυτάτῳ τὴν ἁμαρτίαν καταλῦσαι. σκέ- 2

fers to take ὅστις as used by Diodotus c. 42. 7; 48. 7, and to construe πολλῆς εὐηθείας (sc. ἐστὶ with pers. subj.) as γνώμης τινὸς εἶναι (see on i. 113. 10). Cf. Hdt. i. 107. 13 οἰκίης μὲν ἐόντα ἀγαθῆς, τρόπου δὲ ἡσυχίου. Kr. Spr. 47, 6, 10. —31. ἀποτροπήν τινα ἔχειν: can be deterred. Cf. Dio C.'s imitation of the passage (lv. 16), ἡ φύσις ἡ ἀνθρωπίνη πάντως ἁμαρτάνειν τινὰς ἀναπείθει, καὶ ἀμήχανόν ἐστιν αὐτὴν πρᾶξαί τι ὡρμημένην ἐπισχεῖν.

46. *If therefore we cannot, even by accepting Cleon's proposal, attain certainty for the future, we ought not by pitiless severity to drive those who revolt to desperate resistance, thereby depriving ourselves of the basis of our own power, in that we shall have recovered the cities only after they are ruined.*

1. οὐκ οὖν χρὴ οὔτε τοῦ θανάτου ... βουλεύσασθαι, οὔτε κτέ.: only the first οὔτε clause is strictly a deduction from the argument of c. 45; hence the two οὔτε clauses stand related to each other as the τε ... καὶ clauses in c. 38. 27; ii. 39. 24, the emphasis being on the first. —ἐχεγγύῳ: Schol., βεβαίῳ, ἰσχυρᾷ ὡς ἐγγυῆσαι δυναμένῃ. The word seems to be found elsewhere only in Tragedy and late Greek. Cf. Soph. O. C. 284; Eur. Med. 386; Andr. 191; Phoen. 759; Dio C. xliv. 25 ἐχεγγύῳ πίστει τὸ βέβαιον προνοή-

σετε. Cf. φερεγγυώτατος, viii. 68. 22. —2. χεῖρον βουλεύσασθαι: as in i. 73. 7; here a euphemism for θάνατον ψηφίσασθαι Μυτιληναίων. Cf. εὖ βουλεύεται, c. 48. 7; εὐβουλία, c. 42. 4; 44. 4. —οὔτε ἀνέλπιστον καταστῆσαι ... ὡς οὐκ ἔσται: i.e. οὐκ ἀνέλπιστον ποιῆσαι τὸ μεταγνῶναι. Cf. c. 40. § 8. The const. ἀνέλπιστον καταστῆσαι τοῖς ἀποστᾶσιν, as in i. 140. 30; ii. 89. 47; vii. 44. 26; viii. 66. 24. —3. ὡς οὐκ ἔσται: pleonastic neg. after ἀνέλπιστον. Cf. ἀντίλεγον ὡς οὐ κτέ., i. 77. 13. II. 1029 a; Kr. Spr. 67. 12, 2; Kühn. 516, 3 b. See on c. 32. 13; i. 77. 13. οὐκ ἔσται, it will not be possible. with inf.; in this sense usually with subst. This pregnant force of the verb is freq., esp. after a neg. See on i. 2. 5. —4. ὅτι ἐν βραχυτάτῳ: the prep. regularly stands after ὅτι, ὡς, thus used with a superlative. Kr. Spr. 49, 10, 1; Kühn. 452, N. 3. Cf. ὅτι ἐπ' ἐλάχιστον, l. 26. See on i. 63. 5; ii. 34. 24; and for similar const. in Lat., Madvig on Cic. de Fin. v. 9. 26. —τὴν ἁμαρτίαν καταλῦσαι: suum peccatum eluere. Cf. μεῖζον ἔγκλημα λῦσαι, i. 42.11; ἐγκλήματα καταλῦσαι, i. 82. 24; διαλύσειν τὴν διαβολήν, i. 131. 12; λῦσαι τὰς πρότερον ἁμαρτίας, Ar. Ran. 691. For the act., where the mid. might have been expected, see Kühn. 375, 2.

5 ψάσθε γὰρ ὅτι νῦν μέν, ἤν τις καὶ ἀποστᾶσα πόλις γνῷ
μὴ περιεσομένη, ἔλθοι ἂν ἐς ξύμβασιν δυνατὴ οὖσα
ἔτι τὴν δαπάνην ἀποδοῦναι καὶ τὸ λοιπὸν ὑποτελεῖν·
ἐκείνως δὲ τίνα οἴεσθε ἥντινα οὐκ ἄμεινον μὲν ἢ νῦν
παρασκευάσασθαι, πολιορκίᾳ τε παρατενεῖσθαι ἐς τοὔ-
10 σχατον, εἰ τὸ αὐτὸ δύναται σχολῇ καὶ ταχὺ ξυμβῆναι;
ἡμῖν τε πῶς οὐ βλάβη δαπανᾶν καθημένοις διὰ τὸ ἀξύμ-

5. νῦν μέν: of the present situation, analogous to the more common νῦν δέ, and opp. to ἐκείνως δέ below, as in vi. 11. 9. —καί: emphatic with ἀποστᾶσα. Not, as Kr. and Steup, with ἥν. There is a reference to c. 45. § 2, but the emphasis is here on the tense, *even after it has revolted*. — 6. περιεσομένη: as in c. 45. 4. — ἔλθοι ἄν: softened expression for the regular fut. ind. GMT. 505; H. 901 a. *Cf.* the reverse form of condition, i. 121. 13. —7. ἔτι: belongs to οὖσα. — ἀποδοῦναι, ὑποτελεῖν: aor. of single act of payment of war costs; pres. of regular tribute. — 8. ἐκείνως δέ: as in i. 77. 13; vi. 11. 10. — τίνα ἥντινα οὐκ: see on c. 39. 38. This const., as well as the form of expression throughout, shows that outward similarity to Cleon's words, though with opposite purpose, is sought. — 9. παρασκευάσασθαι: the aor. is the reading of nearly all the Mss. for the vulg. παρασκευάσεσθαι. Steup retains the aor., comparing for similar change of tense, as here from παρασκευάσασθαι to παρατενεῖσθαι, iv. 28. 26, 28; 52. 16, 17; vi. 24. 3, 13; viii. 5. 35. It would seem better, with St., to write the future. See *Qu. Gr.*[2] p. 10 sq. But see App. on this passage and on ii.

3. 8. — πολιορκίᾳ τε παρατενεῖσθαι ἐς τοὔσχατον: *will suffer themselves to be reduced by siege to the last extremity*. *Cf.* Ar. *Nub.* 213 (of Euboea) ὑπὸ γὰρ ἡμῶν παρετάθη καὶ Περικλέους (explained by Schol., ἐξετρυχώθη καὶ κατεπονήθη), Plato *Symp.* 207 b τῷ λιμῷ παρατείνεσθαι. Also Xen. *Cyrop.* i. 3. 11; *Mem.* iii. 13. 6. On fut. mid. used as pass., see Kühn. 376, N. 1; Kr. *Spr.* 40, s. v. *Cf.* vii. 48. 37. The meaning *hold out, resist to the last*, seems not to occur except in Dio C. and other late writers. τε, correl. to μέν joined to an emphatic word, marks a change from an adversative const. to a simple connexion. Kühn. 530, 1. *Cf.* i. 144. 10; ii. 70. 12. — 10. δύναται: valet, means, ξυμβῆναι being subj., τὸ αὐτό object. *Cf.* i. 141. 5; vi. 36. 9.

11. ἡμῖν τε κτέ.: answering and almost parodying c. 39. § 8, hence possibly δέ (for τε) should be written as there. —καθημένοις: *sc.* in tedious siege. *Cf.* iv. 124. 24; v. 6. 22. — διὰ τὸ ἀξύμβατον: *on account of the impossibility of coming to terms*. The ξύμβασις implied has reference to both sides; neither is inclined to it. The final capitulation is here not regarded as a ξύμβασις. The word ἀξύμβατον,

βατον καί, ἢν ἕλωμεν, πόλιν ἐφθαρμένην παραλαβεῖν
καὶ τῆς προσόδου τὸ λοιπὸν ἀπ' αὐτῆς στέρεσθαι· ἰσχύομεν δὲ πρὸς τοὺς πολεμίους τῷδε. ὥστε οὐ δικαστὰς ὄν- 4
15 τας δεῖ ἡμᾶς μᾶλλον τῶν ἐξαμαρτανόντων ἀκριβεῖς βλάπτεσθαι ἢ ὁρᾶν ὅπως ἐς τὸν ἔπειτα χρόνον μετρίως κολάζοντες ταῖς πόλεσιν ἕξομεν ἐς χρημάτων λόγον ἰσχυ-
ούσαις χρῆσθαι, καὶ τὴν φυλακὴν μὴ ἀπὸ τῶν νόμων τῆς
δεινότητος ἀξιοῦν ποιεῖσθαι, ἀλλ' ἀπὸ τῶν ἔργων τῆς

though rare, is sufficiently explained by l. 6 and 10. It seems to be used elsewhere only in late writers, e.g. Polyb. xv. 9. 1. Cf. ἀσυμβάτως ἔχειν, Plut. Cic. 46; Cam. 17; Dion 21. — 12. καὶ ἢν ἕλωμεν: corresponding to τυχόντες in c. 39. 42, and without expressed object. — 13. ἀπ' αὐτῆς: for omission of art. after τῆς προσόδου, see Kr. Spr. 50, 9, 9. Cf. ii. 52. 2. — ἰσχύομεν ... τῷδε: sc. τῷ τὰς προσόδους εὖ ἔχειν. Cf. c. 39. 43; i. 122. 2. With the sentiment of the passage, cf. also v. 93. 2 ἡμεῖς δὲ μὴ διαφθείραντες ὑμᾶς κερδαίνοιμεν ἄν. Jow. quotes Burke's speech on Conciliation with America: 'A further objection to force is, that you impair the object by your very endeavours to preserve it. The thing you fought for is not the thing which you recover; but depreciated, sunk, wasted, and consumed in the contest. Nothing less will content me than whole America. I do not choose to consume its strength along with our own; because in all parts it is the British strength that I consume.'
14. ὥστε οὐ δικαστὰς ὄντας κτέ.: cf. the concluding sent. of c. 44. With δικαστὰς ὄντας βλάπτεσθαι, cf. i. 71. 6

ἀμυνόμενοι μὴ βλάπτεσθαι. βλάπτεσθαι is passive. — 17. ἐς χρημάτων λόγον ἰσχνούσαις: strong in point of money. The unusual form of expression (for χρήμασιν ἰσχνούσαις) is used to emphasize the restriction of the ἰσχύειν of the allied cities to the matter of money, whereas the Athenians πρὸς τοὺς πολεμίους ἰσχύουσιν. With ἐς χρημάτων λόγον, cf. Dem. xix. 142 εἰς ἀρετῆς λόγον καὶ δόξης, Lys. xix. 61 οὐ μόνον πρὸς δόξαν ἀλλὰ καὶ ἐς χρημάτων λόγον λυσιτελεῖ μᾶλλον ὑμῖν ἀποψηφίσασθαι, Hdt. iii. 99. 12; vii. 9. β 13 ἐς τούτου λόγον, iii. 125. 14 ἐν ἀνδραπόδων λόγῳ, vii. 222. 5 ἐν ὁμήρων λόγῳ, also Plut. Lys. 30; Dion. II. v. 34; xi. 17. — 18. τὴν φυλακὴν ποιεῖσθαι: = φυλάττεσθαι, with ἀπό to indicate source. — τῶν νόμων τῆς δεινότητος: for the order, see on c. 23. 27; i. 32. 8. The context shows that the reference is merely to the principle of extreme punishment which would be established by the adoption of Cleon's proposal (cf. § 1 ἀνέλπιστον καταστῆσαι τοῖς ἀποστᾶσιν ... καταλῦσαι). Holzapfel (Rh. Mus. xxxvii. p. 455) therefore wrongly assumes a reference to laws already existing. — 19. ἀπὸ

20 ἐπιμελείας. οὗ νῦν τἀναντία δρῶντες, ἤν τινα ἐλεύθερον καὶ βίᾳ ἀρχόμενον εἰκότως πρὸς αὐτονομίαν ἀποστάντα χειρωσώμεθα, χαλεπῶς οἰόμεθα χρῆναι τιμωρεῖσθαι. χρὴ δὲ τοὺς ἐλευθέρους οὐκ ἀφισταμένους σφόδρα
κολάζειν, ἀλλὰ πρὶν ἀποστῆναι σφόδρα φυλάσσειν καὶ
25 προκαταλαμβάνειν ὅπως μηδ᾽ ἐς ἐπίνοιαν τούτου ἴωσι,
κρατήσαντάς τε ὅτι ἐπ᾽ ἐλάχιστον τὴν αἰτίαν ἐπιφέρειν.
47 "Ὑμεῖς δὲ σκέψασθε ὅσον ἂν καὶ τοῦτο ἁμαρτά-
νοιτε Κλέωνι πειθόμενοι. νῦν μὲν γὰρ ὑμῖν ὁ δῆμος ἐν
πάσαις ταῖς πόλεσιν εὔνους ἐστὶ καὶ ἢ οὐ ξυναφίσταται
τοῖς ὀλίγοις ἤ, ἐὰν βιασθῇ, ὑπάρχει τοῖς ἀποστήσασι πο-

τῶν ἔργων τῆς ἐπιμελείας: *by having care of our own actions*, as explained in l. 23 ff.
20. οὗ: see on c. 39. 1; 43. 1. — ἐλεύθερον καὶ βίᾳ ἀρχόμενον: *i.e.* a state which is free acc. to the terms of alliance, and therefore ὑπήκοος against its will. Diodotus openly acknowledges the true relation (*cf.* c. 10. 18 αὐτόνομοι δὴ ὄντες καὶ ἐλεύθεροι τῷ ὀνόματι), in order to show that the revolt was not unreasonable. —21. εἰκότως: because βίᾳ ἄρχεται. — ἀποστάντα: with πρός elsewhere of the party which revolters join (v. 14. 25; vii. 58. 10), here with πρὸς αὐτονομίαν applied by a sort of word-play to the new political situation.
23. οὐκ ἀφισταμένους: (not ἀποστάντας) to indicate the moment when it is too late, *not when they are revolting.* —24. σφόδρα φυλάσσειν: the adv. repeated, as εὖ in c. 42. 12. —25. προκαταλαμβάνειν: see on c. 2. 15. — ὅπως μηδ᾽ . . . ἴωσι: *that this may not even occur to them. Cf.* iv.

92. 1. τούτου, sc. τοῦ ἀφίστασθαι. —26. ὅτι ἐπ᾽ ἐλάχιστον: of extent, to put the blame on as few as possible. For position of the prep., see on l. 4. The assertion of this principle introduces the argument against Cleon's demand, c. 39. 32 μὴ τοῖς μὲν ὀλίγοις ἡ αἰτία προστεθῇ, τὸν δὲ δῆμον ἀπολύσητε, to which c. 47 is devoted. — τὴν αἰτίαν ἐπιφέρειν: see on c. 42. 17.
47. *We shall also, if we punish the whole population without mercy, turn everywhere the democratic party against us and drive them over to the enemy.*
1. ὅσον: in indir. question, as in i. 78. 3. *Cf.* i. 136. 11 (ὅς), and see on c. 62. 6. On such consts. of the rel. pron., see also Dufour, *Rev. de Philol. N. S.* xiv. p. 57 ff. — τοῦτο: the acc. is cogn., as in c. 37. 5 ὅ τι ἂν ἁμάρτητε.
2. νῦν μὲν γὰρ κτέ.: in answer to c. 39. § 6. —4. ἐὰν βιασθῇ: sc. ξυναφίστασθαι. — ὑπάρχει . . . πολέμιος εὐθύς: *i.e.* as soon as war begins. *Cf.* iv. 78. 14 τοῖς Ἀθηναίοις ἀεὶ ποτε

5 λέμιος εὐθύς, καὶ τῆς ἀντικαθισταμένης πόλεως τὸ πλῆθος ξύμμαχον ἔχοντες ἐς πόλεμον ἐπέρχεσθε. εἰ δὲ δια- 3
φθερεῖτε τὸν δῆμον τῶν Μυτιληναίων, ὃς οὔτε μετέσχε
τῆς ἀποστάσεως, ἐπειδή τε ὅπλων ἐκράτησεν, ἑκὼν παρέδωκε τὴν πόλιν, πρῶτον μὲν ἀδικήσετε τοὺς εὐεργέτας
10 κτείνοντες, ἔπειτα καταστήσετε τοῖς δυνατοῖς τῶν ἀνθρώπων ὃ βούλονται μάλιστα· ἀφιστάντες γὰρ τὰς πόλεις τὸν δῆμον εὐθὺς ξύμμαχον ἕξουσι προδειξάντων
ὑμῶν τὴν αὐτὴν ζημίαν τοῖς τε ἀδικοῦσιν ὁμοίως κεῖσθαι
καὶ τοῖς μή. δεῖ δέ, καὶ εἰ ἠδίκησαν, μὴ προσποιεῖσθαι, 4
15 ὅπως ὃ μόνον ἡμῖν ἔτι ξύμμαχόν ἐστι μὴ πολέμιον γένη-

τὸ πλῆθος τῶν Θεσσαλῶν εὔνουν ὑπῆρχεν.
The result is expressed in καὶ τῆς ἀντικαθισταμένης... ἐπέρχεσθε. τὸ πλῆθος
for τὸν δῆμον to emphasize the numerical superiority.—5. τῆς ἀντικαθισταμένης πόλεως: *of the city opposed
to you*, as in i. 71. 1. —6. ἐς πόλεμον
ἐπέρχεσθε: unusual const., for the
more usual ἐς πόλεμον καθίστασθε (see
on ii. 75. 1), or πρὸς πόλεμον τρέπεσθε
(v. 114. 3). But *cf.* ἐς τιμωρίαν ἐπέρχονται, iv. 25. 35; ἐπεξιέναι ἐς μάχην,
iv. 68. 10. Hence there is no need
to bracket ἐς πόλεμον, with v. H., or
to write ἐς πόλεμον ἔρχεσθε (*cf.* ἰέναι
ἐς τοὺς πολέμους, i. 78. 7; 118. 11),
with Badham and Cobet, *Mnem. N. S.*
viii. p. 137.
8. ἐπειδή τε κτέ.: *cf.* c. 27. § 3; 28.
Diodotus exaggerates somewhat the
services of the demos of Mytilene;
still the course of the democratic
party after arms were received was
the cause of the capitulation. —10.
καταστήσετε ... μάλιστα: *you will
bring to pass what the aristocrats
most wish*. *Cf.* iv. 92. 31 πολλὴν
ἄδειαν τῇ Βοιωτίᾳ μέχρι τοῦδε κατεστήσαμεν. In this sense καθιστάναι
takes, as a rule, a pred. adjective.
See on c. 46. 2. For the part. gen. in
pred. position, *cf.* c. 37. 17; 67. 16;
iv. 17. 14; 28. 25; vii. 61. 7. G. 965;
H. 730 d. —12. προδειξάντων ὑμῶν:
*because you will have taught them
beforehand*. *Cf.* προυδήλου, i. 130. 9.
Or perhaps, as Steup explains, προδεικνύναι, *proclaim*, as προαγορεύειν, i.
26. 20; 29. 3; 43. 2; 140. 22, *etc.* —
14. δεῖ δὲ καὶ ... προσποιεῖσθαι: the
orator, wishing to be as consistent as
possible, assumes the view of his opponent to be true, *you must, even if
they did wrong, ignore it*, lit. pretend
that they did not. The fact is expressed in hypothetical form, as in
c. 43. 19. μὴ προσποιεῖσθαι, *sc.* ἀδικῆσαι αὐτούς. Kr. *Spr.* 67, 1, 5. Schol. μή
τοί γε δεικνύειν τὸ γνῶναι. *Cf.* Theophr.
Char. 1 ἀκούσας τι, μὴ προσποιεῖσθαι,
Diog. Laert. ix. 29 ἐὰν λοιδορούμενος μὴ
προσποιῶμαι.

ται. καὶ τοῦτο πολλῷ ξυμφορώτερον ἡγοῦμαι ἐς τὴν κάθ- 5
εξιν τῆς ἀρχῆς ἑκόντας ἡμᾶς ἀδικηθῆναι ἢ δικαίως οὓς
μὴ δεῖ διαφθεῖραι · καὶ τὸ Κλέωνος τὸ αὐτὸ δίκαιον καὶ
ξύμφορον τῆς τιμωρίας οὐχ εὑρίσκεται ἐν αὐτῷ δυνατὸν
20 ὂν ἅμα γίγνεσθαι.

48   " Ὑμεῖς δὲ γνόντες ἀμείνω τάδε εἶναι καὶ μήτε οἴ- 1
κτῳ πλέον νείμαντες μήτ' ἐπιεικείᾳ, οἷς οὐδὲ ἐγὼ ἐῶ
προσάγεσθαι, ἀπ' αὐτῶν δὲ τῶν παραινουμένων πείθε-

16. καὶ τοῦτο: explained by ἑκόντας
... διαφθεῖραι. Steup explains as
cogn. acc. with ἀδικηθῆναι, referring
to what precedes. Cf. c. 65. 1; i.
38. 10; 67. 10; v. 30. 14; viii. 99. 8.
But its position is against this view.
— κάθεξιν: maintenance, found only
here in Thuc. It means retentio
in Arist. Pol. iv. 15. 6 and Plut. de
Sol. Animal. 968 c. See Lobeck, ad
Phryn. p. 351. — 17. δικαίως: as in
c. 44. 14. — οὓς μὴ δεῖ: i.e. οὓς οὐ
ξυμφέρει τῇ πόλει. — 18. τὸ Κλέωνος τὸ
αὐτὸ δίκαιον καὶ ξύμφορον: "Cleon's
claim of a union of right and justice
in the punishment." Cf. c. 40. 17 ff.
τὸ αὐτό ... ξύμφορον is not appos.,
but the whole expression is closely
connected. τὸ αὐτό in its pred.
sense. Cf. οἱ αὐτοί, as in ii. 40. 12.
— 19. εὑρίσκεται: used of the results
of careful investigation, as in historical inquiry. Cf. i. 21. 7; iv. 62. 2;
vi. 2. 8, and see on i. 1. 11. — ἐν
αὐτῷ: sc. ἐν τῷ διαφθεῖραι αὐτούς.
Not with Dobree ἐν τῷ αὐτῷ, or Kr.
ἐν ταυτῷ; for right and advantage
might often be combined. Since ἐν
αὐτῷ makes τῆς τιμωρίας rather pleonastic, and ἅμα is tautological after
τὸ αὐτὸ δίκαιον καὶ ξύμφορον, Steup

suggests that possibly Thuc. used
οὐχ εὑρίσκεται abs. (is not found),
and that ἐν αὐτῷ ... γίγνεσθαι was a
marginal remark that crept into the
text.

48. Pass judgment calmly on the
instigators of the revolt, but let the
rest continue to live upon their island.
Thus you will best provide for your
own interests.

1. γνόντες ... παραινουμένων: the
motive proposed by Diodotus as the
only right one, and recapitulated
here, is fully expressed in γνόντες
ἀμείνω τάδε εἶναι, having concluded
that this is better for Athens; but Diodotus deems it necessary to disclaim
positively (μήτε ... προσάγεσθαι) the
motives (οἶκτος or ἔλεος and ἐπιείκεια)
imputed by Cleon, c. 40. § 2 f., and
to rest his case solely on the considerations just urged by him (ἀπ' αὐτῶν
τῶν παραινουμένων). — γνόντες: having
decided, followed by the' inf., as in
i. 43. 5; 69. 15. — τάδε: refers to
Μυτιληναίων οὓς ... οἰκεῖν. The connexion is rendered a little obscure
by the intervening clauses, but the
repetition of τάδε in l. 6 makes it
clear. — 2. πλέον νείμαντες: see on
c. 3. 5. — 3. προσάγεσθαι: not pass.

σθέ μοι Μυτιληναίων οὓς μὲν Πάχης ἀπέπεμψεν ὡς ἀδι-
5 κοῦντας κρῖναι καθ᾽ ἡσυχίαν, τοὺς δ᾽ ἄλλους ἐᾶν οἰκεῖν.
τάδε γὰρ ἔς τε τὸ μέλλον ἀγαθὰ καὶ τοῖς πολεμίοις 2
ἤδη φοβερά· ὅστις γὰρ εὖ βουλεύεται, πρὸς τοὺς
ἐναντίους κρείσσων ἐστὶν ἢ μετ᾽ ἔργων ἰσχύος ἀνοίᾳ
ἐπιών."
49   Τοιαῦτα δὲ ὁ Διόδοτος εἶπε.   ῥηθεισῶν δὲ τῶν 1

(as Kr. and Bm.), but mid., as in c. 42. 30; 43. 7, with indef. subject. — ἀπ᾽ αὐτῶν δὲ τῶν παραινουμένων: solely in accordance with the arguments made. For ἀπό in this sense, see on c. 36. 12; 64. 4; i. 21. 11; 91. 28. τῶν παραινουμένων, the word contemptuously used by Cleon, c. 37. 28, is purposely repeated here. — 4. οὓς μὲν Πάχης ἀπέπεμψεν: cf. c. 35. § 1. — 5. καθ᾽ ἡσυχίαν : calmly, i.e. without haste or passion, as in i. 85. 5; vi. 25. 6. Cf. c. 42. 4, where Diodotus designates τάχος τε καὶ ὀργήν as the two worst foes of just decisions. — οἰκεῖν : used in a pregnant sense as antithesis to κρίνεσθαι, as in c. 75. 6. The idea is to let them continue to dwell upon their island without danger to life. Cf. c. 50. § 2.
6. ἤδη : opp. to ἐς τὸ μέλλον, although the emphasizing of τοῖς πολεμίοις has changed the natural order. — 7. ὅστις γὰρ ... ἐπιών : substantiating the words καὶ τοῖς πολεμίοις ἤδη φοβερά. He who deliberates wisely is more formidable toward opponents than he who rushes on inconsiderately with brute force (material strength). Bl. compares Hdt. iii. 127. 13 ἔνθα σοφίης δεῖ, βίης ἔργον οὐδέν. — εὖ βου-

λεύεται : cf. εὐβουλία, c. 42. 4 ; 44. 4, and χεῖρον βουλεύσασθαι, c. 46. 2. — πρὸς τοὺς ἐναντίους : with κρείσσων ἐστίν, as ἰσχύομεν πρὸς τοὺς πολεμίους, c. 46. 14 ; πρὸς τοὺς προσοίκους ἰσχύος, i. 7. 5 ; πρὸς Πελοποννησίους ἰσχύος, vi. 83. 5. It repeats τοῖς πολεμίοις of the preceding line, and is similarly placed first for emphasis. Bk., Kr., and Cl. follow Reiske in connecting πρὸς τοὺς ἐναντίους with εὖ βουλεύεται, but, as Pp. remarks, the deliberation was concerning the Mytileneans who had surrendered, not against the enemy (the Peloponnesians), and the speaker presents in a general truth the idea that good counsel about the former would be profitable against the latter. — 8. κρείσσων ἐστί : as in c. 37. 15. — ἐπιών : Kr. and Cobet would write ὁ ἐπιών, but cf. c. 39. 24 κατὰ λόγον εὐτυχοῦντα. ἐπιέναι as ἐπέρχεσθαι, iv. 86. 21. Cf. also ἐς πόλεμον ἐπέρχεσθε, c. 47. 6.
49. The view of Diodotus having prevailed by a small majority, this decree is immediately despatched to Paches by a trireme, which, making all possible speed, arrives in time to prevent the execution of the first decree.
1. τοιαῦτα δέ : resumptive after μετὰ δ᾽ αὐτόν in c. 41. 1. Cf. c. 68. 1 ; i. 44.

γνωμῶν τούτων μάλιστα ἀντιπάλων πρὸς ἀλλήλας, οἱ
Ἀθηναῖοι ἦλθον μὲν ἐς ἀγῶνα ὅμως τῆς δόξης καὶ ἐγένοντο ἐν τῇ χειροτονίᾳ ἀγχώμαλοι, ἐκράτησε δὲ ἡ τοῦ
5 Διοδότου. καὶ τριήρη εὐθὺς ἄλλην ἀπέστελλον κατὰ 2
σπουδήν, ὅπως μὴ φθασάσης τῆς προτέρας εὕρωσι διεφθαρμένην τὴν πόλιν· προεῖχε δὲ ἡμέρᾳ καὶ νυκτὶ μάλιστα. παρασκευασάντων δὲ τῶν Μυτιληναίων πρέσβεων 3
τῇ νηὶ οἶνον καὶ ἄλφιτα καὶ μεγάλα ὑποσχομένων, εἰ
10 φθάσειαν, ἐγένετο σπουδὴ τοῦ πλοῦ τοιαύτη ὥστε ἤσθιόν

1 ; 79. 1 ; ii. 90. 1 ; vi. 88. 1. See on
vi. 19. 1.— 2. μάλιστα ἀντιπάλων :
pred. to ῥηθεισῶν, *with about equal
weight*. Va., followed by Arn. and
some others, renders, *most opposed to*;
but ἀντίπαλος in Thuc. means everywhere *opposed with equal strength*.
μάλιστα, as in c. 34. 4 ; i. 13. 11. —
3. ἦλθον μὲν ἐς ἀγῶνα ὅμως τῆς δόξης:
the sense seems to be, as most editt.
understand, "in spite of the reaction
(μετάνοια, c. 36. 15), there was a struggle between the two opinions." *Cf.*
vii. 71. 1 ὁ ἐκ τῆς γῆς πεζὸς ... πολὺν
τὸν ἀγῶνα καὶ ξύστασιν τῆς γνώμης εἶχε.
Cl.'s explanation, 'they proceeded
to a vote *nevertheless* (ὅμως, *i.c.* without waiting for further arguments
from either side),' seems untenable,
and the various emendations proposed for ὅμως (ὁμοίως Bredow, ὅλης
Badham, ὁμόσε Weidgen) are unnecessary. St. and Bm. render ἐς ἀγῶνα
τῆς δόξης, in certamen de de-
creto (faciendo). — 4. ἀγχώμαλοι:
nearly equal. This word, which occurs also iv. 134. 7 ; vii. 71. 21, is
found elsewhere only in late writers.
It is called τραχύ by Poll. v. 157. The
choice of expressions here (ἀντίπαλος,

ἀγὼν τῆς δόξης, ἀγχώμαλος) indicates
how precarious was the situation of
the Mytileneans. Everything points
to the concluding words of the chapter, παρὰ τοσοῦτον ... κινδύνου. — ἡ
τοῦ Διοδότου : *sc.* γνώμη.
5. ἄλλην : *cf.* c. 36. 13. — ἀπέστελλον : the impf. combining the notion
of 'continued action' with that of
'outset.' See on i. 10. 34 ; 26. 2. —
6. προτέρας : though in only a few
Mss. (most having δευτέρας or ἑτέρας),
adopted by most editt., and clearly
correct, since προεῖχε necessarily presupposes mention of the first ship.
Cf. l. 15. Va.'s interpretation, non
assecuta haec priorem, also
supports this reading.— 7. μάλιστα :
about. See on l. 2 ; 34. 4 ; i. 13. 11.
8. τῶν Μυτιληναίων πρέσβεων : *cf.*
c. 28. 7 ; 36. 18. — 10. φθάσειαν : as
νομίσειαν, v. 111. 6, for -αιεν of most
of the Mss., since Thuc. has everywhere except in these two passages
only -ειαν in aor. opt. 3rd pl. See
St. *Qu. Gr.*² p. 62 sq. — ὥστε ἤσθιόν
τε κτέ.: as F. Herbst observes (*Wo-
chenschrift f. Kl. Philol.* 1890, p.
788 f.), this passage is against the
view of Breusing (*Lösung d. Tric-*

τε ἅμα ἐλαύνοντες οἴνῳ καὶ ἐλαίῳ ἄλφιτα πεφυραμένα καὶ οἱ μὲν ὕπνον ᾑροῦντο κατὰ μέρος, οἱ δὲ ἤλαυνον. κατὰ τύχην δὲ πνεύματος οὐδενὸς ἐναντιωθέντος καὶ τῆς 4 μὲν προτέρας νεὼς οὐ σπουδῇ πλεούσης ἐπὶ πρᾶγμα ἀλ-
15 λόκοτον, ταύτης δὲ τοιούτῳ τρόπῳ ἐπειγομένης, ἡ μὲν ἔφθασε τοσοῦτον ὅσον Πάχητα ἀνεγνωκέναι τὸ ψήφισμα καὶ μέλλειν δράσειν τὰ δεδογμένα, ἡ δ' ὑστέρα αὐτῆς ἐπικατάγεται καὶ διεκώλυσε μὴ διαφθεῖραι. παρὰ το-

renrätsels, p. 117 f.), that a trireme was always rowed by only one class of rowers, i.e. by the thalamitae or the zygitae or the thranitae. — 11. **οἴνῳ καὶ ἐλαίῳ ἄλφιτα πεφυραμένα**: *barley-cakes kneaded with wine and oil*. Usually the barley meal was kneaded with water and oil. Hesych. (s.v. μᾶζα), μᾶζα ἄλφιτα πεφυραμένη ὕδατι καὶ ἐλαίῳ. *Cf.* Xen. *Cyrop.* vi. 2. 28. — **ὕπνον ᾑροῦντο**: as in ii. 75. 12; σῖτον ᾑροῦντο, iv. 26. 9. — 12. **κατὰ μέρος**: as in iv. 26. 10. *Cf. ἐν τῷ μέρει*, iv. 11. 11. Schol. κατὰ διαδοχὴν μερικήν. Usually all hands slept on shore at night.
13. **τῆς μὲν προτέρας νεὼς ... πλεούσης, ταύτης δὲ ... ἐπειγομένης**: the gen. abs., though the subjs. are the same with those of the leading verbs. GMT. 850; H. 972 d. See on c. 13. 30; 112. 21. — 14. **πρᾶγμα ἀλλόκοτον**: an *unnatural*, and therefore *disagreeable business*. ἀλλόκοτος is of uncertain etymology, not found in Xen. and the orators, and seldom in other Attic authors except Plato. *Cf.* Soph. *Phil.* 1191; Ar. *Vesp.* 47, 71; Plato *Prot.* 346 a; *Legg.* 747 d; *Theaet.* 182 a; *Rep.* 487 d; *Hipp. M.* 292 c. It is common in Plut. and other late

writers. — 16. **ἔφθασε τοσοῦτον**: *cf.* Diod. xii. 55. — **ὅσον**: with inf. with restrictive force, *only so much that*. *Cf.* i. 2. 8. GMT. 759; Kr. *Spr.* 55, 3, 5. — 17. **ἡ δ' ὑστέρα αὐτῆς ἐπικατάγεται**: *while the other comes to land after it*. After the adj., if thus taken pred., the prep. is pleonastic; hence Steup suggests αὐτίκ' for αὐτῆς, comparing c. 22. 24; Hom. B 322; Hdt. i. 79. 1; ii. 181. 16. In that case ἡ δ' ὑστέρα would be subject. — 18. **ἐπικατάγεται**: also viii. 28. 2. *Cf.* Dio C. xlii. 7; Jos. *A. J.* xviii. 7. 2. — **μὴ διαφθεῖραι**: sc. τὴν πόλιν. But Steup finds this complement rather harsh after what has gone before, and suggests that μὴ διαφθεῖραι may have crept into the text from a marginal remark. διεκώλυσε would then be used abs., as in vii. 2. 6; 79. 16. — **παρὰ τοσοῦτον ... κινδύνου**: *such a narrow escape had Mytilene from danger (i.e. destruction)*. This const., which occurs also vii. 2. 23, is to be explained acc. to the analogy of παρὰ τοσοῦτον ἐγένετο or ἦλθε with the inf. (iv. 106. 18; viii. 33. 12; 76. 15). **παρὰ τοσοῦτον**, *within so much, so close*. That to which it had almost come is, when expressed by a clause, in the

50 τοῦτον μὲν ἡ Μυτιλήνη ἦλθε κινδύνου· τοὺς δ' ἄλλους ἄνδρας οὓς ὁ Πάχης ἀπέπεμψεν ὡς αἰτιωτάτους ὄντας τῆς ἀποστάσεως Κλέωνος γνώμῃ διέφθειραν οἱ Ἀθηναῖοι· ἦσαν δὲ ὀλίγῳ πλείους † χιλίων. καὶ Μυτιληναίων τείχη καθεῖλον καὶ ναῦς παρέλαβον. ὕστερον δὲ φόρον μὲν οὐκ ἔταξαν Λεσβίοις, κλήρους δὲ ποιήσαντες τῆς γῆς πλὴν τῆς Μηθυμναίων τρισχιλίους τριακοσίους μὲν τοῖς θεοῖς ἱεροὺς ἐξεῖλον, ἐπὶ δὲ τοὺς ἄλλους σφῶν αὐτῶν κληρούχους τοὺς λαχόντας ἀπέπεμ-

inf.; when by a subst., in the gen., which is to be construed as the gen. with ἐγγύς, etc. G. 1149; H. 757.

50. *The Mytileneans whom Paches had sent to Athens as the most guilty are put to death, the walls of the city pulled down, the ships seized, and the whole of Lesbos except the territory of Methymna given to Attic cleruchs, to whom the Lesbians as tenants paid a yearly rental.*

2. Πάχης: mentioned here for the last time in Thucydides. He was accused of shameful deeds of violence toward Lesbian men and women (Agath. *Epigr.* 57; see Grote, *Hist. of Greece*, ch. 50), and when brought to trial committed suicide in the presence of his judges. *Cf.* Plut. *Arist.* 26; *Nic.* 6 εὐθύνας διδοὺς τῆς στρατηγίας ἐν αὐτῷ τῷ δικαστηρίῳ σπασάμενος ξίφος ἀνεῖλεν ἑαυτόν. — **3.** Κλέωνος γνώμῃ: *on Cleon's motion*, which he doubtless offered in the assembly held for reconsideration. *Cf.* i. 90. 14; 93. 16; vi. 50. 2. — **4.** χιλίων: Steup thinks this number incompatible with what is stated in c. 28. § 1, 2; 35. § 1, and conjectures τριάκοντα (Λ' for Α). See App. —

5. ναῦς παρέλαβον: *i.e.* caused to be delivered to them, corresponding to παραδοῦναι on the part of the Lesbians. *Cf.* i. 19. 5. — **6.** κλήρους δὲ ποιήσαντες τῆς γῆς κτέ.: see App.

8. τριακοσίους τοῖς θεοῖς ἱερούς: *i.e.* the tenth usually consecrated to the gods. 'The portions of land thus assigned to the gods in ancient Greece and Rome were considered a part of the property of the state, and like other public lands were usually let out to individuals, who were bound to keep up the sacred buildings, to provide victims and all things necessary for the sacrifices, and to maintain the priests and inferior ministers of the temples.' Arn. *Cf.* Arist. *Pol.* vii. 10. 11; Xen. *de Vect.* 4. 19, and see Boeckh, *P. E.* book iii. ch. 2. — **9.** τοὺς λαχόντας: *those on whom the lot fell.* The lands were distributed among a definite number of citizens by lot, 'doubtless in such a manner that all who wished to participate in the benefit of the distribution voluntarily announced their desire, and then the lot determined who should receive a share.' Boeckh, *P. E.* p. 548. See also Schoemann,

10 ψαν· οἷς ἀργύριον Λέσβιοι ταξάμενοι τοῦ κλήρου ἑκάστου τοῦ ἐνιαυτοῦ δύο μνᾶς φέρειν αὐτοὶ εἰργάζοντο τὴν γῆν. παρέλαβον δὲ καὶ τὰ ἐν τῇ ἠπείρῳ πολίσματα οἱ Ἀθηναῖοι ὅσων Μυτιληναῖοι ἐκράτουν, καὶ ὑπήκουον ὕστερον Ἀθηναίων.

51 Τὰ μὲν κατὰ Λέσβον οὕτως ἐγένετο· ἐν δὲ τῷ αὐτῷ 1 θέρει μετὰ τὴν Λέσβου ἅλωσιν Ἀθηναῖοι Νικίου τοῦ Νικηράτου στρατηγοῦντος ἐστράτευσαν ἐπὶ Μινῴαν τὴν νῆσον, ἣ κεῖται πρὸ Μεγάρων, ἐχρῶντο δὲ αὐτῇ πύργον 5 ἐνοικοδομήσαντες οἱ Μεγαρῆς φρουρίῳ. ἐβούλετο δὲ 2

Gr. Ant. ii. p. 84 f.; Grote, *Hist. of Gr.* vi. p. 257. Of the 2700 cleruchs thus sent out Boeckh says further (p. 554): 'Undoubtedly many of them returned home. But a part of them must have remained as a garrison, and probably they together with the original inhabitants composed the body politic.' — **10.** ταξάμενοι: *getting themselves rated*, i.e. engaging to pay. See on c. 70. 19; i. 99. 11. — **11.** δύο μνᾶς: so that the whole rent paid to the cleruchs amounted to 90 talents (2 × 2700 = 5400 minas). — φέρειν: as i. 99. 11, with two accusatives, δύο μνᾶς being a sort of part. appos. to ἀργύριον. But it is possible to construe ἀργύριον ταξάμενοι, to which the inf. clause adds a more definite explanation. See Cl.'s note on i. 99. 11.

12. τὰ ἐν τῇ ἠπείρῳ πολίσματα: called in iv. 52. 10 Ἀκταῖαι πόλεις (cf. Kirchhoff, *C.I.A.* i. p. 23), Antandros being mentioned as the most important. — **12.** ὑπήκοον: with change of subj. after καί. See on c. 5. 16.

51. *The Athenians under Nicias occupy the island of Minoa before Megara.*

1. τὰ μὲν ... ἐγένετο: for this formula, see on c. 6. 12. — **2.** Νικίου: already long held in high esteem on account of his wealth and honourable character (Plut. *Nic.* 2), he appears here first in Thuc. as a participant in the war. — **3.** ἐπὶ Μινῴαν: on the ι subscript, see Lobeck, *Pathol. Serm. Gr. Elementa,* i. p. 452. The expedition was occasioned by the experience of the autumn of 429 B.C. (ii. 93, 94). — τὴν νῆσον: already in Strabo's time (p. 391) it had become an ἄκρα of the mainland. See Bursian, i. p. 378 ff. On the situation of the island, see Lolling, *Nisaea u. Minoa (Mitt. d. dtsch. Arch. Inst. i. Athen* v. p. 1 ff.). — **4.** πρὸ Μεγάρων: properly *before* the port of *Megara* (Nisaea), which was eight stades from the city. — ἐχρῶντο δὲ αὐτῇ: directly connected with the preceding rel. clause. For αὐτῇ in second member of a rel. sent., see on i. 42. 2. G. 1040; H. 1005; Kr. *Spr.* 60, 6, 2. — πύργον: Steup thinks the text corrupt. See App. — **5.** φρουρίῳ: in order to protect the port Nisaea.

Νικίας τὴν φυλακὴν αὐτόθεν δι' ἐλάσσονος τοῖς Ἀθηναίοις καὶ μὴ ἀπὸ τοῦ Βουδόρου καὶ τῆς Σαλαμῖνος εἶναι, τούς τε Πελοποννησίους, ὅπως μὴ ποιῶνται ἔκπλους αὐτόθεν λανθάνοντες τριήρων τε, οἷον καὶ τὸ
10 πρὶν γενόμενον, καὶ λῃστῶν ἐκπομπαῖς, τοῖς τε Μεγαρεῦσιν ἅμα μηδὲν ἐσπλεῖν. ἑλὼν οὖν ἀπὸ τῆς Νισαίας 3

6. **αὐτόθεν**: *i.e.* from Minoa. — **δι' ἐλάσσονος**: *at a less distance*, as in vi. 75. 3; vii. 4. 19. — **7. ἀπὸ τοῦ Βουδόρου καὶ τῆς Σαλαμῖνος**: the part is joined to the whole, as ἐπὶ Καύνου καὶ Καρίας, i. 116. 15. See on ii. 69. 9. It seems from this passage that, in consequence of the events of the autumn of 429 B.C., Nisaea was guarded no longer only from Budorum (*cf.* ii. 93. 22; 94. 14), but from several points on Salamis. — **8. εἶναι**: in pregnant sense, almost = ὑπάρχειν. See on i. 2. 5. — **τούς τε Πελοποννησίους**: proleptic for ὅπως μὴ οἱ Πελοποννήσιοι, almost = abs. acc., *as to the Peloponnesians, that they might not* ——. The freedom of const. is perhaps not more striking than τὴν μὲν χαλεπὸν . . . πόλιν ἀντίπαλον παρασκευάσασθαι, i. 142. 6; or τὸν πόνον τὸν κατὰ τὸν πόλεμον, μὴ γένηται . . . ἀρκείτω μὲν ὑμῖν καὶ ἐκεῖνα κτέ., ii. 62. 1. τούς τε Πελοποννησίους seems to have been written as if μὴ ποιεῖσθαι were to follow; but if the sent. had read thus, the inf. clause would have seemed to be co-ord. with φυλακὴν εἶναι, depending on ἐβούλετο (as indeed Kühn. 473, n. 6, following the Schol., construes the ὅπως clause); whereas both ὅπως μὴ ποιῶνται and μηδὲν ἐσπλεῖν depend on τοῖς Ἀθηναίοις τὴν φυλακὴν εἶναι = τοὺς Ἀθηναίους φυ- λάσσειν. τε correl. to τε in l. 9. With this explanation of the const., St.'s conjecture, σκοπῶν before ὅπως, is unnecessary. See *Rh. Mus.* xxiv. p. 629 f. Steup would read, with Hünnekes, πρός τε Πελοποννησίους. See App. — **ποιῶνται λανθάνοντες**: the usual const. is reversed. GMT. 893. *Cf.* λαθόντες διεκομίσθησαν, c. 74. 16; λαθὼν ηὐλίσατο, vii. 29. 10. See on c. 25. 5. — **9. αὐτόθεν**: ἀπὸ τῆς Μινῴας, Schol. Rather from Nisaea, the only Megarian harbour on the Saronic gulf. The fact that αὐτόθεν is used here in a slightly different sense from l. 6 is not sufficient cause for assuming, with C. F. Müller (*N. Jahrbb.* cxli. p. 362), that the text is corrupt. — **οἷον καὶ τὸ πρὶν γενόμενον**: *sc.* ἦν, referring to the attempt of Brasidas described in ii. 93, 94. — **10. λῃστῶν**: taken by Cl. in its literal sense, *plunderers*. But it seems better, with Bl. and Jow., to render it as *privateers*. *Cf.* iv. 9. 7 ἐκ λῃστρικῆς Μεσσηνίων τριακοντόρου καὶ κέλητος. *Cf.* also iv. 67. 11 ἀκάτιον ἀμφηρικὸν ὡς λῃσταί. — **ἐκπομπαῖς**: found only here in Thuc. *Cf.* Plato *Legg.* 740 e. — **τοῖς τε Μεγαρεῦσιν . . . ἐσπλεῖν**: *cf.* ii. 93. 23 νεῶν τριῶν φυλακῇ τοῦ μὴ ἐσπλεῖν Μεγαρεῦσι μηδ' ἐκπλεῖν μηδέν.

11. ἀπὸ τῆς Νισαίας: *away from Nisaea, i.e.* on the side turned from

πρῶτον δύο πύργω προέχοντε μηχαναῖς ἐκ θαλάσσης καὶ τὸν ἔσπλουν ἐς τὸ μεταξὺ τῆς νήσου ἐλευθερώσας ἀπετείχιζε καὶ τὸ ἐκ τῆς ἠπείρου. ᾗ κατὰ γέφυραν διὰ
15 τενάγους ἐπιβοήθεια ἦν τῇ νήσῳ οὐ πολὺ διεχούσῃ τῆς ἠπείρου. ὡς δὲ τοῦτο ἐξειργάσαντο ἐν ἡμέραις ὀλίγαις, 4 ὕστερον δὴ καὶ ἐν τῇ νήσῳ τεῖχος ἐγκαταλιπὼν καὶ φρουρὰν ἀνεχώρησε τῷ στρατῷ.

52   Ὑπὸ δὲ τοὺς αὐτοὺς χρόνους τοῦ θέρους τούτου καὶ 1 οἱ Πλαταιῆς οὐκέτι ἔχοντες σῖτον οὐδὲ δυνάμενοι πολιορκεῖσθαι ξυνέβησαν τοῖς Πελοποννησίοις τοιῷδε τρόπῳ.

Nisaea. *Cf.* i. 7. 6; 46. 10; 99. 10; vi. 64. 20. See App. — 12. **μηχαναῖς**: with reference to this enterprise, *cf.* Ar. *Av.* 363

ὦ σοφώτατ᾽, εὖ γ᾽ ἀνεῦρες αὐτὸ καὶ στρατηγικῶς·
ὑπερακοντίζεις σύ γ᾽ ἤδη Νικίαν ταῖς μηχαναῖς.

— **ἐκ θαλάσσης**: the attack upon the towers was made from the ships. — 13. **καὶ τὸν ἔσπλουν . . . ἐλευθερώσας**: by the capture of the two projecting towers Nicias freed the entrance to (*i.e.* opened to ships) the part of the island lying between these towers. ἐλευθεροῦν in this sense seems not to occur elsewhere in Attic, but *cf.* Dio C. xlii. 12. 2 τὸν ἔσπλουν ἠλευθέρωσε, Procop. *de Aedif.* v. 2 ἐλευθέρας ποιεῖσθαι τῷ ποταμῷ τὰς ἐς τὴν θάλασσαν ἐκβολάς. — **τὸ μεταξύ**: as in vii. 34. 11. — 14. **ἀπετείχιζε καὶ τὸ ἐκ τῆς ἠπείρου**: opp. to ἀπὸ τῆς Νισαίας πρῶτον. After the Athenians had secured a safe landing-place, they walled off (ἀπετείχιζε) the exit from the bridge, which crossed the lagoon at the point nearest the mainland, so that no enemy could

cross over from that quarter. The bridge itself they left for use in further operations. — **διὰ τενάγους**: see on l. 3. — 15. **ἐπιβοήθεια ἦν**: the noun seems to occur in Attic only here and Xen. *Cyrop.* v. 4. 47, though the verb ἐπιβοηθεῖν is common. ἦν (= παρῆν). *Cf.* εἶναι in l. 7.

16. **ἐξειργάσαντο**: transition to the pl. from ἀπετείχιζε. Some Mss. have the sing., but for similar transitions from the general to the army, *cf.* c. 112. 17; ii. 75. 3; iv. 127. 7. — 17. **ὕστερον δὴ . . . στρατῷ**: the text is prob. corrupt. See App. — **φρουράν**: with ἐγκαταλιπών, as in i. 115. 14. *Cf.* φυλακὴν ἐγκαταλιπόντες, iv. 96. 34.

52. *The Plataeans who had remained in the city surrender to the Peloponnesian besieging army, and agree to submit their cause to the Lacedaemonians as judges.*

1. **καὶ οἱ Πλαταιῆς**: *cf.* c. 24. *fin.* καί refers to the similar fate of the Mytileneans, esp. cc. 27, 28. — 2. **πολιορκεῖσθαι**: as in c. 109. 3, = ὑπομένειν τὴν πολιορκίαν, or, as expressed in ii. 70. 2, πολιορκούμενοι ἀντέχειν.

προσέβαλον αὐτῶν τῷ τείχει, οἱ δὲ οὐκ ἐδύναντο ἀμύνεσθαι. 2
5 γνοὺς δὲ ὁ Λακεδαιμόνιος ἄρχων τὴν ἀσθένειαν αὐτῶν
βίᾳ μὲν οὐκ ἐβούλετο ἑλεῖν (εἰρημένον γὰρ ἦν αὐτῷ ἐκ
Λακεδαίμονος, ὅπως, εἰ σπονδαὶ γίγνοιντό ποτε πρὸς
Ἀθηναίους καὶ ξυγχωροῖεν ὅσα πολέμῳ χωρία ἔχουσιν
ἑκάτεροι ἀποδίδοσθαι, μὴ ἀνάδοτος εἴη ἡ Πλάταια ὡς
10 αὐτῶν ἑκόντων προσχωρησάντων), προσπέμπει δὲ αὐτοῖς
κήρυκα λέγοντα, εἰ βούλονται παραδοῦναι τὴν πόλιν ἑκόντες τοῖς Λακεδαιμονίοις καὶ δικασταῖς ἐκείνοις χρήσασθαι,
τούς τε ἀδίκους κολάσειν, παρὰ δίκην δὲ οὐδένα. τo- 3
σαῦτα μὲν ὁ κῆρυξ εἶπεν· οἱ δὲ (ἦσαν γὰρ ἤδη ἐν τῷ

4. **προσέβαλον... οἱ δὲ οὐκ ἐδύναντο**: paratactic connexion, with change of subj. — 5. **ὁ Λακεδαιμόνιος ἄρχων**: the name not given here, nor in c. 20 ff., nor in ii. 78. — 6. **εἰρημένον γὰρ ἦν**: on the reading, see App. **βίᾳ μὴ ἑλεῖν** is to be supplied. *Cf.* Xen. *Cyrop.* iv. 5. 14 οἱ φύλακες, ὥσπερ εἰρημένον ἦν [sc. μὴ εἰσαφεῖναι] ὑπὸ Κύρου, οὐκ εἰσαφῆκαν αὐτούς. — 8. **ξυγχωροῖεν**: sc. οἱ Λακεδαιμόνιοι, since precisely these wish by their present course to secure themselves in advance against a forced concession, such as really was made v. 17. § 2. ἑκάτεροι belongs only to ἔχουσι. So Cl. explains; but it seems equally natural to supply οἱ Λακεδαιμόνιοι καὶ Ἀθηναῖοι from ἑκάτεροι as subj. of ξυγχωροῖεν. — 9. **ἀνάδοτος**: found only here. For the accent and ending, cf. ἀνάγραπτος, i. 129. 14. Kühn. 147 c β. *Cf.* Poll. vii. 2. 13 τὸ μετὰ τὴν πρᾶσιν ἀποδοθὲν ἀνάδοτον ἄν τις εἰπεῖν δύναιτο, εἰπόντος Θουκυδίδου, "μὴ ἀνάδοτος εἴη Πλάταια." —
10. **αὐτῶν**: intensive, which does not, however, make ἑκόντων super-

fluous. — 11. **λέγοντα**: pres. partic., as in vi. 88. 62; vii. 3. 4; 25. 40. On this depends τούς τε ἀδίκους κολάσειν ... οὐδένα, which is apod. to εἰ βούλονται ... χρήσασθαι. The const. is exactly the same as in vii. 3. 4 προπέμπει αὐτοῖς λέγοντα, εἰ βούλονται ἐξιέναι ἐκ τῆς Σικελίας πέντε ἡμερῶν λαβόντες τὰ σφέτερα αὐτῶν, ἑτοῖμος εἶναι σπένδεσθαι. — 13. **τούς τε ἀδίκους**: τε correl. to the following δέ, as i. 11. 2; 25. 11; v. 9. 35; vii. 81. 12; viii. 16. 12. Hence C. F. Müller's conjecture (*N. Jahrbb.* cxli. p. 363 f.), τούς γε ἀδίκους, is unnecessary. Kr. *Spr.* 69, 16, 6; Kühn. 520, s. 3. — **κολάσειν**: the subj. is τοὺς Λακεδαιμονίους or τοὺς δικαστὰς τῶν Λακεδαιμονίων. The fut. has been correctly restored by Kr. for κολάζειν of the Mss., since it depends on λέγοντα. See Kr.'s note and St. *Qu. Gr.*² p. 13.
14. **ἐν τῷ ἀσθενεστάτῳ**: *in the last stage of weakness*. *Cf.* Dio C. lxxiv. 12. 52 ἐν τῷ ἀσθενεστάτῳ ἐγένοντο, Paus. ix. 7. 4 ἐς τὸ ἀσθενέστατον προήχθησαν.

15 ἀσθενεστάτῳ) παρέδοσαν τὴν πόλιν. καὶ τοὺς Πλαταιᾶς ἔτρεφον οἱ Πελοποννήσιοι ἡμέρας τινάς, ἐν ὅσῳ οἱ ἐκ τῆς Λακεδαίμονος δικασταί, πέντε ἄνδρες, ἀφίκοντο. ἐλθόντων δὲ αὐτῶν κατηγορία μὲν οὐδεμία προετέθη, 4 ἠρώτων δὲ αὐτοὺς ἐπικαλεσάμενοι τοσοῦτον μόνον, εἴ τι 20 Λακεδαιμονίους καὶ τοὺς ξυμμάχους ἐν τῷ πολέμῳ τῷ καθεστῶτι ἀγαθὸν [τι] εἰργασμένοι εἰσίν. οἱ δ' ἔλεγον 5 αἰτησάμενοι μακρότερα εἰπεῖν καὶ προτάξαντες σφῶν αὐτῶν Ἀστύμαχόν τε τὸν Ἀσωπολάου καὶ Λάκωνα τὸν Ἀἱειμνήστου, πρόξενον ὄντα Λακεδαιμονίων· καὶ ἐπελθόντες 25 ἔλεγον τοιάδε·

— **15. Πλαταιᾶς**: (not Πλαταιέας) acc. to analogy of 'Ἀλιᾶς. i. 105. 1; Δωριᾶς, i. 107. 4; Ἑστιαιᾶς, i. 114. 16. *Cf.* v. 51. 3. — **16. ἐν ὅσῳ**: *until*. See on c. 28. 8. — **17. πέντε ἄνδρες**: one of whom is named by Paus. iii. 9. 1.
18. προετέθη: *cf.* γνώμας προτιθέναι, c. 36. 21; i. 139. 18; vi. 14. 3; διαγνώμην προθεῖναι, c. 42. 1. — **19. ἐπικαλεσάμενοι**: *calling forth*. In this sense found only here in Thuc. *Cf.* Hdt. v. 39. 7. — **τοσοῦτον μόνον**: *cf.* τοσοῦτοι μόνοι, iv. 110. 12. — **21. ἀγαθὸν [τι] εἰργασμένοι**: *cf.* the question of the Romans on the capture of Capua, Liv. xxvi. 33 ecquis Campanorum bene meritus de republica nostra esset. As in the three other passages where this formula is repeated (c. 54. 7; 68. 3 and 11) a second τι is not found, it has been rightly rejected here by Bm., Cl., and St.
οἱ δ' ἔλεγον: the subj. is all the Plataeans, while in l. 25 the subj. is Astymachus and Laco. — **22. αἰτησάμενοι**: *cf.* c. 53. 10. — **μακρότερα εἰπεῖν**: instead of simply answering 'no,' as they did when asked a second time (c. 68. 12). — **προτάξαντες σφῶν αὐτῶν**: *having appointed as their advocates*. — **23. Ἀϊειμνήστου**: leader of the Plataeans at Marathon and Plataea. See Valck. on Hdt. ix. 64. 7, and Siebel on Plut. *Aristid.* 19. — **ἐπελθόντες**: as in i. 72. 15; 90. 29; 91. 16; 119. 9, of appearing before an assembly or magistrate, particularly of foreigners. παριέναι, of coming forward to speak. See on i. 72. 15. — **25. ἔλεγον**: on the tense, see GMT. 57; II. 831. 'The impf. has only to do with the vision of the narrator.' Gildersleeve (*Am. J. of Ph.* iv. p. 160). See on i. 72. 15. Thuc. introduces extended speeches twenty-two times with impf. (i. 72. 15; 119. 10; 139. 25; ii. 10. 11; 34. 25; 71. 6; iii. 36. 28; 41. 4; 52. 25; 60. 6; iv. 84. 9; 91. 13; 94. 12; v. 8. 19; vi. 8. 23; 15. 21; 19. 8; 32. 21; 35. 10; 67. 19; 75. 23; vii. 76. 3), eighteen times with aor. (i. 31. 16; 36. 22; 67. 18; 79. 8; 85. 14; ii. 59. 14; 86. 26; 88. 14; iii. 8. 6; 29. 11; iv. 9. 23; 16. 24; 58. 9; 125. 22; vi. 81. 2; 88. 65; vii. 60. 30; 65. 10).

53 "Τὴν μὲν παράδοσιν τῆς πόλεως, ὦ Λακεδαιμό- 1
νιοι, πιστεύσαντες ὑμῖν ἐποιησάμεθα οὐ τοιάνδε δίκην
οἰόμενοι ὑφέξειν, νομιμωτέραν δέ τινα ἔσεσθαι καὶ ἐν
δικασταῖς οὐκ ἐν ἄλλοις δεξάμενοι, ὥσπερ καὶ ἐσμέν, γε-

DEFENCE OF THE PLATAEANS.

c. 53–59.

53. *The form of procedure begun and the composition of the court cause us anxiety, lest we may have deceived ourselves in the expectations with which we surrendered; but we dare not even under unfavourable circumstances and hostile influences refrain from trying to defend ourselves.*

On this famous and beautiful oration, cf. Dion. H. *de Thuc. hist. iudic.* 42 ὑπὲρ ἁπάσας τὰς ἐν ταῖς ἑπτὰ βίβλοις φερομένας (δημηγορίας) τὴν Πλαταιέων ἀπολογίαν τεθαύμακα, παρ' οὐδὲν οὕτως ἕτερον, ὡς τὸ μὴ βεβασανίσθαι μηδὲ κατεπιτετηδεῦσθαι, ἀληθεῖ δέ τινι καὶ φυσικῷ κεκοσμῆσθαι χρώματι. τά τε γὰρ ἐνθυμήματα πάθους ἐστὶ μεστά, καὶ ἡ λέξις οὐκ ἀποστρέφουσα τὰς ἀκοάς· ἥ τε γὰρ σύνθεσις εὐεπής, καὶ τὰ σχήματα τῶν πραγμάτων ἴδια.

1. τὴν μὲν παράδοσιν ... ἐποιησάμεθα ... οἰόμενοι: the emphasis of the sent. is on the partics., οἰόμενοι and ἡγούμενοι, opp. to which is νῦν δὲ φοβούμεθα, l. 6, although μέν is joined with the decisive fact (τὴν παράδοσιν ἐποιησάμεθα) placed first in the sent. for emphasis. —2. πιστεύσαντες ὑμῖν: as in c. 59. 22. *Cf.* also c. 59. 27 ἐκ τῆς ὑμετέρας πίστεως. The aor. as in c. 38. 11; 46. 2. Steup takes πιστεύσαντες as dependent on οἰόμενοι, but enticing as is the parallelism which he suggests between πιστεύ-σαντες οἰόμενοι and δεξάμενοι ἡγούμενοι, its position shows that the partic. is to be closely connected with ἐποιησάμεθα. οἰόμενοι and ἡγούμενοι contain the twofold grounds of πιστεύσαντες ὑμῖν τὴν παράδοσιν ἐποιησάμεθα, i.e. expecting due process of law and impartial judges. — τοιάνδε: sc. οἵαν ὑπέχομεν, i.e. by the question, εἴ τι Λακεδαιμονίους ἀγαθὸν εἰργάσμεθα. — δίκην ὑφέξειν: iudicium subituros, as in c. 81. 12. *Cf.* τὴν τιμωρίαν ὑφέξετε, vi. 80. 24. —3. ἐν δικασταῖς οὐκ ἐν ἄλλοις: on the repetition of the prep., see Herbst, *Gegen Cobet*, p. 31. Kühn. 451, 2. *Cf.* vi. 82. 18. For the const. (ἐν δικασταῖς γενέσθαι), St. compares Plato *Legg.* 916 b; Soph. *Ant.* 459. *Cf.* also i. 73. 5 παρὰ δικασταῖς ὑμῖν ... οἱ λόγοι ἂν γίγνοιντο. —4. δεξάμενοι: i.e. εἰ δεξαίμεθα, prob. to μάλιστα ἂν φέρεσθαι, both dependent on ἡγούμενοι. "Since we believed that, if we agreed to appear before a court of Lacedaemonians, we should receive an impartial decision." Steup explains δεξάμενοι as causal to ἡγούμενοι, which is admissible; for an actual stipulation may have been ἐν δικασταῖς οὐκ ἐν ἄλλοις γενέσθαι ἢ ὑμῖν. δέχεσθαι with inf. (γενέσθαι), as i. 143. 8; v. 94. 3; Plato *Rep.* 606 b. — ὥσπερ καὶ ἐσμέν: *as we now are*. εἶναι is the result of γενέσθαι. By emphasizing the outward fulfillment of their expectation, or perhaps of the condition of the sur-

5 νέσθαι ἢ ὑμῖν ἡγούμενοι τὸ ἴσον μάλιστ᾽ ἂν φέρεσθαι. νῦν δὲ φοβούμεθα μὴ ἀμφοτέρων ἅμα ἡμαρτήκαμεν· τόν 3 τε γὰρ ἀγῶνα περὶ τῶν δεινοτάτων εἶναι εἰκότως ὑποπτεύομεν καὶ ὑμᾶς μὴ οὐ κοινοὶ ἀποβῆτε, τεκμαιρόμενοι προκατηγορίας τε ἡμῶν οὐ προγεγενημένης ᾗ χρὴ ἀντει-
10 πεῖν (ἀλλ᾽ αὐτοὶ λόγον ᾐτησάμεθα) τό τε ἐπερώτημα βραχὺ ὄν, ᾧ τὰ μὲν ἀληθῆ ἀποκρίνασθαι ἐναντία γίγνεται, τὰ δὲ ψευδῆ ἔλεγχον ἔχει. πανταχόθεν δὲ ἄποροι 3 καθεστῶτες ἀναγκαζόμεθα καὶ ἀσφαλέστερον δοκεῖ εἶναι

render, they indicate their anxiety lest they may be deceived in the result. — 5. τὸ ἴσον: aequum ius, as i. 34. 7; ii. 37. 5. *Cf.* c. 67. 21. — φέρεσθαι: with τὸ ἴσον, as τὴν ἀξίωσιν φέρεσθαι, i. 69. 7; δόξαν φέρεσθαι, ii. 11. 36; αἰτίαν φέρεσθαι, ii. 60. 25. 6. φοβούμεθα μὴ ἡμαρτήκαμεν: for μή with pf. ind. after verb of fearing, see GMT. 369, 2; H. 888; Kr. *Spr.* 54, 8, 12; Kühn. 589, 6. — ἀμφοτέρων ἡμαρτήκαμεν: *cf.* δυοῖν ἁμάρτωσιν, i. 33. 23. ἀμφότερα, *i.e.* a δίκη νομιμωτέρα and impartial judges. Their disappointment in the first respect is expressed by περὶ τῶν δεινοτάτων (Schol. περὶ τοῦ θανάτου), for there could be no thought of this in a δίκη νομιμωτέρα. — 8. ὑμᾶς: proleptic const., as ii. 21. 3; 67. 23. — κοινοί: *impartial. Cf.* c. 68. 7; iv. 83. 16. — ἀποβῆτε: evadatis, as Xen. *Mem.* iv. 8. 8; Plato *Legg.* 878 c. — 9. προκατηγορίας . . . οὐ προγεγενημένης: for similar pleonasms, *cf.* i. 23. 21; ii. 36. 1; vi. 57. 10; viii. 66. 6. — ᾗ χρὴ ἀντειπεῖν: see on c. 11. 18. — 10. λόγον ᾐτησάμεθα: *sc.* a μακρότερος λόγος. *Cf.* c. 52. 22; 60. 5; 61. 1. *Cf.* λόγον διδόναι, Dem. ii. 29, 31. —

τό τε ἐπερώτημα βραχὺ ὄν: the acc. after the parenthesis in loose connexion with the preceding gen., as if not τεκμαιρόμενοι, but λογιζόμενοι or σκοποῦντες had preceded; or perhaps better, with Pp., to explain as acc. abs., τὸ ἐπερώτημα with βραχὺ ὄν being construed as ἄλλο τι δόξαν, v. 65. 10; κυρωθὲν οὐδέν, iv. 125. 5. Kühn. 487, 8. — 11. ᾧ τὰ μὲν . . . γίγνεται: *to answer which truly is adverse to our interests.* τὰ ἀληθῆ, as well as τὰ ψευδῆ, is obj. of ἀποκρίνασθαι, which is subj. of ἐναντία γίγνεται and of ἔλεγχον ἔχει. ἐναντία is used instead of ἐναντίον, perhaps by assimilation to ἀληθῆ, or the neut. pl. may be compared with ἀδύνατα, c. 88. 4; i. 59. 4; 125. 5; vii. 43. 13. Kr. and Cl. take τὰ ἀληθῆ and τὰ ψευδῆ as subj., and ἀποκρίνασθαι as epexegetic of τὰ ἀληθῆ (see on i. 50. 25). St. and v. H. write ἐναντίον. — 12. ἔλεγχον ἔχει: *refutes itself.* ἔχει = παρέχει, as i. 97. 13; ii. 41. 9; 61. 9; 87. 3; iv. 95. 3. πανταχόθεν ἄποροι καθεστῶτες: *cf.* ii. 59. 8 πανταχόθεν τῇ γνώμῃ ἄποροι καθεστῶτες. — 13. καὶ ἀσφαλέστερον δοκεῖ εἶναι: this second reason, though almost parenthetically inserted, de-

εἰπόντας τι κινδυνεύειν · καὶ γὰρ ὁ μὴ ῥηθεὶς λόγος τοῖς
15 ὧδ' ἔχουσιν αἰτίαν ἂν παράσχοι ὡς, εἰ ἐλέχθη, σωτήριος
ἂν ἦν. χαλεπῶς δὲ ἔχει-ἡμῖν πρὸς τοῖς ἄλλοις καὶ ἡ 4
πειθώ. ἀγνῶτες μὲν γὰρ ὄντες ἀλλήλων ἐπεσενεγκάμενοι
μαρτύρια ὧν ἄπειροι ἦτε ὠφελούμεθ' ἄν · νῦν δὲ πρὸς
εἰδότας πάντα λελέξεται, καὶ δέδιμεν οὐχὶ μὴ προκατα-
20 γνόντες ἡμῶν τὰς ἀρετὰς ἥσσους εἶναι τῶν ὑμετέρων

termines the const. of the following inf. — 14. **εἰπόντας τι κινδυνεύειν**: *i.e.* not to risk our lives without having said something. *Cf.* i. 20. 12 δράσαντές τι κινδυνεῦσαι. The emphasis is on the participle. *Cf.* c. 105. 1; i. 23. 25; 82. 10; 144. 6; ii. 61. 3; vii. 14. 1. — **ὁ μὴ ῥηθεὶς λόγος** : = τὸ τὸν λόγον μὴ ῥηθῆναι. *Cf.* c. 36. 11; 66. 15; Xen. *Cyrop.* iii. 3. 51. — **τοῖς ὧδ' ἔχουσιν**: as in c. 59. 18; Plato *Crito*, 46 d. — 15. **αἰτίαν**: *reproach*, or, more exactly, *ground for reproach*, as i. 140. 26.
16. **ἡ πειθώ**: "the possibility of persuading you." Only here in Thuc. — 17. **ἀγνῶτες... ὠφελούμεθ' ἄν**: the subj. of ἀγνῶτες is ἡμεῖς τε καὶ ὑμεῖς, but with ἐπεσενεγκάμενοι and ὠφελούμεθ' ἄν it is ἡμεῖς. See on c. 10. 17; i. 18. 21. — **ἐπεσενεγκάμενοι**: 'dynamic middle,' implying that the powers of the subject are exerted, as παρέχεσθαι, c. 54. 1; i. 32. 9. Kr. *Spr.* 52, 8, 2. — 18. **ἦτε**: impf. through the influence of the cond. partic. (ἐπεσενεγκάμενοι = εἰ ἐπεσηνεγκάμεθα. — **πρὸς εἰδότας πάντα**: *to men who know all*, and hence without hope of effect. πρὸς εἰδότας, as ii. 43. 5; Aesch. *Agam.* 1402; or ἐν εἰδόσι, ii. 36. 14; iv. 59. 5; vi. 77. 2. — 19. **λελέξεται**: the fut. pf.

is required by the context, and not λέξεται (the reading of Laur., preferred by Hude), which the Tragic writers use for the fut. passive (Soph. *O. C.* 1186; Eur. *Alc.* 322; *Hec.* 906). St. See Kr. *Spr.* 53, 9, 3. — **οὐχὶ**: used by Thuc. six times (c. 67. 22; i. 120. 6; ii. 87. 4; vi. 40. 16; vii. 56. 17), always as emphatic neg., generally to intensify the adversative idea. Here the Plataeans reject emphatically the thought that the Lacedaemonians might consider the merits of the Plataeans in the Persian wars less than their own. — **προκαταγνόντες**: cum praedamnaveritis nos statuentes. St. The same brachylogy as in καταφρονοῦντες, c. 83. 13. Or the meaning may be, *having already formed the unfavourable judgment against*. *Cf.* c. 16. 1; 45. 4. With the former view, ἡμῶν would be taken with τὰς ἀρετάς alone; with the latter, it would belong also to προκαταγνόντες. — 20. **ἥσσους εἶναι τῶν ὑμετέρων**: *are inferior to yours*. Steup suggests that as the Plataeans acknowledge in c. 57. 6 the superiority of the Lacedaemonians (ἀνδρῶν ἀγαθῶν πέρι αὐτοὺς ἀμείνους ὄντας), τῶν ὑμετέρων may be an interpolation, in which case ἥσσους would mean *in-*

ἔγκλημα αὐτὸ ποιῆτε, ἀλλὰ μὴ ἄλλοις χάριν φέροντες ἐπὶ
54 διεγνωσμένην κρίσιν καθιστώμεθα. παρεχόμενοι δὲ ὅμως 1
ἃ ἔχομεν δίκαια πρός τε τὰ Θηβαίων διάφορα καὶ ἐς
ὑμᾶς καὶ τοὺς ἄλλους Ἕλληνας, τῶν εὖ δεδρασμένων ὑπόμνησιν ποιησόμεθα καὶ πείθειν πειρασόμεθα.
5   " Φαμὲν γὰρ πρὸς τὸ ἐρώτημα τὸ βραχύ, εἴ τι Λακε- 2
δαιμονίους καὶ τοὺς ξυμμάχους ἐν τῷ πολέμῳ τῷδε
ἀγαθὸν πεποιήκαμεν, εἰ μὲν ὡς πολεμίους ἐρωτᾶτε,
οὐκ ἀδικεῖσθαι ὑμᾶς μὴ εὖ παθόντας, φίλους δὲ νομίζοντας αὐτοὺς ἁμαρτάνειν μᾶλλον τοὺς ἡμῖν ἐπιστρατεύ-

sufficient, as in c. 45. 6. — **21. αὐτό :** referring to the whole preceding clause. *Cf.* i. 2. 11 ; 68. 3. — **ἀλλὰ ... καθιστώμεθα :** *but lest we to gratify others appear before a court that has already decided against us.* With bitter irony, in view of the foregone conclusion of the trial, the Plataeans ascribe to themselves the evident purpose of the Lacedaemonians. **καθίστασθαι ἐπὶ κρίσιν**, with the κριταί in mind, as **καταστὰς ἐπὶ τὸ πλῆθος**, iv. 84. 8 ; ἐπὶ Ἀθηναίους, iv. 97. 9. **καθίστασθαι** is not passive (*cf.* c. 92. 14 ; 93. 3 ; v. 51. 6), but middle. For διεγνωσμένην, see on c. 42. 1.

54. 1. παρεχόμενοι : *bringing forward.* *Cf.* ἐπεσενεγκάμενοι, c. 53. 17. Bl. compares Dion. H. *Ant.* vii. 32 δίκαια . . . παρεχόμενοι πρὸς ὑμᾶς μεγάλα. — **2. δίκαια :** *just claims*, as c. 44. 16. — **πρός, ἐς :** change of prep., as in c. 37. 4, 5 ; i. 32. 10, 11 ; 38. 1 ; Dem. iii. 1. — **τὰ Θηβαίων διάφορα :** *the quarrels with the Thebans.* *Cf.* iv. 79. 10 τὰ παλαιὰ διάφορα τῶν Ἀθηναίων, ii. 27. 9 τὸ Ἀθηναίων διάφορον. — **3. δεδρασμένων :** this unusual pf. form, found in most Mss., for δεδραμένων, is after the analogy of δρασθέν, c. 38. 19 ; vi. 53. 8. St., Bm., and v. H. write, with two inferior Mss., the usual form δεδραμένων, after the analogy of δρᾶμα. — **ὑπόμνησιν ποιησόμεθα :** as in i. 72. 9 ; ii. 88. 12.

54. § 2-5. *To your unfair question as to our services rendered to you during the war, we reply that we did not break the peace, and not only in the Persian war supported the Hellenes, but also in the uprising of the Helots vigorously aided you.*

5. τὸ βραχύ : the emphatic position betrays indignation at the wicked intention. — **7. εἰ μὲν ὡς πολεμίους κτέ. :** by referring to the possible conditions affecting the question a direct reply is evaded, it is true, but its unwarrantableness in either case is shown. — **8. μὴ εὖ παθόντας :** these words, notwithstanding their hypothetical character, contain an indirect confession that οὐδὲν ἀγαθὸν πεποιήκασι τοὺς Λακεδαιμονίους, but in the apod., οὐκ ἀδικεῖσθαι ὑμᾶς, any guilt from such conduct is denied. — **φίλους δὲ νομίζοντας :** *i.e.* εἰ δὲ φίλους (ἡμᾶς) νομίζετε. — **9. αὐτούς :** sc. ὑμᾶς. —

10 σαντας. τὰ δ' ἐν τῇ εἰρήνῃ καὶ πρὸς τὸν Μῆδον ἀγαθοὶ 3
γεγενήμεθα, τὴν μὲν οὐ λύσαντες νῦν πρότεροι, τῷ δὲ
ξυνεπιθέμενοι τότε ἐς ἐλευθερίαν τῆς Ἑλλάδος μόνοι
Βοιωτῶν. καὶ γὰρ ἠπειρῶταί τε ὄντες ἐναυμαχήσαμεν 4
ἐπ' Ἀρτεμισίῳ, μάχῃ τε τῇ ἐν τῇ ἡμετέρᾳ γῇ γενομένῃ
15 παρεγενόμεθα ὑμῖν τε καὶ Παυσανίᾳ, εἴ τέ τι ἄλλο κατ'
ἐκεῖνον τὸν χρόνον ἐγένετο ἐπικίνδυνον τοῖς Ἕλλησι,
πάντων παρὰ δύναμιν μετέσχομεν, καὶ ὑμῖν, ὦ Λακεδαι- 5
μόνιοι, ἰδίᾳ, ὅτεπερ δὴ μέγιστος φόβος περιέστη τὴν
Σπάρτην μετὰ τὸν σεισμὸν τῶν ἐς Ἰθώμην Εἱλώτων ἀπο-

ἁμαρτάνειν: for the approach to the pf. sense, see GMT. 27; Kr. Spr. 53, 1, 3. Cf. c. 67. 30. — τοὺς ἡμῖν ἐπιστρατεύσαντας: appos. to αὐτούς. Kr. Spr. 50, 7, 12.

10. τὰ δ' ἐν τῇ εἰρήνῃ καὶ πρὸς τὸν Μῆδον: the pl. τά indicates the particular events in a considerable period. Cf. τὰ πρὸ Ἕλληνος, i. 3. 4. The order of time is reversed, as in i. 97. 4; 118. 6. — 11. νῦν: as opp. to the following τότε, refers to the beginning of the πόλεμος ὅδε (ii. 2). — 12. μόνοι Βοιωτῶν: rhetorical inaccuracy, for the Thespians did the same (Hdt. vii. 132. 4; viii. 50. 8), and acc. to Pausanias (ix. 32. 4) the Haliartians also. Cf. c. 62. 2; 64. 2.

13. καὶ γάρ: nam et. καί correl. to καί in l. 17. Kr. Spr. 69, 32, 21. — ἠπειρῶταί τε κτέ.: τε which is joined to the emphatic ἠπειρῶται rather than to ἐναυμαχήσαμεν, where it strictly belongs, is correl. to τε in l. 14, while τε in εἴ τέ τι ἄλλο introduces the third member. See App. Since καὶ ὑμῖν ... ἐπικουρίαν cannot be an explanation of τὴν μὲν ... πρότεροι, as καὶ

γάρ ... μετέσχομεν is of τῷ δὲ ... Βοιωτῶν, the former clause (καὶ ὑμῖν κτέ.) must be considered as rather loosely connected with the main sent., τὰ δὲ ... γεγενήμεθα. — 14. μάχῃ τε γενομένῃ: for the dat. without prep. denoting time when, see G. 1192; H. 782; Kr. Spr. 48, 2, 9. Cf. i. 44. 3; 128. 17; ii. 20. 3. For the order, see on c. 9. 3. — 15. παρεγενόμεθα ... Παυσανίᾳ: cf. Hdt. ix. 28. 26; Plut. Aristid. 20; Diod. xi. 32. — 17. πάντων: connected κατὰ ξύνεσιν with εἴ τι ἄλλο. — παρὰ δύναμιν: beyond our strength, as c. 57. 18; i. 70. 9; viii. 2. 12.

18. ὅτεπερ δή: just when. — περιέστη: with acc., also iv. 10. 3; 55. 10; v. 73. 6; viii. 2. 22; 15. 3; without expressed obj., iv. 34. 24; viii. 1. 9. Cf. Dem. xviii. 195 τοσοῦτος κίνδυνος καὶ φόβος περιέστη τὴν πόλιν, Tac. Hist. iv. 79 circumsteterat Civilem et alius metus. — 19. τῶν ἐς Ἰθώμην Εἱλώτων ἀποστάντων: obj. gen. after φόβος. Kr. Spr. 47, 7, 2. The attrib. partic. is placed after its noun when attended by other modi-

20 στάντων, τὸ τρίτον μέρος ἡμῶν αὐτῶν ἐξεπέμψαμεν ἐς
ἐπικουρίαν· ὧν οὐκ εἰκὸς ἀμνημονεῖν.

55 "Καὶ τὰ μὲν παλαιὰ καὶ μέγιστα τοιοῦτοι ἠξιώ- 1
σαμεν εἶναι, πολέμιοι δὲ ἐγενόμεθα ὕστερον. ὑμεῖς δὲ
αἴτιοι· δεομένων γὰρ ξυμμαχίας ὅτε Θηβαῖοι ἡμᾶς ἐβιάσαντο, ὑμεῖς ἀπεώσασθε καὶ πρὸς Ἀθηναίους ἐκελεύετε
5 τραπέσθαι ὡς ἐγγὺς ὄντας, ὑμῶν δὲ μακρὰν ἀποικούντων. ἐν μέντοι τῷ πολέμῳ οὐδὲν ἐκπρεπέστερον ὑπὸ 2
ἡμῶν οὔτε ἐπάθετε οὔτε ἐμελλήσατε. εἰ δ' ἀποστῆναι 3
Ἀθηναίων οὐκ ἠθελήσαμεν ὑμῶν κελευσάντων, οὐκ ἠδι-
κοῦμεν. καὶ γὰρ ἐκεῖνοι ἐβοήθουν ἡμῖν ἐναντία Θηβαίοις,
10 ὅτε ὑμεῖς ἀπωκνεῖτε, καὶ προδοῦναι αὐτοὺς οὐκέτι ἦν

liers, as often in Thuc. G. 969; Kühn. 464, 8. See on i. 11. 19. For the facts, cf. i. 101. § 2. — 20. **ἡμῶν αὐτῶν**: i.e. of our citizens. Cf. ii. 39. 16. — 21. **ὧν**: the rel. serves as an emphatic connective. Cf. i. 9. 19; 33. 13, etc.

55. *The alliance with the Athenians we sought only when you had rejected our appeal for aid against Thebes and referred us to them; to abandon it would have been shameful. The responsibility, furthermore, for what happens in war belongs to the leaders.*

1. ἠξιώσαμεν: we regarded it our duty, as in i. 22. 9. — **3. δεομένων**: sc. ἡμῶν. For subj. of gen. abs. thus freq. omitted, see on c. 34. 17. — **ἐβιάσαντο**: did violence to, with acc. as in i. 38. 12; viii. 53. 9. This account of the occurrence, which acc. to c. 68. 31, happened in 520 or 519 B.C., is corroborated by Hdt. vi. 108. 6 πιεζεύμενοι ὑπὸ Θηβαίων οἱ Πλαταιέες ἐδίδοσαν... σφέας αὐτούς. — **5. ὑμῶν ... ἀποικούντων**: gen. abs., co-ord. with ὡς ἐγγὺς ὄντας, though ὑμεῖς precedes. See on c. 13. 30; 112. 21. — **μακρὰν ἀποικούντων**: cf. μακρὰν ἀπεῖναι, c. 13. 23; ἡμεῖς ἑκαστέρω οἰκέομεν, Hdt. vi. 108. 9.

6. οὐδὲν ἐκπρεπέστερον: *nothing very unusual.* Cf. ἐκπρεπῶς, i. 38. 9. — **7. ἐμελλήσατε**: sc. παθεῖν. Cf. c. 11. 4; 20. 16.

εἰ δὲ ... οὐκ ἠθελήσαμεν: the fact in hypothetical form. See on c. 32. 6. οὐ belongs to the verb only. GMT. 384; Kr. Spr. 67, 4, 1; Kühn. 513, 4. — **8. ὑμῶν κελευσάντων**: referring to the demand of Archidamus, ii. 72. Cf. c. 64. 13; 68. 6. — **9. ἐναντία**: acc. of inner obj. as adv., as in i. 29. 6. Cf. ὁμοῖα, i. 25. 18; ἀγχώμαλα, vii. 71. 21; βοηθῆσαί μοι τὰ δίκαια, Dem. xxxviii. 2. Kühn. 410, x. 5. — **10. ἀπωκνεῖτε**: *you held back*, abs., as iv. 11. 16; vi. 18. 1; vii. 21. 23; with acc. c. 20. 10; 30. 12; vi. 92. 23;

καλόν, ἄλλως τε καὶ οὓς εὖ παθών τις καὶ αὐτὸς δεόμενος προσηγάγετο ξυμμάχους καὶ πολιτείας μετέλαβεν, ἰέναι δὲ ἐς τὰ παραγγελλόμενα εἰκὸς ἦν προθύμως. ἃ δὲ 4 ἑκάτεροι ἐξηγεῖσθε τοῖς ξυμμάχοις, οὐχ οἱ ἑπόμενοι αἴ- 15 τιοι εἴ τι μὴ καλῶς ἑδρᾶτο, ἀλλ' οἱ ἄγοντες ἐπὶ τὰ μὴ ὀρθῶς ἔχοντα.

56 "Θηβαῖοι δὲ πολλὰ μὲν καὶ ἄλλα ἡμᾶς ἠδίκησαν, 1 τὸ δὲ τελευταῖον αὐτοὶ ξύνιστε, δι' ὅπερ καὶ τάδε πάσχομεν. πόλιν γὰρ αὐτοὺς τὴν ἡμετέραν καταλαμβάνοντας 2 ἐν σπονδαῖς καὶ προσέτι ἱερομηνίᾳ ὀρθῶς ἐτιμωρησάμεθα

viii. 12. 2. — 11. τις: here for ἡμεῖς. *Cf. on* in French Comedy. Kr. *Spr.* 51, 16, 8. — **12. καὶ πολιτείας μετέλαβεν**: sc. αὐτῶν. In Greek, when the rel. would appear in successive clauses in different cases, it is usually omitted in the second, often being represented by a dem. or pers. pronoun. *Cf.* i. 10. 20; 42. 2; ii. 4. 25; 84. 9. G. 1040; H. 1005; Kr. *Spr.* 60, 6, 2; Kühn. 561, 1. The reference is to the relation of ἰσοπολιτεία, acc. to which a citizen of the one city on removing to the other immediately became a citizen of the latter. See Niebuhr, *Hist. of Rome*, ii.[2] p. 58 ff. — **ἰέναι ἐς τὰ παραγγελλόμενα**: as in i. 121. 5. τὰ παραγγελλόμενα is used esp. of military orders. *Cf.* ii. 11. 39; 84. 18; 89. 40; iv. 34. 23. — **13. προθύμως**: placed last for emphasis. *Cf.* i. 77. 19.

ἃ δὲ ἑκάτεροι ἐξηγεῖσθε: *whatsoever each of you directed as 'Hegemones.'* ἅ is cogn. acc. *Cf.* c. 93. 15; v. 66. 10.
— **15. ἑδρᾶτο**: Reiske's conjecture from Bk.'s *Anecd.* p. 145; preferable to ἑδρᾶτε of the Mss., since here in

the prot. an impersonal reference to acts in general suits the context better and is more forcible. For the thought, *cf.* c. 65. 10.

56. *The Thebans have wronged us in many other respects, and now finally by the wanton surprise of our city, for which we have justly punished them. It would not be right that we should now suffer on their account. If you regard justice and your own true interests, you cannot permit this.*

2. ξύνιστε: i.e. of your own knowledge. *Cf.* i. 73. 13; ii. 35. 10; iv. 68. 24. — **δι' ὅπερ**: Pp.'s conjecture, for δι' ἅπερ of the Mss., is necessary, since it refers to τὸ τελευταῖον, which, as opp. to πολλὰ καὶ ἄλλα, is clearly not adv., but the obj. of ξύνιστε.

3. πόλιν γὰρ αὐτοὺς κτέ.: *cf.* ii. 2–6; iii. 65, 66. For the order (πόλιν τὴν ἡμετέραν), see on c. 9. 3; 54. 14.
— **καταλαμβάνοντας**: pres. partic., of the unsuccessful attempt. *Cf.* ii. 3. 3; 5. 21. — **4. ἐν σπονδαῖς**: temporal, as c. 65. 2; i. 55. 14; ii. 5. 20; vii. 18. 13. *Cf. ἐν τῷ πολέμῳ*, c. 52. 20; 54. 6; 68. 11. — **ἱερομηνίᾳ**: *on a holi-*

5 κατὰ τὸν πᾶσι νόμον καθεστῶτα, τὸν ἐπιόντα πολέμιον ὅσιον εἶναι ἀμύνεσθαι. καὶ νῦν οὐκ ἂν εἰκότως δι' αὐτοὺς βλαπτοίμεθα. εἰ γὰρ τῷ αὐτίκα χρησίμῳ ὑμῶν 3 τε καὶ ἐκείνων πολεμίῳ τὸ δίκαιον λήψεσθε, τοῦ μὲν ὀρθοῦ φανεῖσθε οὐκ ἀληθεῖς κριταὶ ὄντες, τὸ δὲ ξυμφέρον
10 μᾶλλον θεραπεύοντες. καίτοι εἰ νῦν ὑμῖν ὠφέλιμοι δο- 4 κοῦσιν εἶναι, πολὺ καὶ ἡμεῖς καὶ οἱ ἄλλοι Ἕλληνες μᾶλλον τότε ὅτε ἐν μείζονι κινδύνῳ ἦτε. νῦν μὲν γὰρ ἑτέροις ὑμεῖς ἐπέρχεσθε δεινοί· ἐν ἐκείνῳ δὲ τῷ καιρῷ, ὅτε πᾶσι δουλείαν ἐπέφερεν ὁ βάρβαρος, οἵδε μετ' αὐτοῦ

day, as in c. 65. 2: This circumstance is not mentioned in the detailed account of the event, ii. 2. ff.— ὀρθῶς ἐτιμωρησάμεθα : the Plataeans pass lightly over the especial charge concerning their conduct, while the Thebans emphasize just this point most strongly, c. 66. § 2. — 5. τὸν ... καθεστῶτα : for the order, see on c. 54. 19. For the thought, *cf.* vii. 68. 3 ff. — πολέμιον : emphatic pred., *as an enemy*. *Cf.* c. 65. 6 ; 66. 1. — 6. οὐκ εἰκότως : *cf.* c. 58. 9 εἰκότως τιμωρήσεσθε, and c. 57. 2 εἰ δὲ περὶ ἡμῶν γνώσεσθε μὴ τὰ εἰκότα. — δι' αὐτούς : *cf.* c. 57. 12 διὰ Θηβαίους.

7. εἰ γὰρ ... τὸ δίκαιον λήψεσθε : τὸ δίκαιον (see on c. 10. 1 ; v. 86. 6) λαμβάνειν, *measure justice*, with which the dat. is connected, as with μετρεῖν, τεκμαίρεσθαί τί τινι. The unworthy motive for such a decision is indicated by the closely connected τῷ αὐτίκα χρησίμῳ ὑμῶν τε καὶ ἐκείνων πολεμίῳ, in which one art. covers both subst. phrases (see on c. 2. 6 ; i. 6. 1 ; 120. 10). *Cf.* Dem. xviii. 31 τὸ ... ἐν τῇ πρεσβείᾳ πρῶτον κλέμμα μὲν Φιλίππου, δωροδόκημα δὲ τῶν ἀδίκων τούτων ἀνθρώπων. The chiastic arrangement (χρησίμῳ ὑμῶν ... ἐκείνων πολεμίῳ), by which the close connexion of the prons. with the adjs. is shown, accounts for the unusual position of τε καί. " If you, influenced by your present advantage and their hostility, shall decide the question of right." — 9. τὸ ξυμφέρον : in the sense of immediate advantage, expediency (*cf.* ii. 40. 23), as opp. to ὀρθόν, which here and c. 66. 20 (τὰ ὀρθά) is the result at once of right judgment and honest intention. In v. 90. 2 τὸ ξυμφέρον is similarly opp. to τὸ δίκαιον. In l. 25 it means *true advantage*. For the const. with θεραπεύειν, *cf.* vi. 79. 1 τὸ δίκαιον ... θεραπεύσετε, Soph. *Phil.* 149 τὸ παρὸν θεραπεύειν, Polyb. xi. 4. 2 καιρὸν πάντα θεραπεύειν.

10. νῦν : sharply contrasted with τότε in l. 12, both occupying emphatic positions at the beginning and end of their respective clauses. *Cf.* c. 54. 11, 12. — 11. μᾶλλον τότε : *sc.* ὠφέλιμοι ἦμεν. *Cf.* c. 40. 5 ; i. 86. 7 ; vi. 60. 13.

THUCYDIDES III. 56.

ἦσαν. καὶ δίκαιον ἡμῶν τῆς νῦν ἁμαρτίας, εἰ ἄρα ἡμάρ- 5
τηται, ἀντιθεῖναι τὴν τότε προθυμίαν, καὶ μείζω τε πρὸς
ἐλάσσω εὑρήσετε καὶ ἐν καιροῖς οἷς σπάνιον ἦν τῶν Ἑλλήνων τινὰ ἀρετὴν τῇ Ξέρξου δυνάμει ἀντιτάξασθαι,
ἐπῃνοῦντό τε μᾶλλον οἱ μὴ τὰ ξύμφορα πρὸς τὴν ἔφο-
δον αὐτοῖς ἀσφαλείᾳ πράσσοντες, ἐθέλοντες δὲ τολμᾶν
μετὰ κινδύνων τὰ βέλτιστα. ὧν ἡμεῖς γενόμενοι καὶ τι- 6
μηθέντες ἐς τὰ πρῶτα νῦν ἐπὶ τοῖς αὐτοῖς δέδιμεν μὴ
διαφθαρῶμεν, Ἀθηναίους ἑλόμενοι δικαίως μᾶλλον ἢ ὑμᾶς
κερδαλέως. καίτοι χρὴ ταὐτὰ περὶ τῶν αὐτῶν ὁμοίως 7

15. **ἡμῶν**: belongs to both τῆς νῦν ἁμαρτίας and τὴν τότε προθυμίαν, and by its position acquires almost the force of a dat. of interest. See on i. 30. 14. — **ἁμαρτίας** . . . **ἀντιθεῖναι**: the gen. as in ii. 85. 9. Kr. *Spr.* 47, 23, 2. — **ἄρα**: intimating doubt, a force retained from its interr. use, it is here, as c. 67. 4, rather negatively inclined (*if indeed*); but generally after εἰ and ἤν it is positive in force (*if perhaps*, c. 30. 10; i. 27. 9; 70. 23; 84. 9; 93. 30; 123. 5; 136. 12; 140. 7, etc.). — **ἡμάρτηται**: impers. pass., as παραβαίνεται, c. 45. 14. — 16. **ἀντιθεῖναι**: as in ii. 85. 8. — **μείζω πρὸς ἐλάσσω**: Schol. μείζω προθυμίαν πρὸς ἐλάσσω ἁμαρτίαν. πρός, as *against*; see on c. 43. 15. — 18. **ἀντιτάξασθαι**: *to array against*. Here lit., in ii. 87. 22 it is fig. — 19. **ἐπῃνοῦντό τε** . . . **πράσσοντες**: *and they were more commended who did not with respect to the attack seek their own advantage in security*. πράσσοντες has reference to negotiations with the enemy. ἀσφαλείᾳ, as opp. to μετὰ κινδύνων, equiv. to δι' ἀσφαλείας, i. 17. 3. It is used adv.

also Soph. *O. R.* 51. Some editt. take it with αὐτοῖς, *for their own security*. — 20. **ἐθέλοντες δὲ** . . . **τὰ βέλτιστα**: the order is chiastic with regard to the preceding clause. The open ἐθέλοντες τολμᾶν is opposed to the secret πράσσοντες, μετὰ κινδύνων to ἀσφαλείᾳ, τὰ βέλτιστα ("what was wholesomest for all") to τὰ ξύμφορα αὐτοῖς. 21. **ὧν**: partitive genitive with γενόμενοι. G. 1094, 7; H. 732 a; Kr. *Spr.* 47, 9, 2. — **τιμηθέντες ἐς τὰ πρῶτα**: as in c. 39. 9. On the matter, *cf.* ii. 71. § 2 f., and Plut. *Aristid.* 20, who says that the ἀριστεῖα were adjudged to the Plataeans. — 22. **ἐπὶ τοῖς αὐτοῖς**: *for the same conduct*, to be taken with διαφθαρῶμεν. Cf. ἐπὶ προδοσίᾳ, i. 138. 31; ἐπὶ βραχείᾳ προφάσει, i. 141. 4. — 23. **ἑλόμενοι**: with acc. (τινα or τά τινος) of party attitude, as c. 63. 11; 64. 6; ii. 7. 9. — 24. **κερδαλέως**: for mere *advantage*, as κερδαλέον, ii. 53. 11. It is contrasted with δικαίως, as τὸ ξυμφέρον above (9) with τὸ δίκαιον.

καίτοι . . . **καθιστῆται**: these words are directed (see Stahl, *N. Jahrbb.* xcvii. p. 117 f.) against a change of

25 φαίνεσθαι γιγνώσκοντας καὶ τὸ ξυμφέρον μὴ ἄλλο τι νομίσαι. ἢ τῶν ξυμμάχων τοῖς ἀγαθοῖς ὅταν αἰεὶ βέβαιον τὴν χάριν τῆς ἀρετῆς ἔχουσι καὶ τὸ παραυτίκα που ὑμῖν ὠφέλιμον καθιστῆται.

57 "Προσσκέψασθέ τε ὅτι νῦν μὲν παράδειγμα τοῖς πολ- 1

judgment on the part of the Lacedaemonians with regard to the consistent conduct of the Plataeans, which would have the saddest results for them (ἐπὶ τοῖς αὐτοῖς δέδιμεν μὴ διαφθαρῶμεν, as quite similarly in the transition from c. 57 to c. 58, καίτοι ἀξιοῦμέν γε κτέ. is opp. to δέδιμεν μὴ οὐ βέβαιοι ἦτε). They are, therefore, not a justification of the Plataeans, but an admonition to the Lacedaemonians. This view necessitates Heilmann's conjecture ἔχουσι (agreeing with ὑμῖν) for ἔχωσι. "You must, however, show yourselves consistent in your judgments concerning the same course of conduct, and consider your true advantage to be only this — to have an ever-enduring sense of gratitude toward good allies for their virtue, while your own immediate interest is secured," i.e. your true interest is subserved only where the advantage of the moment comports with lasting gratitude to deserving allies. From the first general claim (χρὴ ... ὁμοίως φαίνεσθαι γιγνώσκοντας) there is a transition with the aor. νομίσαι to the present case, and with ὑμῖν definitely to the Lacedaemonians. While τῶν ξυμμάχων οἱ ἀγαθοί is a general term for all deserving allies, the Plataeans have esp. in mind the ἀρετή displayed by themselves in the Persian wars (as just described in § 5),

for which they claim αἰεὶ βέβαιον τὴν χάριν. The matter of present advantage (καὶ τὸ παραυτίκα ὠφέλιμον) is placed in the background by the emphatic position of αἰεὶ βέβαιον τὴν χάριν, by the particle καί (also), and by που. — 25. μὴ ἄλλο τι νομίσαι: see on c. 30. 12. — 27. ἔχουσι: for the position, cf. i. 39. 9 διαφόρους ὄντας ἡμῖν δέχεσθαι σφᾶς. — τὸ παραυτίκα που ὠφέλιμον: that these words belong together seems clear from τῷ αὐτίκα χρησίμῳ (7), and from the consideration that, from l. 7 on, above all the narrow regard for immediate advantage is to be proved inadmissible. παραυτίκα, as in ii. 64. 27; vii. 57. 46. For the emphatic position of ὑμῖν, cf. i. 68. 1; 70. 5; v. 82. 23; vii. 78. 26. — 28. καθιστῆται: cf. i. 73. 19; 96. 6; 102. 22; 109. 2; iv. 86. 16.

57. *And if Sparta should for the sake of Thebes inflict upon Plataea a cruel punishment, it would be universally regarded as an unnatural deed, and your present reputation among the Hellenes for justice would be gone.*

1. **προσσκέψασθε**: praeterea considerate, which Meineke (*Herm.* iii. p. 364) and v. H. (*Stud. Thuc.* p. 44) conjecture and St. adopts, is preferable here, where the orators pass to a new consideration, to προσκέψασθε of the Mss. Nor is

λοῖς τῶν Ἑλλήνων ἀνδραγαθίας νομίζεσθε· εἰ δὲ περὶ
ἡμῶν γνώσεσθε μὴ τὰ εἰκότα, (οὐ γὰρ ἀφανῆ κρινεῖτε
τὴν δίκην τήνδε, ἐπαινούμενοι δὲ περὶ οὐδ' ἡμῶν μεμ-
5 πτῶν) ὁρᾶτε ὅπως μὴ οὐκ ἀποδέξωνται ἀνδρῶν ἀγαθῶν
πέρι αὐτοὺς ἀμείνους ὄντας ἀπρεπές τι ἐπιγνῶναι, οὐδὲ
πρὸς ἱεροῖς τοῖς κοινοῖς σκῦλα ἀπὸ ἡμῶν τῶν εὐεργετῶν
τῆς Ἑλλάδος ἀνατεθῆναι. δεινὸν δὲ δόξει εἶναι Πλάταιαν 2

the *look into the future*, which Cl. considers the main thought here, expressed in (5) ὁρᾶτε ὅπως μὴ οὐκ ἀποδέξωνται and (8) δεινὸν δὲ δόξει, any more than in c. 56. 8 τοῦ μὲν ὀρθοῦ φανεῖσθε οὐκ ἀληθεῖς κριταὶ ὄντες. — παράδειγμα: an *example*, as ii. 37. 2. See on c. 40. 37. — 2. ἀνδραγαθίας: here in the general sense of *uprightness* (not *bravery*, as c. 64. 16; ii. 42. 11; v. 101. 2), and ἀνδρῶν ἀγαθῶν and ἀμείνους follow in the same general signification. — 3. μὴ τὰ εἰκότα: cf. c. 56. 6. The neg. here, as well as in οὐδ' ἡμῶν μεμπτῶν below, is out of its regular place, since μή belongs to εἰκότα, οὐδ' to μεμπτῶν. Cf. c. 67. 7; i. 5. 5; 78. 1; ii. 67. 34; 102. 22. — οὐ γὰρ ... μεμπτῶν: the causal clause, thus placed in parataxis before the main one, is not rare in Thuc. See on i. 31. 7. For the sentiment, cf. Sall. *Cat.* 51. 12. — ἀφανῆ: pred. adj. with adv. force, as c. 30. 4. — 4. ἐπαινούμενοι ... μεμπτῶν: sc. κρινεῖτε τὴν δίκην τήνδε. The antithesis, if strictly carried out, would have been perhaps ἐπιφανεστάτην δὲ ἐπαινούμενοι οὐδὲ ἡμᾶς μεμπτοὺς κρινοῦντες. Against the assumption of an ἀφανὴς δίκη two grounds are advanced, the nature of the judges and that of those to be judged. —

περὶ οὐδ' ἡμῶν μεμπτῶν: this order, since in independent const. the sent. would have been οὐδ' ἡμεῖς μεμπτοί ἐσμεν. As to resemblances here and elsewhere in this and the following chapter to expressions in the *Palamedes* (§ 35 f.) attributed to Gorgias, see Maass, *Herm.* xxii. p. 580 f.; also Scheel, *de Gorg. discipl. vestigiis*, 1890, p. 55 ff. — 5. οὐκ ἀποδέξωνται: 'litotes,' for μέμφωνται, as vii. 48. 18. With dependent inf., as δέχεσθαι, c. 53. 4. — 6. αὐτούς: for ὑμᾶς αὐτούς. Cf. c. 54. 9. — ἀπρεπές τι: cf. c. 67. 16. — ἐπιγνῶναι: seems to have reference to the preliminary decision made at the surrender of the city, *decide farther* or *afterwards*. Cf. i. 70. 8; ii. 65. 48. But as it is used of judicial decision in Dion. H. *Ant.* xi. 52 ἢν αὐτοὶ μεθ' ὅρκον δικάσαντες ἑτέρων ἐπέγνωσαν εἶναι (cf. also *C. I. G.* ii. 1845, l. 71 f. περὶ δὲ τοῦ ἀδυνάτου βουλὰ καὶ ἁλία ἐπιγιγνωσκέτω), this may be the meaning here. — οὐδέ: sc. ἀποδέξωνται. — 7. ἱεροῖς τοῖς κοινοῖς: order, as in c. 54. 14; 56. 3. As in v. 18. 3, the temples at Olympia and Delphi are esp. meant.

8. Πλάταιαν Λακεδαιμονίους πορθῆσαι: that *Lacedaemonians lay waste Plataea*. The use of the proper name

Λακεδαιμονίους πορθῆσαι, καὶ τοὺς μὲν πατέρας ἀνα-
10 γράψαι ἐς τὸν τρίποδα τὸν ἐν Δελφοῖς δι' ἀρετὴν τὴν
πόλιν, ὑμᾶς δὲ καὶ ἐκ παντὸς τοῦ Ἑλληνικοῦ πανοικεσίᾳ διὰ Θηβαίους ἐξαλεῖψαι. ἐς τοῦτο γὰρ δὴ ξυμ- 3
φορᾶς προκεχωρήκαμεν, οἵτινες Μήδων τε κρατησάντων

instead of ὑμᾶς emphasizes the un-naturalness (δεινόν) of the deed, since the mind recurs at once to the Spartan claim to be the liberators of Greece (see on c. 13. 35), as well as to the honour they had once paid to Plataea. So in l. 12 the mere word Θηβαίους recalls their betrayal of the Greek cause in the Persian wars (cf. Hdt. vii. 132. 4).—9. καὶ κτέ.: in the double clause introduced by καί as a further element of the δεινόν, the former (τοὺς μὲν ... τὴν πόλιν), though in parataxis, is subord. to the latter (ὑμᾶς δὲ ... ἐξαλεῖψαι). Cf. i. 28. 15.
—10. τὸν τρίποδα τὸν ἐν Δελφοῖς: cf. i. 132. 10 τὸν τρίποδά ποτε τὸν ἐν Δελφοῖς, ὃν ἀνέθεσαν οἱ Ἕλληνες ἀπὸ τῶν Μήδων ἀκροθίνιον, Hdt. ix. 81. 3 ὁ τρίπους ὁ χρύσεος ἀνετέθη ὁ ἐπὶ τοῦ τρικαρήνου ὄφιος τοῦ χαλκέου ἐπεστεὼς ἄγχιστα τοῦ βωμοῦ. The gold tripod was carried off by the Phocians in the sacred war (Paus. x. 13. 5). The bronze column of three intertwined snakes, which was removed by Constantine to Byzantium and placed in the hippodrome, the modern Atmeidan (Gibbon, chap. 17, note 48), was brought to light in 1856. It bears the names of all the Greek states which took part in the Persian war.
—11. παντὸς τοῦ Ἑλληνικοῦ: sc. ἔθνους, as in c. 82. 3. Cf. i. 1. 6; 6. 23. — πανοικεσίᾳ: cf. ii. 16. 4; Dio C. xli. 7. For the form, see St. Qu.

Gr.[2] p. 46. The word is generally considered to mean here, house and all, 'root and branch'; but Steup, who renders 'with all its houses,' maintains that both this expression and Πλάταιαν Λακεδαιμονίους πορθῆσαι refer to the fate of the city (cf. 68. 19), not of its inhabitants, since the women, children, old people, and other non-combatants, besides nearly half of the original defenders, were in Athens (cf. 24. § 2; ii. 6. 18; 72. 17; 78. § 3).—12. διὰ Θηβαίους: cf. δι' αὐτούς, c. 56. 6. — ἐξαλεῖψαι: to blot out, forms with ἐκ παντὸς τοῦ Ἑλληνικοῦ a striking antithesis to ἀναγράψαι ἐς τὸν τρίποδα. There is the same antithesis in the examples compared by Bl., Ar. Pax 1181 τοὺς μὲν ἐγγράφοντας ἡμῶν, τοὺς δ' ἐξαλείφοντας, Eur. Pel. (frg. 4) ὅν γ' ἐξαλείφει ῥᾷον, ἢ γράφει, θεός. The same literal and fig. use obtains in ἐξαλείφειν as in delere. In the fig. sense as here used, it seems to be mainly Tragic and Ionic. Cf. Aesch. Choeph. 503; Sept. 15; Eur. Hec. 590; Hel. 262; Hipp. 1241; I. T. 698; Hdt. vii. 220. 10; Plato Theaet. 187 b, Plut. de Fort. 4, and Aristides's imitation (ii. 857), ἐξαλεῖψαι Λακεδαιμονίους ἐκ τῆς Ἑλλάδος.
ἐς τοῦτο ξυμφορᾶς: cf. ἐς τοῦτο ἀνάγκης, i. 49. 31; Plato Theaet. 170 d; ἐς τοῦτο δυστυχίας, vii. 86. 25; ἐν τούτῳ παρασκευῆς, ii. 18. 1; εἰς τοῦθ' ὕβρεως, Dem. iv. 34; xxii. 16. G.

ἀπωλλύμεθα καὶ νῦν ἐν ὑμῖν τοῖς πρὶν φιλτάτοις Θηβαίων
15 ἡσσώμεθα καὶ δύο ἀγῶνας τοὺς μεγίστους ὑπέστημεν,
τότε μέν, τὴν πόλιν εἰ μὴ παρέδομεν, λιμῷ διαφθαρῆναι, νῦν δὲ θανάτου κρίνεσθαι. καὶ περιεώσμεθα ἐκ 4
πάντων Πλαταιῆς οἱ παρὰ δύναμιν πρόθυμοι ἐς τοὺς
Ἕλληνας ἐρῆμοι καὶ ἀτιμώρητοι· καὶ οὔτε τῶν τότε ξυμ-
20 μάχων ὠφελεῖ οὐδείς, ὑμεῖς τε, ὦ Λακεδαιμόνιοι, ἡ μόνη
ἐλπίς, δέδιμεν μὴ οὐ βέβαιοι ἦτε.

1088; H. 730 c. — **14. ἀπωλλύμεθα:** Steup renders *were ruined*, since the reference is to the burning of their city by Xerxes (Hdt. viii. 50). Even with this reference, however, the rendering *were all but ruined* is admissible. GMT. 38. — **καὶ νῦν κτέ.**: Steup explains that καί co-ordinates ἀπωλλύμεθα with both the following clauses, and that νῦν ἐν ὑμῖν does not refer to the present trial, but is more general. But surely the evident reference in c. 67. 27 to this very passage shows that the present case is meant. — **ἐν ὑμῖν**: *before you* (as judges). For the prep., see on c. 53. 3. — **Θηβαίων**: the mere name here implies τῶν ἐχθίστων πάντων. See on l. 8. — **15. ἡσσώμεθα**: used in a forensic sense. — **δύο ἀγῶνας τοὺς μεγίστους**: for the order, see on c. 42. 4. — **16. τότε μέν**: *i.e.* before we decided to surrender. Cf. c. 52. § 1, 3; 59. 20. τότε is often thus used of a time assumed as well known. Cf. c. 69. 2; i. 101. 8; vii. 31. 12. — **εἰ μὴ παρέδομεν**: nisi tradidissemus, the apod. being ἀγῶνας ὑπέστημεν (= ἐκινδυνεύσαμεν) διαφθαρῆναι. GMT. 427 a. Cf. c. 74. 11. — **17. θανάτου κρίνεσθαι**: *to be tried on a capital charge.* For the gen., see G. 1133; H. 745 b; Kr.

Spr. 47, 22, 1; Kühn. 419, n. 11. Cf. Xen. *Cyrop.* i. 2. 14 θανάτου οὗτοι κρίνουσιν, Hdt. vi. 136. 4 θανάτου ὑπαγαγὼν ὑπὸ τὸν δῆμον Μιλτιάδεα ἐδίωκε τῆς Ἀθηναίων ἀπάτης εἵνεκεν. Steup thinks that δίκη, which is found in all the best Mss. except Vat., should be inserted after θανάτου. Cf. δίκῃ κρίνεσθαι, i. 39. 1; iv. 122. 16, and θανάτου δίκην ἀπολογησάμενος, viii. 68. 16.

περιεώσμεθα ἐκ πάντων: *we have been spurned by all*, lit. *thrust out from all.* Cf. c. 67. 27; Arist. *Pol.* 1304 a, 1306 a. Note the wonderful pathos of the sent., brought out esp. by the antithesis Πλαταιεῖς ... Ἕλληνας (cf. c. 59. 25). See on l. 8 and 14. — **18. παρὰ δύναμιν**: cf. c. 54. 17. — **19. ἐρῆμοι καὶ ἀτιμώρητοι**: *deserted and unaided* (cf. τιμωρία, c. 20. 4), pred. of effect after περιεώσμεθα. Cf. i. 90. 20; ii. 75. 22; vii. 4. 11; 29. 17. — **τῶν τότε ... οὐδείς**: *i.e.* none of the other members of the alliance formed at the time of the Persian war. — **20. οὐδείς, ὑμεῖς τε κτέ.**: the chiastic order produces a fine effect, as also the antithesis ἡ μόνη ἐλπίς, δέδιμεν. — **ἡ μόνη ἐλπίς**: cf. ἡ μεγίστη ἐλπίς, Luc. *Piscat.* 3; unica spes, Liv. xxi. 11; Curt. iii. 8. 1. — **21. οὐ βέβαιοι**: *not to be*

58

"Καίτοι ἀξιοῦμέν γε καὶ θεῶν ἕνεκα τῶν ξυμμαχι-
κῶν ποτε γενομένων καὶ τῆς ἀρετῆς τῆς ἐς τοὺς Ἕλληνας καμφθῆναι ὑμᾶς καὶ μεταγνῶναι εἴ τι ὑπὸ Θηβαίων ἐπείσθητε, τήν τε δωρεὰν ἀνταπαιτῆσαι αὐτοὺς
μὴ κτείνειν οὓς μὴ ὑμῖν πρέπει, σώφρονά τε ἀντὶ αἰσχρᾶς
κομίσασθαι χάριν, καὶ μὴ ἡδονὴν δόντας ἄλλοις κακίαν

depended on, i.e. not faithful to the old alliance and its consequences, μὴ οὐ βέβαιον τὴν χάριν τῆς ἀρετῆς ἔχητε. Cf. c. 56. 26.

58. Instead of Theban hate, let rather the thought of our former close association with you, the recollection of our merits, and the simple instincts of humanity influence you.

1. καίτοι ἀξιοῦμέν γε κτέ.: the chief emphasis is on καὶ θεῶν ἕνεκα ... Ἕλληνας. Over against the anxiety just expressed are now placed those weighty considerations, which should induce the Lacedaemonians not to pass sentence against the Plataeans.— θεῶν ἕνεκα ... γενομένων: for the sake of the gods that once protected our alliance. The order as in c. 57. 7 ἱεροῖς τοῖς κοινοῖς. — 2. τῆς ἀρετῆς: Schol. sc. τῆς ἡμετέρας. Cf. c. 54. § 4; 56. 16; 57. 10, 18. — 3. καμφθῆναι: found only here in Thuc. (cf. Aesch. Prom. 237, 306; Plato Prot. 320 b; Rep. 494 c; Plut. Per. 36), = ἐπι-κλασθῆναι, c. 59. 5; 67. 5; iv. 37. 5. — 4. τήν τε δωρεὰν ... πρέπει: ὑμᾶς is the subj. of κτείνειν, as shown by οὓς μὴ ὑμῖν πρέπει, as well as of ἀνταπ-αιτῆσαι, κομίσασθαι, and ἀντιλαβεῖν, that you in turn ask of them the boon that you should not kill those whom you ought not, i.e. as the Thebans have asked the favour of our death

(as hinted in εἴ τι ὑπὸ Θηβαίων ἐπεί-σθητε — cf. also c. 53. 21 ἄλλοις χάριν φέροντες), do you demand as a counter-favour, etc. Cl. explains, "that you request of them (in return for much favour shown them) the counter-favour, etc." But in that case there should be some explanation of the favours that had been shown by the Lacedaemonians to the Thebans. St. and Kr. explain ἀντι-, "in return for our former merits." Kr. makes αὐτούς, sc. ὑμᾶς, subj. of κτείνειν. But to this is opposed the fact that all the rest of the infs. have ὑμᾶς as subject. For the inf. limiting τὴν δωρεάν, cf. c. 66. 16 τὴν περὶ αὐτῶν ἡμῖν μὴ κτεί-νειν ψευσθεῖσαν ὑπόσχεσιν. — αὐτούς: i.e. τοὺς Θηβαίους, pers. obj. of ἀνταπ-αιτῆσαι. — 5. σώφρονά τε ... χάριν: that you receive an honest gratitude (from us) instead of a disgraceful gratitude (from them). While the Plataeans designate the gratitude that would be acquired from the Thebans by the Lacedaemonians for their destruction as an αἰσχρὰ χάρις, the Thebans, c. 67. 26, demand the death of the Plataeans as a χάρις δίκαια for their merits. κομίζεσθαι is used commonly of good things, as i. 43. 3; iv. 98. 25. Cf. Dem. xxi. 171 κεκόμισται χάριν παρ' ὑμῶν. —
6. κακίαν: as in c. 61. 7, the result

THUCYDIDES III. 58.

αὐτοὺς ἀντιλαβεῖν· βραχὺ γὰρ τὸ τὰ ἡμέτερα σώματα 2
διαφθεῖραι, ἐπίπονον δὲ τὴν δύσκλειαν αὐτοῦ ἀφανίσαι·
οὐκ ἐχθροὺς γὰρ ἡμᾶς εἰκότως τιμωρήσεσθε, ἀλλ' εὔ-
10 νους, κατ' ἀνάγκην πολεμήσαντας. ὥστε καὶ τῶν σωμά- 3
των ἄδειαν ποιοῦντες ὅσια ἂν δικάζοιτε καὶ προνοοῦντες
ὅτι ἑκόντας τε ἐλάβετε καὶ χεῖρας προϊσχομένους (ὁ δὲ
νόμος τοῖς Ἕλλησι μὴ κτείνειν τούτους), ἔτι δὲ καὶ εὐεργέτας γεγενημένους διὰ παντός. ἀποβλέψατε γὰρ ἐς πα- 4
15 τέρων τῶν ὑμετέρων θήκας, οὓς ἀποθανόντας ὑπὸ Μήδων καὶ ταφέντας ἐν τῇ ἡμετέρᾳ ἐτιμῶμεν κατὰ ἔτος
ἕκαστον δημοσίᾳ ἐσθήμασί τε καὶ τοῖς ἄλλοις νομίμοις.

of unworthy conduct, shame, more plainly expressed in δύσκλειαν below. *Cf.* φέρειν ἀρετήν, i. 33. 11.
7. βραχύ: *a small matter*, as i. 140. 23, 27; viii. 76. 25. — **8. αὐτοῦ**: *i.e.* τοῦ διαφθεῖραι. αὐτό thus emphatically used c. 59. 20; i. 68. 9; 74. 3; 122. 20; 138. 11. — **9. εἰκότως**: see on c. 56. 6. — **10. κατ' ἀνάγκην**: as shown c. 55. For the asyndeton, which Cl. was inclined to remove by inserting καί, *cf.* c. 43. 10.
ὥστε καὶ τῶν σωμάτων κτέ.: see App. — **11. ἄδειαν ποιοῦντες**: (*sc.* ἡμῖν) as in viii. 76. 34. *Cf.* vi. 60. 15 ἄδειαν ποιησάμενον, *obtaining security for one's self*. — **ὅσια ἂν δικάζοιτε**: *you would render a righteous judgment, i.e.* in accordance with divine law. — **προνοοῦντες**: rendered by Cl., St., Jow., and others, *if you consider beforehand, i.e.* before you decide. But Steup follows Pp. and Kr. in supplying ἡμῶν with προνοοῦντες (as ἡμῖν with ποιοῦντες). *Cf.* Xen. *Cyrop.* viii. 1. 1; 7. 15; and προνοεῖσθαι with gen., Thuc. vi. 9. 10. — **12. ἑκόντας τε ἐλά-**

βετε κτέ.: the Plataeans would have their voluntary surrender regarded as a ἱκετεία. — **χεῖρας προϊσχομένους**: Schol., ἱκετεύσαντας. *Cf.* c. 66. 12; 67. 22. — **ὁ νόμος**: *i.e.* the international custom based on religion. *Cf.* c. 59. 2 τὰ κοινὰ τῶν Ἑλλήνων νόμιμα, 67. 24 ὁ τῶν Ἑλλήνων νόμος, iv. 97. 10 τὰ νόμιμα τῶν Ἑλλήνων. See Hermann, *Staats-Alt.*[6] p. 70, N. 3. — **13. εὐεργέτας γεγενημένους**: see on c. 2. 11. — **14. διὰ παντός**: *constantly*, of time as usual. See on i. 38. 2.
15. θήκας: see on c. 104. 5; ii. 52. 14. The place of the art. is supplied by the preceding gen., as often. *Cf.* c. 59. 6; i. 1. 11; 3. 1; 11. 2. As to these sepulchres, *cf.* Hdt. ix. 85; Paus. ix. 2. 5. In the sense of *tomb*, the word seems to occur, outside of Thuc., mainly in Hdt. (ii. 67. 4; ix. 85. 4) and Tragedy (Aesch. *Agam.* 453; Pers. 405; Soph. *O. C.* 1763; *El.* 896). *Cf.* Xen. *Cyrop.* vii. 3. 5. — **17. ἐσθήμασί τε ... ὅσα τε**: over against the honours usually paid to the dead is placed as something espe-

ὅσα τε ἡ γῆ ἡμῶν ἀνεδίδου ὡραῖα, πάντων ἀπαρχὰς ἐπιφέροντες, εὖνοι μὲν ἐκ φιλίας χώρας, ξύμμαχοι δὲ ὁμαίχ-
20 μοις ποτὲ γενομένοις. ὧν ὑμεῖς τοὐναντίον ἂν δράσαιτε
μὴ ὀρθῶς γνόντες. σκέψασθε δέ· Παυσανίας μὲν γὰρ 5
ἔθαπτεν αὐτοὺς νομίζων ἐν γῇ τε φιλίᾳ τιθέναι καὶ παρ᾽
ἀνδράσι τοιούτοις· ὑμεῖς δὲ εἰ κτενεῖτε ἡμᾶς καὶ χώραν
τὴν Πλαταιίδα Θηβαΐδα ποιήσετε, τί ἄλλο ἢ ἐν πολεμίᾳ
25 τε καὶ παρὰ τοῖς αὐθένταις πατέρας τοὺς ὑμετέρους καὶ

cial the offering of the first fruits of the land, and instead of continuing with the dat. there is a change of const. to the participle. — ἐσθήμασι : this much, but unjustly, suspected word seems, as Duker explained, to refer to the garments that were offered to the dead. Cf. Soph. *El.* 452; Eur. *Or.* 123, 1436. See Pasanisi, *Rivista di Filol. Class.* xv. p. 518 ff. As to the view of Cl. and St., that ἐσθήμασι refers to the mourning clothes of the participants in the festival, no reason can be conceived why among the honours publicly paid every year to the dead especial mention should be made of the mourning garments. Nor is the difficulty removed by the circumstance emphasized by St., that, acc. to Plut. *Aristid.* 21, the archon of Plataea only at this annual festival put on χιτῶνα φοινικοῦν. Plut.'s omission, in his description of the festival, of any mention of the offering of garments may be explained on the assumption that the custom was obsolete in his time. ἔσθημα is a poetic word, acc. to the Schol. on Soph. *El.* 270. Cf. Aesch. *Ag.* 562; *Pers.* 536; Soph. *El.* 270; Eur. *Troad.* 991. Elsewhere only in late prose. — τοῖς ἄλλοις νομίμοις : Plut. *l.c.* mentions the slaughter of a bull, a drink-offering, *etc.* — 18. ἀνεδίδου : just as in Xen. *Mem.* iv. 3. 5. — ὡραῖα : *products of the land*, as in i. 120. 10. — ἐπιφέροντες : of offerings to the dead, as in ii. 34. 5. — 19. ἐκ φιλίας χώρας : *sc.* τῆς ἡμετέρας ἐπιφέροντες. — ὁμαίχμοις : found only here in Thucydides. Cf. ὁμαιχμία, i. 18. 25; Hdt. vii. 145. 12; viii. 140 a 21. 21. σκέψασθε δέ : as in i. 143. 21, introduces an explanatory addition. Cf. c. 46. 4 σκέψασθε γάρ, i. 33. 7 καὶ σκέψασθε. — 22. ἔθαπτεν : for the force of the impf., see GMT. 35, and compare 56. Cf. ἀπεδίδου οἰκεῖν, ii. 71. 14. — 23. τοιούτοις : *sc.* φιλίοις, as τοιοῦτος often represents a preceding adjective; *cf.* Plato *Phaedo* 108 b τὴν ἀκάθαρτον (ψυχὴν) καί τι πεποιηκυῖαν τοιοῦτον. Esp. is this the case with ἕτερος and ἄλλος. Cf. Plato *Phaedo* 58 d. — 24. Θηβαΐδα ποιήσετε : acc. to c. 68. § 3, the territory of the Plataeans was after a year rented to the Thebans. — τί ἄλλο ἤ : see on c. 39. 10. — 25. τοῖς αὐθένταις : τοῖς φονεῦσι· αὐθένται κυρίως οἱ αὐτόχειρες καὶ πολέμιοι, Schol. See Lobeck *ad*

ξυγγενεῖς ἀτίμους γερῶν ὧν νῦν ἴσχουσι καταλείψετε·
πρὸς δὲ καὶ γῆν ἐν ᾗ ἠλευθερώθησαν οἱ Ἕλληνες δου-
λώσετε, ἱερά τε θεῶν οἷς εὐξάμενοι Μήδων ἐκράτησαν
ἐρημοῦτε, καὶ θυσίας τὰς πατρίους τῶν ἐσσαμένων καὶ
30 κτισάντων ἀφαιρήσεσθε.

59 "Οὐ πρὸς τῆς ὑμετέρας δόξης, ὦ Λακεδαιμόνιοι, 1
τάδε, οὔτε ἐς τὰ κοινὰ τῶν Ἑλλήνων νόμιμα καὶ ἐς τοὺς

Phryn. p. 120. The Thebans are called αὐθένται, because they had sided with the Persians. — 26. ἀτίμους γερῶν: as ii. 65. 32 χρημάτων ἀδωρότατος. G. 1141; H. 753 c; Kr. *Spr.* 47, 26, 10. γέρα, as in i. 13. 5; 25. 15, of honours based on ancient precedent and sacred usage. — ἴσχουσι: *possess, enjoy*, as in ii. 68. 17; Hdt. i. 62. 3. — 27. πρὸς δέ: *moreover*, adv. only here in Thuc., but found also in Xen., Plato, and Demosthenes. Kühn. 443, 2; Kr. *Spr.* 68, 2, 2. — 28. ἱερά τε ... ἀφαιρήσεσθε: *and you desolate the temples of the gods to whom they prayed when they conquered the Medes, and you will take away the hereditary sacrifices from those who founded and built* (the temples). As to the last clause, where ἱερά is supplied, with St. and Bm., as obj. of the partics., Cl. explains, '*you will take away the hereditary sacrifices from those who founded and established them*, where one would expect, "you will take from the sacrifices their founders," *i.e.* the citizens of Plataea, who also in later generations were regarded as founders of those sacrifices.' Steup suggests that as Thuc. in i. 40. 7 uses ἀποστερεῖν (τινά τινος) in the sense

'withdraw,' not as usual 'deprive' (c. 42. 19; i. 69. 3; 136. 19), so here, on the contrary, ἀφαιρεῖσθαί (τινά τινος) may mean not 'withdraw,' but 'deprive.' *Cf.* Dem. xx. 82 τῆς δωρεᾶς ἀφῃρέθη. Also Xen. *Cyneg.* 6. 4; Lys. xxiv. 6; Plut. *Aem. Paul.* 31; *Anton.* 60. But see App. — 29. ἐρημοῦτε: the pres. between two futs. is rather remarkable. For the pres. thus co-ord. with a single fut., *cf.* ii. 44. 2; iv. 10. 11. Cl. considers this a contracted future form. See App. — ἐσσαμένων: with the best Mss.; a few, εἰσαμένων or ἐσαμένων. See Curtius, *Verbum.* I.² p. 129. The archaic form is due possibly to some old formulary usage. — 30. ἀφαιρήσεσθε: with acc. and gen. also c. 43. 4; viii. 46. 33.

59. *By all that is sacred to gods and men, we beg you to spare us. But if you will not do this, then place us again in the position in which we were when we surrendered.*

1. πρὸς τῆς ... δόξης: *for your glory.* See on c. 38. 3. — **2.** τάδε, οὔτε ... ἁμαρτάνειν οὔτε ... διαφθεῖραι: τάδε sums up the various features of an unfavourable decision as developed in the foregoing, and the special points of view to be con-

προγόνους ἁμαρτάνειν οὔτε ἡμᾶς τοὺς εὐεργέτας ἀλλοτρίας ἕνεκα ἔχθρας μὴ αὐτοὺς ἀδικηθέντας διαφθεῖραι,
5 φείσασθαι δὲ καὶ ἐπικλασθῆναι τῇ γνώμῃ οἴκτῳ σώφρονι λαβόντας, μὴ ὧν πεισόμεθα μόνον δεινότητα κατανοοῦντας, ἀλλ' οἷοί τε ἂν ὄντες πάθοιμεν καὶ ὡς ἀστάθμητον τὸ τῆς ξυμφορᾶς ᾧ τινί ποτ' ἂν καὶ ἀναξίῳ ξυμπέσοι. ἡμεῖς τε, ὡς πρέπον ἡμῖν καὶ ὡς ἡ χρεία προάγει, αἰτού- 2
10 μεθα ὑμᾶς, θεοὺς τοὺς ὁμοβωμίους καὶ κοινοὺς τῶν Ἑλ-

sidered are epexegetically added in the οὔτε, οὔτε clauses. — ἐς τὰ κοινὰ . . . νόμιμα . . . ἁμαρτάνειν: see on c. 58. 12. ἁμαρτάνειν ἐς with neut. acc., as Plato *Legg.* 759 c τὰ εἰς τὰ θεῖα ἁμαρτανόμενα. — ἐς τοὺς προγόνους: acc. to c. 58. § 4 f., the graves of the Spartans who fell at Plataea, and the gods who then aided the victors, would be neglected. — 3. τοὺς εὐεργέτας: cf. c. 58. 13. — 4. μὴ αὐτοὺς ἀδικηθέντας: in cond. form, though referring to the present case. For the asyndeton, see on c. 43. 10. — 5. φείσασθαι δέ: sc. πρὸς τῆς ὑμετέρας δόξης ἐστί. — ἐπικλασθῆναι τῇ γνώμῃ: as iv. 37. 5; without τῇ γνώμῃ, c. 67. 5 — 6. λαβόντας: with reference to the wretched condition of the Plataeans, *taking* (i.e. regarding) our case, *judging*. The use of λαβεῖν similar to that in c. 56. 8; iv. 17. 8; vi. 27. 9; 53. 18. In vi. 61. 3 likewise without obj. expressed, περὶ τοῦ Ἀλκιβιάδου . . . χαλεπῶς οἱ Ἀθηναῖοι ἐλάμβανον. To the adv. χαλεπῶς there corresponds in the present passage οἴκτῳ σώφρονι, *with reasonable compassion,* 'reasonable, a) because we are innocent, b) because all men are liable to the same.' (Jow.) — μὴ

μόνον . . . ἀλλά: without καί, as in iv. 60. 1. — κατανοοῦντας: explanatory of οἴκτῳ σώφρονι λαβόντας. St. construes μὴ ὧν δεινότητα with λαβόντας, and considers κατανοοῦντας a gloss. — 7. ὡς ἀστάθμητον . . . ξυμπέσοι: *how uncertain it is on whom misfortune may fall, however (καί) undeserving he may be.* (Jow.) Bl. compares Herodian v. 1. 11 τὰ τῆς τύχης δῶρα καὶ ἀναξίοις περιπίπτει. τὸ τῆς ξυμφορᾶς as τὸ τῆς τύχης, iv. 18. 9; vii. 61. 12; τὸ τῆς ἐπιστήμης, vii. 62. 8. II. 730 c; Kr. *Spr.* 47, 5, 10. The phrase is placed proleptically before ᾧτινι (Kr. and others, with one Ms., ὅ τινι).
9. ἡμεῖς τε: opp. to τῆς ὑμετέρας δόξης above. "As your reputation is at stake, so there remains for us only the prayer ——." — πρέπον: without ἐστί, as δίκαιον (23). ξυμφέρον (c. 44. 5), χρεών (i. 77. 13). εἰκός, αἰσχρόν, δεινόν, etc. — προάγει: *draws us on,* as in c. 45. 26. — 10. ὁμοβωμίους: i.e. having altars both among you and among us, as the context seems to require. *Cf.* ii. 71. 21 θεοὺς τοὺς ὑμετέρους πατρῴους καὶ ἡμετέρους ἐγχωρίους. Most editt. explain, those deities who were worshipped together at the same altar, called ὁμωχέται, iv. 97. 17; σύμβωμοι,

λήνων ἐπιβοώμενοι πεῖσαι τάδε, προφερόμενοί (θ') ὅρκους
οὓς οἱ πατέρες ὑμῶν ὤμοσαν μὴ ἀμνημονεῖν ἱκέται γιγνόμεθα ὑμῶν τῶν πατρῴων τάφων καὶ ἐπικαλούμεθα

Strabo, p. 512. Arn. supposes these to be the magni dii (οἱ δώδεκα). Goell. explains, those gods at whose altars all Greece might jointly sacrifice, e.g. Olympian Jupiter and Pythian Apollo. — 11. ἐπιβοώμενοι: signifies, as Bl. says, like ἐπικαλούμενοι, magna voce invocantes ad auxilium. Cf. c. 67. 9; vii. (69. 20); 75. 15; viii. 92. 50. The word seems to be Ionic and poetic. Cf. Hdt. i. 87. 4; ix. 23. 3; Hom. K 463; a 378; β 143; Eur. Med. 168. Elsewhere only in late writers. — πεῖσαι τάδε: which Kr. and v. H. bracket, is to be construed with ἐπι-βοώμενοι. Just so in l. 14 the purpose of ἐπικαλούμεθα τοὺς κεκμηῶτας is expressed by μὴ γενέσθαι ὑπὸ Θηβαίοις κτέ. The subj. of both infs. is the Plataeans. If πεῖσαι τάδε be taken with αἰτούμεθα ὑμᾶς, as Cl., St., and Jow. explain, πεῖσαι is not only superfluous, but out of place. On the other hand, αἰτούμεθα ὑμᾶς can dispense with the neuter object (cf. iv. 18. 4). τάδε refers to the course which the speakers beg the Lacedaemonians to take (l. 5, φείσασθαι καὶ ἐπικλα-σθῆναι τῇ γνώμῃ). To refer τάδε to what follows, as Cl. does, and make the request proper begin with προ-φερόμενοι is impossible, because the invocation of the gods could not thus be separated from that of the oaths. — προφερόμενοι (θ') ὅρκους: θ' is added, against the Mss., with St.,

who rightly judges that Thuc. could not have let the second part of the invocation follow the first without a connective. — προφερόμενοι: the mid. emphasizes personal interest. "Bringing forward the oaths for our protection." Cf. Plato Phil. 57 a. Elsewhere in Thuc., either act. (c. 64. 7; vi. 7. 11; 31. 21), or passive (v. 26. 22; vii. 69. 19). Most of the Mss. have προσφερόμενοι, but the examples just cited seem sufficiently to establish the vulgate. — 12. μὴ ἀμνημονεῖν: explanatory of ὤμοσαν, unless the words be considered, with Stenp (following Cobet and v. H.), a marginal explanation of ὤμοσαν. Cf. ii. 73. 14, where the purport of the oath is not given. To connect μὴ ἀμνημονεῖν with προφερόμενοι, as Cl., or with ἱκέται γιγνόμεθα, as St., is inadmissible, since the Plataeans cannot be the subj. of this inf., as of πεῖσαι and μὴ γενέσθαι. — ἱκέται γιγνόμεθα: see on c. 2. 11. — 13. ὑμῶν τῶν πατρῴων τάφων: joined with pathetic effect to ἱκέται γιγνό-μεθα, ὑμῶν receiving special emphasis from its position. "We put ourselves under the protection of the graves in which your fathers rest." Cf. i. 136. 9 τῆς γυναικὸς ἱκέτης γενό-μενος, Hdt. i. 73. 28. Ἀλυάττεω ἱκέται ἐγένοντο, Isocr. vi. 23 ἱκέται κατέστησαν ταύτης τῆς πόλεως, Cic. Tusc. i. 29 iudicibus supplex fuit. Cobet, N. L. p. 346, conjectures ὑμῶν πρὸς τῶν πατρῴων τάφων, which would

τοὺς κεκμηῶτας μὴ γενέσθαι ὑπὸ Θηβαίοις μηδὲ τοῖς
15 ἐχθίστοις φίλτατοι ὄντες παραδοθῆναι, ἡμέρας τε ἀναμιμνῄσκομεν ἐκείνης ᾗ τὰ λαμπρότατα μετ' αὐτῶν πράξαντες νῦν ἐν τῇδε τὰ δεινότατα κινδυνεύομεν παθεῖν.
ὅπερ δὲ ἀναγκαῖόν τε καὶ χαλεπώτατον τοῖς ὧδε ἔχουσι,
λόγου τελευτᾶν, διότι καὶ τοῦ βίου ὁ κίνδυνος ἐγγὺς μετ'
20 αὐτοῦ, παυόμενοι λέγομεν ἤδη ὅτι οὐ Θηβαίοις παρεδο-
μεν τὴν πόλιν (εἱλόμεθα γὰρ ἂν πρό γε τούτου τῷ αἰ-

weaken the effect. — 14. **τοὺς κεκμηῶτας**: euphemism for τοὺς τεθνεῶτας, as in Plato *Legg.* 718 a; 927 b; and often in Tragedy, *e.g.* Aesch. *Suppl.* 158; Eur. *Suppl.* 756; *Troad.* 96. The archaic poetic form, which is retained with most of the Mss., like ἐσσαμένων in c. 58. 29, is more appropriate to the solemn invocation. — **ὑπὸ Θηβαίοις**: with γενέσθαι as ὑπὸ Συρακοσίοις, vi. 86. 3; vii. 64. 7. *Cf.* ὑφ' αὑτοῖς ποιεῖσθαι, c. 62. 19. For the const., see G. 1219, 2; H. 808, 2; Kr. *Spr.* 68, 44. — **τοῖς ἐχθίστοις φίλτατοι ὄντες**: sc. τοῖς κεκμηῶσι. *Cf.* c. 58. 25 παρὰ τοῖς αὐθένταις. — 15. **ἡμέρας τε** ... **ἐκείνης**: for the art. omitted, *cf.* γῆν τήνδε, ii. 74. 11; στρατιᾷ τῇδε, iv. 85. 25. Kühn. 465, N. 6 a. — **ἀναμιμνῄσκομεν**: sc. τοὺς κεκμηῶτας. — 16. **ᾗ τὰ λαμπρότατα ... παθεῖν**: two clauses are united in one; the full form would be ᾗ ... ἐπράξαμεν, ὅμως δὲ νῦν κτέ. In πράξαντες the Plataeans identify themselves with their ancestors. — **μετ' αὐτῶν**: sc. τῶν κεκμηώτων. The best Mss. have αὐτῶν or ἑαυτῶν, which is impossible. — 17. **ἐν τῇδε**: the prep. is added to emphasize the important point.

18. **ὅπερ δέ**: for the rel. sent., where παυόμενοι δέ, ὅπερ ἀναγκαῖον κτέ. would seem more natural, see Kr. *Spr.* 51, 13, 13; Kühn. 562, 2. — **τοῖς ὧδε ἔχουσι**: see on c. 53. 14. — 19. **λόγου τελευτᾶν**: epexegesis of ὅπερ, as iv. 125. 8 ἀσαφῶς ἐκπλήγνυσθαι. The gen. as in c. 104. 28; Xen. *Cyrop.* viii. 7. 17 τοῦ ἀνθρωπίνου βίου τελευτήσω. Kr, *Spr.* 47, 13, 7; Kühn. 421, 3. — **μετ' αὐτοῦ**: *i.e.* τοῦ τελευτᾶν. See on c. 58. 8. — 20. **παυόμενοι λέγομεν ἤδη**: repeating the idea of the rel. clause, and more forcible than τοῦτο νῦν ποιοῦντες. — 21. **τῷ αἰσχίστῳ ὀλέθρῳ λιμῷ**: connected as θάνατον ζημίαν, c. 44. 10. See note there. *Cf.* Hom. μ 342 λιμῷ δ' οἴκτιστον θανέειν καὶ πότμον ἐπισπεῖν, Dion. H. *Ant.* vi. 86 τῷ κακίστῳ τῶν μόρων λιμῷ, Sall. *Ep. Pomp.* 1 fame, miserrima omnium morte, Liv. xxi. 41 ultimo supplicio humanorum, fame, xxvii. 44 fame et frigore, quae miserrima mortis genera sunt, Amm. Marcell. xvii. 9 fame ignavissimo mortis genere tabescentes. **αἴσχιστον**, *most shameful*, because manly resistance is impossible. *Cf.* App. *Hisp.* 97 τῷ λιμῷ σφᾶς κατεργαζομένους, ἀμάχῳ

σχίστῳ ὀλέθρῳ λιμῷ τελευτῆσαι), ὑμῖν δὲ πιστεύσαντες προσήλθομεν, καὶ δίκαιον, εἰ μὴ πείθομεν, ἐς τὰ αὐτὰ καταστήσαντας τὸν ξυντυχόντα κίνδυνον ἐᾶσαι ἡμᾶς αὐ-
25 τοὺς ἑλέσθαι. ἐπισκήπτομέν τε ἅμα μὴ Πλαταιῆς ὄντες 4 οἱ προθυμότατοι περὶ τοὺς Ἕλληνας γενόμενοι Θηβαίοις τοῖς ἡμῖν ἐχθίστοις ἐκ τῶν ὑμετέρων χειρῶν καὶ τῆς ὑμετέρας πίστεως ἱκέται ὄντες, ὦ Λακεδαιμόνιοι, παραδοθῆναι, γενέσθαι δὲ σωτῆρας ἡμῶν καὶ μὴ τοὺς ἄλλους
30 Ἕλληνας ἐλευθεροῦντας ἡμᾶς διολέσαι."
60 Τοιαῦτα μὲν οἱ Πλαταιῆς εἶπον. οἱ δὲ Θηβαῖοι 1 δείσαντες πρὸς τὸν λόγον αὐτῶν μὴ οἱ Λακεδαιμόνιοί τι

κακῷ. — **22.** ὑμῖν πιστεύσαντες : *cf.* 53. 2. — **23.** προσήλθομεν : *cf.* c. 52. 10 ὡς αὐτῶν ἑκόντων προσχωρησάντων, v. 17. 15 ὁμολογίᾳ αὐτῶν προσχωρησάντων. — ἐς τὰ αὐτὰ καταστήσαντας : *cf.* c. 34. 14. — **24.** τὸν ξυντυχόντα κίνδυνον : *the first danger that presents itself* (ὃς ἂν ξυντύχῃ, *fut. ex.*, Kr.). *Cf.* τοῖς ἐντυχοῦσιν ἐπιτρέπειν, iv. 132. 18 ; ἐκ τοῦ παρατυχόντος πυνθανόμενος, i. 22. 8. — ἐᾶσαι : *sc.* as subj. ὑμᾶς. **25.** ἐπισκήπτομέν τε ἅμα κτέ. : even after the last despairing request they cannot refrain from summing up once more in a solemn adjuration (ἐπισκήπτομεν, as in ii. 73. 13) all the grounds for mercy already advanced, and, with the appeal ὦ Λακεδαιμόνιοι, bringing these motives home to the consciences of the Lacedaemonians. 'The conclusion of the speech is confused with the accumulation of most passionate admonitions, ἐπισκήπτομέν τε ἅμα μή, 1) Πλαταιῆς ὄντες οἱ προθυμότατοι περὶ τοὺς Ἕλληνας γενόμενοι, 2) Θηβαίοις, 3) τοῖς ἡμῖν ἐχθίστοις, 4) ἐκ τῶν ὑμετέρων χειρῶν καὶ τῆς ὑμετέρας πίστεως, 5) ἱκέται ὄντες, ὦ Λακεδαιμόνιοι, παραδοθῆναι ... διολέσαι, where the anxiety and perplexity of the speaker are well depicted, and the minds of the readers greatly moved by the unusual position of the voc. (ὦ Λακεδαιμόνιοι), by the omission of the acc. ὑμᾶς with γενέσθαι, although ὑμᾶς would naturally be expressed since a different subj. immediately precedes, and by the two phrases ἐκ τῶν ὑμετέρων χειρῶν καὶ τῆς ὑμετέρας πίστεως.' Heilmann. — **26. οἱ προθυμότατοι** : as in c. 57. 18, of a disposition ready for any sacrifice. *Cf.* c. 56. 16; ii. 71. 18. — **Θηβαίοις τοῖς ἡμῖν ἐχθίστοις** : *cf.* ii. 71. 20. — **27. τῆς ὑμετέρας πίστεως** : *cf.* πιστεύσαντες ὑμῖν, l. 22 and c. 53. 2 ; διὰ πονηρῶν ἀνθρώπων πίστιν, vi. 53. 10. — **29. γενέσθαι δέ**: *sc.* ὑμᾶς, the abrupt change of subj. is induced by the address, ὦ Λακεδαιμόνιοι. *Cf.* i. 43. 4. — **τοὺς ἄλλους Ἕλληνας ἐλευθεροῦντας** : see on c. 13. 35 ; 32. 5.
60. *The Thebans ask permission to reply to the speech of the Plataeans.*
2. πρὸς τὸν λόγον : *in view of the*

ἐνδῶσι. παρελθόντες ἔφασαν καὶ αὐτοὶ βούλεσθαι εἰπεῖν, ἐπειδὴ καὶ ἐκείνοις παρὰ γνώμην τὴν αὐτῶν μα-
5 κρότερος λόγος ἐδόθη τῆς πρὸς τὸ ἐρώτημα ἀποκρίσεως.
ὡς δ' ἐκέλευσαν, ἔλεγον τοιάδε·

61 "Τοὺς μὲν λόγους οὐκ ἂν ᾐτησάμεθα εἰπεῖν, εἰ 1
καὶ αὐτοὶ βραχέως τὸ ἐρωτηθὲν ἀπεκρίναντο καὶ μὴ ἐπὶ
ἡμᾶς τραπόμενοι κατηγορίαν ἐποιήσαντο καὶ περὶ αὑτῶν

speech. *Cf.* πρὸς τὸ παρόν, c. 40. 35; ii. 22. 1; v. 9. 14. It belongs to δείσαντες. To connect it also with ἐνδῶσι, as Cl. does, is unnecessary, since ἐνδῶσι depends on δείσαντες. — 3. παρελθόντες : regularly used of orators coming forward to speak. *Cf.* i. 67. 16; 72. 15, etc. Ullrich's suggestion, προσελθόντες (*Beitr.* iii. 7), approved by Cl., is inappropriate, since the Thebans had attended the trial from the beginning. — εἰπεῖν : *i.e.* to make a set speech. *Cf.* 53. 10 λόγον ᾐτησάμεθα, 61. 1 τοὺς λόγους οὐκ ἂν ᾐτησάμεθα εἰπεῖν. — 4. γνώμην τὴν αὐτῶν : order as in c. 56. 3; 58. 14. — 6. ὡς ἐκέλευσαν : sc. the five Lacedaemonian judges. *Cf.* c. 52. 17.

REPLY OF THE THEBANS.
.c. 61-67.

61. *Since the Plataeans, instead of simply answering the question propounded, have in a lengthy speech attacked us and glorified themselves, we too must make a fuller statement.*

The Plataeans early renounced the Boeotian alliance and our hegemony, and placed themselves with hostile intent under the protection of Athens.

1. τοὺς λόγους : const. with εἰπεῖν. "These (lengthy) speeches," implying

the reluctance with which they have recourse to them. The effect of the art. seems to be similar to that of the appos. τοὺς πολλούς in i. 86. 1 τοὺς λόγους τοὺς πολλούς. *Cf.* c. 53. 10 λόγον ᾐτησάμεθα, and c. 60. 3 ἔφασαν καὶ αὐτοὶ βούλεσθαι εἰπεῖν. — 2. καὶ αὐτοί : *i.e.* οὗτοι καὶ αὐτοί, et isti. *Cf.* i. 50. 18; 51. 6. Hude (*Comm. Crit.* p. 106) suggests καὶ οὗτοι. But to refer καὶ αὐτοί . . . ἀπεκρίναντο to the Plataeans is not harder than in c. 60. 6 ὡς δ' ἐκέλευσαν, to understand the Lacedaemonians. — τὸ ἐρωτηθὲν ἀπεκρίναντο : 'such an acc. with ἀποκρίνεσθαι is not found elsewhere in Thuc., though freq. in Plato. This const. seems, however, to be confined to neut. prons. (τόδε, τοῦτο, etc.) and τὸ (τὰ) ἐρωτώμενον (a).' Bm. See Kr. *Spr.* 46, 6, 3; Matth. 409, 6. — 3. καὶ περὶ αὑτῶν . . . ἀπολογίαν : *and had not made concerning themselves a long defence aside from the question, and especially of points which were never charged.* As to the matter, *cf.* c. 52. 18 κατηγορία οὐδεμία προετέθη, and c. 53. 9 προκατηγορίας ἡμῶν οὐ προγεγενημένης. περὶ αὑτῶν opp. to ἐπὶ ἡμᾶς. With ἔξω τῶν προκειμένων (*i.e.* τὸ ἐρώτημα τὸ βραχύ, c. 54. 5) *cf.* ii. 65. 26 ἔξω τοῦ πολέμου, Dem. xviii. 9 τοῖς

ἔξω τῶν προκειμένων καὶ ἅμα οὐδὲ ᾐτιαμένων πολλὴν
5 τὴν ἀπολογίαν καὶ ἔπαινον ὧν οὐδεὶς ἐμέμψατο. νῦν δὲ
πρὸς μὲν τὰ ἀντειπεῖν δεῖ, τῶν δὲ ἔλεγχον ποιήσασθαι,
ἵνα μήτε ἡ ἡμετέρα αὐτοὺς κακία ὠφελῇ μήτε ἡ τούτων
δόξα, τὸ δ' ἀληθὲς περὶ ἀμφοτέρων ἀκούσαντες κρίνητε.

"Ἡμεῖς δὲ αὐτοῖς διάφοροι ἐγενόμεθα πρῶτον ὅτι 2
10 ἡμῶν κτισάντων Πλάταιαν ὕστερον τῆς ἄλλης Βοιωτίας
καὶ ἄλλα χωρία μετ' αὐτῆς, ἃ ξυμμίκτους ἀνθρώπους ἐξελά-
σαντες ἔσχομεν. οὐκ ἠξίουν οὗτοι, ὥσπερ ἐτάχθη τὸ πρῶ-

ἔξωθεν λόγοις. — **4. καὶ ἅμα**: not a simple copula, but, like ἄλλως τε καί, introducing an esp. important circumstance. See on i. 2. 8. — **ᾐτιαμένων**: pass. of dep. verb. II. 819 d; Kr. Spr. 39, 14, 3; Kühn. 377, 4 a. Cf. αἰτιαθείς, vi. 53. 14; viii. 68. 15. It depends on ἀπολογία, as ὧν upon ἔπαινον. Steup follows Cl. in connecting ᾐτιαμένων with αὐτῶν, though he suggests that ᾐτιαμένων may have been a slip of the copyist for ᾐτιαμένοι, due to the influence of the preceding genitives. πολλὴν τὴν ἀπολογίαν καὶ ἔπαινον he takes together (both limited by ὧν), about as οἱ αὐτοὶ ὅρκοι καὶ ξυμμαχία, i. 102. 21, comparing further vi. 49. 21 οὔτε πλοῦν πολὺν οὔτε ὁδόν, 92. 17 ἐς κίνδυνον καὶ ἐς ταλαιπωρίαν πᾶσαν, 97. 8 οὔτε πλοῦν οὔτε ὁδὸν πολλήν. — **6. πρὸς μὲν τά**: order as in c. 82. 52; vi. 45. 5; 66. 6; vii. 12. 4. Cf. Soph. Ant. 557 καλῶς σὺ μὲν τοῖς, τοῖς δ' ἐγώ 'δόκουν φρονεῖν. Kr. Spr. 50, 1, 13; Matth. 288, N. 3. τὰ μέν refers to κατηγορίαν (cf. c. 53. 9), τὰ δέ to τὴν ἀπολογίαν καὶ ἔπαινον. — **ἀντειπεῖν, ἔλεγχον ποιήσασθαι**: cf. c. 53. 9, 12. The former is done in c. 62, the latter in c. 63, 64. — **7. ἡ ἡμε-**
τέρα κακία: refers ironically (cf. c. 58. 6) to the effect of the κατηγορία, and ἡ τούτων (cf. l. 12 οὗτοι) δόξα to that of the ἀπολογία and of the ἔπαινος. — **αὐτούς**: for the position, cf. v. 82. 23; vii. 78. 26, and see on c. 63. 8.
9. ἡμεῖς δέ: the δέ marks the transition from the general introduction to the matter in hand, and should not be altered, with Kr., to δή either here or in i. 37. 7. See on c. 10. 7, and vi. 89. 3. — **διάφοροι ἐγενόμεθα πρῶτον**: (Mss. AC τὸ πρῶτον) as c. 10 7 ξυμμαχία ἐγένετο πρῶτον. — **10. ἡμῶν κτισάντων**: the Thebans substitute themselves for the Boeotians, who were driven out of Thessaly and occupied the country of the Cadmeans (afterwards called Boeotia), about sixty years after the Trojan war, acc. to Thuc. i. 12. § 3. Cf. Strabo ix. 2. 3 ff. See Muenscher, de Reb. Plataeens. p. 27 sqq. — **11. ἄλλα χωρία**: i.e. 'the region below Cithaeron toward the Euripus,' Muensch. ibid. p. 27. — **ἅ**: includes Plataea also. See Muensch. ibid. p. 29. — **ξυμμίκτους ἀνθρώπους**: Strabo l.c. mentions Pelasgians, Thracians, Hyantians. — **12. οὐκ ἠξίουν**: were indignant at.

τον, ἡγεμονεύεσθαι ὑφ' ἡμῶν, ἔξω δὲ τῶν ἄλλων Βοιωτῶν παραβαίνοντες τὰ πάτρια, ἐπειδὴ προσηναγκάζοντο, 15 προσεχώρησαν πρὸς Ἀθηναίους. καὶ μετ' αὐτῶν πολλὰ ἡμᾶς ἔβλαπτον, ἀνθ' ὧν καὶ ἀντέπασχον.

62 " Ἐπειδὴ δὲ καὶ ὁ βάρβαρος ἦλθεν ἐπὶ τὴν Ἑλλάδα, 1 φασὶ μόνοι Βοιωτῶν οὐ μηδίσαι, καὶ τούτῳ μάλιστα αὐτοί τε ἀγάλλονται καὶ ἡμᾶς λοιδοροῦσιν. ἡμεῖς δὲ μηδίσαι 2 μὲν αὐτοὺς οὐ φαμὲν διότι οὐδ' Ἀθηναίους, τῇ μέντοι 5 αὐτῇ ἰδέᾳ ὕστερον ἰόντων Ἀθηναίων ἐπὶ τοὺς Ἕλληνας μόνους αὖ Βοιωτῶν ἀττικίσαι. καίτοι σκέψασθε ἐν οἴῳ 3

Cf. i. 102. 17; iv. 86. 7. — **ὥσπερ ἐτάχθη τὸ πρῶτον**: prob. taken for granted, rather than based on historical tradition. — 13. **ἡγεμονεύεσθαι**: found only here in pass., a sort of milder ἄρχεσθαι (c. 36. 9; 37. 10; ii. 41. 11). G. 1236; H. 819a; Kr. *Spr.* 52, 4, 1; Kühn. 378, 7. — **ἔξω**: *apart from*. See on l. 4. — 14. **παραβαίνοντες τὰ πάτρια**: *i.e.* renouncing the Boeotian alliance. *Cf.* c. 65. 8; 66. 3; ii. 2. 27. — **προσηναγκάζοντο**: *were forced to it*, *i.e.* πρὸς τὸ μὴ παραβαίνειν τὰ πάτρια. *Cf.* iv. 87. 8; v. 42. 19; viii. 76. 32. For the strengthening force of πρός, see on i. 106. 2; vii. 18. 31. — 15. **προσεχώρησαν πρὸς Ἀθηναίους**: *cf.* c. 55. § 1. The simple dat. is more common, as in i. 74. 24; 103. 11; ii. 2. 29; v. 32. 14. — **μετ' αὐτῶν... ἔβλαπτον**: *cf.* Hdt. vi. 108. 5 πόνους ὑπὲρ αὐτῶν (*i.e.* τῶν Πλαταιέων) οἱ Ἀθηναῖοι συχνοὺς ἤδη ἀναιρέοντο.

62. *Only on account of their alliance with Athens did they oppose the Persians. We Thebans, however, were then under the rule of oligarchs,* *who expected advantage from the Persians. Afterwards at Coronea we won Boeotia's independence from Athens.*

1. **καί**: introduces the second point of consideration. — **ἦλθεν ἐπί**: as in l. 5; freq. of going to war. See on i. 78. 7. — 2. **μόνοι**: see on c. 54. 12. — 3. **λοιδοροῦσιν**: Schol. μηδίσαντας δηλονότι, which is implied in τούτῳ.
ἡμεῖς δέ... οὐ φαμέν: *but we say that they did not medize*. For the position of οὐ, which Cl. accents (οὔ) to show that it belongs to μηδίσαι αὐτούς, see Kr. *Spr.* 67, 1, 2. *Cf.* c. 64. 2. — 4. **Ἀθηναίους**: assimilated to the case of αὐτούς, as after ὥσπερ, i. 69. 2.3; v. 99. 4; vi. 68. 9, and, after a rel. pron., vii. 21. 14. — **τῇ αὐτῇ ἰδέᾳ**: *on the same principle*. *Cf.* vi. 76. 12. It belongs with μόνους ἀττικίσαι.

6. **ἐν οἵῳ εἴδει**: *i.e.* τρόπῳ πολιτείας, in quo statu. *Cf.* viii. 90. 2. ἰδέα and εἶδος are here contrasted as representing internal and external conditions, but the meaning common to both words, *form, appearance*, causes sometimes an interchange of use.

εἴδει ἑκάτεροι ἡμῶν τοῦτο ἔπραξαν. ἡμῖν μὲν γὰρ ἡ πόλις τότε ἐτύγχανεν οὔτε κατ' ὀλιγαρχίαν ἰσόνομον πολιτεύουσα οὔτε κατὰ δημοκρατίαν· ὅπερ δέ ἐστι νόμοις
10 μὲν καὶ τῷ σωφρονεστάτῳ ἐναντιώτατον, ἐγγυτάτω δὲ τυράννου, δυναστεία ὀλίγων ἀνδρῶν εἶχε τὰ πράγματα. καὶ οὗτοι ἰδίας δυνάμεις ἐλπίσαντες ἔτι μᾶλλον σχήσειν, 4 εἰ τὰ τοῦ Μήδου κρατήσειε, κατέχοντες ἰσχύι τὸ πλῆθος ἐπηγάγοντο αὐτόν. καὶ ἡ ξύμπασα πόλις οὔτ' αὐτοκράτωρ

Cf. i. 109. 2, where ἰδέα means *outward appearance;* vi. 77. 15; viii. 56. 7, where εἶδος means *mode of action.* οἷος in indir. ques., as i. 69. 12; vii. 64. 8. See on c. 47. 1. — **7. ἑκάτεροι ἡμῶν τοῦτο ἔπραξαν**: *i.e.* we sided with the Persians, they with the Athenians. *Cf.* l. 15. — **ἡμῖν μὲν κτέ.**: the remainder of the chapter contains the first part of the explanation announced in καίτοι σκέψασθε κτέ., c. 63, 64 the second. — **8. κατ' ὀλιγαρχίαν ἰσόνομον πολιτεύουσα**: the const. πολιτεύειν κατά, as in c. 66. 3; i. 19. 2. An oligarchy is meant, in which all the nobles were ὁμότιμοι or ὅμοιοι. *Cf.* Arist. *Pol.* iv. (vi.) 5, who likewise contrasts it with the δυναστεία. — **10. τῷ σωφρονεστάτῳ**: not (= τοῖς σώφροσιν ἀνδράσιν, Schol.), but the ideal of a well-ordered constitution (respublica optime constituta et temperata), to which is opposed, as the extreme of arbitrariness, the τύραννος. — **ἐγγυτάτω δὲ τυράννου κτέ.**: *cf.* Tac. *Ann.* vi. 42 paucorum dominatio regiae libidini propior est. Note the bold use of the concrete (τύραννος) for the abstract. — **11. δυναστεία ὀλίγων ἀνδρῶν**: *cf.* Arist. *Pol.* iv.

(vi.) 5 ὅταν ... ἀρχῃ μὴ ὁ νόμος, ἀλλ' οἱ ἄρχοντες ..., καλοῦσι δὴ τὴν τοιαύτην ὀλιγαρχίαν δυναστείαν. Hdt. (ix. 86. 4) names ἐν πρώτοισι τῶν μηδισάντων Timagenides and Attaginus. — **εἶχε τὰ πράγματα**: as c. 72. 3. *Cf.* ἔχειν τὴν πόλιν, viii. 66. 2; τὴν πολιτείαν, viii. 74. 14; τὴν ἀρχήν, viii. 46. 6; τὴν ἡγεμονίαν, v. 47. 41. See on c. 11. 11; 28. 1.

12. ἰδίας δυνάμεις ... σχήσειν: *expecting that they will win power of their own in still greater measure.* See Lupus, *N. Jahrbb.* cxi. p. 167. — **13. εἰ ... κρατήσειε**: *cf.* Hdt. iv. 137. — **κατέχοντες ἰσχύι τὸ πλῆθος**: *cf.* the reverse in ii. 65. 33 κατεῖχε τὸ πλῆθος ἐλευθέρως. ἰσχύς of brute force, as in c. 39. 20; i. 76. 15. On the matter, *cf.* Plut. *Aristid.* 18. — **14. ἐπηγάγοντο**: the verb is regularly used of inviting strangers into one's country. *Cf.* i. 3. 8; 104. 5; 114. 6; ii. 2. 12; Plato *Menex.* 243 b. — **καὶ ἡ ξύμπασα πόλις οὔτ' αὐτοκράτωρ ... ἔπραξεν, οὔτ' ἄξιον κτέ.**: the vulg. is οὐκ αὐτοκράτωρ and οὐδ' ἄξιον. But the second clause must be a formal antithesis to the first, unless the speakers, in turning from the authorities to the *state* of Thebes, take into

15 οὖσα ἑαυτῆς τοῦτ' ἔπραξεν, οὔτ' ἄξιον αὐτῇ ὀνειδίσαι
ὧν μὴ μετὰ νόμων ἥμαρτεν. ἐπειδὴ γοῦν ὅ τε Μῆδος
ἀπῆλθε καὶ τοὺς νόμους ἔλαβε, σκέψασθαι χρή, Ἀθηναίων
ὕστερον ἐπιόντων τήν τε ἄλλην Ἑλλάδα καὶ τὴν ἡμετέραν χώραν πειρωμένων ὑφ' αὑτοῖς ποιεῖσθαι καὶ κατὰ
20 στάσιν ἤδη ἐχόντων αὐτῆς τὰ πολλὰ εἰ μαχόμενοι ἐν
Κορωνείᾳ καὶ νικήσαντες αὐτοὺς ἠλευθερώσαμεν τὴν
Βοιωτίαν καὶ τοὺς ἄλλους νῦν προθύμως ξυνελευθεροῦμεν,
ἵππους τε παρέχοντες καὶ παρασκευὴν ὅσην οὐκ ἄλλοι
τῶν ξυμμάχων.

consideration along with the facts also the decision, *i.e.* pass to something new. Cobet conjectures (*Mnem. N. S.* viii. p. 140), καὶ οὐχ ἡ ξύμπασα πόλις αὐτοκράτωρ ... οὐδ' ἄξιον κτέ. But this is inadmissible, since ὧν μὴ μετὰ νόμων ἥμαρτεν requires a positive subject (ἡ ξύμπασα πόλις). — **15. τοῦτ' ἔπραξεν**: *i.e.* took the side of the Persians — a mild way of referring to their shameful conduct. As to the matter, see Plutarch's apology for the Thebans, *de Malig. Herod.* 31. 3. — **16. ὧν**: *i.e.* τούτων ἅ. The gen. with ὀνειδίσαι is rare. In Hdt. i. 90. 16 τούτου ὀνειδίσαι, Stein writes τοῦτο. G. 1126; H. 744; Kr. *Spr.* 47, 21; Matth. 368. — **μὴ μετὰ νόμων**: *i.e.* ἄνευ νόμων. *Cf.* c. 40. 30 μὴ ξὺν ἀνάγκῃ. For the effect of the neg., see on i. 91. 28; 141. 24. Kr. *Spr.* 67, 9 and 10, 4.
17. τοὺς νόμους ἔλαβε: *sc.* ἡ πόλις, *received its own laws, i.e.* a constitution based on laws. *Cf.* c. 64. 11. —
18. ἐπιόντων τήν τε ἄλλην ... τὰ πολλά: the particles. πειρωμένων and ἐχόντων are both subord. to and ex-

planatory of ἐπιόντων. Steup thinks there is a slight anacoluthon, comparing c. 67. 24; 86. 16; ii. 46. 1. — **19. κατὰ στάσιν ... τὰ πολλά**: after the battle at Oenophyta, 458 B.C. *Cf.* i. 108. § 2, 3. For κατὰ στάσιν, see on c. 2. 10. — **20. εἰ**: in indir. ques., as ii. 53. 10. G. 1605; H. 1016; Kr. *Spr.* 65, 1, 8. — **μαχόμενοι**: see on c. 113. 13. — **ἐν Κορωνείᾳ**: 446 B.C. *Cf.* i. 113. § 2. — **21. ἠλευθερώσαμεν ... ξυνελευθεροῦμεν**: corresponds chiastically to l. 18 above. — **22. προθύμως ξυνελευθεροῦμεν**: προθύμως, which, with its cognate forms, is used everywhere by Thuc. of a self-sacrificing spirit (*cf.* c. 57. 18; i. 74. 5), is here put into the mouths of the Thebans in order to indicate their hypocritical self-satisfaction. In like manner, ξυνελευθεροῦμεν (*cf.* c. 13. 10; ii. 72. 4) also claims a share in the doubtful Spartan boast of being the liberators of Greece (see on c. 13. 35; 32. 5; 59. 30). — **23. ἵππους τε παρέχοντες καὶ παρασκευὴν κτέ.**: *cf.* ii. 100. 7 ἵπποις καὶ ὅπλοις καὶ τῇ ἄλλῃ παρασκευῇ. — **ἵππους παρέχοντες**: Thuc. uses the

25   "Καὶ τὰ μὲν ἐς τὸν μηδισμὸν τοσαῦτα ἀπολογού-
63 μεθα. ὡς δὲ ὑμεῖς μᾶλλόν τε ἠδικήκατε τοὺς Ἕλληνας
καὶ ἀξιώτεροί ἐστε πάσης ζημίας, πειρασόμεθα ἀποφαίνειν. ἐγένεσθε ἐπὶ τῇ ἡμετέρᾳ τιμωρίᾳ, ὥς φατέ,
Ἀθηναίων ξύμμαχοι καὶ πολῖται. οὐκοῦν χρῆν τὰ πρὸς
5 ἡμᾶς μόνον ὑμᾶς ἐπάγεσθαι αὐτοὺς καὶ μὴ ξυνεπιέναι
μετ' αὐτῶν ἄλλοις, ὑπάρχον γε ὑμῖν, εἴ τι καὶ ἄκοντες
προσήγεσθε ὑπ' Ἀθηναίων, τῆς τῶν Λακεδαιμονίων
τῶνδε ἤδη ἐπὶ τῷ Μήδῳ ξυμμαχίας γεγενημένης, ἣν αὐ-

mid. παρέχεσθαί τι, or the act. παρέχειν τι, according as stress is to be laid on the part of the performer or upon the value and extent of the performance, — the mid. twenty-nine times, the act. ninety-one times. See on ii. 9. 9. For the cavalry of the Boeotians, cf. ii. 9. 11; 12. 18; 22. 11. The matter is mentioned here with a view to its effect on the Lacedaemonian judges. — 25. καὶ τὰ μὲν ... ἀπολογούμεθα: cf. c. 64. 20.

63. You Plataeans have misused your alliance with the Athenians by sharing in all their deeds of violence against other Hellenes, thereby voluntarily incurring a heavy burden of guilt.

1. ὡς δὲ ὑμεῖς κτέ.: beginning of the second part of the explanation announced c. 62. 6. From here to the end of c. 66 the Plataeans are directly addressed. — μᾶλλον ἠδικήκατε τοὺς Ἕλληνας: cf. c. 56. 1. — **2.** ἀξιώτεροι: i.e. μᾶλλον ἄξιοι. "You rather than we are worthy of every penalty." Cf. i. 122. 11.

3. ἐγένεσθε: the asyndeton shows the earnestness of the speaker. —

ἐπὶ τῇ ἡμετέρᾳ τιμωρίᾳ: for our punishment, i.e. for your protection against us. Cf. ii. 42. 17; vi. 76. 15. ἡμετέρᾳ stands for the obj. gen. — ὥς φατέ: c. 55. § 1. — **4.** πολῖται: see on c. 55. 12. — οὐκοῦν κτέ.: Cl. writes οὐκ οὖν, and makes the sent. (ending with προβάλλεσθε) a question. — τὰ πρὸς ἡμᾶς μόνον: only in that which pertains to us, i.e. only against us. — **5.** αὐτούς: i.e. τοὺς Ἀθηναίους. — **6.** ὑπάρχον γε ὑμῖν: when it was certainly open to you, sc. μὴ ξυνεπιέναι. ὑπάρχειν in this sense also c. 109. 20; i. 82. 26; vii. 63. 6. See on i. 124. 1. For the acc. abs., see GMT. 851; H. 973. — ἄκοντες προσήγεσθε: = ἠναγκάζεσθε, as ii. 89. 14. Cf. vi. 54. 13 βίᾳ προσαγάγηται. — **7.** τῶν Λακεδαιμονίων τῶνδε: the art. preceding the dem. τῶνδε is unusual, but prob. the pron. was added with esp. reference to the judges. Kr. Spr. 50, 11, 19. — **8.** ἤδη ἐπὶ τῷ Μήδῳ: placed before ξυμμαχίας, as αὐτούς before κακία in c. 61. 7. ἐπὶ τῷ Μήδῳ, as in c. 13. 18; i. 102. 19, in hostile sense, for the more usual acc. Kühn. 438, ii. d. This const. with the dat. is the rule in epic, and is freq. also in Attic

τοὶ μάλιστα προβάλλεσθε· ἱκανή γε ἦν ἡμᾶς τε ὑμῶν
10 ἀποτρέπειν καί, τὸ μέγιστον, ἀδεῶς παρέχειν βουλεύεσθαι. ἀλλ' ἑκόντες καὶ οὐ βιαζόμενοι ἔτι εἵλεσθε μᾶλλον τὰ Ἀθηναίων. καὶ λέγετε ὡς αἰσχρὸν ἦν προδοῦναι 3
τοὺς εὐεργέτας· πολὺ δέ γε αἴσχιον καὶ ἀδικώτερον τοὺς
πάντας Ἕλληνας καταπροδοῦναι, οἷς ξυνωμόσατε, ἢ
15 Ἀθηναίους μόνους, τοὺς μὲν καταδουλουμένους τὴν
Ἑλλάδα, τοὺς δὲ ἐλευθεροῦντας. καὶ οὐκ ἴσην αὐτοῖς 4
τὴν χάριν ἀνταπέδοτε οὐδὲ αἰσχύνης ἀπηλλαγμένην.
ὑμεῖς μὲν γὰρ ἀδικούμενοι αὐτούς, ὡς φατέ, ἐπηγάγεσθε,
τοῖς δὲ ἀδικοῦσιν ἄλλους ξυνεργοὶ κατέστητε· καίτοι τὰς

poets. — 9. **προβάλλεσθε**: put forward as a cloak. Cf. i. 37. 16; ii. 87. 14. On the matter, cf. esp. c. 58. § 1; iv. 59. § 2. — **ἱκανή γε**: the asyndeton is justified by the order of the words. See on c. 37. 10. St. explains, 'Particula γε sententias iungit hic et i. 40. 15; 70. 6; vi. 86. 8.' Kr. proposes, after Reiske and Va., ἢ ἱκανή γε, or ἱκανήν γε ἡμᾶς. — 10. **ἀποτρέπειν**: as c. 39. 1, doubtless only in the mild sense of restrain, not ward off. — **τὸ μέγιστον**: what is most important. Appos. to the inf. clause. II. 626 b; Kr. Spr. 57, 10, 12. See on i. 142. 1. — **παρέχειν**: sc. ὑμῖν. — 11. **οὐ βιαζόμενοι κτέ.**: in answer to c. 55. 3 ὅτε Θηβαῖοι ἡμᾶς ἐβιάσαντο. — **εἵλεσθε ... τὰ Ἀθηναίων**: cf. c. 56. 23. The formula is similar to φρονεῖν τά τινος, c. 68. 17; βούλεσθαι τά τινος, vi. 50. 12.

12. **καὶ λέγετε**: cf. c. 55. § 3. — **αἰσχρόν, αἴσχιον**: as in ii. 40. 4. — 14. **καταπροδοῦναι**: κατα- with intensive force, as in c. 109. 18; i. 86. 19; iv. 10. 10; vii. 48. 26; and κατα-

δουλουμένους below. — **οἷς ξυνωμόσατε**: i.e. πρὸς οὓς ξυμμαχίαν ἐποιήσασθε. Cf. c. 64. 7, 10; i. 71. 23; ii. 72. 5; 74. 11. — 15. **τοὺς μὲν καταδουλουμένους, τοὺς δὲ ἐλευθεροῦντας**: joined chiastically to the preceding. — 16. **τοὺς δὲ ἐλευθεροῦντας**: as in i. 124. 19 Corinthian speakers address to the representatives of the Peloponnesian alliance the words, τοὺς νῦν δεδουλωμένους Ἕλληνας ἐλευθερώσωμεν, so here the whole Peloponnesian alliance, not merely the ἡγεμόνες, are represented as the liberators of Greece.

οὐκ ἴσην τὴν χάριν: the order and effect as in c. 30. 4 **πολὺ τὸ ἀφύλακτον**, i. 34. 10 ἐλαχίστας τὰς μεταμελείας, the pred. adj. supplying the place of an adverb. — 19. **τοῖς δέ**: sc. τοῖς Ἀθηναίοις, ἀδικοῦσιν ἄλλους being pred. Jow. takes τοῖς ἀδικοῦσιν together in a general sense, wrongdoers, on the ground that τοῖς δέ as dem. would introduce an opposition between it and αὐτούς, while both really refer to the same persons. — **καίτοι τὰς ὁμοίας κτέ.**: "and indeed it

20 ὁμοίας χάριτας μὴ ἀντιδιδόναι αἰσχρὸν μᾶλλον ἢ τὰς μετὰ δικαιοσύνης μὲν ὀφειληθείσας, ἐς ἀδικίαν δὲ ἀποδιδομένας.

64 "Δῆλόν τε ἐποιήσατε οὐδὲ τότε τῶν Ἑλλήνων 1 ἕνεκα μόνοι οὐ μηδίσαντες, ἀλλ' ὅτι οὐδ' Ἀθηναῖοι, ἡμεῖς δέ, τοῖς μὲν ταὐτὰ βουλόμενοι ποιεῖν, τοῖς δὲ τἀναντία. καὶ νῦν ἀξιοῦτε, ἀφ' ὧν δι' ἑτέρους ἐγένεσθε 2

is a shame to refuse to repay favours with like favours, not however to omit the repayment of favours which, though justly due, cannot be returned without injustice." *Cf.* Cic. *de Off.* i. 15. 48 non reddere bono non licet, modo id facere possit sine iniuria. — καίτοι: as in c. 39. 13; ii. 39. 19. — 20. μὴ ἀντιδιδόναι: *cf.* i. 41. 4. The words are to be supplied in the second clause. — μᾶλλον ἤ: as in c. 37. 12; 64. 9, completely subordinates the second member, so that αἰσχρόν applies only to the first. — 21. ὀφειληθείσας, ἀποδιδομένας: the change of time corresponds to the service already rendered and the still doubtful requital. The whole sentence serves to substantiate the words οὐδὲ αἰσχύνης ἀπηλλαγμένην (l. 17), the charge τὰς ὁμοίας χάριτας μὴ ἀντιδιδόναι being, according to the Theban speakers, applicable to the Plataeans. — ἐς ἀδικίαν: *cf.* c. 37. 7; ii. 40. 22.

64. *You have, therefore, no right on your earlier alliance with the Hellenes to base claims which you have forfeited by later conduct, that reveals your real sentiments.*

1. δηλόν τε ἐποιήσατε κτέ.: *and so you showed that not even then was it for the sake of the Hellenes that you*

did not medize, but because the Athenians did not and we did, since you preferred to act with them and to oppose us. So St. and Cl., who adopt ἡμεῖς (sc. ἐμηδίσαμεν), the reading of several of the best Mss., for ὑμεῖς, and put a comma after ἡμεῖς δέ. *Cf.* Plato *Rep.* 422 d οὐδ' ἡμῖν θέμις, ὑμῖν δέ. The other editt. all retain the vulg. ὑμεῖς, which must be explained as a repetition on account of the intervening Ἀθηναῖοι. If ὑμεῖς be read, supply οὐκ ἐμηδίσατε (Arn., Kr.), or οὐ μηδίσαντες (Bm.). The general sense is clear, "only attachment for Athens and hatred of us are the motives of your boasted patriotism." *Cf.* c. 62. § 2. — 2. μηδίσαντες: const. with δῆλον ἐποιήσατε. *Cf.* c. 84. 12; i. 21. 12; ii. 50. 4; Hdt. vi. 21. 8, and see on c. 40. 37. GMT. 904; H. 981; Kühn. 482, 2. — ὅτι οὐδ' Ἀθηναῖοι: sc. ἐμήδισαν. *Cf.* App. *Bell. Civ.* i. 121 τὸν στρατὸν οὐ μεθίει, διότι μηδὲ Πομπήιος. — 3. τοῖς μέν: i.e. the Athenians. — τοῖς δέ: i.e. the Thebans.

4. ἀφ' ὧν: this alone (=ἀπὸ τούτων ἅ) would have been grammatically sufficient. For the epanaleptic dem., notwithstanding the assimilation, see Kr. *Spr.* 51, 11, 2; Kühn. 555, N. 1. *Cf.* Dem. viii. 23 καὶ περὶ ὧν φασι μέλλειν αὐτὸν ποιεῖν, καὶ περὶ

5 ἀγαθοί, ἀπὸ τούτων ὠφελεῖσθαι. ἀλλ' οὐκ εἰκός· ὥσπερ δὲ Ἀθηναίους εἵλεσθε, τούτοις ξυναγωνίζεσθε. καὶ μὴ προφέρετε τὴν τότε γενομένην ξυνωμοσίαν ὡς χρὴ ἀπ' αὐτῆς νῦν σῴζεσθαι. ἀπελίπετε γὰρ αὐτὴν καὶ παρα- 3
βάντες ξυγκατεδουλοῦσθε μᾶλλον Αἰγινήτας καὶ ἄλλους
10 τινὰς τῶν ξυνομοσάντων ἢ διεκωλύετε, καὶ ταῦτα οὔτε ἄκοντες ἔχοντές τε τοὺς νόμους οὕσπερ μέχρι τοῦ δεῦρο καὶ οὐδενὸς ὑμᾶς βιασαμένου, ὥσπερ ἡμᾶς. τὴν τελευταίαν τε πρὶν περιτειχίζεσθαι πρόκλησιν ἐς ἡσυχίαν ὑμῶν, ὥστε μηδ' ἑτέροις ἀμύνειν, οὐκ ἐδέχεσθε. τίνες 4
15 ἂν οὖν ὑμῶν δικαιότερον πᾶσι τοῖς Ἕλλησι μισοῖντο, οἵτινες ἐπὶ τῷ ἐκείνων κακῷ ἀνδραγαθίαν προύθεσθε;

τούτων προκατηγορούντων ἀκροᾶσθε, ibid. 26 ἀφ' ὧν... δανείζεται, ἀπὸ τούτων διάγει. — δι' ἑτέρους : i.e. τοὺς Ἀθηναίους, whereby the merit of ἐγένεσθε ἀγαθοί is annulled. — 5. ἀπὸ τούτων : *from that source*, mockingly added to indicate the groundlessness of the claim. *Cf.* l. 7, and see on c. 36. 12; 48. 3. — 6. εἵλεσθε : *cf.* c. 56. 23; 63. 11. — τούτοις ξυναγωνίζεσθε : *continue as allies with them*. — 7. προφέρετε : as the mid., c. 59. 11. As to the matter, *cf.* c. 57. § 4; 58. § 1; 59. § 2. — τότε : often used of a time assumed to be well known. See on i. 101. 8. — ξυνωμοσίαν : of an alliance also v. 83. 16. *Cf.* l. 10 and c. 63. 14.
8. ἀπελίπετε : *cf.* c. 9. 3. — 9. μᾶλλον : see on c. 37. 12; 63. 20. — Αἰγινήτας : *cf.* i. 105; 108; ii. 27. — ἄλλους τινάς : it cannot be certainly determined who are meant. Pp. thinks the Euboeans, and possibly the Naxians (i. 98). — 10. ξυνομοσάντων : see on c. 63. 14. — διεκωλύετε : *sc.* τὸ ἑτέρους καταδουλοῦσθαι αὐτούς. — 11.

τοὺς νόμους : as in 62. 17. From this it may perhaps be inferred that the Plataeans even at the time of the Aeginetan war had a popular form of government. See Muenscher, p. 78 ff. — μέχρι τοῦ δεῦρο : elsewhere μέχρι δεῦρο. See Kr. *Spr.* 66, 1, 4. — 12. ὥσπερ ἡμᾶς : *cf.* c. 62. § 3, 4. — τὴν τελευταίαν τε... ἀμύνειν : exactly the demand made by Archidamus, ii. 72. 10 (*cf.* c. 68. 6); hence ὑμῶν (obj. gen.) is to be preferred to ἡμῶν (of most Mss.), since the Thebans did not make the proclamation.
15. οὖν : wanting in most of the best Mss., but the asyndeton would be harsh, and οὖν has not infreq. dropped out after ἄν. — τοῖς Ἕλλησι : dat. of agent with the pass., as in c. 70. 4; 82. 45; 85. 10; i. 44. 7; 51. 3; ii. 35. 17; 41. 12; 77. 7; 101. 17; 102. 33; iv. 109. 10; vi. 2. 5; and see Steup, *Thuk. Stud.* ii. p. 55 f. G. 1186, 1187; H. 769. — 16. οἵτινες : refers to ὑμῶν. ὅστις, esp. used in reproach or praise. *Cf.* Soph. *Aj.*

καὶ ἃ μέν ποτε χρηστοὶ ἐγένεσθε, ὡς φατέ, οὐ προσήκοντα
νῦν ἐπεδείξατε, ἃ δὲ ἡ φύσις αἰεὶ ἐβούλετο, ἐξηλέγχθη
ἐς τὸ ἀληθές· μετὰ γὰρ Ἀθηναίων ἄδικον ὁδὸν ἰόντων
20 ἐχωρήσατε.

" Τὰ μὲν οὖν ἐς τὸν ἡμέτερόν τε ἀκούσιον μηδισμὸν 5
καὶ τὸν ὑμέτερον ἑκούσιον ἀττικισμὸν τοιαῦτα ἀποφαί-
65 νομεν. ἃ δὲ τελευταῖά φατε ἀδικηθῆναι (παρανόμως 1
γὰρ ἐλθεῖν ἡμᾶς ἐν σπονδαῖς καὶ ἱερομηνίᾳ ἐπὶ τὴν
ὑμετέραν πόλιν), οὐ νομίζομεν οὐδ' ἐν τούτοις ὑμῶν
μᾶλλον ἁμαρτεῖν. εἰ μὲν γὰρ ἡμεῖς αὐτοὶ πρός τε τὴν 2

1055; El. 587; Ant. 696. — ἀνδραγαθίαν: cf. c. 53. § 4; 55. § 3; 56. § 6;
57. § 1. — προύθεσθε : displayed. Cf.
viii. 85. 20. — 17. ἃ χρηστοὶ ἐγένεσθε :
cf. c. 67. 26 ὧν πρόθυμοι γεγενήμεθα. —
ὡς φατέ : cf. c. 54. § 3, 4. — οὐ προσήκοντα νῦν ἐπεδείξατε : you have now
shown not to belong to you. προσ-
ήκων, as in c. 67. 7 ; ii. 61. 20; 89. 7 ;
iv. 92. 35. In support of ἐπεδείξατε,
meaning show, prove, St. cites Dem.
xxi. 7 ἐὰν ἐπιδείξω Μειδίαν τουτονὶ...
ὑβρικότα, Plato Rep. 391 e ἐπεδείξαμεν
γάρ που, ὅτι ἐκ θεῶν κακὰ γίγνεσθαι
ἀδύνατον. But Steup maintains that,
acc. to Thuc.'s usage, this idea would
have to be expressed either by the
simple verb ἐδείξατε (cf. iv. 73. 8;
v. 9. 40; 72. 10, and with ὅτι, i. 143.
32; iv. 92. 39; vi. 77. 8; vii. 63. 21),
or by ἀπεδείξατε, as Cl. wrote (cf. i.
6. 23; 25. 8; ii. 62. 3). He renders
ἐπεδείξατε, showed afterwards, comparing ἐπικατάγεται, c. 49. 18; ἐπιγνῶναι, c. 57. 6; ἐπιμαθών, i. 138. 13.
In Thuc. ἐπιδεικνύναι occurs (outside
of the documentary v. 77. 19, where
it means lay before, communicate)
certainly only twice, vi. 46. 13; 47. 8,

meaning exhibit, display. In i. 26. 13
it is a doubtful reading, meaning
point to. — 19. ἐς τὸ ἀληθές: this
adv. phrase seems to occur only here,
though Bl. compares Isa. xlii. 3 εἰς
ἀληθῆ. Cf. ἐς τὸ φανερόν, i. 6. 17;
23. 26; ἐς τὸ ἀκριβές, vi. 82. 15. —
ἄδικον ὁδὸν ἰόντων : for the acc.,
see G. 1057. Cf. Soph. O. R. 67
πολλὰς δ' ὁδοὺς ἐλθόντα φροντίδος πλά-
νοις. — 22. τὰ μὲν οὖν . . . ἀποφαίνο-
μεν: cf. c. 62. 25.

65. We undertook to surprise your
city at the call of prominent men
among you, who wished to bring you
back into the Boeotian alliance, where
you naturally and rightly belonged.

1. ἃ δὲ τελευταῖά φατε κτέ.: cf. c.
56. § 1, 2. — 2. ἱερομηνίᾳ : the sing.
as in c. 56. 4, adopted by Cl., St.,
Bm., following Meineke (Hermes iii.
p. 364) and v. H. (Stud. Thuc. p. 46),
for the pl. of all the Mss. The pl. is
due to a slip of the pen after σπονδαῖς,
as in v. 27. 2 αἱ ξυμμαχίαι after αἱ
σπονδαί. Arn. thinks the pl. indicates
that the festival lasted several days.

4. εἰ μὲν . . . ἐμαχόμεθα . . . ἐδηοῦ-
μεν : represented as a possible case,

5 πόλιν ἐλθόντες ἐμαχόμεθα καὶ τὴν γῆν ἐδῃοῦμεν ὡς πολέμιοι, ἀδικοῦμεν· εἰ δὲ ἄνδρες ὑμῶν οἱ πρῶτοι καὶ χρήμασι καὶ γένει, βουλόμενοι τῆς μὲν ἔξω ξυμμαχίας ὑμᾶς παῦσαι, ἐς δὲ τὰ κοινὰ τῶν πάντων Βοιωτῶν πάτρια καταστῆσαι, ἐπεκαλέσαντο ἑκόντες, τί ἀδικοῦμεν;
10 οἱ γὰρ ἄγοντες παρανομοῦσι μᾶλλον τῶν ἑπομένων. ἀλλ᾽ οὔτ᾽ ἐκεῖνοι, ὡς ἡμεῖς κρίνομεν, οὔθ᾽ ἡμεῖς· πολῖ- 3 ται δὲ ὄντες ὥσπερ ὑμεῖς καὶ πλείω παραβαλλόμενοι, τὸ ἑαυτῶν τεῖχος ἀνοίξαντες καὶ ἐς τὴν αὐτῶν πόλιν φιλίους, οὐ πολεμίους κομίσαντες, ἐβούλοντο τούς τε ὑμῶν χείρους

as opp. to εἰ δὲ ... ἐπεκαλέσαντο, which introduces the real case in hypothetical form. αὐτοί, nostra sponte. *Cf.* iv. 60. 11. — **6. ἀδικοῦμεν**: for the pf. force, see GMT. 27; Kr. *Spr.* 53, 1, 3. — **εἰ δὲ ἄνδρες κτέ.**: *cf.* ii. 2. § 2. — **7. τῆς ἔξω ξυμμαχίας**: of the alliance with a foreign, non-Boeotian state. — **8. ἐς τὰ κοινὰ ... καταστῆσαι**: *cf.* c. 34. 14; 59. 23; also iv. 74. 16 ἐς ὀλιγαρχίαν τὰ μάλιστα κατέστησαν τὴν πόλιν, v. 81. 6 τὰ ἐν Σικυῶνι ἐς ὀλίγους μᾶλλον κατέστησαν. — **τὰ κοινὰ ... πάτρια**: τὰ πάτρια, as in c. 61. 14; 66.3; ii. 2. 27. κοινά strengthens τῶν πάντων Βοιωτῶν. *Cf.* iv. 78. 19 ἄνευ τοῦ πάντων κοινοῦ. — **10. οἱ γὰρ ἄγοντες κτέ.**: parody on c. 55. § 4.
11. ὡς ἡμεῖς κρίνομεν: *cf.* ὡς ἐγὼ κρίνω, iv. 60. 3. — **12. πλείω παραβαλλόμενοι**: because they were the richest and most prominent. As to παραβάλλεσθαι, see on c. 14. 5, and *cf.* Xen. *Cyrop.* ii. 3. 11 οὐκ ἴσα παραβάλλεσθαι. — **τὸ ἑαυτῶν τεῖχος ... τὴν αὐτῶν πόλιν**: the repetition emphasizes the idea that the city belonged to the oligarchs as much as to the demos. — **13. φιλίους, οὐ πολεμίους**: so Steup (see *Qu. Thuc.* p. 34) emends the reading of the Mss. φιλίως, οὐ πολεμίως ("with friendly, not with hostile intent"). His grounds are, viz.: not only does κομίσαντες require an obj., but it was necessary to be said here of those admitted into the city, that they were not enemies of Plataea; for it was an important point in this attempt to justify the action of the boeotizing Plataeans that at the time under consideration a state of hostilities did not exist between Thebes and Plataea. Besides, the terms used cannot be applied to the relations of citizens to their own state. Since the reference is to persons, φίλους, it is true, not φιλίους, was to be expected, acc. to Thuc.'s usage; but in c. 58. 22 ἐν γῇ τε φιλίᾳ καὶ παρ᾽ ἀνδράσι τοιούτοις, it is generally agreed that τοιούτοις represents φιλίοις. Hude (*Comm. Crit.* p. 108), who adopts Steup's conjecture, cites also Plato *Symp.* 221 b; Dem. xxiii. 56. — **14. κομίσαντες**: as in viii. 57.

15 μηκέτι μᾶλλον γενέσθαι, τούς τε ἀμείνους τὰ ἄξια ἔχειν, σωφρονισταὶ ὄντες τῆς γνώμης καὶ τῶν σωμάτων τὴν πόλιν οὐκ ἀλλοτριοῦντες, ἀλλ' ἐς τὴν ξυγγένειαν οἰκειοῦντες, ἐχθροὺς οὐδενὶ καθιστάντες, ἅπασι δ' ὁμοίως ἐνσπόνδους.

66   "Τεκμήριον δὲ ὡς οὐ πολεμίως ἐπράσσομεν · οὔτε 1 γὰρ ἠδικήσαμεν οὐδένα, προείπομέν τε τὸν βουλόμενον κατὰ τὰ πάντων Βοιωτῶν πάτρια πολιτεύειν ἰέναι

3. — τοὺς ὑμῶν χείρους : part. gen. in attrib. position. G. 965; H. 730 d. See on c. 22. 26. — 15. μηκέτι μᾶλλον : sc. χείρους. But since the adj. is not repeated, it is the positive that is really had in mind. — 16. σωφρονισταί: *regulators*, or moderators, as in vi. 87. 11; viii. 48. 43. *Cf.* Plato *Rep.* 471 a εὐμενῶς σωφρονοῦσιν, οὐκ ἐπὶ δουλείᾳ κολάζοντες, οὐδ' ἐπ' ὀλέθρῳ, σωφρονισταὶ ὄντες, οὐ πολέμιοι. The intrinsic falseness of the party attitude here maintained, Thucydides doubtless intended to intimate by the unusual forms of expression. — τῶν σωμάτων τὴν πόλιν οὐκ ἀλλοτριοῦντες : chiastically arranged with reference to the preceding. τὰ σώματα, *their persons*, is here contrasted with ἡ γνώμη, as in i. 70. 19. ἀλλοτριοῦντες, *depriving*, chosen prob. on acc. of the antithesis to οἰκειοῦντες (*cf.* c. 13. 22; i. 36. 10; 70. 19; 78. 2), the natural expression being τὴν πόλιν τῶν σωμάτων ἀποστεροῦντες. Kühn. 421, 3.   Abresch compares Sirach xi. 35 ἀπαλλοτριώσει σε τῶν ἰδίων σου. — 17. ἐς τὴν ξυγγένειαν οἰκειοῦντες : "bringing them back into a natural union with their own kindred." *Cf.* l. 8 above, ἐς τὰ κοινὰ ... πάτρια κατα-

στῆσαι. — 18. καθιστάντες : sc. ὑμᾶς. But Steup objects that, as the Plataeans were already ἅπασιν ἔνσπονδοι, ἐχθροὺς οὐδενί must refer to the Thebans admitted into the city, and would understand ἐς τὴν πόλιν with καθιστάντες (*cf.* iv. 78. 35; 103. 16).

66. *You, however, when you discovered how small was the number of the Thebans, treacherously and cruelly took vengeance on them; so that even for this alone you deserve punishment.*

1. τεκμήριον δέ ... γάρ : as in ii. 15. 19; 39. 10; without γάρ in ii. 50. 7. See on i. 8. 3. — ὡς οὐ πολεμίως ἐπράσσομεν : bracketed by St. and v. H., following Meineke (*Hermes* iii. p. 365), on the ground that τεκμήριον refers to what immediately precedes, ἐχθροὺς οὐδενὶ καθιστάντες, ἅπασι δ' ὁμοίως ἐνσπόνδους. But there the reference is to the attitude of the traitorous party in Plataea, here to the Thebans again, esp. to the idea expressed in c. 65. 4 εἰ μὲν ... πολέμιοι. Besides, the sent. οὔτε γὰρ ἠδικήσαμεν κτέ. would not answer for a proof of the concluding words of c. 65 ἐχθροὺς ... ἐνσπόνδους. — οὔτε γὰρ κτέ.: *cf.* ii. 2. — 3. τὰ πάντων Βοιωτῶν πάτρια : Hude (*Comm. Crit.* p.

πρὸς ἡμᾶς. καὶ ὑμεῖς ἄσμενοι χωρήσαντες καὶ ξύμβασιν 2
ποιησάμενοι τὸ μὲν πρῶτον ἡσυχάζετε, ὕστερον δὲ κατανοήσαντες ἡμᾶς ὀλίγους ὄντας, εἰ ἄρα καὶ ἐδοκοῦμέν τι ἀνεπιεικέστερον πρᾶξαι οὐ μετὰ τοῦ πλήθους ὑμῶν ἐσελθόντες, τὰ μὲν ὁμοῖα οὐκ ἀνταπέδοτε ἡμῖν, μήτε νεωτερίσαι ἔργῳ, λόγοις τε πείθειν ὥστε ἐξελθεῖν, ἐπιθέμενοι δὲ παρὰ τὴν ξύμβασιν οὓς μὲν ἐν χερσὶν ἀπεκτείνατε, οὐχ ὁμοίως ἀλγοῦμεν (κατὰ νόμον γὰρ δή τινα ἔπασχον), οὓς δὲ χεῖρας προϊσχομένους καὶ ζωγρήσαντες

108) would insert (with Laur.) τῶν before πάντων, as in c. 65. 8; ii. 2. 27; Cf. also οἱ πάντες "Ελληνες, c. 63. 13; iv. 78. 11; τοὺς ἄπαντας Μυτιληναίους, c. 36. 6; τοὺς ἄπαντας Μεγαρέας, iv. 68. 7. But against these, cf. βοηθείας γενομένης πάντων Βοιωτῶν, iv. 89. 11; ξυμπάντων Σικελιωτῶν, vi. 18. 28; Ἀκαρνᾶσι πᾶσιν, c. 94. 6. — κατὰ ... πολιτεύειν : see on c. 62. 8.
4. χωρήσαντες : sc. πρὸς ἡμᾶς. Cf. ii. 3. 5 πρὸς ξύμβασιν ἐχώρησαν. — 5. κατανοήσαντες κτέ.: cf. ii. 3. § 2. — 6. εἰ ἄρα καὶ ἐδοκοῦμεν ... πρᾶξαι : i.e. εἰ ἐκρίνετε ἡμᾶς πρᾶξαι, to which corresponds the apod. οὐκ ἀνταπέδοτε ἡμῖν κτέ. For εἰ ἄρα, if possibly, see on c. 56. 15. — 7. ἀνεπιεικέστερον : found elsewhere only in late writers, like Dio C. and Arrian. — οὐ μετὰ τοῦ πλήθους : without the consent of the majority. οὐ μετὰ (cf. μὴ μετὰ νόμων, c. 62. 16) = ἄνευ, as in i. 98. 5; 128. 11, etc. Kühn. 515, N. 2. — 8. μήτε νεωτερίσαι ... πείθειν : explanatory of ὁμοῖα. The pres. inf., πείθειν, is necessary to indicate the attempt to persuade — not πεῖσαι (one Ms.) or πείσειν (all the rest). νεωτερίσαι, resort to violence, as in c. 79. 3;

ii. 3. 7. — 9. ὥστε : see on c. 31. 10. — ἐπιθέμενοι δὲ κτέ.: antithesis to τὰ μὲν ὁμοῖα οὐκ ἀνταπέδοτε ἡμῖν. Instead of simply stating the facts, the speakers express also their judgment of them, and an involved const. results. A more natural const. would have been ἐπέθεσθε δὲ παρὰ τὴν ξύμβασιν ἐν ᾧ οὓς μὲν κτέ. (St.), or ἐπιθέμενοι δὲ παρὰ τὴν ξύμβασιν τοὺς μὲν ἡμῶν ἐν χερσὶν ἀπεκτείνατε, τοὺς δὲ χεῖρας προϊσχομένους ... διεφθείρατε (Steup). Kr. thinks the rel. sents. are respectively the objs. of ἀλγοῦμεν and εἴργασθε, comparing for ἀλγεῖν the const. ἀλγεῖν πάθος. But it seems better, with Bm., to supply περὶ τούτων from οὓς μέν, or, with Cl., to consider that both the rel. clauses hold rather the relation of loosely connected protases, "as to those whom, etc." — 10. ἐν χερσίν : in battle, i.e. with arms in their hands. The phrase is here applied to the combatants, as in iv. 96. 14; 113. 6; v. 72. 10; vii. 5. 6; to the combat (hand to hand), iv. 43. 8, 14; vi. 70. 1. — 12. χεῖρας προϊσχομένους κτέ.: the three grounds on which the Thebans base the guilt of the Plataeans are expressed by three

ὑποσχόμενοί τε ἡμῖν ὕστερον μὴ κτενεῖν παρανόμως
διεφθείρατε, πῶς οὐ δεινὰ εἴργασθε; κἀνταῦθα τρεῖς 3
15 ἀδικίας ἐν ὀλίγῳ πράξαντες, τήν τε λυθεῖσαν ὁμολογίαν
καὶ τῶν ἀνδρῶν τὸν ὕστερον θάνατον καὶ τὴν περὶ αὐτῶν ἡμῖν μὴ κτείνειν ψευσθεῖσαν ὑπόσχεσιν, ἢν τὰ ἐν
τοῖς ἀγροῖς ὑμῖν μὴ ἀδικῶμεν, ὅμως φατὲ ἡμᾶς παρανομῆσαι καὶ αὐτοὶ ἀξιοῦτε μὴ ἀντιδοῦναι δίκην. οὔκ, ἤν 4

partics., the first agreeing with the obj., the two last with the subj., and these are connected by καί (Kr. *Spr.* 56, 14, 2) and τε (introducing third member). The Thebans ignore, of course, the contrary assertions of the Plataeans, as stated by Thuc. ii. 5. § 6. See on c. 56. 4. For the expression χεῖρας προϊσχομένους, *cf.* c. 58. 12; 67. 22; and for the facts, *cf.* ii. 4. § 7. — ζωγρήσαντες ὑποσχόμενοί τε: ζωγρήσαντες, as opp. to ἀπεκτείνατε, implies the intention not to kill the captives, while ὑποσχόμενοι adds the express promise, which the Plataeans, it is true, deny. — **13.** ὕστερον: Hude (*l.c.*) would put after μὴ κτενεῖν and const. with διεφθείρατε, comparing ὕστερον θάνατον in l. 16. But the reference to the ὕστερος θάνατος does not exclude, of course, the possibility of the promise having been made ὕστερον. — παρανόμως: *i.e.* παρὰ τὸν τῶν Ἑλλήνων νόμον. *Cf.* c. 67. 25.
14. κἀνταῦθα . . . πράξαντες κτέ.: κἀνταῦθα is Naber's conjecture (*Mnem. N. S.* xiv. p. 137) for καὶ ταῦτα of the Mss. If the common reading be retained, Cl. is prob. right in explaining ταῦτα as obj. of πράξαντες and τρεῖς ἀδικίας as pred., *and committing these three wrongs in a short space*.

But parallel expressions seem to be wanting. Besides, ταῦτα can refer only to the acts of the Plataeans, whereas, in the foregoing, judgments also are expressed (*cf.* l. 14 πῶς οὐ δεινὰ εἴργασθε;). *Cf.* c. 45. 14, where a similar slip of the copyist occurs. — **15.** τήν τε λυθεῖσαν ὁμολογίαν: *cf.* l. 9 ἐπιθέμενοι παρὰ τὴν ξύμβασιν, and for the const. of the partic. here and in l. 17, *cf.* c. 53. 14 ὁ μὴ ῥηθεὶς λόγος. — **17.** ἡμῖν: for which Badham proposed ἢ μήν, is construed with the verbal subst. ὑπόσχεσιν, not with ψευσθεῖσαν. Kr. *Spr.* 48, 12, 4; Kühn. 424. See on i. 63. 9; 122. 3. — μὴ κτείνειν: with ὑπόσχεσιν, as c. 58. 5 with δωρεάν. St. writes, with v. H. *Stud. Thuc.* p. 46, μὴ κτενεῖν, on the ground that everywhere else in Thuc. ὑπισχνεῖσθαι is followed by the fut. inf., though he does not consider it absolutely necessary here. See *Qu. Gr.²* p. 11. — ἢν τὰ . . . ἀδικῶμεν: *cf.* ii. 5. 21 τὰ ἔξω ἔλεγον αὐτοῖς μὴ ἀδικεῖν.
19. οὔκ: abs., as in v. 101. 1, *i.e.* οὐ τοῦτο γενήσεται (ὑμᾶς μὴ δοῦναι δίκην). Kr. *Spr.* 67, 13, 1. — ἤν γε οὗτοι τὰ ὀρθὰ γιγνώσκωσι: answering to c. 56. 8 τοῦ ὀρθοῦ φανεῖσθε οὐκ ἀληθεῖς κριταὶ ὄντες, c. 57. 2 εἰ . . . γνώσεσθε μὴ τὰ εἰκότα, and c. 58. 21 μὴ ὀρθῶς

20 γε οὗτοι τὰ ὀρθὰ γιγνώσκωσι, πάντων δὲ αὐτῶν ἕνεκα κολασθήσεσθε.

67 "Καὶ ταῦτα, ὦ Λακεδαιμόνιοι, τούτου ἕνεκα ἐπεξήλ- 1 θομεν καὶ ὑπὲρ ὑμῶν καὶ ἡμῶν, ἵνα ὑμεῖς μὲν εἰδῆτε δικαίως αὐτῶν καταγνωσόμενοι, ἡμεῖς δὲ ἔτι ὁσιώτερον τετιμωρημένοι. καὶ μὴ παλαιὰς ἀρετάς, εἴ τις ἄρα καὶ 2
5 ἐγένετο, ἀκούοντες ἐπικλασθῆτε, ἃς χρὴ τοῖς μὲν ἀδικουμένοις ἐπικούρους εἶναι, τοῖς δὲ αἰσχρόν τι δρῶσι διπλασίας ζημίας, ὅτι οὐκ ἐκ προσηκόντων ἁμαρτάνουσι. μηδὲ ὀλοφυρμῷ καὶ οἴκτῳ ὠφελείσθων πατέρων τε

γνόντες. — **20. αὐτῶν** : emphatic, of the matters under discussion, as often. See on i. 1. 10.

67. *You judges must, therefore, be influenced neither by inopportune pity nor by misrepresentations, and inflict just punishment.*

1. ὦ Λακεδαιμόνιοι: the speakers address themselves again to the judges. *Cf.* l. 24. — **ταῦτα ἐπεξήλθομεν** : *we have gone over these things.* Of statement here, as of inquiry in i. 22. 11. *Cf.* Aesch. *Prom.* 870 μακροῦ λόγου δεῖ ταῦτ' ἐπεξελθεῖν τορῶς. — **3. ἡμεῖς δὲ ἔτι ὁσιώτερον τετιμωρημένοι** : *sc.* εἰδῶμεν, as grammatical consistency demands; but logically rather a pass. or intr. verb, like φαινώμεθα, seems to be in the mind of the speaker. Kr. conjectures either ἡμᾶς . . . τετιμωρημένους, or ἡμεῖς δὲ δείξωμεν. Rauchenstein proposes (*Philol.* xxxv. ♦. 588 f.), ὑμεῖς μὲν φανῆτε (l. 2). Steup also thinks the fault lies in l. 2, and conjectures that the original was ὑμεῖς μὲν ἔνδηλοι ἦτε, which was first corrupted into ὑμεῖς μὲν ἐνδῆτε, then changed to ὑμεῖς μὲν εἰδῆτε.

The pf. τετιμωρημένοι expresses confident anticipation of the fulfillment of the wish. — **4. καὶ μὴ κτέ.** : it seems best, with Pp. and Kr., to begin here a new sent., for καὶ μὴ ἐπικλασθῆτε can be appropriately taken neither as co-ord. with ἐπεξήλθομεν nor as a third clause dependent on ἵνα. After summing up the result of their previous arguments, the Theban speakers take up here the Plataean appeal for pity, continuing in μηδὲ ὀλοφυρμῷ κτέ. (l. 8). — **μὴ . . . ἐπικλασθῆτε** : answering to c. 59. 5. — **παλαιὰς ἀρετάς** : cf. c. 53. § 4; 56. § 5, 7; 57. § 2; 58. § 1. — **εἴ τις ἄρα καὶ ἐγένετο** : *if indeed there was any.* See on c. 56. 15. — **6. ἐπικούρους** : pred. adj., as βοηθοί, c. 69. 2; τιμωροί, iv. 2. 12. — **7. διπλασίας ζημίας** : the same idea also i. 86. 5. — **οὐκ ἐκ προσηκόντων** : *i.e.* ἐξ οὐ προσηκόντων = οὐ προσηκόντως. *Cf.* c. 43. 5; i. 34. 10; 35.·7; ii. 44. 16. For the order, see on c. 57. 3.

8. ὀλοφυρμῷ : *sc.* ἐκείνων. — **οἴκτῳ** : *sc.* ὑμῶν αὐτῶν. — **ὠφελείσθων** : on the form, see App. on c. 39. 31. — **πατέ-**

τάφους τῶν ὑμετέρων ἐπιβοώμενοι καὶ τὴν σφετέραν
10 ἐρημίαν. καὶ γὰρ ἡμεῖς ἀνταποφαίνομεν πολλῷ δεινό- 3
τερα παθοῦσαν τὴν ὑπὸ τούτων ἡλικίαν ἡμῶν διεφθαρμένην, ὧν πατέρες οἱ μὲν πρὸς ὑμᾶς τὴν Βοιωτίαν ἄγοντες ἀπέθανον ἐν Κορωνείᾳ, οἱ δὲ πρεσβῦται λελειμμένοι
κατ' οἰκίας ἐρῆμοι πολλῷ δικαιοτέραν ὑμῶν ἱκετείαν
15 ποιοῦνται τούσδε τιμωρήσασθαι. οἴκτου τε ἀξιώτεροι 4
τυγχάνειν οἱ ἀπρεπές τι πάσχοντες τῶν ἀνθρώπων, οἱ
δὲ δικαίως, ὥσπερ οἵδε, τὰ ἐναντία ἐπίχαρτοι εἶναι. καὶ 5

ρων τε ... ἐπιβοώμενοι κτέ.: the participial clause co-ord. as third member with ὀλοφυρμῷ καὶ οἴκτῳ. — 9. τάφους ... ἐπιβοώμενοι: cf. c. 59. § 2. — 10. ἐρημίαν: isolation, as in i. 71. 22. Cf. c. 57. § 4. — πολλῷ δεινότερα παθοῦσαν: cf. c. 59. 6 ὧν πεισόμεθα δεινότητα, 59. 17 νῦν τὰ δεινότατα κινδυνεύομεν παθεῖν.
11. τὴν ὑπὸ τούτων ... διεφθαρμένην: cf. ii. 5. § 7. For the order, see on c. 54. 19. ἡλικία concrete (iuventus), like νεότης, ii. 8. 3. — 12. ὧν: referring to the collective noun, ἡλικίαν. Cf. στρατιὰν ... οὕς, vii. 1. 9; στρατεύματι ... οἷς, vii. 75. 39. G. 1021 b; II. 629. — πατέρες οἱ μὲν ... οἱ δέ: part. apposition. See on c. 13. 17. — πρὸς ὑμᾶς ... ἄγοντες: cf. viii. 24. 33 ἐνεχείρησάν τινες πρὸς Ἀθηναίους ἀγαγεῖν τὴν πόλιν. — 13. ἐν Κορωνείᾳ: as in c. 62. 20, a reminder flattering to the Lacedaemonians, which would increase the effect intended to be produced by πρὸς ὑμᾶς τὴν Βοιωτίαν ἄγοντες. — οἱ δὲ πρεσβῦται λελειμμένοι κατ' οἰκίας ἐρῆμοι: while others left behind as desolate (sonless) old men in their homes. κατ' οἰκίας is St.'s conjecture for καὶ οἰκίαι of the Mss. Cl.'s explanation of the vulg., "left behind in old age and their houses desolate," would require καὶ αἱ οἰκίαι, as Kr. proposed. Besides, the bringing together here of aged fathers and desolate houses, where after ὧν πατέρες only the fathers should be spoken of, is quite unnatural. Bm.'s explanation, that οἰκίαι ἐρῆμοι is a bold expression, pred., just as πρεσβῦται, to πατέρες, "left behind as old men and as desolate households," lacks the support of sure parallels for such an expression. — 14. ὑμῶν: obj. gen. to ἱκετείαν. Cf. c. 59. 13, 29.
16. ἀπρεπές τι: cf. c. 57. 6. — οἱ δὲ δικαίως: sc. πάσχοντές τι. — 17. τὰ ἐναντία: adv., as in vi. 79. 15, and in the sing. iv. 86. 6; vii. 87. 5. — ἐπίχαρτοι εἶναι: sc. ἄξιοί εἰσι, from ἀξιώτεροι. ἐπίχαρτοι, objects of rejoicing, i.e. those over whose sufferings men may rejoice. Cf. Aesch. Prom. 164 ἐχθροῖς ἐπίχαρτα πέπονθα, Dem. xlv. 85 μὴ ὑπερίδητέ με καὶ τὰς θυγατέρας δι' ἔνδειαν τοῖς ἐμαυτοῦ δούλοις τούτου κόλαξιν ἐπίχαρτον γενόμενον, Solomon, Prov. xi. 3 ἐπίχαρτος ἀσεβῶν ἀπώλεια. Cf. also Aesch. Agam. 722; Soph. Trach. 1262. ἐπιχαίρειν also generally

τὴν νῦν ἐρημίαν δι' ἑαυτοὺς ἔχουσι· τοὺς γὰρ ἀμείνους
ξυμμάχους ἑκόντες ἀπεώσαντο. παρενόμησάν τε οὐ προ-
20 παθόντες ὑφ' ἡμῶν. μίσει δὲ πλέον ἢ δίκῃ κρίναντες.
καὶ † οὐκ ἀνταποδόντες νῦν τὴν ἴσην τιμωρίαν· ἔννομα
γὰρ πείσονται καὶ οὐχὶ ἐκ μάχης χεῖρας προϊσχόμενοι,
ὥσπερ φασίν. ἀλλ' ἀπὸ ξυμβάσεως ἐς δίκην σφᾶς αὐτοὺς
παραδόντες. ἀμύνατε οὖν, ὦ Λακεδαιμόνιοι, καὶ τῷ 6
25 τῶν Ἑλλήνων νόμῳ ὑπὸ τῶνδε παραβαθέντι, καὶ ἡμῖν
ἄνομα παθοῦσιν ἀνταπόδοτε χάριν δικαίαν ὧν πρόθυμοι
γεγενήμεθα, καὶ μὴ τοῖς τῶνδε λόγοις περιωσθῶμεν ἐν
ὑμῖν, ποιήσατε δὲ τοῖς Ἕλλησι παράδειγμα οὐ λόγων

has this sense. *Cf.* Soph. *Aj.* 961;
Ar. *Pax*, 1015; Dem. ix. 61; xxi. 134.
Cf. also ἐπίχαρις, Aesch. *Sept.* 910,
and ἐπίχαρμα, Eur. *H. F.* 459; *Phoen.*
1555; Theocr. ii. 20.
18. τὴν νῦν ἐρημίαν: see on l. 9.—
19. παρενόμησαν: on the reading,
see App. — 20. πλέον ἤ: as in c. 12.
6; ii. 89. 21; v. 9. 18 = μᾶλλον ἤ.
Kr. *Spr.* 49, 2, 5. — 21. οὐκ ἀνταποδόντες ... τιμωρίαν: on the reading,
see App. — 22. οὐχί: see on c. 53. 19.
— 23. ὥσπερ φασίν: *cf.* c. 58. § 3. —
ἀπὸ ξυμβάσεως ... παραδόντες: *cf.*
c. 52. § 1. 2; 53. § 1.
24. ἀμύνατε κτέ.: a slight anacoluthon. The first καί anticipates a
second obj. corresponding to τῷ ...
νόμῳ, but the introduction of the new
verb ἀνταπόδοτε changes the const.
For similar irregularity of const., *cf.*
c. 71. 2; iv. 105. 2; v. 88. 3, and see on
ii. 46. 1. For similar irregularity after
τε, see on c. 94. 17; i. 16. 2. — τῷ ...
νόμῳ ... παραβαθέντι: *cf.* c. 66. § 2,
3; 67. § 5. For the expression ἀμύνατε τῷ νόμῳ, *cf.* Eur. *Or.* 523 ἀμυνῶ,

ὅσονπερ δυνατός εἰμι, τῷ νόμῳ. βοηθεῖν
is so used Plato *Apol.* 32 c; Aeschin.
i. 33. — 26. ὧν πρόθυμοι γεγενήμεθα:
referring to the service rendered at
Coronea. Both πρόθυμοι and περιωσθῶμεν in parody of c. 57. 17, 18. —
27. μὴ ... περιωσθῶμεν ἐν ὑμῖν: *let
us not be repulsed by you on account
of their words.* See on c. 57. 17. ἐν
ὑμῖν seems to be used with reference
to c. 57. 14. — 28. ποιήσατε ... παράδειγμα ... προθήσοντες: *show that
you will institute* (set forth) *contests
not of words, but of deeds. Cf.*
Gorg. *Palam.* 34 ὑμᾶς δὲ χρὴ μὴ τοῖς
λόγοις μᾶλλον ἢ τοῖς ἔργοις προσέχειν
τὸν νοῦν. For the const., see on c. 40.
37. The art. is not pleonastic, the
sense being, "the contests that you
will set forth, you will set forth not
of words, but of deeds." (Bl.) ἀγῶνας προθήσοντες as στέφανον προτιθεῖσα,
ii. 46. 4. The reference is to the
oratorical gymnastics to which Cleon
alludes in c. 37. § 4; 38. § 3, 4. *Cf.*
Isoc. iv. 45 παρ' ἡμῖν ἔστιν ἀγῶνας
ἰδεῖν μὴ μόνον τάχους καὶ ῥώμης, ἀλλὰ

τοὺς ἀγῶνας προθήσοντες ἀλλ' ἔργων, ὧν ἀγαθῶν μὲν
30 ὄντων βραχεῖα ἡ ἀπαγγελία ἀρκεῖ, ἁμαρτανομένων δὲ
λόγοι ἔπεσι κοσμηθέντες προκαλύμματα γίγνονται. ἀλλ' 7
ἦν οἱ ἡγεμόνες, ὥσπερ νῦν ὑμεῖς, κεφαλαιώσαντες πρὸς
τοὺς ξύμπαντας διαγνώμας ποιήσησθε, ἧσσόν τις ἐπ'
ἀδίκοις ἔργοις λόγους καλοὺς ζητήσει."

καὶ λόγων καὶ γνώμης, and Dem. xviii.
226 ῥητόρων ἀγῶνα. — 29. ὧν: with the
appos. partics. ἀγαθῶν μὲν ὄντων and
ἁμαρτανομένων δέ, dependent on ἡ
ἀπαγγελία and προκαλύμματα. Cf. ii.
65. 28 ἃ κατορθούμενα μὲν ... ὠφελία
ἦν, σφαλέντα δὲ ... βλάβη καθίστατο.
— 30. βραχεῖα: in pred. position,
"though it be short." See on c.
63. 16. The speakers once more (cf.
c. 61. 2) hint reprovingly at the length
of the speech of the Plataeans. —
ἁμαρτανομένων: pass., as in ii. 65. 45;
vii. 18. 25; the act. ἁμαρτάνειν τι in
i. 38. 13; 39. 7; iv. 114. 26. G. 1240;
H. 819 c; Kühn. 378, 10. Cf. Plato
Prot. 357 c ἡ ἐξαμαρτανομένη πρᾶξις,
Xen. Anab. v. 8. 26 μικρὰ ἁμαρτηθέντα.
For the pres. approaching the force
of the pf., cf. c. 54. 9, and see GMT.
27; Kr. Spr. 53, 1, 3. — 31. λόγοι
ἔπεσι κοσμηθέντες: speeches adorned
with fine sentiments. Cf. ii. 41. 14,
and Plato Apol. 17 b κεκαλλιεπημένους
λόγους'. . . ῥήμασί τε καὶ ὀνόμασιν. —
προκαλύμματα: cf. Luc. Pseudol. 31
προκάλυμμα τῆς βδελυρίας, de Merc.
Cond. 5 προκάλυμμα τῆς αὐτομολίας,
Dion. H. Ant. vi. 77 προκάλυμμα τῆς
ἀπάτης. With the sentiment of the
passage, cf. Sall. Jug. 85. 31 ipsa
se virtus satis ostendit: illis
artificio opus est, ut turpia
facta oratione tegant.

ἀλλ' ἦν οἱ ἡγεμόνες ... ζητήσει :
"but if leaders, as now you, sum up
in a short question and make decisions that apply to all, men will strive
less with fair words to justify wrong
deeds." The verb ποιήσησθε is construed with ὑμεῖς instead of ἡγεμόνες.
For similar const., cf. i. 82. 9; Xen.
Cyrop. iv. 1. 3; Dem. iv. 2. — 32. κεφαλαιώσαντες: the reference is to the
βραχὺ ἐπερώτημα of c. 52. § 4. — πρὸς
τοὺς ξύμπαντας : Cl., who construes
these words with διαγνώμας ποιήσησθε,
explains, "as a warning example to
all." Jow. thinks the reference is
to the question being asked of all the
captives without distinction. Steup
thinks best to connect πρὸς τοὺς ξύμπαντας with κεφαλαιώσαντες, comparing i. 36. 14 βραχυτάτῳ κεφαλαίῳ τοῖς
τε ξύμπασι καὶ καθ' ἕκαστον, which he
renders, "with a very short summary
for all as well as for each." In that
case the meaning would be, "having
settled the main point (here the
βραχὺ ἐπερώτημα) with reference to
the interests of all the members of
the alliance." H. Weil (Revue de
Philol. N. S. ii. p. 91 f.) would emend
the passage so as to read, κεφαλαιώσαντες πρὸς τὸ ξύμπαν τὰς διαγνώμας
ποιήσησθε, and this is adopted by v.
H. — 33. διαγνώμας ποιήσησθε : cf.
c. 36. 4 περὶ τῶν ἀνδρῶν γνώμας ἐποι-

68 Τοιαῦτα δὲ οἱ Θηβαῖοι εἶπον. οἱ δὲ Λακεδαιμό- 1
νιοι δικασταὶ νομίζοντες τὸ ἐπερώτημα σφίσιν ὀρθῶς
ἕξειν, εἴ τι ἐν τῷ πολέμῳ ὑπ᾿ αὐτῶν ἀγαθὸν πεπόνθασι,
διότι τόν τε ἄλλον χρόνον ἠξίουν δῆθεν αὐτοὺς κατὰ
5 τὰς παλαιὰς Παυσανίου μετὰ τὸν Μῆδον σπονδὰς ἡσυχάζειν καὶ ὅτε ὕστερον [ἅ] πρὸ τοῦ περιτειχίζεσθαι προεί-

οῦντο. For διαγνώμας, see on c. 42. 1.
—ἐπ᾿ ἀδίκοις ἔργοις : ἐπί with dat. of
conditioning circumstances, similar
to ἐπὶ φανεροῖς, i. 69. 9; ἐπὶ τοῖς δεινοῖς,
i. 70. 10.
68. *In accordance with the decision
of the Lacedaemonian judges, the Plataean and Athenian captives are put
to death, the women enslaved, the city
razed to the ground, and the lands
leased to the Thebans.*
1. τοσαῦτα δέ: see on c. 49. 1. —
2. σφίσιν ὀρθῶς ἕξειν : the emphatic
position of σφίσιν indicates the effort
of the Lacedaemonians to put their
cruel decision in as fair a light as
possible. "The question whether
they have received any good at the
hands of the Plataeans in the war
would be in order for them." — **4.
διότι . . . κατ᾿ ἐκεῖνα, ὡς οὐκ ἐδέξαντο
. . . πεπονθέναι :** these words should
express the ground of the confidence
of the Lacedaemonians in the justice
of their question, but the traditional
reading cannot be construed. The
simplest remedy is, with Heilmann,
Cl., St., Bm., and others, to bracket ἅ
in l. 6. The sense then is: "Because
they not only at all other times
had, forsooth, urged the Plataeans to
neutrality according to the ancient
agreements with Pausanias after the
Persian wars, but especially when
afterwards before the circumvallation they had proposed to them to
be neutral according to those agreements, since the Plataeans did not
accept (the proposals), considering
that by their own just demand
they themselves were now ἔκσπονδοι
(*i.e.* released from treaty obligations)
and had been wronged by the Plataeans." With the view here taken
of the relation of ἡγούμενοι to the
preceding (*i.e.* that ὡς οὐκ ἐδέξαντο,
ἡγούμενοι . . . κακῶς πεπονθέναι is an
epexegetical explanation of νομίζοντες
. . . διότι κτέ.), any emendation of ὡς
οὐκ ἐδέξαντο is perhaps unnecessary.
Cl. and Bm. follow St. (*Jahrbb.* 1868,
p. 111) in inserting δ᾿ (ὡς δ᾿ οὐκ ἐδέξαντο). Küppers (*Curae Crit.* p. 12
sq.) proposes καὶ ὥς. The simplest
change would be οὐδ᾿ ὥς (v. 55. 11;
115. 6). For possible interpretations
of the text as it stands, see Jow. —
4. τόν τε ἄλλον χρόνον ἠξίουν κτέ.:
cf. the words of Archidamus ii. 72. 9
ἅπερ καὶ τὸ πρότερον ἤδη προυκαλεσάμεθα, ἡσυχίαν ἄγετε κτέ. — **ἠξίουν
αὐτοὺς ἡσυχάζειν :** belongs to both
τόν τε ἄλλον χρόνον and καὶ ὅτε ὕστερον κτέ. — **δῆθεν :** ironical, indicating
Thuc.'s doubt of the sincerity of the
admonitions here mentioned. — **5.
Παυσανίου:** cf. ii. 71. § 2 ff.; 72. § 1.
— **μετὰ τὸν Μῆδον:** *i.e.* μετὰ τὰ Μη-
δικά. — **6. ὅτε ὕστερον κτέ.:** refers to
the demand of Archidamus (c. 64. 13;

χοντο αὐτοῖς κοινοὺς εἶναι κατ' ἐκεῖνα, ὡς οὐκ ἐδέξαντο, ἡγούμενοι τῇ ἑαυτῶν δικαίᾳ βουλήσει ἔκσπονδοι ἤδη ὑπ' αὐτῶν κακῶς πεπονθέναι, αὖθις τὸ αὐτὸ ἕνα ἕκαστον
10 παραγαγόντες καὶ ἐρωτῶντες. εἴ τι Λακεδαιμονίους καὶ τοὺς ξυμμάχους ἀγαθὸν ἐν τῷ πολέμῳ δεδρακότες εἰσίν. ὁπότε μὴ φαῖεν, ἀπάγοντες ἀπέκτεινον, καὶ ἐξαίρετον ἐποιήσαντο οὐδένα. διέφθειραν δὲ Πλαταιῶν μὲν αὐτῶν 2 οὐκ ἐλάσσους διακοσίων, Ἀθηναίων δὲ πέντε καὶ εἴκοσιν,
15 οἳ ξυνεπολιορκοῦντο · γυναῖκας δὲ ἠνδραπόδισαν. τὴν 3

ii. 72. 10). — προείχοντο: as i. 140.
24. Schol. προεβάλλοντο. — 7. κοινούς: neutral, as in c. 53. 8. — κατ' ἐκεῖνα: i.e. κατὰ τὰς παλαιὰς σπονδάς. — 8. βουλήσει: as the word occurs nowhere else in Thuc. in the sense of demand, it may be better to render it by intention (voluntas), as Bl. does. Cf. v. 105. 4. Arn. considers the text (τῇ ἑαυτῶν δικαίᾳ βουλήσει) to be either corrupt or else a scholium. St. proposes τῇ ἑαυτῶν δικαιώσει, of which he thinks τῇ δικαίᾳ βουλήσει was prob. a gloss. Cf. i. 141. 6; iv. 86. 21; v. 17. 11. Rauchenstein (Philol. xxxv. p. 589) suggests τῇ αὐτῶν δικαιώσει. — ἔκσπονδοι ἤδη: cf. ii. 74. § 3. These words contain the main point of the whole sentence. The result of Plataean obstinacy is at the same time the excuse for the Lacedaemonians not sparing them. — 9. ἕνα ἕκαστον παραγαγόντες καί: inserted between τὸ αὐτό and ἐρωτῶντες. For similar breaks in the const., Cl. compares ii. 4. 20; ii. 9, and Bm. vi. 68. 17. But Steup, who objects that none of these is exactly parallel, and the first not above suspicion, thinks that καί is possibly to

be bracketed, with Reiske and v. II. — 10. παραγαγόντες: bringing forward. Cf. v. 45. 19; 46. 34; viii. 53. 13; Dem. xviii. 170; xxvi. 17. — 12. ὁπότε μὴ φαῖεν: when they answered 'no.' μὴ φάναι, as in viii. 53. 19. For the opt. of general cond., see GMT. 532; H. 914, B 2. — καὶ ἐξαίρετον ἐποιήσαντο οὐδένα: cf. ii. 24. 5, 10.
13. Πλαταιῶν μὲν αὐτῶν οὐκ ἐλάσσους διακοσίων, Ἀθηναίων δὲ πέντε καὶ εἴκοσιν: originally 400 Plataeans and 80 Athenians were besieged (ii. 78. § 3). Of these 480 defenders, 212 escaped in the sortie (c. 24. 11), and one was captured (c. 24. 13). Since now, acc. to the present passage, not less than 225 were killed after the surrender, about 42 must have perished during the siege, the most of these prob. before the sortie, for in c. 20. § 2 the Plataeans and Athenians who attempt to break out are represented as ἐς ἄνδρας διακοσίους καὶ εἴκοσι μάλιστα, and also as the half of the beleaguered men still surviving. — 15. ξυνεπολιορκοῦντο: impf., from the beginning of the siege till this time. Kr. Spr. 53, 2, 8. Hence Meineke's conjecture, ξυνεπεπολιόρκηντο,

δὲ πόλιν ἐνιαυτὸν μέν τινα [Θηβαῖοι] Μεγαρέων ἀνδράσι κατὰ στάσιν ἐκπεπτωκόσι καὶ ὅσοι τὰ σφέτερα φρονοῦντες Πλαταιῶν περιῆσαν ἔδοσαν ἐνοικεῖν· ὕστερον δὲ καθελόντες αὐτὴν ἐς ἔδαφος πᾶσαν ἐκ τῶν θεμε-
20 λίων ᾠκοδόμησαν πρὸς τῷ Ἡραίῳ καταγώγιον διακοσίων

is unnecessary.—**γυναῖκας** : *i.e.* those remaining of the 110, who had stayed as σιτοποιοί in the city (ii. 78. 13). Müller-Strübing (*Aristoph. etc.* p. 44 f. and *Thuk. Forsch.* p. 138 ff.) objected to the words γυναῖκας δὲ ἠνδραπόδισαν, because the women in question were already slaves and not now first made so. But as v. Velsen replied (*Philol. Anz.* vii. p. 372), ἠνδραπόδισαν is only the antithesis to ἀπέκτεινον (*cf.* c. 28. 9, 10; 36. 6, 8), and it makes no difference whether the captured women were slaves before or not. Indeed, ἀνδραποδίζειν may be rendered here, with St. (*Gött. Gel. Anz.* 1882, p. 99), "to sell as prisoners of war." That the women were slaves before, a view held already by Grote, is now generally accepted, and seems to be supported by ii. 78. § 4, where, after giving the number of the defendants and of the σιτοποιοί, Thuc. says, τοσοῦτοι ἦσαν οἱ ξύμπαντες ὅτε ἐς τὴν πολιορκίαν καθίσταντο, καὶ ἄλλος οὐδεὶς ἦν ἐν τῷ τείχει οὔτε δοῦλος οὔτε ἐλεύθερος. But even if the women were only slaves, a remark about their fate was still by no means superfluous, as Müller-Strübing asserts.—**16. τινα**: "about," with the definite period of time ἐνιαυτόν, as elsewhere with numbers. Kr. *Spr.* 51, 10, 4. *Cf.* c. 111. 7; vii. 34. 10; 87. 15; viii. 21. 4. — **[Θηβαῖοι]**: St.,

Bm., and v. II. rightly follow Cl. in bracketing this word, for it seems clear from the context that the general subj. down to ἀπεμίσθωσαν inclusive is the Lacedaemonian leaders. See App. — **17. κατὰ στάσιν**: *in consequence of a sedition.* See on c. 2. 10. — **ἐκπεπτωκόσι**: *cf.* iv. 66. § 1 ff.; 74. § 2. — **τὰ σφέτερα φρονοῦντες**: *cf.* v. 84. 3; vi. 51. 7; viii. 31. 7. — **19. ἐς ἔδαφος**: also iv. 109. 2; here strengthened by ἐκ τῶν θεμελίων, f u n d i t u s. So Cl. explains, with most editors. *Cf.* Procop. *de Aedif.* p. 12 d καθεῖλε μὲν αὐτὸ ἐς τὸ ἔδαφος ἐκ τῶν θεμελίων, Jos. *Ant.* 174, 29 ἐξ αὐτῶν ἀνασπᾶν θεμελίων καὶ μηδὲ ἔδαφος καταλιπεῖν. But Steup follows St. in connecting ἐκ τῶν θεμελίων with ᾠκοδόμησαν, *built out of the foundation-stones* (of the ruined houses). *Cf.* i. 93. 3. — **20. πρὸς τῷ Ἡραίῳ**: *cf.* Hdt. ix. 52. 9; Plut. *Aristid.* 18; Paus. ix. 2. 7. The temples must have been left standing, and served doubtless as a starting-point for the rebuilding after the peace of Antalcidas (387 B.C.). — **καταγώγιον**: *i.e.* a πανδοκεῖον for the accommodation of those who came to worship at the temple. This building, as well as the νεὼς ἑκατόμποδος mentioned below, was evidently meant to propitiate the patron goddess of the land. Concerning such inns connected with temples, see

ποδῶν πανταχῇ, κύκλῳ οἰκήματα ἔχον κάτωθεν καὶ ἄνωθεν, καὶ ὀροφαῖς καὶ θυρώμασι τοῖς τῶν Πλαταιῶν ἐχρήσαντο, καὶ τοῖς ἄλλοις ἃ ἦν ἐν τῷ τείχει ἔπιπλα, χαλκὸς καὶ σίδηρος, κλίνας κατασκευάσαντες ἀνέθεσαν τῇ Ἥρᾳ, 25 καὶ νεὼν ἑκατόμποδον λίθινον ᾠκοδόμησαν αὐτῇ. τὴν δὲ γῆν δημοσιώσαντες ἀπεμίσθωσαν ἐπὶ δέκα ἔτη, καὶ ἐνέμοντο Θηβαῖοι. σχεδὸν δέ τι καὶ τὸ ξύμπαν περὶ Πλα- 4 ταιῶν οἱ Λακεδαιμόνιοι οὕτως ἀποτετραμμένοι ἐγένοντο Θηβαίων ἕνεκα, νομίζοντες ἐς τὸν πόλεμον αὐτοὺς ἄρτι 30 τότε καθιστάμενον ὠφελίμους εἶναι.

Καὶ τὰ μὲν κατὰ Πλάταιαν ἔτει τρίτῳ καὶ ἐνενηκοστῷ 5

Becker, *Charicles* (ed. Göll), ii. p. 5 f. — 21. πανταχῇ: on every side, doubtless more prop. connected with διακοσίων ποδῶν, *200 feet square*, than with κύκλῳ, though in vii. 79. 19 it is joined with κύκλῳ. — κάτωθεν καὶ ἄνωθεν: i.e. κάτω καὶ ἄνω. The designation has reference to the starting-point. See on ii. 102. 14. — 22. ὀροφαῖς καὶ θυρώμασι: including all the woodwork of the buildings. — 23. τοῖς ἄλλοις: connect with κατασκευάσαντες. — ἔπιπλα, χαλκὸς καὶ σίδηρος: i.e. everything of metal found within the ruined city (ἐν τῷ τείχει, cf. ii. 78. 15) that could be applied to any use. — 24. κλίνας: *couches* for the καταγώγιον. — 27. ἐνέμοντο Θηβαῖοι: the Thebans leased (ἐμισθώσαντο) and used the land. νέμεσθαι refers to occupation of the soil in any way. *Cf*. i. 2. 6. See App. on Θηβαῖοι, l. 16.

σχεδὸν δέ τι καὶ τὸ ξύμπαν: *pretty nearly or altogether*. σχεδόν τι, as in v. 66. 16; vii. 33. 6. Kr. *Spr*. 51, 16, 5. For τὸ ξύμπαν, see Kr. *Spr*. 46, 3,

3. The advantage conceded to the Thebans in the usufruct of the Plataean territory induces the general remark, that in their whole conduct toward the Plataeans the Lacedaemonians were determined by regard for the Thebans, Θηβαίων ἕνεκα, on which the stress of the sent.° rests. — 28. ἀποτετραμμένοι ἐγένοντο: this periphrasis is unusual in good prose. Kr. *Di*. 56, 1, 5. — 29. ἄρτι τότε καθιστάμενον: see on c. 3. 2. — 30. ὠφελίμους εἶναι: *cf*. c. 62. § 5.

31. ἔτει τρίτῳ καὶ ἐνενηκοστῷ: i.e. 520 or 519 B.C. *Cf*. c. 55. 3. Grote (chap. 31) charges Thuc. with error, on the strength of Hdt. vi. 108, and thinks that the alliance of Plataea with Athens could not have been formed before the expulsion of Hippias in 510 B.C. But see, *per contra*, Curtius, *Gr. Gesch*. i.⁶ p. 678, N. '65. It does not seem necessary to assume here, with Gutschmid and others (see Busolt, *Die Laked*. i. p. 307, N. 49, and *Gr. Gesch*. i. p. 609, N. 3), even a slip of the copyist for

ἐπειδὴ Ἀθηναίων ξύμμαχοι ἐγένοντο οὕτως ἐτελεύτησεν·
69 αἱ δὲ τεσσαράκοντα νῆες τῶν Πελοποννησίων αἱ Λεσβίοις 1
βοηθοὶ ἐλθοῦσαι, ὡς τότε φεύγουσαι διὰ τοῦ πελάγους
ἔκ τε τῶν Ἀθηναίων ἐπιδιωχθεῖσαι καὶ πρὸς τῇ Κρήτῃ
χειμασθεῖσαι καὶ ἀπ' αὐτῆς σποράδες πρὸς τὴν Πελο-
5 πόννησον κατηνέχθησαν, καταλαμβάνουσιν ἐν τῇ Κυλλήνῃ τρεῖς καὶ δέκα τριήρεις Λευκαδίων καὶ Ἀμπρακιωτῶν καὶ Βρασίδαν τὸν Τέλλιδος, ξύμβουλον Ἀλκίδᾳ
ἐπεληλυθότα. ἐβούλοντο γὰρ οἱ Λακεδαιμόνιοι, ὡς τῆς 2
Λέσβου ἡμαρτήκεσαν, πλέον τὸ ναυτικὸν ποιήσαντες ἐς

τρίτῳ καὶ ὀγδοηκοστῷ. — 32. **ἐπειδὴ Ἀθηναίων ξύμμαχοι ἐγένοντο**: cf. ii. 73. 10 ἀφ' οὗ ξύμμαχοι ἐγενόμεθα. — **ἐπειδή**: after. Cf. c. 70. 1; i. 6. 9, 20; viii. 68. 27.

69. *Alcidas and Brasidas join in an expedition against Corcyra.*

1. αἱ δὲ τεσσαράκοντα νῆες κτέ.: the account of the fleet of Alcidas, interrupted at c. 33. § 1, is here resumed. For the number of ships, see on c. 26. 2. — **Λεσβίοις βοηθοὶ ἐλθοῦσαι**: const. as in i. 53. 14. See on c. 67. 6. — 2. **τότε φεύγουσαι διὰ τοῦ πελάγους**: i.e. in a southwesterly direction from Ephesus. Cf. c. 33. 1. τότε is freq. used of a time assumed to be well known. See on i. 101. 8. — 3. **ἐκ τῶν Ἀθηναίων**: ἐκ for ὑπό, as i. 20. 10; ii. 49. 1; vi. 36. 9; Plato Theaet. 171 b; Xen. Anab. ii. 6. 1. II. 798 c; Kühn. 430, 2, 3 c. — **ἐπιδιωχθεῖσαι**: sc. as far as Patmos, c. 33. 13. — **πρὸς τῇ Κρήτῃ ... κατηνέχθησαν**: σποράδες is correl. to the preceding parties. = σποράδες γενόμεναι, i.e. διασπαρεῖσαι. Kühn. 491. Cf. c. 82. 6 οὐκ ἂν ἐχόντων πρόφασιν οὐδ'

ἑτοίμων παρακαλεῖν αὐτούς, v. 64. 17 οὐ ῥᾴδιον ἦν μὴ ἀθρόοις καὶ ἀλλήλους περιμείνασι διελθεῖν τὴν πολεμίαν. So most of the editors explain, but Cl. and St. take σποράδες with κατενέχθησαν, and consider καί after χειμασθεῖσαι an interpolation. — 5. **καταλαμβάνουσι**: without partic. (see on i. 59. 3), as in ii. 18. 17; 94. 19. — 5. **ἐν τῇ Κυλλήνῃ**: the naval station of the Eleans (τὸ Ἠλείων ἐπινεῖον, i. 30. 9; ii. 84. 33). It was prob. designated as the place of rendezvous. — 7. **Βρασίδαν**: first mentioned ii. 25. 7, and referred to everywhere by Thuc. with marked respect as the ablest Spartan leader. — **ξύμβουλον Ἀλκίδᾳ ἐπεληλυθότα**: *who had arrived as adviser to Alcidas.* For the const., cf. viii. 20. 7 ναύαρχος αὐτοῖς ἐκ Λακεδαίμονος Ἀστύοχος ἐπῆλθεν. The ξύμβουλος was a commissioner with irregular powers sent to advise the nauarch. Three ξύμβουλοι are given to the nauarch in ii. 85. 1; eleven in viii. 39. 7. For the ten ξύμβουλοι assigned to king Agis, see on v. 63. 15. See also on c. 42. 19.

10 τὴν Κέρκυραν πλεῦσαι στασιάζουσαν, δώδεκα μὲν ναυσὶ μόναις παρόντων Ἀθηναίων περὶ Ναύπακτον, πρὶν δὲ πλέον τι ἐπιβοηθῆσαι ἐκ τῶν Ἀθηνῶν ναυτικόν, ὅπως προφθάσωσι· καὶ παρεσκευάζοντο ὅ τε Βρασίδας καὶ ὁ Ἀλκίδας πρὸς ταῦτα.

70 Οἱ γὰρ Κερκυραῖοι ἐστασίαζον, ἐπειδὴ οἱ αἰχμά- 1 λωτοι ἦλθον αὐτοῖς οἱ ἐκ τῶν περὶ Ἐπίδαμνον ναυμαχιῶν ὑπὸ Κορινθίων ἀφεθέντες, τῷ μὲν λόγῳ ὀκτακο-

10. δώδεκα ναυσί: cf. 75. 3; 77. 11. Twelve was the number under the command of Asopius at Naupactus (c. 7. 3). — 11. πρὶν δὲ ... προφθάσωσι: the natural const. would have been ὅπως δέ, πρὶν ... ναυτικόν, προφθάσωσι, but ὅπως is placed after the πρίν clause, in order that the clauses δώδεκα μὲν ... περὶ Ναύπακτον and πρὶν δὲ ... ναυτικόν may be in direct antithesis. For the co-ordination of the different kinds of clauses, see Kr. Spr. 59, 2, 3. — 13. παρεσκευάζοντο: were making preparation. The undertaking is described in c. 76 ff. — 14. πρὸς ταῦτα: cf. ii. 77. 4 πρὸς τὴν περιτείχισιν παρεσκευάζοντο.

HISTORY OF THE POLITICAL CONFLICTS IN CORCYRA. c. 70–85.

70. The bitter struggle between the Athenian and Corinthian parties in Corcyra from the beginning until the murder of the Athenian proxenus Pithias.

1. ἐστασίαζον: cf. c. 69. 10 ἐς τὴν Κέρκυραν πλεῦσαι στασιάζουσαν. — ἐπειδή: see on c. 68. 32. — 2. ἦλθον αὐτοῖς: for dat. with ἐλθεῖν, see on c. 5. 12; 39. 22; i. 13. 12. — ἐκ τῶν περὶ Ἐπίδαμνον ναυμαχιῶν: more accurately,

from the second of the two sea-fights, that at Sybota. Cf. i. 47–55. Acc. to i. 55. 6, the number of captives was 250, of whom it is said ἐτύγχανον δυνάμει αὐτῶν οἱ πλείους πρῶτοι ὄντες τῆς πόλεως. — 3. ὑπὸ Κορινθίων ἀφεθέντες: as may be inferred from the context, not before the winter of 428–427 B.C., so that their captivity (ἐν θεραπείᾳ εἶχον πολλῇ) must have lasted about five years. See App. — ὀκτακοσίων ταλάντων: gen. of price. The ransom of each man would be 3⅕ talents, which seems enormous, even though the most of the captives were among the first men of the state (see above), and so would be, as a body of 250, a most valuable pledge in the hands of the Corinthians. Jow. thinks that the unusual amount is not a matter of much importance, as the sum was never meant to be paid. But Steup thinks that, even in a sham transaction, the demand would have to seem reasonable, in order not to excite suspicion. He cites from Philip's letter, Dem. xii. 3, a ransom of nine talents for a single man, and urges here the importance to the Corinthians of a body of 250 Corcy-

σίων ταλάντων τοῖς προξένοις διηγγυημένοι, ἔργῳ δὲ
5 πεπεισμένοι Κορινθίοις Κέρκυραν προσποιῆσαι. καὶ
ἔπρασσον οὗτοι ἕκαστον τῶν πολιτῶν μετιόντες, ὅπως
ἀποστήσωσιν Ἀθηναίων τὴν πόλιν. καὶ ἀφικομένης Ἀτ- 2
τικῆς τε νεὼς καὶ Κορινθίας πρέσβεις ἀγουσῶν καὶ ἐς
λόγους καταστάντων ἐψηφίσαντο Κερκυραῖοι Ἀθηναίοις
10 μὲν ξύμμαχοι εἶναι κατὰ τὰ ξυγκείμενα, Πελοποννησίοις
δὲ φίλοι ὥσπερ καὶ πρότερον. καὶ (ἦν γὰρ Πειθίας ἐθε- 3

raean captives of such prominence, referring to the advantage which the Athenians derived from the 292 Spartans captured at Sphacteria (iv. 41. § 1; 117). For the ordinary ransom, see Boeckh, p. 99 f. — **4. τοῖς προξένοις διηγγυημένοι**: *bailed on the security of their proxeni*, i.e. of Corinthian citizens who were the representatives of Corcyra at Corinth. For the dat., see on c. 64. 15. As to the relation of πρόξενος, see Schoemann, *Gr. Ant.* ii. p. 25. — **5. πεπεισμένοι ... προσποιῆσαι**: cf. i. 55. 5 (οἱ Κορίνθιοι) τῶν Κερκυραίων ... πεντήκοντα καὶ διακοσίους δήσαντες ἐφύλασσον καὶ ἐν θεραπείᾳ εἶχον πολλῇ, ὅπως αὐτοῖς τὴν Κέρκυραν ἀναχωρήσαντες προσποιήσειαν. — **προσποιῆσαι**: *to win over*, as in i. 55. 8; ii. 8. 15. — **7. ἀποστήσωσιν**: subjv. after past tense of verb of striving, as in i. 57. 9. GMT. 339; II. 885 b.
ἀφικομένης: sing. before two nouns, **ἀγουσῶν** following them. G. 901; H. 607. *Cf.* i. 29. 6. — **8. ἐς λόγους καταστάντων**: sc. τῶν πρέσβεων ἑκατέρων τοῖς Κερκυραίοις. — **10. ξύμμαχοι εἶναι κατὰ τὰ ξυγκείμενα**: i.e. an ἐπιμαχία, *defensive alliance*, as described i. 44.8. — **11. ὥσπερ καὶ πρότερον**: i.e. as

before the conflict with Corinth and other members of the Peloponnesian alliance about Epidamnus. *Cf.* i. 28. 10, where Corcyraean ambassadors, warning the Corinthians against going to war about Epidamnus, remark, εἰ δὲ μή, καὶ αὐτοὶ ἀναγκασθήσεσθαι ἔφασαν, ἐκείνων βιαζομένων, φίλους ποιεῖσθαι οὓς οὐ βούλονται, ἑτέρους τῶν νῦν ὄντων μᾶλλον, ὠφελίας ἕνεκα. So that, although Corcyra had never belonged to the Peloponnesian alliance, she had had, before the contention about Epidamnus, not only peaceful, but even friendly, relations with the Peloponnesians. These were now to be renewed without affecting the treaty obligations of Corcyra to Athens. The whole decision was a kind of first triumph of the Corinthian party, since Corcyra's conflicts with Corinth and her allies about Epidamnus, and her participation in the ravaging of the Peloponnesian coasts in the summer of 425 B.C. (ii. 25. § 1), were disregarded, while the connexion with Athens was expressly restricted to existing conditions, ἐπιμαχία τῇ ἀλλήλων βοηθεῖν, ἐάν τις ἐπὶ Κέρκυραν ἴῃ ἢ Ἀθήνας ἢ τοὺς τούτων ξυμμάχους (i. 44. 8).

λοπρόξενός τε τῶν Ἀθηναίων καὶ τοῦ δήμου προειστήκει) ὑπάγουσιν αὐτὸν οὗτοι οἱ ἄνδρες ἐς δίκην, λέγοντες
Ἀθηναίοις τὴν Κέρκυραν καταδουλοῦν. ὁ δὲ ἀποφυγὼν 4
15 ἀνθυπάγει αὐτῶν τοὺς πλουσιωτάτους πέντε ἄνδρας,
φάσκων τέμνειν χάρακας ἐκ τοῦ τε Διὸς τοῦ τεμένους
καὶ τοῦ Ἀλκίνου· ζημία δὲ καθ' ἑκάστην χάρακα ἐπέκειτο στατήρ. ὀφλόντων δὲ αὐτῶν καὶ πρὸς τὰ ἱερὰ ἱκε- 5

καὶ (ἦν γὰρ ... προειστήκει): a causal sent. thus placed in parataxis before the main one is common in Hdt. and not rare in Thuc. For const. and punctuation, see on i. 31. 7. — Πειθίας: this name occurs in a late Corcyraean epitaph, in the form Πειθείας (C. I. G. ii. 1911). — ἐθελο-πρόξενος: Schol. ἀφ' ἑαυτοῦ γενόμενος καὶ μὴ κελευσθεὶς ἐκ τῆς πόλεως. οἱ γὰρ πρόξενοι κελευόμενοι ἐκ τῆς ἑαυτῶν πόλεως ἐγένοντο, i.e. as Boeckh (C. I. G. i. p. 731) explains, non a Corcyracis constitutus. But Steup thinks that others prob. more correctly explain, non ab Atheniensibus declaratus. The word and the office occur only here and in the comments of the grammarians on this passage. — 12. προειστήκει: i.e. προστάτης ἦν τοῦ δήμου. Cf. c. 75. 9; iv. 46. 14. — 13. ὑπάγουσιν: used with and without ἐς δίκην. Cf. Hdt. vi. 136. 4; Xen. Hell. ii. 3. 12, 33; v. 4. 24. — οὗτοι οἱ ἄνδρες: Schol. οἱ ἀπὸ Κορίνθου ἐπανελθόντες. — 14. καταδουλοῦν: i.e. trying to enslave. GMT. 25; H. 825.
ἀποφυγών: acquitted, as in c. 13. 34. — 16. τέμνειν χάρακας: acc. to the remark of the grammarians (χάραξ θηλυκῶς ἐπὶ τῶν ἀμπέλων, ἀρσενικῶς δὲ ἐπὶ τῶν πρὸς πολιορκίαν), the χάρακες

are the stakes that support the vines. Cf. Phryn. Ecl. p. 61 ἡ χάραξ τὸ τῆς ἀμπέλου στήριγμα. See Lobeck ad loc. cit. Probably the more prominent citizens had the oversight and management of the temple and groves, and were now accused of having used these for their own private advantage. The pres. τέμνειν indicates that the transgression charged had been a constant practice; and this may explain the large amount of the fine, which manifestly threatened their existence. — ἐκ τοῦ τε Διὸς τοῦ τεμένους καὶ τοῦ Ἀλκίνου: these were doubtless two τεμένη, as is clear both from the position of καὶ τοῦ Ἀλκίνου and the correlation with τε ... καί. For ἐκ τοῦ Διὸς τοῦ τεμένους, cf. c. 81. 27; 96. 1; v. 47. 65. The reading of Vat. ἐκ τοῦ τε Διὸς τεμένους is prob. due to a slip of the copyist, and Cobet's conjecture ἔκ τε τοῦ Διὸς τεμένους (Mnem. N. S. viii. p. 142) is hardly to be accepted. The sites of the two τεμένη are unknown. See B. Schmidt, p. 32 f. — 17. τοῦ Ἀλκίνου: the Homeric king of 'Scheria,' who was worshipped as a ἥρως. — ἐπέκειτο: here and viii. 15. 6, pf. pass. of ἐπιτιθέναι (viii. 67. 13). — 18. στατήρ: whether a gold coin worth twenty drachmae, or a silver coin worth two

τῶν καθεζομένων διὰ πλῆθος τῆς ζημίας, ὅπως ταξάμε-
20 νοι ἀποδῶσιν, ὁ Πειθίας (ἐτύγχανε γὰρ καὶ βουλῆς ὢν)
πείθει ὥστε τῷ νόμῳ χρήσασθαι. οἱ δ᾽, ἐπειδὴ τῷ τε νόμῳ
ἐξείργοντο καὶ ἅμα ἐπυνθάνοντο τὸν Πειθίαν, ἕως ἔτι
βουλῆς ἐστι, μέλλειν τὸ πλῆθος ἀναπείσειν τοὺς αὐτοὺς
Ἀθηναίοις φίλους τε καὶ ἐχθροὺς νομίζειν, ξυνίσταντό τε
25 καὶ λαβόντες ἐγχειρίδια ἐξαπιναίως ἐς τὴν βουλὴν ἐσελθόντες τόν τε Πειθίαν κτείνουσι καὶ ἄλλους τῶν τε βουλευ-
τῶν καὶ ἰδιωτῶν ἐς ἑξήκοντα· οἱ δέ τινες τῆς αὐτῆς γνώμης

drachmae, is meant, is doubtful. The context favours the former, as otherwise too large a number of χάρακες must be assumed in order to bring the amount of the fine up to a sum that would make intelligible the conduct of the accused rich men. In the inscription cited by B. Schmidt, p. 71 (*C. I. A.* ii. 841), which belongs prob. to the beginning of the third century B.C., a fine of fifty drachmae is imposed, ἄν τις ληφθῇ κόπτων ἢ φέρων τι τῶν ἀπειρημένων ἐκ τοῦ ἱεροῦ. ὀφλόντων: *condemned*, as in v. 101. 3; Plato *Legg.* 754 c. — πρὸς τὰ ἱερά: cf. ii. 47. 16 πρὸς ἱεροῖς ἱκέτευσαν, and c. 81. 25 πρὸς αὐτοῖς (*i.e.* τοῖς ἱεροῖς) ἐκτείνοντο. — ἱκετῶν καθεζομένων: see on c. 28. 13; i. 24. 19. — 19. διὰ πλῆθος τῆς ζημίας: πλῆθος for μέγεθος, with reference perhaps to the large number of the χάρακες. Cf. στρατιᾶς πλήθει, i. 129. 17. — ταξάμενοι: *getting themselves rated*, *i.e.* arranging for payment by instalments. Cf. the use of τάξις as a technical expression for such an arrangement with creditors, Plato *Legg.* 844 b. Cf. c. 50. 10; i. 99. 11, and see B. Schmidt, p. 71 f.

— 20. καὶ βουλῆς: cf. l. 12 τοῦ δήμου προεστήκει. Both parties were represented in the βουλή. In l. 23 also βουλή occurs without the article. Cf. Dio C. xxxvi. 11 βουλῆς γεγονώς, Plut. *Coriol.* 30 ἀπὸ βουλῆς. — 21. πείθει ὥστε: see on c. 31. 10. τῷ νόμῳ ἐξείργοντο: sc. τοῦ ταξάμενοι ἀποδοῦναι. — 23. μέλλειν . . . νομίζειν: whereby the relation with Athens would be effected, which the Athenians themselves had rejected, i. 44. § 1. — 24. ξυνίσταντο: of conspirators also ii. 88. 4; v. 82. 4; viii. 65. 6. The subj. is the five *with their followers*. — 26. καὶ ἄλλους: *i.e.* the leaders of the democratic party. — 27. καὶ ἰδιωτῶν: perhaps partisans of Pithias, who had come to his rescue. — οἱ δέ τινες . . . ὀλίγοι: *i.e.* some few of the partisans of Pithias who were present in the βουλευτήριον, not of the democratic factions in general; for while most of the leaders doubtless perished at this time, the faction itself was not almost entirely destroyed. For τινες ὀλίγοι, cf. i. 63. 7; iv. 46. 17; 56. 7. — τῆς αὐτῆς γνώμης: as in i. 113. 10; v. 46. 26. For the pred. gen., see G. 1094; H. 732;

τῷ Πειθίᾳ ὀλίγοι ἐς τὴν Ἀττικὴν τριήρη κατέφυγον ἔτι παρ-
71 οῦσαν. δράσαντες δὲ τοῦτο καὶ ξυγκαλέσαντες Κερκυ- 1
ραίους εἶπον ὅτι ταῦτα καὶ βέλτιστα εἴη καὶ ἥκιστ᾽ ἂν
δουλωθεῖεν ὑπ᾽ Ἀθηναίων, τό τε λοιπὸν μηδετέρους
δέχεσθαι ἀλλ᾽ ἢ μιᾷ νηὶ ἡσυχάζοντας, τὸ δὲ πλέον πο-
5 λέμιον ἡγεῖσθαι. ὡς δὲ εἶπον, καὶ ἐπικυρῶσαι ἠνάγκασαν τὴν γνώμην. πέμπουσι δὲ καὶ ἐς τὰς Ἀθήνας εὐθὺς 2
πρέσβεις περί τε τῶν πεπραγμένων διδάξοντας ὡς ξυνέφερε καὶ τοὺς ἐκεῖ καταπεφευγότας πείσοντας μηδὲν
ἀνεπιτήδειον πράσσειν, ὅπως μή τις ἐπιστροφὴ γένηται.

Kr. *Spr.* 47, 6, 10. — 28. **ἐς τὴν Ἀττικὴν τριήρη** : *cf.* l. 7.

71. *The victorious oligarchs take precautions for their security.*

2. ταῦτα... δουλωθεῖεν: ταῦτα refers to what has already happened, the murder of the democratic leaders, hence εἴη is used without ἂν of the past, but ἥκιστ᾽ ἂν δουλωθεῖεν of the future. For the position of καὶ before βέλτιστα, see on c. 67. 24. — **3. τό τε λοιπὸν κτέ.**: τε introduces a third member, of which the verbs, as expressing a proposal after εἰπεῖν, are in the inf., as ii. 13. 14. GMT. 99; II. 946 b; Kr. *Spr.* 55, 3, 13. — **μηδετέρους δέχεσθαι ἀλλ᾽ ἢ μιᾷ νηί**: similar formulae also ii. 7. 13; vi. 52. 7. ἀλλ᾽ ἢ, nisi, as in v. 60. 5; 80. 6; vii. 50. 23; viii. 28. 9. II. 1046, 2 c; Kr. *Spr.* 69, 4, 6. — **4. ἡσυχάζοντας**: remaining quiet, *i.e.* taking neither side; to be construed with τοὺς Κερκυραίους, as a comparison with ii. 7. 13 shows. — **τὸ δὲ πλέον**: *any larger number*. *Cf.* c. 108. 13; ii. 100. 26.

7. ὡς ξυνέφερε: "where their interest lay," *i.e.* to put matters in the most favourable light for themselves. — **8. τοὺς ἐκεῖ καταπεφευγότας**: *i.e.* those who had taken refuge first on the Attic trireme (c. 70. 28), and afterwards had fled to Athens. ἐκεῖ instead of ἐκεῖσε, because of the force of the pf. G. 1226; II. 788 b. *Cf.* ἐν for ἐς after pf., i. 87. 18; iv. 14. 7; vii. 71. 40; 87. 13. Kr. *Spr.* 68, 12, 2. — **9. ὅπως μή τις ἐπιστροφὴ γένηται**: *that vengeance may not be taken* on Corcyra, *i.e.* by the Athenians. ἐπιστροφή (lit. animadversio, ἄμυνα Suid. s.v.) in this sense also Polyb. iv. 4. 4 καὶ κοινῆς αὐτοὺς ἐπιστροφῆς ἔφη τεύξεσθαι, xxii. 17. 7 καὶ ἐπιστροφῆς εἶναι καὶ κολάσεως. It expresses the purpose of πέμπουσι πρέσβεις, not a warning μηδὲν ἀνεπιτήδειον πράσσειν. So also Kr. and Bm. explain. St. renders *revolution* (rerum conversio), comparing Soph. *O. C.* 537 ἰὼ δῆτα μυρίων γ᾽ ἐπιστροφαὶ κακῶν, and Polyb. xxii. 13. 15 καὶ τὰ μὲν κατὰ τοὺς Αἰτωλοὺς καὶ καθόλου τοὺς Ἕλληνας τοιαύτην ἔσχε τὴν ἐπιστροφήν (Ursinus's conjecture). Arn. and Jow. prefer *counter-revolution*.

72 ἐλθόντων δὲ οἱ Ἀθηναῖοι τούς τε πρέσβεις ὡς νεω- 1
τερίζοντας ξυλλαβόντες καὶ ὅσους ἔπεισαν κατέθεντο ἐς
Λίγιναν. ἐν δὲ τούτῳ τῶν Κερκυραίων οἱ ἔχοντες τὰ 2
πράγματα ἐλθούσης τριήρους Κορινθίας καὶ Λακεδαιμονίων πρέσβεων ἐπιτίθενται τῷ δήμῳ, καὶ μαχόμενοι ἐνί-
κησαν. ἀφικομένης δὲ νυκτὸς ὁ μὲν δῆμος ἐς τὴν ἀκρό- 3
πολιν καὶ τὰ μετέωρα τῆς πόλεως καταφεύγει, καὶ αὐτοῦ
ξυλλεγεὶς ἱδρύθη καὶ τὸν Ὑλλαϊκὸν λιμένα εἶχον· οἱ δὲ
τήν τε ἀγορὰν κατέλαβον, οὗπερ οἱ πολλοὶ ᾤκουν αὐτῶν,
καὶ τὸν λιμένα τὸν πρὸς αὐτῇ καὶ πρὸς τὴν ἤπειρον.

72. *The demos, attacked by the oligarchs, seizes the Acropolis and other high points, as well as the Hyllaic harbour. Their opponents take possession of the agora and the adjacent harbour.*

1. **ἐλθόντων**: sc. τῶν πρέσβεων. For gen. abs. without expressed subj., when this can be easily supplied from the context, see on i. 2. 8. GMT. 818; II. 972 a. — 2. **ὅσους ἔπεισαν**: sc. of the ἐκεῖ καταπεφευγότες. — **κατέθεντο**: see on c. 28. 14.
3. **οἱ ἔχοντες τὰ πράγματα**: see on c. 11. 11; 28. 1. — 4. **ἐλθούσης**: placed first in agreement with the nearest noun, but belonging also to πρέσβεων. See on c. 70. 7. — 5. **ἐπιτίθενται τῷ δήμῳ**: the oligarchs thought they could not carry out their further plans without a second and greater butchery.
6. **ἀφικομένης νυκτός**: Kr. conjectures ἐφικομένης, acc. to analogy of ἐπιέναι, ἐφήκειν (iv. 129. 28; viii. 67. 7; 94. 1). But ἀφικνεῖσθαι can be used with νύξ, as with νόσος ii. 48. 9, and with ἀγγελία v. 64. 1; viii. 15. 1.

ἐφικνεῖσθαι is not found in Thuc. The approach of night is usually expressed by ἐπιγίγνεσθαι (c. 112. 3; iv. 25. 9; 48. 16; 125. 6). — **ἐς τὴν ἀκρόπολιν**: regarding the site, see B. Schmidt, p. 27 f. — 7. **τὰ μετέωρα**: *the higher points.* Cf. c. 89. 11; iv. 44. 11; 57. 9; 112. 8; 124. 19. — 8. **ἱδρύθη**: of a temporary occupation also iv. 44. 11; 131. 2. — **τὸν Ὑλλαϊκὸν λιμένα**: Leake (in Bloomfield's ed.), after careful investigation, concludes the Hyllaic harbour to be the now shallow bay which extends inward west of the southward projecting promontory on which the acropolis lay (now called the bay of Chalikiopulos). The harbour 'by the agora and toward the mainland' (l. 10), where the νεώριον was (c. 74. 6), Leake considers to be the modern bay of Kastrades at the northern end of the peninsula. See also J. Partsch, *die Insel Korfu*, p. 65, and B. Schmidt, p. 22 ff. — **εἶχον**: easy transition to the plural. Cf. i. 13 6; 34. 5. Kühn. 359, 2. — 9. **οὗπερ**: *where*, i.e. adjacent to which. See on c. 75. 19.

73 τῇ δ' ὑστεραίᾳ ἠκροβολίσαντό τε ὀλίγα καὶ ἐς τοὺς ἀγροὺς περιέπεμπον ἀμφότεροι, τοὺς δούλους παρακαλοῦντές τε καὶ ἐλευθερίαν ὑπισχνούμενοι· καὶ τῷ μὲν δήμῳ τῶν οἰκετῶν τὸ πλῆθος παρεγένετο ξύμμα-
5 χον, τοῖς δ' ἑτέροις ἐκ τῆς ἠπείρου ἐπίκουροι ὀκτακόσιοι.
74 διαλιπούσης δ' ἡμέρας μάχη αὖθις γίγνεται, καὶ νικᾷ 1 ὁ δῆμος χωρίων τε ἰσχύι καὶ πλήθει προέχων, αἵ τε γυναῖκες αὐτοῖς τολμηρῶς ξυνεπελάβοντο βάλλουσαι ἀπὸ τῶν οἰκιῶν τῷ κεράμῳ καὶ παρὰ φύσιν ὑπομένουσαι
5 τὸν θόρυβον. γενομένης δὲ τῆς τροπῆς περὶ δείλην ὀψίαν 2 δείσαντες οἱ ὀλίγοι μὴ αὐτοβοεὶ ὁ δῆμος τοῦ τε νεωρίου

73. *Both parties get reinforcements.*

1. ἠκροβολίσαντο: of light skirmishing as a prelude to severer fighting, also iv. 34. 2; ἀκροβολισμός, vii. 25. 19, 37. — **ὀλίγα**: acc. neut. pl. of inner obj., approximating to an adverb. See on c. 40. 12; i. 38. 6; vii. 34. 23. — **2. τοὺς δούλους**: in the case required by the nearest partic., but belonging to both. — **4. τὸ πλῆθος**: *the majority*, as in i. 106. 8; 125. 4; iv. 96. 32; viii. 81. 4. — **5. ἐπίκουροι**: see on c. 18. 3; i. 115. 18.

74. *In a bitter conflict in the city itself, in which the oligarchs for their own protection set fire to all the houses about the agora, the demos is victorious.*

1. διαλιπούσης: intr., of time, as in i. 112. 1. The day between the two μάχαι is the one whose events have just been described in c. 73. — **2. αἵ τε γυναῖκες κτέ.**: *cf.* ii. 4. 5. — **3. ξυνεπελάβοντο**: intr., the obj. of the common effort being implied in the context. *Cf.* i. 115. 9;

viii. 92. 31. — **βάλλουσαι ἀπὸ τῶν οἰκιῶν κτέ.**: as at Plataea, ii. 4. 7. — **4. τῷ κεράμῳ**: collective, as in ii. 4. 7; iv. 48. 10. — **παρὰ φύσιν**: as in vi. 17. 1.

5. περὶ δείλην ὀψίαν: as in viii. 26. 1. Schol. τοῦ ἡλίου περὶ δυσμὰς ὄντος. — **6. αὐτοβοεί**: *with a sudden rush*, lit. *at the first cry. Cf.* Liv. i. 11 primo impetu et clamore, vi. 4 primo clamore atque impetu. The word occurs also c. 113. 27; ii. 81. 21; v. 3. 9; viii. 23. 11; 62. 8; 71. 12, but is not found elsewhere except in late writers. Acc. to Marcell. *Vit.* 52, it is ἀρχαιότερον τῶν κατ' αὐτὸν χρόνων. Kr. quotes Bekker's *Anecd.* p. 214 and 465, ταχέως καὶ ἅμα τῷ πολεμικῷ ἀλαλαγμῷ. οὕτω Θουκυδίδης, παρὰ Θεοπόμπῳ δὲ ἀντὶ τοῦ κατὰ κράτος. — **τοῦ νεωρίου**: apparently the strongest of the points occupied by the oligarchs (c. 72. § 3). The νεώρια were usually enclosed by walls. See Hermann, *Gr. Ant.* ii. 2, p. 277. Thuc.'s silence as to the site of this νεώριον would seem to indicate that he re-

κρατήσειεν ἐπελθὼν καὶ σφᾶς διαφθείρειεν, ἐμπιπρᾶσι τὰς οἰκίας τὰς ἐν κύκλῳ τῆς ἀγορᾶς καὶ τὰς ξυνοικίας, ὅπως μὴ ᾖ ἔφοδος, φειδόμενοι οὔτε οἰκείας οὔτε ἀλλο-
10 τρίας, ὥστε καὶ χρήματα πολλὰ ἐμπόρων κατεκαύθη καὶ ἡ πόλις ἐκινδύνευσε πᾶσα διαφθαρῆναι, εἰ ἄνεμος ἐπεγένετο τῇ φλογὶ ἐπίφορος ἐς αὐτήν.

Καὶ οἱ μὲν παυσάμενοι τῆς μάχης ὡς ἑκάτεροι ἡσυ- 3 χάσαντες τὴν νύκτα ἐν φυλακῇ ἦσαν, καὶ ἡ Κορινθία
15 ναῦς τοῦ δήμου κεκρατηκότος ὑπεξανήγετο, καὶ τῶν ἐπικούρων οἱ πολλοὶ ἐς τὴν ἤπειρον λαθόντες διεκομίσθησαν.

75 τῇ δ' ἐπιγιγνομένῃ ἡμέρᾳ Νικόστρατος ὁ Διειτρέφους, 1 Ἀθηναίων στρατηγός, παραγίγνεται βοηθῶν ἐκ Ναυ-

garded a νεώριον as part of every harbour. See on c. 81. 8. — 8. τῆς ἀγορᾶς : *cf*. 72. 9. — τὰς ξυνοικίας : *i.e.* large tenement houses (= insulae at Rome). *Cf*. Aeschin. i. 124 ὅπου μὲν πολλοὶ μισθωσάμενοι μίαν οἴκησιν διελόμενοι ἔχουσι ξυνοικίαν καλοῦμεν, ὅπου δ' εἷς ἐνοικεῖ οἰκίαν. Also Ar. *Eq*. 1001; (Xen.) de *Rep. Athen.* 1. 17. — 10. χρήματα : *wares*, as vi. 97. 27 ; vii. 24. 9 ; 25. 7. — 11. εἰ ἄνεμος ἐπεγένετο ... ἐπίφορος : *cf*. ii. 77. 20 πνεῦμα εἰ ἐπεγένετο αὐτῇ ἐπίφορον. — εἰ ἐπεγένετο : si ingruisset, since ἐκινδύνευσε διαφθαρῆναι is about equiv. to διεφθάρη ἄν. See on c. 10. 20. GMT. 427 a ; Kühn. 392[b], 5.
13. ὡς ἑκάτεροι : utrique pro se (as ὡς ἕκαστοι, i. 3. 19), to be construed with ἡσυχάσαντες. — ἡσυχάσαντες : *after they had become quiet*, *i.e.* gone to rest again. — 14. ἐν φυλακῇ ἦσαν : *cf*. ii. 13. 52 ; iv. 55. 6. See on c. 75. 11. — ἡ Κορινθία ναῦς : *cf*. c. 72. 4. — 15. ὑπεξανήγετο :

slipped out to sea. The word seems to occur only here. — τῶν ἐπικούρων : *cf*. c. 73. 5. — 16. λαθόντες διεκομίσθησαν : *cf*. c. 51. 9 ; vii. 29. 10. GMT. 893.

75. *The Athenian strategus, Nicostratus, arriving at Corcyra from Naupactus with twelve ships, makes an unsuccessful effort to effect an adjustment.*

1. Νικόστρατος : mentioned as general also iv. 53. 5 ; 119. 10 ; 129. 11 ; v. 61. 3. — Διειτρέφους : so acc. to inscriptions, although the Mss. have Διιτρέφους. See St. *Qu. Gr.*[2] p. 38 ; Meisterhans,[2] p. 40. — 2. παραγίγνεται βοηθῶν κτἑ. : a crisis in the στάσις of the Corcyraeans is now reached, inasmuch as after this there is outside interference in the conflicts. Nicostratus prob. reached Corcyra (see App. on c. 70. 3) about the time when Alcidas arrived in Cyllene (c. 69. § 1 ; *cf*. c. 76), and Müller-Strübing is doubtless right in con-

πάκτου δώδεκα ναυσὶ καὶ Μεσσηνίων πεντακοσίοις ὁπλίταις· ξύμβασίν τε ἔπρασσε καὶ πείθει ὥστε ξυγχωρῆσαι ἀλλήλοις δέκα μὲν ἄνδρας τοὺς αἰτιωτάτους κρῖναι (οἳ οὐκέτι ἔμειναν), τοὺς δ' ἄλλους οἰκεῖν σπονδὰς πρὸς ἀλλήλους ποιησαμένους καὶ πρὸς Ἀθηναίους ὥστε τοὺς αὐτοὺς ἐχθροὺς καὶ φίλους νομίζειν. καὶ ὁ μὲν ταῦτα 2 πράξας ἔμελλεν ἀποπλεύσεσθαι, οἱ δὲ τοῦ δήμου προστάται πείθουσιν αὐτὸν πέντε μὲν ναῦς τῶν αὐτοῦ σφίσι καταλιπεῖν, ὅπως ἧσσόν τι ἐν κινήσει ὦσιν οἱ ἐναντίοι, ἴσας δὲ αὐτοὶ πληρώσαντες ἐκ σφῶν αὐτῶν ξυμπέμψειν. καὶ ὁ μὲν ξυνεχώρησεν, οἱ δὲ τοὺς ἐχθροὺς κατέλεγον ἐς 3

jecturing (N. *Jahrbb.* cxxxiii. p. 597), that his appearance was due to the news of the murder of Pithias (c. 70. 26), and that this intelligence was the occasion also of the voyage of the Peloponnesians to Corcyra (c. 69. § 2). — **ἐκ Ναυπάκτου δώδεκα ναυσί**: *cf.* c. 69. 10, and see App. on c. 77. **12. — 4. ξύμβασιν ἔπρασσε**: *tried to effect an agreement.* — **ὥστε**: see on c. 31. 10. — **5. δέκα μὲν ἄνδρας ... οἰκεῖν**: see on c. 48. 5. — **δέκα ἄνδρας τοὺς αἰτιωτάτους**; for the order, see on c. 42. 4. — **αἰτιωτάτους**: *most to blame*, sc. for the bloody conflicts that had occurred. This expression proves that all the ten men belonged to the ὀλίγοι, and this is confirmed by the circumstances under which the agreement was effected. See B. Schmidt, p. 73. — **οἳ οὐκέτι ἔμειναν**: parenthetical, "who no longer remained, after the conclusion of the agreement, but made off." — **6. σπονδὰς ποιησαμένους ὥστε**: *cf.* i. 44. 4 ξυμμαχίαν ποιήσασθαι ὥστε. — **7. ὥστε ... νομίζειν**: belongs only to πρὸς Ἀθηναίους, not to πρὸς ἀλλήλους. For ὥστε, *on condition that*, see on c. 28. 4; i. 28. 18. The formula τοὺς αὐτοὺς ἐχθροὺς καὶ φίλους νομίζειν also c. 70. 23; i. 44. 5; vii. 33. 29. *Cf.* also v. 48. 6 τοῖς αὐτοῖς πολεμεῖν καὶ εἰρήνην ἄγειν. **8. ὁ μὲν ἔμελλεν..., οἱ δὲ ... πείθουσι**: paratactic connexion, where a dependent const. in the first clause might have been expected. — **11. ὅπως ... οἱ ἐναντίοι**: *that their opponents might be less inclined to stir.* For ἧσσόν τι, see on c. 45. 29. — **ἐν κινήσει ὦσιν**: a periphrasis indicating an enduring condition, as ἐν ταραχῇ καὶ ἀπορίᾳ ἐγίγνοντο, vii. 44. 1; ἐν ἐλπίδι εἶναι, i. 74. 22; iv. 70. 20; vii. 25. 4, 43; 46. 6; ἐν φυλακῇ εἶναι, c. 74. 14; ii. 13. 52; iv. 55. 6. — **12. ἴσας**: after numerals, *an equal number of*. See on i. 115. 13. — **ξυμπέμψειν**: depends on ἐπαγγέλλονται, or some such word, to be supplied from πείθουσιν. For similar const., *cf.* c. 94. 19. Kr. *Spr.* 65, 11, 7.

13. καὶ ὁ μὲν ξυνεχώρησεν κτέ.: the objections urged by Müller-Strü-

τὰς ναῦς. δείσαντες δὲ ἐκεῖνοι μὴ ἐς τὰς Ἀθήνας ἀπο-
15 πεμφθῶσι καθίζουσιν ἐς τὸ τῶν Διοσκόρων ἱερόν. Νι- 4
κόστρατος δὲ αὐτοὺς ἀνίστη τε καὶ παρεμυθεῖτο. ὡς δ᾽
οὐκ ἔπειθεν, ὁ δῆμος ὁπλισθεὶς ἐπὶ τῇ προφάσει ταύτῃ,
ὡς οὐδὲν αὐτῶν ὑγιὲς διανοουμένων τῇ τοῦ μὴ ξυμπλεῖν
ἀπιστίᾳ, τά τε ὅπλα αὐτῶν ἐκ τῶν οἰκιῶν ἔλαβε καὶ
20 αὐτῶν τινας οἷς ἐπέτυχον, εἰ μὴ Νικόστρατος ἐκώλυσε,
διέφθειραν ἄν. ὁρῶντες δ᾽ οἱ ἄλλοι τὰ γιγνόμενα καθί- 5
ζουσιν ἐς τὸ Ἥραιον ἱκέται καὶ γίγνονται οὐκ ἐλάσσους

bing (ibid. p. 598) against the credibility of what is here related are refuted by B. Schmidt, p. 74 f. — κατέλεγον: of levying troops for military or naval service. *Cf.* vii. 31. 27; viii. 31. 2, both in mid., the commander being subject. — **15. καθίζουσιν**: see on c. 28. 13. — **τὸ τῶν Διοσκόρων ἱερόν**: Διοσκόρων (not Διοσκούρων) with Bk. and others, acc. to Laur. See St. *Qu. Gr.*[2] p. 46; Meisterhans,[2] p. 21. The site of the sanctuary is unknown. See B. Schmidt, p. 33 f. — **16. ἀνίστη**: the regular word for this action. *Cf.* l. 24; 28. 13; i. 126. 33; 128. 3; 137. 1. Acc. to the following narrative, ἀνίστη must be understood, with B. Schmidt, p. 75, not of the mere attempt, but of the actual accomplishment. The correlation τε καί also supports this view. As Schmidt rightly observes (p. 73), ἀνίστη carries the idea of pledging the security of the ἱκέται.
17. ἐπὶ τῇ προφάσει ταύτῃ: on this ground. *Cf.* i. 141. 3; iv. 80. 7; v. 42. 7. — **18. οὐδὲν ὑγιὲς διανοουμένων**: lit. *planning nothing wholesome for the state.* They view the matter, of course, from a party point of view.

Cf. iv. 22. 9; Dem. xli. 22 τὰ μηδὲν ὑγιὲς ὄντα μηδ᾽ ἀληθῆ γράμματα, Plut. *Otho* 3 οὐδὲν ὑγιὲς διανοεῖσθαι. — **τῇ τοῦ μὴ ξυμπλεῖν ἀπιστίᾳ**: by their refusal to sail. For μή with inf. after ἀπιστίᾳ, which gets from the context the force of *refusal* arising from *mistrust*, see on c. 32. 13. *Cf.* i. 10. 3 ἀπιστοίη μὴ γενέσθαι τὸν στόλον τοσοῦτον. — **19. ἐκ τῶν οἰκιῶν**: acc. to Müller-Strübing (ibid. p. 599), this mention of the houses of the ὀλίγοι is incompatible with c. 72. 8 οἱ δὲ (*i.e.* οἱ ὀλίγοι) τήν τε ἀγορὰν κατέλαβον, οὗπερ οἱ πολλοὶ ᾤκουν αὐτῶν, and c. 74. 7 (οἱ ὀλίγοι) ἐμπιπρᾶσι τὰς οἰκίας τὰς ἐν κύκλῳ τῆς ἀγορᾶς καὶ τὰς ξυνοικίας. But Schmidt rightly observes (p. 75), that in c. 72. 8 only the most, not *all*, of the oligarchs are meant. Besides, it is not necessary to restrict οὗπερ there to the immediate environment of the agora. — **20. αὐτῶν τινας οἷς ἐπέτυχον**: these had doubtless left the place where Nicostratus had treated with the ἱκέται, and gone home.
21. καθίζουσιν . . . ἱκέται: see on c. 28. 13; i. 24. 19. — **22. ἐς τὸ Ἥραιον**: Bl. thinks that they removed from the temple of Castor and Pollux to

τετρακοσίων. ὁ δὲ δῆμος δείσας μή τι νεωτερίσωσιν, ἀνίστησί τε αὐτοὺς πείσας καὶ διακομίζει ἐς τὴν πρὸ τοῦ
25 Ἡραίου νῆσον, καὶ τὰ ἐπιτήδεια ἐκεῖσε αὐτοῖς διεπέμπετο.
76 Τῆς δὲ στάσεως ἐν τούτῳ οὔσης τετάρτῃ ἢ πέμπτῃ ἡμέρᾳ μετὰ τὴν τῶν ἀνδρῶν ἐς τὴν νῆσον διακομιδὴν αἱ ἐκ τῆς Κυλλήνης Πελοποννησίων νῆες, μετὰ τὸν ἐκ τῆς Ἰωνίας πλοῦν ἐφ' ὅρμῳ οὖσαι, παραγίγνονται τρεῖς

that of Hera, because the greater sanctity of the latter offered a surer asylum.— **γίγνονται**: with numerals, as in i. 107. 24; ii. 13. 27; 20. 11; 98. 14; iv. 9. 10. — **23. τετρακοσίων**: from the largeness of the number B. Schmidt concludes (p. 75 f.) that οἱ ἄλλοι in l. 21 refers to the rest of the oligarchs in general, not simply to the rest of those that refused to go upon the ships. But the latter view seems tenable. For, besides the substitutes for the proportional part of the 500 Messenian hoplites of Nicostratus (forty-two men for each ship), there may be reckoned for the five ships all the usual crew of Attic triremes, except the rowers, i.e. acc. to Boeckh i.[2] p. 389, thirty men each. And even of the oarsmen some may not have been slaves or mercenaries.— **νεωτερίσωσιν**: applied to any innovation in established order, esp. to harsh and violent changes. Cf. c. 66. 9; i. 58. 3; ii. 3. 7; iv. 51. 3. — **24. διακομίζει . . . νῆσον**: cf. iv. 46. 11 αὐτοὺς ἐς τὴν νῆσον οἱ στρατηγοὶ τὴν Πτυχίαν ἐς φυλακὴν διεκόμισαν. — **ἐς τὴν πρὸ τοῦ Ἡραίου νῆσον**: Leake (in Bloomfield's ed., c. 72. 8) thinks the Heraeum stood on the esplanade between the modern city (Corfu) and its citadel on the opposite island; and this island,

not Ptychia-Vido, as others think, he considers to be the νῆσος πρὸ τοῦ Ἡραίου. B. Schmidt (p. 34 ff.) follows Leake with reference to the island, but locates the Heraeum near the southern shore of the bay of Kastrades, on the hill where now is the monastery of Euphemia. The Heraeum seems certainly to have been on the mainland (see on c. 79. 4), though Partsch (die Insel Korfu, p. 66 ff.), who decides for Vido as the νῆσος, locates the temple on the modern citadel-island. See also Partsch, Wochenschr. f. kl. Phil. 1891, p. 593 ff.
76. Fifty-three Peloponnesian ships under Alcidas and Brasidas appear before Corcyra.
3. αἱ ἐκ τῆς Κυλλήνης . . . . νῆες: cf. c. 69. 6. For ἐκ τῆς, the usual prolepsis, see on c. 5. 1. — **4. ἐφ' ὅρμῳ**: with St. (Rh. Mus. xxvi. p. 345 f.), for ἔφορμοι of the Mss., which the Schol. explains by ἐν ὅρμῳ διατρίβουσαι. ἔφορμος as adj. seems not to be found; as a noun, it is found in c. 6. 6; iv. 27. 7; 32. 4. ὅρμος is a place of safe anchorage, not a harbour proper. Cf. iv. 26. 9; vi. 44. 12; vii. 41. 4. The expression ἐφ' ὅρμῳ εἶναι is not found elsewhere. Kr. conjectured ἐν ἐφόρμῳ οὖσαι, Meineke and v. H. ἐφορμοῦσαι. That ἔφορμος

5 καὶ πεντήκοντα· ἦρχε δὲ αὐτῶν Ἀλκίδας, ὅσπερ καὶ πρότερον, καὶ Βρασίδας αὐτῷ ξύμβουλος ἐπέπλει. ὁρμισάμενοι δὲ ἐς Σύβοτα λιμένα τῆς ἠπείρου ἅμα ἕῳ ἐπέπλεον
77 τῇ Κερκύρᾳ. οἱ δὲ πολλῷ θορύβῳ καὶ πεφοβημένοι τά τ' 1
ἐν τῇ πόλει καὶ τὸν ἐπίπλουν παρεσκευάζοντό τε ἅμα
ἑξήκοντα ναῦς καὶ τὰς αἰεὶ πληρουμένας ἐξέπεμπον πρὸς
τοὺς ἐναντίους, παραινούντων Ἀθηναίων σφᾶς τε ἐᾶσαι
5 πρῶτον ἐκπλεῦσαι καὶ ὕστερον πάσαις ἅμα ἐκείνους ἐπιγενέσθαι. ὡς δὲ αὐτοῖς πρὸς τοῖς πολεμίοις ἦσαν σπο- 2
ράδες αἱ νῆες, δύο μὲν εὐθὺς ηὐτομόλησαν, ἐν ἑτέραις
δὲ ἀλλήλοις οἱ ἐμπλέοντες ἐμάχοντο, ἦν δὲ οὐδεὶς κόσμος τῶν ποιουμένων. ἰδόντες δὲ οἱ Πελοποννήσιοι τὴν 3
10 ταραχὴν εἴκοσι μὲν ναυσὶ πρὸς τοὺς Κερκυραίους ἐτάξαντο, ταῖς δὲ λοιπαῖς πρὸς τὰς δώδεκα ναῦς τῶν Ἀθη-

and ἐφορμεῖν do not always refer to a blockade is shown by the use of ἐφόρμησις in vi. 48. 9. After the forty ships of Alcidas had returned from the Ionian coast and united with the thirteen of Brasidas, the fleet lay for some time at anchor at Cyllene, occupied with preparations for the voyage to Corcyra, c. 69. 13. — 6. ξύμβουλος: see on c. 69. 7. — ἐπέπλει: *was on board*. See on c. 16. 17. It is quite different from ἐπέπλεον in the next line. — 7. Σύβοτα: name of islands, promontory, and harbour on the Thesprotian coast (*cf.* i. 47. 4; 50. 14; 54. 4); still existing in *S. Nicolo di Sivota*.

77, 78. *In a sea-fight the Corcyraean ships, advancing in disorder, are thrown into confusion. Their retreat is covered by the twelve Attic ships, which after an indecisive conflict retire before superior numbers.*

1. οἱ δέ: *i.e.* the democratic authorities in Corcyra. — πολλῷ θορύβῳ καὶ πεφοβημένοι: unlike elements combined in the same pred. relation. Kr. *Spr.* 59, 2, 3. *Cf.* c. 25. 8; 34. 17; 42. 23; i. 63. 7. — 3. τὰς αἰεὶ πληρουμένας ἐξέπεμπον: both impf. and pres. partic. are necessary with the iterative αἰεί. See on c. 23. 11. — 4. παραινούντων Ἀθηναίων: *although the Athenians advised. Cf.* c. 79. 10. — 5. πάσαις ἅμα: *i.e.* with all at once, not ταῖς αἰεὶ πληρουμέναις. — ἐπιγενέσθαι: *to follow after. Cf.* ii. 44. 12. 6. αὐτοῖς: the dat. placed first in the most general relation to the whole. *Cf.* i. 6. 8; 48. 9. — 8. οἱ ἐμπλέοντες: only here = οἱ ἐπιβάται. — 9. τῶν ποιουμένων: *cf.* vi. 87. 10; viii. 43. 14; 46. 27; 69. 9. 10. ἐτάξαντο: 'direct middle,' as in i. 48. 9; iv. 11. 2, etc. G. 1242, 1; H. 812. *Cf.* κύκλον τάξασθαι, c. 78. 7;

78 ναίων, ὧν ἦσαν αἱ δύο Σαλαμινία καὶ Πάραλος. καὶ 1
οἱ μὲν Κερκυραῖοι κακῶς τε καὶ κατ' ὀλίγας προσπίπτοντες ἐταλαιπωροῦντο ⟨τὸ⟩ καθ' αὑτούς· οἱ δ' Ἀθηναῖοι φοβούμενοι τὸ πλῆθος καὶ τὴν περικύκλωσιν ἁθρό-
5 αις μὲν οὐ προσέπιπτον οὐδὲ κατὰ μέσον ταῖς ἐφ' ἑαυτοὺς τεταγμέναις, προσβαλόντες δὲ κατὰ κέρας καταδύ-
ουσι μίαν ναῦν. καὶ μετὰ ταῦτα κύκλον ταξαμένων
αὐτῶν περιέπλεον καὶ ἐπειρῶντο θορυβεῖν. γνόντες δὲ οἱ 2
πρὸς τοῖς Κερκυραίοις καὶ δείσαντες, μὴ ὅπερ ἐν Ναυ-
10 πάκτῳ γένοιτο, ἐπιβοηθοῦσι· καὶ γενόμεναι ἁθρόαι αἱ
νῆες ἅμα τὸν ἐπίπλουν τοῖς Ἀθηναίοις ἐποιοῦντο. οἱ δ' 3
ὑπεχώρουν ἤδη πρύμναν κρουόμενοι καὶ ἅμα τὰς τῶν Κερ-

ii. 83. 23.—12. ὧν ἦσαν κτέ.: cf. i.
116. 8 ὧν ἦσαν αἱ εἴκοσι στρατιώτιδες.
See App.—Σαλαμινία καὶ Πάραλος:
see on c. 33. 2.
78. 2. κακῶς: referring to οὐδεὶς
κόσμος of c. 77. 8. — κατ' ὀλίγας: as
described c. 77. § 1. — 3. ἐταλαιπωροῦντο: see on c. 3. 1. — ⟨τὸ⟩ καθ'
αὑτούς: in sua parte, Haase's conjecture (Lucubr. p. 44), adopted by
Cl. and St., for the vulg. καθ' αὑτούς,
suits the context better. Cf. c. 108.
10; i. 62. 24. The vulg. would mean
either of themselves, inter se, i.e.
without the enemy's help (cf. ii. 88.
4; iv. 71. 5), or alone, per se (cf. c.
39. 14; ii. 99. 6). — 4. τὸ πλῆθος: the
superior number, as ii. 89. 5. — ἁθρό-
αις: like κατὰ μέσον, referring to the
hostile ships, ταῖς ἐφ' ἑαυτοὺς τεταγμέναις. Both expressions supplement
each other with this sense: The Athenians fear to attack the whole fleet of
thirty-three ships in the centre, but
throwing themselves with their whole
strength upon one wing, κατὰ κέρας,

sink one ship; whereupon the Peloponnesians concentrate (κύκλον ταξαμένων) their ships in the same manner
as described in ii. 83. § 5, and the
Attic ships repeat the movement that
was so successful on the former occasion (περιέπλεον καὶ ἐπειρῶντο θορυβεῖν),
but a like result is prevented by
timely aid to the Peloponnesians
from the other division. — 5. μέσον:
the art. omitted as often. H. 661.
Cf. i. 62. 14; ii. 81. 11; iv. 31. 8;
96. 10. — ἐφ' ἑαυτούς: Palat. has ἐφ'
ἑαυτοῖς, which is supported by the
const. of c. 13. 18; ii. 70. 8. But for
the acc., cf. l. 14; 77. 10.
8. οἱ πρὸς τοῖς Κερκυραίοις: i.e.
οἱ πρὸς τοὺς Κερκυραίους τεταγμένοι τῶν
Πελοποννησίων. Cf. c. 77. 10. For
the const., cf. c. 77. 6. — 9. ὅπερ ἐν
Ναυπάκτῳ: sc. ἐγένετο. Cf. ii. 84.—
10. ἁθρόαι: i.e. the hitherto separate
divisions.
12. πρύμναν κρουόμενοι: backing
water. i.e. withdrawing without turning the vessel. See on i. 50. 21; vii.

κυραίων ἐβούλοντο προκαταφυγεῖν ὅτι μάλιστα, ἑαυτῶν
σχολῇ τε ὑποχωρούντων καὶ πρὸς σφᾶς τεταγμένων τῶν
15 ἐναντίων.

Ἡ μὲν οὖν ναυμαχία τοιαύτη γενομένη ἐτελεύτα 4
79 ἐς ἡλίου δύσιν, καὶ οἱ Κερκυραῖοι δείσαντες, μὴ σφίσιν 1
ἐπιπλεύσαντες ἐπὶ τὴν πόλιν ὡς κρατοῦντες οἱ πολέμιοι ἢ
τοὺς ἐκ τῆς νήσου ἀναλάβωσιν ἢ καὶ ἄλλο τι νεωτερίσωσι,
τούς τε ἐκ τῆς νήσου πάλιν ἐς τὸ Ἥραιον διεκόμισαν καὶ
5 τὴν πόλιν ἐφύλασσον. οἱ δ' ἐπὶ μὲν τὴν πόλιν οὐκ ἐτόλ- 2
μησαν πλεῦσαι κρατοῦντες τῇ ναυμαχίᾳ, τρισκαίδεκα δὲ

40. 2. — 13. προκαταφυγεῖν ὅτι μάλιστα, ἑαυτῶν σχολῇ κτέ.: Cl. wrote, with Vat., προκαταφυγεῖν, ἑαυτῶν ὅτι μάλιστα, remarking that it was unimportant whether or not the Corcyraeans outstripped the enemy *as far as possible* (ὅτι μάλιστα), if only they gained time to reach their harbour. But there is no need to take ὅτι μάλιστα (*cf*. i. 44. 13; v. 36. 9) in this sense. On the contrary, the fact that the Corcyraeans lost altogether thirteen ships (c. 79. 6) seems to indicate that ὅτι μάλιστα means *as much as possible*, *i.e.* as many ships as possible. St. construes ὅτι μάλιστα with ἐβούλοντο, comparing c. 47. 11; i. 141. 29; ii. 90. 17; iv. 79. 11; v. 36. 8; vi. 9. 11; viii. 91. 15. — 14. ὑποχωρούντων: gen. abs. instead of ὑποχωροῦντες, on account of the parallelism with the following clause. See also on c. 13. 30. — τεταγμένων: *cf*. l. 6; 77. 10. Hude's conjecture (p. 110) τετραμμένων is unnecessary.

16. τοιαύτη γενομένη: tacitly implying the success of the Athenian plan, — not only that they finished their retreat without loss, but also that the Corcyraeans reached the harbour, though with a loss, it is true, of thirteen ships (c. 79. § 2). — ἐτελεύτα ἐς ἡλίου δύσιν: *lasted till sunset. Cf.* c. 108. 18; i. 51. 9.

79. *The Peloponnesians, afraid to attack the city, sail away with thirteen captured Corcyraean ships, and disembarking next day at Leucimme ravage the island.*

3. τοὺς ἐκ τῆς νήσου: proleptic, as c. 76. 3. *Cf*. c. 75. 24. — νεωτερίσωσι: *resort to violence*, as in c. 66. 9; ii. 3. 7. See on c. 75. 23. — 4. τούς τε . . . ἐφύλασσον: from these words in connexion with the foregoing, B. Schmidt (p. 43) rightly infers that the Heraeum was inside of the city walls. — 5. ἐφύλασσον: = ἐν φυλακῇ or διὰ φυλακῆς εἶχον.

ἐπὶ μὲν τὴν πόλιν: the real antithesis is not τρισκαίδεκα δὲ ναῦς ἔχοντες, but, after the repetition of ἐπὶ μὲν τὴν πόλιν in l. 8, ἐπὶ δὲ τὴν Λευκίμμην (l. 11). — 6. κρατοῦντες τῇ ναυμαχίᾳ: *although superior in the naval battle*. These words, wrongly rejected by

ναῦς ἔχοντες τῶν Κερκυραίων ἀπέπλευσαν ἐς τὴν ἤπειρον ὅθενπερ ἀνηγάγοντο. τῇ δ᾽ ὑστεραίᾳ ἐπὶ μὲν τὴν 3
πόλιν οὐδὲν μᾶλλον ἐπέπλεον, καίπερ ἐν πολλῇ ταραχῇ
10 καὶ φόβῳ ὄντας καὶ Βρασίδου παραινοῦντος, ὥς λέγεται, Ἀλκίδᾳ, ἰσοψήφου δὲ οὐκ ὄντος· ἐπὶ δὲ τὴν Λευκίμμην τὸ ἀκρωτήριον ἀποβάντες ἐπόρθουν τοὺς ἀγρούς.
80 ὁ δὲ δῆμος τῶν Κερκυραίων ἐν τούτῳ, περιδεὴς γενό- 1
μενος μὴ ἐπιπλεύσωσιν αἱ νῆες, τοῖς τε ἱκέταις ἦσαν ἐς
λόγους καὶ τοῖς ἄλλοις ὅπως σωθήσεται ἡ πόλις, καί τινας
αὐτῶν ἔπεισαν ἐς τὰς ναῦς ἐσβῆναι· ἐπλήρωσαν γὰρ ὅμως
5 τριάκοντα [προσδεχόμενοι τὸν ἐπίπλουν]. οἱ δὲ Πελοποννή- 2
σιοι μέχρι μέσου ἡμέρας δῃώσαντες τὴν γῆν ἀπέπλευσαν.

Kr. as an unnecessary repetition, are added in order that πλεῦσαι ἐπὶ τὴν πόλιν may appear as the natural result of the advantage won. The indecision of Alcidas appears here, as in l. 9, in an unfavourable light. — τρισκαίδεκα δὲ ναῦς: cf. viii. 22. 5 τρισκαίδεκα ναυσίν. — 8. ὅθενπερ ἀνηγάγοντο: cf. c. 76. 7.

10. ὄντας: agreeing κατὰ ξύνεσιν with πόλιν. See on c. 2. 2. — ὥς λέγεται: shows the prudence of the historian, who is not sure of the matter, and the special mention of Brasidas indicates the interest everywhere manifested by Thuc. in the Spartan leader. See on c. 69. 7; ii. 25. 7. — 11. ἰσοψήφου οὐκ ὄντος: sc. as ξύμβουλος of the ναύαρχος. Cf. c. 69. 7; 76. 6. — τὴν Λευκίμμην: the S.E. promontory of Corcyra, now Leukimo. Cf. i. 30. 2.

80. At nightfall news comes of the approach of an Athenian fleet of sixty ships, under the command of Eurymedon.

1. ὁ δῆμος ἦσαν: collective noun with pl. verb, as in c. 75. 20; v. 82. 5. G. 900; H. 609. — 3. τοῖς ἄλλοις: the ἱκέται of c. 75. 22, who were brought back to the Heraeum (c. 79. 4), formed only a part of the aristocratic party, the ὀλίγοι of c. 7.4. 6. — καί τινας αὐτῶν ἔπεισαν: with better success than before, c. 75. § 3. — 4. ὅμως: i.e. in spite of the sad experiences of c. 77, 78. — 5. [προσδεχόμενοι τὸν ἐπίπλουν]: these words which are wanting in most Mss., and found on the margin of a few, state correctly the motive of ἐπλήρωσαν... τριάκοντα, but were doubtless added by an attentive reader from the preceding περιδεὴς γενόμενος μὴ ἐπιπλεύσωσιν.

6. μέχρι μέσου ἡμέρας: μέσον (neut.) with the gen. of a subst. seems to be found only here and vii. 52. 9 in Thuc.; for μέσος is an adj. in iv. 96. 2 μέχρι μέσου τοῦ στρατοπέδου, vi. 101. 7 διὰ μέσου τοῦ ἕλους, just as in ii. 83. 20 κατὰ μέσον τὸν πορθμόν, v. 9. 22 κατὰ

καὶ ὑπὸ νύκτα αὐτοῖς ἐφρυκτωρήθησαν ἑξήκοντα νῆες Ἀθηναίων προσπλέουσαι ἀπὸ Λευκάδος, ἃς οἱ Ἀθηναῖοι πυνθανόμενοι τὴν στάσιν καὶ τὰς μετ᾽ Ἀλκίδου ναῦς ἐπὶ Κέρ-
10 κυραν μελλούσας πλεῖν ἀπέστειλαν καὶ Εὐρυμέδοντα τὸν
81 Θουκλέους στρατηγόν. οἱ μὲν οὖν Πελοποννήσιοι τῆς νυ- 1
κτὸς εὐθὺς κατὰ τάχος ἐκομίζοντο ἐπ᾽ οἴκου παρὰ τὴν γῆν,

μέσον τὸ στράτευμα. As a noun, it is freq. in Xenophon. Kühn. 403, a γ. See on c. 78. 5.—7. ἐφρυκτωρήθησαν: i.e. by the φρυκτωροί appointed for the purpose (viii. 102. 2). See on c. 22. 34, and ii. 94. 1. This verb is found only here. — 8. ἀπὸ Λευκάδος: from its position more naturally connected, as Cl. and Bm. explain, with προσπλέουσαι than with ἐφρυκτωρήθησαν, but most editt. construe with the latter, on the ground, as some express it, that if the Athenian fleet had been already under way from Leucas it would have been at Corcyra before the Peloponnesian fleet could have escaped, or, as others, that the Athenian fleet would have got so far north by the time Alcidas reached Leucas that his fleet, even if it had sailed round Leucas, could hardly have been seen by Eurymedon's ships (c. 81. 4). For Steup's view, see App. It seems reasonable to infer from this passage that the number, as well as the approach, of the fleet was signalled, though ἑξήκοντα may be only an anticipatory explanation of the author. — 10. μελλούσας πλεῖν: pred., so that πυνθανόμενοι has the double const. of the simple obj. acc. and of the supplem. partic. Between the coming of the first information and of the second

there was prob. a slight interval; for the Peloponnesians doubtless decided upon the voyage to Corcyra (c. 69. § 2) only after the murder of Pithias (see on c. 75. 2), while the Athenians, as B. Schmidt (p. 77) rightly observes, had already learned of the outbreak of the στάσις from the Attic trireme mentioned in c. 70. 7, 28, which must have returned immediately thereafter to Athens. It is to be noticed that, although in c. 72. § 1 mention is made of precautions taken in consequence of the στάσις, here still the announcement of the outbreak is spoken of. This inconsistency would doubtless have been removed could the historian have revised his work. — Εὐρυμέδοντα: first mentioned here, but after this time freq. in active service until his death in Sicily, vii. 52. 11.

81. *Hereupon the Peloponnesians sail homewards, and the democratic party in Corcyra, falling upon its defenceless enemies, perpetrates with all the horrors of hate and revenge a terrible butchery among them.*

1. τῆς νυκτὸς εὐθὺς κατὰ τάχος: the sarcastic tone noted at c. 29. 2 ; 31. 11, is perhaps observable here also. To flee with fifty-three ships at the approach of sixty is not very creditable. — τῆς νυκτός, παρὰ τὴν γῆν: these two circumstances may account

καὶ ὑπερενεγκόντες τὸν Λευκαδίων ἰσθμὸν τὰς ναῦς, ὅπως
μὴ περιπλέοντες ὀφθῶσιν, ἀποκομίζονται. Κερκυραῖοι 2
5 δὲ αἰσθόμενοι τάς τε Ἀττικὰς ναῦς προσπλεούσας τάς τε
τῶν πολεμίων οἰχομένας, λαβόντες τούς τε Μεσσηνίους
ἐς τὴν πόλιν ἤγαγον πρότερον ἔξω ὄντας, καὶ τὰς ναῦς
περιπλεῦσαι κελεύσαντες ἃς ἐπλήρωσαν ἐς τὸν Ὑλλαϊκὸν
λιμένα, ἐν ὅσῳ περιεκομίζοντο, τῶν ἐχθρῶν εἴ τινα λά-

for Alcidas not having been seen by Eurymedon, even if the Athenian fleet when announced was advancing from Leucas. See B. Schmidt, p. 78. —3. ὑπερενεγκόντες... τὰς ναῦς: sc. with the aid of ὁλκοί, such as are mentioned c. 15.7. τὸν ἰσθμόν is governed by ὑπερ-, τὰς ναῦς by the verb. Kühn. 411, 7. Cf. iv. 8. 8; viii. 7. 7. This isthmus (cf. iv. 8.8), which then connected the island with the mainland, had been previously cut through by the Corinthians (Strab. p. 452 c). But the canal (ὁ Διόρυκτος, Polyb. v. 12) became filled with sand (Plin. Hist. Nat. iv. 1. 2, 5), and remained so until the Romans again opened it for a short time. Liv. xxxiii. 17. See Oberhummer, Akarnanien im Alterthum, p. 7 ff., and Partsch, Die Insel Leukas, p. 2 ff. (Petermann's Mitteilungen, Ergänzungsheft 95). — ὅπως ... ὀφθῶσιν: see App. on c. 80. 8. — 4. ἀποκομίζονται: sc. to Cyllene or Gytheum; and thus ended the activity of the Peloponnesian fleet for this year.

6. λαβόντες: bracketed by Cl., following Kr., on the ground that it was prob. a gloss of εἴ τινα λάβοιεν that crept into the text. But it is better to retain it, with St., for even though ii. 67. 21 οἱ δὲ λαβόντες ἐκόμισαν ἐς τὰς

Ἀθήνας may not be quite parallel, since there λαβόντες means having received, yet cf. Ar. Vesp. 1379 ἄγειν ταύτην λαβών, Lysist. 1115, 1128; Thesm. 212; Ran. 888. — τοὺς Μεσσηνίους: i.e. the 500 whom Nicostratus had brought with him, c. 75. 3. The object in bringing them into the city was doubtless merely the intimidation of the oligarchs; that they participated directly in the butchery that followed, as Cl. thought, seems probable neither from Thuc.'s narrative nor in itself. See B. Schmidt, p. 78. — 8. ἃς ἐπλήρωσαν: cf. c. 80. 4. — ἐς τὸν Ὑλλαϊκὸν λιμένα: the ships had been therefore in the harbour near the agora (c. 72. 10), which was esp. exposed to the attacks of enemies from without, since its entrance was not narrow like that of the Hyllaic harbour. They were ordered round to the Hyllaic harbour in order that the oligarchs on them might be cut off from their friends in the neighbourhood of the agora (c. 72. 9) and in the Heraeum. The matter is intelligible only if a νεώριον be assumed also for the Hyllaic harbour. See on c. 74. 6. — 9. ἐν ὅσῳ: while, as in viii. 61. 5; 87. 23. — εἴ τινα λάβοιεν: the oligarchs perhaps tried to conceal

10 βοιεν, ἀπέκτεινον. καὶ ἐκ τῶν νεῶν ὅσους ἔπεισαν ἐσ-
βῆναι ἐκβιβάζοντες ἀπεχρῶντο, ἐς τὸ Ἡραιόν τε ἐλθόντες τῶν ἱκετῶν ὡς πεντήκοντα ἄνδρας δίκην ὑποσχεῖν
ἔπεισαν καὶ κατέγνωσαν πάντων θάνατον. οἱ δὲ πολλοὶ 3
τῶν ἱκετῶν, ὅσοι οὐκ ἐπείσθησαν, ὡς ἑώρων τὰ γιγνό-
15 μενα, διέφθειρον αὐτοῦ ἐν τῷ ἱερῷ ἀλλήλους καὶ ἐκ τῶν
δένδρων τινὲς ἀπήγχοντο, οἱ δ' ὡς ἕκαστοι ἐδύναντο ἀνη-

themselves. — 10. ἐκ τῶν νεῶν: these words, which belong to ἐκβιβάζοντες, imply that it was those that had remained in the city who were killed before this. — ὅσους ἔπεισαν: cf. c. 80. 4. — 11. ἀπεχρῶντο: for which the most and best Mss. have ἀπεχώρησαν, is sufficiently protected by the remark of ancient grammarians (Suidas, Zonaras, and in Bekker's *Anecd.* p. 423 Θουκυδίδης ἀπεχρῶντο ἀντὶ τοῦ ἀνῄρουν), and is indispensable to the sense; for those on the ships were certainly killed immediately, not, as Kr. thinks, first tried along with the fifty ἱκέται. Besides, τε introduces the next clause (ἐς τὸ Ἡραιόν τε) as the *third* act in this drama of horrors. ἀποχρῆσθαι meaning *to kill* is supported only by a citation from Aristophanes in Suidas (s.v. ἀπεχρήσαντο) and Pollux ix. 153 (τοὺς ἄνδρας ἀπεχρήσαντο). But the analogy of διαχρῆσθαι (c. 36. 15; i. 126. 38, where some Mss. have ἀπεχρήσαντο; vi. 61. 17; Antiph. i. 23; Hdt. i. 24. 12; 110. 18) and καταχρῆσθαι (Hdt. i. 82. 42; 117. 5; iii. 36. 28; iv. 146. 7; vi. 135. 9, and late writers) is in its favour. The strong expression doubtless indicates the feeling of horror of the historian. The portion of the demos to be understood as subj. of ἀπεχρῶντο was of course different from that implied in ἀπέκτεινον. See B. Schmidt, p. 79. — 11. ἐς τὸ Ἡραιόν τε: cf. c. 79. 4. The particle is similarly placed also in vii. 84. 15 ἐς τὰ ἐπὶ θάτερά τε. Kühn. 520, N. 5. — 13. ἔπεισαν καὶ κατέγνωσαν: aors. to indicate summary process. That the sentence was immediately executed is plain from the following ὡς ἑώρων τὰ γιγνόμενα (partic. impf.). In all the rest of the description of the horrors, the impf. (ἀπέκτεινον, ἀπεχρῶντο, ἀπήγχοντο, ἀνηλοῦντο, ἐφόνευον, etc.) prevails, and hence in l. 15 διέφθειρον (three Mss.) is to be preferred to διέφθειραν, which most Mss. have, since there is no sufficient reason for the change of tense.

14. ὡς ἑώρων τὰ γιγνόμενα: these words, which are suspected by Müller-Strübing, p. 602 f., are quite in order, if, with B. Schmidt, p. 42 and 78 f., a high site be assumed for the Heraeum. — 15. αὐτοῦ ἐν τῷ ἱερῷ: emphatic combination. Cf. c. 98. 11; ii. 25. 18; v. 22. 2; 83. 4. See Herbst, *Gegen Cobet*, p. 58 ff. — 16. ἀνηλοῦντο: = σφᾶς αὐτοὺς ἀνήλουν. Cf. iv. 48. 17. ἀναλοῦν, which Thuc. prefers to ἀναλίσκειν, is, like ἀποχρῆσθαι, unusual in this sense. Cf. Aesch. *Agam.* 570;

λοῦντο. ἡμέρας τε ἑπτά, ἃς ἀφικόμενος ὁ Εὐρυμέδων 4
ταῖς ἑξήκοντα ναυσὶ παρέμεινε, Κερκυραῖοι σφῶν αὐτῶν
τοὺς ἐχθροὺς δοκοῦντας εἶναι ἐφόνευον, τὴν μὲν αἰτίαν
20 ἐπιφέροντες τοῖς τὸν δῆμον καταλύουσιν, ἀπέθανον δέ
τινες καὶ ἰδίας ἔχθρας ἕνεκα, καὶ ἄλλοι χρημάτων σφίσιν ὀφειλομένων ὑπὸ τῶν λαβόντων. πᾶσά τε ἰδέα κατ- 5
έστη θανάτου, καὶ οἷον φιλεῖ ἐν τῷ τοιούτῳ γίγνεσθαι,
οὐδὲν ὅ τι οὐ ξυνέβη καὶ ἔτι περαιτέρω. καὶ γὰρ πατὴρ

Soph. O. T. 1174; Eur. El. 681. From c. 75. 23 ὁ δὲ δῆμος δείσας μή τι νεωτερίσωσιν κτἑ., it may be inferred that the ἱκέται had arms.

17. ὁ Εὐρυμέδων: seems to have arrived during the first act of the horrors here related (1. 7 τὰς ναῦς ... ἀπέκτεινον); hence the butchery of the oligarchs might be reckoned from his coming. Nicostratus prob. left Corcyra before the seven days ended (cf. c. 75. 9, and see on l. 6). — 19. ἐφόνευον: slaughtered, as in i. 50. 3; vii. 29. 20; 85. 8; viii. 95. 29. It is classed by Rutherford (New. Phryn. p. 15) among the old Ionisms that survived in Tragedy. It occurs, in this sense, also in legal language in Plato (Legg. 871 d; 873 e), and is freq. in late writers. — τὴν μὲν αἰτίαν ... καταλύουσιν: i.e. λόγῳ μὲν αἰτιώμενοι τοὺς τὸν δῆμον καταλύοντας. The following clause, if regular, would have been ἔργῳ δὲ ἀποκτείνοντες καί τινας κτἑ., but there is a transition to the finite verb, owing to the moral significance of the individual occurrences. For similar change of const., cf. c. 87. § 1; ii. 47. § 3; vii. 47. § 2. "Though they asserted that they wished to bring to trial only the subverters of the democracy, yet many were killed also from other motives." καταλύειν τὸν δῆμον also v. 76. 5; viii. 54. 17; 86. 8; καταλύειν τὴν δημοκρατίαν, viii. 47. 17. καταλύειν is the technical word for this idea in Attic. Cf. Ar. Eccles. 453; Andoc. i. 95; Lys. xiii. 4; Dem. xviii. 182. — 22. ὑπὸ τῶν λαβόντων: sc. τὰ χρήματα, τῶν δανεισαμένων, Schol. So also most editt. explain, doubtless correctly, since thus the baseness of the motive is made manifest. Bm. renders by their captors.

πᾶσά τε ἰδέα: as in c. 83. 1; 98. 15; 112. 23; ii. 19. 1; 77. 7; vii. 29. 26. For τε in a résumé, see on c. 40. 16.
— 23. ἐν τῷ τοιούτῳ: "in times like those just described." ὁ τοιοῦτος as in iv. 56. 4; vii. 81. 13. See on c. 43. 12.
— 24. οὐδὲν ὅ τι οὐ: as in vii. 87. 14, 25, for the fuller form οὐδέν ἐστιν ὅ τι οὐ. Cf. ii. 62. 13. II. 1003 a; Kr. Spr. 51, 10, 11; Kühn. 555, 5. See on c. 39. 38. — καὶ ἔτι περαιτέρω: in this hyperbolical expression the adv. has the force of an adj., as in Ar. Thesm. 705 δεινὰ πράγματ᾽ ἐστὶ καὶ περαιτέρω, Av. 416 ἄπιστα καὶ πέρα κλύειν, Soph. Epig. (ap. Stob. Flor. 73, 51) ὦ πᾶν σὺ τολμήσασα καὶ πέρα γυνή. Cf. Sall.

25 παῖδα ἀπέκτεινε καὶ ἀπὸ τῶν ἱερῶν ἀπεσπῶντο καὶ πρὸς αὐτοῖς ἐκτείνοντο. οἱ δέ τινες καὶ περιοικοδομηθέντες ἐν τοῦ Διονύσου τῷ ἱερῷ ἀπέθανον.

82 Οὕτως ὠμὴ ⟨ἡ⟩ στάσις προυχώρησε, καὶ ἔδοξε μᾶλ- 1 λον, διότι ἐν τοῖς πρώτη ἐγένετο· ἐπεὶ ὕστερόν γε καὶ πᾶν ὡς εἰπεῖν τὸ Ἑλληνικὸν ἐκινήθη, διαφορῶν οὐσῶν ἑκασταχοῦ τοῖς τε τῶν δήμων προστάταις τοὺς Ἀθηναίους 5 ἐπάγεσθαι καὶ τοῖς ὀλίγοις τοὺς Λακεδαιμονίους. καὶ ἐν μὲν εἰρήνῃ οὐκ ἂν ἐχόντων πρόφασιν οὐδ' ἑτοίμων παρακαλεῖν αὐτούς, πολεμουμένων δὲ καὶ ξυμμαχίας ἅμα

Jug. 44 cuncta fuere et alia amplius. — 25. πρὸς αὐτοῖς: see on c. 70. 18. — 26. περιοικοδομηθέντες : = ἀποικοδομηθέντες (i. 134. 13 ; vii. 73. 8). Found only here in Thuc. *Cf.* Hdt. vii. 60. 11 ; Xen. *Cyrop.* i. 4. 11. — ἐν τοῦ Διονύσου τῷ ἱερῷ: see on c. 70. 16. The site of this sanctuary is unknown. See B. Schmidt, p. 33.

82, 83. *General reflections on the fearful results of party struggles, which the war produced everywhere in the Hellenic world.*

1. οὕτως ὠμή: pred. to προυχώρησε, as in i. 23. 4 μέγα to προύβη. — **ἡ στάσις**: Kr.'s restoration of the art., which could easily have been lost after ὠμή, seems necessary. since the reference is to the sedition just described. — **ἔδοξε μᾶλλον**: Schol. μᾶλλον ὠμὴ ἔδοξεν ἤπερ ἐγένετο. — 2. **ἐν τοῖς πρώτη**: see on c. 17. 2. — 3. **ὡς εἰπεῖν**: so always in Thuc., not ὡς ἔπος εἰπεῖν, as in Plato and the orators. GMT. 777, 1; II. 956. See on i. 1. 9. *Cf.* i. 138. 18; vii. 49. 18. — **τὸ Ἑλληνικόν**: as in c. 57. 11; i. 1. 6; 6. 23; including all Hellenic states, even those outside of Greece proper. —

ἐκινήθη: as in iv. 76. 21, of profound political disturbance. See on κίνησις, i. 1. 8. — **διαφορῶν οὐσῶν . . . τοὺς Λακεδαιμονίους**: "since everywhere the chiefs of the democracy and of the oligarchy were struggling, the one to bring in the Athenians, the other the Lacedaemonians." Jow. **ἐπάγεσθαι** in loose connexion with διαφορῶν οὐσῶν expresses the result. This verb is regularly used of inviting strangers into one's country. See on i. 3. 8. — 5. **καὶ ἐν μὲν εἰρήνῃ . . . ἐπορίζοντο**: *and while, in time of peace, they would have no pretext, and were not even ready to call them in, being at war, those on either side who wished a revolution easily procured allies both to harass their enemies and to acquire for themselves power from the same source.* See App. — 6. **οὐκ ἂν ἐχόντων**: gen. abs. without expressed subj., as often in Thuc. when it can be easily supplied from the context. GMT. 848; II. 972 a. See on c. 34. 17. — **ἑτοίμων**: for omission of ὄντων, *cf.* v. 64. 18, and see on c. 69. 4. — 7. **πολεμουμένων δέ**: corresponds to ἐν μὲν εἰρήνῃ. Instead of a

ἑκατέροις τῇ τῶν ἐναντίων κακώσει καὶ σφίσιν αὐτοῖς
ἐκ τοῦ αὐτοῦ προσποιήσει ῥᾳδίως αἱ ἐπαγωγαὶ τοῖς νεω-
10 τερίζειν τι βουλομένοις ἐπορίζοντο. καὶ ἐπέπεσε πολλὰ 2
καὶ χαλεπὰ κατὰ στάσιν ταῖς πόλεσι, γιγνόμενα μὲν καὶ
αἰεὶ ἐσόμενα, ἕως ἂν ἡ αὐτὴ φύσις τῶν ἀνθρώπων ᾖ,
μᾶλλον δὲ καὶ ἡσυχαίτερα καὶ τοῖς εἴδεσι διηλλαγμένα,

gen. abs. answering to οὐκ ἂν ἐχόντων
... οὐδ' ἑτοίμων, the const. changes
to a finite verb, ἐπορίζοντο. St. compares vi. 69. 9. Kr. Spr. 69, 16, 4. —
καὶ ξυμμαχίας ἅμα: depends on αἱ
ἐπαγωγαί, but is thus emphatically
placed as containing the main idea
and in order that the ξυμμαχία may
appear as the natural result of the
state of war (πολεμουμένων). ξυμμαχία,
"help of allies," as i. 32. 2; 42. 12;
vi. 73. 5. — 8. ἑκατέροις: (i.e. the demo-
crats and the oligarchs) restricted by
τοῖς νεωτερίζειν τι βουλομένοις, and
having therefore the force of ἑκατέρων. But Steup, who considers the
Athenians and Lacedaemonians to
be the subj. of πολεμουμένων, holds
that ἑκατέροις also refers to those
states. In that case, ἑκατέροις would
be dat. of agent with ἐπορίζοντο (see
on c. 64. 15) and τοῖς ... βουλομένοις
dat. of advantage. — τῇ τῶν ἐναντίων
κακώσει καὶ ... προσποιήσει: the
two substs. with common art. closely
connected. See on c. 2. 6; 56. 7.
The dats. express purpose, as πλεονεξίᾳ, l. 39; ὠφελίᾳ, l. 38; i. 123. 10;
ξυμμαχίᾳ, vi. 33. 9. προσποίησις from
the mid. προσποιεῖσθαι, which is used
esp. of the acquisition of allies (i. 8.
16; ii. 30. 6; iv. 77. 13). The verbal
subst. governs σφίσιν αὐτοῖς. Kr. Spr.
48, 12, 4; Kühn. 424, 1. Cf. i. 63. 9;

73. 1. — 9. αἱ ἐπαγωγαί: the unusual
subst. used on account of ἐπάγεσθαι
above. See on c. 100. 6. Cf. v. 82.
24 ἐπαγωγὴ τῶν ἐπιτηδείων.
10. καὶ ἐπέπεσε κτέ.: and so befell,
etc., i.e. after outside help was called
in. — 11. κατὰ στάσιν: see on c. 2.
10; 68. 17. — γιγνόμενα μὲν καὶ αἰεὶ
ἐσόμενα: = οἷα γίγνεται καὶ αἰεὶ ἔσται.
Cf. Dio C.'s imitation (xxxvi. 20) οὐ
γὰρ ἔστιν ὅτε ταῦτ' οὐκ ἐγένετο, οὐδ'
ἂν παύσαιτό ποτε ἕως ἂν ἡ αὐτὴ φύσις
ἀνθρώπων ᾖ, Tac. Hist. iv. 74 vitia
erunt, donec homines. For other
passages expressing the same sentiment, see notes of Pp. and Bl. Steup
thinks the simple γιγνόμενα with αἰεὶ
ἐσόμενα κτέ. strange, and suggests that
ἐσόμενα may be an interpolation, comparing iv. 132. 2 βουλόμενοι μὲν καὶ
αἰεί, παρεστηκὸς κτέ. — 12. τῶν ἀνθρώπων: so with two Mss. (Vat. and H.)
for ἀνθρώπων of the rest. Cf. i. 20. 2;
77. 15; 140. 2; ii. 61. 19, etc. But
the art. is wanting in i. 41. 11; iv. 97.
13; v. 111. 12, and even in the imitation of Dio C. just quoted. — 13.
μᾶλλον: in a higher degree, referring
to χαλεπά. Supply γιγνόμενα. For
adv. and adj. (ἡσυχαίτερα) thus co-ord.
as preds. to verb, see on c. 4. 4. Cf.
Xen. Anab. iv. 7. 23 ἐπειδὴ δὲ βοὴ
πλείων τε ἐγίγνετο καὶ ἐγγύτερον. —
καὶ ἡσυχαίτερα: for καί, cf. iv. 63. 10

ὡς ἂν ἕκασται αἱ μεταβολαὶ τῶν ξυντυχιῶν ἐφιστῶνται. ἐν 15 μὲν γὰρ εἰρήνῃ καὶ ἀγαθοῖς πράγμασιν αἵ τε πόλεις καὶ οἱ ἰδιῶται ἀμείνους τὰς γνώμας ἔχουσι διὰ τὸ μὴ ἐς ἀκουσίους ἀνάγκας πίπτειν· ὁ δὲ πόλεμος ὑφελὼν τὴν εὐπορίαν τοῦ καθ᾽ ἡμέραν βίαιος διδάσκαλος καὶ πρὸς τὰ παρόντα τὰς ὀργὰς τῶν πολλῶν ὁμοιοῖ. ἐστασίαζέ τε οὖν 3

τὸν εὖ καὶ κακῶς δρῶντα. — τοῖς εἴδεσι: in their manifestations. — διηλλαγμένα: pass. only here in Thuc. Bl. cites Dion. II. xxiii. 17 ταῖς φωναῖς αὐτῶν διηλλαγμέναις. For the act. in same sense, see on c. 10. 5. — 14. ὡς: according as. Cf. c. 45. 18. — τῶν ξυντυχιῶν: of conditions of life, circumstances, as in c. 45. 18. — ἐφιστῶνται: present themselves, occur. Schol. πίπτωσι. Cf. Soph. O. R. 776 πρίν μοι τύχη τοιάδ᾽ ἐπέστη, Eur. Hipp. 819 ὦ τύχα, ὥς μοι βαρεῖα καὶ δόμοις ἐπεστάθης, Med. 331 ὅπως ἂν παραστῶσιν τύχαι. — ἐν μὲν γὰρ εἰρήνῃ κτέ.: in proof of the asserted influence of changed circumstances. — 15. ἀγαθοῖς πράγμασιν: rebus secundis; the phrase is prob. not found elsewhere. — 16. τὰς γνώμας: convictions, as in i. 140. 4. See Introd. to Book I. p. 32. — ἐς ἀκουσίους ἀνάγκας πίπτειν: "to fall under the dominion of imperious necessities, in which free choice is impossible." Cf. l. 18 βίαιος διδάσκαλος, and see on i. 84. 24. — 17. ὑφελών: see on c. 13. 32. — τὴν εὐπορίαν τοῦ καθ᾽ ἡμέραν: the comfortable provision of daily life. As τοῦ καθ᾽ ἡμέραν is unusual for τῶν καθ᾽ ἡμέραν, Kr. would insert, with the Schol., βίου before βίαιος. — 18. βίαιος διδάσκαλος: Bl. compares, for the sentiment, Theophyl. Hist. i. 15 (p.

63 Bk.) ὁ πόλεμος ... τῶν ἀνθρωπίνων κακῶν ἀρχηγέτης καὶ διδάσκαλος αὐτοδίδακτος. — πρὸς τὰ παρόντα: instead of the dat. Cf. viii. 57. 11 ἐπανισοῦν τοὺς Ἕλληνας πρὸς ἀλλήλους. Cf. i. 140. 4; vi. 34. 47. — 19. τὰς ὀργάς: dispositions, the old, chiefly poetic sense. Schol. νῦν ὀργὰς τὰς γνώμας καὶ τοὺς τρόπους ἐκάλεσεν. Cf. i. 130. 11; 140. 3; viii. 83. 10; Hdt. iii. 131. 3; vi. 128. 5; Theog. 963. See Diener, De Serm. Thuc. p. 15 ff.; C. F. Smith, Proc. Amer. Phil. Assoc. xxii. p. xix.

ἐστασίαζέ τε οὖν κτέ.: οὖν resumptive and τε correl. to following καί. Therefore both the cities were disturbed by factions, and those which revolted later, through hearing of what had been done before, went much further still in the extravagance of their revolutionary spirit, both in the over-ingenuity of their enterprises and the strangeness of their revenges. With the sentiment, cf. Eur. Hipp. 939 ὁ δ᾽ ὕστερος τοῦ πρόσθεν εἰς ὑπερβολὴν πανοῦργος ἔσται. — ἐστασίαζε τὰ τῶν πόλεων: cf. Dem. xix. 320 ἐστασίαζε τὰ τῶν Θετταλῶν. τὰ τῶν πόλεων is a periphrasis for αἱ πόλεις. See on c. 59. 7. Steup would have expected here ἐστασίαζε τὰ τῶν πόλεων τῶν πολλῶν, or ἐστασίαζε τὰ τῶν πόλεων ἐπὶ πολύ (cf. l. 2 ὕστερόν γε καὶ πᾶν ὡς εἰπεῖν τὸ Ἑλληνικὸν ἐκινήθη). Hampke conjec-

20 τὰ τῶν πόλεων καὶ τὰ ἐφυστερίζοντά που πύστει τῶν προγενομένων πολὺ ἐπέφερε τὴν ὑπερβολὴν τοῦ καινοῦσθαι τὰς διανοίας τῶν τ' ἐπιχειρήσεων περιτεχνήσει καὶ τῶν τιμωριῶν ἀτοπίᾳ. καὶ τὴν εἰωθυῖαν ἀξίωσιν τῶν ὀνο- 4 μάτων ἐς τὰ ἔργα ἀντήλλαξαν τῇ δικαιώσει. τόλμα μὲν 25 γὰρ ἀλόγιστος ἀνδρία φιλέταιρος ἐνομίσθη, μέλλησις δὲ προμηθὴς δειλία εὐπρεπής, τὸ δὲ σῶφρον τοῦ ἀνάνδρου πρόσχημα, καὶ τὸ πρὸς ἅπαν ξυνετὸν ἐπὶ πᾶν ἀργόν· τὸ δ' ἐμπλήκτως ὀξὺ ἀνδρὸς μοίρᾳ προσετέθη, ἀσφαλείᾳ δὲ

tured (Ztschr. f. d. Gymnasialw. xxxii. p. 396 f.) τὰ τῶν πολλῶν. — 20. τὰ ἐφυστερίζοντά που: αἱ πόλεις αἱ ὕστερον τῶν ἄλλων στασιάζουσαι, Schol. — 21. πολύ: Schol. κατὰ πολύ. Cf. Xen. Anab. iii. 4. 33 πολὺ περιῆσαν. Kr. Spr. 48, 15, 13. For the text, see App. — 22. τὰς διανοίας: see Introd. to Book_I. p. 82. — περιτεχνήσει: κακουργίᾳ, περινοίᾳ, Schol. Only here in Thuc.; elsewhere only in Dio C. (xlvi. 19; liii. 11). See on c. 43. 9. — 23. ἀτοπίᾳ: τῷ δήθει, τῇ δεινότητι, Schol. ἀξίωσιν: value, or generally received meaning; the objective meaning, as opp. to τῇ δικαιώσει, subjective interpretation. This meaning of ἀξίωσις seems to be rare. Bl. cites Dion. II. Ant. vi. 73 τὴν ἀξίωσιν τῶν δικαίων ἀναστρέφοντες, Heliod. Aeth. viii. 4 ἡ τῶν ὀνομάτων ἀξίωσις. — 24. ἐς τὰ ἔργα: in relation to things, belonging to ἀξίωσιν. ὀνόματα and ἔργα in the same relation also vi. 78. 19. — τῇ δικαιώσει: "as they thought fit." τῇ ἑαυτῶν δικαίᾳ κρίσει, Schol. The noun is Thucydidean (i. 141. 6; iv. 86. 21; v. 17. 11). See on i. 141. 6. As to Thuc.'s fondness for verbal nouns in -σις, see on c. 23. 27. — 25. ἐνομίσθη:

single characteristic examples are expressed by (empirical) aors. (cf. προσετέθη in l. 28; ἐγένετο, l. 37); general conduct by impfs. (cf. ἐπηνεῖτο in l. 35; ἐκρατύνοντο, l. 40, etc.). — φιλέταιρος: i.e. ready to sacrifice one's self for one's friends; the political signification of ἑταῖροι, as it appears below in ἑταιρία and ἑταιρικόν, being esp. prominent. Found only here in Thuc. — 26. εὐπρεπής: fair-seeming. Cf. c. 11. 10; 38. 12; i. 39. 6. — τὸ δὲ σῶφρον τοῦ ἀνάνδρου πρόσχημα: cf. Plato Rep. 560 d σωφροσύνην ἀνανδρίαν καλοῦντές τε καὶ προπηλακίζοντες. — 27. καὶ τὸ . . . ἀργόν: for the sentiment, cf. Eur. Oed. (frg. 556) πότερα γενέσθαι δῆτα χρησιμώτερον συνετὸν ἄτολμον ἢ θρασύν τε κάμαθῇ; — ἐπὶ πᾶν ἀργόν: cf. vii. 67. 18 ἀργότεραι ἐς τὸ δρᾶν τι. — τὸ δ' ἐμπλήκτως ὀξὺ ἀνδρὸς μοίρᾳ προσετέθη: inconsiderate rashness was held to be the part of a man. For ἐμπλήκτως, cf. Soph. Aj. 1358; Plato Gorg. 482 a. ἀνδρὸς μοίρᾳ προσετέθη = ἐν ἀνδρὸς μοίρᾳ (or ἐν μέρει, Dem. ii. 14; iii. 31) ἐτέθη. — 28. ἀσφαλείᾳ δὲ τὸ ἐπιβουλεύσασθαι . . . εὔλογος: prudent reflexion a specious pretext for yielding, lit. in security

τὸ ἐπιβουλεύσασθαι ἀποτροπῆς πρόφασις εὔλογος. καὶ 5
ὁ μὲν χαλεπαίνων πιστὸς αἰεί, ὁ δ᾽ ἀντιλέγων αὐτῷ ὕποπτος. ἐπιβουλεύσας δέ τις τυχὼν ξυνετὸς καὶ ὑπονοήσας ἔτι δεινότερος· προβουλεύσας δὲ ὅπως μηδὲν αὐτῶν δεήσει, τῆς τε ἑταιρίας διαλυτὴς καὶ τοὺς ἐναντίους ἐκπεπληγμένος. ἁπλῶς τε ὁ φθάσας τὸν μέλλοντα κακόν τι
δρᾶν ἐπῃνεῖτο, καὶ ὁ ἐπικελεύσας τὸν μὴ διανοούμενον.
καὶ μὴν καὶ τὸ ξυγγενὲς τοῦ ἑταιρικοῦ ἀλλοτριώτερον 6

to take further thought, a specious pretext for turning away. So St. explains; but see App. ἐνομίσθη is to be supplied here, as well as with the following predicates (πιστός and ὕποπτος). See on c. 107. 25. ἀσφαλείᾳ adv., as in c. 56. 20. ἐπιβουλεύσασθαι, *further deliberate, reflect.* ἐπι- as in ἐπιγνῶναι, c. 57. 6; i. 70. 8; ii. 65. 48. See on ἐπιταλαιπωρεῖν, i. 123. 3. ἀποτροπή not act., as in c. 45. 31, but belonging rather to the mid. ἀποτρέπεσθαι (ii. 40. 17; iv. 59. 7; viii. 10. 10), as ἀποστροφή (iv. 76. 25) to ἀποστρέφεσθαι, ἐπαγωγή (l. 9; 100. 6) to ἐπάγεσθαι, ἀποκομιδή (l. 137. 26) to ἀποκομίζεσθαι, ξυναλλαγή (l. 45) to ξυναλλάσσεσθαι. (St.)

30. ὁ μὲν χαλεπαίνων πιστὸς αἰεί: *the hot-headed man was always trusted.* Rauchenstein (*Philol.* xxxv. p. 590) conjectures ὁ μὲν πάντ᾽ ἐπαινῶν, Hampke *ibid.* p. 398 ὁ μὲν χαλεπὰ ἐπαινῶν. — 31. ἐπιβουλεύσας τυχών: ἐπιβουλεύσας is subord. to τυχών (for which St. and Widmann read τυχών τε, after Dion. H. p. 889), *if one had succeeded in any plot.* For the paronomasia, ἐπιβουλεύσας, προβουλεύσας, see on c. 39. 10; i. 33. 26. — ὑπονοήσας ἔτι δεινότερος: *if any one had sus-*pected *a plot* (he was considered) *still more clever.* τις is understood with ὑπονοήσας as with προβουλεύσας in the next line. δεινότερος = ξυνετώτερος. —
32. αὐτῶν: *i.e.* τοῦ τε ἐπιβουλεύειν καὶ ὑπονοεῖν. — 33. τῆς τε ἑταιρίας διαλυτὴς κτέ.: *sc.* because he took no part in the plots of his faction against their opponents. — ἐκπεπληγμένος : *smitten with fear of,* pass. with acc. as in v. 10. 30; vi. 11. 14; 33. 16. All other examples of this const. seem to be Ionic or Tragic. *Cf.* Hdt. ix. 82. 11; Soph. *Aj.* 33; *El.* 1045; *Phil.* 1026. See *Proc. Amer. Phil. Assoc.* xxii. p. xviii. — 34. ἁπλῶς τε : Haase's conjecture (*Lucubr.* p. 75) for ἁπλῶς δέ. See on c. 40. 16; iv. 64. 11; vi. 37. 18. — τὸν μέλλοντα κακόν τι δρᾶν: refers, as τὸν μὴ διανοούμενον in the next clause, to an associate, not an opponent. — 35. ὁ ἐπικελεύσας τὸν μὴ διανοούμενον: with both parties. κακόν τι δρᾶν is understood. Kr. *Spr.* 55, 4, 11. ἐπικελεύσας, as Xen *Cyrop.* iii. 3. 41, a strengthened κελεύσας, ἐπι- having the same force as in ἐπιβουλεύσασθαι, l. 29. *Cf.* ἐπιδιώκειν, c. 33. 14; ἐπιχρῆσθαι, i. 41. 4.
36. τὸ ξυγγενὲς . . . ἐγένετο : *the tie of blood was weaker than that of party.*

ἐγένετο διὰ τὸ ἑτοιμότερον εἶναι ἀπροφασίστως τολμᾶν·
οὐ γὰρ μετὰ τῶν κειμένων νόμων ὠφελίᾳ αἱ τοιαῦται
ξύνοδοι, ἀλλὰ παρὰ τοὺς καθεστῶτας πλεονεξίᾳ. καὶ τὰς
40 ἐς σφᾶς αὐτοὺς πίστεις οὐ τῷ θείῳ νόμῳ μᾶλλον ἐκρατύνοντο ἢ τῷ κοινῇ τι παρανομῆσαι. τά τε ἀπὸ τῶν ἐναν- 7
τίων καλῶς λεγόμενα ἐνεδέχοντο ἔργων φυλακῇ, εἰ προύχοιεν, καὶ οὐ γενναιότητι. ἀντιτιμωρήσασθαί τέ τινα περὶ
πλείονος ἦν ἢ αὐτὸν μὴ προπαθεῖν. καὶ ὅρκοι εἴ που ἄρα
45 γένοιντο ξυναλλαγῆς, ἐν τῷ αὐτίκα πρὸς τὸ ἄπορον ἑκα-

τοῦ ἑταιρικοῦ, as in viii. 48. 18. — 37. διὰ τὸ ἑτοιμότερον εἶναι : (sc. τὸ ἑταιρικόν) i.e. because restrained by no scruples. On account of the harshness of the ellipsis, Badham conjectured, and v. H. writes, ἀνετοιμότερον. If any change is to be made, Steup would rather insert τὸ ἑταιρικόν after ἑτοιμότερον. — 38. οὐ γὰρ . . . πλεονεξίᾳ: for such associations were not formed in accordance with the established laws for the (public) good, but contrary to the established laws for private advantage. — ὠφελίᾳ : correctly restored by St., for ὠφελίας of the Mss., since it is evidently opp. to πλεονεξίᾳ, as μετὰ τῶν κειμένων νόμων to παρὰ τοὺς καθεστῶτας. The emendation is supported not only by Valla's rendering of the passage, non enim huiusmodi conventus per leges ob utilitatem, sed contra leges ob avaritiam fiebant, but by Dion. H.'s paraphrase (p. 891), οὐ γὰρ ἐπὶ ταῖς κατὰ νόμον ὠφελίαις αἱ τῶν ἑταιριῶν ἐγίγνοντο σύνοδοι, ἀλλ' ἐπὶ τῷ παρὰ τοὺς νόμους τι πλεονεκτεῖν. ὠφελίᾳ and πλεονεξίᾳ are dats. of purpose. See on l. 8. — 39. ξύνοδοι : Schol. συστάσεις καὶ ἑται-
ρίαι. Cf. Plut. Ages. 32 ἐμηνύθη συνωμοσία καὶ σύνοδος ἀνδρῶν Σπαρτιατῶν· ἐπὶ πράγμασι νεωτέροις εἰς οἰκίαν κρύφα συνερχομένων. — 40. ἐς σφᾶς αὐτούς : i.e. ἐς ἀλλήλους. G. 996; H. 686 b. — οὐ τῷ θείῳ νόμῳ : on the decay of awe of the divine as a symptom of demoralization in society, see Introd. to Book I. p. 28. — ἐκρατύνοντο : see on c. 18. 7.
41. ἀπὸ τῶν ἐναντίων . . . γενναιότητι : i.e. fair words (here definite proposals) were not relied on ; they were accepted, if the momentary superiority of opponents (εἰ προύχοιεν, sc. οἱ ἐναντίοι) made this necessary, but only guardedly, not in a spirit of generous confidence. For ἀπό with the pass., see on c. 36. 24. Steup considers the subj. of προύχοιεν to be the same as that of ἐνεδέχοντο, comparing c. 83. 6 κρείσσους δὲ ὄντες κτέ. — 42. ἔργων φυλακῇ : cf. τῶν ἔργων τῆς ἐπιμελείας, c. 46. 19; ἔργῳ φυλασσομένη, vi. 40. 17. — 43. γενναιότητι: like τὸ γενναῖον, c. 83. 2. — ἀντιτιμωρήσασθαι : though the simple verb expresses the idea of retaliation, this is intensified by ἀντι-. — 45. ξυναλλαγῆς : so far removed from ὅρκοι

τέρῳ διδόμενοι ἴσχυον οὐκ ἐχόντων ἄλλοθεν δύναμιν·
ἐν δὲ τῷ παρατυχόντι ὁ φθάσας θαρσῆσαι, εἰ ἴδοι ἄφρακτον, ἥδιον διὰ τὴν πίστιν ἐτιμωρεῖτο ἢ ἀπὸ τοῦ προφανοῦς, καὶ τό τε ἀσφαλὲς ἐλογίζετο καὶ ὅτι ἀπάτῃ περιγε-
50 νόμενος ξυνέσεως ἀγώνισμα προσελάμβανε. ῥᾷον δ' οἱ

that the connexion is rather loose, with a view to reconciliation. — **πρὸς τὸ ἄπορον**: *in view of their perplexity*; more expressive than κατά τι ἄπορον, i. 136. 6. πρός as in πρὸς τὸ παρόν, c. 40. 35; ii. 22. 1; v. 9. 14. — **ἑκατέρῳ διδόμενοι**: for the dat. of agent with pass., see on c. 64. 15. — **46. οὐκ ἐχόντων**: without expressed subj. as in l. 6 above, but αὐτῶν is easily supplied from ἑκατέρῳ, *as they had no power from any other source*. Hampke (*ibid.* p. 400) refers οὐκ ἐχόντων to ὅρκοι, *having authority for no other reason*, sc. than their present helplessness. Steup, not satisfied with any interpretation that has been offered, suggests that the words have crept into the text from a marginal explanation of πρὸς τὸ ἄπορον ἑκατέρῳ διδόμενοι. — **47. ἐν τῷ παρατυχόντι**: as in v. 38. 3, "in any event that might chance." παρα- with the force of αἰεί, of what presents itself from time to time; hence the sing. *Cf.* i. 122. 6 πρὸς τὸ παρατυγχάνον. — **ὁ φθάσας θαρσῆσαι**: *he who first made bold*, i.e. without the help of oaths. As Thuc. nowhere else construes the inf. with φθάνειν, θαρσήσας was rather to be expected. *Cf.* c. 23. 21; 83. 11; 89. 11; 112. 5; ii. 91. 5; iv. 4. 11; v. 3. 5, 8; 10. 13; vi. 61. 11; 97. 11; vii. 6. 16; 42. 19; viii. 12. 3; 92. 3. The const. with inf. is rare in Attic, more freq. in late writers. Kr. *Spr.* 56,

5, 5. The inf. is doubtless used here to avoid the concurrence of two parties. — **ἄφρακτον**: (sc. τὸν ἐναντίον) *unguarded, off his guard*. *Cf.* c. 39. 8; vi. 33. 14. — **48. διὰ τὴν πίστιν**: i.e. because his enemy relied on the oath, and so was ἄφρακτος. — **ἀπὸ τοῦ προφανοῦς**: adv., as in i. 35. 17; 66. 7; ii. 93. 15; v. 9. 13. The phrase seems to be peculiar to Thuc. *Cf.* ἐκ τοῦ προφανοῦς, c. 43. 10; 109. 10. — **49. καὶ τό τε ἀσφαλὲς ἐλογίζετο . . . προσελάμβανε**: *and he reckoned not only the safety* (of such a course), *but also that proving superior by means of deceit he was winning besides the prize of shrewdness*. λογίζεσθαι as in i. 76. 13; ii. 89. 24. — **50. ξυνέσεως ἀγώνισμα**: *cf.* c. 37. 27 ξυνέσεως ἀγών. — **ῥᾷον δ' οἱ πολλοί . . . ἀγαθοί**: "men in general, when dishonest, more easily gain credit for cleverness, than, when simple, for goodness." ῥᾷον κέκληνται, lit. *are more readily called*. This is the view of Arn., Jow., and St. But Cl. and Steup follow Kr. in rendering, *prefer to be called*, which makes τῷ μὲν αἰσχύνονται . . . ἀγάλλονται a mere repetition. The pf. κέκληνται as in ii. 37. 4; v. 9. 35. GMT. 49 a; H. 849. Steup brackets ὄντες, on the ground that predicates follow καλεῖσθαι without ὤν, and sees in it a marginal explanation of some one who mistook κακοῦργοι as equiv. to κακοῦργοι ὄντες.

πολλοὶ κακοῦργοι ὄντες δεξιοὶ κέκληνται ἢ ἀμαθεῖς ἀγαθοί, καὶ τῷ μὲν αἰσχύνονται, ἐπὶ δὲ τῷ ἀγάλλονται. πάν- 8
των δ' αὐτῶν αἴτιον ἀρχὴ ἡ διὰ πλεονεξίαν καὶ φιλοτιμίαν· ἐκ δ' αὐτῶν καὶ ἐς τὸ φιλονικεῖν καθισταμένων
55 τὸ πρόθυμον. οἱ γὰρ ἐν ταῖς πόλεσι προστάντες μετ' ὀνόματος ἑκάτεροι εὐπρεποῦς, πλήθους τε ἰσονομίας πολιτικῆς καὶ ἀριστοκρατίας σώφρονος προτιμήσει, τὰ μὲν κοινὰ λόγῳ θεραπεύοντες ἆθλα ἐποιοῦντο, παντὶ δὲ τρόπῳ ἀγωνιζόμενοι ἀλλήλων περιγίγνεσθαι ἐτόλμησάν τε τὰ

— **51. κακοῦργοι ὄντες δέξιοι ... ἀμαθεῖς ἀγαθοί**: observe the chiasmus. — **52. τῷ μὲν ... ἀγάλλονται**: chiastic with regard to the preceding. "They are ashamed of simple goodness, but glory in clever dishonesty." Jow. Cf. Plut. de Garrul. 4 ἥδιόν γε τοῖς πονηροῖς ὁμιλοῦσιν ἐπιδεξίοις, ἢ χρηστοῖς ἀδολέσχαις. For the order ἐπὶ δὲ τῷ, see on c. 61. 6.
53. αἴτιον: used as pred. subst., as often, without regard to gender of subj. See on i. 11. 1. G. 925; H. 617. Madvig (Adv. i. p. 317) and Hampke (ibid. p. 400 f.) would bracket αἴτιον, Hude (p. 113 sq.) both αἴτιον and ἡ. H. Weil (Rev. de Philol. N. S. ii. p. 92) conjectures πάντων δ' αὐτῶν ἀρχὴ ἡ λίαν πλεονεξία καὶ φιλοτιμία. — **ἀρχή**: Schol. ἡ ἐπιθυμία τοῦ βούλεσθαι ἄρχειν. Cf. gloria = gloriae cupiditas. As to the order, ἀρχὴ ἡ διὰ πλεονεξίαν, cf. i. 41. 15 φιλονικίας ἕνεκα τῆς αὐτίκα, 75. 1 προθυμίας ἕνεκα τῆς τότε, 77. 9 δυνάμει τῇ διὰ τὴν ἀρχήν. — **54. ἐκ δ' αὐτῶν**: i.e. τῆς πλεονεξίας καὶ φιλοτιμίας. — **καὶ ἐς τὸ φιλονικεῖν καθισταμένων**: with indef. pers. subj. (as in l. 6). *When men were once embarked in strife*. — **55. τὸ πρόθυμον**: sc. ἦν.

sprang zealous party-spirit. — **οἱ γὰρ ... προστάντες**: aor., *those who had become leaders in the cities*. — **μετ' ὀνόματος εὐπρεποῦς**: Sallust's (Cat. 38) honestis nominibus. — **56. πλήθους τε ... προτιμήσει**: explanation of μετ' ὀνόματος ... εὐπρεποῦς, the dat. προτιμήσει being a variation of μετά with the gen. The one party laid stress on the designation πλήθους ἰσονομία πολιτική (*the political equality of the many*), rather than the objectionable δημοκρατία, — the other on ἀριστοκρατία σώφρων (*a moderate aristocracy*), rather than the hated ὀλιγαρχία. On the ἰσονομία πολιτική, see Schoemann, Antiq. Jur. p. 95; Niebuhr, Hist. of Rome, i. p. 315. — **57. ἀριστοκρατίας σώφρονος**: the ὀλίγοι were given to boasting of their σωφροσύνη. Cf. c. 65. 16; viii. 53. 21; 64. 21. — **τὰ μὲν κοινὰ ... ἐποιοῦντο**: *in name devoted to the public interests they made them prizes (for which they strove)*. τὰ κοινά, as in i. 120. 4; 141. 31, obj. of θεραπεύοντες, as well as of ἆθλα ἐποιοῦντο. — **59. ἀγωνιζόμενοι ... μείζους**: for the sentiment, cf. Sall. Jug. 42. 4. — **περιγίγνεσθαι**: for the inf. dependent on

60 δεινότατα, ἐπεξῇσάν τε τὰς τιμωρίας ἔτι μείζους, οὐ
μέχρι τοῦ δικαίου καὶ τῇ πόλει ξυμφόρου προτιθέντες,
ἐς δὲ τὸ ἑκατέροις που αἰεὶ ἡδονὴν ἔχον ὁρίζοντες, καὶ ἢ
μετὰ ψήφου ἀδίκου καταγνώσεως ἢ χειρὶ κτώμενοι τὸ
κρατεῖν ἑτοῖμοι ἦσαν τὴν αὐτίκα φιλονικίαν ἐκπιμπλά-
65 ναι. ὥστε εὐσεβείᾳ μὲν οὐδέτεροι ἐνόμιζον, εὐπρεπείᾳ
δὲ λόγου, οἷς ξυμβαίη ἐπιφθόνως τι διαπράξασθαι, ἄμει-

ἀγωνιζόμενοι, see on c. 38. 10. — 60. ἐπεξῇσαν τὰς τιμωρίας: pursued revenges. Cf. c. 40. 28; v. 100. 5. Hampke's conjecture (ibid. p. 401 f.) ἐπεξήνεγκαν, increased, seems unnecessary. — ἔτι μείζους: pred., still greater, sc. than the δεινότατα τολμήματα. — οὐ μέχρι . . . προτιθέντες: not stretching their revenges up to the limits of right and the advantage of the state, i.e. not setting this limit to them. So Cl. explains, retaining the Vulg. But the signification of προτιθέναι which he gives seems to be without parallel. The ordinary meaning of προτιθέντες, when referring to punishments, i.e. proponentes, does not suit the verb ἐπεξῇσαν. The reading προστιθέντες (Dion. H.) though slightly supported, is adopted by Kr., St., and Bm., and gives the best sense, — inflicting punishments (or revenges). Cf. c. 39. 38. — 62. ἐς δὲ τὸ ἑκατέροις που αἰεὶ ἡδονὴν ἔχον ὁρίζοντες: limiting them according to what at any time afforded pleasure to either party. ἔχον = παρέχον. See on c. 53. 12; i. 97. 13. — 63. μετὰ ψήφου ἀδίκου καταγνώσεως: καταψηφιζόμενοι ἀδίκως, Schol. For the order of the words, cf. ii. 39. 20 μετὰ νόμων τὸ πλεῖον ἢ τρόπων ἀνδρείας. See on c. 23. 27; 46. 18. ψήφου ἀδίκου is subjective (not as c. 16. 2 ἀσθενείας obj.) gen. Cf. i. 87. 17 ἡ διαγνώμη αὕτη τῆς ἐκκλησίας. A fraudulent count is prob. not meant, but a vote influenced by hate and thirst for revenge. — ἢ χειρὶ κτώμενοι τὸ κρατεῖν: the combination of a prepositional phrase with a partic. const. is freq. Cf. c. 25. 9; 42. 23; i. 39. 2; ii. 89. 22. — χειρί: by force, only here. Cf. ii. 13. 19 διὰ χειρὸς ἔχειν. — 64. ἑτοῖμοι ἦσαν: were ready, i.e. unscrupulous as to the means employed (ἢ μετὰ ψήφου ἀδίκου καταγνώσεως ἢ χειρί). — τὴν αὐτίκα φιλονικίαν: also i. 41. 15. — ἐκπιμπλάναι: explere, as ἀποπλῆσαι, vii. 68. 5. — 65. ὥστε . . . ἄμεινον ἤκουον: εὐπρεπείᾳ δὲ λόγου, as antithesis to εὐσεβείᾳ μέν, is the ground of ἄμεινον ἤκουον. "On piety neither side placed any value, but by fair pretences those had a better name who succeeded in accomplishing some odious purpose." Many editors construe εὐπρεπείᾳ λόγου with the rel. clause (see on c. 39. 5; i. 5. 11). — ἐνόμιζον: = ἐχρῶντο, with dat. also i. 77. 26; ii. 38. 3; Hdt. ii. 50. 14. Kühn. 425, 5. — 66. ἐπιφθόνως: as in i. 75. 3; Xen. Cyrop. vii. 5. 37. — ἄμεινον ἤκουον: i.e. were more praised

νον ἤκουον. τὰ δὲ μέσα τῶν πολιτῶν ὑπ' ἀμφοτέρων
ἢ ὅτι οὐ ξυνηγωνίζοντο ἢ φθόνῳ τοῦ περιεῖναι διεφθεί-
83 ροντο. οὕτω πᾶσα ἰδέα κατέστη κακοτροπίας διὰ τὰς 1
στάσεις τῷ Ἑλληνικῷ, καὶ τὸ εὔηθες, οὗ τὸ γενναῖον
πλεῖστον μετέχει, καταγελασθὲν ἠφανίσθη, τὸ δὲ ἀντιτετάχθαι ἀλλήλοις τῇ γνώμῃ ἀπίστως ἐπὶ πολὺ διήνεγ-
5 κεν· οὐ γὰρ ἦν ὁ διαλύσων οὔτε λόγος ἐχυρὸς οὔτε ὅρ- 2

for plausibility of speech than for piety. — 67. **τὰ μέσα τῶν πολιτῶν**: οἱ μηδετέρῳ μέρει προστιθέμενοι, Schol. *Cf.* viii. 75. 4 οἱ διὰ μέσου, iv. 83. 9 ἑτοῖμος ὧν Βρασίδᾳ μέσῳ δικαστῇ ἐπιτρέπειν, Dio C. xliv. 29 καὶ οὕτω καὶ τὰ μέσα τῶν πολιτῶν στασιάζειν παράγεται. — 68. **ὅτι οὐ ξυνηγωνίζοντο**: *i.e.* because they did not furnish the aid demanded. — **φθόνῳ τοῦ περιεῖναι**: = ὅτι ἐφθονοῦντο διὰ τὸ περιεῖναι. Kr. compares Eur. *I. T.* 352

οἱ δυστυχεῖς γὰρ τοῖσιν εὐτυχεστέροις
αὐτοὶ κακῶς πράξαντες οὐ φρονοῦσιν
εὖ.

—**διεφθείροντο**: for the pl. verb with neut. pl. subj., see G. 899, 2; II. 604 a; Kr. *Spr.* 63, 2, 1; Kühn. 365 a. *Cf.* iv. 88. 6; vii. 57. 04.

83. 1. πᾶσα ἰδέα: see on c. 81. 22.
— **κακοτροπίας**: *of wickedness, i.e.* baseness of the whole mode of thought and conduct (*i.e.* τρόποι, ii. 36. 16; 39. 21; 41. 7). The word occurs elsewhere only in Dio C., Jos., and other late writers. — 2. **τῷ Ἑλληνικῷ**: *cf.* c. 82. 3. — **καὶ τὸ εὔηθες ... ἠφανίσθη**: *and simplicity, of which nobility partakes most largely, was laughed at and disappeared.* τὸ εὐηθές as εὐήθεια, c. 45. 30. This passage is cited by grammarians (Photius, Thomas Mag., Moeris) as furnishing a characteristic example of the original meaning of the word. — **τὸ γενναῖον**: *cf.* c. 82. 43 γενναιότητι. — 3. **πλεῖστον μετέχει**: *cf.* i. 84. 12 αἰδὼς σωφροσύνης πλεῖστον μετέχει. — **τὸ δὲ ἀντιτετάχθαι ... διήνεγκεν**: *but to be in mind distrustfully arrayed against each other prevailed far and wide. Cf.* c. 82. 41 ff. — **ἀντιτετάχθαι**: as in war, v. 55. 7. — 4. **ἐπὶ πολύ**: of space, as in i. 62. 24; ii. 75. 8; v. 73. 25; vi. 37. 18; 70. 12; viii. 10. 9. — **διήνεγκε**: Schol. κρεῖττον ἐγένετο.

5. **οὐ γὰρ ἦν ... φοβερός**: "for there was no word binding enough, no oath terrible enough, to bring about an adjustment." Lit. *for there was, that could bring about an adjustment, neither binding word nor fearful oath.* ὁ διαλύσων (qui dirimeret) is construed by most editt. as pred. (see Kr. *Spr.* 50, 4, 4). But Steup objects that the implication would then be, that there was not indeed λόγος ἐχυρός or ὅρκος φοβερός, but something else, ὁ διαλύσων. He makes therefore διαλύσων attrib., and the complete subj. ὁ διαλύσων ... φοβερός. *Cf.* ii. 62. 13 οὐκ ἔστιν ὅστις οὔτε βασιλεὺς κωλύσει οὔτε ἄλλο οὐδὲν ἔθνος. —

κος φοβερός, κρείσσους δὲ ὄντες ἅπαντες λογισμῷ ἐς τὸ
ἀνέλπιστον τοῦ βεβαίου μὴ παθεῖν μᾶλλον προεσκόπουν
ἢ πιστεῦσαι ἐδύναντο. καὶ οἱ φαυλότεροι γνώμην ὡς τὰ 3
πλείω περιεγίγνοντο· τῷ γὰρ δεδιέναι τό τε αὐτῶν ἐν-
10 δεὲς καὶ τὸ τῶν ἐναντίων ξυνετόν, μὴ λόγοις τε ἥσσους
ὦσι καὶ ἐκ τοῦ πολυτρόπου αὐτῶν τῆς γνώμης φθάσωσι
προεπιβουλευόμενοι, τολμηρῶς πρὸς τὰ ἔργα ἐχώρουν. οἱ 4

6. **κρείσσους δὲ ὄντες ... μᾶλλον προεσκόπουν ἢ κτέ.**: *all men when stronger* (than their enemies), *by consideration of the hopelessness of security* (in word and oath), *rather made provision not to suffer, than were able to trust others.* This seems to be the meaning of this much discussed passage. κρείσσους ὄντες = εἰ προύχοιεν, c. 82. 42. ἐς, "with reference to." St.'s explanation (*Rh. Mus.* xv. p. 475), adopted by Cl., is: "all men found more strength in calculations providing against the unexpected than in pledges of security (such as promises and oaths), and looked rather to suffering no ill, than were able to trust others." With this view, τοῦ βεβαίου, depending on κρείσσους, = ἢ τῷ βεβαίῳ. *Cf.* vi. 1 μείζονι παρασκευῇ τῆς μετὰ Λάχητος, and Xen. *Anab.* ii. 5. 13. Dobree supplies τοῦ λόγου καὶ τοῦ ὅρκου with κρείσσους (*cf.* c. 84. 12 κρείσσων τοῦ δικαίου), which Kr. rightly thinks harsh. The explanation of the Schol. is, ῥέποντες δὲ οἱ ἄνθρωποι τοῖς λογισμοῖς πρὸς τὸ μὴ ἐλπίζειν τινὰ πίστιν καὶ βεβαιότητα ("the thoughts of all men tended to despair of security"), which Bl., Jow., and Hude prefer. Dio C.'s imitation of the passage (frg. 49) is

viz. κρείττους ἐς τὸ ἀφανὲς τοῦ προδήλου (*i.e.* ἢ ἐς τὸ πρόδηλον) τῷ λογισμῷ γιγνόμενοι.
8. **οἱ φαυλότεροι γνώμην**: *those inferior in intellect. Cf.* c. 37. 17. — **ὡς τὰ πλείω**: = ὡς ἐπὶ τὸ πλεῖον, c. 37. 18. — 9. **τὸ ἐνδεές**: Schol. τὴν ἔλλειψιν τῆς γνώμης. — 10. **μὴ ... φθάσωσι προεπιβουλευόμενοι**: epexegetical explanation of τό τε αὐτῶν ἐνδεὲς κτέ. — 11. **ἐκ τοῦ πολυτρόπου αὐτῶν**: *in consequence of their versatility.* ἐκ as in i. 2. 17; 75. 7. τὸ πολύτροπον as πολυτροπίη, Hdt. ii. 121. ε 12. *Cf.* πολύτροπος, Hom. a 1. As noun not found elsewhere. αὐτῶν, *i.e.* τῶν ἐναντίων.
— **φθάσωσι προεπιβουλευόμενοι**: the pres. partic. with φθάνειν as in vi. 99. 12, elsewhere in Thuc. always the aor. partic. (c. 23. 21; 89. 11; 112. 5; ii. 91. 5; iv. 4. 11; 104. 20; v. 3. 5; 10. 13; vi. 61. 11; 97. 11; 101. 34; vii. 6. 16; 23. 3; 25. 45; 42. 19; viii. 12. 3; 17. 7; 95. 20; 100. 3), except possibly viii. 92. 4, where Vat. has the pf. See Gildersleeve, *Amer. J. of Ph.* xii. p. 76.
12. **οἱ δέ**: *their opponents*, already characterized as οἱ ξυνετώτεροι. — 13. **καταφρονοῦντες**: in causal relation to ἄφρακτοι, *arrogantly presuming.* Schol. διὰ καταφρόνησιν πεποιθότες.

δὲ καταφρονοῦντες κἂν προαισθέσθαι καὶ ἔργῳ οὐδὲν σφᾶς δεῖν λαμβάνειν ἃ γνώμῃ ἔξεστιν ἄφρακτοι μᾶλλον
15 διεφθείροντο.

84 [Ἐν δ' οὖν τῇ Κερκύρᾳ τὰ πολλὰ αὐτῶν προε- 1
τολμήθη, καὶ ὁπόσα ὕβρει μὲν ἀρχόμενοι τὸ πλέον ἢ σωφροσύνῃ ὑπὸ τῶν τὴν τιμωρίαν παρασχόντων οἱ ἀντ-

On καταφρονοῦντες depend both κἂν προαισθέσθαι and ἔργῳ οὐδὲν δεῖν λαμβάνειν. Kr. Spr. 65, 11, 7; Kühn. 473, 1. Cf. Hdt. i. 66. 6 καταφρονήσαντες Ἀρκάδων κρέσσονες εἶναι, Xen. Hell. iv. 5. 12 κατεφρόνουν διὰ τὰς ἔμπροσθεν τύχας μηδένα ἂν ἐπιχειρῆσαι σφίσιν. — προαισθέσθαι: Cl. adopted from Vat. and Aug. προαίσθεσθαι (as pres.). But since the only mark of distinction from the aor. is the accent, as to which the better Mss. agree hardly anywhere, it is best to consider this aor. here, as well as in ii. 93. 17; v. 26. 29; vi. 40. 9; vii. 75. 8. See Steup, App. on ii. 93. 17; St. Qu. Gr.² p. 66. — **14. ἄφρακτοι**: see on c. 82. 47. — **μᾶλλον**: i.e. in greater numbers. Cf. ii. 7. 15. Junghahn (N. Jahrbb. cxix. p. 367 f.) unnecessarily objects to the statement in § 3, 4 that in the στάσεις inferior intellects generally got the better of the cleverer sort. Steup infers from the striking transitions and repetitions of c. 82 and 83 (cf. e.g. c. 83. § 1 f. with c. 82. § 7), that these two chapters are composed of reflexions written at several different times.

84. *Reflexions of a later moralist on the contents of the two preceding chapters.*

(As to the authenticity of the chapter, see App.)

1. δ' οὖν: acc. to Thuc.'s usage, resumptive after a digression. See on i. 3. 19. — **αὐτῶν**: referring with emphasis to the ills described in the two preceding chapters, or perhaps, as Arn. explains, to τὰ ἔργα in c. 83. 12. See on i. 1. 10. — **προετολμήθη**: cf. c. 82. 2 ἐν τοῖς πρώτη ἐγένετο. The word is not found elsewhere except in late authors. Cf. Dio C. xlvii. 4; Herodian vi. 7. See Steph. Thes. s.v. — **2. καὶ ὁπόσα κτέ.**: explanatory of ἃ πολλά, both whatsoever ——. 'The three principal causes of the crimes committed in civil disturbances: 1st, the desire of vengeance for oppression and insolence in the ruling party; 2nd, the thirst of plunder, which urges the needy to covet the property of the rich; 3rd, the mere bitterness of party spirit, which men contract by being habitually opposed to one another.' Arn. The const. is, ὁπόσα . . . δράσειαν . . . γιγνώσκοιεν . . . ἐπέλθοιεν. After καὶ ὁπόσα ὕβρει the natural const. would have been καὶ ὁπόσα πενίας, but the insertion of μέν causes the slight change. — **ὕβρει μὲν** . . . **παρασχόντων**: "ruled more with insolence than with moderation by those who had now afforded them opportunity for revenge." With τὴν τιμωρίαν παρασχεῖν, cf. δίκην παρασχεῖν, Hes. Op. 710; Eur. Andr. 1107; Phoen.

ἀμυνόμενοι δράσειαν, πενίας δὲ τῆς εἰωθυίας ἀπαλλα-
ξείοντές τινες, μάλιστα δ' ἂν διὰ πάθους ἐπιθυμοῦντες
τὰ τῶν πέλας ἔχειν παρὰ δίκην γιγνώσκοιεν, οἵ τε μὴ
ἐπὶ πλεονεξίᾳ, ἀπὸ ἴσου δὲ μάλιστα ἐπιόντες ἀπαιδευσίᾳ ὀργῆς πλεῖστον ἐκφερόμενοι ὠμῶς καὶ ἀπαραιτήτως
ἐπέλθοιεν. ξυνταραχθέντος τε τοῦ βίου ἐς τὸν καιρὸν 2
τοῦτον τῇ πόλει καὶ τῶν νόμων κρατήσασα ἡ ἀνθρωπεία
φύσις, εἰωθυῖα καὶ παρὰ τοὺς νόμους ἀδικεῖν, ἀσμένη

1654. — 4. δράσειαν: the opt. may be explained as that of general rel. cond. (*all that men would naturally have done who*). GMT. 532; H. 914, B 2. Cf. vii. 71. 22 ἄλλα ὅσα ἐν μεγάλῳ κινδύνῳ μέγα στρατόπεδον πολυειδῆ ἀναγκάζοιτο φθέγγεσθαι. If this explanation be adopted, the ἄν of l. 5 must be construed not with γιγνώσκοιεν, but with the partic. ἐπιθυμοῦντες, forming with it a sort of parenthesis, as Kr. explains, μάλιστα δ' ἂν διὰ πάθους ἐπεθύμουν τὰ τῶν πέλας ἔχειν, and *who would be above all men passionately covetous of their neighbour's goods*. Or ἄν may be taken with γιγνώσκοιεν and supplied with δράσειαν and ἐπέλθοιεν. It might indeed have easily dropped out after δράσειαν. — ἀπαλλαξείοντες: found only here and i. 95. 24. — 5. διὰ πάθους: in *passion*, a use of the word which seems not to occur elsewhere before Aristotle. Nor does it seem appropriate to the context. Why should avarice of all the desires be esp. mentioned as passionate? For the const., cf. δι' ὀργῆς, viii. 43. 24. — 6. γιγνώσκοιεν: *determine on, purpose*. Cf. i. 70. 7, 27. — οἵ τε: the particle introduces, acc. to Thuc.'s usage, the *third* member.

— 7. ἀπὸ ἴσου δὲ μάλιστα ἐπιόντες: *i.e.* 'those who enter into revolution on an equality with their adversaries — not as oppressed men thirsting for vengeance, nor as needy men desiring plunder — and whose cruelties are owing merely to the fury of party spirit which they acquire in the course of the contest.' Arn. — ἀπαιδευσίᾳ ὀργῆς πλεῖστον ἐκφερόμενοι: *carried away for the most part by the ungovernableness of their passions*. Cf. Eur. (apud Stob. *Flor.* 20. 12) πόλλ' ἔστιν ὀργῆς ἐξ ἀπαιδεύτου κακά, Jos. *Antiq.* xvii. 11. 3 ἀπαιδευσίᾳ τοῦ πείθεσθαι τοῖς νόμοις, xix. 2. 2 ἀπαίδευτον τὴν ὀργὴν ἐπαφιείς. See on ἀπαιδευσία γνώμης, c. 42. 6.

9. ἐς τὸν καιρὸν τοῦτον: *at this crisis*. For similar use of ἐς, cf. iv. 89. 6; vi. 16. 33. Or can the sense be, *to this point, degree?* — 10. καὶ τῶν νόμων κρατήσασα: *having got a complete mastery over the laws*, i.e. no longer regarding them. For parties, in different cases thus co-ord., see on c. 66. 12; i. 65. 2. Kr. *Spr.* 56, 14, 2. — 11. εἰωθυῖα καὶ παρὰ τοὺς νόμους ἀδικεῖν: cf. Dio C. lii. 34. 6 ἡ φύσις καὶ παρὰ τὸν νόμον πολλοὺς ἁμαρτάνειν ἐξάγει, 34. 7 ὁ νόμος ... οὐ δύνα-

ἐδήλωσεν ἀκρατὴς μὲν ὀργῆς οὖσα, κρείσσων δὲ τοῦ δικαίου, πολεμία δὲ τοῦ προύχοντος· οὐ γὰρ ἂν τοῦ τε ὁσίου τὸ τιμωρεῖσθαι προυτίθεσαν τοῦ τε μὴ ἀδικεῖν τὸ
15 κερδαίνειν, ἐν ᾧ μὴ βλάπτουσαν ἰσχὺν εἶχε τὸ φθονεῖν. ἀξιοῦσί τε τοὺς κοινοὺς περὶ τῶν τοιούτων οἱ ἄνθρωποι 3 νόμους, ἀφ' ὧν ἅπασιν ἐλπὶς ὑπόκειται σφαλεῖσι κἂν αὐτοὺς διασῴζεσθαι, ἐν ἄλλων τιμωρίαις προκαταλύειν καὶ μὴ ὑπολείπεσθαι, εἴ ποτε ἄρα τις κινδυνεύσας τινὸς
20 δεήσεται αὐτῶν.]

85 Οἱ μὲν οὖν κατὰ τὴν πόλιν Κερκυραῖοι τοιαύταις 1

ται τῆς φύσεως ἀεὶ κρατεῖν. — **ἀσμένη ἐδήλωσεν ... τοῦ δικαίου**: took delight in showing that its passions were ungovernable, that it was stronger than justice. Cf. c. 45. § 7. Bl. cites, as imitations of this passage, Jos. Antiq. xvii. 8. 1 (of Herod) ἀνὴρ ὡμὸς μὲν εἰς πάντας ὁμοίως, καὶ ὀργῆς μὲν ἥσσων, κρείσσων δὲ τοῦ δικαίου, xix. 2. 2 κρείσσων μὲν τοῦ δικαίου γενόμενος, ἥσσων δὲ τοῦ κατ' ἰδίαν ἡδονήν, and xviii. 8. 8. But, as St. says, this imitation is uncertain, since such use of κρείσσων is freq. — 13. **πολεμία δὲ τοῦ προύχοντος**: cf. ii. 35. 16 τῷ δ' ὑπερβάλλοντι αὐτῶν φθονοῦντες ἤδη καὶ ἀπιστοῦσιν, Hdt. vii. 236. 7 τοῦ τε εὐτυχέειν φθονέουσι καὶ τὸ κρέσσον στυγέουσι. — 14. **προυτίθεσαν**: for the const., see on c. 39. 20. — 15. **ἐν ᾧ ... τὸ φθονεῖν**: when (lit. in a case where) envy had not its fatal power. ἐν ᾧ μή = εἰ μὴ ἐν τούτῳ. Cl. renders, "in which case envy would have had not its fatal effect." But with this view, though the omission of ἄν would give no trouble (cf. vi. 55. 18; viii. 86. 22), it requires a strained interpretation to justify μή.

16. **ἀξιοῦσί τε κτέ.**: Arn. well expresses the sense, "Men in their violence set the example of doing away with those common laws of humanity which all parties alike might have appealed to in their adversity, and by their own previous conduct put themselves out of the pale of these laws, when they themselves might have occasion to solicit their protection." ἀξιοῦσι, presume, as in i. 42. 2; 74. 12; iv. 66. 9; vii. 63. 21. — 17. **ἐλπὶς ὑπόκειται**: cf. vi. 87. 18 ὑπεῖναι ἐλπίδα, Dem. xix. 24 πάντα [τἆλλ'] οἶμαι τότε δεύτερ' ἦν τῶν ὑποκειμένων προσδοκιῶν καὶ τῶν ἐλπίδων. — **σφαλεῖσι**: in case they should be unfortunate. — 18. **αὐτούς**: after preceding dat. G. 928, 1; H. 941; Kühn. 475, 2 a. See on i. 31. 10. — 19. **ὑπολείπεσθαι**: mid., to let them stand, i.e. the laws. — **εἴ ποτε ἄρα**: if ever perchance.

85. *Eurymedon leaves Corcyra. Those of the oligarchical party in Corcyra who had escaped establish themselves first on the mainland opposite, then on Mount Istone, and harass their opponents.*

1. **οἱ κατὰ τὴν πόλιν Κερκυραῖοι**:

ὀργαῖς ταῖς πρώταις ἐς ἀλλήλους ἐχρήσαντο, καὶ ὁ Εὐρυμέδων καὶ οἱ Ἀθηναῖοι ἀπέπλευσαν ταῖς ναυσίν. ὕστερον δὲ οἱ φεύγοντες τῶν Κερκυραίων (διεσώθησαν 2 γὰρ αὐτῶν ἐς πεντακοσίους) τείχη τε λαβόντες, ἃ ἦν ἐν τῇ ἠπείρῳ, ἐκράτουν τῆς πέραν οἰκείας γῆς καὶ ἐξ αὐτῆς ὁρμώμενοι ἐλῄζοντο τοὺς ἐν τῇ νήσῳ καὶ πολλὰ ἔβλαπτον, καὶ λιμὸς ἰσχυρὸς ἐγένετο ἐν τῇ πόλει. ἐπρεσβεύοντο δὲ 3 καὶ ἐς τὴν Λακεδαίμονα καὶ Κόρινθον περὶ καθόδου· καὶ ὡς οὐδὲν αὐτοῖς ἐπράσσετο, ὕστερον χρόνῳ πλοῖα καὶ

opp. to οἱ φεύγοντες τῶν Κερκυραίων in l. 4. But since these fugitives were such as the result of the events described in c. 81, to which events also, in explanation of their existence, the parenthesis διεσώθησαν... ἐς πεντακοσίους refers back, Steup suspects κατὰ τὴν πόλιν to be an interpolation. — τοιαύταις ὀργαῖς ταῖς πρώταις: i.e. outbreaks of party passion. τοιαύταις, pred. referring to c. 81. Cf. vi. 44. 1 τοσαύτη ἡ πρώτη πρὸς τὸν πόλεμον διέπλει. — 2. ταῖς πρώταις: usually understood as contrasted with the cruelties described in iv. 46 ff. But Cl. and Jow. think it more natural to consider the words a repetition of c. 82. 2 ἐν τοῖς πρώτῃ (i.e. ἡ στάσις) ἐγένετο, supplying πασῶν. St. takes ταῖς πρώταις as opp. to ὕστερον in l. 4. But ὕστερον prob. refers only to the departure of Eurymedon with his ships, after which the fugitives could make their venture. Besides, this seizure by the oligarchs of a point on the mainland does not come under the notion of the ὀργαί above. — 3. ἀπέπλευσαν: sc. after remaining seven days, c. 81. 17.

4. διεσώθησαν: sc. ναυσὶ ἐς τὴν ἤπει-

ρον. — 5. ἐς πεντακοσίους: see on c. 20. 11. — 6. τῆς πέραν οἰκείας γῆς: i.e. the territory belonging to Corcyra on the mainland opposite. — 7. ἐλῄζοντο: (not ἔληζον) with Bk. and most Mss., all of which have the mid. in i. 5. 15; 24. 14; v. 56. 12; 115. 7; and only in iv. 41. 8 all have the active. See on iv. 41. 8. — 8. καὶ λιμὸς ἰσχυρὸς κτέ.: cf. iv. 2. 12. Müller-Strübing's objections to this statement are refuted by B. Schmidt, p. 80 f.

9. περὶ καθόδου: of fugitives, as in v. 16. 18; viii. 47. 3. — 10. οὐδὲν αὐτοῖς ἐπράσσετο: dat. of agent, as in ii. 101. 17. See on c. 64. 15. οὐδὲν πράσσεσθαι in this sense also v. 46. 31; 50. 26. — ὕστερον χρόνῳ: denotes always a considerable interval. See on i. 8. 17. The conjectures of Köhler, Hermes xxvi. p. 45 ff., that the fugitives did not cross over to Corcyra till 425 B.C., and that in the winter of 426–25 they took part in the Amphilochian war, are very improbable. In the first case, Thuc. would hardly have mentioned the crossing over to the island until iv. 2; in the second, he could surely not have passed over

ἐπικούρους παρασκευασάμενοι διέβησαν ἐς τὴν νῆσον,
ἑξακόσιοι μάλιστα οἱ πάντες, καὶ τὰ πλοῖα ἐμπρήσαντες, 4
ὅπως ἀπόγνοια ᾖ τοῦ ἄλλο τι ἢ κρατεῖν τῆς γῆς, ἀνα-
βάντες ἐς τὸ ὄρος τὴν Ἰστώνην τεῖχος ἐνοικοδομησάμε-
15 νοι ἔφθειρον τοὺς ἐν τῇ πόλει καὶ τῆς γῆς ἐκράτουν.
86 Τοῦ δ' αὐτοῦ θέρους τελευτῶντος Ἀθηναῖοι εἴ- 1
κοσι ναῦς ἔστειλαν ἐς Σικελίαν καὶ Λάχητα τὸν Μελα-

the matter in complete silence here, and still less in the detailed account of the Amphilochian war (c. 105 ff.). Köhler bases his assumption, that the 500 Corcyraeans belonged to those who were conquered by the Athenians in the Amphilochian war, forming part of the 3000 Ambracian hoplites of c. 105. § 1, on the very fragmentary remains of a popular decree, in which the word Κερκυραίων occurs. But it is quite possible, of course, that in this decree Κερκυραίων had a very different application from the one which Köhler assumes. —
πλοῖα: i.e. transports, not warships.
— 11. ἐπικούρους: see on c. 18. 3. —
12. ἑξακόσιοι: compared with ἐς πεντακοσίους, l. 5, this number seems rather small. — οἱ πάντες: in all. See on i. 60. 6; vii. 1. 31. Kr. Spr. 50, 11, 13.
13. ἀπόγνοια: not found elsewhere. — ἄλλο τι ἤ: as in v. 87. 2. After the negative ἀπόγνοια there is the same ellipse of ποιεῖν as with οὐδὲν ἄλλο ἤ, ii. 16. 10; iv. 14. 18; vii. 75. 25; viii. 5. 1. See on c. 39. 10. —
κρατεῖν τῆς γῆς: the words τῆς γῆς are bracketed by Kr., as borrowed from τῆς γῆς ἐκράτουν, l. 15, with the approval of B. Schmidt, p. 81, who thinks that Thuc. could not have used

κρατεῖν τῆς γῆς in two different senses in the same sentence. But τῆς γῆς may be understood in both places of the open country as opp. to the πόλις. For the oligarchical Corcyraeans it sufficed for the time to establish themselves on the island and to get the upper hand in the open field; hence we need not think here, with the Schol., of the whole of Corcyra. κρατεῖν τῆς γῆς occurs also in c. 6. 8; 18. 13; i. 111. 5; iv. 46. 6; vi. 23. 7; 37. 10; vii. 4. 31. Cf. also l. 6 above, and c. 115. 9 τῆς γῆς αὐτῶν ἐκράτουν. — 14. τὴν Ἰστώνην: also iv. 46. 5. The situation is uncertain. See App. — τεῖχος ἐνοικοδομησάμενοι: Cf. iv. 46. 4 τοὺς ἐν τῷ ὄρει ... καθιδρυμένους. — 15. ἔφθειρον ... καὶ ... ἐκράτουν: the impfs. represent the action as in progress. This state of affairs is to be regarded as lasting until the further events related in iv. 46. Cf. also iv. 2. § 3.

86. At the request of the Leontines the Athenians send to aid them against the Syracusans a fleet of twenty ships, which take their station at Rhegium.
2. ἐς Σικελίαν: first fateful participation of Athens in Sicilian quarrels. — Λάχητα: from this his first appearance, in constant activity (c. 90. 8; 103. 12; 115. 7; iv. 118. 45;

νώπου στρατηγὸν αὐτῶν καὶ Χαροιάδην τὸν Εὐφιλήτου. οἱ γὰρ Συρακόσιοι καὶ Λεοντῖνοι ἐς πόλεμον ἀλλήλοις 2
5 καθέστασαν. ξύμμαχοι δὲ τοῖς μὲν Συρακοσίοις ἦσαν πλὴν Καμαριναίων αἱ ἄλλαι Δωρίδες πόλεις, αἵπερ καὶ πρὸς τὴν τῶν Λακεδαιμονίων τὸ πρῶτον ἀρχομένου τοῦ πολέμου ξυμμαχίαν ἐτάχθησαν, οὐ μέντοι ξυνεπολέμησάν γε, τοῖς δὲ Λεοντίνοις αἱ Χαλκιδικαὶ πόλεις καὶ
10 Καμάρινα· τῆς δὲ Ἰταλίας Λοκροὶ μὲν Συρακοσίων ἦσαν, Ῥηγῖνοι δὲ κατὰ τὸ ξυγγενὲς Λεοντίνων. ἐς οὖν τὰς Ἀθή- 3
νας πέμψαντες οἱ τῶν Λεοντίνων ξύμμαχοι κατά τε παλαιὰν ξυμμαχίαν καὶ ὅτι Ἴωνες ἦσαν πείθουσι τοὺς Ἀθηναίους πέμψαι σφίσι ναῦς· ὑπὸ γὰρ τῶν Συρακοσίων

v. 19. 9; 24. 6; 43. 9) untill his death at Mantinea 418 B.C. (cf. v. 61. 2; 74. 10). He is one of the speakers in Plato's *Laches.*—3. Χαροιάδην: killed in this campaign in Sicily, c. 90. 7.

6. αἱ ἄλλαι Δωρίδες πόλεις : for particulars of these, as well as of the Χαλκιδικαὶ πόλεις (l. 9), cf. vi. 3–5.—

7. πρὸς τὴν τῶν Λακεδαιμονίων . . . ξυμμαχίαν : see on ii. 7. 9. — τὸ πρῶτον ἀρχομένου τοῦ πολέμου : at the very beginning of the war, to be construed with ἐτάχθησαν. See on c. 63. 8. πρῶτον is often joined with ἀρχομένου to emphasize the moment of beginning. See on i. 103. 16. — 8. οὐ μέντοι ξυνεπολέμησάν γε : referring to πρὸς τὴν ξυμμαχίαν ἐτάχθησαν. They had joined the alliance, but, in spite of the great things expected from them (ii. 7. § 2), had so far taken no active part in the war. —10. Καμάρινα : founded 599 B.C. by the Syracusans, who afterwards expelled the inhabitants for revolting. Later Hippocrates, the tyrant of Gela, having received the place as the ransom of some Syracusan captives, colonized it anew. But the inhabitants having been again driven out by Gelo, the city was colonized for the third time by the Geloans. See vi. 5. § 3. — Συρακοσίων, Λεοντίνων : it is not necessary to understand ξύμμαχοι. Cf. v. 84. 13 οὐδετέρων ὄντες.

— 11. κατὰ τὸ ξυγγενές : since both were Chalcidians. Cf. vi. 44. 19.

12. οἱ τῶν Λεοντίνων ξύμμαχοι : including the Leontines themselves. At the head of this embassy was the celebrated rhetorician Gorgias. Diod. xii. 53; [Plato] *Hipp. Maj.* 282 b. See on c. 38. 31. — κατά τε παλαιὰν ξυμμαχίαν κτέ. : belongs to πείθουσι πέμψαι. — κατὰ παλαιὰν ξυμμαχίαν : in *C. I. A.* i. 33 (cf. Kirchhoff iv. p. 13) and iv. 33 a, there are fragments of treaties of alliance concluded under the archon Apsendes (433–32 B.C.) between Athens and the Rhegians and Leontines; probably there were still older treaties than these.—13. Ἴωνες:

15 τῆς τε γῆς εἴργοντο καὶ τῆς θαλάσσης. καὶ ἔπεμψαν 4 οἱ Ἀθηναῖοι τῆς μὲν οἰκειότητος προφάσει, βουλόμενοι δὲ μήτε σῖτον ἐς τὴν Πελοπόννησον ἄγεσθαι αὐτόθεν, πρόπειράν τε ποιούμενοι, εἰ σφίσι δυνατὰ εἴη τὰ ἐν τῇ Σικελίᾳ πράγματα ὑποχείρια γενέσθαι. καταστάντες οὖν 5
20 ἐς Ῥήγιον τῆς Ἰταλίας τὸν πόλεμον ἐποιοῦντο μετὰ τῶν ξυμμάχων, καὶ τὸ θέρος ἐτελεύτα.

87 Τοῦ δ' ἐπιγιγνομένου χειμῶνος ἡ νόσος τὸ δεύ- 1 τερον ἐπέπεσε τοῖς Ἀθηναίοις, ἐκλιποῦσα μὲν οὐδένα χρόνον τὸ παντάπασιν, ἐγένετο δέ τις ὅμως διοκωχή. παρέμεινε δὲ τὸ μὲν ὕστερον οὐκ ἔλασσον ἐνιαυτοῦ, τὸ 2
5 δὲ πρότερον καὶ δύο ἔτη, ὥστε Ἀθηναίων γε μὴ εἶναι ὅ τι

like the Athenians. *Cf.* iv. 61. 10; Strabo, p. 446 f. — **15. τῆς γῆς εἴργοντο**: *cf.* c. 6. 7; 115. 10; i. 141. 16; ii. 85. 4.
16. τῆς μὲν οἰκειότητος προφάσει: *on the pretext of relationship. Cf.* iv. 61. 10; vi. 6. 5; 76. 10. — **18. πρόπειράν τε ποιούμενοι**: the natural const. would have been πρόπειράν τε ποιεῖσθαι, but the sent. continues as if τὸ δ' ἀληθὲς οὔτε βουλόμενοι had gone before. (St.) See on c. 67. 24. πρόπειρα, *a first trial*, only here in Thuc. *Cf.* Hdt. ix. 48. 10 *ἐν Ἀθηναίοισι τὴν πρόπειραν ποιευμένους*. — **σφίσι**: belongs to *ὑποχείρια*. — **δυνατὰ εἴη**: as *δυνατὰ εἶναι* in viii. 106. 22, in personal const. with τὰ *πράγματα*.
19. καταστάντες ἐς Ῥήγιον: *when they had arrived at Rhegium. Cf.* iv. 14. 23 *καταστάντες ἐς τὸ στρατόπεδον*, iv. 75. 8 *ἔνθα οἱ φεύγοντες τῶν Σαμίων καταστάντες*. See on i. 49. 10. They made Rhegium their base of operations. *Cf.* c. 88. 13; 115. 5. — **20. τὸν πόλεμον ἐποιοῦντο κτἑ.**: for further account of events in Sicily, see c. 88, 90, 99, 103, 115.

87. *In the winter of 427–6 the plague breaks out a second time in Athens, and at the same time numerous earthquakes occur at various places.*

(On the contents of this chapter, *cf.* Diod. xii. 58.)

1. **ἡ νόσος**: *i.e.* that described ii. 47 ff. — **2. ἐπέπεσε**: as in ii. 48. 14. — **ἐκλιποῦσα**: *eclipsing*, as of the sun, ii. 28. 2; of the moon, vii. 50. 27. — **3. τὸ παντάπασιν**: found with the art. only here, but protected by τὸ *παράπαν*, vi. 80. 4. — **ἐγένετο δέ**: for like change to finite verb, *cf.* c. 81. 20; i. 53. 8; 57. 10; ii. 47. 12; vii. 13. 10; 15. 15; 47. 8. — **διοκωχή**: Schol. διάλειψις, ἀναβολή, *intermission, pause*. It is not found elsewhere before Dio C. (xxxix. 47; xli. 25; xlvii. 27). On the form, see St. *Qu. Gr.*[2] p. 43 sq. See on c. 4. 12.
5. **ὥστε ... τὴν δύναμιν**: as was

μᾶλλον ἐκάκωσε τὴν δύναμιν. τετρακοσίων γὰρ ὁπλιτῶν 3
καὶ τετρακισχιλίων οὐκ ἐλάσσους ἀπέθανον ἐκ τῶν τάξεων καὶ τριακοσίων ἱππέων, τοῦ δὲ ἄλλου ὄχλου ἀνεξεύρετος ἀριθμός. ἐγένοντο δὲ καὶ οἱ πολλοὶ τότε σεισμοὶ 4
10 τῆς γῆς ἔν τε Ἀθήναις καὶ ἐν Εὐβοίᾳ καὶ ἐν Βοιωτοῖς καὶ
μάλιστα ἐν Ὀρχομενῷ τῷ Βοιωτίῳ.

recognized by Ullrich (*Beitr.* p. 90 ff.), these words could not have been written after the end of the Peloponnesian war. The reference, in explanation of this remark, to the losses of Athenian men-at-arms caused by the plague (§ 3) by no means justifies taking δύναμις here in a narrower sense than *power* (*cf.* i. 118. 13; iv. 108. 20; v. 14. 14; vii. 28. 17); for the remaining bases of Athenian power (money, ships, allies) suffered little or nothing from the plague. But if δύναμις does mean here *power*, there can be no doubt that this sent. was written without a knowledge of the later events of the war, esp. of the unhappy issue of the Sicilian expedition. Regarding this expedition, *cf.* vi. 43; 44. § 1; 94. § 4; vii. 16. § 2; 20. § 2; 42. § 1; 75. § 5; 87. § 4, 6; viii. i. § 2. Moreover, the remark is a general one, and not confined to the war which began in the spring of 431 B.C. — Ἀθηναίων γε: placed first with esp. emphasis because, as stated ii. 54. 19, no place in Greece had suffered so much as Athens.

6. τετρακοσίων γὰρ κτέ.: Diod. xii. 58 gives the numbers as follows, στρατιωτῶν ὑπὲρ τοὺς τετρακισχιλίους, ἱππεῖς δὲ τετρακοσίους. τῶν δὲ ἄλλων ἐλευθέρων τε καὶ δούλων ὑπὲρ τοὺς μυρίους. But in the absence of further proof, Thuc.'s statement is to be preferred. — 7. ἐκ τῶν τάξεων : = ἐκ καταλόγου (vi. 43. 9; vii. 16. 7; 20. 8), *i.e.* all the men liable to military service of the three upper census-classes. — 8. τοῦ ἄλλου ὄχλου : *i.e.* θῆτες, μέτοικοι, and δοῦλοι. — ἀνεξεύρετος : *not to be found out*, because there were no lists. *Cf.* Arist. de Mundo ii. 8. The word seems not to occur elsewhere except in late authors.

9. ἐγένοντο: often used of natural phenomena. See on i. 54. 6. — οἱ πολλοὶ τότε σεισμοί : the art. because the reference is to events well known. Acc. to c. 89, the earthquakes continued till the summer of 426 B.C. *Cf.* i. 23. 12 σεισμῶν τε πέρι, οἳ ἐπὶ πλεῖστον ἅμα μέρος γῆς καὶ ἰσχυρότατοι οἱ αὐτοὶ ἐπέσχον. — 10. καὶ ἐν Εὐβοίᾳ : this reading of Vat. and Laur. is to be preferred, with earlier editt. and Hude, to καὶ Εὐβοίᾳ of most of the better Mss., since in an enumeration of the places visited by earthquakes a hint of the political connexion between Athens and Euboea would be out of place. — 11. τῷ Βοιωτίῳ : as opp. to the Arcadian Orchomenos, v. 61. 13.

88 Καὶ οἱ μὲν ἐν Σικελίᾳ Ἀθηναῖοι καὶ Ῥηγῖνοι τοῦ αὐτοῦ χειμῶνος τριάκοντα ναυσὶ στρατεύουσιν ἐπὶ τὰς Αἰόλου νήσους καλουμένας· θέρους γὰρ δι' ἀνυδρίαν ἀδύνατα ἦν ἐπιστρατεύειν. νέμονται δὲ Λιπαραῖοι αὐτάς, Κνιδίων ἄποικοι ὄντες. οἰκοῦσι δ' ἐν μιᾷ τῶν νήσων οὐ μεγάλῃ, καλεῖται δὲ Λιπάρα· τὰς δὲ ἄλλας ἐκ ταύτης ὁρμώμενοι γεωργοῦσι, Διδύμην καὶ Στρογγύλην καὶ Ἱεράν. νομίζουσι δὲ οἱ ἐκείνῃ ἄνθρωποι ἐν τῇ Ἱερᾷ ὡς ὁ Ἥφαιστος χαλκεύει, ὅτι τὴν νύκτα φαίνεται πῦρ ἀναδιδοῦσα πολὺ καὶ τὴν ἡμέραν καπνόν. κεῖνται δὲ αἱ νῆσοι αὗται κατὰ τὴν Σικελῶν καὶ Μεσσηνίων γῆν, ξύμμαχοι

88. *The Attic fleet sails from Rhegium on an expedition against the Aeolian islands.*

1. καὶ οἱ μὲν κτέ.: the anticipated δέ clause seems not to have been expressed in what follows. II. 10.46, 1 b. —**2. τριάκοντα ναυσί**: the Rhegians had doubtless added ten to the Attic twenty. Cf. c. 86. 1. — **3. Αἰόλου νήσους**: as in c. 115. 5. Cf. Strabo 275 c *ai Λιπαραίων νῆσοι ἅς Αἰόλου τινὲς προσαγορεύουσι*, Plin. *N. H.* iii. 8. 92 Aeoliae, appellatae eaedem Liparaeorum, Hephaestiades a Graecis, a nostris Volcaniae. The islands are now called the Liparian or Aeolian. — **καλουμένας**: for this position of the attrib. partic., see on c. 54. 19. — **4. ἀδύνατα ἦν**: as to the use of the neut. pl. of the adj., see on c. 16. 10; i. 7. 2.

νέμονται: implies possession or occupation of the soil in any way. See on i. 2. 6. Here = γεωργεῖν, not οἰκεῖν. — **5. Κνιδίων ἄποικοι**: cf. also Paus. x. 11. 3; Diod. v. 9. — **6. καλεῖται δέ**: paratactic connexion, as ἐπίκειται δέ, iv. 53. 6. Kühn. 518, 7. — **Λιπάρα**: from the adj. λιπαρά, with change of accent. — **7. Διδύμην κτέ.**: to the four islands here named, Strabo and Pliny add three others, Erikussa or Erikodes, Phoenikussa or Phoenikodes, and Euonymos. Modern geographers mention eleven or twelve. See Holm, *Gesch. Siciliens*, i. p. 37 ff., 348 ff. — **Ἱεράν**: acc. to Diod. v. 7. 1, the full name seems to have been Ἱερὰ Ἡφαίστου. Strabo, *l.c.*, calls it Thermessa, but remarks, ἣν νῦν Ἱερὰν Ἡφαίστου καλοῦσι, and Pliny, iii. 8. 93, says, antea Therasia appellata, nunc Hiera.

8. ἐν τῇ Ἱερᾷ: before the conj. See on i. 77. 4. Kr. *Spr.* 54, 17, 7; Kühn. 606, 6. — **ὡς**: note the unusual const. after νομίζω. Kr. *Spr.* 65, 1, 4; Kühn. 550, N. 1. Cf. ἐλπίζειν ὡς, v. 9. 8; οἴεσθαι ὡς, Xen. *Mem.* iii. 3. 14. — **9. ἀναδιδοῦσα**: *sending up*. See on c. 58. 18. Cf. Diod. v. 7 αὗται δὲ (i.e. αἱ νῆσοι) πᾶσαι πυρὸς ἐσχήκασιν ἀναφυσήματα μεγάλα, ὧν κρατῆρες γεγενημένοι καὶ τὰ στόματα μέχρι τοῦ νῦν εἰσὶ φανερά. — **11. κατά**: *over against*.

δ' ἦσαν Συρακοσίων. τεμόντες δ' οἱ Ἀθηναῖοι τὴν γῆν, 4
ὡς οὐ προσεχώρουν, ἀπέπλευσαν ἐς τὸ Ῥήγιον. καὶ ὁ
χειμὼν ἐτελεύτα, καὶ πέμπτον ἔτος τῷ πολέμῳ ἐτελεύτα
τῷδε ὃν Θουκυδίδης ξυνέγραψεν.

89 *Τοῦ δ' ἐπιγιγνομένου θέρους Πελοποννήσιοι καὶ 1
οἱ ξύμμαχοι μέχρι μὲν τοῦ Ἰσθμοῦ ἦλθον ὡς ἐς τὴν
Ἀττικὴν ἐσβαλοῦντες Ἄγιδος τοῦ Ἀρχιδάμου ἡγουμένου,
Λακεδαιμονίων βασιλέως, σεισμῶν δὲ γενομένων πολλῶν
ἀπετράποντο πάλιν καὶ οὐκ ἐγένετο ἐσβολή. καὶ περὶ 2
τούτους τοὺς χρόνους, τῶν σεισμῶν κατεχόντων, τῆς
Εὐβοίας ἐν Ὀροβίαις ἡ θάλασσα ἐπανελθοῦσα ἀπὸ τῆς
τότε οὔσης γῆς καὶ κυματωθεῖσα ἐπῆλθε τῆς πόλεως

Cf. i. 46. 8; 48. 12; ii. 30. 8. — **Μεσσηνίων**: since the territory of Messene included also a part of the north coast, which was mostly occupied by native Sicels. — **ξύμμαχοι Συρακοσίων**: since they were Dorians, being descendants of the Cnidians. *Cf.* c. 86. 6.
13. **προσεχώρουν**: sc. οἱ Λιπαραῖοι. *Cf.* c. 7. 12; 91. 8. — **ἐς τὸ Ῥήγιον**: *cf.* c. 86. 20. — 14. **τῷ πολέμῳ ἐτελεύτα**: so, acc. to the best Mss., instead of ἐτελεύτα τῷ πολέμῳ. The former is the regular order; only in ii. 70. 22, where, however, ὁ χειμὼν ἐτελεύτα does not precede, all Mss. offer ἐτελεύτα τῷ πολέμῳ τῷδε. See on viii. 60. 17.

SIXTH YEAR OF THE WAR.
c. 89–116.

89. *The proposed invasion of Attica by the Peloponnesians is prevented by earthquakes. Other remarkable natural phenomena connected therewith.*
3. **Ἄγιδος**: his father Archidamus,

the leader of the three first, ἐσβολαί (c. 1. 3; ii. 10. 9; 47. 5), had died prob. not long before. See on c. 26. 7. — 4. **σεισμῶν πολλῶν**: *cf.* c. 87. 9. — 5. **ἀπετράποντο πάλιν**: *turned back*, as v. 13. 4 ἀπετράποντο ἐπ' οἴκου. *Cf.* vi. 95. 2.
6. **κατεχόντων**: *prevailing*, abs., as i. 10. 5; 11. 19. — **τῆς Εὐβοίας**: position as in c. 19. 6. — 7. **ἐν Ὀροβίαις**: on the northwest coast of the island, still recognizable in the village Rovias. See Bursian ii. p. 411. — **ἐπανελθοῦσα**: with the Schol. against all the Mss., which have ἐπ ελθοῦσα. *Cf.* κύματος ἐπαναχώρησις, l. 16. See App. Arn. gives the sense of the passage correctly: 'The sea first retired from what was then the line of the coast, and afterwards rising in a heap or head of water it invaded a part of the city.' For a similar description, see Plin. *Epist.* vi. 20. 9, and concerning the earthquake at Lisbon, Schaefer, *Gesch. v. Portugal* v. p. 246. — 8. **κυματωθεῖσα**: prob. coined by Thuc.

μέρος τι, καὶ τὸ μὲν κατέκλυσε, τὸ δ' ὑπενόστησε, καὶ
10 θάλασσα νῦν ἐστι πρότερον οὖσα γῆ· καὶ ἀνθρώπους
διέφθειρεν ὅσοι μὴ ἐδύναντο φθῆναι πρὸς τὰ μετέωρα
ἀναδραμόντες. καὶ περὶ Ἀταλάντην τὴν ἐπὶ Λοκροῖς τοῖς 3
Ὀπουντίοις νῆσον παραπλησία γίγνεται ἐπίκλυσις, καὶ
τοῦ τε φρουρίου τῶν Ἀθηναίων παρεῖλε καὶ δύο νεῶν
15 ἀνειλκυσμένων τὴν ἑτέραν κατέαξεν. ἐγένετο δὲ καὶ ἐν 4
Πεπαρήθῳ κύματος ἐπαναχώρησίς τις, οὐ μέντοι ἐπέκλυσέ
γε· καὶ σεισμὸς τοῦ τείχους τι κατέβαλε καὶ τὸ πρυ-
τανεῖον καὶ ἄλλας οἰκίας ὀλίγας. αἴτιον δ' ἔγωγε νομίζω 5
τοῦ τοιούτου, ᾗ ἰσχυρότατος ὁ σεισμὸς ἐγένετο, κατὰ
20 τοῦτο ἀποστέλλειν τε τὴν θάλασσαν καὶ ἐξαπίνης πάλιν

and occurring elsewhere only in late writers. — 9. τὸ μὲν κατέκλυσε, τὸ δ' ὑπενόστησε : one part of the tide made a (permanent) inundation, the other receded. ὑπονοστεῖν only here in Thuc., as in Hdt. i. 191. 14 ; unusual in Attic.
— 11. διέφθειρεν : sc. ἡ θάλασσα. — τὰ μετέωρα : see on c. 72. 7.
12. Ἀταλάντην : this had been fortified by the Athenians (ii. 32. 1), ἐρήμη πρότερον οὖσα. See Bursian i. p. 191. — ἐπὶ Λοκροῖς : as in ii. 32. 3.
— 13. παραπλησία γίγνεται ἐπίκλυσις κτέ.: on the occurrence, see Lolling, Mitt. Arch. Inst. Athen. i. p. 253 f. The passage is treated inexactly by Sen. Nat. Qu. vi. 24. — 14. τοῦ φρουρίου : part. gen., as in v. 2. 14. G. 1091; H. 736; Kühn. 416, 1, N. 2. —
15. ἀνειλκυσμένων: drawn up on shore, because not at the moment in use. Cf. vii. 24. 11. — κατέαξεν : of ships also iv. 11. 20.
16. Πεπαρήθῳ : northeast of Euboea. See Bursian ii. p. 387. — κύματος ἐπαναχώρησις : return of a

wave. ἐπαναχώρησις, corresponding to ἐπανελθοῦσα above, seems to occur elsewhere only in Diod. Excerpt. 510, 31 ; the verb is found in i. 131. 5. κῦμα is used in a collective sense. See on κέραμος c. 74. 4. — ἐπέκλυσε : more definite expression for ἐπῆλθε (8), with τὸ κῦμα as subj. — 18. αἴτιον νομίζω : with inf., without art. as obj., as i. 23. 23 τὴν ἀληθεστάτην πρόφασιν τοὺς Ἀθηναίους ἡγοῦμαι ἀναγκάσαι.
— 19. τοῦ τοιούτου : i.e. the recoil of the sea followed by an inundation.
— κατὰ τοῦτο : after ᾗ=ταύτῃ, at this point. — 20. ἀποστέλλειν τε ... καὶ ... τὴν ἐπίκλυσιν ποιεῖν : Jowett's explanation is doubtless correct. 'Thuc. is pointing out the connexion between the earthquake and the inundation. Where the earthquake was most violent, there the inundation was greatest. But the effect was indirect, being immediately caused by the recoil of the sea after the earthquake was over; hence τὴν θάλασσαν, and not, as we might expect,

ἐπισπωμένην βιαιότερον τὴν ἐπίκλυσιν ποιεῖν· ἄνευ δὲ σεισμοῦ οὐκ ἄν μοι δοκεῖ τὸ τοιοῦτο ξυμβῆναι γενέσθαι.

90 Τοῦ δ' αὐτοῦ θέρους ἐπολέμουν μὲν καὶ ἄλλοι, ὡς ἑκάστοις ξυνέβαινεν, ἐν τῇ Σικελίᾳ, καὶ αὐτοὶ οἱ Σικελιῶται ἐπ' ἀλλήλους στρατεύοντες καὶ οἱ Ἀθηναῖοι ξὺν τοῖς σφετέροις ξυμμάχοις· ἃ δὲ λόγου μάλιστα ἄξια ἢ

τὸν σεισμόν, is the subj. of ποιεῖν. ἀποστέλλειν, either active or neuter.' ἀποστέλλειν and ποιεῖν are impf. infs. See App. — 21. βιαιότερον: with the masc. ending of the positive, as δυσεσβολώτατος, c. 101. 9; ἀπορώτερος, v. 110. 2. ἐννομωτέρου παιδιᾶς, Plato Rep. 424 e. Kühn.³ 152 x. — ἄνευ σεισμοῦ: after ᾗ ... ἐγένετο (19). = εἰ μὴ σεισμὸς ἐγένετο. — 22. ἄν: belongs to ξυμβῆναι. The independent const. would have been ἂν ξυνέβη. — ξυμβῆναι γενέσθαι: the pleonasm as in i. 56. 1; ii. 8. 12; viii. 73. 2.

90. *In Sicily Messene is forced to join the Athenian alliance.*

1. καὶ ἄλλοι κτέ.: if the text is in order, καὶ ἄλλοι must be regarded as the antithesis to καὶ αὐτοὶ οἱ Σικελιῶται καὶ οἱ Ἀθηναῖοι ξὺν τοῖς σφετέροις ξυμμάχοις, and as referring to the Sicels (see on c. 103. 2). But supposing that Thuc. really intended to speak of the Sicels, it would be strange that he should have designated these so vaguely. Besides, a consideration of the especial warlike undertakings of the Sicels — and only of these could one think, since below it is said, καὶ οἱ Ἀθηναῖοι ξὺν τοῖς σφετέροις ξυμμάχοις (*cf.* c. 103. 3) — would be quite out of place. Against Pp.'s conjecture (approved by Cl. and others), καὶ ἄλλα, it may be urged that, aside from the fact that τὰ ἄλλα ξυνεπολέμει in i. 65. 10 is not sufficient support for such a const. as ἄλλα πολεμεῖν, even in Pp.'s text the subj. of the following rel. clause (ἃ δὲ ... ἀντιπόλεμοι) does not agree with that of the first clause; whereas only with identity of subj. could the antithesis between less important and more important events have been emphasized in the manner assumed by Pp. As it seems, in the traditional text two separate sentences of Thucydides are united in one, namely, ἐπολέμουν μὲν καὶ ἄλλοι, ὡς ἑκάστοις ξυνέβαινεν, ἐν τῇ Σικελίᾳ καὶ οἱ Ἀθηναῖοι ξὺν τοῖς σφετέροις ξυμμάχοις and ἐπολέμουν μὲν ἐν τῇ Σικελίᾳ καὶ αὐτοὶ οἱ Σικελιῶται ἐπ' ἀλλήλους στρατεύοντες ("there warred indeed in Sicily also the Siceliots themselves, fighting against one another"). The latter sent., which, though shorter, is clearer, and with which ἃ δὲ κτέ. more naturally connects, seems to be the author's later conception. — **2. ξυνέβαινεν:** sc. πολεμεῖν. Kr. *Spr.* 55, 4, 11. — **αὐτοὶ οἱ Σικελιῶται ἐπ' ἀλλήλους στρατεύοντες**: there is no account of such conflicts in Thuc., not even in iv. 25. 53 μετὰ δὲ τοῦτο οἱ μὲν ἐν τῇ Σικελίᾳ Ἕλληνες ἄνευ τῶν Ἀθηναίων κατὰ γῆν ἐστράτευον ἐπ' ἀλλήλους. — **4. λόγου μάλιστα ἄξια**: that Thuc. did not communicate all even of the former

THUCYDIDES III. 90.

μετὰ τῶν Ἀθηναίων οἱ ξύμμαχοι ἔπραξαν ἢ πρὸς τοὺς Ἀθηναίους οἱ ἀντιπόλεμοι, τούτων μνησθήσομαι. Χα- 2 ροιάδου γὰρ ἤδη τοῦ Ἀθηναίων στρατηγοῦ τεθνηκότος ὑπὸ Συρακοσίων πολέμῳ Λάχης ἅπασαν ἔχων τῶν νεῶν τὴν ἀρχὴν ἐστράτευσε μετὰ τῶν ξυμμάχων ἐπὶ Μυλὰς τὰς τῶν Μεσσηνίων. ἔτυχον δὲ δύο φυλαὶ ἐν ταῖς Μυλαῖς τῶν Μεσσηνίων φρουροῦσαι καί τινα καὶ ἐνέδραν πεποιημέναι τοῖς ἀπὸ τῶν νεῶν. οἱ δὲ Ἀθηναῖοι καὶ οἱ 3 ξύμμαχοι τούς τε ἐκ τῆς ἐνέδρας τρέπουσι καὶ διαφθείρουσι πολλούς, καὶ τῷ ἐρύματι προσβαλόντες ἠνάγκασαν ὁμολογίᾳ τήν τε ἀκρόπολιν παραδοῦναι καὶ ἐπὶ Μεσσήνην ξυστρατεῦσαι. καὶ μετὰ τοῦτο ἐπελθόντων οἱ Μεσσήνιοι 4 τῶν τε Ἀθηναίων καὶ τῶν ξυμμάχων προσεχώρησαν καὶ

events in Sicily, in which the Athenians took part, but only certain selected ones, may be inferred from his remark about the death of Charoeades (7). — 5. **πρὸς τοὺς Ἀθηναίους οἱ ἀντιπόλεμοι**: in spite of this announcement there is neither in this chapter. nor in c. 99, an account of these undertakings. — 6. **ἀντιπόλεμοι**: rightly restored by St. (for ἀντιπολέμιοι of the Mss.) acc. to the statement of Pollux i. 150 τὸ τῶν ἀντιπολέμων ὄνομα, εἰ καὶ Θουκυδίδης αὐτῷ κέχρηται, σκληρόν ἐστι. In Hdt. (iv. 134. 7; 140. 10; vii. 236. 17; viii. 68. β 2) this form has been generally adopted (by Stein in the last two places). **Χαροιάδου**: cf. c. 86. 3. — 7. **τεθνηκότος**: prob. his death did not seem to Thuc. important enough to be stated among the events of the winter of 426-7, where it belonged. See on l. 4. — 8. **πολέμῳ**: in war. Cf.

περιέσεσθαι τῷ πολέμῳ, ii. 13. 59; περιγενέσθαι τῷ πολέμῳ, ii. 65. 61; περιγίγνεται τῷ πολέμῳ τῶν Κορινθίων, i. 55. 11, and, on the other hand, τῶν ἐν τῷδε τῷ πολέμῳ πρώτων ἀποθανόντων, ii. 34. 2. — 9. **μετὰ τῶν ξυμμάχων**: as c. 86. 20. — **Μυλάς**: on the northern coast, now Milazzo. — 10. **φυλαί**: borrowed by the military from the civil classification, as also, in Athens and Syracuse, φυλή occurs for τάξις (vi. 98. 17; 100. 6). — 12. **τοῖς ἀπὸ τῶν νεῶν**: of disembarked troops also c. 91. 10; 94. 2; viii. 23. 20, etc.

14. **τῷ ἐρύματι**: Schol. τῷ φρουρίῳ. Cf. iv. 31. 13; 35. 3; v. 4. 14; vi. 94. 7. — 15. **ὁμολογίᾳ**: by capitulation, as i. 29. 22; 107. 10; 114. 15; 117. 13, etc.

16. **οἱ Μεσσήνιοι**: the position is rather unusual. But compare the similar arrangement in ii. 86. 12; iv. 135. 1; v. 47. 1; vi. 6. 13. — 17. **καὶ αὐτοί**: also themselves, as before the garrison of Mylae. Cf. c. 61. 2;

αὐτοί, ὁμήρους τε δόντες καὶ τὰ ἄλλα πιστὰ παρασχόμενοι.

91 Τοῦ δ' αὐτοῦ θέρους οἱ Ἀθηναῖοι τριάκοντα μὲν 1 ναῦς ἔστειλαν περὶ Πελοπόννησον, ὧν ἐστρατήγει Δημοσθένης τε ὁ Ἀλκισθένους καὶ Προκλῆς ὁ Θεοδώρου, ἑξήκοντα δὲ ἐς Μῆλον καὶ δισχιλίους ὁπλίτας· ἐστρατήγει 5 δὲ αὐτῶν Νικίας ὁ Νικηράτου. τοὺς γὰρ Μηλίους ὄντας 2 νησιώτας καὶ οὐκ ἐθέλοντας ὑπακούειν οὐδὲ ἐς τὸ αὐτῶν ξυμμαχικὸν ἰέναι ἐβούλοντο προσαγαγέσθαι. ὡς δὲ αὐ- 3 τοῖς δῃουμένης τῆς γῆς οὐ προσεχώρουν, ἄραντες ἐκ τῆς Μήλου αὐτοὶ μὲν ἔπλευσαν ἐς Ὠρωπὸν τῆς Γραϊκῆς,

i. 50. 18; 51. 6. — 18. καὶ τὰ ἄλλα πιστὰ παρασχόμενοι: *arranging other matters in a trustworthy manner*, i.e. satisfactory to the Athenians. πιστά is not a subst. (*pledges*), but pred. to τὰ ἄλλα. *Cf.* i. 32. 8 καὶ ταῦτα πιστεύοντες ἐχυρὰ ὑμῖν παρέξεσθαι ἀπέστειλαν ἡμᾶς. The further occurrences in Sicily are related in c. 99, 103, and 115.

91. *Operations of the Athenians on the Peloponnesian coast and against the island of Melos. Incursion of Boeotia and victory at Tanagra. Devastation of the coast of eastern Locris.*

2. ναῦς ἔστειλαν περὶ Πελοπόννησον: *cf.* c. 3. 10; 7. 3; 16. 12. The operations of this fleet are narrated c. 99 ff. — Δημοσθένης: from this his first appearance until his death in Sicily (vii. 82, 86), one of the most active and enterprising generals of the war. See Curtius, *Hist. of Greece*, iii. p. 137 ff.; Holm, *Gr. Gesch.* ii. p. 399 and 444. — 3. Προκλῆς: perishes this very summer in the campaign against the Aetolians, c. 98. 23.

—5. Νικίας: already mentioned, c. 51, and henceforth of predominant influence in Athenian home, as well as foreign, affairs, until he also perishes in the Sicilian expedition (vii. 85, 86).

τοὺς Μηλίους: who, with the inhabitants of Thera, had, as Laconian colonists (v. 84. § 2), alone of all the Cyclades, held aloof from the Attic alliance. *Cf.* ii. 9. 19. — 6. ἐς τὸ αὐτῶν ξυμμαχικὸν ἰέναι: *to come into their alliance*. *Cf.* ἐς τὰς Ἀττικὰς σπονδὰς ἐσελθεῖν, v. 36. 13; ἐς τὰς σπονδὰς ἐσαγαγεῖν, v. 35. 24. αὐτῶν, for αὐτῶν of the Mss., is required both by its position and reference to the subj. of ἐβούλοντο. See on c. 22. 31. ἐς τὸ ξυμμαχικόν is found only here and viii. 9. 10; elsewhere κατὰ τὸ ξυμμαχικόν. See on c. 3. 19. — 7. προσαγαγέσθαι: *to bring over*, causative to προσχωρεῖν, in the same sense also ii. 30. 7; iv. 86. 3; vii. 7. 8.

9. τῆς Γραϊκῆς: so, with St., for the Vulg. τῆς πέραν γῆς, acc. to the correct reading, as testified by Steph.

10 ὑπὸ νύκτα δὲ σχόντες εὐθὺς ἐπορεύοντο οἱ ὁπλῖται ἀπὸ
τῶν νεῶν πεζῇ ἐς Τάναγραν τῆς Βοιωτίας. οἱ δ' ἐκ τῆς 4
πόλεως πανδημεὶ Ἀθηναῖοι, Ἱππονίκου τε τοῦ Καλλίου
στρατηγοῦντος καὶ Εὐρυμέδοντος τοῦ Θουκλέους, ἀπὸ
σημείου ἐς τὸ αὐτὸ κατὰ γῆν ἀπήντων. καὶ στρατοπε- 5
15 δευσάμενοι ταύτην τὴν ἡμέραν ἐν τῇ Ταναγρᾳ ἐδῄουν
καὶ ἐνηυλίσαντο. καὶ τῇ ὑστεραίᾳ μάχῃ κρατήσαντες τοὺς
ἐπεξελθόντας τῶν Ταναγραίων καὶ Θηβαίων τινὰς προσ-
βεβοηθηκότας καὶ ὅπλα λαβόντες καὶ τροπαῖον στήσαν-

Byz. (s.v. Ὠρωπός), of ii. 23. 12 τὴν γῆν τὴν Γραϊκὴν καλουμένην, ἣν νέμονται Ὠρώπιοι. For the assumption that ἡ πέραν γῆ was originally a local (Euboean), then a general designation for the territory of Oropos, there is no ground. — 10. σχόντες : *putting in*. See on c. 29. 5; vii. 1. 14. — οἱ ὁπλῖται ἀπὸ τῶν νεῶν: to be construed together. See on c. 90. 12. For the order of the words, *cf.* ii. 80. 10 τὸ μὲν ναυτικὸν ἔκ τε Κορίνθου καὶ Σικυῶνος. —11. πεζῇ: *i.e.* along the valley of the Asopus. — ἐς Τάναγραν : *into the territory of Tanagra*. See on l. 15 ; 102. 19 ; 106. 8; ii. 18. 2. — οἱ ἐκ τῆς πόλεως Ἀθηναῖοι : proleptic, as c. 79. 4 τοὺς ἐκ τῆς νήσου. See on c. 5. 1. —12. Ἱππονίκου : son of Callias, head of the well-known aristocratic and wealthy family, particulars of which are given by Boeckh, *P. E.* p.623 ff., and Welzel, *Kallias* (Gymn.-Progr. Breslau, 1888). His daughter Hipparete was the wife of Alcibiades. — 13. Εὐρυμέδοντος : see on c. 80. 10. — ἀπὸ σημείου : implying that the action was concerted. *Cf.* ii. 90. 18.
15. ἐν τῇ Ταναγρᾳ : *i.e.* in the territory of Tanagra. Cl. wrote ἐν τῇ

Ταναγραίᾳ, on the ground that, with ἐδῄουν καὶ ἐνηυλίσαντο, ἐν with the name of the city is inadmissible. But the Vulg., which corresponds exactly to ἐς Τάναγραν above (11), is sufficiently supported by such passages as ii. 31. 6 τοὺς ἐκ τῆς πόλεως πανστρατιᾷ ἐν Μεγάροις ὄντας, iv. 5. 4 ὁ στρατὸς ἔτι ἐν ταῖς Ἀθήναις ὤν, v. 55. 1 καθ' ὃν χρόνον ἐν τῇ Ἐπιδαύρῳ οἱ Ἀργεῖοι ἦσαν. *Cf.* also c. 67. 13 ; i. 100. 15 ; iv. 118. 16 ; v. 58. 7 ; vii. 1. 18.
— 16. τῇ ὑστεραίᾳ μάχῃ : the adj. is always fem. in Thuc., and most freq. signifies the following *day*, though ἡμέρᾳ is never expressed. It accords best with the context to construe it independently here, and not with μάχῃ. But see on i. 44. 4 and Herbst, *Gegen Cobet*, p. 34. — μάχῃ κρατήσαντες : κρατεῖν takes the acc. in Thuc. when joined with μάχῃ or μαχόμενος (c. 103. 15 ; i. 108. 18 ; ii. 39. 14 ; iv. 67. 29), or, more rarely, when the connexion clearly implies this (c. 99. 3 ; ii. 39. 18) ; otherwise always with the gen. See on i. 108. 19. — 18. καὶ ὅπλα λαβόντες καὶ τροπαῖον στήσαντες: the first καὶ does not connect what follows with κρατήσαντες, *when they had con-*

τες ἀνεχώρησαν, οἱ μὲν ἐς τὴν πόλιν, οἱ δὲ ἐπὶ τὰς ναῦς.
20 καὶ παραπλεύσας ὁ Νικίας ταῖς ἑξήκοντα ναυσὶ τῆς 6
Λοκρίδος τὰ ἐπιθαλάσσια ἔτεμε καὶ ἀνεχώρησεν ἐπ' οἴκου.
92 Ὑπὸ δὲ τὸν χρόνον τοῦτον Λακεδαιμόνιοι Ἡράκλειαν 1
τὴν ἐν Τραχινίοις ἀποικίαν καθίσταντο ἀπὸ τοιᾶσδε

quered, but the two co-ord. λαβόντες and στήσαντες (both... and). That the Athenians did not retire without the usual tokens of victory is emphasized. — ὅπλα λαβόντες : sc. of the slain or of those who had lost their arms, as in c. 103. 15; vii. 45. 5. — 20. παραπλεύσας... ἔτεμε : cf. c. 7. 6 παραπλέουσαι αἱ νῆες τῆς Λακωνικῆς τὰ ἐπιθαλάσσια χωρία ἐπόρθησαν. παραπλεύσας, *sailing along the coast.* See on c. 7. 6. — τῆς Λοκρίδος : *i.e.* Eastern Locris. The terms Λοκροί and Λοκρίς seem to refer in Thuc., without further designation, to the Eastern or Opuntian and Epicnemidian Locrians, unless the context fixes the reference to the Ozolian or Epizephyrian Locrians. See on ii. 9. 8.
92. *The Lacedaemonians, for the protection of the Trachinians and Dorians, re-found the Trachinian Heraclea in the territory of Malis.*
1. τὸν χρόνον τοῦτον : as viii. 78. 1. Cl. wrote, with Vat., τοῦτον τὸν χρόνον (cf. viii. 63. 9). The episode in this and the following chapter, which interrupts the narrative begun at c. 91, is inserted here because the re-settlement of Heraclea occurred without doubt immediately after the withdrawal of Nicias from the Locrian coast. — 2. τὴν ἐν Τραχινίοις ἀποικίαν καθίσταντο : Τραχινίοις seems to be the correct form. Cf. τὰς ἐν

Παρρασίοις πόλεις, v. 33. 11; ἐν Βοιωτοῖς or ἐν τοῖς Βοιωτοῖς, c. 87. 10; i. 107. 18; iv. 89. 3; 108. 24; ἐν Χαλκιδεῦσιν, i. 65. 9; ii. 101. 25. Most, and nearly all good, Mss. have Τραχινίαις, which Bernhardy (*Syntax*, p. 64) considers a secondary form of Τραχίς, and Cl. as a local name borrowed from the Τραχίνιαι πέτραι ("precipitate cliffs"), at whose foot the old Trachis lay (see Hdt. vii. 198. 7; Bursian i. p. 94). But neither view is probable. The reading of Laur., Τραχινίᾳ, would be acceptable in itself (cf. Diod. xv. 57. 2); only it would be difficult to explain how the vulg. originated from it. Against the conjectures Τραχινίᾳ ἐς and Τραχῖνι ἐς, Pp. rightly objects that one would expect as obj. of ἐς ἀποικίαν καθίσταντο, not Ἡράκλειαν, but Τραχῖνα, the name of the old city, as well as of the district. The fact that all the Mss. agree in ἐν Τραχῖνι in the four other passages where the name of the city occurs (Ἡράκλεια ἡ ἐν Τραχῖνι, c. 100. 8; iv. 78. 3; v. 12. 4; Ἡρακλεῶται οἱ ἐν Τραχῖνι, v. 51. 1), does not exclude the assumption here of a slightly different designation of the city. — ἀποικίαν καθίσταντο : *established as their colony. Cf.* the pass. καθίστασθαι, 1. 14; 93. 3; v. 51. 6. On the significance of the whole enterprise, see Curtius, *Hist. of Greece*, iii. p. 135. — καθίσταντο : the intro-

γνώμης· Μηλιῆς οἱ ξύμπαντες εἰσὶ μὲν τρία μέρη, Πάρ- 2
άλιοι, Ἱερῆς, Τραχίνιοι· τούτων δὲ οἱ Τραχίνιοι πολέμῳ
5 ἐφθαρμένοι ὑπὸ Οἰταίων ὁμόρων ὄντων, τὸ πρῶτον μελλήσαντες Ἀθηναίοις προσθεῖναι σφᾶς αὐτούς, δείσαντες
δὲ μὴ οὐ σφίσι πιστοὶ ὦσι, πέμπουσιν ἐς Λακεδαίμονα,
ἑλόμενοι πρεσβευτὴν Τεισαμενόν. ξυνεπρεσβεύοντο δὲ 3
αὐτοῖς καὶ Δωριῆς ἡ μητρόπολις τῶν Λακεδαιμονίων,
10 τῶν αὐτῶν δεόμενοι· ὑπὸ γὰρ τῶν Οἰταίων καὶ αὐτοὶ
ἐφθείροντο. ἀκούσαντες δὲ οἱ Λακεδαιμόνιοι γνώμην 4
εἶχον τὴν ἀποικίαν ἐκπέμπειν, τοῖς τε Τραχινίοις βουλόμενοι καὶ τοῖς Δωριεῦσι τιμωρεῖν. καὶ ἅμα τοῦ πρὸς
Ἀθηναίους πολέμου καλῶς αὐτοῖς ἐδόκει ἡ πόλις καθί-
15 στασθαι· ἐπί τε γὰρ τῇ Εὐβοίᾳ ναυτικὸν παρασκευα-

ductory impf. of the whole; the details follow, from § 5 on, in aors. See on c. 107. 15. — ἀπὸ τοιᾶσδε : the following clause, as usual in Thuc., is without γάρ. See on i. 89. 2.

3. Μηλιῆς οἱ ξύμπαντες κτέ. : *of the Malians all together there are three parts.* Cf. Caes. B. G. i. 1. 1. The natural position of μέν would be after Μηλιῆς. — 4. Ἱερῆς : both name and place uncertain. See Bursian i. p. 95 f. Steph. Byz. mentions Ἱρά, with the gentile noun Ἱριεύς, as a πόλις Μαλιέων. — 5. Οἰταίων : here, l. 10, and viii. 3. 4, as well as Hdt. vii. 217. 4; Xen. Hell. i. 2. 18, etc., mentioned as an independent mountain tribe. See Niebuhr, Vortr. ü. A. L. u. V.-K. p. 173, and Weil, Hermes vii. p. 380 ff. —τὸ πρῶτον μελλήσαντες: *having been at first about* ——. — 6. προσθεῖναι σφᾶς αὐτούς : with the dat. also viii. 46. 29; 50. 10. — 8. Τεισαμενόν : not Τισαμενόν of the Mss., acc. to the con-

stant usage of inscriptions. See St. Qu. Gr.[2] p. 38; Meisterhans,[2] p. 41. On the accent, see Goettling, p. 199.

9. Δωριῆς : applied to both district and inhabitants; hence the appos. ἡ μητρόπολις, as in i. 107. 4. Cf. Hdt. viii. 31. 7. ἡ μητρόπολις τῶν Λακεδαιμονίων distinguishes the Dorians here meant from the Δωριῆς Καρσὶ πρόσοικοι (ii. 9. 10), and from the Dorians as a race.

11. γνώμην εἶχον : *determined*, with the inf., as in c. 31. 11; ii. 86. 17, 19; iv. 125. 20; viii. 44. 2. — 13. καὶ ἅμα ... καθίστασθαι : *and at the same time the city seemed to be conveniently situated for the war against Athens.* — τοῦ πρὸς Ἀθηναίους πολέμου : governed by καλῶς καθίστασθαι. Cf. i. 36. 11; 75. 3. See on 17 below. — 14. ἡ πόλις : *i.e.* the colony to be planted; hence the inf. pres. pass., as in c. 93. 3. Cf. also v. 51. 5 εὐθὺς καθισταμένῃ τῇ πόλει. — 15. ἐπί τε γὰρ ... χρησίμως ἕξειν : the two

σθῆναι ἄν, ὥστ' ἐκ βραχέος τὴν διάβασιν γίγνεσθαι, τῆς τε ἐπὶ Θρᾴκης παρόδου χρησίμως ἕξειν. τό τε ξύμπαν ὥρμηντο τὸ χωρίον κτίζειν. πρῶτον μὲν οὖν ἐν Δελφοῖς τὸν θεὸν ἐπήροντο, κελεύοντος δὲ ἐξέπεμψαν τοὺς οἰκήτορας αὐτῶν τε καὶ τῶν περιοίκων, καὶ τῶν ἄλλων Ἑλλήνων τὸν βουλόμενον ἐκέλευον ἕπεσθαι πλὴν Ἰώνων καὶ Ἀχαιῶν καὶ ἔστιν ὧν ἄλλων ἐθνῶν. οἰκισταὶ δὲ τρεῖς Λακεδαιμονίων ἡγήσαντο, Λέων καὶ Ἀλκίδας καὶ Δα-

reasons explanatory of τοῦ πρὸς Ἀθηναίους καλῶς καθίστασθαι, co-ordinated by τε, τε, to which is added, by way of summing up, τό τε ξύμπαν... κτίζειν. — ἐπὶ τῇ Εὐβοίᾳ : *against Euboea*. For the force of the prep., see on c. 13. 18. Cf. c. 93. 2, 7 ; v. 51. 4. — 16. ὥστε ... γίγνεσθαι : cf. c. 93. 3. — τῆς ἐπὶ Θρᾴκης παρόδου : const. with χρησίμως ἕξειν. G. 1092, II. 757 a ; Kühn. 419, 5. See on i. 22. 13. ἡ πάροδος, *the march along the coast*, as iv. 82. 3. Cf. iv. 78. § 1 ; v. 12. § 1. The minds of the Lacedaemonians were already turned, for Athens's hurt, toward Thrace. Cf. iv. 78 ff. — 17. τό τε ξύμπαν : see on c. 40. 16. — 18. ὥρμηντο : *were eager*. Cf. ii. 59. 6 ; iv. 27. 21 ; 29. 8 ; v. 29. 21 ; vi. 6. 3 ; viii. 73. 15.

ἐν Δελφοῖς : as to the influence of the Delphic oracle on Hellenic colonization, see Curtius, *Hist. of Greece*, ii. p. 37 ff. — 19. κελεύοντος : sc. αὐτοῦ. The subj. is not expressed, as in viii. 6. 23. See on i. 2. 8. Jow. calls attention to the fact that 'in this instance the god is stated to give his sanction to an enterprise which ends in complete failure.' — τοὺς οἰκήτορας αὐτῶν τε καὶ τῶν περιοίκων : *the settlers who belonged to themselves and to the Perioeci*. Cf. c. 93. 12, οἱ ἄρχοντες αὐτῶν τῶν Λακεδαιμονίων, and c. 109. 12 μετὰ τῶν ξυστρατήγων Ἀκαρνάνων. — 20. τῶν περιοίκων : i.e. the old inhabitants, chiefly of Achaean stock, who had been reduced to a condition of dependence (not slavery) by the Dorians. See Müller, *Dor.* Book III. p. 16 ff. Cf. i. 101. 6. — 21. τὸν βουλόμενον ἐκέλευον ἕπεσθαι : cf. i. 26. 3. — πλὴν Ἰώνων καὶ Ἀχαιῶν : the Ionians were excepted on account of the difference of race, but the Achaeans, in spite of their federal relations (see on ii. 9. 7), from political aversion. See Curtius, *Pelop.* i. p. 415. The same will apply also to the ἄλλα ἔθνη that are not named. — 22. ἔστιν ὧν : G. 1029 ; H. 998. Cf. vi. 88. 34 ; vii. 11. 7. — ἐθνῶν : used even of small states, but always with regard to race individuality. Cf. vi. 6. 1 ; vii. 58. 8. In Xen. *Hell.* i. 2. 18 those inhabitants of the new city who had previously occupied the district are called Ἀχαιοί in contrast with the ἔποικοι. — τρεῖς : the number *three*, as often in important undertakings of the Lacedaemonians, c. 100. 3 ; iv. 132. 13 ; v. 12. 2. — 23. Ἀλκίδας : without doubt the

μάγων. καταστάντες δὲ ἐτείχισαν τὴν πόλιν ἐκ καινῆς, ὃ
25 ἡ νῦν Ἡράκλεια καλεῖται, ἀπέχουσα Θερμοπυλῶν σταδίους μάλιστα τεσσαράκοντα, τῆς δὲ θαλάσσης εἴκοσι,
νεώριά τε παρεσκευάζοντο καὶ εἶρξαν τὸ κατὰ Θερμοπύλας κατ' αὐτὸ τὸ στενόν, ὅπως εὐφύλακτα αὐτοῖς εἴη.
93 οἱ δὲ Ἀθηναῖοι τῆς πόλεως ταύτης ξυνοικιζομένης 1
τὸ πρῶτον ἔδεισάν τε καὶ ἐνόμισαν ἐπὶ τῇ Εὐβοίᾳ
μάλιστα καθίστασθαι, ὅτι βραχύς ἐστιν ὁ διάπλους πρὸς
τὸ Κήναιον τῆς Εὐβοίας. ἔπειτα μέντοι παρὰ δόξαν
5 αὐτοῖς ἀπέβη· οὐ γὰρ ἐγένετο ἀπ' αὐτῆς δεινὸν οὐδέν.

nauarch already mentioned, c. 16, 26, 31, 76, 80. § 2.
24. καταστάντες: *having established themselves*, abs. with ἐτείχισαν τὴν πόλιν, as with ἐμάχοντο, i. 49. 10; with ἐπολέμουν, i. 59. 7; v. 4. 15. See on c. 86. 19. — **ἐκ καινῆς**: *anew*. Cf. ἐκ νέης, Hdt. i. 60. 6. For similar ellipses, see on i. 14. 15. Kr. Spr. 43, 3, 8. The new town was built on the site of the old. Cf. Strabo ix. 4. 13 Ἡράκλεια ἡ Τραχὶν καλουμένη πρότερον, Λακεδαιμονίων κτίσμα. Acc. to tradition, Trachis had been founded by Heracles, hence the new name. — **25. ἀπέχουσα**: the partic. construed with the rel., rather than with the main clause.
— **27. εἶρξαν τὸ κατὰ Θερμοπύλας**: *they closed the side toward* (the approach from) *Thermopylae, i.e.* they repaired the old fortifications, which, acc. to Hdt. vii. 176. 19 ff., the Phocians had built as a protection against the Thessalians, and which Leonidas used in his struggle with the Persians (Hdt. vii. 208, 223, 225). εἵργειν, which usually has a personal obj. in Thuc., is here construed as in c. 18. 21; viii.

40. 6; Hom. η 88. **τὸ κατὰ Θερμοπύλας** as τὸ ἐκ τῆς ἠπείρου, c. 51. 13. See App. — **28. εὐφύλακτα**: cf. viii. 55. 8 εὐφυλακτότερα. For the use of the neut. pl. of the adj., see on c. 16. 10; i. 7. 2.
93. *The new colony falls into a decline, owing to the hostility of its neighbours and the bad administration of the Lacedaemonians.*
1. ξυνοικιζομένης: rare use of the compound instead of the simple οἰκιζομένης. Bl. compares Eur. *Hec.* 1138 f.,

ἔδεισα μὴ σοὶ πολέμιος ληφθεὶς ὁ παῖς
Τροίαν ἀθροῖσαι καὶ ξυνοικίσαι πάλιν.

Cl. thinks that the compound is used on account of the various nationalities represented, c. 92. § 5. — **3. καθίστασθαι**: cf. c. 92. 14. — **βραχύς ἐστιν** . . . **Εὐβοίας**: cf. c. 92. 16. — **4. τὸ Κήναιον**: the N. W. promontory of the island. See Bursian ii. p. 401.
— **5. ἀπέβη**: only here impers., elsewhere with general subj., as οὐδὲν ἀπέβαινεν αὐτοῖς ὧν προσεδέχοντο, c. 26. 15. Cf. iv. 104. 10. Here the subj. to

αἴτιον δὲ ἦν· οἵ τε Θεσσαλοὶ ἐν δυνάμει ὄντες τῶν ταύτῃ 2
χωρίων καὶ ὧν ἐπὶ τῇ γῇ ἐκτίζετο, φοβούμενοι μὴ σφίσι
μεγάλῃ ἰσχύι παροικῶσιν. ἔφθειρον καὶ διὰ παντὸς ἐπολέμουν ἀνθρώποις νεοκαταστάτοις, ἕως ἐξετρύχωσαν
10 γενομένους τὸ πρῶτον καὶ πάνυ πολλούς (πᾶς γάρ τις

be understood from the context is τὸ τὴν πόλιν καθίστασθαι. — ἀπ' αὐτῆς: i.e. τῆς πόλεως ταύτης. 6. αἴτιον δὲ ἦν · οἵ τε Θεσσαλοὶ κτέ.: instead of a ὅτι clause, as in ii. 65. 31, or a partic. sent., as in iv. 26. 14; viii. 9. 12, the explanatory clause is added without connective, as in ii. 50. 7 after τεκμήριον δέ. *Cf.* Dem. viii. 32 αἴτιον δὲ τούτων, παρεσκευάκασιν ὑμᾶς, xviii. 108 τὸ αἴτιον, ἐν τοῖς πένησιν ἦν τὸ λειτουργεῖν. Hence it is not necessary, with Cobet *ad Hyper.*[2] p. 43, to write οἱ γάρ for οἵ τε, nor indeed to bracket ἦν. For the analogy of the elliptical const. of τεκμήριον or μαρτύριον δέ (see on i. 8. 3) is not necessarily to be transferred to αἴτιον, which Thuc. construes with ἦν in i. 11. 1; ii. 65. 31; iv. 26. 14, and with ἐγένετο in viii. 9. 11, although the verb is omitted in c. 82. 53. — οἵ τε Θεσσαλοί: to τε answers irregularly οὐ μέντοι ἥκιστα in l. 12. Thuc. had in mind from the start, doubtless, the two chief points of the αἴτιον, — hostile neighbours and the bad administration of the Lacedaemonian governors. Between τε and καί, there is, therefore, no connexion. — ἐν δυνάμει ὄντες τῶν ταύτῃ χωρίων: *who were predominant in that region*. With this unusual expression, *cf.* Plato *Rep.* 328 c εἰ μὲν γὰρ ἐγὼ ἔτι ἐν δυνάμει ἦν τοῦ ῥᾳδίως πορεύεσθαι πρὸς τὸ ἄστυ. — 7. καὶ ὧν ... ἐκτίζετο: sc.

ἡ πόλις, this clause also explanatory of οἱ Θεσσαλοί, *and against whose territory it was being founded*. Kr. took καὶ ὧν, with the Schol., in the sense of κἀκεῖνοι ὧν, i.e. as a second subject. But acc. to v. 51. 1 ff., there can be no doubt that, along with the Aenianians, Dolopians, and Malians, the Thessalians also considered themselves threatened by the new city: Ἡρακλεώταις μάχη ἐγένετο πρὸς Αἰνιᾶνας καὶ Δόλοπας καὶ Μηλιᾶς καὶ Θεσσαλῶν τινας· προσοικοῦντα γὰρ τὰ ἔθνη ταῦτα τῇ πόλει πολέμια ἦν· οὐ γὰρ ἐπ' ἄλλῃ τινὶ γῇ ἢ τῇ τούτων τὸ χωρίον ἐτειχίσθη. Besides, after emphasizing the predominant position of the Thessalians in those regions, there would be little reason in referring still to the hostility of the little tribes of Aenianians, Dolopians, Malians, Oetaeans (v. 51. 2; viii. 3. 4 ff.), even though these tribes, as is clear from ii. 101. § 2, were not all actually ὑπήκοοι to the Thessalians. — ἐπὶ τῇ γῇ: see on c. 92. 15. — 8. παροικῶσιν: sc. οἱ Ἡρακλεῶται. — διὰ παντός: *continually*, of time as usual. See on i. 38. 2. — 9. νεοκαταστάτοις: not found elsewhere except in late writers *Cf.* νεόκτιστος, c. 100. 9. — ἐξετρύχωσαν: as in vii. 48. 11; elsewhere only in late writers. The simple verb occurs in i. 126. 24; iv. 60. 13; vii. 28. 23. — 10. καὶ πάνυ πολλούς: Diod., xii. 59, gives the number as 4000

Λακεδαιμονίων οἰκιζόντων θαρσαλέως ᾔει, βέβαιον νομίζων τὴν πόλιν)· οὐ μέντοι ἥκιστα οἱ ἄρχοντες αὐτῶν 3
τῶν Λακεδαιμονίων οἱ ἀφικνούμενοι τὰ πράγματά τε
ἔφθειρον καὶ ἐς ὀλιγανθρωπίαν κατέστησαν, ἐκφοβήσαν-
15 τες τοὺς πολλοὺς χαλεπῶς τε καὶ ἔστιν ἃ οὐ καλῶς ἐξηγούμενοι, ὥστε ῥᾷον ἤδη αὐτῶν οἱ πρόσοικοι ἐπεκράτουν.

94 Τοῦ δ' αὐτοῦ θέρους, καὶ περὶ τὸν αὐτὸν χρόνον 1
ὃν ἐν τῇ Μήλῳ οἱ Ἀθηναῖοι κατείχοντο, καὶ οἱ ἀπὸ
τῶν τριάκοντα νεῶν Ἀθηναῖοι περὶ Πελοπόννησον ὄντες
πρῶτον ἐν Ἑλλομενῷ τῆς Λευκαδίας φρουρούς τινας λο-

Peloponnesians and 6000 other Hellenes. — πᾶς τις: see on c. 13. 33. —
11. Λακεδαιμονίων οἰκιζόντων· "since the Lacedaemonians were the colonizers."
12. οἱ ἄρχοντες αὐτῶν τῶν Λακεδαιμονίων: for the expression, see on c. 92. 19; for the matter, cf. v. 51. § 2; 52. § 1. St. compares these governors with the ἐπιδημιουργοί, whom Potidaea received from her mother-city, Corinth, i. 56. 8. — 13.
ἀφικνούμενοι: placed after in apposition, as i. 95. 11 τῶν Ἑλλήνων τῶν ἀφικνουμένων. — 14. κατέστησαν: sc. τὴν πόλιν. —15. χαλεπῶς . . . οὐ καλῶς: cf. the example of Hegesippidas, v. 52. § 1. χαλεπῶς, oppressively, as in c. 46. 22. For ἔστιν ἅ, see on c. 92. 22. ἅ is cognate acc., as in c. 55.
13. — ἐξηγούμενοι: abs., exercising supremacy, as in i. 76. 3; 95. 26; ii. 65. 17.
94. Demosthenes with thirty ships first attacks Leucas; but is persuaded by the Messenians to turn against Aetolia.
(On this and the following chapters, cf. Diod. xii. 60.)

1. καὶ περὶ τὸν αὐτὸν χρόνον κτέ.: this reference to c. 91. § 3 is the more necessary because the episode of the two preceding chaps. (see on c. 92. 1) has reached a point of time considerably in advance. — 2. κατείχοντο: as in ii. 86. 2, and referring to the vain attempt of c. 91. § 2, 3. — οἱ ἀπὸ τῶν τριάκοντα νεῶν: see on c. 90. 12.
— 3. τῶν τριάκοντα νεῶν: cf. c. 91. 1.
— περὶ Πελοπόννησον ὄντες: placed after the noun, without article. Cf. i. 51. 11; ii. 31. 4; 100. 8. G. 968. —
4. ἐν Ἑλλομενῷ: so, not Ἑλλομένῳ with the Mss., acc. to the analogy of Ὀρχομενός. See St. Qu. Gr.² p. 33 f. Acc. to Dodwell, Classical Tour, ii. p. 49, this place still retains its ancient name (Llomeno, identical with Ἑλλόμενος), and is situated on the east coast of Leucadia, a little inland. But as the name occurs nowhere else in the ancient writers, Forchhammer (Hellenica, p. 102) conjectures ἐν Κλυμένῳ, the real name being preserved in Klimeno, situated on a bay on the east coast of S. Maura. So also Leake; and Kiepert has adopted this form. But see Bursian i. p. 117.

5 χήσαντες διέφθειραν, ἔπειτα ὕστερον ἐπὶ Λευκάδα μείζονι στόλῳ ἦλθον, Ἀκαρνᾶσί τε πᾶσιν, οἳ πανδημεὶ πλὴν
Οἰνιαδῶν ξυνέσποντο, καὶ Ζακυνθίοις καὶ Κεφαλλῆσι
καὶ Κερκυραίων πεντεκαίδεκα ναυσί. καὶ οἱ μὲν Λευκά- 2
διοι τῆς τε ἔξω γῆς δῃουμένης καὶ τῆς ἐντὸς τοῦ ἰσθμοῦ,
10 ἐν ᾗ καὶ ἡ Λευκάς ἐστι καὶ τὸ ἱερὸν τοῦ Ἀπόλλωνος,
πλήθει βιαζόμενοι ἡσύχαζον· οἱ δὲ Ἀκαρνᾶνες ἠξίουν
Δημοσθένην τὸν στρατηγὸν τῶν Ἀθηναίων ἀποτειχίζειν
αὐτούς, νομίζοντες ῥᾳδίως τ' ἂν ἐκπολιορκῆσαι πόλεώς
τε αἰεὶ σφίσι πολεμίας ἀπαλλαγῆναι. Δημοσθένης δ' ἀνα- 3
15 πείθεται κατὰ τὸν χρόνον τοῦτον ὑπὸ Μεσσηνίων ὡς
καλὸν αὐτῷ στρατιᾶς τοσαύτης ξυνειλεγμένης Αἰτωλοῖς
ἐπιθέσθαι, Ναυπάκτῳ τε πολεμίοις οὖσι, καὶ ἢν κρατήσῃ

—τῆς Λευκαδίας : Thuc. uses the form
Λευκαδία of the territory of the Leucadians, which, acc. to what follows,
included, besides the peninsula (see
on c. 81. 3), also a part of the neighbouring mainland. *Cf.* iv. 42. 17;
viii. 13. 3. — **φρουρούς τινας** : *cf.* c. 7.
16; iv. 42. 17. — **λοχήσαντες διέφθειραν**: as in i. 65. 10. — 5. **ἔπειτα ὕστερον**: as in ii. 9. 7; v. 61. 15; vi. 66.
14; 88. 54; vii. 82. 7. — **ἐπὶ Λευκάδα**:
against the city of *Leucas*, which was
situated on the peninsula near the
isthmus (*cf.* l. 10). — 6. **Ἀκαρνᾶσί τε
πᾶσιν**: as to the omission of the art.,
see on c. 66. 3; ii. 9. § 2. — **πλὴν Οἰνιαδῶν**: *cf.* ii. 102. 10.
9. **ἔξω** : *sc.* τοῦ ἰσθμοῦ. See on c.
81. 3. — 10. **τὸ ἱερὸν τοῦ Ἀπόλλωνος** :
this sanctuary was on the promontory of Leucatas, the southernmost
point of the peninsula. — 11. **πλήθει
βιαζόμενοι** : *forced by superior numbers*, the cause of ἡσύχαζον. — 12.

Δημοσθένην: see on c. 91. 2. — **ἀποτειχίζειν αὐτούς** : *to wall them off*,
i.e. τοὺς Λευκαδίους. That a complete
circumvallation is meant (*cf.* i. 65. 2 ;
vii. 1. 4 ; viii. 26. 20), is clear from
c. 95. 12 διὰ τῆς Λευκάδος τὴν οὐ περιτείχισιν.
14. **ἀναπείθεται**: stronger term than
the simple verb. *Cf.* c. 70. 23, and see
on i. 84. 10. — 15. **ὑπὸ Μεσσηνίων** :
sc. τῶν ἐν Ναυπάκτῳ. *Cf.* c. 107. 5 ;
ii. 25. 22 ; iv. 9. 8 ; v. 35. 31. — **ὡς
καλὸν αὐτῷ** : *sc.* ἐστίν. *Cf.* Plato *Rep.*
p. 327 c ἢν πείσωμεν ὑμᾶς ὡς χρὴ ἡμᾶς
ἀφεῖναι. πείθειν with inf. means *persuade to do something* ; with ὡς,
convince, induce to believe, that. Kr.
Spr. 65, 1, 4. — 16. **ξυνειλεγμένης** : note
the force of the perf. partic., *already
collected*, and not just with a view to
the ἐπιθέσθαι. GMT. 142. — 17. **Ναυπάκτῳ τε . . . οὖσι, καὶ . . . προσποιήσειν**: the two motives (co-ord. by τε,
καί) for the attack on the Aetolians

αὐτῶν, ῥᾳδίως καὶ τὸ ἄλλο ἠπειρωτικὸν τὸ ταύτῃ Ἀθηναίοις προσποιήσειν. τὸ γὰρ ἔθνος μέγα μὲν εἶναι τὸ 4
τῶν Αἰτωλῶν καὶ μάχιμον, οἰκοῦν δὲ κατὰ κώμας ἀτειχίστους, καὶ ταύτας διὰ πολλοῦ, καὶ σκευῇ ψιλῇ χρώμενον οὐ χαλεπὸν ἀπέφαινον, πρὶν ξυμβοηθῆσαι, καταστραφῆναι. ἐπιχειρεῖν δ' ἐκέλευον πρῶτον μὲν Ἀποδω- 5
τοῖς, ἔπειτα δὲ Ὀφιονεῦσι, καὶ μετὰ τούτους Εὐρυτᾶσιν, ὅπερ μέγιστον μέρος ἐστὶ τῶν Αἰτωλῶν, ἀγνωστότατοι δὲ γλῶσσαν καὶ ὠμοφάγοι εἰσίν, ὡς λέγονται· τούτων γὰρ ληφθέντων ῥᾳδίως καὶ τἆλλα προσχωρήσειν.
95 ὁ δὲ τῶν Μεσσηνίων χάριτι πεισθεὶς καὶ μάλιστα 1

stand in different grammatical relations to the main clause. For similar irregularities of const., cf. i. 129. 5; ii. 5. 21; iv. 3. 19, and see on i. 16. 2. προσποιήσειν and the following infs. depend on ἀναπείθεται, or some verb like ἔλεγον to be supplied from it. Kr. *Spr.* 65, 11, 7; Kühn. 593, N. 1. —
18. τὸ ἄλλο ἠπειρωτικὸν τὸ ταύτῃ : i.e. all the Lacedaemonian allies on this coast, as the Ambraciots, Oeniadae, Leucadians, etc.
20. κατὰ κώμας : cf. i. 5. 7; 10. 12. — 21. διὰ πολλοῦ : *far apart*. Cf. διὰ τοσούτου, ii. 29. 17; δι' ὀλίγου, ii. 89. 41; δι' ἐλάσσονος, vi. 75. 3; vii. 4. 19. οὔσας is omitted, as ὤν in ii. 29. 19 βασιλεὺς πρῶτος ἐν κράτει. — σκευῇ : as in i. 8. 6, the equipment, dress, etc., of individuals. See on i. 2. 12. — 22. οὐ χαλεπὸν ἀπέφαινον : χαλεπόν pred. without ὄν, as is often the case with adjs. after ὁρᾶν. Cf. ii. 45. 2; iv. 24. 8; 25. 14; viii. 16. 8. — χαλεπὸν καταστραφῆναι : the less usual pass. inf. after an adj., as ἀπρεπῆ λεχθῆναι, ii. 36. 19; λόγον προσήκοντα ῥηθῆναι, Plato *Legg.* 751 b; κάλλιστος ὀφθῆναι, Plut. *Dem.* 16. See on c. 40. 8.
23. Ἀποδωτοῖς : the accent acc. to Steph. Byz. s.v. See St. *Qu. Gr.*² p. 34. The Aetolian tribes here named dwelt in the so-called Αἰτωλία ἐπίκτητος, above Naupactus. — 25. ὅπερ : assimilated to the pred. H. 631; Kr. *Spr.* 61, 7, 8. — ἀγνωστότατοι γλῶσσαν : because they had remained semi-barbarians (οὐκ ἔχοντες τὴν διάλεκτον εὐκολον γνωσθῆναι, Schol.). Cf. Polyb. xviii. 5 Αἰτωλῶν οὐκ εἰσὶν Ἕλληνες οἱ πλεῖστοι. — 26. ὠμοφάγοι : Niebuhr (*Vortr. etc.* p. 138) refers this to the custom of eating flesh smoked or dried. Regarding the Aetolians, cf. also i. 5. § 3. — 27. ῥᾳδίως . . . προσχωρήσειν : as viii. 25. 28. The inf. depends on ἔλεγον to be supplied from ἐκέλευον. See on προσποιήσειν above.
95. *Having been joined by the Messenians, Cephallenians, and Zacynthians, Demosthenes advances into the interior.*
1. τῶν Μεσσηνίων χάριτι πεισθείς :

νομίσας ἄνευ τῆς τῶν Ἀθηναίων δυνάμεως τοῖς ἠπειρώταις ξυμμάχοις μετὰ τῶν Αἰτωλῶν δύνασθαι ἂν κατὰ γῆν ἐλθεῖν ἐπὶ Βοιωτοὺς διὰ Λοκρῶν τῶν Ὀζολῶν 5 ἐς Κυτίνιον τὸ Δωρικόν, ἐν δεξιᾷ ἔχων τὸν Παρνασσόν, ἕως καταβαίη ἐς Φωκέας, οἳ προθύμως ἐδόκουν κατὰ τὴν Ἀθηναίων αἰεί ποτε φιλίαν ξυστρατεύειν ἢ κἂν βίᾳ προσαχθῆναι (καὶ Φωκεῦσιν ἤδη ὅμορος ἡ Βοιωτία ἐστίν),

induced by regard for the Messenians, as vi. 11. 10 without πεισθείς. — 2. τοῖς ἠπειρώταις ξυμμάχοις: with the continental allies. Cf. i. 35. 21 ἠπειρώτιδος τῆς ξυμμαχίας διδομένης, and see on c. 103. 2. — 3. μετὰ τῶν Αἰτωλῶν: in agreement (alliance) with the Aetolians. Cf. c. 66. 7; vi. 86. 8. Dem. thought that the alliance of the Aetolians with Athens would enable him, with an army composed solely of continental allies, to attack Boeotia from the west. With this view, the sent. offers no difficulty, and hence there is no occasion for bracketing, with St., μετὰ τῶν Αἰτωλῶν, the most important words of the whole sent.— 4. ἐλθεῖν ἐπὶ Βοιωτούς: Demosthenes here first conceives the plan of attacking in the rear the most hated enemy of Athens, Boeotia. This plan is not now executed, owing to the failure of the attempt to subdue the Aetolians (c. 95. § 2–98), but is revived in another form in the eighth year of the war (iv. 76 f.), though without success (iv. 89). The goal (Boeotia) being named, the proposed route, through Locris, Doris, and along the northern slopes of Parnassus, is given in detail (though not accomplished), without doubt in order that the excellence of Demosthenes's plan might be recognized. — διὰ Λοκρῶν τῶν Ὀζολῶν: these Locrians were at that time allies of Athens. Cf. l. 17; 97. 7; 101. 2. See on ii. 9. 8. — 5. Κυτίνιον: at the northern outlet of the pass leading from the plain of Amphissa in Locris into the valley of the river Pindus. See Bursian i. p. 155; Lolling, Mitt. d. arch. Inst. in Athen ix. p. 313 ff. — 6. ἕως καταβαίη: donec descenderet. For the opt., see GMT. 613, 4; H. 921 b. — κατὰ τὴν φιλίαν: the Phocians, though mentioned among the Lacedaemonian allies, ii. 9. 8, seem to have continued to favour the Athenians. — 7. αἰεί ποτε: expresses forcibly the continual existence of a state of things, esp. of a friendly or hostile relation. See on i. 13. 16; ii. 102. 10. — ξυστρατεύειν ἢ κἂν βίᾳ προσαχθῆναι: the pres. of a relation confidently looked forward to as enduring, as l. 20, ὠφελία ἐδόκουν εἶναι, the aor. with ἄν of a case possible, but hardly to be expected. So Cl. and Steup explain, but it would seem better to write, with St., ξυστρατεύσειν. See Qu. Gr.² p. 11. — 8. ἤδη: local, as in ii. 96. 17; viii. 101. 15; Eur. Hipp. 1200 πρὸς πόντον ἤδη κειμένη Σαρωνικόν.

ἄρας οὖν ξύμπαντι τῷ στρατεύματι ἀπὸ τῆς Λευκάδος
10 ἀκόντων Ἀκαρνάνων παρέπλευσεν ἐς Σόλλιον. κοινώσας 2
δὲ τὴν ἐπίνοιαν τοῖς Ἀκαρνᾶσιν, ὡς οὐ προσεδέξαντο διὰ
τῆς Λευκάδος τὴν οὐ περιτείχισιν, αὐτὸς τῇ λοιπῇ στρατιᾷ, Κεφαλλῆσι καὶ Μεσσηνίοις καὶ Ζακυνθίοις καὶ Ἀθηναίων τριακοσίοις τοῖς ἐπιβάταις τῶν σφετέρων νεῶν
15 (αἱ γὰρ πεντεκαίδεκα τῶν Κερκυραίων ἀπῆλθον νῆες)
ἐστράτευσεν ἐπ᾽ Αἰτωλούς. ὡρμᾶτο δὲ ἐξ Οἰνεῶνος 3
τῆς Λοκρίδος. οἱ δὲ Ὀζόλαι οὗτοι Λοκροὶ ξύμμαχοι
ἦσαν, καὶ ἔδει αὐτοὺς πανστρατιᾷ ἀπαντῆσαι τοῖς Ἀθηναίοις ἐς τὴν μεσόγειαν· ὄντες γὰρ ὅμοροι τοῖς Αἰ-
20 τωλοῖς καὶ ὁμόσκευοι μεγάλη ὠφελία ἐδόκουν εἶναι
ξυστρατεύοντες μάχης τε ἐμπειρίᾳ τῆς ἐκείνων καὶ χω-
96 ρίων. αὐλισάμενος δὲ τῷ στρατῷ ἐν τοῦ Διὸς τοῦ Νε- 1
μείου τῷ ἱερῷ, ἐν ᾧ Ἡσίοδος ὁ ποιητὴς λέγεται ὑπὸ

Kühn. 499, 2. — 9. οὖν: resumes the narrative after the explanation and parenthesis. *Cf.* vi. 64. 13; vii. 6. 7; 42. 24. — 10. Σόλλιον: *cf.* ii. 30. 2. See Bursian i. p. 115.
11. οὐ προσεδέξαντο: did not approve. *Cf.* c. 15. 2; ii. 70. 10. — 12. τὴν οὐ περιτείχισιν: see on c. 94. 12. For the adv. qualifying the subst., see G. 952, 1; H. 600; Kühn. 461, 6; Kr. *Spr.* 50, 8, 4. *Cf.* i. 137. 29; v. 35. 6; 50. 17; vii. 34. 26; 44. 42.
— 14. τριακοσίοις τοῖς ἐπιβάταις: on thirty triremes (c. 94. 3), as iv. 76. 2; 101. 13 there are 400 on forty. 'In the Peloponnesian war only ten heavy-armed epibatae used to be put on board of a trireme.' Boeckh, *P. E.* p. 384. See on i. 49. 4. — 15. τῶν Κερκυραίων: *cf.* c. 94. 8.
16. Οἰνεῶνος: northeast of Naupactus, on or near the coast. Steph.

Byz. Οἰνεών, Λοκρίδος λιμήν. *Cf.* c. 98. 17; 102. 4. See Bursian i. p. 148. — 17. ξύμμαχοι: *cf.* l. 3; ii. 9. 8. — 18. ἔδει αὐτοὺς κτέ.: *i.e.* acc. to agreement. *Cf.* c. 2. 7; ii. 5. 1; 92. 24; 95. 16; vi. 56. 11. — 19. ὅμοροι καὶ ὁμόσκευοι: connected as in ii. 96. 7.
— 21. μάχης: *manner of fighting*, as in iv. 34. 15.

96. *All the Aetolian peoples unite to repel the invasion.*
1. αὐλισάμενος: doubtless after the first day's march. The temple of Nemean Zeus, in whose neighbourhood the troops first rested, was situated in Locris (possibly in the territory of Oeneon, Bursian i. p. 148), so that the enumeration of the days (l. 5 ff.) begins from the advance into Aetolia. — ἐν τοῦ Διὸς . . . τῷ ἱερῷ: for the order, see on c. 70. 16.
— 2. λέγεται: for the particulars of

τῶν ταύτῃ ἀποθανεῖν, χρησθὲν αὐτῷ ἐν Νεμέᾳ τοῦτο παθεῖν, ἅμα τῇ ἕῳ ἄρας ἐπορεύετο ἐς τὴν Αἰτωλίαν. 5 καὶ αἱρεῖ τῇ πρώτῃ ἡμέρᾳ Ποτιδανίαν καὶ τῇ δευ- 2 τέρᾳ Κροκύλειον καὶ τῇ τρίτῃ Τείχιον, ἔμενέ τε αὐτοῦ καὶ τὴν λείαν ἐς Εὐπάλιον τῆς Λοκρίδος ἀπέπεμψε· τὴν γὰρ γνώμην εἶχε τἆλλα καταστρεψάμενος οὕτως ἐπὶ Ὀφιονέας, εἰ μὴ βούλοιντο ξυγχωρεῖν, ἐς Ναύπακτον ἐπ-10 αναχωρήσας στρατεῦσαι ὕστερον. τοὺς δὲ Αἰτωλοὺς οὐκ 3 ἐλάνθανεν αὕτη ἡ παρασκευὴ οὔτε ὅτε τὸ πρῶτον ἐπεβουλεύετο, ἐπειδή τε ὁ στρατὸς ἐσεβεβλήκει, πολλῇ χειρὶ

the tradition, cf. Plut. Sept. Sap. Conv. 19. See O. Friedl, Die Sage vom Tode Hesiods (Fleckeisens Jahrbb., Suppl. Bd. x. p. 233 ff.). — ὑπὸ τῶν ταύτῃ: const. with ἀποθανεῖν. Cf. c. 90. 8; i. 9. 10. — 3. χρησθέν: neut. pass. partic. in acc. abs. GMT. 851; H. 973; Kr. Spr. 56, 9, 5. Cf. i. 140. 13; vii. 18. 14. The cause of this mention is doubtless Thuc.'s critical interest in oracles which admitted of different interpretations. Cf. ii. 17. 11; 54. 6. This verb, in the sense give an oracle, occurs in Thuc. only in aor., act. five times, pass. once; to consult an oracle, once (χρώμενος, i. 126. 9). This use of the word seems to be mainly Ionic and poetic. See Diener, De Serm. Thuc. etc. p. 42. — τοῦτο παθεῖν: for the aor. inf. with χρησθέν, cf. Hdt. vii. 220. 10 ἐκέχρηστο γὰρ ὑπὸ τῆς Πυθίης . . ., ἢ Λακεδαίμονα ἀνάστατον γενέσθαι ὑπὸ τῶν βαρβάρων, ἢ τὸν βασιλέα σφέων ἀπολέσθαι.

5. Ποτιδανίαν, Κροκύλειον, Τείχιον: places of the Apodotians, whose situations cannot be definitely fixed (Bursian i. p. 142), any more than the Locrian Εὐπάλιον mentioned in l. 7 and c. 102. 4 (Bursian, i. p. 148). — 8. τὴν γνώμην εἶχε: see on c. 92. 11. — τἆλλα: for which a less general expression might have been expected, must be understood prob. only of the territory of the Apodotians (c. 94. 23). — οὕτως: resumes emphatically τἆλλα καταστρεψάμενος. H. 976 b; Kühn. 486, N. 5. Cf. i. 37. 4. The goal of the expedition was the distant Ophioneans (c. 94. 24), but his purpose was, after first subduing the intervening country, to advance from Naupactus with fresh forces.

11. οὔτε ὅτε . . ., ἐπειδή τε κτέ.: the sent. has an anacoluthon, for instead of a second dependent temporal clause introduced by οὔτε, an independent and positive clause follows. See on c. 39. 14. — ἐπεβουλεύετο: pass. with ἡ παρασκευή, as subj. (cf. vi. 88. 43); often with pers. subj., as in c. 109. 21. — 12. χειρί: in the sense of a military force only here in Thuc. but freq. in Hdt. Cf. also Aesch. Suppl. 958; Eur. Heracl. 337; El. 629. It occurs also in Xen.

ἐπεβοήθουν πάντες, ὥστε καὶ οἱ ἔσχατοι Ὀφιονέων οἱ πρὸς τὸν Μηλιακὸν κόλπον καθήκοντες, Βωμιῆς καὶ Καλλιῆς, 97 ἐβοήθησαν. τῷ δὲ Δημοσθένει τοιόνδε τι οἱ Μεσσήνιοι 1 παρῄνουν, ὅπερ καὶ τὸ πρῶτον· ἀναδιδάσκοντες αὐτὸν τῶν Αἰτωλῶν ὡς εἴη ῥᾳδία. ἡ αἵρεσις, ἰέναι ἐκέλευον ὅτι τάχιστα ἐπὶ τὰς κώμας καὶ μὴ μένειν ἕως ἂν ξύμπαντες 5 ἀθροισθέντες ἀντιτάξωνται, τὴν δ᾽ ἐν ποσὶν αἰεὶ πειρᾶσθαι αἱρεῖν. ὁ δὲ τούτοις τε πεισθεὶς καὶ τῇ τύχῃ ἐλπί- 2 σας, ὅτι οὐδὲν αὐτῷ ἠναντιοῦτο, τοὺς Λοκροὺς οὐκ ἀναμείνας οὓς αὐτῷ ἔδει προσβοηθῆσαι (ψιλῶν γὰρ ἀκοντιστῶν ἐνδεὴς ἦν μάλιστα) ἐχώρει ἐπὶ Αἰγιτίου, καὶ κατὰ

Occ. 21. 8, and late writers. — 13. πρὸς τὸν Μηλιακὸν κόλπον: *towards the Malian gulf.* — 14. Βωμιῆς καὶ Καλλιῆς: for the little that is known of the seats of these peoples, see Bursian i. p. 141 f.

97. *Pressing forward without waiting for the Locrians, Demosthenes is attacked at Aegitium by the Aetolians with superior numbers.*

1. τοιόνδε τι : without following γάρ, as in ii. 75. 23; viii. 50. 5. See on c. 92. 2. In such connexions, Thuc. uses also the simple τοιόνδε, τόδε and τάδε. See on ii. 75. 23. —
2. ὅπερ καὶ τὸ πρῶτον: *cf.* c. 94. § 3 ff. Steup removes the colon after τὸ πρῶτον, on the ground that the words ἀναδιδάσκοντες . . . αἵρεσις are confusing if connected with what follows rather than with τὸ πρῶτον. — ἀναδιδάσκοντες : = διδάσκοντες, *teaching*, as in i. 32. 4 ; viii. 86. 4, not *teaching otherwise* or *better*. Nothing indicates that Dem. had held a different opinion with regard to an attack upon the Aetolians. — τῶν Αἰτωλῶν . . . αἵρεσις : *cf.* c. 94. § 4.

— τῶν Αἰτωλῶν: emphatic position before the conj. See on c. 88. 8. — 4. τὰς κώμας : *cf.* c̄. 94. 20. — 5. τὴν ἐν ποσὶν αἰεί : *the first village in his way.* κώμην can be supplied the more easily, since καὶ μὴ μένειν . . . ἀντιτάξωνται is only inserted as an explanation of ὅτι τάχιστα. For the expression τὴν ἐν ποσίν, *cf.* Hdt. iii. 79. 7 ἔκτεινον πάντα τινὰ τῶν Μάγων τὸν ἐν ποσὶ γινόμενον, Soph. *Ant.* 1327 βράχιστα γὰρ κράτιστα τἀν ποσὶν κακά, Eur. *Alc.* 739 τοὺν ποσὶν γὰρ οἰστέον κακόν, also *Androm.* 397 ; Pind. *Pyth.* 8. 33. It is used also by Dio C. and Lucian.
6. τῇ τύχῃ ἐλπίσας : *confident on account of his good fortune.* The dat. with ἐλπίζειν gives the ground of the hope, as in c. 98. 27; ii. 89. 24 with φοβεῖσθαι ; iv. 85. 9 ; vii. 63. 13 with θαυμάζειν, and freq. with πιστεύειν (c. 46. 1, *etc.*). — 7. τοὺς Λοκρούς : *cf.* c. 95. 17. — 8. ψιλῶν ἀκοντιστῶν : of this kind of ψιλοί consisted, acc. to the following account, the army of the Aetolians. *Cf.* c. 94. 21 σκευῇ ψιλῇ χρώμενον. — 9. Αἰγιτίου : in the territory of the Apodotians. See

10 κράτος αἱρεῖ ἐπιών. ὑπέφυγον γὰρ οἱ ἄνθρωποι καὶ ἐκάθηντο ἐπὶ τῶν λόφων τῶν ὑπὲρ τῆς πόλεως· ἦν γὰρ ἐφ᾽ ὑψηλῶν χωρίων ἀπέχουσα τῆς θαλάσσης ὀγδοήκοντα σταδίους μάλιστα. οἱ δὲ Λἰτωλοί (βεβοηθηκότες γὰρ ἤδη 3 ἦσαν ἐπὶ τὸ Αἰγίτιον) προσέβαλλον τοῖς Ἀθηναίοις καὶ
15 τοῖς ξυμμάχοις καταθέοντες ἀπὸ τῶν λόφων ἄλλοι ἄλλοθεν καὶ ἐσηκόντιζον, καὶ ὅτε μὲν ἐπίοι τὸ τῶν Ἀθηναίων στρατόπεδον, ὑπεχώρουν, ἀναχωροῦσι δὲ ἐπέκειντο. καὶ ἦν ἐπὶ πολὺ τοιαύτη ἡ μάχη, διώξεις τε καὶ ὑπαγωγαί, ἐν οἷς ἀμφοτέροις ἥσσους ἦσαν οἱ Ἀθη-
98 ναῖοι. μέχρι μὲν οὖν οἱ τοξόται εἶχόν τε τὰ βέλη αὐ- 1

Bursian i. p. 142. — κατὰ κράτος: *by storm*, as in c. 18. 19; 103. 3, etc. See on i. 64. 14. — **10.** ἐπιών: *at the first onset*. — ὑπέφυγον: *had stolen away*. So, with v. H., for ὑπέφευγον of the Mss. After the impf., καὶ ἐκάθηντο would be unsuitable, since it denotes the holding, not the taking, of a position. — οἱ ἄνθρωποι: i.e. the inhabitants of Aegitium. — **12.** ἐφ᾽ ὑψηλῶν χωρίων: *cf.* c. 105. 5. The pl. is doubtless to be explained by κατὰ κώμας οἰκεῖν, c. 94. 20 (*cf.* l. 4), i.e. the open place consisted of a number of villages scattered over the hills. Steup explains, *near, in the neighbourhood of, high points*, comparing ἐπὶ Θρᾴκης (i. 56. 11, etc.) and v. 34. 7 κείμενον ἐπὶ τῆς Λακωνικῆς καὶ τῆς Ἠλείας. Kr. would omit χωρίων. But for χωρίον in this sense, *cf.* v. 65. 2 χωρίον ἐρυμνὸν καὶ δυσπρόσοδον, ibid. 6 χωρίον καρτερόν, vii. 73. 9 τὰ στενόπορα τῶν χωρίων. **13.** βεβοηθηκότες ἦσαν: on the periphrasis, see on c. 2. 8 and App. on i. 1. 5. — **14.** ἐπὶ τὸ Αἰγίτιον: for the const. βοηθεῖν ἐπὶ τόπον, *carry aid to a place*, *cf.* iv. 8. 3; 72. 2; vi. 65. 20; Hdt. iv. 125. 18; βοηθεῖν ἐς τόπον, iv. 42. 15; vii. 18. 4; viii. 60. 15; Hdt. vi. 103. 2. βοηθεῖν ἐπί τινα = *carry aid against one*, as c. 110. 8; i. 107. 21; 126. 22, etc. — **16.** ὅτε μὲν ἐπίοι . . . ἐπέκειντο: const. of sent. and tactics as in ii. 79. 24; vii. 79. 21. — **19.** ὑπαγωγαί: ἀναχωρήσεις, Schol. Only here in Thuc. For this signification, which seems not to occur elsewhere in the earlier Greek writers, *cf.* the use of the verb ὑπάγειν in iv. 126. 34; v. 10. 15; viii. 10. 8. — οἷς ἀμφοτέροις: neut. after two fem. substs., as in vi. 72. 20. *Cf.* Dem. xviii. 171; Sall. *Cat.* 5 inopia rei familiaris et conscientia scelerum, *quae utraque* his artibus auxerat. Kr. *Spr.* 58, 3, 5.

98. *Demosthenes is forced to retreat and suffers heavy losses in his flight. On that account he avoids returning to Athens for some time.*

1. μέχρι: here and c. 10. 12 with the impf., *so long as*; iv. 4. 3, with aor.

τοῖς καὶ οἷοί τε ἦσαν χρῆσθαι, οἱ δὲ ἀντεῖχον· τοξευόμενοι γὰρ οἱ Αἰτωλοί, ἄνθρωποι ψιλοί, ἀνεστέλλοντο. ἐπειδὴ δὲ τοῦ τε τοξάρχου ἀποθανόντος οὗτοι διεσκεδάσθησαν
5 καὶ αὐτοὶ ἐκεκμήκεσαν καὶ ἐπὶ πολὺ τῷ αὐτῷ πόνῳ ξυνεχόμενοι, οἵ τε Αἰτωλοὶ ἐνέκειντο καὶ ἐσηκόντιζον, οὕτω δὴ τραπόμενοι ἔφευγον, καὶ ἐσπίπτοντες ἔς τε χαράδρας ἀνεκβάτους καὶ χωρία ὧν οὐκ ἦσαν ἔμπειροι διεφθείροντο· καὶ γὰρ ὁ ἡγεμὼν αὐτοῖς τῶν ὁδῶν, Χρόμων ὁ
10 Μεσσήνιος, ἐτύγχανε τεθνηκώς. οἱ δὲ Αἰτωλοὶ ἐσακοντί- 2 ζοντες πολλοὺς μὲν αὐτοῦ ἐν τῇ τροπῇ κατὰ πόδας αἱροῦντες, ἄνθρωποι ποδώκεις καὶ ψιλοί, διέφθειρον, τοὺς

ind. of an historical, and i. 137. 13 with the aor. subjv. of a hypothetical, case. There are no other instances of the simple μέχρι as conj. in Thuc.; for μέχρι οὗ, however, see on c. 28. 15. — αὐτοῖς: on their side, dat. of interest in loose relation, as in l. 9; i. 6. 8; 48. 9. G. 1170; H. 771. Schol. ἀντὶ τοῦ οἱ τοξόται αὐτῶν. Reiske's proposed change in the order, καὶ αὐτοῖς ... χρῆσθαι, is unnecessary. — 2. οἱ δέ: δέ in apod. as in ii. 46. 6; 65. 19. G. 1422; H. 1046, 1 c; Kühn. 533, 1. See on i. 11. 6; 37. 20. — τοξευόμενοι ... ἀνεστέλλοντο: i.e. so long as they were exposed to the arrows of the archers they were driven back. ἀνεστέλλοντο, as in vi. 70. 15. — 3. ἄνθρωποι ψιλοί: cf. c. 94. 21. The words are bracketed by v. H., as a gloss from l. 12 ἄνθρωποι ποδώκεις καὶ ψιλοί, on the ground that hoplites also could have been wounded with arrows, and that the archers were ψιλοί as well as the Aetolians. But hoplites could, at any rate, protect themselves far better, and the τοξόται are not reckoned among the ψιλοί also in iv. 36. 3; 94. 4; v. 47. 39; viii. 71. 18. — 4. οὗτοι: οἱ τοξόται. — 5. αὐτοί: the main body of the army, esp. the hoplites. — καὶ ἐπὶ πολύ: for quite a long time. καί, as in καὶ μάλα or καὶ πάνυ. Cf. i. 91. 3 καὶ σαφῶς, quite positively. Kr. Spr. 69, 32, 18. ἐπὶ πολύ, as c. 97. 18; i. 6. 12. — τῷ αὐτῷ πόνῳ: referring to the manner of fighting described in c. 97. § 3. — ξυνεχόμενοι: hard pressed, as in ii. 49. 24. — 6. οἵ τε Αἰτωλοί: τε introducing third cause. — οὕτω δή: introducing the decisive moment, as in i. 131. 8; ii. 12. 16; 19. 3. Cf. τότε δή, i. 49. 30; 58. 9. — 7. ἐσπίπτοντες ... διεφθείροντο: cf. c. 112. 22. — χαράδρας: here, as in c. 25. 4; 107. 14; 112. 22, the deep beds of mountain streams, whether filled with water or not. — 10. ἐτύγχανε τεθνηκώς: i.e. in the preceding battle.

11. αὐτοῦ ἐν τῇ τροπῇ: see on αὐτοῦ ἐν τῷ ἱερῷ, c. 81. 15. — κατὰ πόδας αἱροῦντες: Schol. συντόμως. Cf. iv. 126. 38; v. 64. 8; viii. 17. 15. — 12. πο-

δὲ πλείους τῶν ὁδῶν ἁμαρτάνοντας καὶ ἐς τὴν ὕλην ἐσφερομένους, ὅθεν διέξοδοι οὐκ ἦσαν, πῦρ κομισάμενοι
15 περιεπίμπρασαν. πᾶσά τε ἰδέα κατέστη τῆς φυγῆς καὶ 3 τοῦ ὀλέθρου τῷ στρατοπέδῳ τῶν Ἀθηναίων, μόλις τε ἐπὶ τὴν θάλασσαν καὶ τὸν Οἰνεῶνα τῆς Λοκρίδος, ὅθενπερ καὶ ὡρμήθησαν, οἱ περιγενόμενοι κατέφυγον. ἀπέ- 4 θανον δὲ τῶν τε ξυμμάχων πολλοὶ καὶ αὐτῶν Ἀθηναίων
20 ὁπλῖται περὶ εἴκοσι μάλιστα καὶ ἑκατόν. τοσοῦτοι μὲν τὸ πλῆθος καὶ ἡλικία ἡ αὐτὴ οὗτοι βέλτιστοι δὴ ἄνδρες ἐν τῷ πολέμῳ τῷδε ἐκ τῆς Ἀθηναίων πόλεως διεφθάρησαν. ἀπέθανε δὲ καὶ ὁ ἕτερος στρατηγὸς Προκλῆς. τοὺς δὲ νεκροὺς ὑποσπόνδους ἀνελόμενοι παρὰ τῶν Αἰτωλῶν
25 καὶ ἀναχωρήσαντες ἐς Ναύπακτον ὕστερον ἐς τὰς Ἀθή-

δώκεις : poetic word, found also in Plato *Rep.* 467 e; Xen. *Mem.* iii. 11. 8; *de Eq.* 3. 12. — 14. ἐσφερομένους : *falling into*. Bk. proposed ἐκφερομένους, which Cobet (*Mnem. N. S.* viii. p. 144) approves as the proper expression for those who have lost their way.

15. πᾶσα ἰδέα : see on c. 81. 22. — 16. τῷ στρατοπέδῳ : Reiske's emendation, for τῶν στρατοπέδων of all the Mss., restores the proper number (c. 97. 17) and case (c. 83. 2). — 17. τὸν Οἰνεῶνα : *cf.* c. 95. 16. The masc., as τὸν Κρομμυῶνα in iv. 42. 22. See Göttling, p. 266.

20. τοσοῦτοι μὲν ... διεφθάρησαν : the removal of the colon before οὗτοι, as Haase suggested (*Lucubr.* p. 7), brings the two modifiers, of number and age, into a pred. relation to οὗτοι. "So many in number and all of the same age, these were the best men from the city of Athens that perished in this war." ἡλικία ἡ αὐτή collective and pregnant in meaning = ἴσοι τὴν ἡλικίαν. Arn. prob. rightly infers from this remark, 'that the epibatae on this occasion were not taken solely from the class of the Thetes, but that some young men of higher families had been induced to serve on this expedition.' See on c. 16. 5. The emphasis laid by Thuc. upon the greatness of the Athenian loss makes strongly against the view of Swoboda (*Thuk. Quellenstud.* p. 50 ff.), approved by Köhler (*Hermes* xxvi. p. 46), that Thuc.'s account of the Aetolian campaign and its results is too favourable to Demosthenes. — 21. βέλτιστοι δὴ ἄνδρες : since Thuc. gives no explanation of this high praise, it is left uncertain whether ἐν τῷ πολέμῳ τῷδε refers to the ten years', or to the twenty-seven years', war.

23. Προκλῆς : *cf.* c. 91. 3. — 24. ὑποσπόνδους ἀνελόμενοι : an acknowl-

νας ταῖς ναυσὶν ἐκομίσθησαν. Δημοσθένης δὲ περὶ Ναύπακτον καὶ τὰ χωρία ταῦτα ὑπελείφθη, τοῖς πεπραγμένοις φοβούμενος τοὺς Ἀθηναίους.

99 Κατὰ δὲ τοὺς αὐτοὺς χρόνους καὶ οἱ περὶ Σικελίαν Ἀθηναῖοι πλεύσαντες ἐς τὴν Λοκρίδα ἐν ἀποβάσει τέ τινι τοὺς προσβοηθήσαντας Λοκρῶν ἐκράτησαν καὶ περιπόλιον αἱροῦσιν ὃ ἦν ἐπὶ τῷ Ἄληκι ποταμῷ.

100 Τοῦ δ' αὐτοῦ θέρους Αἰτωλοὶ προπέμψαντες πρότερον ἔς τε Κόρινθον καὶ ἐς Λακεδαίμονα πρέσβεις, Τόλοφόν τε τὸν Ὀφιονέα καὶ Βοριάδην τὸν Εὐρυτᾶνα

edgment of defeat. In ii. 22. 15, the words ἀνείλοντο αὐτοὺς ἀσπόνδους show that the defeat was not decisive. See on i. 63. 17. — 27. ὑπελείφθη : sc. until he returned to Athens with the booty from the Amphilochian campaign, c. 114. § 1. — τοῖς πεπραγμένοις . . . Ἀθηναίους: cf. c. 114. 7. For the causal dat., see on c. 97. 6.

99. *The Attic ships in the Sicilian waters make a landing in the territory of the Italian Locri.*

1. οἱ περὶ Σικελίαν Ἀθηναῖοι: cf. c. 90. — 3. τοὺς προσβοηθήσαντας : one of the few cases where κρατεῖν takes the acc. without μάχῃ. See on c. 91. 16. — 4. περιπόλιον: i.e. a fort for the protection of the plain, called φρούριον c. 115. 21. Cf. vi. 45. 6; vii. 48. 32. — τῷ Ἄληκι ποταμῷ : cf. Strabo, p. 260 c ὁ διορίζων τὴν Ῥηγίνην ἀπὸ τῆς Λοκρίδος.

100. *At the request of the Aetolians the Spartans send an army under Eurylochus against Naupactus.*

1. προπέμψαντες πρότερον : the pleonasm as in c. 53. 9; i. 23. 21; vi. 57. 10. The reference is generally explained to be to the time before the invasion of Dem., the hostility of the Aetolians to Naupactus being assumed to have been of long standing (cf. c. 94. 17). But Steup urges against this view the absence of any definite date, as well as of any statement as to the object of the embassy; further, that no one has explained how Corinthians, as well as Lacedaemonians, are the implied object of πείθουσιν, although the πέμψαι στρατιάν seems to have been the business of the Lacedaemonians alone (cf. l. 6 καὶ ἐξέπεμψαν Λακεδαιμόνιοι κτέ.). He assumes, therefore, that the text is corrupt, and that originally perhaps it was said, that the Aetolians, before sending to Sparta, had already asked Corinth and some other state for help, viz.: Αἰτωλοί, προπέμψαντες πρότερον ἔς τε Κόρινθον καὶ ἐς Βοιωτούς, ἀποστείλαντες ἐς Λακεδαίμονα πρέσβεις κτέ. — 3. Τόλοφόν τε τὸν Ὀφιονέα κτέ. : sc. as the representatives of the chief tribes, c. 94. § 5. For the art. with these names, see on l. 11. —

καὶ Τείσανδρον τὸν Ἀποδωτόν, πείθουσιν ὥστε σφίσι
5 πέμψαι στρατιὰν ἐπὶ Ναύπακτον διὰ τὴν τῶν Ἀθηναίων
ἐπαγωγήν. καὶ ἐξέπεμψαν Λακεδαιμόνιοι περὶ τὸ φθι- 2
νόπωρον τρισχιλίους ὁπλίτας τῶν ξυμμάχων (τούτων
ἦσαν πεντακόσιοι ἐξ Ἡρακλείας τῆς ἐν Τραχῖνι πόλεως,
τότε νεοκτίστου οὔσης)· Σπαρτιάτης δ' ἦρχεν Εὐρύλοχος
10 τῆς στρατιᾶς, καὶ ξυνηκολούθουν αὐτῷ Μακάριος καὶ
101 Μενεδάιος οἱ Σπαρτιᾶται. ξυλλεγέντος δὲ τοῦ στρατεύμα- 1
τος ἐς Δελφοὺς ἐπεκηρυκεύετο Εὐρύλοχος Λοκροῖς τοῖς Ὀζό-
λαις· διὰ τούτων γὰρ ἡ ὁδὸς ἦν ἐς Ναύπακτον, καὶ ἅμα τῶν
Ἀθηναίων ἐβούλετο ἀποστῆσαι αὐτούς. ξυνέπρασσον δὲ 2
5 μάλιστα αὐτῷ τῶν Λοκρῶν Ἀμφισσῆς, διὰ τὸ τῶν Φωκέων

4. Τείσανδρον: for the form, see St. *Qu. Gr.*[2] p. 38; Meisterhans,[2] p. 41, 144. See on c. 92. 8. — **πείθουσιν ὥστε**: see on c. 31. 10. — **5. διὰ τὴν τῶν Ἀθηναίων ἐπαγωγήν**: *on account of their bringing on the Athenians* against the Aetolians. *Cf.* c. 94. § 3 ff.; 95. § 2; 97. § 1; 98. § 1. ἐπαγωγή is from the act. ἐπάγειν, not the mid. ἐπάγεσθαι. See on c. 82. 9.
6. περὶ τὸ φθινόπωρον: see on c. 18. 15; ii. 31. 1.—**8. ἐξ Ἡρακλείας... οὔσης**: *cf.* c. 92 f. A mention of the Mantineans might have been expected here (*cf.* c. 107. 27; 108. 16; 109. 12; 111. 2, 14; 113. 4), esp. as there is no further mention of the 500 Heracleots. — **τῆς ἐν Τραχῖνι**: see on c. 92. 2.
— **9. νεοκτίστου**: found only here in Thuc. *Cf.* Hdt. v. 24. 20; Pind. *Nem.* 9. 3. *Cf.* νεοκατάστατος, c. 93. 9. —
10. ξυνηκολούθουν: acc. to the law, ἄρχειν, εἴ τι ἐκεῖνος πάσχοι (iv. 38. 9), as it really happened in this case, c. 109. § 1. As to the usual number of three, see on c. 92. 22. — **11. Μενε-**
δάιος: doubtless the correct form, restored by Dind. in Steph. *Thes.* (not Μενέδαιος, or Μενέδατος). It is Doric for Μενεδήιος. — **οἱ Σπαρτιᾶται**: for the art., *cf.* ll. 3, 4; 25. 2; 98. 9; i. 126. 41; iv. 132. 6; viii. 26. 8; 35. 2. Acc. to L. Herbst (*Philol.* xl. p. 281), the art. is used here on account of the antithesis between the leaders and an army composed only of allies. But that Thuc. should have stressed this antithesis in the case of the associates of Eurylochus more than of the chief commander, is not probable.

101. *The army of Eurylochus collects at Delphi and compels most of the tribes of the Ozolian Locrians to join the expedition.*

2. ἐς Δελφούς: at that time on the Lacedaemonian side. *Cf.* i. 118. § 3; 123. § 1 f.; ii. 54. § 4. — **3. διὰ τούτων**: i.e. through their territory. *Cf.* c. 110. 4. —**τῶν Ἀθηναίων ἀποστῆσαι**: *cf.* c. 95. § 3.
5. τῶν Λοκρῶν: depends not upon μάλιστα, but upon Ἀμφισσῆς. *Cf.* i.

ἔχθος δεδιότες· καὶ αὐτοὶ πρῶτοι δόντες ὁμήρους καὶ
τοὺς ἄλλους ἔπεισαν δοῦναι φοβουμένους τὸν ἐπιόντα
στρατόν, πρῶτον μὲν οὖν τοὺς ὁμόρους αὐτοῖς Μυονέας
(ταύτῃ γὰρ δυσεσβολώτατος ἡ Λοκρίς), ἔπειτα Ἰπνέας καὶ
10 Μεσσαπίους καὶ Τριταιᾶς καὶ Χαλαίους καὶ Τολοφωνίους

27. 11 Παλῆς Κεφαλλήνων, v. 67. 7 Ἀρκάδων Ἡραιῆς. There is no ground for the assumption that other Locrian tribes besides the Amphissians had from the beginning supported the efforts of Eurylochus. One might have expected, too, from the context, to find the relation of the Amphissians to the Locrians more sharply emphasized; hence possibly the text should read αὐτῶν τῶν Λοκρῶν. With ξυνέπρασσον it would be easy to supply αὐτῷ. Cf. iv. 76. 13; 103. 9; v. 43. 21; viii. 60. 2. — διὰ τὸ τῶν Φωκέων ἔχθος δεδιότες: i.e. because they feared, if they did not join the expedition, it would go hard with them, on account of their hostility to their Phocian neighbours, who were in alliance with Sparta. That the Phocians, as a state, were in alliance with Sparta, may be inferred from ii. 9. 8; iv. 118. 5, and from the whole manner of Eurylochus's expedition against Naupactus. The fact that Demosthenes, acc. to c. 95. 6, had hoped that the Phocians would join him, in an attack upon Boeotia from the west, προθύμως κατὰ τὴν Ἀθηναίων αἰεί ποτε φιλίαν, is scarcely applicable in explanation of the present passage, since in c. 95. 7 it is added ἢ κἂν βίᾳ προσαχθῆναι. Besides, the state of affairs in those regions at that time was not such as to excite fear of the Athenians. — 6. καὶ αὐτοὶ πρῶτοι δόντες: see App.

— 7. τοὺς ἄλλους φοβουμένους τὸν ἐπιόντα στρατόν: the const. as in i. 44. 15 τοῖς ἄλλοις ναυτικὸν ἔχουσιν, i. 91. 2 τῶν ἄλλων ἀφικνουμένων. That not all the rest of the Locrians are meant, is clear from c. 102. § 1. — ἔπεισαν δοῦναι: for the position, see on c. 63. 8. — 8. μὲν οὖν: in explanation of τοὺς ἄλλους φοβουμένους unusual, since no new finite verb follows. But cf. iv. 104. 20. — Μυονέας: this form is attested for Thuc. not only by the Mss., but also by Paus. vi. 19. 5 and Steph. Byz. s.v. Μυονία. The Delphian inscriptions have always Μυανεύς. The forms Μυᾶνες (Paus.) and Μύονες (Steph. Byz.) seem to be due to misconceptions. See Dittenberger, Sylloge Inscr. no. 462 N. The place is called Μυωνία in Paus. x. 38. 8, but in Steph. Byz. Μυονία and Μύων. As to its site, see Bursian i. p. 152. — 9. δυσεσβολώτατος: fem., see on c. 89. 21. The Amphilochians seem to have given a first proof of their zeal for their new allies by winning over the inhabitants of the region which in nature and situation was most important for the proposed expedition of the Peloponnesians. — ἔπειτα Ἰπνέας κτέ.: for the Locrian tribes mentioned in the remainder of the chapter, whose locality generally cannot be exactly determined, see Bursian i. p. 149 f. and 152. — 10. Μεσσαπίους: cf. Steph. Byz. s.v. Χά-

καὶ Ἡσσίους καὶ Οἰανθέας. οὗτοι καὶ ξυνεστράτευον πάντες. Ὀλπαῖοι δὲ ὁμήρους μὲν ἔδοσαν, ἠκολούθουν δὲ οὔ· καὶ Ταῖοι οὐκ ἔδοσαν ὁμήρους, πρὶν αὐτῶν εἷλον κώμην
102 Πόλιν ὄνομα ἔχουσαν. ἐπειδὴ δὲ παρεσκεύαστο πάντα καὶ 1 τοὺς ὁμήρους κατέθετο ἐς Κυτίνιον τὸ Δωρικόν, ἐχώρει τῷ στρατῷ ἐπὶ τὴν Ναύπακτον διὰ τῶν Λοκρῶν, καὶ πορευόμενος Οἰνεῶνα αἱρεῖ αὐτῶν καὶ Εὐπάλιον· οὐ γὰρ προσ-
5 εχώρησαν. γενόμενοι δ᾽ ἐν τῇ Ναυπακτίᾳ καὶ οἱ Αἰτωλοὶ 2 ἅμα ἤδη προσβεβοηθηκότες ἐδῄουν τὴν γῆν καὶ τὸ προάστειον ἀτείχιστον ὂν εἷλον· ἐπί τε Μολύκρειον ἐλθόν-

λαιον, where, citing the words from Μεσσαπίους to Οἰανθέας, the Mss. read Μεταπίους. But since several of the following names are unquestionably cited incorrectly in Steph., the preference can hardly be given here to the Mss. of Steph., as Niese claims in *Hermes* xiv. p. 427 f. — Τριταιᾶς: as Πλαταιᾶς, c. 52. 15. The Mss. of Thuc. have Τριταιέας, those of Steph. Byz. *l.c.* Τριταίους. St. read Τριτειέας, acc. to Steph. Byz. *s.v.* Τρίτεια, but in *Qu. Gr.*[2] p. 43 has declared for Meineke's conjecture Τριτέας, which is based on Hdt. viii. 33. 4 and Hesych. Τριτῆες γενεήν. The city seems to have been called Τρίτεια as well as Τρίταια. — 12. Ὀλπαῖοι: these Locrians are prob. to be distinguished from the inhabitants of the Amphilochian Ὄλπαι or Ὄλπη, mentioned c. 105. 5 and freq.— 13. Ταῖοι: Steph. Byz. Ταία· πόλις Λοκρῶν Ὀζολῶν. τὸ ἐθνικὸν Ταῖος.
102. *The attack on Naupactus fails, because Demosthenes throws Acarnanian reinforcements into the town. Eurylochus then turns, at the*

request of the Ambraciots, against the Amphilochian Argos.
2. κατέθετο: *sc.* Εὐρύλοχος, c. 101. 2. See on c. 28. 14. — Κυτίνιον: see on c. 95. 5; i. 107. 5. — 4. Οἰνεῶνα... καὶ Εὐπάλιον: the reverse of the geographical order. See on c. 29. 6. For the former place, see on c. 95. 16; 98. 17; for the latter, c. 96. 7. — αὐτῶν: for the part. gen., *cf.* 101. 5 τῶν Λοκρῶν, 86. 10 τῆς Ἰταλίας Λοκροὶ μὲν κτέ.
5. καὶ ... προσβεβοηθηκότες: supplementary addition to γενόμενοι ἐν τῇ Ναυπακτίᾳ (*sc.* οἱ ξὺν Εὐρυλόχῳ). The pf. partic. has reference to the union already effected before the entry into the territory of Naupactus. The undeniable harshness of the const. involved in joining by means of καί ... ἅμα a second subject to one merely implied in an appositive partic. (γενόμενοι) would be removed by assuming, with Steup (*Quaest. Thuc.* p. 50 sq.), that αὐτοί has been lost before καὶ οἱ. *Cf.* iv. 90. 2; 131. 1. — 6. ἤδη προσβεβοηθηκότες: *cf.* c. 6. 10. — 7. Μολύκρειον: *cf.* ii. 84. 28.

τες, τὴν Κορινθίων μὲν ἀποικίαν, Ἀθηναίων δὲ ὑπήκοον, αἱροῦσι. Δημοσθένης δὲ ὁ Ἀθηναῖος (ἔτι γὰρ ἐτύγχανεν 3 ὢν μετὰ τὰ ἐκ τῆς Αἰτωλίας περὶ Ναύπακτον) προαισθόμενος τοῦ στρατοῦ καὶ δείσας περὶ αὐτῆς, ἐλθὼν πείθει Ἀκαρνᾶνας, χαλεπῶς διὰ τὴν ἐκ τῆς Λευκάδος ἀναχώρησιν, βοηθῆσαι Ναυπάκτῳ. καὶ πέμπουσι μετ' αὐτοῦ 4 ἐπὶ τῶν νεῶν χιλίους ὁπλίτας, οἳ ἐσελθόντες περιεποίησαν τὸ χωρίον· δεινὸν γὰρ ἦν μή, μεγάλου ὄντος τοῦ τείχους, ὀλίγων δὲ τῶν ἀμυνομένων, οὐκ ἀντίσχωσιν. Εὐρύ- 5 λοχος δὲ καὶ οἱ μετ' αὐτοῦ, ὡς ᾔσθοντο τὴν στρατιὰν ἐσεληλυθυῖαν καὶ ἀδύνατον ὂν τὴν πόλιν βίᾳ ἑλεῖν, ἀνεχώρησαν, οὐκ ἐπὶ Πελοποννήσου, ἀλλ' ἐς τὴν Αἰολίδα

—8. τὴν Κορινθίων μὲν ἀποικίαν κτέ.: concerning Potidaea, cf. i. 56. 6. — ὑπήκοον: sc. πόλιν. Doubtless to be construed subst., as ξυμμαχίδα, ii. 2 11, and ξύμμαχον, v. 35. 2.
9. ὁ Ἀθηναῖος: the mention of Demosthenes among the distant ξύμμαχοι causes the addition of the ἐθνικόν. — 10. μετὰ τὰ ἐκ τῆς Αἰτωλίας: for μετὰ τὰ ἐν τῇ Αἰτωλίᾳ, with reference to the retreat, c. 98. Cf. iv. 81. 9 ἐς τὸν μετὰ τὰ ἐκ Σικελίας πόλεμον, vi. 89. 5 περὶ τὴν ἐκ Πύλου ξυμφοράν, viii. 2. 1 πρὸς τὴν ἐκ τῆς Σικελίας . . . κακοπραγίαν. Kr. Spr. 50, 8, 13. For the attraction of the prep., see also on c. 5. 1. — περὶ Ναύπακτον: c. 98. 26. — 11. τοῦ στρατοῦ: the gen. with προαισθόμενος, as with the simple verb. See on i. 57. 14. G. 1102; H. 742. — περὶ αὐτῆς: sc. τῆς Ναυπάκτου, as viii. 93. 17 ἐφοβεῖτο περὶ τοῦ πολιτικοῦ. Elsewhere περί after verbs of fear takes the dat. See on i. 60. 3. — 12. χαλεπῶς διὰ τὴν . . . ἀναχώρησιν: inserted almost parenthetically. As to the matter, cf. c. 95. § 1.

14. ἐπὶ τῶν νεῶν: can refer only to ships of the Acarnanians, for the thirty Athenian ships, which Dem. had commanded in the spring and summer, had returned to Athens (c. 98. 25), and the twenty mentioned c. 105. 15 sailed later. The fifteen Corcyraean ships (c. 94. 8), to which Müller-Strübing refers (Aristoph. etc. p. 491 N.), had also returned home (c. 95. 15). That the Acarnanians possessed ships is, with their extensive coast, altogether probable, even though there be a lack of good harbours. Since these ships are not mentioned before, and their number cannot have been great (cf. ii. 9. § 4, 5), Steup proposes ἐπί τινων νεῶν, comparing, for the order of the words, iv. 76. 5; viii. 32. 12. — περιεποίησαν: cf. ii. 25. 13. — 15. δεινὸν γὰρ ἦν: sc. before aid came. δεινόν, as in iv. 75. 7; vii. 25. 31.
18. ἐσεληλυθυῖαν: the pf. partic. emphasizes the fact that it was now too late for an attack. — 19. Αἰολίδα: this ancient name of the district is not

20 τὴν νῦν καλουμένην Καλυδῶνα καὶ Πλευρῶνα καὶ ἐς τὰ
ταύτῃ χωρία καὶ ἐς Πρόσχιον τῆς Αἰτωλίας. οἱ γὰρ Ἀμ- 6
πρακιῶται ἐλθόντες πρὸς αὐτοὺς πείθουσιν ὥστε μετὰ
σφῶν Ἄργει τε τῷ Ἀμφιλοχικῷ καὶ Ἀμφιλοχίᾳ τῇ ἄλλῃ
ἐπιχειρῆσαι καὶ Ἀκαρνανίᾳ ἅμα, λέγοντες ὅτι, ἢν τούτων
25 κρατήσωσι, πᾶν τὸ ἠπειρωτικὸν Λακεδαιμονίοις ξύμμαχον καθεστήξει. καὶ ὁ μὲν Εὐρύλοχος πεισθεὶς καὶ τοὺς 7
Αἰτωλοὺς ἀφεὶς ἡσύχαζε τῷ στρατῷ περὶ τοὺς χώρους
τούτους, ἕως τοῖς Ἀμπρακιώταις ἐκστρατευσαμένοις περὶ
τὸ Ἄργος δέοι βοηθεῖν. καὶ τὸ θέρος ἐτελεύτα.

103 Οἱ δ' ἐν τῇ Σικελίᾳ Ἀθηναῖοι τοῦ ἐπιγιγνομένου 1
χειμῶνος ἐπελθόντες μετὰ τῶν Ἑλλήνων ξυμμάχων

found elsewhere in ancient writers, but is supported by Strabo's remark (p. 464 c), τὴν Πλευρωνίαν ὑπὸ Κουρήτων οἰκουμένην Αἰολεῖς ἐπελθόντες ἀφείλοντο. *Cf.* also the remark of Hesychius, ἡ γὰρ Καλυδὼν Αἰολὶς ἐκαλεῖτο. See Niebuhr, *Vortr. etc.* p. 146; Bursian i. p. 130. On the text, see App. — **20. Καλυδῶνα καὶ Πλευρῶνα**: see Bursian i. p. 129 ff. — **21. Πρόσχιον**: on the site of the Homeric Pylene (B 639). Bursian i. p. 131.

23. Ἄργει τε... καὶ Ἀκαρνανίᾳ: the Ambraciots recur to their plans of the year 430 and 429 B.C. *Cf.* ii. 68, and 80–82. — **24. καὶ Ἀκαρνανίᾳ ἅμα, λέγοντες κτέ.**: so with Bk., Pp., and Kr., not καὶ Ἀκαρνανίᾳ, ἅμα λέγοντες κτέ., since ἅμα would be out of place in a statement of the means by which the Ambraciots persuaded Eurylochus over to their plans, whereas the correlation τε, καὶ ἅμα occurs often in Thuc. (c. 40. 17; v. 69. 4; vi. 15. 8; vii. 19. 3). *Cf.* ii. 80. § 1, where the const. πείθουσι..., λέγοντες ὅτι occurs in a similar passage. — **25. πᾶν τὸ ἠπειρωτικὸν κτέ.**: similar promises were made ii. 80. § 1. τὸ ἠπειρωτικόν, as in c. 94. 18. — **ξύμμαχον καθεστήξει**: see on c. 37. 13.

26. τοὺς Αἰτωλοὺς ἀφείς: thus abandoning the enterprise undertaken at their instance. *Cf.* c. 7. 13; ii. 78. 3; v. 75. 2. The Locrians also (*cf.* c. 101. § 2) seem to have been dismissed at that time by Eurylochus. — **28. ἕως ... δέοι βοηθεῖν**: "until the right moment should have come to lend aid," which is expressed by the aor. partic. ἐκστρατευσαμένοις, "when the Ambraciots should have taken the field." This occurs c. 105. 1, Ἀμπρακιῶται ... ἐκστρατεύονται ἐπὶ Ἄργος. For the opt., see GMT. 614; H. 921. — **περὶ τὸ Ἄργος**: const. with βοηθεῖν.

103. *Beginning of the winter of 426–25 B.C. Further operations of the Athenians in Sicily and on the Italian coast.*

1. οἱ ἐν τῇ Σικελίᾳ Ἀθηναῖοι: continuation of c. 90 and 99. — **2. μετὰ**

καὶ ὅσοι Σικελῶν κατὰ κράτος ἀρχόμενοι ὑπὸ Συρακοσίων καὶ ξύμμαχοι ὄντες ἀποστάντες αὐτοῖς [ἀπὸ Συρα-
5 κοσίων] ξυνεπολέμουν, ἐπ' Ἴνησσαν τὸ Σικελικὸν πόλισμα, οὗ τὴν ἀκρόπολιν Συρακόσιοι εἶχον, προσέβαλον, καὶ ὡς οὐκ ἐδύναντο ἑλεῖν, ἀπῇσαν. ἐν δὲ τῇ ἀναχω- 2 ρήσει ὑστέροις Ἀθηναίων τοῖς ξυμμάχοις ἀναχωροῦσιν ἐπιτίθενται οἱ ἐκ τοῦ τειχίσματος Συρακόσιοι, καὶ προσ-
10 πεσόντες τρέπουσί τε μέρος τι τοῦ στρατοῦ καὶ ἀπέκτειναν οὐκ ὀλίγους. καὶ μετὰ τοῦτο ἀπὸ τῶν νεῶν ὁ 3 Λάχης καὶ οἱ Ἀθηναῖοι ἐς τὴν Λοκρίδα ἀποβάσεις τινὰς ποιησάμενοι κατὰ τὸν Καικῖνον ποταμὸν τοὺς προσβοη-

τῶν Ἑλλήνων ξυμμάχων : sc. τῶν Σικελιωτῶν, who are enumerated c. 86. § 2. For the adj. use of Ἑλλήνων, cf. i. 62. 10; iv. 25. 34; v. 6. 21, and see on c. 95. 2; ii. 36. 13; vi. 62. 9. See Rutherford, *New Phrynichus*, p. 21; Diener, *De Serm. Thuc.* p. 43 sq. — 3. καὶ ὅσοι Σικελῶν: i.e. καὶ μετὰ τούτων τῶν Σικελῶν, ὅσοι ———. The Sicels were the barbarian aborigines; the Siceliots the inhabitants of the Greek cities in Sicily. — κατὰ κράτος ἀρχόμενοι : = βίᾳ ἀρχόμενοι (c. 46. 21). Cf. Plut. *Lyc. et Num.* 3, [αἱ γυναῖκες] τῶν οἴκων ἄρχουσαι κατὰ κράτος. — ἀρχόμενοι καὶ ξύμμαχοι ὄντες: partics. impf., and as such preceding ἀποστάντες, "being subjects and allies of the Syracusans had now revolted from them." Regarding the matter, cf. vi. 88. 21. — 4. αὐτοῖς : sc. τοῖς Ἀθηναίοις, with ξυνεπολέμουν. This connexion becomes clearer if, with v. H. (*Stud. Thuc.* p. 147) ἀπὸ Συρακοσίων be bracketed as an unnecessary gloss. — 5. ἐπ' Ἴνησσαν: const. with ἐπελθόντες. This was situated

not far from Catana, acc. to Strab. p. 268 c. Cf. vi. 94. 15. — 6. προσέβαλον, ἀπῇσαν: προσέβαλον, with Bk. and some inferior Mss., for προσέβαλον, since the context requires the comprehensive aor. But ἀπῇσαν is quite in place, since in what follows matters are narrated which occurred during the retreat.

8. ὑστέροις Ἀθηναίων: *after the Athenians*. Cf. c. 49. 17. — 11. μετὰ τοῦτο : includes the return to the coast and the voyage back to Rhegium (c. 86. 19; 88. 13; 115. 5), whence the following expeditions set out. — 12. Λάχης: cf. c. 90. 8. — ἀποβάσεις τινάς: as already c. 99. 2. — 13. κατὰ τὸν Καικῖνον ποταμόν: on the accent of Καικῖνος, see Göttling, p. 203. This river is without doubt to be distinguished from the Halex (c. 99. 4), although Pausanias (vi. 6. 4) says the same thing of it as Strabo of the Halex, τὴν Λοκρίδα καὶ Ῥηγίνην ὁρίζων. Either the courses of the rivers must have changed, or the boundary must have been different at different times.

θοῦντας Λοκρῶν μετὰ Προξένου τοῦ Καπάτωνος ὡς τριακο-
15 σίους μάχῃ ἐκράτησαν καὶ ὅπλα λαβόντες ἀπεχώρησαν.
104 Τοῦ δ' αὐτοῦ χειμῶνος καὶ Δῆλον ἐκάθηραν Ἀθη- 1
ναῖοι κατὰ χρησμὸν δή τινα. ἐκάθηρε μὲν γὰρ καὶ
Πεισίστρατος ὁ τύραννος πρότερον αὐτήν, οὐχ ἅπασαν,
ἀλλ' ὅσον ἀπὸ τοῦ ἱεροῦ ἐφεωρᾶτο τῆς νήσου· τότε δὲ
5 πᾶσα ἐκαθάρθη τοιῷδε τρόπῳ· θῆκαι ὅσαι ἦσαν τῶν 2

104. The *Athenians purify the island of Delos, and institute the Delian Penteteris.*
1. Δῆλον ἐκάθηραν: cf. i. 8. 3; Diod. xii. 58; Strab. p. 486, and see Curtius, *Hist. of Greece,* iii. p. 142. The occasion of this extraordinary homage to Apollo was doubtless the pestilence, which had reappeared in 427-26 B.C. (c. 87. § 1-3) with undiminished force, and the object of the festival seems to have been, not to give thanks to the god for the cessation of the plague, but to bring about its cessation. So at least Diodorus, *l.c.*, represents the matter, and the narrative of Thuc. seems compatible with this view. For there is no reason why the beginning of the period during which the pestilence raged the second time (οὐκ ἔλασσον ἐνιαυτοῦ, c. 87. 4) should not be put far back into the winter of 427-26 B.C., whereas the purification of Delos must have been taken in hand early in the winter of 426-25, since acc. to c. 102. § 7; 105. § 1 the irruption of the Ambraciots into the territory of Argos (c. 105. § 1) could have happened only shortly after the end of the preceding summer. So it was deemed proper to propitiate the wrath of the god, to which many had ascribed the pestilence (cf. ii. 54. § 4 f.), in esp. solemn wise. The oracle directing the purification may have had some connexion with Nicias's influence at that time. Cf. Thuc. vii. 50. 30 ἦν γάρ τι καὶ ἄγαν θειασμῷ τε καὶ τῷ τοιούτῳ προσκείμενος. The interest manifested by Thuc. in the occurrence was prob. due not only to its historical importance, but also to the wish to correct erroneous views of his contemporaries with regard to earlier and later Δήλια. Hence here, as in vi. 54 ff., the digression with all its details is justifiable. See A. Baumeister, *Hymn. Hom.* p. 113, against G. Hermann, *Philol.* i. p. 372 (= *Opusc.* viii. p. 388 f.). — **2. δή:** in a supplementary explanation (cf. i. 24. 5; ii. 102. 28); not ironical, as Bl. thought possible. — **3. Πεισίστρατος ... οὐχ ἅπασαν:** cf. Hdt. i. 64. 10 καθήρας δὲ ὧδε· ἐπ' ὅσον ἔποψις τοῦ ἱροῦ εἶχε, ἐκ τούτου τοῦ χώρου παντὸς ἐξορύξας τοὺς νεκροὺς μετεφόρεε ἐς ἄλλον χῶρον τῆς Δήλου. — **4. ὅσον ... τῆς νήσου:** cf. ἐπ' ὅσον ... τοῦ ἱροῦ, just cited from Hdt., and Thuc. vii. 37. 6 προσῆγε τῷ τείχει τῶν Ἀθηναίων, καθ' ὅσον πρὸς τὴν πόλιν αὐτοῦ ἑώρα.
5. θῆκαι ὅσαι: without γάρ after τοιῷδε. See on c. 92. 2; 97. 1. The subst. thus placed acquires a char-

τεθνεώτων ἐν Δήλῳ, πάσας ἀνεῖλον, καὶ τὸ λοιπὸν προεῖπον μήτε ἐναποθνήσκειν ἐν τῇ νήσῳ μήτε ἐντίκτειν,
ἀλλ' ἐς τὴν Ῥήνειαν διακομίζεσθαι. ἀπέχει δὲ ἡ Ῥήνεια
τῆς Δήλου οὕτως ὀλίγον ὥστε Πολυκράτης ὁ Σαμίων
10 τύραννος, ἰσχύσας τινὰ χρόνον ναυτικῷ καὶ τῶν τε ἄλλων Νήσων ἄρξας καὶ τὴν Ῥήνειαν ἑλών, ἀνέθηκε τῷ
Ἀπόλλωνι τῷ Δηλίῳ ἁλύσει δήσας πρὸς τὴν Δῆλον. καὶ
τὴν πεντετηρίδα τότε πρῶτον μετὰ τὴν κάθαρσιν ἐποίη-

acter of generality, with nearly the effect of a part. gen. *Cf.* c. 113. 21, and see on i. 1. 8. θῆκαι means here, doubtless, movable *coffins*, as in i. 8. 4; v. 1. 6, not "graves," as in c. 58. 15. As to such coffins, see Müller, *Handbuch* iv. p. 463 b. — **6. ἀνεῖλον**: as in i. 8. 4; v. 1. 6. — **τὸ λοιπόν**: to be construed with ἐναποθνήσκειν and ἐντίκτειν. *Cf.* Diod. *l.c.* μήτε τίκτειν ἐν Δήλῳ μήτε θάπτειν, Strabo 486 c οὐ γὰρ ἔξεστιν ἐν αὐτῇ τῇ Δήλῳ θάπτειν οὐδὲ καίειν νεκρόν. — **προεῖπον**: of a distinctly expressed order, as i. 45. 6. — **8. ἐς τὴν Ῥήνειαν**: *cf.* Strabo *l.c.* ὅπου τὰ μνήματα τοῖς Δηλίοις ἐστίν. — **διακομίζεσθαι**: sc. τούς τε ἀποθνήσκοντας καὶ τὰς τικτούσας. — **9. οὕτως ὀλίγον**: four stadia, acc. to Strabo *l.c.* — **Πολυκράτης** . . . **τῷ Ἀπόλλωνι τῷ Δηλίῳ**: *cf.* i. 13. § 6. — **10. ἰσχύσας τινὰ χρόνον ναυτικῷ**: *who for some time was powerful in naval affairs.* *Cf.* ναυτικῷ ἰσχύων, i. 13. 28. The temporal modifier (τινα χρόνον) makes the above rendering seem necessary (*cf.* ἐκράτησάν τινα χρόνον, i. 13. 27); though Cl., Kr., and Bm. take the aor. partic. as ingressive, like ἄρξας in l. 11. — **11. Νήσων**: for the vulg. νήσων, since here, as in i. 13. 29; vii. 57. 15, and freq., not islands in general, but only the Cyclades are to be understood. See Steup, *Rh. Mus.* xxv. p. 328, n. — **ἄρξας** : = ὑπηκόους ποιησάμενος (i. 13. 29), as the connexion with ἑλών shows. *Cf.* i. 4. 3. This *ingressive* force is nearly confined to the first aor. GMT. 55; H. 841. — **12. ἁλύσει δήσας πρὸς τὴν Δῆλον**: the chief stress of the sent. is on these words. The chaining of Rhenea to Delos indicates the proximity of the two islands. — **ἁλύσει δήσας**: 'as a symbolical expression of indissoluble union.' Curtius, ii. p. 142. Weiske (*N. Jahrbb.* cxxxvii. p. 555 f.) explains the ἁλύσει δήσας as symbolically indicating the hanging up or setting up of an offering in the precincts of the temple of the god (ἀνατιθέναι). But that ἀνατιθέναι does not necessarily imply a hanging up or setting up of something in a sacred precinct, or indeed any local connexion with such a precinct, but may have the general meaning "consecrate," is clear from i. 13. 29 Ῥήνειαν ἑλὼν ἀνέθηκε τῷ Ἀπόλλωνι τῷ Δηλίῳ, where the manner of the consecration must have been stated, had ἀνατιθέναι only the narrower meaning claimed by Weiske. *Cf.* Hdt. i. 26. 5 ἀνέθεσαν τὴν πόλιν τῇ Ἀρτέμιδι. — **13. τὴν πεντετηρίδα** . . .

σαν οἱ Ἀθηναῖοι [τὰ Δήλια]. ἦν δέ ποτε καὶ τὸ πάλαι
15 μεγάλη ξύνοδος ἐς τὴν Δῆλον τῶν Ἰώνων τε καὶ περικτιόνων νησιωτῶν· ξύν τε γὰρ γυναιξὶ καὶ παισὶν ἐθεώρουν,
ὥσπερ νῦν ἐς τὰ Ἐφέσια Ἴωνες, καὶ ἀγὼν ἐποιεῖτο
αὐτόθι καὶ γυμνικὸς καὶ μουσικός, χορούς τε ἀνῆγον
αἱ πόλεις. δηλοῖ δὲ μάλιστα Ὅμηρος ὅτι τοιαῦτα 4

οἱ Ἀθηναῖοι: the quadrennial festival was celebrated by the Athenians then for the first time after the purification. τὴν πεντετηρίδα, cf. Poll. viii. 107. ποιεῖν, not the mid., of the celebration of a festival, as in ii. 15. 17; Plato Rep. 327 a. Cf. also l. 17; ii. 15. 24; v. 80. 18; vi. 28. 4; 58. 10. Since the celebration of the festival, acc. to the present passage, followed directly upon the purification undertaken at the beginning of the winter (see on l. 1), it could not have occurred, as Boeckh thinks (Sthlt. d. Athen. ii.² p. 82), in the Attic month Thargelion, and hardly, as C. Robert conjectures (Hermes xxi. p. 161 ff.), in Anthesterion. — 14. [τὰ Δήλια]: rightly bracketed by v. H., Stud. Thuc. p. 48, as a gloss to τὴν πεντετηρίδα. The context renders the addition unnecessary; besides, the term τὰ Δήλια was not restricted to the πεντετηρίς. Cf. Xen. Mem. iv. 8. 2.

15. ξύνοδος ἐς τὴν Δῆλον: as i. 96. 10 ξύνοδοι ἐς τὸ ἱερὸν ἐγίγνοντο, and, similarly, l. 17 ἐς τὰ Ἐφέσια, sc. ἐθεώρουν (cf. viii. 10. 2). — τῶν Ἰώνων κτέ.: acc. to l. 40, mention of the Athenians might have been expected here. Possibly Ἀθηναίων καὶ has dropped out after καὶ. Ἰώνων refers, as Ἴωνες in l. 17, to the Ionians of Asia Minor. These Ionians, whose participation in the older festival was one of the chief distinctions between that and the later (l. 39 ff.), are esp. emphasized by τε, which would naturally follow directly after the art. belonging to both nouns. Cf. i. 6. 2. — περικτιόνων νησιωτῶν: i.e. the inhabitants of the Cyclades. περικτίονες, found only here in Thuc., is poetic (Hom. P 220; Σ 212; β 65), and possibly taken from some ancient hymn. — 16. ξύν τε γὰρ κτέ.: in explanation of μεγάλη ξύνοδος (cf. l. 39). — ἐθεώρουν: of the whole celebration of the festival, as in v. 18. 4; 50. 8. θεωρεῖν ἐς also viii. 10. 2; Ar. Vesp. 1183; Luc. Tim. 50. — 17. τὰ Ἐφέσια: sc. at the temple of Artemis; of which Dion. H. (iv. 25) gives a similar description. — ἀγὼν ἐποιεῖτο: a contest was instituted. Cf. l. 43; v. 80. 17, and see on l. 13. — 18. χορούς ἀνῆγον: brought out, conducted, choral dances. Cf. Hes. Sc. 280; Callim. Del. 279 πᾶσαι δὲ χορούς ἀνάγουσι, Eur. Troad. 325 πάλλε πόδ' αἰθέριον, ἄναγε χορόν, 332 χόρευε, μᾶτερ, ἄναγε. Hdt. has ὁρτὴν ἀνάγειν (ii. 40. 4; 48. 4; 61. 2). Cf. ὀρτάζουσι μεγάλας ἀνάγοντες θυσίας, Hdt. ii. 60. 13.

19. Ὅμηρος: clearly regarded by Thuc. as the author of the hymn here cited. How definite a personality he was to Thuc., is shown esp. by l. 29. See Sengebusch, Hom. Diss.

20 ἦν ἐν τοῖς ἔπεσι τοῖσδε, ἅ ἐστιν ἐκ προοιμίου Ἀπόλλωνος·

ἀλλ' ὅτε Δήλῳ, Φοῖβε, μάλιστά γε θυμὸν ἐτέρφθης,
ἔνθα τοι ἑλκεχίτωνες Ἰάονες ἠγερέθονται
σὺν σφοῖσιν τεκέεσσι γυναιξί τε σὴν ἐς ἄγυιαν·
ἔνθα σε πυγμαχίῃ τε καὶ ὀρχηστυῖ καὶ ἀοιδῇ
25 μνησάμενοι τέρπουσιν, ὅταν καθέσωσιν ἀγῶνα.

ὅτι δὲ καὶ μουσικῆς ἀγὼν ἦν καὶ ἀγωνιούμενοι ἐφοίτων, 5
ἐν τοῖσδε αὖ δηλοῖ, ἅ ἐστιν ἐκ τοῦ αὐτοῦ προοιμίου· τὸν
γὰρ Δηλιακὸν χορὸν τῶν γυναικῶν ὑμνήσας ἐτελεύτα τοῦ
ἐπαίνου ἐς τάδε τὰ ἔπη, ἐν οἷς καὶ ἑαυτοῦ ἐπεμνήσθη·

30 ἀλλ' ἄγεθ', ἱλήκοι μὲν Ἀπόλλων Ἀρτέμιδι ξύν,
χαίρετε δ' ὑμεῖς πᾶσαι. ἐμεῖο δὲ καὶ μετόπισθε

i. p. 140. — ἐν τοῖς ἔπεσι: τὰ ἔπη used by Thuc. only of verses or poetic expressions. Cf. i. 3. 16; ii. 41. 14; 54. 4, and see on c. 67. 31. — 20. ἐκ προοιμίου: Schol. ἐξ ὕμνου· τοὺς γὰρ ὕμνους προοίμια ἐκάλουν, i.e. introductions to the recitation of other songs. See Wolf, Proleg. ad Hom. p. cvii. The two following citations are from the hymn to the Delian Apollo, 146 ff. and 165 ff. Several deviations in Thuc.'s version from that of the hymn are due without doubt to his following a different original, not to quoting from memory. See Baumeister, ibid. p. 141; Guttmann, de Hymn. Hom. Hist. Crit. p. 17 sq.; Bücheler, Coniectanea (Index Schol., Bonn, W. 1878-79), p. 3 sq. — 21. ἀλλ' ὅτε: most recent editors write ἄλλοτε, with Camerarius; but even thus, Steup thinks, no proper connexion with the preceding verses is established (see Gemoll, Hom. Hymnen, p. 143). He proposes, therefore, ἀλλ' ὅτι, and to take ἔνθα of l. 22 not as rel., but dem., as in l. 24. — 23. ἄγυιαν: i.e. the street leading to the temple. — 25. καθέσωσιν ἀγῶνα: certamen instituant. Guttmann, p. 22, compares Hom. Ψ 258 ἵζανεν εὐρὺν ἀγῶνα.

26. καὶ μουσικῆς ἀγών: in l. 24 f. only a γυμνικὸς ἀγών (πυγμαχίῃ) was implied beyond all doubt, since ὀρχηστυῖ καὶ ἀοιδῇ might refer to the χοροὶ of l. 18 (cf. l. 40). Thuc. adds, therefore, special testimony for the musical contests. — ἀγωνιούμενοι: sc. μουσικήν. Cf. l. 34 f. — 27. τὸν ... χορὸν τῶν γυναικῶν: hymn v. 156-164. — 28. ἐτελεύτα ... ἐς τάδε τὰ ἔπη: cf. ii. 51. 5; iv. 48. 23 ἐς τοῦτο ἐτελεύτα, Soph. O. C. 476 τὸ δ' ἔνθεν ποῖ τελευτῆσαί με χρή; — τοῦ ἐπαίνου: sc. τοῦ τῶν γυναικῶν. For the gen. with τελευτᾶν, see on c. 59. 19.

μνήσασθ', ὁππότε κέν τις ἐπιχθονίων ἀνθρώπων
ἐνθάδ' ἀνείρηται ταλαπείριος ἄλλος ἐπελθών·
"Ὦ κοῦραι, τίς δ' ὔμμιν ἀνὴρ ἥδιστος ἀοιδῶν
35 ἐνθάδε πωλεῖται, καὶ τέῳ τέρπεσθε μάλιστα;"
ὑμεῖς δ' εὖ μάλα πᾶσαι ὑποκρίνασθ' εὐφήμως·
"Τυφλὸς ἀνήρ, οἰκεῖ δὲ Χίῳ ἐνὶ παιπαλοέσσῃ."

τοσαῦτα μὲν Ὅμηρος ἐτεκμηρίωσεν ὅτι ἦν καὶ τὸ πάλαι 6
μεγάλη ξύνοδος καὶ ἑορτὴ ἐν τῇ Δήλῳ· ὕστερον δὲ τοὺς
40 μὲν χοροὺς οἱ Νησιῶται καὶ οἱ Ἀθηναῖοι μεθ' ἱερῶν ἔπεμ-
πον, τὰ δὲ περὶ τοὺς ἀγῶνας καὶ τὰ πλεῖστα κατελύθη
ὑπὸ ξυμφορῶν, ὡς εἰκός, πρὶν δὴ οἱ Ἀθηναῖοι τότε τὸν
ἀγῶνα ἐποίησαν καὶ ἱπποδρομίας, ὃ πρότερον οὐκ ἦν.

105 Τοῦ δ' αὐτοῦ χειμῶνος Ἀμπρακιῶται, ὥσπερ ὑπο- 1
σχόμενοι Εὐρυλόχῳ τὴν στρατιὰν κατέσχον, ἐκστρατεύ-

— **33. ἄλλος ἐπελθών**: Bücheler, ibid. p. 4, proposes ἄλλοθεν ἐλθών.
38. τοσαῦτα μέν: adv. so far. — ἐτεκμηρίωσεν: used by Thuc. alone of Attic writers, and only of Homer's evidence. Cf. i. 3. 12; 9. 24. It is common in the writers of the κοινὴ διάλεκτος. — **40. μεθ' ἱερῶν**: i.e. with the sacrifices and all that pertained to the festal offerings. — **41. καὶ τὰ πλεῖστα**: and indeed most things, as Bm. explains. Not only did the contests fall into disuse, but the Ionians came no more, women and children were no longer brought along, and otherwise the number of participants seems to have greatly diminished. Cl. explained as = vel plurima, with St., a sort of limiting appos. to τὰ περὶ τοὺς ἀγῶνας. But the ἀγῶνες unquestionably ceased entirely. For this reason Kr. is certainly wrong in bracketing καί. — **42. πρὶν δή**: until,

see on c. 29. 5. — **τὸν ἀγῶνα**: i.e. the contest held afterwards every four years. — **43. ἐποίησαν**: see on l. 17.
105. The Ambraciots, in order to bring the Amphilochian Argos to terms, occupy Olpae in its territory: the Acarnanians summon to the protection of the place Demosthenes and twenty Athenian ships, which happened to be on the Peloponnesian coast.
1. ὥσπερ ὑποσχόμενοι: cf. c. 102. § 6, 7. — **2. ἐκστρατεύονται**: to be construed only with ὥσπερ ὑποσχόμενοι Εὐρυλόχῳ, for τὴν στρατιὰν κατέσχον expresses merely the result of the promise, and has no effect on ἐκστρατεύονται. The chief emphasis of the sent. is on the partic., as in c. 53. 14. The sense of the passage is, as Jow. renders, "in fulfilment of the promise by which they had induced Eurylochus and his army to remain, the Ambraciots make an expedition ——."

ονται ἐπὶ Ἄργος τὸ Ἀμφιλοχικὸν τρισχιλίοις ὁπλίταις, καὶ ἐσβαλόντες ἐς τὴν Ἀργείαν καταλαμβάνουσιν
5 Ὄλπας, τεῖχος ἐπὶ λόφου ἰσχυρὸν πρὸς τῇ θαλάσσῃ, ὅ ποτε Ἀκαρνᾶνες τειχισάμενοι κοινῷ δικαστηρίῳ ἐχρῶντο· ἀπέχει δὲ ἀπὸ τῆς Ἀργείων πόλεως ἐπιθαλασσίας οὔσης πέντε καὶ εἴκοσι σταδίους μάλιστα. οἱ δὲ Ἀκαρ- 2 νᾶνες οἱ μὲν ἐς Ἄργος ξυνεβοήθουν, οἱ δὲ τῆς Ἀμφιλο-
10 χίας ἐν τούτῳ τῷ χωρίῳ ὃ Κρῆναι καλεῖται, φυλάσσοντες τοὺς μετὰ Εὐρυλόχου Πελοποννησίους μὴ λάθωσι πρὸς τοὺς Ἀμπρακιώτας διελθόντες, ἐστρατοπεδεύσαντο. πέμπουσι δὲ καὶ ἐπὶ Δημοσθένην τὸν ἐς τὴν Αἰτωλίαν 3

— 3. Ἄργος τὸ Ἀμφιλοχικόν: on the inmost recess of the Ambracian gulf. On its relation to Ambracia, cf. ii. 68. § 1. — 5. Ὄλπας: the sing. in c. 107. 13; 111. 5; 113. 2. Cf. Ἰδομενή (c. 112. 2; 113. 14) and Ἰδομεναί (113. 10); Πλαταιαί (ii. 7. 1; 10. 1) and Πλαταιά (everywhere in Thuc. except the two places just cited); Κεγχρειαί (viii. 10. 5; 20. 6; 23. 2), Κεγχρειά (iv. 42. 21; 44. 14). As to the site of this fortress, with which the Ὀλπαῖοι of c. 101. 12 have nothing to do, as well as of Κρῆναι (l. 10), see Bursian i. p. 38, and Oberhummer, *Akarnanien*, p. 27 f. — ὅ . . . ἐχρῶντο: ὅ with τειχισάμενοι, from which ᾧ is to be supplied with ἐχρῶντο. The sent. is best explained with Schoemann, *Gr. Alterth.* ii.[3] p. 76, that the Acarnanians after fortifying Olpae had once used it as a common place of justice for their alliance. For the impf. with ποτε expressing what formerly existed for some time, cf. ii. 44. 8; viii. 52. 12; 62. 13, and the pres. partic., i. 132. 30; v. 43. 11; vi. 92. 5. Prob. the occupation of the Amphilochian Olpae by the Acarnanians fell in the time of the ξυμφοραί of the Amphilochian Argos, mentioned in ii. 68. 12. After the Amphilochians had joined the Acarnanians (διδόασιν ἑαυτοὺς Ἀκαρνᾶσι, ii. 68. 18), the place was doubtless restored to its former possessors and the federal court removed elsewhere. See App.

8. οἱ Ἀκαρνᾶνες οἱ μὲν . . . οἱ δέ: part. appos. See on c. 13. 17. — 9. ξυνεβοήθουν: the impf. represents continuance, whereas ἐστρατοπεδεύσαντο in l. 12 simply states the matter as a fact. — τῆς Ἀμφιλοχίας: the name of the country precedes that of the place, as in c. 19. 6; 89. 7; i. 100. 15. — 10. φυλάσσοντες τοὺς . . . Πελοποννησίους μὴ λάθωσι: proleptic const. as in i. 26. 6; ii. 67. 22. Kr. *Spr.* 61, 6, 5. — 11. μὴ λάθωσι . . . διελθόντες: 'for Crenae, now Παλαιὸ Αὐλί, guarded the entrance to the district from the south.' Bursian (*l.c.*), after Heuzey, *Le Mont Olympe et l'Acarnanie*, p. 290. Cf. c. 106. 14. — 13. Δημοσθένην τὸν . . . στρατηγήσαντα: the designation recalls indeed

Ἀθηναίων στρατηγήσαντα, ὅπως σφίσιν ἡγεμὼν γίγνηται,
15 καὶ ἐπὶ τὰς εἴκοσι ναῦς Ἀθηναίων αἳ ἔτυχον περὶ Πελοπόννησον οὖσαι, ὧν ἦρχεν Ἀριστοτέλης τε ὁ Τιμοκράτους καὶ Ἱεροφῶν ὁ Ἀντιμνήστου. ἀπέστειλαν δὲ καὶ ἄγγελον 4
οἱ περὶ τὰς Ὄλπας Ἀμπρακιῶται ἐς τὴν πόλιν κελεύοντες
σφίσι βοηθεῖν πανδημεί, δεδιότες μὴ οἱ μετ᾽ Εὐρυλόχου οὐ
20 δύνωνται διελθεῖν τοὺς Ἀκαρνᾶνας καὶ σφίσιν ἢ μονωθεῖσιν
ἡ μάχη γένηται ἢ ἀναχωρεῖν βουλομένοις οὐκ ᾖ ἀσφαλές.
106 Οἱ μὲν οὖν μετ᾽ Εὐρυλόχου Πελοποννήσιοι, ὡς 1

an undertaking unwelcome to the Acarnanians (c. 95. § 1 f.), but better relations had been already restored (c. 102. § 3 f.). Further, the aor. partic. refers only to what had happened in the summer of 426 B.C. (*who had led the army of the Athenians to Aetolia*), and does not indicate the expiration of the office of strategus. Had Demosthenes been at that time no longer strategus, he could hardly have obeyed the here mentioned invitation of the Acarnanians and hastened with 200 Messenian hoplites and sixty Athenian bowmen to the scene of action (c. 107. 6), and at any rate it could not have been said of him, in iv. 2. 14, ὄντι ἰδιώτῃ μετὰ τὴν ἀναχώρησιν τὴν ἐξ Ἀκαρνανίας. For clearly, acc. to these words, his term of office did not expire before his return from Acarnania to Athens (c. 114. § 1). — 14. ἡγεμὼν γίγνηται: *cf.* c. 107. 11, and see on c. 2. 11. — 15. ἐπὶ τὰς εἴκοσι ναῦς Ἀθηναίων: which, after the return of the thirty ships (c. 98. 25), had been sent out again, under the generals named, περὶ Πελοπόννησον, prob. in consequence of news of the operations of Eurylochus against

the Ozolian Locrians and Naupactus (c. 101 f.). Their real goal was Naupactus (*cf.* c. 114. 8), but they turned aside for the moment, in consequence of the appeal of the Acarnanians, to the Ambracian gulf (c. 107. 4). — 16. ἦρχεν: Bm. proposed ἦρχον. But *cf.* iv. 37. 1; 38. 9, and see Kr. *Spr.* 63, 4. — Ἀριστοτέλης: later prob. one of the Thirty. *Cf.* Xen. *Hell.* ii. 3. 2.
17. ἀπέστειλαν δὲ καί: emphatic repetition after πέμπουσι (l. 13). See on c. 18. 8; i. 28. 8; ii. 7. 3. — 18. ἐς τὴν πόλιν: *sc.* τὴν Ἀμπρακίαν. — 19. πανδημεί: *i.e.* with all the forces which they could raise after sending out the 3000 hoplites (l. 3). For the execution of this request, *cf.* c. 110. — 21. (μὴ) ἡ μάχη γένηται: *cf.* i. 63. 10; v. 51. 2; 59. 18; viii. 80. 19. — οὐκ ᾖ ἀσφαλές: with indef. subj., as iv. 36. 1 ἀπέραντον ἦν, viii. 105. 7 ἀφανὲς ἦν.

106. *Eurylochus, with the Peloponnesians, marches safely from Proschium in Aetolia through Acarnania and Agrais to Amphilochia, and unites with the Ambraciots in Olpae.*

1. οἱ μετ᾽ Εὐρυλόχου Πελοποννή-

ᾔσθοντο τοὺς ἐν Ὄλπαις Ἀμπρακιώτας ἥκοντας, ἄραντες
ἐκ τοῦ Προσχίου ἐβοήθουν κατὰ τάχος, καὶ διαβάντες
τὸν Ἀχελῷον ἐχώρουν δι' Ἀκαρνανίας, οὔσης ἐρήμου
5 διὰ τὴν ἐς Ἄργος βοήθειαν, ἐν δεξιᾷ μὲν ἔχοντες
τὴν Στρατίων πόλιν καὶ τὴν φρουρὰν αὐτῶν, ἐν ἀρι-
στερᾷ δὲ τὴν ἄλλην Ἀκαρνανίαν. καὶ διελθόντες τὴν 2
Στρατίων γῆν ἐχώρουν διὰ τῆς Φυτίας καὶ αὖθις Μεδεῶνος παρ' ἔσχατα, ἔπειτα διὰ Λιμναίας· καὶ ἐπέβησαν
10 τῆς Ἀγραίων, οὐκέτι Ἀκαρνανίας, φιλίας δὲ σφίσι. λαβό- 3

σιοι: cf. c. 102. 26. — 2. τοὺς ἐν Ὄλπαις... ἥκοντας: that the Ambraciots
had arrived at Olpae, lit. that the
Ambraciots in Olpae had arrived.
This is a case of anticipation. Kühn.
447, N. 4. — 3. ἐκ τοῦ Προσχίου: sc.
τῆς Αἰτωλίας. Cf. c. 102. 21. — 4. τὸν
Ἀχελῷον: i.e. the boundary of Acarnania. — οὔσης ἐρήμου: i.e. without
military protection, since the population able to bear arms had gone to
Argos. Cf. ii. 81. 7 (where the adj. has
the fem. ending). — 6. τὴν Στρατίων
πόλιν: μεγίστην τῆς Ἀκαρνανίας, ii. 80.
38. — τὴν φρουρὰν αὐτῶν: sc. τῶν
Στρατίων, i.e. the garrison of the
city.
8. τῆς Φυτίας: the reading of all
the Mss., though Polyb. (iv. 63. 7, 10)
has Φοιτίαι and Steph. Byz. Φοιτίαι
and Φοίτιον. Several inscriptions, too,
read Φοι- (see Oberhummer, Akarnanien, p. 38), though local coins have
ΦΥ- (see Head, Hist. Numorum, p.
281). The reference is to the territory belonging to the place, as also
in the case of Μεδεῶνος and Λιμναίας.
See on c. 91. 11, 15. — Μεδεῶνος:
Polybius calls the place Μεδίων (Steph.
Byz.), the inhabitants Μεδιώνιοι,

the district Μεδιωνία, and Livy also
(xxxvi. 11 sq.) has Medion and
Medionii. — 9. παρ' ἔσχατα: i.e.
to the frontier. Cf. viii. 95. 19 ἐπ'
ἔσχατα. — διὰ Λιμναίας: cf. ii. 80. 37.
This is the name both of a place and
of the whole swampy lowland on
the southern slopes of the Thyamus
mountains. See Bursian i. p. 110.
— 10. τῆς Ἀγραίων: this district,
which in c. 111. 18 is called ἡ Ἀγραΐς,
and had a king of its own, Salynthius, must be sought, acc. to ii. 102.
13 (where the Agraeans are placed
between the Dolopians and Amphilochians), north of the road followed
up to this point. Eurylochus made,
evidently to avoid the Acarnanian
garrison at Crenae (c. 105. 10), a
detour through the mountains and
from there descended into the Argive
district, and thence marched along
the coast to Olpae. — οὐκέτι Ἀκαρνανίας: chorographic gen., to which in
the next clause an adj. corresponds.
Strabo, p. 449 c, calls the Agraeans
Αἰτωλικὸν ἔθνος. They belonged to
the ἐπίκτητος Αἰτωλία. See Bursian i.
p. 140.
λαβόμενοι τοῦ... ὄρους: see on

μένοι δὲ τοῦ Θυάμου ὄρους, ὅ ἐστιν Ἀγραϊκόν, ἐχώρουν δι' αὐτοῦ καὶ κατέβησαν ἐς τὴν Ἀργείαν νυκτὸς ἤδη, καὶ διεξελθόντες μεταξὺ τῆς τε Ἀργείων πόλεως καὶ τῆς ἐπὶ Κρήναις Ἀκαρνάνων φυλακῆς ἔλαθον καὶ προσέμειξαν τοῖς 107 ἐν Ὄλπαις Ἀμπρακιώταις. γενόμενοι δὲ ἀθρόοι ἅμα τῇ 1 ἡμέρᾳ καθίζουσιν ἐπὶ τὴν Μητρόπολιν καλουμένην καὶ στρατόπεδον ἐποιήσαντο. Ἀθηναῖοι δὲ ταῖς εἴκοσι ναυσὶν οὐ πολλῷ ὕστερον παραγίγνονται ἐς τὸν Ἀμπρακικὸν βοη- 5 θοῦντες τοῖς Ἀργείοις, καὶ Δημοσθένης Μεσσηνίων μὲν ἔχων διακοσίους ὁπλίτας, ἑξήκοντα δὲ τοξότας Ἀθηναίων.

c. 24. 10. — 11. **τοῦ Θυάμου ὄρους**: now Σπαρτοβοῦνι, forming the northeast boundary of Acarnania toward Aetolia, but belonging for the most part to the Agraean district. Hence O. Müller's conjecture (*Dorians* ii.[2] p. 529; see Bursian i. p. 105, n. 1), Ἀγραϊκόν, has been adopted for ἀγροῖκον of the Mss. See App. — 12. **νυκτὸς ἤδη**: *already night*. For other examples of ἤδη thus used, see on i. 30. 20. — 13. **τῆς ... φυλακῆς**: sc. which awaited the advance of Eurylochus on the direct road from Limnaea to Argos. *Cf.* c. 105. § 2. — 14. **προσέμειξαν τοῖς ... Ἀμπρακιώταις**: *joined the Ambraciots in Olpae*. *Cf.* v. 58. 3 βουλόμενοι τοῖς ἄλλοις προσμεῖξαι.

107, 108. *Demosthenes, elected commander-in-chief by the Acarnanians, by means of a skilfully-planned ambush wins a decisive victory over the Peloponnesians and Ambraciots*.

1. **γενόμενοι ἀθρόοι**: sc. the Ambraciots and Peloponnesians. — 2. **καθίζουσιν**: *encamp*, intr. as in iv. 93. 5. The const. καθίζειν στρατόν is more freq. in Thuc. (ii. 71. 4; iv. 90. 5; v. 7. 14; vi. 66. 2; vii. 82. 16). — **τὴν Μητρόπολιν**: seems from the context (*cf.* l. 13) to have been a place very near Olpae. — 3. **ταῖς εἴκοσι ναυσίν**: *cf.* c. 105. 15. — 4. **τὸν Ἀμπρακικόν**: *sc.* κόλπον, which a few Mss. have in the text. But a copyist would be much more likely to add than omit it. ὁ Ἀμπρακικός alternates with ὁ Ἀμπρακικὸς κόλπος (i. 29. 11; 55. 3; ii. 68. 9; iv. 49. 3), as ὁ Ἰόνιος (vi. 30. 6; 34. 24; 104. 10; vii. 33. 14) with ὁ Ἰόνιος κόλπος (i. 24. 1; ii. 97. 26; vi. 13. 11; 44. 8; vii. 57. 57). See also App. on ii. 92. 22. — 5. **καὶ Δημοσθένης κτέ.**: Demosthenes (sc. παραγίγνεται ἐς τὸν Ἀμπρακικόν) came from Naupactus (*cf.* c. 102. § 3) with two hundred Messenian hoplites and sixty Athenian bowmen. As was remarked on c. 105. 13, he could hardly have brought these troops, if he was no longer general. From the manner in which he is mentioned here after the twenty ships, it seems impossible that his sixty bowmen were taken from these ships. Probably there was at that time an Athenian garrison *permanently* stationed at Naupactus, so that he, even after the return (c.

καὶ αἱ μὲν νῆες περὶ τὰς Ὄλπας τὸν λόφον ἐκ θαλάσσης
ἐφώρμουν· οἱ δὲ Ἀκαρνᾶνες καὶ Ἀμφιλόχων ὀλίγοι
(οἱ γὰρ πλείους ὑπὸ Ἀμπρακιωτῶν βίᾳ κατείχοντο)
ἐς τὸ Ἄργος ἤδη ξυνεληλυθότες παρεσκευάζοντο ὡς
μαχούμενοι τοῖς ἐναντίοις, καὶ ἡγεμόνα τοῦ παντὸς ξυμμαχικοῦ αἱροῦνται Δημοσθένην μετὰ τῶν σφετέρων στρατηγῶν. ὁ δὲ προσαγαγὼν ἐγγὺς τῆς Ὄλπης ἐστρατοπε- 3
δεύσατο, χαράδρα δ᾽ αὐτοὺς μεγάλη διεῖργε. καὶ ἡμέρας
μὲν πέντε ἡσύχαζον, τῇ δ᾽ ἕκτῃ ἐτάσσοντο ἀμφότεροι ὡς
ἐς μάχην. καὶ (μεῖζον γὰρ ἐγένετο καὶ περιέσχε τὸ τῶν

98. 25) of the thirty ships of c. 91. 1, had control of some Athenian forces. — **Μεσσηνίων**: see on c. 94. 15.

7. τὰς Ὄλπας τὸν λόφον: = τὸ τεῖχος ἐπὶ τοῦ λόφου (c. 105. 5), τὸν λόφον being appos. to τὰς Ὄλπας. Kr. *Spr.* 50, 7, 2. Steup follows v. H. in bracketing τὸν λόφον, on the ground that, after c. 105. 4 καταλαμβάνουσιν Ὄλπας, τεῖχος ἐπὶ λόφου ἰσχυρὸν πρὸς τῇ θαλάσσῃ), the expression περὶ τὰς Ὄλπας ἐκ θαλάσσης ἐφώρμουν needs no explanation, and, if it did, that this would hardly be added in the form of a simple appositive (τὸν λόφον). — **8. Ἀμφιλόχων**: the inhabitants of the whole district, whose chief city was Argos. They remained βάρβαροι even after Argos had become hellenized, ii. 68. 14. — **9. οἱ πλείους ... κατείχοντο**: they were kept from taking part in the war by the fact that the Ambraciots had seized their territory or taken hostages from them. *Cf.* c. 114. 19. — **10. ἤδη ξυνεληλυθότες**: the Acarnanians of Crenae (c. 105. 10; 106. 14) had also meanwhile gone to Argos, to whose aid the rest of the Acarnanians marched at the outset (c. 105. 9 οἱ μὲν ἐς Ἄργος ξυνεβοήθουν). — **11. τοῦ παντὸς ξυμμαχικοῦ**: *of the whole allied army*, i.e. of all the Acarnanian and Amphilochian forces. *Cf.* i. 62. 5 στρατηγὸν τοῦ πεζοῦ παντὸς οἱ ξύμμαχοι ᾕρηντο Ἀριστέα. — **12. Δημοσθένην**: the form Δημοσθένη, of the most and best Mss., is against the usage of Thuc. — **μετὰ τῶν σφετέρων στρατηγῶν**: i.e. these commanded the various contingents under Demosthenes as general-in-chief.

13. προσαγαγών: without obj., as ducere, only here in Thuc. — **τῆς Ὄλπης**: see on c. 105. 5. — **14. χαράδρα**: see on c. 25. 4; 98. 7. — **15. ἐτάσσοντο**: introductory impf., the details following. *Cf.* l. 22 ᾖσαν ἐς χεῖρας. See on c. 92. 2. — **ὡς ἐς μάχην**: *with the intention to fight*, as i. 62. 20; iv. 93. 6; vi. 67. 2. *Cf.* ὡς ἐπὶ ναυμαχίαν, i. 48. 2, and see on c. 4. 6. — **16. καὶ (μεῖζον γὰρ κτέ.)**: paratactic structure of the period, just as in c. 70. 11; i. 31. 7; hence here too the causal sent. must be regarded as parenthetical. — **περιέσχε**: intr. *extended beyond, out-flanked*, as in c. 108. 1; v. 71. 12,

Πελοποννησίων στρατόπεδον) ὁ Δημοσθένης δείσας μὴ κυκλωθῇ λοχίζει ἐς ὁδόν τινα κοίλην καὶ λοχμώδη ὁπλίτας καὶ ψιλοὺς ξυναμφοτέρους ἐς τετρακοσίους, ὅπως 20 κατὰ τὸ ὑπερέχον τῶν ἐναντίων ἐν τῇ ξυνόδῳ αὐτῇ ἐξαναστάντες οὗτοι κατὰ νώτου γίγνωνται. ἐπεὶ δὲ παρε- 4 σκεύαστο ἀμφοτέροις, ἦσαν ἐς χεῖρας, Δημοσθένης μὲν τὸ δεξιὸν κέρας ἔχων μετὰ Μεσσηνίων καὶ Ἀθηναίων ὀλίγων, τὸ δὲ ἄλλο Ἀκαρνᾶνες ὡς ἕκαστοι τεταγμένοι 25 ἐπεῖχον καὶ Ἀμφιλόχων οἱ παρόντες ἀκοντισταί· Πελο-

16, and περιίσχειν, v. 71. 4. Schol. ὑπερέτεινεν, ὑπερέσχεν. The aors. ἐγένετο and περιέσχε express a result of the drawing up (ἐτάσσοντο). — 18. λοχίζει: in insidiis collocat. ἐνέδραν καθίζει, Schol. Cf. λοχισθέντες (ambushed), v. 115. 2; Dio C. xli. 51; ἐλόχισε, distributed into companies, Hdt. i. 103. 4. — κοίλην καὶ λοχμώδη: cf. Dio C. 13, 9 ἐν κοίλῳ τινὶ καὶ λοχμώδει τόπῳ, 1279, 17 ἐς κοῖλόν τινα καὶ λοχμώδη τόπον, Polyaen. iii. 1. 2 ἐς τὸ κοῖλον καὶ λοχμῶδες ἐνελόχισεν ὁπλίτας καὶ ψιλοὺς τετρακοσίους. λοχμώδης occurs only here in Thuc. — 20. κατὰ τὸ ὑπερέχον: i.e. at the part of the enemy's line which extended beyond their own and threatened to outflank them. Cf. Polyaen. l.c. ὅπως ἐπειδὰν ὑπερφαλαγγήσωσιν οἱ ἐναντίοι κατὰ τὸ ὑπερβάλλον αὐτῶν, ἐξαναστάντες κατὰ νώτου γένοιντο. For similar consts., cf. l. 29; i. 48. 10, 12; 62. 24; iv. 36. 7; v. 71. 22. For ὑπερέχον, cf. viii. 104. 15. Acc. to c. 108. 2, it was the left wing, not, as was usually the case, the right (cf. v. 71. § 1). — ἐξαναστάντες: rushing out from their ambush. Cf. Xen. Hell. iv. 8. 37. — 21. οὗτοι: for which Hude (Comm.

Crit. p. 116 sq.) proposed οὕτω, is opposed to the remaining troops of Demosthenes. — κατὰ νώτου: as in c. 108. 4; i. 62. 13, etc. κατὰ νῶτον, which some good Mss. have, is contrary to Thuc.'s usage.
ἐπεὶ δὲ παρεσκεύαστο ἀμφοτέροις: for the impers. pass., see on c. 22. 1.
— 22. ἦσαν ἐς χεῖρας: see on l. 15.
— 23. ἔχων: the regular verb in such tactical statements. See on i. 48. 10.
— Ἀθηναίων ὀλίγων: Steup thinks that, as the small number of Athenian bowmen (sixty) has already been stated in l. 6, and there was no cause for emphasizing their fewness here, whereas one might have expected some mention of the Amphilochians that were not ἀκοντισταί, prob. some words have been lost between Ἀθηναίων and ὀλίγων, — perhaps καὶ Ἀμφιλόχων ὁπλιτῶν or καὶ Ἀμφιλόχων σφενδονητῶν. That the main body of the Amphilochians were ψιλοί, is clear from c. 112. 20. — 24. τὸ ἄλλο: i.e. the centre and left. — 24. ὡς ἕκαστοι τεταγμένοι: i.e. arrayed by tribes and under their own leaders (l. 12).
— 25. ἐπεῖχον: occupied, as in i. 48. 7; Hdt. ix. 31. 7. — Πελοποννήσιοι

ποννήσιοι δὲ καὶ Ἀμπρακιῶται ἀναμὶξ τεταγμένοι πλὴν
Μαντινέων· οὗτοι δὲ ἐν τῷ εὐωνύμῳ μᾶλλον καὶ οὐ τὸ
κέρας ἄκρον ἔχοντες ἀθρόοι ἦσαν, ἀλλ᾽ Εὐρύλοχος ἔσχατον εἶχε τὸ εὐώνυμον καὶ οἱ μετ᾽ αὐτοῦ, κατὰ Μεσσηνίους
108 καὶ Δημοσθένην. ὡς δ᾽ ἐν χερσὶν ἤδη ὄντες περιέσχον 1
τῷ κέρᾳ οἱ Πελοποννήσιοι καὶ ἐκυκλοῦντο τὸ δεξιὸν τῶν
ἐναντίων, οἱ ἐκ τῆς ἐνέδρας Ἀκαρνᾶνες ἐπιγενόμενοι αὐτοῖς
κατὰ νώτου προσπίπτουσί τε καὶ τρέπουσιν, ὥστε μήτε
5 ἐς ἀλκὴν ὑπομεῖναι φοβηθέντας τε ἐς φυγὴν καὶ τὸ πλέον
τοῦ στρατεύματος καταστῆσαι· ἐπειδὴ γὰρ εἶδον τὸ κατ᾽
Εὐρύλοχον καὶ ὃ κράτιστον ἦν διαφθειρόμενον, πολλῷ
μᾶλλον ἐφοβοῦντο. καὶ οἱ Μεσσήνιοι ὄντες ταύτῃ μετὰ

δὲ καὶ Ἀμπρακιῶται: sc. ἦσαν ἐς χεῖρας, not the nearest but the most important verb being understood. — **26. ἀναμίξ**: only here in Thuc. *Cf.* Hdt. i. 103. 6; vii. 40. 4. — **26. πλὴν Μαντινέων** ... ἦσαν: acc. to these words, as well as c. 108. 16; 109. 12; 111. 2, 14; 113. 4, a considerable portion of the Peloponnesians under Eurylochus must have been Mantineans. — **27. οὗτοι δέ**: epexegetical, as in c. 34. 4; i. 26. 23; 143. 20. — **οὐ τὸ κέρας ἄκρον ἔχοντες**: pred., like ἔσχατον, *having not the extreme point of the wing.* G. 978, 1; H. 671; Kr. *Spr.* 50, 11, 5. — **29. οἱ μετ᾽ αὐτοῦ**: this part of the army, which in c. 108. 6 is described as τὸ κατ᾽ Εὐρύλοχον καὶ ὃ κράτιστον ἦν, acc. to what goes before must have consisted of contingents from various states. Some statement as to its composition might have been expected. — **κατὰ Μεσσηνίους**: see on l. 20.

108. 1. περιέσχον: see on c. 107. 16.
— **2. τῷ κέρᾳ**: *i.e.* τῷ ἑαυτῶν εὐωνύμῳ

κέρᾳ. — **3. ἐπιγενόμενοι**: see on c. 30. 6. — **αὐτοῖς κατὰ νώτου**: const. with ἐπιγενόμενοι. *Cf.* c. 107. 21. — **5. ἐς ἀλκὴν ὑπομεῖναι**: *cf.* ἐς χεῖρας ὑπομεῖναι, v. 72. 23; εἰς χεῖρας δέχεσθαι, Xen. *Hell.* ii. 4. 34; *An.* iv. 3. 31; ἐς ἀλκὴν τρέπεσθαι, ii. 84. 24; Hdt. ii. 45. 7; iii. 78. 5; iv. 125. 21; ix. 102. 18. See on c. 30. 7. — **φοβηθέντας τε** ... **καταστῆσαι**: *and in their panic put to flight also the greater part of the army.* — **ἐς φυγὴν καταστῆσαι**: as in iv. 14. 4; vii. 43. 47. *Cf. ἐς ἀπόνοιαν καταστῆσαι,* i. 82. 20; vii. 67. 22; ἐς ἀπορίαν, ii. 81. 37; vii. 75. 14; ἐς ὑποψίαν, v. 29. 18; ἐς ταραχήν, iv. 75. 10; ἐς ἔκπληξιν, vi. 36. 7; ἐς κίνδυνον, ii. 100. 25; ἐς λογισμόν, vi. 34. 25. — **6. τὸ κατ᾽ Εὐρύλοχον**: *i.e.* the part of the army with him and under his personal command (οἱ μετ᾽ αὐτοῦ, c. 107. 29), characterized also as τὸ κράτιστον. *Cf.* iv. 33. 1 οἱ περὶ τὸν Ἐπιτάδαν καὶ ὅπερ ἦν πλεῖστον. κατά, as in l. 10; in a different sense from c. 107. 20, 29. — **8. ταύτῃ**: *i.e.* on the

τοῦ Δημοσθένους τὸ πολὺ τοῦ ἔργου ἐξῆλθον. οἱ δὲ 2 Ἀμπρακιῶται καὶ οἱ κατὰ τὸ δεξιὸν κέρας ἐνίκων τὸ καθ' ἑαυτοὺς καὶ πρὸς τὸ Ἄργος ἀπεδίωξαν· καὶ γὰρ μαχιμώτατοι τῶν περὶ ἐκεῖνα τὰ χωρία τυγχάνουσιν ὄντες. ἐπ- 3 αναχωροῦντες δέ, ὡς ἑώρων τὸ πλέον νενικημένον καὶ οἱ ἄλλοι Ἀκαρνᾶνες σφίσι προσέκειντο, χαλεπῶς διεσώζοντο ἐς τὰς Ὄλπας, καὶ πολλοὶ ἀπέθανον αὐτῶν, ἀτάκτως καὶ οὐδενὶ κόσμῳ προσπίπτοντες πλὴν Μαντινέων· οὗτοι δὲ μάλιστα ξυντεταγμένοι παντὸς τοῦ στρατοῦ ἀνεχώρησαν. καὶ ἡ μὲν μάχη ἐτελεύτα ἐς ὀψέ.

right wing, c. 107. 23. — 9. τὸ πολὺ τοῦ ἔργου ἐξῆλθον: *performed the chief part of the work.* Cf. i. 70. 21 ἃ μὲν ἂν ἐπινοήσαντες μὴ ἐξέλθωσιν, Soph. Tr. 505 ἐξῆλθον ἄεθλ' ἀγώνων, i. 70. 9 τἀναγκαῖα ἐξικέσθαι. Hence ἐξῆλθον, of Vat. and other good Mss., is adopted instead of ἐπεξῆλθον of most Mss., which Haase prefers (Lucubr. p. 100).
οἱ δὲ Ἀμπρακιῶται κτἑ.: see App.
— 10. ἐνίκων τὸ καθ' ἑαυτούς: *were victorious in their own quarter.* Cf. c. 78. 3. — 11. ἀπεδίωξαν: i.e. pursued from their position. Cf. vi. 102. 15 τῶν Ἀθηναίων ἀποδιωξάντων τοὺς ἐκεῖ, also Xen. Hell. iv. 5. 14; vi. 2. 20; Ar. Nub. 1296. These passages support the Mss. reading sufficiently against Haase's conjecture (Lucubr. p. 62) ἐπεδίωξαν.
12. ἐπαναχωροῦντες . . . νενικημένον: cf. i. 63. 1. ἐπαναχωροῦντες, *returning, sc.* from the pursuit (i. 63. 1 ἐπαναχωρῶν ἀπὸ τῆς διώξεως), during which the flight of the greater part of the army (l. 5) had occurred; hence the pf. partic. νενικημένον.—
14. διεσώζοντο: as in c. 85. 4; 109.

5; i. 82. 10; ii. 60. 10; iv. 96. 33. — 15. αὐτῶν: if the text be sound, it seems necessary to adopt Jowett's explanation, that αὐτῶν is used not of the right wing of the Peloponnesian army just mentioned, for the Mantineans were on the left, but generally "of their army." But see App. — ἀτάκτως καὶ οὐδενὶ κόσμῳ προσπίπτοντες: cf. vi. 97. 17 προσπεσόντες ἀτακτότερον. Vat. and other Mss. read ἀφυλάκτως, prob. because ἀτάκτως and οὐδενὶ κόσμῳ are so nearly synonymous, but the reading of the text is supported by iv. 126. 34 κόσμῳ καὶ τάξει, Herod. ii. 4 τὸ κόσμιον καὶ εὔτακτον. — 16. προσπίπτοντες: sc. τῷ τείχει, *rushing to the fort*, as in vi. 97. 17; viii. 84. 5. The Schol. wrongly explains, τοῖς ἐναντίοις δηλονότι. — 17. τοῦ στρατοῦ: dependent on μάλιστα. G. 1088; Kr. Spr. 47, 28, 8. — 18. ἐς ὀψέ: as viii. 23. 7; Dem. lvii. 15; μέχρι ὀψέ, vii. 83. 13. Cf. c. 78. 16 ἐτελεύτα ἐς ἡλίου δύσιν, i. 51. 9 ἡ ναυμαχία ἐτελεύτα ἐς νύκτα. Kühn. 446 b; Kr. Spr. 66, 1, 4. The reading of Vat. and other good Mss., ἕως ὀψέ, is explained by Lobeck, ad Phryn.

109 Μενεδάιος δὲ τῇ ὑστεραίᾳ Εὐρυλόχου τεθνεῶτος 1
καὶ Μακαρίου αὐτὸς παρειληφὼς τὴν ἀρχὴν καὶ ἀπορῶν
μεγάλης ἥσσης γεγενημένης ὅτῳ τρόπῳ ἢ μένων πολιορκήσεται, ἔκ τε γῆς καὶ ἐκ θαλάσσης ταῖς Ἀττικαῖς
5 ναυσὶν ἀποκεκλημένος, ἢ καὶ ἀναχωρῶν διασωθήσεται,
προσφέρει λόγον περὶ σπονδῶν καὶ ἀναχωρήσεως Δημοσθένει καὶ τοῖς Ἀκαρνάνων στρατηγοῖς καὶ περὶ νεκρῶν
ἅμα ἀναιρέσεως. οἱ δὲ νεκροὺς μὲν ἀπέδοσαν καὶ τρο- 2
παῖον αὐτοὶ ἔστησαν καὶ τοὺς ἑαυτῶν τριακοσίους μάλι-
10 στα ἀποθανόντας ἀνείλοντο· ἀναχώρησιν δὲ ἐκ μὲν τοῦ
προφανοῦς οὐκ ἐσπείσαντο ἅπασι, κρύφα δὲ Δημοσθένης
μετὰ τῶν ξυστρατήγων Ἀκαρνάνων σπένδονται Μαντι-

p. 47, παρέτεινε ἕως ὀψὲ καὶ ὀψὲ ἐτελεύτα,—which seems too artificial.

109. *Menedaius, who assumes command after the death of Eurylochus and Macarius, makes a secret agreement by which he and a part of the Peloponnesians are allowed to withdraw undisturbed.*

1. **Μενεδάϊος**: see on c. 100. 11. — 2. **αὐτός**: *alone*. Cf. c. 27. 9; i. 139. 15; iv. 49. 5; v. 60. 4; vi. 37. 3. — **παρειληφώς**: not παραλαβών, since this act stands for itself, without causal connexion with προσφέρει λόγον. — 3. **μεγάλης ἥσσης γεγενημένης**: the art., though it would be in order, is not necessary. Cf. i. 18. 15, and see on ii. 5. 13. — **ὅτῳ τρόπῳ**: with fut. ind. for the more usual ὅπως. See on i. 107. 18. — **πολιορκήσεται**: pass. and with the same meaning, as in c. 52. 2. — 4. **ἔκ τε γῆς καὶ ἐκ θαλάσσης**: answers to πανταχόθεν, v. 60. 12; viii. 42. 14. — 5. **ἀποκεκλημένος**: pf. partic. because he is already in this situation. — 6. **προσφέρει λόγον**: as in

viii. 32. 12; Hdt. iii. 134. 3; v. 30. 15; more freq. λόγους, c. 4. 8; i. 57. 11; ii. 70. 6.

9. **τοὺς ἀποθανόντας**: *the fallen*, almost a subst., as in c. 113. 23; ii. 34. 2. It is a relic of the Hom. usage; cf. Il 457 τὸ γὰρ γέρας ἐστὶ θανόντων. See Classen, *Beob. über den Hom. Sprachgebrauch*, p. 57 ff. — **μάλιστα**: see on c. 21. 4. — 10. **ἀναχώρησιν**: for acc. with σπένδεσθαι, see on c. 24. 19. — **ἐκ τοῦ προφανοῦς**: as c. 43. 10; viii. 68. 2. See on c. 43. 5; 82. 48. — 12. **μετὰ τῶν ξυστρατήγων Ἀκαρνάνων**: cf. c. 107. 12. For the gen. Ἀκαρνάνων, see on c. 92. 19. On the recessive accent here and ll. 58. 2, see Göttling, p. 321. — **σπένδονται**: pl. after Δημοσθένης μετὰ τῶν ξυστρατήγων. A rare const., the more striking since βουλόμενος (l. 15) agrees only with Δημοσθένης. Kr. *Spr.* 63, 4, 3; Kühn. 359, x. 5. Cf. Xen. *Hell.* i. 1. 10 Ἀλκιβιάδης ἐκ Σάρδεων μετὰ Μαντιθέου ἵππων εὐπορήσαντες ἀπέδρασαν. Steup would prefer σπένδεται, on the

νεῦσι καὶ Μενεδαΐῳ καὶ τοῖς ἄλλοις ἄρχουσι τῶν Πελοποννησίων καὶ ὅσοι αὐτῶν ἦσαν ἀξιολογώτατοι ἀποχω-
15 ρεῖν κατὰ τάχος, βουλόμενος ψιλῶσαι τοὺς Ἀμπρακιώτας τε καὶ τὸν μισθοφόρον ὄχλον [τὸν ξενικόν], μάλιστα δὲ

ground that the pl. conflicts with the manifest intention to emphasize Demosthenes, as shown by the addition of Δημοσθένης μετὰ τῶν ξυστρατήγων Ἀκαρνάνων after ἐσπείσαντο. — 13. τοῖς ἄλλοις ἄρχουσι: i.e. the higher officers. Cf. c. 30. 1; v. 9. 33; vi. 32. 7. — 14. ἀξιολογώτατοι: most influential, as ii. 10. 11. — ἀποχωρεῖν: inf. after σπένδονται, as iv. 114. 9; vii. 83. 4; σπείσασθαι ... ἢ μὴν ἐμμενεῖν, iv. 118. 57. — 15. ψιλῶσαι: only here in Thuc. μονῶσαι, ψιλοὺς τῶν ξυμμάχων ποιῆσαι, Schol. Cf. Hdt. ii. 151. 17; Xen. Cyr. iv. 5. 12. The synonymous μονοῦν is used in Attic only in the passive. — 16. τὸν μισθοφόρον ὄχλον: understood by Bl., Cl., and Jow. as mercenaries in the pay of the Ambraciots, prob. from the neighbouring Epirot tribes, and constituting part of the 3000 hoplites of c. 105. 3. This view assumes that the Peloponnesians were all included in the secret agreement. 'The subject of ἀποχωρεῖν is "the Peloponnesians" to be supplied from "the leaders of the Peloponnesians." Demosthenes negotiated with the Mantineans, Menedaius, and the leaders of the Peloponnesians, not for their personal safety only, but for the safe withdrawal of their forces; the Ambraciots, their allies, being left to their fate.' (Jow.) But Steup holds that τὸν μισθοφόρον ὄχλον covers all the army of Menedaius that were not

Mantineans or ἄρχοντες or ἀξιολογώτατοι. His grounds are viz.: that not all the Peloponnesians were included in the agreement is clear both from the plain meaning of l. 12 ff. and from the expressions οἷς ἐδέδοτο ἡ ἀποχώρησις, l. 21, and οἱ Μαντινῆς καὶ οἷς ἔσπειστο, c. 111. 2. Later, it is true, those entitled to withdraw are designated simply as οἱ Πελοποννήσιοι (c. 111. 10), or οἱ Μαντινῆς καὶ οἱ Πελοποννήσιοι (c. 111. 14), but again in c. 113. 4 they are called οἱ Μαντινῆς καὶ οἱ ὑπόσπονδοι, and in c. 114. 10 the remnants of the other part of the army are spoken of as οἱ ὡς Σαλύνθιον καταφυγόντες Ἀμπρακιῶται καὶ Πελοποννήσιοι. A comparison with vii. 57. 48 makes it prob. that the Mantineans also were mercenaries. The τρισχίλιοι ὁπλῖται τῶν ξυμμάχων under Eurylochus's command (c. 100. 7) seem, then, to have been all mercenaries, just as Brasidas led, along with 700 Helots, also 1000 Peloponnesian mercenaries to the Thracian coast (iv. 78. 2; 80. 21). That the passage assumes as known that the Peloponnesian army was composed of mercenaries, though no mention is made of this fact, must be attributed, doubtless, to the lack of a final revision of his work by the author. — [τὸν ξενικόν]: rightly bracketed by v. H. (Stud. Thuc. p. 49) as a gloss (see on viii. 25. 10). If τὸν μισθοφόρον ὄχλον includes a part of the Peloponnesians, ξενικόν is unin-

Λακεδαιμονίους καὶ Πελοποννησίους διαβαλεῖν ἐς τοὺς ἐκείνῃ χρῄζων, Ἕλληνας ὡς καταπροδόντες τὸ ἑαυτῶν προυργιαίτερον ἐποιήσαντο. καὶ οἱ μὲν τούς τε νεκροὺς 3
20 ἀνείλοντο καὶ διὰ τάχους ἔθαπτον, ὥσπερ ὑπῆρχε, καὶ τὴν ἀποχώρησιν κρύφα οἷς ἐδέδοτο ἐπεβούλευον·

telligible. Cl., who retains τὸν ξενικόν, thinks that Thuc. wished possibly to define both features (mercenary and foreign) of a military relation then still rare. — 17. Λακεδαιμονίους καὶ Πελοποννησίους: the two names connected, because the shameful agreement affected Peloponnesians commanded by a Spartan. — διαβαλεῖν ἐς τοὺς ἐκείνῃ: *to bring into discredit with those in that quarter*, as in iv. 22. 12. διαβάλλειν, in this sense, with the dat., viii. 88. 9; 109. 4. — 18. χρῄζων: *wishing*, only here in Thuc., and indeed seldom in Attic prose. Cf. Xen. Cyrop. i. 6. 15; Arist. Plant. i. 1. 21. It occurs several times in Aristophanes and numberless times in Tragedy. — Ἕλληνας ὡς καταπροδόντες κτέ.: *because they had betrayed Hellenes and considered their own advantage more important*. See Steup, Quaest. Thuc. p. 29 sq. Usually Ἕλληνας is connected with ἐς τοὺς ἐκείνῃ. But, first, there is no reason why regard should have been had only to the Hellenes of that quarter, when the barbarian Amphilochians were participants in the war (cf. c. 112. 29; ii. 68. 16); secondly, καταπροδόντες requires an obj., and the thought of the ὡς clause is greatly strengthened by making Ἕλληνας this object. For thus it is esp. emphasized, that while Sparta proclaimed that the whole war was waged for the freedom of the Hellenes (see on c. 13. 35; 32. 5), now Hellenes (*i.e.* the Ambraciots and the Peloponnesian μισθοφόρος ὄχλος) are betrayed by Lacedaemonians and Peloponnesians. For the emphatic position of Ἕλληνας before the conj., cf. ii. 64. 17, and see on c. 88. 8. The objection of St., that the treachery had been committed, non in omnes Graecos, sed in illorum socios, would be admissible only if not Ἕλληνας, but τοὺς Ἕλληνας were to be connected with καταπροδόντες. — 19. προυργιαίτερον ἐποιήσαντο: cf. Isoc. vi. 35; Isae. ix. 25; Polyb. i. 1. 6. The comp. προυργιαίτερον from the adv. προύργου (iv. 17. 8), as πλησιαίτερον from πλησίον.

20. ὥσπερ ὑπῆρχε: "as well as possible under the circumstances," = ἐκ τῶν ὑπαρχόντων or παρόντων. Cf. Xen. Anab. vi. 4. 9 ἔθαψαν ἐκ τῶν ὑπαρχόντων ὡς ἐδύναντο κάλλιστα. — 21. τὴν ἀποχώρησιν... ἐπεβούλευον: *those to whom it had been granted were making secret preparations for retreat*. With τὴν ἀποχώρησιν ἐπεβούλευον, cf. vii. 51. 5 τὸν ἔκπλουν ἐπιβουλεῦσαι, vi. 54. 14 ἐπιβουλεύει κατάλυσιν τῇ τυραννίδι, viii. 60. 4 ἐπιβουλεύοντες ἀπόστασιν. See on c. 96. 11. οἷς ἐδέδοτο, *i.e.* ἐκεῖνοι οἷς, those named above, l. 12 ff.

110 τῷ δὲ Δημοσθένει καὶ τοῖς Ἀκαρνᾶσιν ἀγγέλλεται 1
τοὺς Ἀμπρακιώτας τοὺς ἐκ τῆς πόλεως πανδημεὶ κατὰ
τὴν πρώτην ἐκ τῶν Ὀλπῶν ἀγγελίαν ἐπιβοηθεῖν διὰ
τῶν Ἀμφιλόχων, βουλομένους τοῖς ἐν Ὄλπαις ξυμμεῖξαι, εἰδότας οὐδὲν τῶν γεγενημένων, καὶ πέμπει εὐθὺς 2
τοῦ στρατοῦ μέρος τι τὰς ὁδοὺς προλοχιοῦντας καὶ
τὰ καρτερὰ προκαταληψομένους, καὶ τῇ ἄλλῃ στρατιᾷ
111 ἅμα παρεσκευάζετο βοηθεῖν ἐπ' αὐτούς. ἐν τούτῳ 1
δ' οἱ Μαντινῆς καὶ οἷς ἔσπειστο πρόφασιν ἐπὶ λαχανισμὸν καὶ φρυγάνων ξυλλογὴν ἐξελθόντες ὑπαπῆσαν
κατ' ὀλίγους, ἅμα ξυλλέγοντες ἐφ' ἃ ἐξῆλθον δῆθεν·
προκεχωρηκότες δὲ ἤδη ἄπωθεν τῆς Ὄλπης θᾶσσον

110. *Advance of fresh auxiliaries from Ambracia.*

1. ἀγγέλλεται, (5) καὶ πέμπει: parataxis, by which cause and effect are brought into close connexion, as in i. 61. 1, 2. — **2. τοὺς ἐκ τῆς πόλεως**: sc. Ἀμπρακίας, as distinguished from those who after the battle were shut up in Olpae (c. 108. 14; 111. § 2). — **κατὰ τὴν πρώτην ... ἀγγελίαν**: cf. c. 105. § 4. — **3. διὰ τῶν Ἀμφιλόχων**: i.e. through the hostile Amphilochian territory. Cf. c. 101. 3. — **4. ξυμμεῖξαι**: as in ii. 84. 34; vii. 26. 4. For the form, see on c. 22. 4.
6. προλοχιοῦντας: pl. after μέρος τι. See on c. 2. 2; 79. 10; 80. 1. The word occurs also in c. 112. 22; ii. 81. 24; elsewhere prob. only in late writers. — **7. τὰ καρτερά**: i.e. natural strongholds, as in c. 18. 19; ii. 100. 3. — **τῇ ἄλλῃ στρατιᾷ**: dat. of means with βοηθεῖν. Cf. i. 81. 5. — **8. βοηθεῖν ἐπ' αὐτούς**: as in i. 107. 22; 126. 22. See on c. 97. 14.

111. *Meanwhile the Acarnanians fall upon the Ambraciots, who are trying to join the fleeing Peloponnesians, and kill many of them.*

2. οἷς ἔσπειστο: *with whom the agreement had been made,* not *for whom.* Cf. l. 12; 109. 11. — **πρόφασιν**: adv. *on the pretext,* as in v. 80. 17; vi. 33. 9; Eur. I. A. 362; Dem. xviii. 77. Kr. Spr. 46, 3, 5; Kühn. 462 i. — **λαχανισμόν**: ἅπαξ in Thuc. λαχάνων συνάθροισιν, Schol. Cf. Poll. i. 162 ἐξῆλθον ἐπὶ λαχανισμόν, ἐπὶ φρυγανισμόν. λάχανα are wild cabbage, still used in Greece. Gell, Morea, p. 191. See also Leake, Northern Greece, iv. p. 248. — **3. φρυγάνων ξυλλογήν**: = φρυγανισμόν, vii. 4. 30; 13. 7. Cf. φρύγανα συλλέγειν, Lycurg. 86. — **ὑπαπῆσαν**: *withdrew gradually.* Cf. v. 9. 17. — **4. κατ' ὀλίγους**: *a few at a time.* Cf. c. 78. 2; Hdt. viii. 113. 14. — **δῆθεν**: "as they pretended." Cf. c. 68. 4; i. 92. 3; 127. 2; iv. 99. 7. — **5. θᾶσσον ἀπεχώρουν**: cf. c. 109. 14 ἀποχωρεῖν

ἀπεχώρουν. οἱ δ' Ἀμπρακιῶται καὶ οἱ ἄλλοι ὅσοι 2
μὲν † ἐτύγχανον οὕτως, ἁθρόοι ξυνελθόντες, ὡς ἔγνωσαν ἀπιόντας, ὥρμησαν καὶ αὐτοὶ καὶ ἔθεον δρόμῳ, ἐπικαταλαβεῖν βουλόμενοι. οἱ δὲ Ἀκαρνᾶνες τὸ μὲν πρῶτον 3
10 καὶ πάντας ἐνόμισαν ἀπιέναι ἀσπόνδους ὁμοίως καὶ τοὺς
Πελοποννησίους ἐπεδίωκον (καί τινας αὐτῶν τῶν στρατηγῶν κωλύοντας καὶ φάσκοντας ἐσπεῖσθαι αὐτοῖς ἠκόν-
τισέ τις, νομίσας καταπροδίδοσθαι σφᾶς)· ἔπειτα μέντοι
τοὺς μὲν Μαντινέας καὶ τοὺς Πελοποννησίους ἀφίεσαν,

κατὰ τάχος. ἀπεχώρουν, impf., covers the time in which the following events occurred.
6. οἱ ἄλλοι ὅσοι κτέ.: the μισθοφόρος ὄχλος of c. 109. 16. — ὅσοι μὲν † ἐτύγχανον οὕτως : the passage is certainly corrupt. See App. — **7. ἁθρόοι ξυνελθόντες** : in their critical situation they first came together to take counsel, but when they learned that the Peloponnesians were already withdrawing, they set off *also themselves* (καὶ αὐτοί), and were hastening to overtake them. But see App. — **8. ἔθεον δρόμῳ** : = ἐχώρουν δρόμῳ, v. 3. 7. *Cf.* iv. 67. 21; 112. 2; v. 10. 26; vi. 100. 14; Xen. *Anab.* i. 8. 8; iv. 6. 25. — **ἐπικαταλαβεῖν**: *overtake*, as in ii. 90. 23. *Cf.* Plato *Tim.* 39 c; Jos. *Antiq.* xviii. 9. 5; Polyb. i. 66. 4; Diod. xviii. 71.
9. οἱ δὲ Ἀκαρνᾶνες: since Dem. had let only their leaders into the secret. — **10. καὶ πάντας**: *i.e.* not merely the Ambraciots. — **τοὺς Πελοποννησίους**: this and τοὺς Μαντινέας καὶ τοὺς Πελοποννησίους (l. 14) are not quite exact expressions for τοὺς Μαντινέας καὶ οἷς ἔσπειστο (l. 2). See on c. 109. 16. The Ἀμπρακιῶται καὶ οἱ ἄλλοι of l. 6 are not mentioned, perhaps because reference is not yet had to the time when they too set off from Olpae (ὥρμησαν καὶ αὐτοὶ κτέ.). — **11. αὐτῶν τῶν στρατηγῶν**: *of the generals themselves*, indicating a great degree of excitement, on which account alone indeed the whole occurrence is narrated. — **12. ἠκόντισε**: with acc. without prep. Kr. *Spr.* 47, 14, 1. — **13. τις**: the sing. of the partic. νομίσας is against taking τις here in the sense of *one and another*, as Arn., Goell., and St. do. In Xen. *An.* i. 8. 20 τοξευθῆναί τις ἐλέγετο, which Arn. compares, τις doubtless refers to a single person. — **σφᾶς**: refers to the subj. of the leading clause (τις), though including more than this. For the pl. thus used after a sing. subj., *cf.* iv. 36. 3; vi. 49. 9. Kr. *Spr.* 58, 4, 3. — **14. τοὺς Μαντινέας καὶ τοὺς Πελοποννησίους**: the same emphasis of the part beside the whole, as in l. 2 οἱ Μαντινῆς καὶ οἷς ἔσπειστο. — **ἀφίεσαν**: the use of the augment of this verb in Thuc., as well as in other Attic writers, is inconstant. *Cf.* ἤφιει, ii. 49. 8; ἀφίει, iv. 122. 11; viii. 41. 13. See Kr. on

15 τοὺς δ' Ἀμπρακιώτας ἔκτεινον. καὶ ἦν πολλὴ ἔρις καὶ 4
ἄγνοια εἴτε Ἀμπρακιώτης τίς ἐστιν εἴτε Πελοποννήσιος.
καὶ ἐς διακοσίους μέν τινας αὐτῶν ἀπέκτειναν· οἱ δ'
ἄλλοι διέφυγον ἐς τὴν Ἀγραΐδα ὅμορον οὖσαν, καὶ Σαλύν-
θιος αὐτοὺς ὁ βασιλεὺς τῶν Ἀγραίων φίλος ὢν ὑπεδέξατο.
112 Οἱ δ' ἐκ τῆς πόλεως Ἀμπρακιῶται ἀφικνοῦνται 1
ἐπ' Ἰδομενήν. ἐστὸν δὲ δύο λόφω ἡ Ἰδομενὴ ὑψηλώ·
τούτοιν τὸν μὲν μείζω νυκτὸς ἐπιγενομένης οἱ προαποσταλέντες ὑπὸ τοῦ Δημοσθένους ἀπὸ τοῦ στρατοπέδου
5 ἔλαθόν τε καὶ ἔφθασαν προκαταλαβόντες, τὸν δ' ἐλάσσω
ἔτυχον οἱ Ἀμπρακιῶται προαναβάντες καὶ ηὐλίσαντο. ὁ 2

ii. 49. 8. The impf. here, as well as ἔκτεινον (15), because the action is represented as in progress. Cf. ἀπε-χώρουν (6), ἔθεον (8), ἐπεδίωκον (11). But in l. 17 the aor. (ἀπέκτειναν) occurs, because only the result is to be stated.
17. ἐς διακοσίους μέν τινας: *about two hundred*, as in viii. 21. 4. For the force of τινας, see on c. 68. 16. The prepositional phrase represents the obj., as in c. 114. 22. See on c. 20. 11. — αὐτῶν: refers only to the Ambraciots, as is clear from οἱ δ' ἄλλοι διέφυγον κτἑ. — 18. ἐς τὴν Ἀγραΐδα: see on c. 106. 10.
112. *The Ambraciots from the city coming to bring aid to their friends are surprised by Demosthenes before daybreak and most of them destroyed.*
1. οἱ ἐκ τῆς πόλεως Ἀμπρακιῶται: cf. c. 110. — 2. ἐπ' Ἰδομενήν: in c. 113. 10 Ἰδομεναί. See on c. 105. 5. The Mss. have Ἰδομένη and Ἰδομέναι, but see St. *Qu. Gr.*² p. 34, and on c. 94. 4. For the position of these two heights, which acc. to l. 20 and c. 110. 3, are to be sought on Amphilochian territory, see Bursian i. p. 39, and Oberhummer, *Akarnanien*, p. 110. — ἐστόν: construed with the pred. Cf. iv. 102. 13; Hdt. vi. 112. 3. G. 904; H. 610; Kr. *Spr.* 63, 6; Kühn. 369, 3. — ἡ Ἰδομενή: rejected as a gloss by v. H. and St.; but *cf*. ii. 18. 3, 5; 30. 6, 8. — 3. οἱ προαποσταλέντες: *cf*. c. 110. 5. — 4. ἀπὸ τοῦ στρατοπέδου: *i.e.* detached from the main army. — 5. ἔφθασαν προκαταλαβόντες: *cf*. φθάσαντες προκατέλαβον, iv. 127. 14. For similar pleonasms, see on c. 53. 9. προκαταλαβόντες belongs to ἔλαθον as well as to ἔφθασαν. — τὸν ἐλάσσω: the const. with προαναβάντες without prep. is rather surprising, since Thuc. never construes ἀναβαίνειν with the simple acc.; but this const. is found in Plato *Phaedo* 113 d, and later authors, *e.g.* Dio C. lx. 23; App. i. p. 175; Paus. vi. 16. 9. Kr. conjectured ἐς τὸν δ' ἐλάσσω, and Rauchenstein (*Philol.* xxxv. p. 592) proposed εἶχον for ἔτυχον.

THUCYDIDES III. 112.   251

δὲ Δημοσθένης δειπνήσας ἐχώρει καὶ τὸ ἄλλο στράτευμα ἀπὸ ἑσπέρας εὐθύς, αὐτὸς μὲν τὸ ἥμισυ ἔχων ἐπὶ τῆς ἐσβολῆς, τὸ δ' ἄλλο διὰ τῶν Ἀμφιλοχικῶν ὀρῶν. καὶ ἅμα 3
10 ὄρθρῳ ἐπιπίπτει τοῖς Ἀμπρακιώταις ἔτι ἐν ταῖς εὐναῖς καὶ οὐ προῃσθημένοις τὰ γεγενημένα, ἀλλὰ πολὺ μᾶλλον νομίσασι τοὺς ἑαυτῶν εἶναι· καὶ γὰρ τοὺς Μεσσηνίους 4 πρώτους ἐπίτηδες ὁ Δημοσθένης προύταξε καὶ προσαγορεύειν ἐκέλευε, Δωρίδα τε γλῶσσαν ἱέντας καὶ τοῖς
15 προφύλαξι πίστιν παρεχομένους, ἅμα δὲ καὶ οὐ καθορωμένους τῇ ὄψει νυκτὸς ἔτι οὔσης. ὡς οὖν ἐπέπεσε τῷ 5

7. **ἐχώρει**: *went forward;* the decisive events following in the pres., ἐπιπίπτει (10) τρέπουσι (17), and the narration continuing in the aor. — **καὶ τὸ ἄλλο στράτευμα**: opp. to οἱ προαποσταλέντες (3). *Cf.* τῇ ἄλλῃ στρατιᾷ, c. 110. 7. — 8. **ἀπὸ ἑσπέρας εὐθύς**: *immediately after nightfall,* as in viii. 27. 27 (without εὐθύς, vii. 29. 8). *Cf.* ἀπὸ πρώτου ὕπνου, vii. 43. 17. The march lasted, therefore, all night. — **ἐπὶ τῆς ἐσβολῆς**: with ἐχώρει, *toward the pass,* which led up from the plain between the two hills, and so to the ascent to that occupied by the Ambraciots. ἐσβολή, as in iv. 83. 6; 127. 13; Hdt. vii. 172. 9; 175. 10; Xen. *Anab.* i. 2. 21; *Hell.* v. 4. 48.
9. **ἅμα ὄρθρῳ**: *at daybreak,* which comports with νυκτὸς ἔτι οὔσης, 1. 16. *Cf.* ii. 3. 17 ἔτι νύκτα καὶ αὐτὸ τὸ περίορθρον, iv. 110. 4 νυκτὸς ἔτι καὶ περὶ ὄρθρον, vi. 101. 13 περὶ ὄρθρον, Plato *Prot.* 310 a τῆς παρελθούσης νυκτὸς ταυτησὶ ἔτι βαθέος ὄρθρου. On the meaning of ὄρθρος (the interval between the first cock-crow and morning twilight), see Unger, *Philol.* xliii. p. 594 f. — 10. **ἔτι ἐν ταῖς εὐναῖς**: as in iv. 32.

2. *Cf.* Tac. *Ann.* i. 50 strati etiam tum per cubilia. — 12. **τοὺς ἑαυτῶν εἶναι**: sc. τοὺς ἐπιπίπτοντας.
τοὺς Μεσσηνίους: *cf.* c. 107. 5, 23; 108. 8. — 13. **πρώτους προύταξε**: for the pleonasm, see on l. 5. — **ἐπίτηδες**: *prudently.* Schol. ἐσκεμμένως. The adv. is found only here in Thuc. — 14. **ἐκέλευε**: for the impf. where the aor. would seem more natural, see GMT. 57; Kr. *Spr.* 53, 2, 8; Kühn. 383, 3. — **Δωρίδα γλῶσσαν**: *cf.* i. 138. 4; ii. 68. 14; and vi. 5. 5 Δωρὶς φωνή. See on c. 103. 2. — **γλῶσσαν ἱέντας**: as in Hdt. i. 57. 1; ix. 16. 13; Soph. *El.* 596. The const., which occurs only here in Thuc., is common in Hom., Hdt., and the Attic poets. *Cf.* ὄπα ἱέναι, Hom. Γ 152, 221; μ 192; φωνὴν ἱέναι, Hdt. ii. 2. 11; iv. 23. 7; 135. 15; Ar. *Acharn.* 747; *Eq.* 522; *Vesp.* 562; Aesch. *Choeph.* 563; γῆρυν ἱέναι, Ar. *Aves* 233; φθογγὰς ἱέναι, Eur. *Hec.* 338; κωκυτὸν ἱέναι, Soph. *Aj.* 851. It occurs twice in Plato (*Legg.* 890 d; *Phileb.* 51 d). *Cf.* Lat. vocem mittere. — 15. **πίστιν παρεχομένους**: *inspiring confidence.* *Cf.* vi. 17. 3. — 16. **τῇ ὄψει**: *by sight,* with

στρατεύματι αὐτῶν, τρέπουσι. καὶ τοὺς μὲν πολλοὺς αὐτοῦ διέφθειραν, οἱ δὲ λοιποὶ κατὰ τὰ ὄρη ἐς φυγὴν ὥρμησαν. προκατειλημμένων δὲ τῶν ὁδῶν, καὶ ἅμα τῶν 6
20 μὲν Ἀμφιλόχων ἐμπείρων ὄντων τῆς ἑαυτῶν γῆς καὶ ψιλῶν πρὸς ὁπλίτας, τῶν δὲ ἀπείρων καὶ ἀνεπιστημόνων ὅπῃ τράπωνται, ἐσπίπτοντες ἔς τε χαράδρας καὶ τὰς προλελοχισμένας ἐνέδρας διεφθείροντο. καὶ ἐς πᾶσαν ἰδέαν 7
χωρήσαντες τῆς φυγῆς ἐτράποντό τινες καὶ ἐς τὴν θά-
25 λασσαν οὐ πολὺ ἀπέχουσαν, καὶ ὡς εἶδον τὰς Ἀττικὰς ναῦς παραπλεούσας ἅμα τοῦ ἔργου τῇ ξυντυχίᾳ, προσένευσαν, ἡγησάμενοι ἐν τῷ αὐτίκα φόβῳ κρεῖσσον εἶναι σφίσιν ὑπὸ τῶν ἐν ταῖς ναυσίν, εἰ δεῖ, διαφθαρῆναι ἢ

the eyes (cf. c. 38. 20; iv. 34. 5; 126. 32; vii. 75. 8), added here because the antithesis ἀκονομένους μὲν τῇ ἀκοῇ is in mind. For similar pleonasms, cf. ἔθεον δρόμῳ, c. 111. 8; λόγῳ εἶπον, i. 23. 1; προλοχίζουσι ἐνέδραις, ii. 81. 24 (cf. l. 22 below). Others render "not distinguished by their appearance."
17. τρέπουσι : sudden transition from the general to his troops. See on c. 51. 16, and cf. Xen. An. iii. 3. 7.
— αὐτοῦ: on the spot. Cf. c. 81. 15; 98. 11.
19. προκατειλημμένων τῶν ὁδῶν: cf. l. 5; 110. 7. — τῶν Ἀμφιλόχων : cf. c. 107. 8, 25. — 21. πρὸς ὁπλίτας: cf. c. 105. 3. For πρός, against, see on c. 43. 15. — τῶν δὲ ἀπείρων καὶ ἀνεπιστημόνων : closely connected with and balancing τῶν μὲν . . . ἐμπείρων ὄντων, and hence also in gen. abs., although the subj. is the same as that of the leading verb. Cf. c. 49. 13; 55. 5, and see on c. 13. 30. —

22. ἐσπίπτοντες . . . διεφθείροντο : cf. c. 98. 7. — τὰς προλελοχισμένας : cf. c. 110. 6.
23. πᾶσαν ἰδέαν : see on c. 81. 22.
— 24. ἐτράποντό τινες : the partial subj. is separated from the general one contained in χωρήσαντες, as in i. 49. 14. — 25. τὰς Ἀττικὰς ναῦς : cf. c. 107. 3, 7. — 26. ἅμα τοῦ ἔργου τῇ ξυντυχίᾳ: to be taken with παραπλεούσαις, sailing along the coast at the moment of the occurrence of the action. Cf. i. 33. 1 ἡ ξυντυχία . . . τῆς ἡμετέρας χρείας. τὸ ἔργον in this sense also i. 105. 24; 107. 28; ii. 89. 42; iv. 32. 24; 72. 21; viii. 42. 12. — προσένευσαν: the verb, which is found only here in Thuc., occurs also in Plut. Mar. 37; Luc. Bis Acc. 21; Ael. V. H. i. 1. — 28. εἰ δεῖ, if it must be, as in ii. 74. 3; vii. 48. 30; Dem. xx. 53. Thuc. does not tell the fate of these fugitives, but the expression εἰ δεῖ, διαφθαρῆναι favours the inference that they received no mercy from the

ὑπὸ τῶν βαρβάρων καὶ ἐχθίστων Ἀμφιλόχων. οἱ μὲν οὖν 8
30 Ἀμπρακιῶται τοιούτῳ τρόπῳ κακωθέντες ὀλίγοι ἀπὸ
πολλῶν ἐσώθησαν ἐς τὴν πόλιν · Ἀκαρνᾶνες δὲ σκυλεύ-
σαντες τοὺς νεκροὺς καὶ τροπαῖα στήσαντες ἀπεχώρησαν
113 ἐς Ἄργος. καὶ αὐτοῖς τῇ ὑστεραίᾳ ἦλθε κῆρυξ ἀπὸ τῶν 1
ἐς Ἀγραίους καταφυγόντων ἐκ τῆς Ὄλπης Ἀμπρακιωτῶν,
ἀναίρεσιν αἰτήσων τῶν νεκρῶν οὓς ἀπέκτειναν ὕστερον
τῆς πρώτης μάχης, ὅτε μετὰ τῶν Μαντινέων καὶ τῶν
5 ὑποσπόνδων ξυνεξῇσαν ἄσπονδοι. ἰδὼν δ' ὁ κῆρυξ τὰ 2
ὅπλα τῶν ἀπὸ τῆς πόλεως Ἀμπρακιωτῶν ἐθαύμαζε τὸ
πλῆθος · οὐ γὰρ ᾔδει τὸ πάθος, ἀλλ' ᾤετο τῶν μετὰ σφῶν
εἶναι. καί τις αὐτὸν ἤρετο ὅ τι θαυμάζοι καὶ ὁπόσοι αὐ- 3
τῶν τεθνᾶσιν, οἰόμενος αὖ ὁ ἐρωτῶν εἶναι τὸν κήρυκα

Athenian crew. — **29. τῶν βαρβάρων**: adj. *Cf.* ii. 68. 15 οἱ δὲ ἄλλοι Ἀμφίλοχοι βάρβαροί εἰσιν. 'The Ambraciots affected to regard the Amphilochians as barbarians, because they were in reality a mixed race.' Arn.
30. ὀλίγοι ἀπὸ πολλῶν ἐσώθησαν: this formula as in i. 110. 2; vii. 87. 26. Kühn. 414, N. 4. See on c. 24. 12. — **32. τροπαῖα**: the pl. as in v. 3. 10; vii. 24. 3; 41. 12; 45. 1. Here to be accounted for prob. by the divisions of the army mentioned in c. 110. § 2; 112. § 2.
113. *The severity of the blow to Ambracia is vividly portrayed in the demeanor of the herald at Argos.*
1. αὐτοῖς ἦλθε: *cf.* c. 5. 12; 39. 22; 70. 2, and see on i. 13. 12. — **2. ἐς Ἀγραίους**: *cf.* c. 111. 18. — **3. τῶν νεκρῶν οὓς ἀπέκτειναν**: "the corpses of those whom they killed." *Cf.* c. 111. 17. v. H. (*Stud. Thuc.* p. 49) unnecessarily objects to the ple-

onasm. — **4. τῆς πρώτης μάχης**: near Olpae, c. 108; not προτέρας, because it is the first of the three battles, c. 108, 111, and 112. — **τῶν ὑποσπόνδων**: = οἷς ἔσπειστο, c. 111. 2. The part joined to the whole, as in c. 111. 2, 14. Kr. *Spr.* 69, 32, 2. *Cf.* c. 109. § 2. — **5. ξυνεξῇσαν**: *attempted to depart with*. Steup thinks the impf. is used with reference to the continuance of the occurrence, as in c. 34. 5; 68. 12; 96. 11. Regarding the matter, *cf.* c. 111. § 1.
6. τῶν ἀπὸ τῆς πόλεως: *cf.* c. 112. 1. — **7. τὸ πάθος**: *i.e.* the fatal night-battle of Idomene. — **τῶν μετὰ σφῶν**: *i.e.* τῶν ἐς Ἀγραίους καταφυγόντων, the messenger representing those by whom he was sent. *Cf.* τῶν μεθ' ἡμῶν μαχομένων, l. 13. — **8. εἶναι**: sc. τὰ ὅπλα.
θαυμάζοι καὶ . . . τεθνᾶσιν: change of mood, as in ii. 80. 9. GMT. 670 a. *Cf.* c. 22. 38; vi. 96. 18. — **9. αὖ**: *in*

10 ἀπὸ τῶν ἐν Ἰδομεναῖς. ὁ δ' ἔφη διακοσίους μάλιστα. ὑπολαβὼν δ' ὁ ἐρωτῶν εἶπεν · "Οὐκ οὖν τὰ ὅπλα ταυτὶ 4 διακοσίων φαίνεται, ἀλλὰ πλέον ἢ χιλίων." αὖθις δὲ εἶπεν ἐκεῖνος · "Οὐκ ἄρα τῶν μεθ' ἡμῶν μαχομένων ἐστίν." ὁ δ' ἀπεκρίνατο · "Εἴπερ γε ὑμεῖς ἐν Ἰδομενῇ χθὲς ἐμάχεσθε."
15 " Ἀλλ' ἡμεῖς γε οὐδενὶ ἐμαχόμεθα χθές, ἀλλὰ πρώην ἐν τῇ ἀποχωρήσει." "Καὶ μὲν δὴ τούτοις γε ἡμεῖς χθὲς ἀπὸ τῆς πόλεως βοηθήσασι τῆς Ἀμπρακιωτῶν ἐμαχόμεθα." ὁ δὲ κῆρυξ, ὡς ἤκουσε καὶ ἔγνω ὅτι ἡ ἀπὸ τῆς πόλεως 5 βοήθεια διέφθαρται, ἀνοιμώξας καὶ ἐκπλαγεὶς τῷ μεγέ-
20 θει τῶν παρόντων κακῶν ἀπῆλθεν εὐθὺς ἄπρακτος καὶ οὐκέτι ἀπῄτει τοὺς νεκρούς. πάθος γὰρ τοῦτο μιᾷ πόλει 6

turn. The emphasizing of this antithesis causes the repetition of the subj. ὁ ἐρωτῶν. — **10.** τῶν ἐν Ἰδομεναῖς: as ii. 34. 14 τοὺς ἐν Μαραθῶνι. For the pl. alternating with the sing. (l. 14; 112. 2), see on c. 105. 5. — διακοσίους μάλιστα: *cf.* c. 111. 17. The statement of the number answers indirectly also the first question of the Acarnanian (ὅ τι θαυμάζοι). For μάλιστα, see on c. 21. 4.

11. οὐκ οὖν τὰ ὅπλα ταυτὶ ... χιλίων: *you see, then, that these here are not the arms of two hundred, but of more than a thousand.* Cl. adopted into his text, and Steup retains, διακοσίων, on Kr.'s conjecture that σ' had dropped out. But this seems unnecessary. St. renders, apparet vero haec non esse arma corum, *etc.* The Schol. says, λείπει τὸ διακοσίων εἶναι μόνων. οὐκ οὖν, as οὐκ ἄρα (13), draws an inference from what lies before the eye. Kalinka, *Diss. Phil. Vindobon.* ii. p. 184 would understand οὐκ οὖν = οὐδαμῶς. — **13.** μαχομένων:

partic. impf., which tense follows in l. 14. The aor. might have been expected; but in Thuc. ἐμαχόμην is used also in an aoristic sense, ἐμαχεσάμην occurring only in v. 34. 4. See Steup, *Thuk. Stud.* ii. p. 44. — **14.** εἴπερ γε: sc. ἔστι μέντοι before these words. — **15.** πρῴην: *day before yesterday*, as appears from c. 112. § 2 f. and c. 113. § 1. *Cf.* Plato *Prot.* 309 a, and the formula χθὲς καὶ πρῴην. — **16.** καὶ μὲν δή: at vero, in strong asseveration, as often καὶ μήν. Kr. *Spr.* 69, 35, 1; Kühn. 503, 3 f.

19. διέφθαρται: pf. ind., expressing hopeless certainty. — **20.** ἄπρακτος: *without doing his errand*. With ἀπελθεῖν also iv. 61. 28; 99. 10; v. 38. 21; 56. 19; 85. 15; 86. 23. — **21.** οὐκέτι ἀπῄτει: in the desperation of grief, just as in the case of the Athenians, vii. 72. § 2.

πάθος ... μέγιστον δὴ κτέ.: Thuc. often puts a pronominal subj., as τοῦτο, after a pred. subst. and before a sup. adj. which belongs to it. This posi-

Ἑλληνίδι ἐν ἴσαις ἡμέραις μέγιστον δὴ τῶν κατὰ τὸν πόλεμον τόνδε ἐγένετο. καὶ ἀριθμὸν οὐκ ἔγραψα τῶν ἀποθανόντων, διότι ἄπιστον τὸ πλῆθος λέγεται ἀπολέ-
25 σθαι ὡς πρὸς τὸ μέγεθος τῆς πόλεως. Ἀμπρακίαν μέντοι οἶδα ὅτι εἰ ἐβουλήθησαν Ἀκαρνᾶνες καὶ Ἀμφίλοχοι

tion of the subst. gives it a character of generality with nearly the effect of a part. gen. See on i. 1. 8. For similar concluding formulae, cf. vii. 29. 29; 30. 19. Whether this remark of Thuc.'s — in which the restrictive expressions, μιᾷ πόλει Ἑλληνίδι and ἐν ἴσαις ἡμέραις, are to be esp. noted —refers to the ten years', or to the twenty-seven years' war, cannot be determined; for neither here is the number of the total loss of the Ambraciots given, nor in regard to all the great losses of the later periods of the Peloponnesian war are definite numbers for individual states known. L. Herbst (Philol. xxxviii. p. 521 f.) cites vii. 29 f. in favour of understanding κατὰ τὸν πόλεμον τόνδε only of the ten years' war. But since Mycalessus is called in vii. 29. 12 a πόλις οὐ μεγάλη (cf. vii. 30. 20 ὡς ἐπὶ μεγέθει, sc. τῆς πόλεως), the number of Mycalessians, including even women and children, slain by the Thracians, may very well have been less than the number of the Ambraciots that fell in the three days. — 22. ἐν ἴσαις ἡμέραις: i.e. in three days. See on c. 75. 12. — 23. ἀριθμόν: i.e. the sum-total of the fallen. As this number has not been directly stated, it is not possible to make an approximately accurate estimate of it from c. 108. 15 (πολλοὶ ἀπέθανον), c. 111. 17, and the dialogue here (§ 3, 4). Grote, Hist. of Greece, c. 51, on an arbitrarily assumed ratio between the 300 πανοπλίαι assigned to Demosthenes (c. 114. 5) and those set apart for the Athenian government (namely 1 : 6), and without taking into consideration the fact that a part of the booty had been taken from the Peloponnesians, reckons the loss of the Ambraciots at about 6000, which is certainly too high. — τῶν ἀποθανόντων: see on c. 109. 9. — 24. ἄπιστον τὸ πλῆθος: the pred. adj. has the effect of a rel. clause, ἄπιστον τὸ πλῆθός ἐστι, ὃ λέγεται. Cf. c. 30. 4; 57. 3; 63. 16. With the sentiment, cf. Xen. Hier. 2. 16 χαλεπὸν εὑρεῖν, ὅπου οὐχὶ καὶ ἐπιψεύδονται, πλέονας φάσκοντες ἀπεκτονέναι ἢ ὅσοι ἂν τῷ ὄντι ἀποθάνωσιν. — 25. ὡς πρὸς τὸ μέγεθος: in proportion to the size. Cf. vii. 30. 20 ὡς ἐπὶ μεγέθει. ὡς, as in i. 10. 34; 21. 8; ii. 65. 44; iv. 34. 10. Kr. Spr. 69, 63, 4 and 6; Kühn. 581, 5. — Ἀμπρακίαν: placed first, almost abs. See on c. 15. 4; i. 32. 17. — 26. οἶδα: the confidence of the assertion perhaps justifies the inference that Thuc. made careful inquiry in Ambracia itself. See Köhler, Hermes xxvi. p. 47. How weak Ambracia was even after the return of the remnants of the 3000 hoplites of c. 105. 3 (c. 114. § 2), may be inferred from c. 114. § 4. —

Ἀθηναίοις καὶ Δημοσθένει πειθόμενοι ἐξελεῖν, αὐτοβοεὶ
ἂν εἷλον· νῦν δ' ἔδεισαν μὴ οἱ Ἀθηναῖοι ἔχοντες αὐτὴν
χαλεπώτεροι σφίσι πάροικοι ὦσι.

114 Μετὰ δὲ ταῦτα τρίτον μέρος νείμαντες τῶν σκύ- 1
λων τοῖς Ἀθηναίοις τὰ ἄλλα κατὰ τὰς πόλεις διείλοντο.
καὶ τὰ μὲν τῶν Ἀθηναίων πλέοντα ἑάλω, τὰ δὲ νῦν
ἀνακείμενα ἐν τοῖς Ἀττικοῖς ἱεροῖς Δημοσθένει ἐξῃρέθη-
5 σαν τριακόσιαι πανοπλίαι, καὶ ἄγων αὐτὰς κατέπλευσε·
καὶ ἐγένετο ἅμα αὐτῷ μετὰ τὴν τῆς Αἰτωλίας ξυμφορὰν ἀπὸ

27. ἐξελεῖν: a stronger term than ἑλεῖν. Cf. iv. 69. 5; 122. 24; v. 43. 16; viii. 100. 12; Dem. ii. 7. — αὐτοβοεί: see on c. 74. 6. — 28. νῦν δέ: introduces the real state of the case, as in i. 71. 8. — 29. πάροικοι: only here in Thuc., and elsewhere mostly in the poets. Cf. Aesch. Pers. 869; Soph. Ant. 1139. It is used fig. in Hdt. vii. 235. 13, as in Dio C. lxxv. 5; St. Paul Eph. ii. 19.

114. *Demosthenes returns with rich booty to Athens. Peace and alliance between the Ambraciots on the one side and the Acarnanians and Amphilochians on the other.*

1. μετὰ ταῦτα: i.e. after the departure of the Ambracian herald, and the rejection of the proposition of Demosthenes to attack Ambracia. — νείμαντες: sc. οἱ Ἀκαρνᾶνες, as the real belligerents. Cf. c. 112. 31. — 2. κατὰ τὰς πόλεις: in ii. 78. 4; v. 114. 4; vii. 19. 5, κατὰ πόλεις is used in the same connexion, and so Cobet (Mnem. N. S. viii. p. 144) would write here. — 3. πλέοντα: of things, as freq. ἐκπλεῖν and ἐσπλεῖν (c. 51. 11; Dem. xx. 31). — ἑάλω: by whom and how the rich booty was taken is not stated, perhaps

because its capture was not strictly an event of the war. — 4. ἀνακείμενα: pf. pass. of ἀνατίθημι. Cf. ξύγκειται, i. 22. 20. — ἐξῃρέθησαν: pl. agreeing with the appos. πανοπλίαι. Kr. Spr. 63, I, 3. This meaning of the word occurs already in Homer (Δ 627; η 10). — 5. ἄγων αὐτὰς κατέπλευσε: sc. ἐς τὰς Ἀθήνας. Cf. ii. 103. 3. These words balance πλέοντα ἑάλω (3). While the ships bearing the rest of the booty were captured, Demosthenes reached Athens safely with his share of the spoils. Since, acc. to l. 8, the twenty Athenian triremes of c. 105. 15 returned to Naupactus, the ships bearing the booty seem to have been insufficiently or not at all protected by war-ships. — 6. καὶ ἐγένετο ἅμα κτέ.: the brilliant success of Demosthenes not only brought him rich spoils, but rendered his return to Athens ἀδεεστέρα. — τῆς Αἰτωλίας: = ἐν τῇ Αἰτωλίᾳ. The fact that in later times the simple gen. was felt to be unusual doubtless caused the readings ἐκ τῆς Αἰτωλίας (Laur. and Palat.; cf. c. 102. 10) and ἐν Αἰτωλίᾳ (inferior Mss.). — ἀπό: in consequence of. Cf. c. 64. 5; ii. 62. 28. —

ταύτης τῆς πράξεως ἀδεεστέρα ἡ κάθοδος. ἀπῆλθον 2
δὲ καὶ οἱ ἐν ταῖς εἴκοσι ναυσὶν Ἀθηναῖοι ἐς Ναύπακτον.
Ἀκαρνᾶνες δὲ καὶ Ἀμφίλοχοι ἀπελθόντων Ἀθηναίων καὶ
10 Δημοσθένους τοῖς ὡς Σαλύνθιον καὶ Ἀγραίους καταφυ-
γοῦσιν Ἀμπρακιώταις καὶ Πελοποννησίοις ἀναχώρησιν
ἐσπείσαντο ἐξ Οἰνιαδῶν οἷπερ καὶ μετανέστησαν παρὰ
Σαλυνθίου. καὶ ἐς τὸν ἔπειτα χρόνον σπονδὰς καὶ ξυμ- 3
μαχίαν ἐποιήσαντο ἑκατὸν ἔτη Ἀκαρνᾶνες καὶ Ἀμφίλοχοι

7. **ταύτης τῆς πράξεως**: πρᾶξις, in Thuc. only here and vi. 88. 57. On πράξεις in the interpolated passage i. 39. § 3, see App. on i. 39. 15. The reference is to the brilliant repulse of the Ambracian-Peloponnesian attack upon Acarnania and Amphilochia. — **ἀδεεστέρα**: *with less apprehension*. Cf. c. 98. 26 Δημοσθένης περὶ Ναύπακτον καὶ τὰ χωρία ταῦτα ὑπελείφθη, τοῖς πεπραγμένοις φοβούμενος τοὺς Ἀθηναίους. The expression ἀδεεστέρα, however, does not necessarily prove that the Aetolian disaster had no unpleasant consequences for Demosthenes. To it may have been due the fact that the next summer Demosthenes was ἰδιώτης (iv. 2. 14). Indeed, if one take literally the words in iv. 2. 14 Δημοσθένει ὄντι ἰδιώτῃ μετὰ τὴν ἀναχώρησιν τὴν ἐξ Ἀκαρνανίας, and add the fact that, acc. to Arist. Ἀθ. πολ. 44 (p. 116 Kenyon), the election of στρατηγοί took place at earliest in the seventh prytany of the year, the inference seems possible that Demosthenes was not left in office even till the usual time of change of στρατηγοί. For since the Amphilochian campaign began early in the winter (cf. c. 102. § 7; 105. § 1) and was of short duration, the return of Demosthenes to Athens must have occurred before mid-winter.

8. **οἱ ἐν ταῖς εἴκοσι ναυσὶν Ἀθηναῖοι**: cf. c. 105. 15; 107. 3; 112. 25. — 10. **τοῖς ὡς Σαλύνθιον κτέ.**: cf. c. 111. 18; 113. 2. — 11. **ἀναχώρησιν**... **παρὰ Σαλυνθίου**: ἀναχώρησιν ἐσπείσαντο, as in c. 109. 10. They now obtained by treaty an unmolested departure by sea. They had already succeeded in reaching, prob. through Aetolian territory, the friendly Oeniadae (c. 7. 11; 94. 7; ii. 102. 10), hoping to be able to embark there. This is the meaning of the passage as happily emended by G. Hermann, οἷπερ (for οὕπερ of the Mss.) καὶ μετανέστησαν παρὰ Σαλυνθίου (Σαλύνθιον, Mss.), *whither they had withdrawn from Salynthius*. καί, as in c. 86. 6; 98. 18. Oberhummer, *Akarnanien*, p. 112, conjectures ἐπ' Οἰνιαδῶν, but does not explain why the Ambraciots should have withdrawn, not home, but to Oeniadae. In ii. 82, which he cites, the situation was quite different, for then there was no difficulty about the withdrawal of the Peloponnesians by sea, since two Peloponnesian fleets were not far from Oeniadae.

14. **ἑκατὸν ἔτη**: without ἐς, as v.

15 πρὸς Ἀμπρακιώτας ἐπὶ τοῖσδε, ὥστε μήτε Ἀμπρακιώτας
μετὰ Ἀκαρνάνων στρατεύειν ἐπὶ Πελοποννησίους μήτε
Ἀκαρνᾶνας μετὰ Ἀμπρακιωτῶν ἐπ' Ἀθηναίους, βοηθεῖν
δὲ τῇ ἀλλήλων, καὶ ἀποδοῦναι Ἀμπρακιώτας ὁπόσα ἢ
χωρία ἢ ὁμήρους Ἀμφιλόχων ἔχουσι, καὶ ἐπὶ Ἀνακτόριον
20 μὴ βοηθεῖν πολέμιον ὂν Ἀκαρνᾶσι. ταῦτα ξυνθέμενοι 4
διέλυσαν τὸν πόλεμον. μετὰ δὲ ταῦτα Κορίνθιοι φυλακὴν ἑαυτῶν ἐς τὴν Ἀμπρακίαν ἀπέστειλαν ἐς τριακοσίους

47. 1. *Cf.* iv. 21. 17 σπονδὰς ποιήσασθαι ὁπόσον ἂν δοκῇ χρόνον ἀμφοτέροις, and ii. 73. 1; vi. 7. 8; iv. 114. 8. — 15. ἐπὶ τοῖσδε: in ii. 70. 13 and Hdt. vi. 108. 25 ἐπὶ τοῖσδε is followed by the inf. without ὥστε, in viii. 18. 1 by the inv. The combination with ὥστε is unusual. *Cf.* Hdt. v. 65. 11 ἐπ' οἷσι... ὥστε, vii. 154. 18 ἐπὶ τοισίδε ... ἐπ' ᾧ. The conditions are those of a defensive alliance, ἐπιμαχία, as in i. 44. 8; v. 48. 8, and were evidently due to the treaties existing between the Ambraciots and Spartans and between the Acarnanians and Athenians. — 16. μετὰ Ἀκαρνάνων, Ἀκαρνᾶνας: without mention of the Amphilochians, which the author seems to have considered superfluous after the words Ἀκαρνᾶνες καὶ Ἀμφίλοχοι πρὸς Ἀμπρακιώτας (14). Besides, the Acarnanians were unquestionably the main force. *Cf.* c. 112. 31, and see on c. 1. 1; ii. 13. 1. — στρατεύειν: as opp. to βοηθεῖν, of the offensive, as rightly recognized by X. in *Philol. Anz.* xiii. p. 303. *Cf.* v. 48. 8 ἀλλήλοις βοηθεῖν, ξυνεπιστρατεύειν δὲ μηδενί, and v. 47. 42 στρατεύεσθαι. — 18. βοηθεῖν τῇ ἀλλήλων: sc. γῇ, as in i. 44. 8. X. (*l.c.*) would supply, "against the Peloponnesians, or the Athenians, as the case might be." Steup, who thinks the idea is, "under all circumstances," suggests that καὶ πάντως (*cf.* v. 41. 19; vi. 20. 1) has dropped out before the following καί. The sense is doubtless as Steup suggests, but it seems unnecessary to suppose that anything has been lost. — 19. ὁμήρους: the reading adopted since Bk. for the meaningless ὁμόρους of most of the Mss. These are included in the ὁπόσα, the hostages being one of the means whereby the Amphilochians ὑπὸ Ἀμπρακιωτῶν βίᾳ κατείχοντο, c. 107. 9. — ἐπὶ Ἀνακτόριον μὴ βοηθεῖν: *not to come to the aid of Anactorium.* See on c. 97. 14. — Ἀνακτόριον: *cf.* i. 55. 2; ii. 9. 9; 80. 18, 24; 81. 12; iv. 49. 2.

21. διέλυσαν τὸν πόλεμον: also viii. 46. 2. — Κορίνθιοι ... ἀπέστειλαν: Corinth was the 'mother-city' of Ambracia (*cf.* ii. 80. 15 ξυμπροθυμούμενοι μάλιστα τοῖς Ἀμπρακιώταις ἀποίκοις οὖσι). The precaution was taken doubtless because Ambracia was so much weakened. See on c. 113. 26. — φυλακήν: i.e. as a garrison. — 22. ἑαυτῶν: i.e. of their own citizens, as in i. 26. 4; 61. 3; 64. 9. — ἐς τριακοσίους

ὁπλίτας καὶ Ξενοκλείδαν τὸν Εὐθυκλέους ἄρχοντα · οἳ κομιζόμενοι χαλεπῶς διὰ τῆς ἠπείρου ἀφίκοντο.

115 Τὰ μὲν κατ' Ἀμπρακίαν οὕτως ἐγένετο · οἱ δ' ἐν τῇ Σικελίᾳ Ἀθηναῖοι τοῦ αὐτοῦ χειμῶνος ἔς τε τὴν Ἱμεραίαν ἀπόβασιν ἐποιήσαντο ἐκ τῶν νεῶν μετὰ τῶν Σικελῶν ἄνωθεν ἐσβεβληκότων ἐς τὰ ἔσχατα τῆς Ἱμεραίας, καὶ
5 ἐπὶ τὰς Αἰόλου νήσους ἔπλευσαν. ἀναχωρήσαντες δὲ ἐς 2 Ῥήγιον Πυθόδωρον τὸν Ἰσολόχου, Ἀθηναίων στρατηγόν,

ὁπλίτας: for the prepositional phrase representing an acc., see on c. 20. 11; 111. 17. — 23. Ξενοκλείδαν: Doric form. Without doubt the στρατηγός of i. 46. 7. — 24. κομιζόμενοι χαλεπῶς: i.e. by a difficult march. — 25. τὰ μὲν κατ' Ἀμπρακίαν οὕτως ἐγένετο: conclusion of the account of the fortunes of Ambracia, which have been carefully followed since ii. 68. § 1. The formula is similar to that with regard to Lesbos c. 50. 15, and Plataea, c. 68. 31. τὰ μέν without καί, as in c. 50. 15.

115. *New enterprises of the Athenians in Sicily. Their strategus Pythodorus is defeated by the Locrians.*

1. οἱ ἐν τῇ Σικελίᾳ Ἀθηναῖοι: resumes the narrative interrupted at c. 103. § 3. — 2. τὴν Ἱμεραίαν: the Himeraean territory, ἥπερ μόνη ἐν τούτῳ τῷ μέρει τῆς Σικελίας Ἑλλὰς πόλις ἐστί, vi. 62. 9 (cf. vi. 5. § 1). — 3. μετὰ τῶν Σικελῶν: Bl.'s conjecture Σικελῶν, for Σικελιωτῶν of the Mss., is adopted by most recent editors. The expression ἄνωθεν ἐσβεβληκότων suits much better the Σικελοί, who lived in the interior (vi. 88. 22), than the more distant Σικελιῶται. Besides, since part of the Siceliots held with the Syracusans

(c. 86. § 2), those that were allied with Athens could not properly be designated simply as οἱ Σικελιῶται. Only a part, it is true, of the Sicels were allied to Athens (c. 103. § 1), but it was the greater part (vii. 57. 61), and in iv. 25. 31 these allies are called simply οἱ Σικελοί. In this last place, too, ὑπὲρ τῶν ἄκρων is doubtless, as St. says, to be compared with ἄνωθεν here. Furthermore, it is not likely that the Siceliot allies of Athens, of whom it is said, l. 9, τῆς μὲν γὰρ γῆς αὐτῶν οἱ Συρακόσιοι ἐκράτουν, would have made this long march across the island at the risk of having their retreat cut off. In vii. 57. 61, the same mistake of Σικελιωτῶν for Σικελῶν, though found in all the Mss. except three, has been corrected by all recent editors. See App. — **4.** ἄνωθεν: *from the interior. Cf.* i. 59. 8; ii. 99. 16. — ἐς τὰ ἔσχατα τῆς Ἱμεραίας: *i.e.* toward the interior. *Cf.* c. 106. 8 Μεδεῶνος παρ' ἔσχατα, Tac. *Ann.* iv. 74 imperii extrema. — **5.** ἐπὶ τὰς Αἰόλου νήσους: as already before, c. 88. 2.

ἐς Ῥήγιον: *cf.* c. 86. 20; 88. 13. — **6.** Πυθόδωρον: this man, whose generalship in Sicily is mentioned also

καταλαμβάνουσιν ἐπὶ τὰς ναῦς διάδοχον ὧν ὁ Λάχης ἦρχεν. οἱ γὰρ ἐν Σικελίᾳ ξύμμαχοι πλεύσαντες ἔπεισαν 3 τοὺς Ἀθηναίους βοηθεῖν σφίσι πλείοσι ναυσί· τῆς μὲν γὰρ γῆς αὐτῶν οἱ Συρακόσιοι ἐκράτουν, τῆς δὲ θαλάσσης ὀλίγαις ναυσὶν εἰργόμενοι παρεσκευάζοντο ναυτικὸν ξυναγείροντες ὡς οὐ περιοψόμενοι. καὶ ἐπλήρουν ναῦς τεσσα- 4 ράκοντα οἱ Ἀθηναῖοι ὡς ἀποστελοῦντες αὐτοῖς, ἅμα μὲν ἡγούμενοι θᾶσσον τὸν ἐκεῖ πόλεμον καταλυθήσεσθαι, ἅμα

in iv. 2. 7; 65. 11, is perhaps the same as the archon mentioned in ii. 2. 5. See also on vi. 105. 12. — **7. ἐπὶ τὰς ναῦς διάδοχον**: taken together as pred. to καταλαμβάνουσιν, which in the sense *find, discover*, usually takes the supplementary partic. (but see on c. 69. 5), and indeed always in the pres. or pf., never aor. (see on i. 59. 3). But here the idea of transition implied in διάδοχον supplies the place of the partic. ἥκοντα (which v. H. thinks has dropped out) or ἐπεληλυθότα (cf. c. 69. 8); and so is explained also ἐπί with the acc., for which St. compares Xen. *Hell.* iii. 4. 20 τούτων Ξενοκλέα μὲν καὶ ἄλλον ἔταξεν ἐπὶ τοὺς ἱππεῖς, and *Cyr.* iv. 5. 58. — **ὁ Λάχης**: see on c. 86. 2. He seems to have been recalled on some charge, prob. of embezzlement, as Bl. shows from Ar. *Vesp.* 240 and the Schol. thereon.

8. οἱ ἐν Σικελίᾳ ξύμμαχοι: i.e. the Hellenic allies of Athens (cf. c. 86. §2; 90. §4). — **πλεύσαντες ἔπεισαν**: these aors., including ἀπέστειλαν in l. 16, give, as in c. 33. 2; ii. 2. 11, the supplementary explanation for the arrival of the new strategus, who was to be followed by two others. "The allies in Sicily *had sent* an embassy to Athens (πλεύσαντες), and there had obtained the promise of more effective assistance (ἔπεισαν τοὺς Ἀθηναίους βοηθεῖν σφίσι πλείοσι ναυσίν." Hude's conjecture (*Comm. Crit.* p. 118) πέμψαντες for πλεύσαντες seems unnecessary. — **9. τῆς μὲν γὰρ γῆς ... ἐκράτουν**: just as before the interference of the Athenians in the conflicts of the Siceliots (c. 86. 14). For τῆς γῆς κρατεῖν, see on c. 85. 13. — **10. τῆς δὲ θαλάσσης κτέ.**: at sea the situation had indeed become quite different from that before the appearance of the Athenians, when the Leontines and their allies were excluded by the Syracusans also from the sea (c. 86. 15); but with the small number of Athenian ships it was to be feared that the Syracusans might, with the preparations they were making, be able to face their opponents even at sea with prospect of success. — **τῆς θαλάσσης ... εἰργόμενοι**: cf. ii. 85. 4 ὑπ᾿ ὀλίγων νεῶν εἴργεσθαι τῆς θαλάσσης, and see on c. 6. 7; 86. 15; i. 141. 16. — **12. ὡς οὐ περιοψόμενοι**: sc. εἰργέσθαι.

καὶ ἐπλήρουν: *and they were manning*. The impf. because the preparation continued beyond the appear-

15 δὲ βουλόμενοι μελέτην τοῦ ναυτικοῦ ποιεῖσθαι. τὸν μὲν 5 οὖν ἕνα τῶν στρατηγῶν ἀπέστειλαν Πυθόδωρον ὀλίγαις ναυσί, Σοφοκλέα δὲ τὸν Σωστρατίδου καὶ Εὐρυμέδοντα τὸν Θουκλέους ἐπὶ τῶν πλειόνων νεῶν ἀποπέμψειν ἔμελλον. ὁ δὲ Πυθόδωρος ἤδη ἔχων τὴν τοῦ Λάχητος τῶν 6
20 νεῶν ἀρχὴν ἔπλευσε τελευτῶντος τοῦ χειμῶνος ἐπὶ τὸ Λοκρῶν φρούριον ὃ πρότερον Λάχης εἷλε· καὶ νικηθεὶς μάχῃ ὑπὸ τῶν Λοκρῶν ἀνεχώρησεν.

116 Ἐρρύη δὲ * περὶ αὐτὸ τὸ ἔαρ τοῦτο ὁ ῥύαξ τοῦ πυ- 1 ρὸς ἐκ τῆς Αἴτνης, ὥσπερ καὶ τὸ πρότερον. καὶ γῆν

ance of Pythodorus in Sicily. — 15. μελέτην... ποιεῖσθαι: cf. i. 18.33.—
16. ἀπέστειλαν; this very winter; the other two follow in the spring. Cf. iv. 2. § 2. — 17. Σοφοκλέα: Roscher conjectures (Leben des Thuk. p. 416) that he was the Sophocles who was afterwards one of the Thirty Tyrants. — Εὐρυμέδοντα: see on c. 80. 10.
19. ἤδη ἔχων: sc. after the ships had returned from the Aeolus islands. — τὴν τοῦ Λάχητος τῶν νεῶν ἀρχήν: subj. and obj. gen. both in attrib. position, whereas the obj. gen. is placed after its noun in c. 12. 10; i. 25.21; vii. 34. 25. v. II.'s bracketing of τῶν νεῶν· is the less to be approved, since in c. 90. 8 it is remarked, concerning the position of Laches after the death of Charoeades, ἅπασαν ἔχων τῶν νεῶν τὴν ἀρχήν. — 21. ὁ Λάχης εἷλε: cf. c. 99. 4; the fort on the Halex, which must therefore meanwhile have been recaptured by the Locrians. — 22. ἀνεχώρησεν: sc. ἐς Ῥήγιον. Cf. l. 5.
116. *Eruption of Aetna.*
1. περὶ αὐτὸ τὸ ἔαρ τοῦτο: "just at the beginning of this spring."

τοῦτο refers to the words τελευτῶντος τοῦ χειμῶνος, c. 115. 20, in which there is a hint of the nearness of spring. On this, as well as the relation of the present passage to ταῦτα μὲν κατὰ τὸν χειμῶνα τοῦτον ἐγένετο (l. 7), see App. on ii. 2. 7. The eruption began doubtless in the last days of winter and extended a little beyond the commencement of spring, i.e. into the summer, as Thuc. uses the term. — ὁ ῥύαξ: used esp., as τὸ ῥεῦμα l. 6, of volcanic eruptions, with and without τοῦ πυρός. Cf. Plato *Phaedo* 111 e; Lycurg. c. *Leocr.* 95; Arist. *de Ause. Mirab.* 38 τὸν δ' ἐν τῇ Αἴτνῃ ῥύακα οὔτε φλογώδη φασὶν οὔτε συνεχῆ, ἀλλὰ διὰ πολλῶν ἐτῶν γίνεσθαι, 40 τὸ ἐν Σικελίᾳ περὶ τὸν ῥύακα γινόμενον. 'The art. is used because the "fire-flood" was a well known phenomenon peculiar to Aetna. So App. *B. C.* v. 117 ἐμπεσεῖσθαι σφίσι καὶ τὸν ῥύακα, and Strabo vi. 2. 3.' Arn. See Kr. *Spr.* 47, 8, 5. — 2. ὥσπερ καὶ τὸ πρότερον: Unger, N. *Jahrbb.* cxli. p. 183, understands the meaning to be, that the two eruptions occurred in the same season of the year. But the τοῦτο added

τινα ἔφθειρε τῶν Καταναίων, οἳ ἐπὶ τῇ Αἴτνῃ τῷ ὄρει
οἰκοῦσιν, ὅπερ μέγιστόν ἐστιν ὄρος ἐν τῇ Σικελίᾳ. λέγε- 2
ται δὲ πεντηκοστῷ ἔτει ῥυῆναι τοῦτο μετὰ τὸ πρότερον

to περὶ αὐτὸ τὸ ἔαρ is against this explanation. Besides, it is incredible that Thuc., who acc. to what follows did not venture a definite statement even with regard to the year of the preceding eruption, should have distinctly designated the season of the year. In ὥσπερ καὶ τὸ πρότερον, as also before (cf. ii. 72. 9 ἅπερ καὶ τὸ πρότερον ἤδη προυκαλεσάμεθα), Thuc. seems to have intended to indicate only that the eruption of 425 B.C. was not the first. This he regards as certain, whereas he does not vouch (λέγεται, l. 4) for the correctness of the statement, that since the Hellenic settlement of Sicily, in all *three* eruptions had occurred, nor for that of his authority as to the interval between the eruption of 425 B.C. and the preceding.—3. ἐπὶ τῇ Αἴτνῃ: near *Aetna*. Cf. c. 89. 12; i. 105. 3, 6; ii. 32. 3; 86. 11; iv. 101. 20; v. 14. 5. The reading of Laur. ὑπὸ τῇ Αἴτνῃ is certainly a gloss. — τῷ ὄρει: considered an interpolation by Cobet, v. ll., and Kallenberg (*Studien über d. griech. Artikel*, ii. p. 21). But the repetition of ὄρος in the following rel. clause should not give offence, since Thuc. is by no means careful to avoid the repetition of a word after a short interval (e.g. cf. ῥυῆναι, l. 5, and ῥεῦμα twice in l. 6). Nor can much weight be laid upon the circumstance that, allowing with Kallenberg that in viii. 108. 16 διὰ τῆς Ἴδης τοῦ ὄρους the gen. τῆς Ἴδης depends upon τοῦ ὄρους, the present passage is the only one in Thuc. in which τὸ ὄρος follows the name of a mountain likewise connected with the art. For, disregarding Hdt. i. 43. 3 ἐς τὸν Ὄλυμπον τὸ ὄρος, the following passages, Thuc. iv. 96. 28 πρὸς Πάρνηθα τὸ ὄρος, ii. 23. 3 μεταξὺ Πάρνηθος καὶ Βριλησσοῦ ὄρους, ii. 102. 12 ἐκ Πίνδου ὄρους, and esp. c. 79. 11 ἐπὶ τὴν Λευκίμμην τὸ ἀκρωτήριον (cf. i. 47. 7), if considered without bias, are not so essentially different from the present passage that one must object to the latter. And, finally, the transition from the simple τῆς Αἴτνης to τῇ Αἴτνῃ τῷ ὄρει does not seem more remarkable than e.g. the change of expression in ii. 23. 3 μεταξὺ Πάρνηθος καὶ Βριλησσοῦ ὄρους. At any rate, objection could more properly be raised, with Badham, against the remark ὅπερ... Σικελίᾳ, since it is not coupled with the first mention of Aetna. But this too may be due to the lack of revision on the part of the historian. — 5. τοῦτο: the present eruption of 425 B.C. — τὸ πρότερον ῥεῦμα: refers without doubt to the eruption of Aetna mentioned in the *Parian Marble* 52, 67 ff. as contemporaneous with the battle of Plataea. But this is not sufficient reason why πεντηκοστῷ ἔτει, which taken strictly would lead to the year 475 or 474 instead of 479 B.C. should either be considered as a *round number* (see Boeckh in *C. I. G.* ii. p. 339), or changed, acc. to Kr.'s conjecture, into πεντηκοστῷ πέμπτῳ (or

ῥεῦμα, τὸ δὲ ξύμπαν τρὶς γεγενῆσθαι τὸ ῥεῦμα ἀφ' οὗ
Σικελία ὑπὸ Ἑλλήνων οἰκεῖται. ταῦτα μὲν κατὰ τὸν χει- 3
μῶνα τοῦτον ἐγένετο, καὶ ἕκτον ἔτος τῷ πολέμῳ ἐτελεύτα
τῷδε ὃν Θουκυδίδης ξυνέγραψεν.

νέ) ἔτει. For unquestionably Thuc. indicates by λέγεται that he does not vouch for the correctness of the number given by him. The expression λέγεται is also decidedly against the assumption of Büdinger, *Poesie und Urkunde bei Thuk.* i. p. 39, that Thuc. chose the date πεντηκοστῷ ἔτει with reference to the first Pythian ode of Pindar (474 B.C.), in which, v. 21 ff., an eruption of Aetna is described. At most, Thuc.'s *authority* may have fixed the date by inference from Pindar's ode. — **6. τρὶς γεγενῆσθαι κτέ.**: from his manner of expression it is clear that Thuc. can have had no knowledge, when he wrote this passage, of an eruption of Aetna later than that of 425 B.C. Otherwise he must have expressed himself definitely as to three eruptions, and not with λέγεται τρὶς γεγενῆσθαι τὸ ῥεῦμα, since acc. to l. 2 two eruptions are regarded by him as facts. Evidently, then, Thuc.'s authority must have mentioned, in addition to the πρότερον ῥεῦμα of l. 5, a still earlier eruption. See Ullrich, *Beitr.* p. 92 f., and Introd. to Book I. p. 18, N. 38. Another eruption is said by Diod. xiv. 59 and Orosius ii. 18 to have occurred in the year 396. Thuc., therefore, must have either died before 396, or never revised this passage. — **ἀφ' οὗ ... οἰκεῖται**: *i.e.* from about the middle of the 8th century B.C. See on vi. 3. 1. — **7. ταῦτα μὲν ... ἐγένετο, καὶ ... ξυνέγραψεν**: *cf.* the similar conclusion of ii. 70. 21.

REFERENCES.

For statement concerning Mss., as also for a full list of complete and partial editions, and for information regarding the literature of Thucydides, see the Appendix to Book I., pp. 304-307. For the convenience of the student, especial reference is made here to those editions and auxiliaries which will be found most helpful in the study of Book III.

Editions.

E. F. Poppo: ed. maior, 11 vols., Leipzig, 1821-40.
E. F. Poppo: ed. minor, vol. ii., sect. 1, with notes in Latin. Revised by J. M. Stahl, Leipzig, 1875.
K. W. Krüger: Band I., Heft 2, with notes in German. Revised (3rd ed.) by W. Pökel, Leipzig, 1885.
G. Boehme: Band I., Heft 2, with brief notes in German. Revised (4th ed.) by S. Widmann, Leipzig, 1885.
S. T. Bloomfield: vol. i., with notes in English and maps. London, 1842-3. Especially full in citation of parallel passages from other authors.
Thomas Arnold: vol. i., with notes in English, appendices, and maps. 8th ed., London and Oxford, 1874.
F. Goeller: vol. i., with notes in Latin, indices, chronological tables, and maps. Leipzig, 1836.
G. A. Simcox: Books III. and IV., with notes in English. London, 1875.
J. M. Stahl: ed. stereotypa, vol. i. Text, with Latin introduction and adnotatio critica. Leipzig, 1873.
H. v. Herwerden: vol. ii. Text, with critical notes in Latin. Utrecht, 1878.

Auxiliaries.

J. D. Heilmann: *Thucydides Geschichte übersetzt und erläutert*, 1760 (1824).
S. T. Bloomfield: *Thucydides translated into English.* (3 vols., with copious annotations.) Vol. i. London, 1829.
G. Boehme: *Thucydides ins Deutsche übersetzt.* Leipzig, 1854.
R. Crawley: *Thucydides translated into English.* London, 1876.
B. Jowett: *Thucydides translated into English.* With introduction, marginal analysis, notes, and indices. Oxford, 1881. (Vol. i. translation, vol. ii. notes.) This is the best translation, and the notes are of great value.
H. M. Wilkins: *Speeches from Thucydides translated into English.* London, 1873.
Jebb: *The Speeches of Thucydides.* In 'Hellenica,' edited by E. Abbott, p. 266-323. London, 1880.

REFERENCES.

Sheppard and Evans: *Notes* (original and compiled) *on Books I., II., and III.*, without text. London, 1876.
E. A. Betant: *Lexicon Thucydideum*, 2 vols. Full treatment, except of particles, prepositions, and pronouns. Geneva, 1843–47. (Out of print.)
v. Essen: *Index Thucydideus*. Thoroughly reliable and, for exact study, indispensable. Berlin, 1887.
K. Bursian: *Geographie von Griechenland*. 2 Bände. Leipzig, 1862–72.
H. Diener: *De Sermone Thucydidis quatenus cum Herodoto congruens differat a scriptoribus Atticis*. Lipsiae, 1889.
M. Büdinger: *Poesie und Urkunde bei Thukydides*. 2 Teile. Wien, 1890–91.

Of other works which merit especial notice for the construction or elucidation of the text, the following deserve mention, in addition to those named in the Appendix to Book I.:

Haase: *Lucubrationes Thucydideae*. Berlin, 1841.
J. M. Stahl: *Quaestiones Grammaticae* (2nd ed.). Leipzig, 1886.
Meisterhans: *Grammatik der Attischen Inschriften*.[2] Berlin, 1888.
L. Herbst: *Ueber Cobets Emendationen im Thukydides*, 1859, and *Zu Thukydides: Erklärungen und Wiederherstellungen*. Leipzig, 1892–93.
F. Junge: *Zur Rede des Kleon*. 1879.
E. Lange: *Kleon bei Thukydides*. Köln, 1886.
Müller-Strübing: *Thukydideische Forschungen*. Wien, 1881. Also on the *Siege of Plataea*, and Κερκυραικά, in N. Jahrbb. f. Philologie, 1885 and 1886.
K. Hude: *Commentarii Critici ad Thucydidem pertinentes*. Copenhagen, 1888.
W. Herbst: *Der Abfall Mytilenes von Athen*. Köln, 1861.
B. Schmidt: *Korkyraeische Studien*. Leipzig, 1890.
J. Partsch: *Die Insel Korfu*, and *Die Insel Leucas* (Petermanns Mitteilungen, Ergänzungshefte 88, 95).
E. Oberhummer: *Akarnanien im Alterthum*.

Numerous references to other critical treatises or articles will be found in the notes under the text or in the Appendix.

APPENDIX.

3. 25. τά τε ἄλλα τῶν τειχῶν καὶ λιμένων (Vat. καὶ τῶν λιμένων) περὶ τὰ ἡμιτέλεστα φραξάμενοι ἐφύλασσον. Steup's critical note is as follows: The peculiarity of Haacke's explanation consists in this, that 1) τὰ ἄλλα = praeterea etiam; 2) τῶν τειχῶν καὶ λιμένων depends on τὰ ἡμιτέλεστα, and τὰ ἡμιτέλεστα τῶν τειχῶν καὶ λιμένων is understood not of a part of the fortifications (so that complete and incomplete parts would be distinguished), but of these fortifications in general; 3) ἐφύλασσον means "kept watch," and with it is construed περὶ τὰ ἡμιτέλεστα τῶν τειχῶν καὶ λιμένων, while with φραξάμενοι is supplied as object αὐτά (i.e. τὰ ἡμιτέλεστα τῶν τειχῶν καὶ λιμένων). For the adv. use of τὰ ἄλλα, Stahl rightly compares iv. 55. 6; vi. 31. 24; viii. 86. 32. Haacke's suggestion, that τὰ ἡμιτέλεστα τῶν τειχῶν καὶ λιμένων refers to the fortifications as a whole (cf. c. 2. 5 τῶν λιμένων τὴν χῶσιν καὶ τειχῶν οἰκοδόμησιν . . . ἐπέμενον τελεσθῆναι), has been urged with especial emphasis by Hude, *Commentarii Critici ad Thuc. pertinentes* (1888), p. 90 sq. φυλάσσειν, meaning *keep watch*, occurs also ii. 13. 43; 24. 3; vii. 17. 5; 53. 7; 70. 3. Bauer's conjecture, τῶν τειχῶν καὶ λιμένων πέρι, approved by Haase (*Lucubr.* p. 48 sq.), Cl., and others, only renders the const. of the passage more difficult; nor would the sent. gain by Meineke's proposal πέριξ. The change, too, suggested by Steup (*Qu. Thuc.* p. 35 sqq.), of ἐφύλασσον to ἐφυλάσσοντο, now seems unnecessary.

4. 15. ἀποστέλλουσι . . ., οἳ ὥρμουν ἐν τῇ Μαλέᾳ πρὸς βορέαν τῆς πόλεως. A. Conze (*Reise auf der Insel Lesbos*, p. 7), H. Lolling (in R. Koldewey's *die antiken Baureste der Insel Lesbos*, p. 14 f.), and others, have rightly recognized that ἡ Μαλέα, mentioned here and c. 6. 12, cannot be the southeastern promontory of Lesbos, which in Strabo, p. 616 f., has the name Μαλία. This promontory was, according to Strabo, seventy stades distant from Mytilene, whereas in c. 6. 8 (τῆς δὲ γῆς τῆς μὲν ἄλλης ἐκράτουν οἱ Μυτιληναῖοι . . ., τὸ δὲ περὶ τὰ στρατόπεδα οὐ πολὺ κατεῖχον οἱ 'Αθηναῖοι, ναύσταθμον δὲ μᾶλλον ἦν αὐτοῖς πλοίων καὶ ἀγορᾶς ἡ Μαλέα) it is not possible that ἡ Μαλέα can refer to a point on the coast of Lesbos so far removed from Mytilene. For the two camps of the Athenians (c. 6. 5 ἐτείχισαν στρατόπεδα δύο) were without doubt quite close to Mytilene. How, then, could a place seventy stades distant from the city be included in τὸ περὶ τὰ στρατόπεδα οὐ πολύ, — all the land that the Athenians had under control? In c. 4, therefore, the reference could be to the southeastern promontory only in case one should, with Hünnekes (*Kl. Beitr. etc.* p. 37), Stahl, and Cl.[2]. construe πρὸς βορέαν τῆς πόλεως, not with the rel. sent., but with the preceding. But this construction, of which even Plehn had thought (*Lesbiaca*, p. 18), is incompatible with the position of the words, whether πρὸς βορέαν τῆς πόλεως be construed with ἀποστέλλουσι — as hitherto all the supporters of this view have construed — or with λαθόντες. Besides, the trireme sent to Sparta would not by a northern course have got so soon into the open sea (*cf.* l. 20 ταλαιπώρως διὰ τοῦ πελάγους κομισθέντες), and the Athenians, acc. to c. 5. 4, about the same time received reinforcements from the north (from Methymna, Imbros, and Lemnos). Further, only the construction of πρὸς βορέαν τῆς πόλεως with ὥρμουν makes it possible, by a slight change of the vulg., to give to c. 6. 4. (καὶ περιορμισάμενοι τὸ πρὸς νότον τῆς πόλεως ἐτείχισαν στρατόπεδα δύο) a sense which agrees admirably with what Thuc. elsewhere says about the operations of the Athenians against Mytilene, whereas St.'s explanation of this passage is exposed to serious objections (see on c. 6. 4). When St. urges against the assumption of a point on the coast north of Mytilene as the first station of the Athenians, that there the Mytileneans would not have effected by the truce the desired removal of the Athenians, it may be replied, that, on the contrary, it would have been very strange if the Athenian ships had during the truce entirely desisted from watching the city. Not so easily disposed of is the circumstance, that the place north of Mytilene is simply called ἡ Μαλέα, as if there had been no second place of the same or a quite similar name near by; — the Laconian promontory, called Μαλέα in iv. 53. 7; 54. 5; viii. 39. 17, no sensible reader, of course, would think of. It is hardly permissible, in order to get over this difficulty, to assume, with Plehn (*l.c.*) and Swoboda (*Thuk. Quellenstudien*, p. 63 ff.), an error on the part of Thuc. Whether the historian knew Lesbos from personal observation, as L. Herbst, *Philol.* xlii. p. 708, thinks probable, or not, one must certainly hesitate to assume that Thuc. confounded the name of the place north of Mytilene, first occupied by the Athenians, with that of the southeastern promontory of the island, at least so long as similar errors with reference to equally important points of the theatre of war have not been proved against our author. Accordingly, perhaps nothing remains but to conjecture the loss of τῇ before πρὸς βορέαν τῆς πόλεως, or to assume that the similarity of the names of the point north of the city and of the promontory is due to obscurity in the vulgate. The southeastern promontory is called in Strabo, *l.c.*, and Ar. *Ran.* 33 Μαλία, in Xen. *Hell.* i. 6. 26 Μαλέα, in Ptolem. v. 2. 29 Μανία. If the last form might be deemed correct, the names would be so different that there would be no danger of confusing the two. Or it may be that the vulg., as Kr. conjectured for the present passage, is corrupt, though his conjectures for τῇ Μαλέᾳ, namely τῷ Μαλόεντι and τῇ παραλίᾳ, manifestly depart too far from the Mss. — L. Herbst, *l.c.*, thinks the Malea of Thuc. is the small island on which "the old Mytilene" was situated, but which at the time of the Peloponnesian war was no longer a part of the city. It is strange that Herbst has herein neglected the fact that Strabo (p. 617) and other late writers (see Conze, *ibid.* p. 6) consider the island a part of Mytilene. But close attention to the statements of Thuc. alone shows Herbst's view to be inadmissible. The Athenian fleet anchored, acc. to c. 4. 17, at Malea during the truce, the first camp of the Athenians was, acc. to c. 5. § 2, accessible by land from Mytilene, and Malea is called in c. 6. 11 the ναύσταθμον πλοίων καί ἀγορᾶς of the Athenians — who would not conclude from such data, that Malea was a point on the coast and not an island. Further, the words of c. 4. 17 οἱ ὥρμουν ἐν τῇ Μαλέᾳ πρὸς βορέαν τῆς πόλεως necessarily presuppose a place only north of the city, whereas the island extended from north to south eastward of the newer portion of the city. — In the inscription of Mytilene given by E. Fabricius, *Mitt. d. dtsch. arch. Inst. in Athen* ix. p. 88 ff. and R. Meister, *Studia Nicol.* p. 3 sqq. (= Hoffmann, *Griech. Dialekte* ii. 90), occur the expressions ἐν Μαλόεντι and ἐμ Μαλείᾳ, but unfortunately no explanation is given as to the site of these places.

6. 4. περιορμισάμενοι τὸ πρὸς νότον τῆς πόλεως κτέ. Stahl objects to the view adopted in the text that it would require ἐπὶ τὸ πρὸς νότον, comparing Dem. li. 4 ὅς ἂν μὴ πρὸ τῆς ἕνης καὶ νέας ἐπὶ χῶμα τὴν ναῦν περιορμίσῃ. He assumes that the Athenians had on their advance first blockaded the southern part of the city, so as not to be hindered by the hostile fleet in those works with which they were about to proceed. To which Steup replies, that in that case Thuc. must certainly have stated in how far the blockading of the southern part of the city could have protected also the works to be prosecuted in the north against the hostile fleet. He thinks it must be doubted, too, whether such a thing was possible. At any rate, it by no means follows from Strabo's remark concerning the southern harbour (p. 617 c), ὁ νότιος κλειστὸς τριηρικὸς (Mss. τριήρει καὶ ἐν) ναυσὶ πεντήκοντα, that triremes had no exit also from the northern harbour. For the triremes drew less water than merchantmen (see E. Assmann in Baumeister's *Denkmäler*, *s.v. Seewesen*, p. 1623); besides, Strabo *l.c.* says, ὁ δὲ βόρειος μέγας καὶ βαθύς, χώματι σκεπαζόμενος.

6. 5. ἐτείχισαν στρατόπεδα δύο ἑκατέρωθεν τῆς πόλεως. Steup thinks that these words, acc. to the analogy of c. 22. 17 ἐξ ἐφ' ἑκάτερον τῶν πύργων and Xen. *Cyrop.* viii. 3. 19 παρείποντο αὐτῷ τρεῖς ἑκατέρωθεν τοῦ ἅρματος, would mean that in all there were, not two, but four camps, and therefore, since Thuc. evidently meant to speak here of only two camps, that the words ἑκατέρωθεν τῆς πόλεως, ' which are altogether unnecessary and contain in τῆς πόλεως a burdensome repetition (see v. II. *Stud. Thuc.* p. 38),' are prob. interpolated. Stahl, following Va., omits τῆς πόλεως.

7. 2. καὶ περὶ Πελοπόννησον. The prep. περί, found in Monac. and (acc. to Hude) Laur., and first advocated by v. II. *Stud. Thuc.* p. 143, Steup thinks necessary, for, as the subsequent narrative shows, the real goal of Asopius was not Peloponnesus but Naupactus. *Cf.* c. 3. 10, where Thuc. says of the forty ships which were sent to Lesbos, but upon the same or a like errand as that of the thirty ships, ἔτυχον περὶ Πελοπόννησον παρεσκευασμέναι πλεῖν. v. II. perhaps rightly conjectures that ἐς, which most Mss. have, was arbitrarily inserted to restore connexion after the loss of περί.

10. 3. εἰδότες οὔτε φιλίαν ἰδιώταις βέβαιον γιγνομένην οὔτε κοινωνίαν πόλεσιν ἐς οὐδέν, εἰ μὴ μετ' ἀρετῆς δοκούσης ἐς ἀλλήλους γίγνοιντο καὶ τἆλλα ὁμοιό-

τρόποι εἶεν. The sense which Cl. gives to γίγνοιντο seems, as Bm. says, doubtful, if not impossible. Kr., Bm., and Jow. supply φιλία καὶ κοινωνία as subj., though of course understanding ἰδιῶται καὶ πόλεις as subj. of εἶεν. Goell. and Bl. supply φίλοι from φιλία. The sent. might be construed as if the main clause had read : εἰδότες ὅτι οὔτε φίλοι ἰδιῶται βέβαιοι γίγνονται οὔτε κοινωνοὶ πόλεις ἐς οὐδέν, in which case the subj. of γίγνοιντο would be φίλοι, or φίλοι καὶ κοινωνοί, the proximity of ἐς ἀλλήλους perhaps inducing the personal const. of γίγνοιντο. The sense would then be : " Knowing that neither individuals become secure friends nor states firm allies, unless they become so (*i.e.* φίλοι, or φίλοι καὶ κοινωνοί) in the belief of mutual honesty of purpose, and are otherwise similar in general character."

10. 15. ἐπειγομένους. Ross' and Bk.'s conjecture, which is adopted by Stahl and Cl. (see *N. Jahrbb.* xcvii. p. 112), is preferred also by Haase, Arn., and Bl. — Funkhaenel renders the Ms. reading, ἐπαγομένους, sibi, suum in usum, adducentes, comparing Soph. *Ant.* 361 Ἅιδα μόνον φεῦξιν οὐκ ἐπάξεται, Dem. xix. 259 αὐθαίρετον αὐτοῖς ἐπάγονται δουλείαν. This view is substantially adopted by Kr., Bm., and Sheppard, while Jow. offers the alternative between this interpretation and "themselves actively bringing subjugation (δούλωσις, not δουλεία) on the allies." Bm. cites v. 82. 20 τὴν τῶν Ἀθηναίων ξυμμαχίαν πάλιν προσαγόμενος, as in some measure supporting the vulgate.

11. 4. καὶ πρὸς τὸ πλεῖον ἤδη εἶκον τοῦ ἡμετέρου ἔτι μόνου ἀντισουμένου. Steup follows Hampke, *Stud. zu Thuk.* p. 16 ff., in bracketing these words. Hampke thinks there can be no reason, after it has once been stated that the Athenians associated with the Mytileneans on an equal footing, for emphasizing the *desire* of the Mytileneans for a status that actually existed, nor again for referring in καὶ πρὸς τὸ πλεῖον ἤδη εἶκον once more to the fact that most of the allies had become subjects of Athens. He remarks also that μόνου is inexact, since the Chians also (c. 10. 17) had maintained their independence. Steup objects further to μόνον, 1) as forming no proper antithesis to τὸ πλεῖον, 2) that, strictly taken, it implies more than is said of the Mytileneans in what follows (ἄλλως τε καὶ ὅσῳ δυνατώτεροι αὐτοὶ αὐτῶν ἐγίγνοντο καὶ ἡμεῖς ἐρημότεροι), while it rather strikingly anticipates the later remark. For τὸ ἡμέτερον, in the sense of "we" or "our state," there is, it is claimed, no parallel in Thuc. For these reasons, Steup considers that the words καὶ . . . ἀντισουμένου were prob. originally a marginal explanation of χαλεπώτερον εἰκότως ἔμελλον οἴσειν, and that by their omission the difficulty in the connexion of ἄλλως τε καὶ κτέ. is relieved.

11. 7. τὸ δὲ ἀντίπαλον δέος μόνον πιστὸν ἐς ξυμμαχίαν. Steup brackets δέος on the following grounds : the interpretation adopted in the text would contradict c. 12. § 1, where the Mytileneans emphasize as a *peculiarity* of their alliance with Athens, that it does not, as other alliances, rest upon εὔνοια and φιλία, but upon φόβος and δέος. Nor would this sentence, and that which follows (ὁ γὰρ παραβαίνειν τι βουλόμενος τῷ μὴ προέχων ἂν ἐπελθεῖν ἀποτρέπεται), agree with what is said c. 9. § 2 and 10. § 1 concerning εὔνοια and ἀρετή as bases of a proper alliance. Assuming that δέος crept into the text from a marginal explanation, the whole passage may be compared with c. 9. § 2, where it is intimated that a proper alliance is possible only between those that are ἀντίπαλοι τῇ παρασκευῇ καὶ δυνάμει.

11. 10. ἐς τὴν ἀρχήν. Bracketed by Steup, on Kr.'s suggestion, on the grounds that, since τὰ πράγματα must be understood of the position sought by the Athenians as against the allies, ἐς τὴν ἀρχήν interferes with the thought, and that nowhere else in the speech of the Mytileneans is mention made of the ἀρχή of the Athenians.

11. 13. ἅμα μὲν γὰρ μαρτυρίῳ ἐχρῶντο ... ξυστρατεύειν. Steup objects to the view adopted in the text, that such a condensed form of statement, as must be assumed with the reading ἄκοντας (of all the Mss.), seems to be without parallel in Thuc., and that the passage of Dem. (liv. 32), cited by Hude (*Comm. Crit.* p. 92), οὐδέποτ' ἂν ... τὰ ψευδῆ μαρτυρεῖν ἠθέλησαν, εἰ μὴ ταῦθ' ἑώρων πεπονθότα, is in so far dissimilar, that the speaker by using the expression τὰ ψευδῆ, as well as πρὸς τὸν οὐδ' ἁψάμενον, simply assumes the point of view of his opponent. ἑκόντας (with both Scholiasts), which older commentators read and Cobet prefers (*Mnem. N. S.* viii. p. 125), gives, Steup thinks, the simple and suitable thought, which Kr. sought in vain in the vulgate, "their voluntary participation is proof of the justice of the cause."

11. 23. ἂν ἐδοκοῦμεν δυνηθῆναι. Steup objects to the impf. on the ground, that the Mytileneans, not merely when they determined to revolt, but also at the time of this speech, were convinced that only the outbreak of the great war had secured the continuance of their independence, and that the present was necessary to the proper effect upon the audience. δοκοῦμεν (= οἰόμεθα) would be appropriately followed by παραδείγμασι χρώμενοι τοῖς ἐς τοὺς ἄλλους, "having as examples what happened to others." He thinks, further, that the context requires, not the idea "for a long time (ἐπὶ πολύ), but "for a long time still," and so suggests ἂν ἔτι δοκοῦμεν δυνηθῆναι.

12. 4. ὅ τε τοῖς ἄλλοις μάλιστα εὔνοια [πίστιν] βεβαιοῖ, ἡμῖν τοῦτο ὁ φόβος ἐχυρὸν παρεῖχε. Cl. objects to Kr.'s interpretation, that his expansion does violence to the const., and that the thought is incorrect; since with this view τοῦτο, strictly taken, stands for τὸ πίστιν βεβαιοῦν, or at least for πίστιν. Can it then be said that from the state of mutual suspicion thus described springs πίστις, *trust*, and that this is strengthened by *fear*? The sentiment on which for good or ill the bond depends being indicated above by εὔνοια and δέος, the effect of the two cannot be another sentiment (πίστις), but the actual relation, the alliance. Striking out πίστιν, then, as the gloss of a superficial reader, the federal relation is indicated in the first clause only, it is true, by the prons. ὅ and τοῦτο, but the second clause is so definitely expressed by δέει τε ... ξύμμαχοι ἦμεν that nothing is wanting to a clear comprehension of the passage. Stahl also brackets πίστιν.

Goell. renders the passage: ac quum (ὅ τε, and whereas) aliis benevolentia maxime fidei vinculum sit, id nobis tantum metus praestat. Bl. also renders ὅ τε, and whereas. Arn. translates: "That which in the case of others takes this shape, namely that faith is secured by love, that in our case takes a different form, namely that faith is secured by fear." Reiske and Haacke take πίστιν in appos. to ὅ. Pp. suggests to take πίστιν βεβαιοῖ, quasi pro uno verbo, the expression governing ὅ. Jow. explains: 'ὅ answers to τοῦτο, and is in apposition either with πίστιν, or better, with πίστιν βεβαιοῖ taken as a single word; τοῦτο, sc il. τὸ βεβαιοῦσθαι τὴν πίστιν.' Sheppard queries, 'Might ὅ be taken as acc. after βεβαιοῖ, and πίστιν as its exegesis?' — Entirely different from this passage is that in ii. 40. § 3, where ὅ covers both the following clauses.

12. 12. εἰ γὰρ δυνατοὶ ἦμεν κτέ. Cl. argues that for a correct understanding of the whole passage one must start from the concluding sent., ἐπ' ἐκείνοις δὲ ... τὸ προαμύνασθαι. The antithesis to the actual relation here expressed is the preceding hypothetical sent. Accordingly, there must be in the first sent., answering to ἐπιχειρεῖν, some similar expression, which, as appropriate to the Athenians, is disallowed to the Mytileneans, and this can only be ἀντεπιβουλεῦσαι, not καὶ ἀντεπιβουλεῦσαι καὶ ἀντιμελλῆσαι. The Mytileneans can indeed wait, but as they cannot, like the Athenians, choose the favourable moment to take the offensive (ἀντεπιβουλεῦσαι), neither can they equally with these (ἐκ τοῦ ὁμοίου) delay indefinitely (ἀντιμελλῆσαί τι) the opening of hostilities (ἐπ' ἐκείνους ἰέναι), but they must be allowed to secure themselves by anticipating attack (προαμύνασθαι). — A misconception of the proleptic καὶ before ἀντεπιβουλεῦσαι prob. induced its correlation with καὶ before ἀντιμελλῆσαι, and thereby the reading τί ἔδει, with change of punctuation. The Ms. ἐπ' ἐκείνοις εἶναι might, as Bm., followed by St., suggests, be dispensed with entirely: "So must we, equally with them, have waited (with our plans)." But the thought is still more precise: "Were we, just as they, able to execute our plans, we also might, just as they, postpone hostilities as long as we pleased." ἐπ' ἐκείνους ἰέναι, which has been adopted from Kr., might easily have been corrupted into ἐπ' ἐκείνοις εἶναι through the influence of the following ἐπ' ἐκείνοις ὄντος. Bm. objects to Kr.'s conjecture, that the Mytileneans could not call their revolt an *attack* (which ἐπ' ἐκείνους ἰέναι must mean), but only a defending of themselves by taking measures in advance (προαμύνασθαι), and brackets ἐπ' ἐκείνοις εἶναι. — Most of the good Mss., including Vat., have, not ἀντιμελλῆσαι, but ἀντεπιμελλῆσαι, some ἀντεπιμελῆσαι. The latter, notwithstanding the Schol.'s explanation, τὴν αὐτὴν ἐπιμέλειαν δέξασθαι, is prob. only a slip of the pen. But ἀντεπιμελλῆσαι seems here, in antithesis, not impossible (referring to τὴν ἐκείνων μέλλησιν, to *counter-delay*), esp. as Thuc. shows a certain fondness for compounds in ἀντεπι- (see Ullrich, *Beitr.* i. p. 10). But see, per contra, Stahl, *N. Jahrbb.* xcvii. p. 105. For other explanations and emendations, see Pp. *ed. maior;* Haase, *Lucubr.* p. 84 ; Kaempf, *Qu. Thuc.* p. 11 ; Krohl, *Qu. Thuc.* i. p. 5; Cobet,

Var. Lect. p. 214 and *Mnem. N. S.* viii. p. 126; Herbst, *Gegen Cobet*, p. 28 ff.; Madvig, *Adv.* i. p. 314 f. Stahl, who in the Tauchnitz edition had followed Cl.'s text, has in the second edition of Poppo adopted Bm.'s view and bracketed ἐπ' ἐκείνοις εἶναι. —Steup adds: Rauchenstein, *Philol.* xxxv. p. 577, would bracket τι after ἀντιμελλῆσαι as 'without sense.' But though ἀντιμελλῆσαι alone would suffice, ἀντιμελλῆσαί τι is by no means impossible, if only one supplies as antithesis on the part of the Athenians not μελλῆσαι, as R. does, but μελλῆσαί τι. Against Stahl's remark, that ἐπ' ἐκείνους ἰέναι is opposed not only to the actual situation, but also to the object of the Mytileneans, who claim for themselves τὸ προαμύνασθαι (15), it may be urged that in the apod. of the cond. sent. regard need not be had also to the actual situation and the real object of the Mytileneans. See Ilude, *Comm. Crit.* p. 93.

13. 13. ᾗ καὶ μᾶλλον χρὴ ξυμμάχους δεξαμένους ἡμᾶς διὰ ταχέων βοήθειαν ἀποστέλλειν. It seems strange, Steup thinks, that the subj. of the inf. is indicated only by δεξαμένους. The speakers turn here from the attitude of their own state to the duty of the Lacedaemonians or Peloponnesians. Hence ὑμᾶς was to be expected. Further, it is surprising, that here the sending of help to Lesbos is demanded (βοήθειαν ἀποστέλλειν, *cf.* c. 4. 21 ἔπρασσον ὅπως τις βοήθεια ἥξει), but in l. 19 ff. (ἢν ὑμεῖς ἐν τῷ θέρει τῷδε ναυσί τε καὶ πεζῷ ἅμα ἐπεσβάλητε τὸ δεύτερον), without any transitional remark, a second invasion of Attica. It is also peculiar that in the latter passage Attica is not mentioned. These things can hardly be ascribed to the fault of the historian. In the continuation of the narrative, c. 15. § 1, the admission of the Mytileneans into the Peloponnesian alliance and a second invasion of Attica are treated as the especial demands of the ambassadors (προσδεξάμενοι τοὺς λόγους ξυμμάχους τε τοὺς Λεσβίους ἐποιήσαντο καὶ τὴν ἐς τὴν Ἀττικὴν ἐσβολὴν κτέ.). Is it not likely that Thuc. connected these points in the speech? If the copyist is to blame, it seems necessary to assume a considerable lacuna. Possibly Thuc. wrote somewhat as follows: ᾗ καὶ μᾶλλον χρὴ ξυμμάχους δεξαμένους ἡμᾶς διὰ ταχέων ⟨ὑμᾶς μάλιστα μὲν ἐς τὴν Ἀττικὴν ναυσί τε καὶ πεζῷ ἅμα ἐσβάλλειν, εἰ δὲ μή, ἐς τὴν Λέσβον νεῶν⟩ βοήθειαν ἀποστέλλειν (*cf.* viii. 80. 18 πέμπουσιν ... νεῶν βοήθειαν ... ἐς τὸν Ἑλλήσποντον). By this, or some similar change, all difficulty in the sent. would be removed (*cf.* c. 16. § 3).

15. 4. παροῦσι. Steup thinks that this word has crept into the text from a marginal explanation, urging against its being *attributive* to τοῖς ξυμμάχοις both its position, and that, acc. to c. 8. 3, representatives of all the allies must be assumed as present in Olympia; against its being *appositive* that such reiteration of the presence of the allies would seem strange in a sent., the subj. of which is οἱ δὲ Λακεδαιμόνιοι καὶ οἱ ξύμμαχοι. Against Lupus's explanation, he objects, that as the ξύμμαχοι were to present themselves on the Isthmus (*cf.* l. 6 αὐτοὶ πρῶτοι ἀφίκοντο ... οἱ δὲ ἄλλοι ξύμμαχοι βραδέως ξυνελέγοντο, and c. 16. 11 ὡς αὐτοῖς καὶ οἱ ξύμμαχοι ἅμα οὐ παρῆσαν), Thuc. might have said παρεῖναι ἐς τὸν Ἰσθμόν, but never παροῦσι ... ἰέναι ἐς τὸν Ἰσθμόν.

16. 12. καὶ ἠγγέλλοντο καὶ αἱ περὶ τὴν Πελοπόννησον [τριάκοντα] νῆες τῶν Ἀθηναίων τὴν περιοικίδα αὐτῶν πορθοῦσαι. The following arguments of Steup against the genuineness of τριάκοντα, which have met the approval of Cl., Stahl., and v. H., have been vigorously combated by Müller-Strübing, Thuk. Forsch. p. 109 ff., but without shaking Steup's conviction of the correctness of his position. See also Stahl, Gött. Gel. Anz. 1882, p. 98.

The mention of thirty ships here cannot be reconciled with what is said of these ships in c. 7. § 2 f. and c. 13. § 3 f. In c. 7. 6 the statement is made of the thirty ships with which Asopius was sent round Peloponnesus, καὶ παραπλέουσαι αἱ νῆες τῆς Λακωνικῆς τὰ ἐπιθαλάσσια χωρία ἐπόρθησαν, and the Mytilenean ambassadors at Olympia say of the Athenians, c. 13. 17, νῆές τε αὐτοῖς αἱ μὲν περὶ τὴν ὑμετέραν (i.e. τὴν Λακωνικήν) εἰσίν, αἱ δ' ἐφ' ἡμῖν τετάχαται, that is, according to the former passage, Asopius on his voyage round Peloponnesus ravaged the Laconian coast; according to the latter, at the time of the Olympian festival he was on this coast. Both passages taken together leave no doubt that the thirty ships were ravaging the Laconian coast at the time of the festival. The federal council in Olympia was followed by the return of the Spartan authorities to Sparta, the calling out of the Spartan army, the march to the Isthmus, and finally a stay of the Spartans there for some time until they were induced, by the delay of the allies and news of the ravages of an Athenian fleet on their own coast, to abandon completely their great plans. The ravages announced at this time could not possibly have been committed by the thirty ships of Asopius, for their passage along the Laconian coast (c. 7. 6) could not have lasted so long. Besides, as the Spartans knew of the matter some time before they marched out, how could it have been announced anew so long afterwards, and how could they have laid so much stress on it? Müller-Strübing would, it is true, have περὶ τὴν ὑμετέραν understood in the sense of περὶ τὴν Πελοπόννησον. But not the whole peninsula belonged to the Peloponnesian alliance, nor was there any reason why the Lesbians, to whom among the allies of Sparta the Boeotians stood nearest, should speak only of the states of the alliance within Peloponnesus. Besides, even if περὶ τὴν Πελοπόννησον had been written in c. 13. 18, bearing in mind that there the thirty ships of Asopius are spoken of, it must be accepted that Asopius at the time of the federal council was on the Laconian coast. For, acc. to c. 7. 7, Asopius, after ravaging the Laconian coast, sent back eighteen of his thirty ships; and as to the voyage before reaching this coast Thuc. says nothing of operations of Asopius; so that the news of the departure of the thirty ships could scarcely have got to Olympia before these ships reached the Laconian coast, to say nothing of the fact that the words of the ambassadors περὶ . . . εἰσιν and ἀπ' ἀμφοτέρων ἀποχωρήσονται, which presuppose a certain tarrying, would suit the voyage of the ships up to the Laconian coast.

Besides the contradiction thus found to c. 7. § 2 f. and 13. § 3 f., one cannot see, with the traditional text of c. 16. 12, why (see note in text) the fleet of

Asopius also is not included under μὴ κινοῦντες in c. 16. 3. Just as little as the thirty ships, can, after the removal of τριάκοντα, the twelve ships be thought of, with which Asopius proceeded from the Laconian coast. For what is narrated of these ships in c. 7. § 3 ff. cannot possibly be compressed into so short a period, that the twelve ships could at the time when the Spartans were on the Isthmus have been already again on the Laconian coast. But τριάκοντα being removed, the αἱ περὶ τὴν Πελοπόννησον νῆες τῶν Ἀθηναίων can very well be the 100 ships with which the Athenians, acc. to § 1, παρὰ τὸν Ἰσθμὸν ἀναγαγόντες ἐπίδειξίν τε ἐποιοῦντο καὶ ἀποβάσεις τῆς Πελοποννήσου ᾗ δοκοίη αὐτοῖς. If it is further a fact that the Spartans, although they saw the 100 ships sail southward — in which quarter certainly the points where the ἀποβάσεις of the Athenians were made must be sought — remained quietly on the Isthmus, there is no difficulty in thinking of them as remaining there until they heard of the 100 ships on their own coast. So bold a movement of the Athenians, in the face of the proposed Peloponnesian invasion of Attica, the Spartans had not reckoned upon. Nor are the concluding words of c. 16 ἀνεχώρησαν δὲ καὶ οἱ Ἀθηναῖοι ταῖς ἑκατὸν ναυσίν, ἐπειδὴ καὶ ἐκείνους εἶδον incompatible with the view here taken, as Müller-Strübing thought. The Athenians on the 100 ships need not be the subject of εἶδον. It may be, or rather probably must be, assumed, that the Athenians, after the great fleet had gone southward, caused the movements on the Isthmus to be watched by a few ships. Besides, the sent., if it read, ἀνεχώρησαν δὲ καὶ οἱ ἐν ταῖς ἑκατὸν ναυσὶν Ἀθηναῖοι, ἐπειδὴ κτέ., would contain no serious difficulty. For nothing is in the way of assuming that the Athenians of the 100 ships on the Laconian coast saw the returned Spartan army.

L. Herbst (Philol. xlii. p. 680 f.) urges against Steup's view that αἱ περὶ Πελοπόννησον νῆες in Thuc. means only ships sailing 'beyond, west of Peloponnesus,' whereas the 100 ships had remained 'this side of Peloponnesus, near the Isthmus.' But the groundlessness of Herbst's assertion can be proved from the very examples which he cites in support of it. A comparison of vii. 20. § 1 with § 2 makes it pretty clear that the goal of the general there sent περὶ Πελοπόννησον was not the west. But the matter becomes quite certain from a still further comparison with c. 26, from which it is seen that the general sent περὶ Πελοπόννησον does not sail at all to the west of Peloponnesus, but only to the point of the coast opposite Cythera, i.e. not even to the southernmost point of the peninsula, Taenarum. In vi. 105. § 2. περὶ τὴν ἄλλην Πελοπόννησον has no reference to the west; rather the rest of the coast of Peloponnesus hostile to the Athenians is opposed to the Laconian coast. So in c. 29. § 1, where it is said of the ships of Alcidas, πλέοντες περί τε αὐτὴν τὴν Πελοπόννησον ἐνδιέτριψαν καὶ κατὰ τὸν ἄλλον πλοῦν σχολαῖοι κομισθέντες κτέ., there is no reference to the west of Peloponnesus, but rather the voyage along the coasts of the peninsula is antithetical to the rest of the voyage. Again, in ii. 67. 29, where it is stated that the Spartans at the beginning of the war τοὺς ἐμπόρους οὓς ἔλαβον Ἀθηναίων καὶ τῶν ξυμμάχων ἐν ὁλκάσι περὶ Πελοπόννησον πλέοντας, no unprejudiced reader would think only of merchant-vessels sailing west of Peloponnesus; besides, the very next sentence makes plain what Thuc. meant by περὶ Πελοπόννησον πλέοντας. Indeed every fleet that was on or near any coast of Peloponnesus was for Thuc. περὶ Πελοπόννησον.

17. Steup's view of the spuriousness of this chapter was accepted by Cl. in his second edition, but has been attacked by Stahl (*Rh. Mus.* xxvii. p. 278 ff. and xxviii. p. 622 ff.) and L. Herbst (*Philol.* xlii. p. 681 ff.). The former, in order to refer the statements of § 2 to the *fourth* year of the war, makes three emendations, while the latter maintains that Thuc. could very well have made those statements concerning the summer of the *first* year. Steup replied to Stahl's first article in *Rh. Mus.* xxvii. p. 637 ff. Reconsideration of the question, in connexion with the articles above mentioned and other expressions of opinion of a more casual nature, has only confirmed Steup in the soundness of his conclusions.

The grounds for the charge of spuriousness are of threefold nature: 1) a looseness and obscurity of statement that is foreign to Thuc. (see notes under the text); 2) a number of linguistic peculiarities (see notes); 3) a lack of agreement with statements elsewhere made by Thuc. This third class of reasons, the most important of all, will now be considered.

At variance with Thuc.'s representation elsewhere is, first, the statement of § 1, that at the beginning of the war, when, acc. to § 2, 250 Attic ships were sent out at one time, about as many ships (παραπλήσιαι) had been at the same time at sea as in the fourth summer. For against the 250 ships one can reckon up from other statements of Thuc. for the year 428 B.C. only a little over 150 ships, viz. forty at Mytilene (c. 3. 10), twelve of Asopius (c. 7. 9), one hundred mentioned c. 16. 5, three stationed at Salamis (*cf.* c. 51. 7; ii. 93. 23; 94. 14), two at Atalante (c. 89. 14), *i.e.* in all at most 157.

Again, though it is said in § 2 that at the beginning of the war τὴν Ἀττικὴν καὶ Εὔβοιαν καὶ Σαλαμῖνα ἑκατὸν νῆες ἐφύλασσον, in the account of the first year of the war there is no mention of these 100 ships. Herbst (*ibid.* p. 687 f.) finds a previous reference to the matter in ii. 13. 15 παρῄνει δὲ (*i.e.* ὁ Περικλῆς τοῖς Ἀθηναίοις) ... τὸ ναυτικὸν ... ἐξαρτύεσθαι, by which he understands that the 300 triremes mentioned ii. 13. 55 are to be 'sent to sea.' But Herbst misinterprets τὸ ναυτικὸν ἐξαρτύεσθαι, the meaning of which is clear from the parallel passage in i. 25. 23. There it is said that the Corcyraeans on account of the naval glory of the ancient Phaeacian inhabitants of their island so much the more ἐξηρτύοντο τὸ ναυτικόν, *i.e.* put their navy in good order. Just so Pericles gives the Athenians the general advice to put their navy in good order. The calling out of 300 triremes would require different treatment, above all a clear and orderly statement. For this number would have been the very utmost the Athenians could have furnished, if indeed they could have furnished that. It is as inconceivable that Thuc. only learned later of the fitting out of a fleet of 100 triremes to guard Attica, Euboea, and Salamis at the opening of the war, as that he

APPENDIX.

should not have considered this worthy of mention in his account of the year 431. There was no lack of opportunity to mention the matter. So e.g. ii. 17. § 4, where the 100 ships sent round Peloponnesus are first mentioned; ii. 22. § 1 f., where Pericles's bearing at the time of the first invasion is described; ii. 24. § 1, where the new method of guarding the land, after the withdrawal of the Peloponnesians, is under discussion. Besides, one fails to understand why the lords of the whole sea should have called out for the protection of their own coasts 100 triremes, and should have kept these at their posts for some time even after despatching other 100 ships round Peloponnesus, to say nothing of of the fact that at this time the Peloponnesians made an invasion of Attica by land, to which even the coasts of Attica, except fortified points, according to Pericles's plan of warfare were left exposed.

Further, the words in l. 6 χωρὶς δὲ αἱ περὶ Ποτείδαιαν καὶ ἐν τοῖς ἄλλοις χωρίοις are strange, inasmuch as the ἄλλα χωρία have not been mentioned before. The thirty ships sent by the Athenians, acc. to ii. 26. 2, περὶ τὴν Λοκρίδα καὶ Εὐβοίας ἅμα φυλακήν, are not meant, because the ships that were περὶ Ποτείδαιαν καὶ ἐν τοῖς ἄλλοις χωρίοις amounted, acc. to our chap., to only 50, but the expression περὶ Ποτείδαιαν καὶ κτέ., at least if Thuc. be its author, presupposes that at none of the ἄλλα χωρία were there more ships than at Potidaea. Nor will any one suppose that Thuc. meant to reckon to Potidaea only twenty ships, or even less, since ἡ Λοκρίς could hardly have been designated by τὰ ἄλλα χωρία. The ἐν τοῖς ἄλλοις χωρίοις νῆες cannot be found in any previous mention any more than the 100 just discussed. Besides, acc. to i. 61. 18, there were originally at Potidaea seventy Athenian ships, and Thuc. nowhere mentions a withdrawal of any part of these. Possibly, however, too much stress must not be laid upon this point, since Thuc.'s work lacked final revision. Stahl finds an intimation that not all of the seventy ships remained at Potidaea in the fact that in i. 64. 15 the art. is wanting with ναυσίν. But in the conclusion of the account of the blockade of Potidaea the indefinite expression, "and at the same time from the sea by means of blockading ships," could certainly be used even if all seventy ships were still at Potidaea. Whether less than seventy ships would suffice for the blockade of a city washed on two sides by the sea may be left undecided; but certainly Stahl's view, that only twenty-five ships were required, is highly improbable, and his argument in proof, that ad ipsos duos Mytilenae portus intercludendos forty ships would have sufficed, is hardly intelligible, since at Mytilene help could be brought from one harbour to the other far quicker than at Potidaea from one sea to the other.

Further, in § 3, after the sent. καὶ τὰ χρήματα τοῦτο μάλιστα ὑπανήλωσε μετὰ Ποτειδαίας, the absence of any mention of the 4000 hoplites and 3000 cavalry of Hagnon and Cleopompus (ii. 58), can be explained only on a rather improbable assumption, unless the chapter be ascribed to an interpolator. It must be assumed that the 4000 hoplites were not δίδραχμοι, but received less pay, and that in explanation of the great expenses occasioned by Potidaea especial stress was laid upon the high pay of two of the armies fitted out for the recapture of the city. This is improbable, inasmuch as the 4000 were with the original besieging army before Potidaea, while the 1600 were there only a short time and not for the purpose of blockading. — Besides, if τὴν Ποτείδαιαν ἐφρούρουν includes also the 1600 men of Phormio, this ill accords with i. 64. 13, where Phormio's work is designated by ἀπετείχισε τὸ ἐκ τῆς Παλλήνης τεῖχος (cf. i. 65. 13), and still less with i. 64. 4, where Phormio's task as τειχίζειν is directly opposed to φρουρεῖν (intr.). Especially troublesome are the words τρισχίλιοι μὲν οἱ πρῶτοι, ὧν οὐκ ἐλάσσους διεπολιόρκησαν. The evident meaning is that the siege of Potidaea was begun by 3000 hoplites, and was prosecuted and completed by no less a number. But acc. to i. 64. 1, the siege was begun by the army which just before (τὸ δ' ἐκ τοῦ ἰσθμοῦ τεῖχος εὐθὺς οἱ Ἀθηναῖοι ἀποτειχίσαντες ἐφρούρουν) had fought the battle near Potidaea, and of the 3000 Athenian hoplites, which had been with this army (i. 61. 15), 150 had, acc. to i. 63. 20, fallen in the battle. Then, acc. to ii. 58. 10, the original besieging army also had been attacked by the plague, whereas there is no mention anywhere of reinforcements by which the number of the army was raised again to 3000 or higher. The only reinforcements mentioned were the troops of Phormio and those of Hagnon and Cleopompus, and these returned as complete corps. The fact that in ii. 31. 11, where the expedition made against Megaris toward the end of the summer is described, one reads χωρὶς δὲ (i.e. besides the μυρίων ὁπλιτῶν οὐκ ἐλάσσους, which invaded Megaris) αὐτοῖς οἱ ἐν Ποτειδαίᾳ τρισχίλιοι ἦσαν, by no means proves that the full number of 3000 hoplites then lay before Potidaea. As the article shows, reference is there made to i. 61. 15, and the loss meanwhile incurred is disregarded, just as the troops of Phormio, which must have suffered losses (cf. i. 65. § 3; ii. 29. § 6), are still designated in ii. 58. 12, where their return home is mentioned, as οἱ ἑξακόσιοι καὶ χίλιοι (cf. i. 64. 8; 65. 13). Although in ii. 31. § 2, where the point was to remove the apparent contradiction with ii. 13. § 6, a round number is unobjectionable, — even the strength of the main body of Athenian hoplites is not exactly stated — here, where it is expressly affirmed that not less than 3000 hoplites had continually blockaded the city, τρισχίλιοι cannot possibly be regarded as a round number. It must be noticed also that, acc. to ii. 79. § 1, the campaign which led to the defeat of the Athenians at Spartalos was undertaken with 2000 hoplites, and that the same Xenophon was general (τρίτος αὐτός), who also is mentioned first among the three generals to whom Potidaea had surrendered the preceding winter (ii. 70. 8), although Thuc. neither mentions an immediate or early return of the Athenian army, nor states how the 2000 hoplites of ii 79. § 1 came to the Thracian coast. Is not the conjecture reasonable that the 2850 hoplites, which were originally before Potidaea, had in consequence of losses through the plague and the hardships of the siege gradually shrunk to 2000 ?

Stahl proposed to strike out δέ after παραπλήσιαι (3), insert ἤ before ἀρχομένου (3), omit περὶ Ποτείδαιαν καὶ (6), and so make it possible to refer the statements in § 2 about Athenian ships simultaneously at sea to the *fourth* year of the war. But even thus the matter is far from clear. For example, if § 2 refers to 428 b.c., the absence of any explanation of ἀρχομένου τοῦ πολέμου is remarkable; the difficulty occasioned by τοῦτο is enhanced, if there is only casual mention of the first year of the war; the difficulty of referring τοῦτο to Potidaea is not relieved; and if, as Stahl assumes, ἐν τοῖς πλεῖσται δὴ νῆες (2) means "among the most ships," then, as Cl. rightly observed, the definite expression νῆες τοσαῦται δὴ πλεῖσται (15), referring to these same ships, seems strangely out of place. Besides, the linguistic peculiarities are not touched by Stahl's emendations; the difficulties in the statements about Potidaea (§ 3) are not relieved; and § 1 and 2, even in the form given them by Stahl, are by no means free from difficulties of fact. The ships of the year 428 b.c., even if they amounted to 250, could hardly be said to be παραπλήσιαι to those of 431. For the latter can be reckoned at highest at 200 (i. 61. 18; ii. 23. 5; 26. 1), or indeed at only 155, if the ships that remained at Potidaea be estimated, with Stahl, at only twenty-five (see note under text). Further, the words τὴν Ἀττικὴν καὶ Εὔβοιαν καὶ Σαλαμῖνα ἑκατὸν νῆες ἐφύλασσον (§ 2) are not less troublesome when referred to 428 than to 431; for there is as little mention elsewhere of such a fleet in the former year as in the latter, and if the Athenians really had raised, as Stahl assumes, two fleets of 100 ships each against a threatened simultaneous attack of the Peloponnesians by land and sea, it is inconceivable that Thuc. should in c. 16. § 1 have mentioned only one.

The occasion for the insertion of this chapter seems to have been the fact that in c. 19. § 1 Thuc. mentions without further details (προσδεόμενοι δὲ οἱ Ἀθηναῖοι χρημάτων ἐς τὴν πολιορκίαν κτέ.) the financial straits of the Athenians, although for observant readers, after c. 3. § 1; ii. 70. § 2; and esp. c. 13. § 3, the fact of this financial pressure could have been no surprise. The chapter is an awkward attempt to fill the supposed gap. The statements of the interpolator, that can be tested, have been proved in many respects either inexact or incorrect. Inexact is what is said in § 3 about the army which opened the siege of Potidaea, and incorrect is the statement concerning the 100 ships called out in 431 to guard Attica, Euboea, and Salamis. There is in this latter case manifestly a misunderstanding of the import of the 100 reserve ships, of which Thuc. speaks in ii. 24. § 2. Further, the expression παραπλήσιαι καὶ ἔτι πλείους (§ 1) is intelligible only if the author has reckoned the number of ships of the year 428 much too high. And indeed he seems to have thought of the 100 reserve ships in the ship-houses as called out also in this fourth year, but to have completely overlooked the twelve ships of c. 7. 9. After the above considerations, the credibility also of those statements which cannot be tested, esp. those about the pay of the Athenian hoplites and seamen, must be designated as extremely doubtful; for here, too, whether through the fault of the interpolator or his authorities, it was easy for inaccuracies and misconceptions to slip in. Not to be approved is therefore L. Holzapfel's course (*Beitr. z. gr.*

Gesch. p. 78 ff. in *Berliner Studien* vii., and *Wochenschr. f. kl. Phil.* 1888, p. 1269 ff.) in making the statements about wages the basis for a calculation of the length of the siege. For Holzapfel's hypothesis that these data originated, 'if not from Thuc. himself, at least from a well-informed source,' is entirely without support.

20. 19. ἀλλὰ ῥᾳδίως καθορωμένου ἐς ὃ ἐβούλοντο τοῦ τείχους. Steup brackets ἐς ὃ ἐβούλοντο, on the following grounds: Whether τοῦ τείχους be construed as subj. of καθορωμένου, or as dependent on ἐς ὅ, the vulg. is unsatisfactory. If it be meant that the *whole* wall was easily overlooked, any addition to τοῦ τείχους which designates τὸ τεῖχος as the wall of circumvallation, is unnecessary. Just such an addition, however, would ἐς ὃ ἐβούλοντο be. For to Hude's explanation (*Comm. Crit.* p. 94) of ἐς ὅ = ὅσον or ἐς ὅσον (*so far as*), sc. καθορᾶν, it must be objected that a parallel to ἐς ὅ in this sense is not to be found in Thuc. (in v. 66. 6, ἐς ὅ = *so long as, since*), and hardly elsewhere. If τοῦ τείχους be taken with καθορωμένου, ἐς ὃ ἐβούλοντο must mean *whither they wished* (sc. ἀναβαίνειν, cf. c. 85. 13). But such a remark would be not only idle, but also, as Pp. saw, in an unnatural position, since one would have expected it after τοῦ τείχους, and it is further surprising that it should have been said, that the Plataeans *wished to ascend*, and not they *wished to cross* (cf. l. 6; 23. 1). The first to call attention to this imperfect designation of the purpose of the Plataeans was Stahl, who, however, construes τοῦ τείχους as part. genitive. If it were meant that the portion of the wall where the Plataeans proposed to place their ladders was sufficiently visible, it is less surprising that only the ascent of the wall is indicated, since the descent might under some circumstances be easier at some other point. But against this Stahl rightly observes, that it would be strange if here the point of ascent were indicated, while before it was the part that enabled the Plataeans to determine the necessary length of the ladders. That these parts were identical was not self-evident, and needed to be indicated by Thucydides. But even if τοῦ τείχους be construed as partitive and the identity of the parts of the wall be assumed, it is not less surprising that the second characteristic of the portion of the wall from which the height could be determined from the city, viz. the nearer approach to the city wall, is not mentioned along with the absence of plaster, but only as a later addition. In this respect nothing is changed by St.'s conjecture ὅσον ἐβούλοντο (sc. καθορᾶν). Besides, what could have induced Thuc. to use the peculiar circumlocution ὅσον ἐβούλοντο τοῦ τείχους to designate the point of the wall in question? See, further, Steup, *Rh. Mus.* xxxiii. p. 250 f.

22. 11. τὸν ἀριστερὸν πόδα μόνον ὑποδεδεμένοι ἀσφαλείας ἕνεκα τῆς πρὸς τὸν πηλόν. The Schol. explains, ὑπεδέδεντο τὸν μὲν ἕνα τῶν ποδῶν δι' ἀσφάλειαν, τὸν δὲ ἕτερον γυμνὸν εἶχον διὰ κουφότητα, and this is essentially the view taken by Kr., Bl., Grote, Sh., while Cl., Steup, Stahl, Arn., Jow., Bm., and Goell. hold the view given in the text. It was doubtless not uncommon for Greek and Roman soldiers to go with one foot shod, the other bare, though there seems to have been no fixed custom as to which foot should be bare. *Cf. e.g.* Eur. frg. 574 (Nauck)

Οἱ δὲ Οἐστίου
κόροι τὸ λαιὸν ἴχνος ἀνάρβυλοι ποδός
τὸν δ' ἐν πεδίλοις. ὡς ἐλαφρίζον γόνυ
ἔχοιεν· ὃς δὴ πᾶσιν Λἰτωλοῖς νόμος.

Cf. also Aristotle frg. 74 (Rose) δεῖ γὰρ οἶμαι τὸν ἡγούμενον (*i.e.* right) ἔχειν ἐλαφρόν, ἀλλ' οὐ τὸν ἐμμένοντα (*i.e.* left). So Livy ix. 40 (of the Samnites) sinistrum crus ocreâ tectum, and Juv. *Sat.* vi. 256 crurisque sinistri dimidium tegmen. But Verg. *Aen.* vii. 690

vestigia nuda sinistri
Instituere pedis, crudus tegit altera pero,

and Vegetius i. 20 pedites autem scutati praeter catafractas et galeas, etiam ferreas ocreas in dextris cruribus cogerentur accipere. So on a pictured vase in Millin ii., No. 30. — It might be disputed whether a bare or a sandaled foot would more easily slip in the mud, though in hand to hand fighting, where the right arm is used and the left foot needs to be firmly planted, the sandal would undoubtedly be of advantage. But here it is a question not of mud only, but of scaling, feeling the way over, and descending from a wall in the darkness, and for such an enterprise the bare foot was better suited. Rauchenstein (*Philol.* xxxv. p. 578) compares J. Müller, *Schweizergesch.* Buch ii. Kap. 7, p. 723.

22. 12. προσέμισγον πρὸς τὰς ἐπάλξεις κτέ. Steup finds here the proximity of κατὰ μεταπύργιον and πρὸς τὰς ἐπάλξεις intolerable, since it would seem from c. 21. § 4, where ἐπάλξεις and πύργοι are placed in antithesis, that the towers had no battlements. He objects, too, to the idea of *approaching the battlements*, which were on top of the wall. Hence he brackets πρός (which in Cisalp. is added by a second hand), as prob. due to a mistaken connexion of τὰς ἐπάλξεις with προσέμισγον, and puts a comma after προσέμισγον, with which can easily be supplied from l. 5 τῷ τείχει τῶν πολεμίων. For the const. τὰς ἐπάλξεις εἰδότες ὅτι κτέ., he compares c. 113. 25 'Αμπρακίαν μέντοι οἶδα ὅτι κτέ. Steup mentions Müller-Strübing's objection to the expression προσέμισγον πρὸς τὰς ἐπάλξεις, but only to express his complete disagreement with Müller-Strübing's treatment (*N. Jahrbb.* cxxxi. p. 327-335) of the account of the sortie of the Plataeans, in support of the assumption that Thucydides's account of the siege of Plataea is merely a theory of the art of siege or of fortress-warfare under the form of an actual siege.

22. 12. πρῶτον μὲν τὰς κλίμακας φέροντες, καὶ προσέθεσαν· ἔπειτα ψιλοὶ δώδεκα ξὺν ξιφιδίῳ καὶ θώρακι ἀνέβαινον, ὧν ἡγεῖτο Ἀμμέας ὁ Κοροίβου, καὶ πρῶτος ἀνέβη (μετὰ δὲ αὐτὸν οἱ ἑπόμενοι ἓξ ἐφ' ἑκάτερον τῶν πύργων ἀνέβαινον)· ἔπειτα ψιλοὶ ἄλλοι μετὰ τούτους ξὺν δορατίοις ἐχώρουν, οἷς ἕτεροι κατόπιν τὰς ἀσπίδας ἔφερον κτέ. Steup's critical note is as follows: The parenthetical clause is marked, in order to indicate its subordinate importance. Cl., followed by Stahl, transposed the second ἀνέβαινον and ἐχώρουν. His reasons were that, after the statement that the first twelve ψιλοί had ascended, and the mention of their leader had induced the supplementary remark καὶ πρῶτος ἀνέβη, there was no occasion for a second ἀνέβαινον, but only for the statement that the twelve had advanced in two divisions against the towers, for which χωρεῖν ἐπί was the fittest expression; that, on the contrary, ἀνέβαινον was quite appropriate for the detachment armed with spears, which was to follow as speedily as possible. Now it is quite certain, as Cl. hints and Stahl says, that it cannot be meant here that the twelve ψιλοί ascended the towers. For acc. to c. 23. 6, the ascent of the towers, on whose roofs there were no guards (*cf.* c. 21. § 4), was not made till control had been got of the passages below; but, as was remarked in the *Rh. Mus.* xxxiii. p. 252, ἐξ ἐφ' ἑκάτερον τῶν πύργων might merely mean that the twelve were intended, after reaching the top of the wall, to turn in equal divisions against the two towers, so that the second ἀνέβαινον would be simply a repetition of the first. Moreover, what follows strongly supports the view that μετὰ δὲ αὐτὸν κτέ. does not refer to an occurrence subsequent to the ascent of the wall by the twelve; for of the spear-bearing division it is said, not ἐν τούτῳ δὲ ψιλοὶ ἄλλοι κτέ., but ἔπειτα ψιλοὶ ἄλλοι κτέ. And the besiegers were not alarmed by the advance of the twelve against the towers, but by the falling of a tile, which a Plataean, while *ascending the wall*, accidentally threw down (l. 22 ff.). Finally, the moment at which the tile fell is stated with reference only to the *ascent* of the wall (l. 21 ὡς δὲ ἄνω πλείους ἐγένοντο). With the fact, now, that in what follows there is no mention of further operations on the part of the twelve, agrees the circumstance, that of the spear-bearing detachment it is merely stated, acc. to the vulg., that they advanced after the others (ἐχώρουν), not that they ascended the wall (ἀνέβαινον); and the words ὡς δὲ ἄνω πλείους ἐγένοντο accord better with c. 23. 2 ὡς οἱ πρῶτοι αὐτῶν ἀνεβεβήκεσαν κτέ., if they refer, not to the spear-bearing detachment, but only to a number of the twelve. Accordingly, it cannot be admitted that the context requires emendation of the vulgate. Nor need the triple occurrence of ἀναβαίνειν in three lines arouse suspicion, since Thuc. by no means avoids the repetition of the same word. More serious might seem the objections of H. Weil (*Rev. de Philol. N. S.* ii. p. 89), that, although at first only twelve ψιλοί are mentioned, acc. to the words μετὰ δὲ αὐτὸν (*i.e.* τὸν Ἀμμέαν) οἱ ἑπόμενοι ἐξ ἐφ' ἑκάτερον τῶν πύργων ἀνέβαινον, if μετὰ αὐτὸν οἱ ἑπόμενοι be taken quite literally, Ammeas was the *thirteenth;* and though Ammeas first ascended the wall, apparently only the destination of his companions is indicated. To obviate these difficulties Weil would put a comma after ἑπόμενοι and bracket the second ἀνέβαινον. But, even disregarding the fact that this would render idle the remark μετὰ δὲ αὐτὸν οἱ ἑπόμενοι (*sc.* ἀνέβαινον), certainly the words ἐξ ἐφ' ἑκάτερον τῶν πύργων, which would have to be construed with the first ἀνέβαινον, would drag intolerably. Besides, it does not seem impossible to take μετὰ αὐτὸν οἱ ἑπόμενοι as including the leader, i.e. "*Ammeas* and his followers after him," after the analogy of the consts., οἱ περί τινα (v. 46. 19; vi. 96. 14; viii. 67. 1), οἱ ἀμφί τινα (viii. 65. 1), οἱ μετά τινος (i. 3. 14; 61. 3).

26. 2. τὰς ἐς τὴν Μυτιλήνην [δύο καὶ τεσσαράκοντα] ναῦς. Since in previous mentions of this fleet, reference to which is indicated by the art., the number of ships is only forty (c. 16. 16; 25. 7), as likewise in the further account till the union with Brasidas (cf. c. 29. 1; 69. 1; 76. 4), the number forty-two can hardly be correct here. v. H. bracketed δύο καί, which Kr. had already suspected. But X (Stahl?) proposed rather (*Philol. Anz.* xiii. p. 302) to bracket all three words, δύο καὶ τεσσαράκοντα, as an addition of some interpreter who added to the forty ships the two mentioned in c. 5. 15 and 25. 3. This latter suggestion, Steup thinks, has the advantage of allowing an easier explanation of the origin of the vulgate. For if the number of ships was mentioned here, there was little occasion for a change. On the other hand, after the number had been given not only in c. 16. 16, but just before in c. 25. 7, there was no reason for its repetition here. And in c. 27. 1 it is simply stated, ὡς αἵ τε νῆες αὐτοῖς (i.e. τοῖς Μυτιληναίοις) οὐχ ἧκον ἀπὸ τῆς Πελοποννήσου κτέ.

26. 3. ἄρχοντα. This conjecture of H. Stephanus (*Thes. s.v. προστάσσειν*) is adopted by Cl. against ἔχοντα of all the Mss. The const. of ἄρχοντα προστάξαντες with a finite verb is so genuinely Thucydidean, as is shown by the four corresponding passages (cf. vi. 93. 8; vii. 19. 23; viii. 23. 21; 39. 13), that the slight change cannot but commend itself, esp. as the usual abbreviations for ἔχειν and ἄρχειν look much alike. With the vulg. the order of words is harsh, and the pleonastic προστάξαντες drags intolerably. No objection can be made against the proximity of ἄρχοντα προστάξαντες, which designates the one appointed to the chief command for the specific enterprise, and ὃς ἦν αὐτοῖς ναύαρχος, which states that Alcidas held the office of nauarch.

26. 6. ταῖς ναυσὶν ἐς τὴν Μυτιλήνην καταπλεύσαις ἐπιβοηθήσουσιν. Steup objects to the instrumental const. of the dat., that thus ἐπιβοηθήσουσιν is strangely left without obj., while the καταπλεῖν of the ships is quite unnecessarily mentioned. He brackets, therefore, καταπλεούσαις, as an explanatory marginal note that has crept into the text, and renders: "that the Athenians, embarrassed in both quarters, might the less with their ships bring aid to Mytilene." Cf. i. 142. 12 ταῖς ναυσὶν ἀμύνεσθαι, c. 96. 12 πολλῇ χειρὶ ἐπεβοήθουν πάντες, vii. 3. 17 ἐπιβοηθοῖεν ἄλλοσε, Xen. *Hell.* vii. 5. 24 ἐπιβοηθῶσιν ἀπὸ τοῦ εὐωνύμου κέρατος ἐπὶ τὸ ἐχόμενον. The arguments of Müller-Strübing (*Thuk. Forsch.* p. 113 ff.) and of Osberger (*Festgruss f. Heerwagen*, p. 85 ff.), to prove the whole final clause spurious, are not convincing. See, further, Steup in *Rh. Mus.* xxxiii. p. 256 f.

26. 9. πατρὸς δὲ ἀδελφὸς ὤν. Though the const. of the preceding words does not grammatically justify δέ, since no other attribute of Cleomenes is mentioned, still it may be retained on the ground, that the words ὑπὲρ Παυσανίου ... νεωτέρου ἔτι imply, with reference to Cleomenes, the idea αὐτὸς μὲν οὐ βασιλεύων. If any change is to be made, Cl. would not omit δέ, with Kr., but write

APPENDIX.

ἦν for ὦν. . Stahl writes δή for δέ acc. to the analogy of iv. 59. 14; vi. 80. 14; vii. 81. 10, which would relieve the difficulty.

26. 10. [καί]. Bracketed, with Dindorf, against all the Mss. The antithesis to τά τε πρότερον τετμημένα is only καὶ ὅσα . . . παρελέλειπτο, and εἴ τι ἐβεβλαστήκει, "if anything had sprouted up," is the necessary explanation of τὰ πρότερον τετμημένα.

29. 3. ἐνδιέτριψαν. Steup would either change to ἐνδιατρίψαντες, or bracket, on the ground that the conduct of the Peloponnesians during the second part of their voyage was not less the opposite of what should have happened (οὓς ἔδει ἐν τάχει παραγενέσθαι), than their conduct during the first part, and that τοὺς μὲν . . . ἑάλωκε was by no means merely the result of the slowness of the Peloponnesians in the *second* part of the voyage. He thinks, too, that the vulg. involves a harsh anacoluthic change from finite verb to participle.

30. 13. τὸ κοινὸν τοῦ πολέμου. Steup's conjecture (*Rh. Mus.* xxxiii. p. 257 ff.) for καινόν or κενόν of the Mss., of which the former has recently been generally accepted. The reference in the rel. sent. is undoubtedly to a mistake in the conduct of the war, to which also the speaker clearly refers in what precedes. Hence it follows that τὸ τοιοῦτον (*cf.* τὰς τοιαύτας ἁμαρτίας, v. 9. 10) must refer to τὸ ἀφύλακτον in l. 4. But unguardedness (τὸ ἀφύλακτον) could not be represented either as the new and surprising (τὸ καινόν), or as the vain and deceptive (τὸ κενόν) in war. On the contrary, the speaker, whose object was to encourage his colleagues, might well say that τὸ κοινὸν τοῦ πολέμου, "that which was common (or impartial) in war," was nothing else but τὸ ἀφύλακτον ("*lack of precaution*"). *Cf.* Hector's ξυνὸς Ἐνυάλιος (Hom. Σ 309), which Aristotle, *Rhet.* ii. 21, calls τεθρυλημένη καὶ κοινὴ γνώμη, and the Lat. communis Mars or communis Mars belli. *Cf.* also Thuc. v. 102. 1, where τὰ τῶν πολέμων ἐστιν ὅτε κοινοτέρας (some Mss. καινοτέρας) τὰς τύχας λαμβάνοντα ἢ κατὰ τὸ διαφέρον ἑκατέρων πλῆθος means, "the fortune of war is sometimes impartial, and not according to superior numbers." See also on ii. 62. 31. Steup still maintains, as formerly (*ibid.* p. 261 f.), that no certain example of τὸ καινὸν or τὰ κοινὰ τοῦ πολέμου has been found, in spite of the fact that Heliodorus (*Aethiop.* ix. 5, p. 355 Kor.) says, καινουργὸς δὲ ὦν ἀεί πως ὁ πόλεμος, and Polybius (i. 4. 5; iv. 2. 4) attributes καινοποιεῖν to τύχη.

31. 7. καὶ τὴν πρόσοδον ταύτην μεγίστην οὖσαν Ἀθηναίων ἣν ὑφέλωσι, καὶ ἅμα, ἣν ἐφορμῶσι σφίσιν, αὐτοῖς δαπάνη γίγνηται. Steup's critical note is as follows: The first part of this from of old (see the Scholia) variously treated passage is given in accordance with the essentially unanimous tradition of the Mss., the second part in agreement with v. H., and with Müller-Strübing, *Thuk. Forsch.* p. 97, after Codex M and a Schol. (τὸ σφίσιν αὐτοῖς οὐχ ἅμα ἀναγνωστέον, ἀλλὰ διαιρετέον, καὶ κατὰ τὸ σφίσιν ὑποστικτέον). Most Mss. have ἐφορμῶσιν αὐτοῖς (or αὐτοὺς) δαπάνη σφίσι γίγνηται (Vat. γίγνεται), G ἐφορμῶσιν αὐτοῖς σφίσι δαπάνη γίγνηται. Numerous emendations have been proposed. Two things seem certain, viz. that σφίσι, whatever its true position, must refer, like ἀποστήσωσι, ἀφῖχθαι, and ψφέλωσι, to the Peloponnesians and their Ionian and Lesbian friends; ἐφορμῶσι, on the other hand, to the Athenians. The former is clear on grammatical grounds; material considerations leave no doubt of the latter. Before the Peloponnesians could have thought of blockading the Athenians in Mytilene or anywhere else, they must have won supremacy at sea. On the other hand, c. 33. 16 οὐδαμοῦ ἐγκαταληφθεῖσαι ἠναγκάσθησαν στρατόπεδον ποιεῖσθαι καὶ φυλακὴν σφίσι καὶ ἐφόρμησιν παρασχεῖν shows very clearly that the immediate result of the occupation of an Ionian or Aeolian city by the Peloponnesians would have been the blockade of this city by the Athenians. But if the Athenians are the subj. of ἐφορμῶσι, and σφίσι refers to the Peloponnesians, the two words must be taken together, — a const. allowed by M alone of traditional readings. The fact that thus along with the loss of the greatest source of revenue of the Athenians is mentioned also the expense that would be caused by the blockade of a coast city, cannot be surprising after c. 13. § 3 and 19. § 1. Nor is there any special difficulty in the fact that σφίσιν αὐτοῖς, though standing together, must be construed apart. Hence it seems unnecessary to write, with Kr. and Cobet (*Mnem. N. S.* viii. p. 131), ἢν ἐφορμῶσι σφίσι, δαπάνη αὐτοῖς γίγνηται, and the reading of M seems the rather to be preferred, as the other readings might so easily have been derived from it. It is only necessary to assume, that in the Ms. to which all the rest go back, σφίσιν was lost after ἐφορμῶσι and written in afterwards above the line or on the margin. To bracket σφίσι, as some suggest, is inadmissible, since it facilitates the understanding of the passage and relieves the harshness of the change of subject in ἐφορμῶσι. If καὶ ἅμα be rendered *also at the same time* (see Stahl, *Rh. Mus.* xvii. p. 620; also Hünnekes, *Kl. Beitr. etc.* 1. p. 2), no change in the first part of the passage is necessary. Hardly to be approved certainly is Dobree's suggestion to change the first ἤν, which follows the emphatically placed words τὴν πρόσοδον . . . 'Αθηναίων, to ἵν', or Cl.'s, to bracket it. Since the revolt of Ionia would involve the immediate loss of the Athenian revenues from that quarter, it was not necessary to emphasize the latter point in the same way as the first, and the parenthesis, which establishes the probability of the revolt of Ionia, certainly does not support the assumption that this had already happened.

32. **11 ff. ὁρῶντες . . . παραβαλεῖν.** Cl. was inclined to transpose this concluding sent. and put it after τοὺς πολλούς in l. 3, rightly recognizing that the first mention of the captives was the proper place for an explanation about them, which this last clause must be admitted to be. But with the order proposed by Cl., Steup thinks clearness would require τοῦ 'Αλκίδου instead of αὐτοῦ in l. 4, and ὁ 'Αλκίδας in c. 33. 1 would, as Rauchenstein recognized (*Philol.* xxxv. p. 584), be unnecessary after ὁ μέν (sc. 'Αλκίδας) in the sent. immediately preceding (c. 32. 10). Besides, it would be difficult to explain how the traditional order originated. Hence prob. it is not safe to go further than to suggest that c. 32 is one of those passages which indicate a lack of final revision on the part of the historian.

APPENDIX.

34. 8. ἐπαγαγόμενοι. So, with Kr., for ἐπαγόμενοι of all the Mss. See on ἀνταναγαγόμενοι, i. 29. 18 (App.), and ἐπαγαγόμενοι, vi. 6. 10. The confusion of the pres. and aor. forms of ἄγειν and its compounds is so common in the Mss., that the correct form must always be determined from the context. Here ἐν διατειχίσματι εἶχον requires the aor. partic. of antecedent action. *Cf.* ξυνεσελθόντες ἐπολίτευον in l. 10. Stahl (adnot. crit. ad vol. ii. p. v.) explains the pres. as in auxilium adhibentes.

36. 9. καὶ ὅτι οὐκ ἀρχόμενοι . . . ἐποιήσαντο. Cl. inserted καί before ὅτι, without Mss. authority, on the ground that only thus is a proper antithesis to τήν τε ἄλλην ἀπόστασιν obtained and the evident sense of the passage secured. "The Athenians reproached the Mytileneans with the revolt in general (τήν τε ἄλλην), and esp. that (καὶ ὅτι) they had revolted, although not subjects like the other allies; and it contributed to increase their fury that Peloponnesian ships should have had the audacity to venture over to Ionia and assist the rebels." *Cf.* c. 39. § 1, 2, where Cleon emphasizes the inexcusableness of the Mytilenean revolt, as compared with that of subject allies. Against Cl.'s view, see Stahl, *N. Jahrbb.* xcvii. p. 108, in answer to which Cl. emphasizes two points: 1) The revolt of a πόλις ξύμμαχος αὐτόνομος, or οὐκ ἀρχομένη, is for the whole political attitude of Athens of such importance, that it must be strongly emphasized. This is accomplished only by setting, by means of καί, the ὅτι οὐκ ἀρχόμενοι feature over against ἀπόστασις in general. If ὅτι οὐκ ἀρχόμενοι . . . ἐποιήσαντο be only epexegetical to ἄλλην ἀπόστασιν, as would be the case without καί, then the inexcusable fault implied in τήν τε ἄλλην must be sought in what follows. 2) ἐπικαλοῦντες τήν τε ἄλλην ἀπόστασιν points (even without καί before ὅτι), both in const. and sense, to a still greater fault of the Mytileneans, and this, could one even allow the anacoluthon assumed by Stahl in καὶ προσξυνεβάλετο κτέ., cannot possibly be the appearance of a Peloponnesian fleet on the Ionian coast, even if this was in answer to the Mytilenean appeal for help. Besides, the very term προσξυνεβάλετο indicates that this was of secondary importance. Steup adds, that the vulg. is the less tenable, since it would seem to convey the notion that the Athenians did not consider every revolt a crime.

36. 24. ἄλλαι τε γνῶμαι ἀφ' ἑκάστων ἐλέγοντο καὶ Κλέων ὁ Κλεαινέτου, ὅσπερ καὶ τὴν προτέραν ἐνενικήκει ὥστε ἀποκτεῖναι κτέ. Steup objects to the vulg., on the ground that from ἄλλαι γνῶμαι, *other views* or *proposals*, γνώμην, *decree*, must be supplied with τὴν προτέραν, and suggests that Thuc. wrote ὅσπερ καὶ τῇ προτέρᾳ ἐνενικήκει ὥστε ἀποκτεῖναι, "who also on the preceding day had carried a motion to put the Mytileneans to death." Thus changed, the passage would better accord with the remark of Diodotus, c. 41. 2 ὅσπερ καὶ ἐν τῇ προτέρᾳ ἐκκλησίᾳ ἀντέλεγε μάλιστα μὴ ἀποκτεῖναι Μυτιληναίους. For τῇ προτέρᾳ, cf. vii. 51. 10, and (with ἡμέρᾳ) v. 75. 14; Hom. π 50, and (with ἡμέρᾳ) Arist. *Polit.* v. 12.

37. 9. πρὸς ἐπιβουλεύοντας αὐτοὺς καὶ ἄκοντας ἀρχομένους · οὐκ ἐξ ὧν κτέ. Stahl (*Rh. Mus.* xxvi. p. 150 ff.) finds the asyndeton intolerable and not justified by the parallel passages cited, which he reads or renders differently, and has incorporated into the text his conjecture, ἐπιβουλεύοντας αὐτοὺς καὶ ἄκοντες ἀρχόμενοι ὡς οὐκ ἐξ ὧν κτέ. But the change seems neither necessary nor appropriate. The passage in c. 63. 9, to say nothing of the others, certainly seems a clear case of asyndeton, the particle γε not having *connective* force, but giving emphasis to the preceding word, such as is conferred here, and possibly also in vi. 36. 9, upon οὐκ by its position. Against ἄκοντες ἀρχόμενοι it may be esp. urged, that since οὐκ ἐξ ὧν . . . περιγένησθε, contains the clear and striking explanation of these words, ἄκοντες ἀρχόμενοι cannot stand in a causal relation to ἀκροῶνται κτέ., as Stahl's const. would require. Besides ἐπιβουλεύοντας αὐτούς alone is not sufficiently clear. Stahl explains that the twofold warning against μαλακίζεσθαι (i.e. ἐπικινδύνως ἐς ὑμᾶς and οὐκ ἐς τὴν τῶν ξυμμάχων χάριν) is established in two clauses (οὐ σκοποῦντες ὅτι . . . αὐτούς and οὐ σκοποῦντες ὡς οὐκ . . . περιγένησθε); but it seems rather that the speaker would only emphatically reject all thought of χάρις τῶν ξυμμάχων, and so would lay esp. stress upon the relation of the τυραννίς with its necessary results, as expressed down to the end of the period. Finally, the slips of the copyist, assumed by Stahl, would be hard to explain.

38. 6. ἀντίπαλον μάλιστα τὴν τιμωρίαν ἀναλαμβάνει. ὅν after ἀντίπαλον is omitted, with Haase (*Lucubr.* p. 115). The superlatives ὅτι ἐγγυτάτω κείμενον and ἀντίπαλον μάλιστα being related as cause and effect must be construed together, whereas ὅν would require ἀντίπαλον to be construed with ἀμύνασθαι.

38. 25. τοῖς τοιαῦτα λέγουσι. Steup considers τοιαῦτα, which Pp. designated as obscurius dictum and v. H. brackets, not explainable. The usual reference to τὰ κοινὰ καὶ ἄτοπα he thinks impossible, since § 5 includes not only καινότης λόγου and τὰ ἄτοπα, but also δεδοκιμασμένος λόγος and τὰ εἰωθότα, and in l. 24 εἰπεῖν refers only to speaking in general. But since it would be hard to understand why τοιαῦτα should have been inserted in a clause already clear (ἀνταγωνιζόμενοι τοῖς λέγουσι κτέ.) and no esp. mention of the speakers is here necessary, Steup brackets, not τοιαῦτα only, but τοῖς τοιαῦτα λέγουσι, as an awkward explanation of ἀνταγωνιζόμενοι. This would remove also, he thinks, the harsh transition from τοῖς λέγουσι to ὀξέως . . . λέγοντος.

38. 27. καὶ προαισθέσθαι τε πρόθυμοι εἶναι . . . ἀποβησόμενα. Steup's view differs from that adopted in the text only in that he makes εἶναι depend, with Haacke, upon δοκεῖν, and in answer to Pp.'s remark, that elsewhere here infs. pres. depend directly only on partices. and adjs., while everything secondary is in the aor., he cites l. 22 ἄριστοι μὴ ξυνέπεσθαι ἐθέλειν. Steup adds, that if εἶναι is to be bracketed, with most recent editors following Pp., the context would require the omission also of καί in l. 27. For προαισθέσθαι τε κτέ. could not be connected as an entirely independent clause with the preceding — as would be necessary if only εἶναι were omitted — since the ideas προεπαινέσαι and προαισθέσθαι are too closely connected, the former not being conceivable without the latter. But with the omission also of καί in l. 27, προαισθέσθαι τε πρόθυμοι κτέ.

APPENDIX.   287

would have the same relation to the preceding, as in l. 23 δοῦλοι ὄντες ... εἰωθότων to ἄριστοι, which would agree very well with the context.

39. 22. αἶς ἂν μάλιστα καὶ δι' ἐλαχίστου ἀπροσδόκητος εὐπραξία ἔλθῃ κτἑ. Gelzer's proposed transposition (*Inaug. Diss.* Gött. 1869), αἶς ἂν μάλιστα ἀπροσδόκητος ἔλθῃ, καὶ δι' ἐλαχίστου ἐς ὕβριν τρέπειν, Cl. thought inviting, but not necessary. The latter, though recognizing the difficulty in the separation of μάλιστα from ἀπροσδόκητος, thought it unadvisable to depart from the vulg., esp. as Clemens Alex. *Strom.* p. 620 c (ed. Sylb.), though often free in this respect, retains the order of the vulg., εἰώθασι δὲ οἱ πολλοὶ τῶν ἀνθρώπων οἷς ἂν μάλιστα καὶ δι' ἐλαχίστου ἀπροσδόκητος εὐπραξία ἔλθῃ, εἰς ὕβριν τρέπεσθαι. But there is a difficulty also, Steup thinks, in understanding the reference to a *sudden* change of fortune on the part of the Mytileneans (see Müller-Strübing, *Thuk. Forsch.* p. 183); for they could have been brought to the conviction that they would be victorious only slowly by the course of the war. Since then Gelzer's conjecture removes both difficulties without violence, Steup considers it probable. The difficulty in regard to δι' ἐλαχίστου is not removed by the transpositions suggested by Weil (*Rev. de Philol. N. S.* ii. p. 90), αἶς ἂν δι' ἐλαχίστου ἀπροσδόκητος εὐπραξία ἔλθῃ, μάλιστα καὶ ἐς ὕβριν τρέπειν, and Hude (p. 98), αἶς ἂν μάλιστα ἀπροσδόκητος καὶ δι' ἐλαχίστου εὐπραξία ἔλθῃ κτἑ.

39. 31. κολασθέντων. The vulg. has κολασθήτωσαν, just as the Mss. have in c. 67. 8 ὠφελείσθωσαν, i. 34. 2 μαθέτωσαν, iv. 92. 40 κτάσθωσαν, viii. 18. 13, 15 ἔστωσαν. The substitution of the shorter for these longer forms, first proposed by v. H. (*Stud. Thuc.* p. 116) on the basis of inscriptions from the period down to 300 B.C., has been adopted by Stahl (see *Qu. Gr.*² p. 63). But Cl. objected that in treaty-documents in Thuc. also (v. 18. 17, 31, 33, 42, 49; 47. 46, 47, 66; viii. 18. 5, 8) the shorter forms appear in the Mss. But viii. 18. 13, 15 belong also to a treaty-document, and if in these two out of the six passages a change must certainly be made, it would surely be better to change also the four others, than to assume an otherwise unsupported deviation of official language from ordinary prose.

39. 43. τῆς ἔπειτα προσόδου, δι' ἣν ἰσχύομεν, τὸ λοιπὸν στερήσεσθε. Steup emphasizes two difficulties here. 1) The undeniable pleonasm (ἔπειτα and τὸ λοιπόν), which Cl. sought to excuse by assuming a proleptic relation of τῆς ἔπειτα προσόδου to στερήσεσθε. 2) The words δι' ἣν ἰσχύομεν, which, since they presuppose a previous general mention of the revenues of the Athenians, are loosely connected with τῆς ἔπειτα προσόδου. The first difficulty would be removed by Ullrich's conjecture (*Beitr.* p. 1 ff.), τῆς ἐκεῖθεν προσόδου, for which he compares c. 46. 12 πόλιν ἐφθαρμένην παραλαβεῖν καὶ τῆς προσόδου τὸ λοιπὸν ἀπ' αὐτῆς στέρεσθαι; ἰσχύομεν δὲ πρὸς τοὺς πολεμίους τῷδε. But even with this reading, the difficulty in δι' ἣν ἰσχύομεν remains, just as it does with Weil's (*Rev. de Philol. N. S.* ii. p. 90) proposed reading, τῆς ἐπετείου προσόδου. For τῆς ἐπετείου προσόδου must be merely equiv. to τῆς ἐκεῖθεν προσόδου, unless perhaps τὸ μέρος be inserted before τὸ λοιπόν. Besides, ἐπέτειος does not occur elsewhere in Thuc., and indeed such a notion would be idle here. Hence Steup thinks that the words δι' ἦν ἰσχύομεν, τὸ λοιπόν have perhaps crept into the text from an explanation of τῆς ἔπειτα ... στερήσεσθε, in which use had been made of c. 46. 12 ff.

40. 15. τοὺς ὁμοίως τε καὶ οὐδὲν ἧσσον πολεμίους ὑπολειπομένους. Cl.'s conjecture (*Symbol.* i. p. 20) ὁμοίως, for ὁμοίους of the Mss., which had already been suggested by Fr. Thiersch, seems necessary, since ὁμοίους without a reference to something preceding seems hardly intelligible, and to omit ὁμοίους τε καί, with Kr., is too violent a remedy. To the embitterment of Cleon, who will allow nothing good to the Mytileneans, corresponds the combination of the affirmative and negative expression for the same idea. For the correlation with τε καί, cf. ἀπροσδοκήτου τε καὶ παρὰ λόγον, ii. 91. 15; τοιαῦτά τε καὶ παραπλήσια, vii. 78. 4.

40. 21. εἰ δὲ δή ... ἀνδραγαθίζεσθαι: Junghahn (*N. Jahrbb.* cxi. p. 662) considers this a clear case of false substantiation by means of a γάρ clause, such as he claims to have found repeatedly in Thuc. He claims that the idea to be substantiated, viz., that the punishment of the Mytileneans is *at once useful and just*, is made void by the following assertion, that in the interest of utility the punishment must be inflicted even *contrary to justice.* But Junge (*ibid.* p. 14) rightly denies the necessity of referring εἰ γὰρ κτέ. to τά τε δίκαια ἐς Μυτιληναίους καὶ τὰ ξύμφορα ἅμα ποιήσετε, and certainly the words εἰ γὰρ οὗτοι ὀρθῶς ἀπέστησαν, ὑμεῖς ἂν οὐ χρεὼν ἄρχοιτε may very well be taken as the substantiation of ὑμᾶς δὲ αὐτοὺς μᾶλλον δικαιώσεσθε. But Steup thinks there is an undeniable difficulty in εἰ δὲ δή ... ἀνδραγαθίζεσθαι, in view of the context, since the thought to be supplied is not quite clear; and, further, that the second clause of the apod. (ἢ παύεσθαι ... ἀνδραγαθίζεσθαι) does not suit the prot., since if the prot. be valid, what is stated in this second apod. cannot occur. Perhaps here too (see App. on c. 32. 11) the lack of a last revision may be recognized.

44. 6. ἤν τε καὶ ... φαίνοιτο. Cl. retains εἶεν, explaining that the apod. which would correspond to ἤν τε ... ξυγγνώμης (i.e. οὐ διὰ τοῦτο ἀπολῦσαι αὐτοὺς κελεύσω) is not expressed, but merely indicated by the concessive εἶεν, εἰ τῇ πόλει μὴ ἀγαθὸν φαίνοιτο. The ἀνταναπόδοτον here is the opp. of that in c. 3. 15. Generally it is the apod. of the first alternative that is suppressed, as in the cases cited on c. 3. 15, and esp. Ar. *Plut.* 468 ff.

κἂν μὲν ἀποφήνω μόνην
ἀγαθῶν ἁπάντων οὖσαν αἰτίαν ἐμὲ
ὑμῖν δι' ἐμέ τε ζῶντας ὑμᾶς, — εἰ δὲ μή,
ποιεῖτον ἤδη τοῦθ' ὅ τι ἂν ὑμῖν δοκῇ.

Here, however, the consequence of the first alternative, being all-important to the speaker, could not be suppressed, while it is quite in accord with his feelings to pass over the painful consequence of the second as lightly as possible. For this purpose εἶεν is quite appropriate, not as a regular apod., but as an exclamation implying resignation. "Very well! I ask no mercy, if it be not to the interest of the state." *Cf.* Soph. *Aj.* 101; *El.* 534. — The various emendations proposed, viz., ἐάν (Lindau and Burgess), ἐλεεῖν (Fittbogen), ἀνεῖναι (Kr.), Cl. objects to, because they all require οὐ κελεύσω to be supplied, which after the new alternative ἤν τε καί he thinks the const. of the context would hardly permit.

45. 14. κἀν τούτῳ ὅμως παραβαίνεται. Cl. explained παραβαίνεσθαι, here and in l. 12, as transferred from the law transgressed to the penalty for the transgression. Accordingly he understood τοῦτο of the death-penalty, which 'no longer opposes any bar,' and in l. 12 supplied τῶν ζημιῶν with παραβαινομένων, so that there after the gen. abs., whose subj. was ζημίαι in general, the more exactly defined subj. αἱ πολλαί (sc. ζημίαι) would follow. To Cl.'s view Lupus (*N. Jahrbb.* cxi. p. 166 f.) offers, Steup thinks, two well-grounded objections. The first is to the force of παραβαίνεσθαι assumed by Cl. παραβαίνειν has, it is true, the more general sense cited by Stahl, neglegere, nihil curare. *Cf.* Aeschin. iii. 204 οὐ τοὺς νόμους μόνον παραβέβηκεν, ἀλλὰ καὶ τὸν καιρὸν τῆς ἀναρρήσεως καὶ τὸν τόπον, Dem. xxiv. 32 παραβὰς τὸν χρόνον τὸν ἐκ τῶν νόμων, Din. i. 36 παραβεβηκὼς ἅπαντας τοὺς παρεληλυθότας καιρούς. But none of these consts. is by any means so strange as παραβαίνειν ζημίαν would be; nor of παραβαίνειν in the more general sense has any example been found in Thuc., although he uses the verb not infrequently. The second objection of Lupus was to the reference of the neut. τοῦτο to ἐς τὸν θάνατον, which Cl. explained as induced by the modified meaning of θάνατος (*death-penalty*). Steup finds a still stronger objection in the ὅμως after τοῦτο, on the ground that, "in course of time most punishments have gone as far as death" cannot properly be continued with "and this punishment is *nevertheless* not regarded."

To St.'s explanation also (see note under the text) Steup objects, on the ground that it neither allows to ὅμως, which is not intensive, its proper force, nor relieves the difficulty in the const. ζημίαι παραβαίνονται, and, further, that "and even this consideration is disregarded" expresses the speaker's meaning by no means so clearly as was to be expected.

If, however, the vulg. is untenable, Kr.'s conjecture κἀν τούτῳ is preferable to bracketing τοῦτο, with Lupus, since no probable explanation can be given as to how τοῦτο could have got into the simple sent. καὶ ὅμως παραβαίνεται. In i. 37. 15 also καὶ τοῦτο is the reading of Laur. for κἀν τούτῳ. See also on c. 66. 14.

45. 16 ff. ἡ μὲν πενία . . . κινδύνους. In this statement, Cl. explains, of the motives which in spite of all deterrents entice men into foolhardy enterprises, the outward circumstances which give the impulse are distinguished from the passions which urge to execution. In the two first clauses definite external and internal conditions are emphasized; in the third all other possible cases are comprehended in general terms. To πενία is opposed ἐξουσία, as furnishing the means for the satisfaction of all desires (*cf.* i. 38. 13; 123. 6), and to the τόλμα occasioned by the former corresponds the πλεονεξία induced by the latter. The likewise contrasted causes of the τόλμα and πλεονεξία, i.e. ἀνάγκη and ὕβρει καὶ φρονήματι, are, it is true, only outwardly parallel, the former residing in outward circumstances, the latter in the perverted disposition of men. In the third comprehensive clause αἱ ἄλλαι ξυντυχίαι, *the other relations of life*, answer to πενία and ἐξουσία of the two first, while to the definite causes there, ἀνάγκη and ὕβρις, corresponds here the indefinite κρεῖσσόν τι, which exercises decisive influence in the individual ξυντυχίαι (ὡς ἑκάστη τις, sc. ξυντυχία, κατέχεται), including, e.g. honor or revenge, or, as in the case of the Mytileneans, freedom and independence; and, finally, to the impelling states of mind there mentioned answers in this third comprehensive clause the general term ὀργή. In this so carefully selected and ordered series of conceptions occurs in the Mss. τῶν ἀνθρώπων, which, whether construed with αἱ ξυντυχίαι or with ὀργῇ, is equally unnecessary, and would be more naturally followed by ἕκαστός τις than by ἑκάστη τις. Hence the change to τὸν ἄνθρωπον, which gives to ἐξάγουσιν its most natural object. To Stahl's change ὀργήν (libidinem), for ὀργῇ, it is objected that the word seems not to have this meaning.

45. 21. ἐπιβουλήν. Cl. and Steup object to ἐπιβολή, on the ground that in the sense *Anschlag, Unternehmen*, it does not occur before Polybius. But it cannot be denied that, as Stahl says, though ἐπιβουλάς, *plots*, suits the context at i. 93. 23, ἐπιβολήν, *attempt*, is more appropriate here, and the verb ἐπιβάλλεσθαι, suscipere, conari, occurs in Plato *Tim.* 48 c; Soph. 264 b. The Schol. renders here by ἐγχείρησιν and in i. 93. 23 by ἐπιθέσεις, and so must have found the word ἐπιβολή in both places. Valla may have read here ἐπιβουλήν (insidiae), but certainly read ἐπιβολάς (incursus) in i. 93. 23.

46. 8. οὐκ ἄμεινον μὲν... παρασκευάσασθαι, πολιορκίᾳ τε παρατενεῖσθαι κτέ. Cl. inserted ἂν before ἄμεινον, but afterwards, in his full discussion of the const. of the aor. inf. referring to the fut. after verba dicendi or putandi (see on ii.[3] 3. 8), expressed a doubt of the correctness of the emendation. Following this suggestion, Steup has restored the vulg., on the ground that if in such consts. there is a freq. transition from the fut. to the aor. inf., the opposite change need not excite surprise. He thinks, further, that the difference in tense in the second clause is here the less striking, because this second clause is not, as originally intended, connected by δέ, but by τε.

50. 4. ἦσαν δὲ ὀλίγῳ πλείους χιλίων. Steup's argument against χιλίων is as follows: Müller-Strübing recognized that the number of the Mytileneans executed in Athens, as given in the vulg., was too large. His conclusion, however (*Thuk. Forsch.* p. 154 ff.), that the whole first part of c. 50 is an 'interpolation of a bloodthirsty grammarian,' must be considered unproved. But, although his discussion contains much that is distorted and useless, its essential correctness cannot be doubted, notwithstanding the arguments of Stahl (*Gött. Gel. Anz.* 1882, p. 99 ff.), Holzapfel (*Rh. Mus.* xxxvii. p. 448 ff.), and L. Herbst (*Philol.* xlii. p. 707 ff.).

The statement that more than 1000 Mytileneans were executed is irreconcilable with the previous narrative. This chief point has been too little emphasized by Müller-Strübing (p. 178 f. and 226). The Mytileneans sent by Paches to Athens, consisted, acc. to c. 35. § 1, partly of the πράξαντες πρὸς τοὺς Λακεδαιμονίους μάλιστα τῶν Μυτιληναίων (c. 28. 10), who on the entry of the Athenians had fled to the altars and then been transferred to Tenedos, where they could be more easily watched (*cf.* c. 2. § 3); partly of any others that seemed to Paches responsible for the revolt. It seems clear from Thuc.'s language (c. 35. 5 καὶ εἴ τις ἄλλος αὐτῷ αἴτιος ἐδόκει εἶναι τῆς ἀποστάσεως), that this second class comprised, as compared with the first, only a small number; so that the πράξαντες πρὸς τοὺς Λακεδαιμονίους μάλιστα τῶν Μυτιληναίων of c. 28. 10 formed the great majority of those sent to Athens. But if the hitherto dominant oligarchical party, in order to avoid danger on the inevitable fall of the city, had with the demos made an agreement with Paches (c. 28. § 1), the great majority of this party could have had no occasion, on the entry of the Athenians, in spite of the agreement to take refuge at the altars. The πράξαντες κτέ., who did this, must have been then only a small part of the oligarchs. And yet acc. to the vulg. these must have been not far from 1000! Besides, the negotiations with the Lacedaemonians *before the revolt* (*cf.* c. 2. § 1, 3; 5. § 4; 13. § 1) — and only to these negotiations can οἱ πράξαντες πρὸς τοὺς Λακεδαιμονίους μάλιστα τῶν Μυτιληναίων refer, acc. to c. 35. 5 καὶ εἴ τις ἄλλος αὐτῷ αἴτιος ἐδόκει εἶναι τῆς ἀποστάσεως, and c. 50. 2 οὓς ὁ Πάχης ἀπέπεμψεν ὡς αἰτιωτάτους ὄντας τῆς ἀποστάσεως — must have been conducted quite secretly. That there should have been nearly 1000 participants in such negotiations is incomprehensible, and, further, the μάλιστα πράξαντες could have been only a small part of the πράξαντες, and so only a small number of men. Such a small number accords best not only with c. 28. § 1, but with all the rest of the narrative, including the speeches, up to c. 50. § 1. Holzapfel and Herbst find support for the number of the vulg. in Cleon's words, c. 39. 31 καὶ μὴ τοῖς μὲν ὀλίγοις ἡ αἰτία προστεθῇ, τὸν δὲ δῆμον ἀπολύσητε, since they refer τοῖς ὀλίγοις only to the Mytileneans sent by Paches to Athens. But that not all the ὀλίγοι were brought to Athens is clear from c. 28. § 1, 2 and 35. § 1, and it is not surprising that Cleon, who wanted all the Mytileneans put to death, takes for granted that at least *all* the oligarchs, not merely those in Athens, are to be punished. Herbst cites also Diodotus's speech in support of χιλίων. But what is said in c. 47 concerning the demos of Mytilene has nothing to do with the number of oligarchs brought to Athens, and in c. 48. § 1, where Diodotus does mention the Mytileneans in Athens, he sets over against them, not the demos, but τοὺς ἄλλους.

Another point of considerable importance is made by Müller-Strübing (p. 161 ff.), that in all the literature of antiquity there is no other mention of this alleged execution of over 1000 prominent Mytileneans. Diod. xiii. 30. 4, where Gylippus says to the Syracusans, ἐπεί τοί γε Ἀθηναῖοι πῶς ἐχρήσαντο Μυτιληναίοις; κρατήσαντες γὰρ αὐτῶν, ἀδικῆσαι μὲν οὐδὲν βουλομένων, ἐπιθυμούντων δὲ τῆς ἐλευθερίας, ἐψηφίσαντο τοὺς ἐν τῇ πόλει κατασφάξαι κτέ., proves of course, as Holzapfel and Herbst recognize, that Diodorus and his authority knew of the execution of the Mytileneans brought to Athens. But it does not follow that either Diodorus or his authority knew the number 1000. As the words τοὺς ἐν τῇ πόλει are intelligible only when one knows the particulars from some other source, it is clear that Diodorus was making only hasty excerpts. It may therefore be conjectured that in Diodorus's authority Gylippus had spoken of both decrees of the Athenians and had cited as a conspicuous example of Athenian cruelty, that the sentence of death first decreed against all the Mytileneans had actually been executed on those in Athens. The number of the latter need not have been emphasized as large, and the assumption that it was not is sustained by the fact, that Diodorus in his own account of the Lesbian revolt (xii. 55) makes no mention of the matter of those chiefly culpable.

For the change of χιλίων to τριάκοντα H. Schütz has declared himself (*Ztschr. f. d. Gymnasialwesen*, xxxv. p. 455 f.). Müller-Strübing thought that ὀλίγῳ πλείους was against this change, since in a number less than 100 Thuc. would have given the units. But against this objection, *cf.* iv. 25. 2 ναυσὶν ὀλίγῳ πλείοσιν ἢ τριάκοντα, iv. 32. 6 νεῶν ἑβδομήκοντα καὶ ὀλίγῳ πλειόνων, iv. 44. 28 ὀλίγῳ ἐλάσσους πεντήκοντα.

50. 6. κλήρους δὲ ποιήσαντες τῆς γῆς πλὴν τῆς Μηθυμναίων κτέ. Steup remarks on this passage, viz.: The objections raised by Müller-Strübing (*Thuk. Forsch.* p. 218 ff.), and approved by Holzapfel (*Rh. Mus.* xxxvii. p. 462 ff. and xxxviii. p. 631 ff.), against what is here narrated, — confirmed, too, by Diod. xii. 55. 10, — are convincingly refuted by Stahl (*Gött. Gel. Anz.*, 1882, p. 106 ff. and *Rh. Mus.* xxxviii. p. 143 ff.). But L. Herbst, in his attempt at refutation (*Philol.* xlii. p. 720 ff.), proceeds from the assumption that the area of Lesbos is only 10 German square miles (= 212 English), whereas it is 1700 square kilometers (= 656 English square miles). The comparatively small rental is very easily explained, if, as may be conjectured, the object of the Athenians was only to furnish to a considerable number of poorer citizens a definite income at the expense of the Lesbians. Besides, there is nothing in the way of assuming that the former landowners were all oligarchs, so that the demos, whom the Athenians had reason to be indulgent with, would be little, if at all, affected. Further, the fact that Antiphon speaks of the course of Athens toward Mytilene in words that remind one of c. 48. § 1 (v. 77 ἐπεὶ δ' ὑμεῖς τοὺς αἰτίους τούτων ἐκολάσατε . . ., τοῖς δ' ἄλλοις Μυτιληναίοις ἄδειαν ἐδώκατε οἰκεῖν τὴν σφετέραν αὐτῶν) is no argument against the confiscation of the whole of the land. For acc. to the present passage the old owners remained as hereditary tenants on their former estates, and the orator would naturally use as mild an expression as possible of the course of the Athenians. Still less difficulty is occasioned by § 79 of the same oration, regarding the consequences of the revolt for the Mytileneans, ἠλλάξαντο μὲν πολλῆς εὐδαιμονίας πολλὴν κακοδαιμονίαν, ἐπεῖδον

APPENDIX. 293

δὲ τὴν ἑαυτῶν πατρίδα ἀνάστατον γενομένην. For, as the citation from § 77 shows, ἀνάστατον must be understood, either of the collapse of the power of Mytilene, or, with Stahl, of the ravages caused by the war.

51. 4. πύργον ἐνοικοδομήσαντες. Steup objects to πύργον on the ground that, acc. to l. 12, there were two πύργοι. Cl. explained πύργον as collective (*fortifications*); but the word seems not to have this force elsewhere, and here at any rate it would be highly improbable, not only on account of δύο πύργω in l. 12, but also because these two towers seem not to have been connected by fortifications. This last consideration is also against Meineke's conjecture (*Hermes* iii. p. 364) πύργωμα. Perhaps πύργους should be restored.

51. 8. τούς τε Πελοποννησίους. Steup thinks that the proleptic const., as explained in the text, would have been preceded by τοὺς 'Αθηναίους φυλάσσεσθαι, not by τὴν φυλακὴν τοῖς 'Αθηναίοις εἶναι. For the conjecture of Hünnekes (*Quaest. Thuc.* p. 32 sqq.), he compares vii. 17. 17 πρὸς τὴν σφετέραν ἀντίταξιν τῶν τριήρων τὴν φυλακὴν ποιούμενοι. The omission of the art. need not excite surprise perhaps, since the Peloponnesians have not been, like the Megarians, mentioned before (*cf.* i. 44. 1), and indeed Thuc.'s use of the article with names of peoples seems often arbitrary (*cf.* i. 28. 12, 16). Badham conjectured ἔς τε Πελοποννησίους.

51. 11. ἑλὼν οὖν ἀπὸ τῆς Νισαίας πρῶτον δύο πύργω προέχοντε μηχαναῖς ἐκ θαλάσσης κτέ. Against the usual explanation of the words ἀπὸ τῆς Νισαίας, *on the side toward Nisaea* (ab ea parte quae Nisaeam spectat), Steup objects: 1) that it has not been proved that the words can mean this, 2) that the reference here must be to a *different* side of the island from that toward Nisaea, of which it is remarked, l. 14, ἀπετείχιζε καὶ τὸ ἐκ τῆς ἠπείρου κτέ., 3) that it would be incomprehensible that Nicias should have first attacked the side toward the near and hostile mainland. Against the explanation of Ullrich (*Quaest. Aristoph.* p. 36 and *Beitr.* iii. p. 28), adopted in the text, no valid objection can be made. Since Thuc. could assume as known that Nisaea was in possession of the enemies of the Athenians, the expression ἀπὸ τῆς Νισαίας, though in itself ambiguous, might very well be connected, in the sense *away from Nisaea*, with ἑλών. Cl.'s objection, that ἐκ θαλάσσης would render ἀπὸ τῆς Νισαίας in this sense superfluous, is valid only if ἐκ θαλάσσης = *from the sea-side* (*cf.* iv. 11. 9; 31. 11), whereas there is no reason why the words may not be taken in their original sense, *from the sea*. Hence there is no need with Cl. to bracket ἀπὸ τῆς Νισαίας, nor with C. F. Müller to transfer it to the place of αὐτόθεν. — There is no reason to doubt, with Arn. and others, that both towers were in Minoa; for the expedition was ἐπὶ Μινῴαν, and if any point on the mainland had been occupied by Nicias this should have been clearly stated. — In l. 13 Cl. proposed κλειθρώσας for ἐλευθερώσας. But if ἐς τὸ μεταξὺ τῆς νήσου be explained as in the text (not as heretofore by supplying καὶ τῆς ἠπείρου), there is no difficulty in the clause, and the fact that ἐλευθεροῦν, in this sense, seems not to occur elsewhere in Attic is not of itself sufficient ground for objection.

294   APPENDIX.

51. 17. ὕστερον δὴ καὶ ἐν τῇ νήσῳ τεῖχος ἐγκαταλιπὼν καὶ φρουρὰν ἀνεχώρησε τῷ στρατῷ. Meineke's objection to καὶ ἐν τῇ νήσῳ τεῖχος ἐγκαταλιπών (*Hermes* iii. p. 364) seems well founded. τεῖχος ἐγκαταλιπών is a strange way to express the construction of further fortifications, as opp. to the walling off of the bridge. Meineke was inclined to consider τεῖχος a gloss to τοῦτο and to bracket both this and the second καί, as indeed Stahl, Cl., and v. H. have done. But Steup thinks that thus the first καί would be rendered unintelligible. Further, he finds strange the omission of any mention of the leaving of a guard of ships (*cf.* ii. 94. 23), and infers from 1. 14 ἤ . . . ἐπιβοήθεια ἦν τῇ νήσῳ, coupled with the lack of any express statement of the capture of the whole island, that at first a part of the island still remained in the hands of the Peloponnesians. Concluding that the passage has suffered from omissions rather than additions, he suggests the following, as possibly the original form of the text: ὕστερον δὴ ⟨καὶ τὴν ἄλλην Μινῴαν ἑλὼν⟩ καὶ ἐν τῇ νήσῳ τεῖχος ⟨ἐγκατοικοδομήσας ναῦς⟩ ἐγκαταλιπὼν καὶ φρουρὰν ἀνεχώρησε τῷ στρατῷ.

52. 6. εἰρημένον γὰρ ἦν κτέ. That the Schol. did not read ἦν is, as Pp. observes, clear from the remark, ἀντίπτωσις, ἤτοι αἰτιατικὴ ἀντὶ γενικῆς · ἀντὶ τοῦ εἰρημένου γὰρ αὐτῷ εἶπεν. Hence Cobet (*ad Hyper.* p. 68) would omit γὰρ ἦν. But the value to be given to the authority of the Schol. may be judged from the fact that he not only let γάρ stand, but failed to recognize the const. of the acc. abs. Though the acc. abs. here might be allowed, if the Mss. so read, it must be remembered, that in the passage compared by Cobet, vii. 18. 14, as well as in i. 140. 14 and Ar. *Lysist.* 13, the abs. εἰρημένον precedes, with the antithesis to the condition therein expressed following. Such is not the case here. Besides, the distinct parenthesis makes clearer the antithesis of the two clauses βίᾳ μὲν οὐκ ἐβούλετο ἑλεῖν and προσπέμπει δὲ αὐτοῖς κήρυκα, and the periphrastic εἰρημένον ἦν, for εἴρητο, is sufficiently well established (Xen. *Cyrop.* iv. 5. 13, *cf.* Xen. *Hell.* vii. 1. 28). Hence the reading of all the Mss. is to be retained against the Schol.

54. 13. καὶ γὰρ ἠπειρῶταί τε κτέ. Stahl renders καὶ γάρ, etenim, but that the words have this force in Thuc. lacks proof. E. Kalinka, *Diss. Philol. Vindob.* ii. p. 168, explains that καί emphasizes the concessive force of ὄντες (*cf.* vi. 16.34), but the position of the words is decidedly against this view (which would require, perhaps, ἐναυμαχήσαμέν τε γὰρ καὶ ἠπειρῶται ὄντες). Cl. correlated καί in l. 13 with τε in εἴτε τι ἄλλο in l. 15, explaining that for the second καί, which was to be expected, the weaker τε was substituted after the vivid statement of the first member. He proposed also ἠπειρῶταί γε, on the ground that thus the difficulty of the first καί would be lessened and the emphatically placed ἠπειρῶται be made more effective.

58. 10. ὥστε καὶ τῶν σωμάτων ἄδειαν ποιοῦντες ὅσια ἂν δικάζοιτε καὶ προνοοῦντες ὅτι κτέ. Steup considers the text unsound here. To Stahl's explanation, that the first καί = etiam, he objects that τῶν σωμάτων ἄδειαν ποιοῦντες is simply the antithesis to τὰ σώματα διαφθεῖραι in l. 7, — for if the *Lacedaemonians*

APPENDIX.   295

did not kill the Plataeans their lives were secure, since they had surrendered to the Lacedaemonians (c. 52. § 2 f.) — and hence καί = etiam is impossible. The co-ordination of the two partic. clauses (καὶ τῶν σωμάτων ... ποιοῦντες and καὶ προνοοῦντες ὅτι κτέ.), both dependent on ὥστε ὅσια ἂν δικάζοιτε, as usually explained, he finds also unsatisfactory; for, taking προνοοῦντες, sc. ἡμῶν = *caring for us*, he thinks that the parenthetical clause, ὁ δὲ νόμος ... τούτους shows this to mean about the same as τῶν σωμάτων ἄδειαν ποιοῦντες. The consideration that ὅτι ἑκόντας τε κτέ. refers to points not before mentioned leads him to conjecture that the original text may have read ὥστε καὶ τῶν ⟨δὲ ἕνεκα τῶν⟩ σωμάτων ἄδειαν ποιοῦντες. Thus would be secured an opposition of different motives and the correlation would be similar to that in c. 38. 27; 46. 1; ii. 39. 24. In Thuc. ὅδε often refers to something mentioned before, as e.g. c. 59. 2. *Cf.* also c. 66. 20 πάντων αὐτῶν ἕνεκα κολασθήσεσθε.

58. 28. ἱερά τε θεῶν ... ἀφαιρήσεσθε. Stahl objected (*N. Jahrbb.* xcvii. p. 119 f.) to Cl.'s explanation of this passage, and substituted ἐρημοῦντες for ἐρημοῦτε, rendering, *desolating the sanctuaries of the gods, to whom they prayed when they conquered the Medes, you will take away also the hereditary sacrifices instituted by those who founded and built them* (sc. τὰ ἱερά). The ἱερά esp. had in view Stahl thought to be the temple of Zeus Eleutherios and the θυσίαι, those common sacrifices which the Hellenes instituted after the battle of Plataea at this sanctuary, which had been founded by them (Plut. *Arist.* 20). Cl. was not convinced by Stahl's arguments, and Steup is even less so. The latter considers the θεοί to be only the ancient gods of the land, as shown by ii. 74. § 3, and, accordingly, that the ἱερά cannot refer to a sanctuary that was not established till after the battle. For the const. which supplies αὐτάς (sc. θυσίας) with ἐσσαμένων καὶ κτισάντων, as Cl. explained, Steup cites Pind. *Ol.* vi. 69 ἑορτὰν κτίζειν, *Ol.* xi. 24 ἀγῶνα κτίζεσθαι, Eratosth. (apud *Athen.* vii. p. 276 a) τοῦ Πτολεμαίου κτίζοντος ἑορτὴν (Kaibel ἑορτῶν) καὶ θυσιῶν παντοδαπῶν γένη, though he doubts whether a parallel can be found for ἐσσαμένων θυσίας. [Not very different is Eur. *I. T.* 945
    ἔστιν γὰρ ὁσία ψῆφος, ἣν Ἄρει ποτὲ
    Ζεὺς εἵσατ᾽ ἐκ τοῦ δὴ χερῶν μιάσματος.]

But he considers the best remedy for all difficulties would be to bracket ἐρημοῦτε, as a marginal explanation which crept into the text, and construe both ἱερά and θυσίας as objects of ἀφαιρήσεσθε, supplying ἱερά with ἐσσαμένων, θυσίας with κτισάντων. In τὰς πατρίους an antithesis may be assumed to those sacrifices established in consequence of the battle. *Cf.* iv. 98. § 2 f., which possibly supports the omission of ἐρημοῦτε.

58. 29. ἐρημοῦτε. Cl. held that ἐρημοῦτε is to be considered, with Buttmann *Gr.* 95, N. 16, not a pres., but a cont. fut. form, as in verbs with a long vowel before -σω, as cited by Buttmann, *l.c.*, and also in Soph. *El.* 1365 κυκλοῦνται, *O. C.* 618 τεκνοῦται, Eur. *Phoen.* 888 δαιμονῶντας, Ar. *Ran.* 472 φρουροῦσι, Plato *Phaedo* 100 b ἐπιχειρῶν, Xen. *Hell.* i. 6. 32 οἰκεῖται, prob. also Thuc. vii. 56. 11 ἐλευθεροῦσθαι, 12 ἀπολύεσθαι.

296   APPENDIX.

67. 19. παρενόμησαν. So Stahl and v. H. following Laur. Cl. and Steup retain, with the rest of the Mss., παρηνόμησαν. The temporal augment is due to false derivation. Stahl says, 'Quam mature verbi originem ignorare coeperint, ostendit παρηνομημένου in *C. I. G.* 2691 c (titulus in Caria factus est a. 355 ante Chr.), nisi lapicidae errorem statuere mavis. . . . Scriptoribus certe hanc qualiscumque est ignorantiam vix recte imputaveris.'

67. 21. καὶ † οὐκ ἀνταποδόντες κτέ. Usually a comma at most is placed before these words, and most recent editt., taking καί . . . τιμωρίαν as part of the period beginning with παρενόμησάν τε, pronounce corrupt the aor. partic. ἀνταποδόντες, which is in the way of such connexion. Pp. would prefer ἀνταποδιδόντες or ἀνταποδώσοντες, Bk. ἀνταποδιδόντες or ἂν ἀποδόντες, while Cl. and v. H. write, after Dobree, ἂν ἀνταποδόντες, Stahl ἀνταποδώσοντες. But Steup argues that, even if the partic. be so emended as to express more or less clearly that the punishment must first be suffered, καί . . . τιμωρίαν cannot be joined to the preceding. In παρενόμησάν τε . . . κρίναντες the speakers refer, after the preceding rather negative statements, to the fact that the Plataeans had acted contrary to law and right without having first been treated thus, as something which must lead to severe punishment. Accordingly, the thought that the death-penalty demanded by the Thebans will not be likewise illegal, as καί . . . τιμωρίαν is usually explained (τὴν ἴσην τιμωρίαν, *the equivalent punishment, i.e.* likewise contrary to law and right), cannot form a part of the same sent. with the preceding, in the manner assumed by most editors. It must have been expressed independently. This Goell. and Hofman recognized, and proposed καὶ οὐκ ἀνταποδόντες τὴν νῦν ἴσην τιμωρίαν (ἔννομα γάρ) πείσονται κτέ. But the parenthesis ἔννομα γάρ would be too harsh, whether πείσονται or ἀνταποδόντες be supplied with it. If now the words καί . . . τιμωρίαν be joined neither with the preceding nor with the following, ἀνταποδόντες must either be changed to a finite verb with fut. or pres. meaning, or, as seems more natural, the loss of such a verb assumed, c.g. δόξουσιν before οὐκ ἀνταποδόντες. Thus, before directing a last appeal to the Spartans (ἀμύνατε οὖν κτέ.), the speakers would assert, still in reply to the statements of c. 57. § 1 f., 58. § 1 ff., that the death-penalty would be just. *Cf.* l. 26 ἀνταπόδοτε χάριν δικαίαν and c. 53. 5 ἡγούμενοι τὸ ἴσον μάλιστ' ἂν φέρεσθαι.

68. 16. [Θηβαῖοι]. Cl.'s reasons for bracketing Θηβαῖοι are as follows. In l. 1 οἱ Λακεδαιμόνιοι δικασταί are represented as the actors; but since these in the explanation of the grounds of their decision (νομίζοντες . . . πεπονθέναι) appear as the representatives of the Lacedaemonian state, from l. 9 on the subject implied is the Peloponnesians in general without special distinction (*cf.* c. 52. 3, 16), the leaders of course being meant. This being the case, it is strange to find in l. 16 the Thebans mentioned as the authors of the further measures. Had they a closer relation to Megara, or any more reason to propitiate the Plataean Hera than the rest of the allies? Above all, how is it that the Thebans τὴν γῆν

APPENDIX. 297

δημοσιώσαντες ἀπεμίσθωσαν (for if they are the subj. of ἔδοσαν in l. 18, then necessarily also of ἀπεμίσθωσαν in l. 26)? Why should they alone reap the fruits of the common victory? Besides, do not the words καὶ ἐνέμοντο Θηβαῖοι (26) presuppose a different subj. for ἀπεμίσθωσαν? Down to ἀπεμίσθωσαν, then, the subj. is the enemies in general of the Plataeans, οἱ Πελοποννήσιοι, but after the mention of the advantage accruing to the Thebans from their proximity, καὶ ἐνέμοντο Θηβαῖοι, the remark follows naturally, that in general the Lacedaemonians for the sake of the Thebans had turned against the Plataeans.

70. 3. ὑπὸ Κορινθίων ἀφεθέντες. In determining the date of the liberation of the 250 Corcyraeans, the following considerations, Steup thinks, are esp. to be noted. When the Lacedaemonians, after the failure of their expedition to Lesbos, conceived the plan of an expedition against Corcyra (c. 69. § 2), Nicostratus (c. 75) was not yet at Corcyra. For one thing that influenced the Lacedaemonians was that the Athenians were περὶ Ναύπακτον with only twelve ships (c. 69. 10). But Nicostratus arrived three days after the victory of the oligarchs over the demos of Corcyra (c. 72. § 2). And this victory, even if ἐν τούτῳ in c. 72. 3 refer only to the measures of the Athenians mentioned in c. 72. § 1, and not also to the voyage of the Corcyraean embassy (c. 71. 6; 72. 1), must have occurred only a few weeks after the murder of Pithias (c. 70. 26). For one can certainly assume as intervening only the voyage of the ambassadors to Athens and a few days before and after. Further, the resolution of the Corcyraeans (c. 70. 9) can hardly have preceded the murder of Pithias by more than two months. For the Attic trireme which brought to Corcyra the ambassadors mentioned c. 70. 8 was, acc. to c. 70. 28, still there at the time of the murder. That resolution therefore was adopted prob. not earlier than the first half of the winter of 428–27. Since, finally, Thuc. makes the στασιάζειν of the Corcyraeans begin with the return of the 250, but the στάσις did not come to light before the negotiations with the Athenian and Corinthian ambassadors (c. 70. § 2), and in c. 80. 8 it is stated, οἱ Ἀθηναῖοι πυνθανόμενοι τὴν στάσιν καὶ τὰς μετ' Ἀλκίδου ναῦς ἐπὶ Κέρκυραν μελλούσας πλεῖν, the efforts of the 250 up to the time of their first success cannot have lasted very long. Accordingly, the 250 returned at earliest in the beginning of the winter of 428–27. That four or five years should have elapsed before the 250 were persuaded to win back Corcyra for the Corinthians and the sham transaction as to their ransom was accomplished, does not seem incomprehensible when one considers the bitterness with which the war was waged between Corinth and Corcyra and their previous relations (cf. i. 25. § 3, 4; 34. § 1; 38. § 1). The fact that the Corcyraeans, after the beginning of the war, had assisted the Athenians, so far as we know, only in the summer of 431, B. Schmidt (*Kork. Stud.* p. 69) thinks due to the activity of the 250 after their return; but there is possibly another explanation. Acc. to the treaty with Athens, the Corcyraeans were bound only to come to the *defense* of Athens or her ξύμμαχοι when summoned. Their participation in the Athenian *attack* upon Peloponnesus in 431 (ii. 25. § 1) was perhaps a free service in recognition of the assistance received in 433 or 432. That they did not further take part unnecessarily in the war was quite in accord with their previous policy (*cf.* i. 32. § 4), though they may have been influenced also by anxiety for the 250 citizens in the hands of the Corinthians (see text-note on ὀκτακοσίων ταλάντων). The obligation to lend aid on demand hardly applied, however, to the conflicts of the Acarnanians and Phormio with the Peloponnesians in the summer of 429 B.C. For the Acarnanians were not ξύμμαχοι of the Athenians in the narrower sense prob. alone contemplated in i. 44. 10, and Naupactus was not directly attacked.

77. 12. ὧν ἦσαν ... Πάραλος. Müller-Strübing (*Polem. Beitr. etc.* p. 35 ff.) attacked the genuineness of these words, but Steup contends that they are open to no well founded objections, chronologically or otherwise. The two state-ships may very well, after fulfilling their missions to Paches (c. 33. § 1, 2), have returned directly to Athens and then sailed straightway to Naupactus. It is therefore not at all impossible that at the time when the Peloponnesians conceived their plan as to Corcyra (c. 69. § 2) these ships were already near Naupactus. Nor need the fact that twelve ships with Asopius are mentioned already at c. 7. 9 be in the way of the assumption that the Salaminia and the Paralos are included in δώδεκα ναυσὶ μόναις παρόντων Ἀθηναίων περὶ Ναύπακτον, c. 69. 10. For of the twelve, two might have returned to Athens or been lost in some way. Besides, since it is said of Nicostratus in c. 75. 2 παραγίγνεται βοηθῶν ἐκ Ναυπάκτου δώδεκα ναυσὶ κτέ., but not ταῖς ἐκ κτέ., it is also conceivable that he had left behind two ships at Naupactus — perhaps with a view to getting speedy information of suspicious movements of the Peloponnesians in the Corinthian Gulf. In that case it must be assumed that at the time to which c. 69. 10 refers the two state-ships had not yet reached the neighbourhood of Naupactus, which in itself is not less possible than the contrary.

80. 8. προσπλέουσαι ἀπὸ Λευκάδος. Steup considers these words irreconcilable with the statement in c. 81. 3, that the Peloponnesians after having sailed along the coast from Sybota to Leucas had transported their ships across the isthmus of the Leucadians, ὅπως μὴ περιπλέοντες ὀφθῶσιν, sc. ὑπὸ τῶν ἑξήκοντα νεῶν Ἀθηναίων. Had the fear indicated by ὅπως κτέ. been, as Schmidt assumes, idle and due merely to the anxiety and cowardice of Alcidas, Thuc. would surely have intimated this. The apprehension then, if the text be sound, must have been not superfluous, *i.e.* the Athenian fleet was, when Alcidas neared the city of Leucas, acc. to c. 81. § 1, not yet past the peninsula. On the other hand, the information received by Alcidas on the evening of the day after the sea-fight was that Eurymedon's fleet *was sailing up from Leucas*. For, acc. to the order of words, Thuc. must have meant to connect ἀπὸ Λευκάδος with προσπλέουσαι. Considering now that, acc. to Hyginus (*apud Charis.* i. p. 134 K), those coming from the north were wont to shorten the voyage by crossing the isthmus of the Leucadians (ibi solent iteris minuendi causa remulco, quem Graeci πάκτωνα dicunt, navem traducere), and that, acc. to iv. 8. 8, a Peloponnesian fleet hastening southwards is transported across this isthmus, the conjecture seems warranted that the words ὅπως ... ὀφθῶσιν in c. 81. 3 are an interpolation. To bracket ἀπὸ Λευκάδος in the present passage would, on the contrary, be inadvisable, since προσπλεῖν could hardly be used of a fleet still at a considerable distance from Leucas, as must be assumed acc. to c. 81. § 1. Alcidas had presumably, in view of the probable appearance of another Athenian fleet (cf. c. 69. 12), erected on Leucas and on the coast of Epirus a series of signal-stations. To signal direct from Leucas to Sybota was hardly possible in the fifth century b.c. See B. Schmidt, p. 76 f.

82. 5. καὶ ἐν μὲν εἰρήνῃ ... αὐτούς. Cl. conjectured for ἑτοίμων (sc. ὄντων) ἐτόλμων, or ἐν ἑτοίμῳ ἦν, or ἑτοῖμ᾽ ἦν. Steup considers the anacoluthon of the vulg. unendurable, and would prefer ἐτόλμων, the subj. being the parties, while the Athenians and Lacedaemonians are the subj. of ἐχόντων.

82. 20. πύστει τῶν προγενομένων πολὺ ἐπέφερε τὴν ὑπερβολὴν τοῦ καινοῦσθαι τὰς διανοίας. Steup's critical note is as follows. In Kr.'s text of Dion. H. *de Thuc. Jud.* p. 886, this passage is given just as in the Mss. of Thuc.; but in the following discussion by Dion. H. it reads, ἐπιπύστει τῶν προγεγενημένων πολλὴν ἐπέφερε τὴν ὑπερβολὴν ἐς τὸ καινοῦσθαι τὰς διανοίας. Stahl adopts this latter form of the text, Widmann ἐπιπύστει and ἐς τὸ καινοῦσθαι, v. H. only ἐπιπύστει. Cl., though considering προγεγενημένων and πολλὴν acceptable, hesitated to adopt them, on the ground that the relation of Dion. H.'s text of Thuc. to the vulg. is too uncertain. Acc. to the explanatory passage which follows in Dion. H., οἱ δὲ ὑστερίζοντες ἐπιπυνθανόμενοι τὰ γεγενημένα παρ᾽ ἑτέρων ἐλάμβανον ὑπερβολὴν ἐπὶ τὸ διανοεῖσθαί τι καινότερον, it can hardly be doubted that he read ἐπιπύστει. But since the word is not found elsewhere, "report" was to be expected, and ἐφυστερίζοντα and ἐπέφερε are close by, it is not prob. that Thuc. wrote ἐπιπύστει. Dion. H. seems to have read also ἐς τὸ καινοῦσθαι, but this has no advantage over the vulg., since the const. of τοῦ καινοῦσθαι τὰς διανοίας with τὴν ὑπερβολὴν offers no difficulty. Even if Dion. H. read προγεγενημένων, and the pf. be the more usual form, the aor. is certainly not at variance with Thuc.'s usage. As to πολλὴν ἐπέφερε, it is hardly to be doubted that Dion. H. did not so read, since acc. to L. Sadee, *de Dion. H. Scriptis Rhet.* p. 164, the Cod. Ambros. has in the second citation, as well as the first, πολὺ ἐπέφερε, and the explanations, ἐλάμβανον ὑπερβολὴν ἐπὶ τὸ διανοεῖσθαί τι καινότερον and πολλὴν τὴν ἐπίδοσιν ἐλάμβανον εἰς τὸ διανοεῖσθαί τι καινότερον are not incompatible with the reading πολὺ ἐπέφερε. Still the adv. use of πολύ is undeniably harsh, and if one considers that even without πολύ a good sense is obtained ("pushed to the extreme their revolutionary spirit"), that Dion. H. found before πύστει a superfluous ἐπι-, and that before καὶ τὰ ἐφυστερίζοντά που some idea like ἐπὶ πολύ seems lacking, the conjecture is natural, that originally after τὰ τῶν πόλεων the words ἐπὶ πολύ were first omitted, then written on the margin, and finally restored to the text in distorted fashion, as in Dion. H.'s text. The reading of Cod. M is ἀποπύστει, in which Stahl finds a trace of ἐπιπύστει. But that may be due to διττογραφία after ἐφυστερίζοντά που, as Hude suggests (*Comm. Crit.* p. 112).

82. 28. ἀσφαλείᾳ δὲ τὸ ἐπιβουλεύσασθαι... εὔλογος. All the better Mss. read ἀσφάλεια, which Goell. and Bk. retain, putting a comma after ἐπιβουλεύσασθαι. Pp., Kr., and Bm. read as in the text, and render, *to deliberate with caution was regarded as a specious pretext for declining.* But to this Cl. makes three objections: 1) that ἀσφαλείᾳ, adv., *with caution*, is strange, not only in position, but also in meaning, since it rather signifies (objective) *security* than (subjective) *caution;* 2) that ἐπιβουλεύσασθαι, *deliberate, reflect*, is without parallel; 3) that ἀποτροπή = *warding off, defense*, often occurs in Attic (Aesch. *Pers.* 217; Plato *Prot.* 354 b; *Rep.* 382 c), but hardly = *declining* (a contest). As opp. to τὸ ἐμπλήκτως ὀξύ, *inconsiderate rashness*, Cl. would render τὸ ἐπιβουλεύσασθαι, "to plot secretly against an enemy," though the use of the mid. seems strange. With this meaning, it would be better to read ἀσφάλεια δὲ τὸ ἐπιβουλεύσασθαι, ἀποτροπῆς πρόφασις εὔλογος, "to plot secretly against an enemy passed for (ἐνομίσθη) self-preservation, a specious pretense of warding off." The reading of the text Cl. would render, "to plot secretly was reckoned the part of self-preservation, a specious pretense of warding off," — construing ἀσφαλείᾳ with προσετέθη. — Steup thinks that after τὸ δ' ἐμπλήκτως ὀξὺ... προσετέθη one must regard ἀσφάλεια as the aim of the opposite demeanour, and prefers therefore ἀσφαλείᾳ, rendering, with Lupus (*N. Jahrbb.* cxi. p. 169 f.), "with a view to security." *Cf.* l. 8 and 38. The order ἀσφαλείᾳ τὸ ἐπιβουλεύσασθαι, however, he finds the more strange since the art. is unnecessary (*cf.* c. 38. 5; 46. 10), and conjectures that Thuc. wrote ἀσφαλείᾳ του ἐπιβουλεύσασθαι, "to deliberate with a view to the security of an enterprise." For ἐπιβουλεύσασθαι = βουλεύσασθαι he compares ἐπιβουλεύειν, as equiv. to βουλεύειν, c. 20. 5. Lupus prefers, with Lindau, ἔτι βουλεύσασθαι, but Steup objects that one would expect rather "before" than "still."— In support of the view adopted in the text, *cf.* Schol. τὸ ἐπιπολὺ βουλεύσασθαι δι' ἀσφάλειαν πρόφασις ἀποτροπῆς ἐνομίζετο. See Stahl, *N. Jahrbb.* xcvii. p. 122.

84. Cl.'s critical note is as follows. Among internal proofs of the spuriousness of this chapter the following deserve consideration: 1) The Schol. remarks, τὰ ὠβελισμένα οὐδενὶ τῶν ἐξηγητῶν ἔδοξε Θουκυδίδου εἶναι· ἀσαφῆ γὰρ καὶ τῷ τύπῳ τῆς ἑρμηνείας καὶ τοῖς διανοήμασι πολὺν ἐμφαίνοντα τὸν νεωτερισμόν. 2) Dion. II., who discusses at length (*de Thuc. Jud.* c. 28–33, p. 885–896) both the matter and form of cc. 81, 82, does not touch c. 84, though it required notice even more than those; hence it may be inferred that it was not in his text.[1] 3) Cod. F obelizes every line of the chapter.

---

[1] It seems worthy of remark that Dion. II., c. 28 and 29, in his discussion of c. 82, passes from l. 5 καὶ τοῖς ὀλίγοις τοὺς Λακεδαιμονίους directly to l. 19 ἐστασίαζέ τε οὖν, although he makes the transition in these words ἃ δὲ τούτοις ἐπιφέρει... ἃ μέλλω νυνὶ λέγειν. It may be conjectured that his text did not contain the intervening passage. On the other hand, as Steup adds, the omission of any consideration of l. 28 τὸ δ' ἐμπλήκτως ὀξὺ ἀνδρὸς μοίρᾳ προσετέθη, and of l. 39–44 καὶ τὰς ἐς σφᾶς αὐτοὺς πίστεις... προπαθεῖν is prob. to be ascribed to the haste of Dion. II., or to the carelessness of copyists.

For added proof furnished by the thought and form of expression, see notes under the text. So far as Thuc.'s usage is followed, this is to be ascribed to intentional imitation on the part of the unknown author.

Since Bk. the great majority of editors have condemned the chapter, but Kämpf (*Quaest. Thuc.* 2) and Jowett defend it. Cobet's conjecture (*Mnem.* N. S. viii. p. 143) that the chapter is from Philistus, has been, as Steup thinks, rightly rejected by Naber (*ibid.* xiv. p. 139). The imitation, cited by Pp., from Dio C. lii. 34. 6, 7 would indicate that Dio C. knew the chapter.

85. 14. ἐs τὸ ὄρος τὴν Ἰστώνην. The location of this mountain near the city, which many have deemed necessary on account of l. 15 ἔφθειρον τοὺς ἐν τῇ πόλει, has been rightly opposed, Steup thinks, by B. Schmidt, *Kork. Stud.* p. 61. In l. 7, where Thuc. speaks of the forays made by the oligarchs from the Corcyraean Peraea, their enemies are designated as τοὺς ἐν τῇ νήσῳ, for which expression, after the transfer of the basis of the oligarchs to the island, a designation of their enemies as τοὺς ἐν τῇ πόλει is quite in order, no matter how far the τεῖχος of the oligarchs was from the city. To a misapprehension is due, acc. to Schmidt p. 97, also the remark of Steph. Byz. Ἰστώνη, ὄρος προσεχὲς τῇ Κερκύρᾳ. Θουκυδίδης τρίτῃ. τὸ ἐθνικὸν Ἰστωναῖος ὡς Τορωναῖος. Schmidt locates the τεῖχος of the oligarchs, with Vischer, *Erinnerungen aus Gr.* p. 19, on Pantokrator — in the northeastern part of the island, and the highest mountain of Corfu — induced esp. by the consideration that the 600 prob. landed in the northeast, where the channel is narrowest and their crossing could not be so easily observed from the city (p. 59). But the forays from the mainland had certainly been directed against various parts of the island ; so that the oligarchs seem not to have been in very great fear of their opponents, esp. as these seem to have been from time to time occupied elsewhere (*cf.* c. 94. 8 ; 95. 15). Hence it is uncertain whether the oligarchs chose the narrowest crossing, or placed their τεῖχος on the mountain nearest to their landing-place. Nor does the fact that a modern village in the northeast of the island is called Vistonas (Βίστωνας) give a sure basis for determining the locality of the τεῖχος and of Mt. Istone. That there is no linguistic objection to the connexion of Ἰστώνη and Βίστωνας Schmidt shows (p. 62), but remarks (p. 64) that no locality of modern Greece seems to have taken its name from an ancient mountain, though the names of ancient districts or islands are sometimes transferred to modern cities or villages. See also *N. Jahrbb.* 1892, p. 317 f., where Schmidt calls attention to a mediaeval document, acc. to which one of the dekarchies into which the island of Corfu (except the capital) was subdivided in the middle ages was called Bistone. For the reason just given, then, together with its probable location in the northeastern part of the island, and the fact that in iv. 46. 4 the text reads ἐπὶ τοὺς ἐν τῷ ὄρει τῆς Ἰστώνης Κερκυραίων καθιδρυμένους, not, as would correspond to this passage, τῇ Ἰστώνῃ, Schmidt conjectures (p. 64 ff.) that the whole of the mountainous district in the north of the island was called Istone. In the conviction, further, that, even though a single mountain might have borne the name Istone, Thuc. would not under identical conditions have mentioned at one time the mountain, at another the range, Schmidt proposes to write here ἐς τὸ ὄρος τῆς Ἰστώνης, holding responsible for the error some grammarian, who, supposing that the mountain Istone was meant, wrote the accus., in order to restore the correct const. In iv. 46. 4, τῆς Ἰστώνης has usually been explained as a rare use of the gen. for the dat. in appos. (see Kr. *Spr.* 50, 7, 7), but the view that it is the name of a district, which also Kallenberg (*Stud. üb. d. gr. Artikel* 2, p. 21) seems to prefer, is perhaps more correct. It is a different question, however, whether Istone is in *both* places the name of a district. *Cf.* i. 105. 13 τὰ ἄκρα τῆς Γερανείας κατέλαβον καὶ ἐς τὴν Μεγαρίδα κατέβησαν, and, on the contrary, iv. 70. 7 ἔστι δὲ κώμη τῆς Μεγαρίδος ὄνομα τοῦτο ἔχουσα ὑπὸ τῷ ὄρει τῇ Γερανείᾳ. At any rate, the location and extent of the district seems uncertain, since the modern Vistonas is not necessarily within the bounds of the ancient district (see Schmidt's observation concerning the modern city Arkadia, p. 64).

89. 20. ἀποστέλλειν τε ... καὶ ... τὴν ἐπίκλυσιν ποιεῖν. Cl. understood τὸν σεισμόν to be the subj. of both infs., and so followed Stahl in adopting the conjecture of Meineke (*Hermes* iii. p. 354) and v. II. (*Stud. Thuc.* p. 146), ἐπισπωμένης. 'The earthquake,' he explained, ·forced the sea back (ἀποστέλλειν, or perhaps ἀναστέλλειν, answering to ἐπανελθεῖν in l. 7 and ἐπαναχώρησις κύματος in l. 16) and, as this suddenly returned, made the inundation more violent.' Madvig, *Adv. Crit.* i. p. 317, preferred, with a Schol., ἐπισπώμενον (*bringing on*), which would be a better antithesis to ἀποστέλλειν. But Steup, finding the chief difficulty of the passage in the fact that here, not simply inundations (*cf.* l. 13 ἐπίκλυσις, l. 16 ἐπέκλυσε), but *more violent* inundations, are mentioned, suggests to bracket τὴν ἐπίκλυσιν as a marginal explanation of this clause, or of τὸ τοιοῦτο in l. 22, and to read ἐπισπώμενον βιαιότερον [τὴν ἐπίκλυσιν] ποιεῖν (sc. αὐτήν, τὴν θάλασσαν).

92. 27. καὶ εἶρξαν τὸ κατὰ Θερμοπύλας. The reading of Pal. εἶρξαν τό, for ἤρξαντο of the rest of the Mss., has been generally adopted. Cl. argues that the vulg. is untenable on several grounds. Is it conceivable that the war-harbour with its νεώρια was located elsewhere than at the nearest point of the sea, twenty stades distant (l. 26)? What protection would harbour and arsenal at the pass have had, unless the latter was fortified? And how can one conceive of the *beginning* of the works at the distance of forty stades? Was the idea to build gradually southwards? What is to be considered, then, the extent of the whole works, understanding the expression *locally*, as seems necessary? Or does the *beginning* have reference to *time?* Why, then, is nothing said of continuation or interruption? While with simply νεώρια παρεσκευάζοντο all these objections would be removed, by the reading adopted is added a circumstance well supported by the context. It was exactly the Thessalians, who regarded the settlement with hostile eyes, that had to be guarded against, and that too by the very means adopted of old by the Phocians when they were still in posses-

APPENDIX. 303

sion of the district. *Cf.* Hdt. vii. 176. 19 ἔδειμαν τὸ τεῖχος δείσαντες, ἐπεὶ Θεσσαλοὶ ἦλθον ἐκ Θεσπρωτῶν οἰκήσοντες γῆν τὴν Αἰολίδα τήν περ νῦν ἐκτέαται. ἄτε δὴ πειρωμένων τῶν Θεσσαλῶν καταστρέφεσθαί σφεας, τοῦτο προεφυλάξαντο οἱ Φωκέες. Considering the varied use and const. of εἴργειν (*cf.* Thom. *Mag.* p. 141, 8 κ.), the concise expression εἶρξαν τὸ κατὰ Θερμοπύλας seems unobjectionable, since Thuc. does not enter into the details of the fortification.

101. 6. καὶ αὐτοὶ πρῶτοι δόντες ὁμήρους καὶ τοὺς ἄλλους ἔπεισαν κτέ. The Mss. read πρῶτον. But, as Steup says, since the antithesis clearly consists, not in actions, but in persons, the adv. is impossible, unless it be assumed, with Kalinka (*Ztschr. f. d. oest. Gymn.* xlii. p. 599 f.), that Thuc. sometimes uses πρῶτον where πρῶτος is demanded. But the examples of the normal const., as against the vulg. here and in ii. 34. 3; vi. 3. 1, are too numerous for Kalinka's assumption. The slight change of πρῶτον to πρῶτοι, first suggested by Kr. and adopted by Stahl and v. H., is decidedly preferable to bracketing it, with Cl., as διττογραφία from l. 8. Cl.'s objection, that πρῶτοι would make the passage unnecessarily diffuse, seems hardly valid. *Cf.* αὐτοὶ πρῶτοι, c. 15. 6.

102. 19. ἐς τὴν Αἰολίδα τὴν νῦν καλουμένην Καλυδῶνα καὶ Πλευρῶνα καὶ ἐς τὰ ταύτῃ χωρία. The usual rendering is, "to Aeolis, which is now called Calydon and Pleuron, and to the regions in that quarter." But Steup finds strange the absence of any immediate characterization of Αἰολίς as a term anciently used, referring for Thuc.'s usage, in comparing archaic and current names, to i. 12. 7; 100. 12; ii. 15. 27; iv. 76. 11; further, that over against the *one* ancient name Αἰολίς are set *two* current designations. Since now the names Calydon and Pleuron occur repeatedly even in the Iliad, Steup thinks that it was prob. not Thuc.'s intention to designate the district at once with an archaic and a current name, and proposes to write ἐς τὴν Αἰολίδα [τὴν] νῦν καλουμένην, Καλυδῶνα καὶ Πλευρῶνα καὶ [ἐς] τὰ ταύτῃ χωρία, καὶ ἐς Πρόσχιον τῆς Αἰτωλίας. Thuc. freq. thus uses the phrase νῦν καλούμενος, even when a second name is not added, *e.g.* i. 2. 1; ii. 29. 12; 99. 19. In the text thus emended the words Καλυδῶνα ... χωρία would be in epexegetical appos., Καλυδῶνα and Πλευρῶνα designating the districts belonging to the like-named cities, and τὰ ταύτῃ χωρία referring to the neighbouring regions. *Cf.* c. 98. 26 περὶ Ναύπακτον καὶ τὰ χωρία ταῦτα, i. 5. 17 περὶ Λοκροὺς τοὺς Ὀζόλας ... καὶ τὴν ταύτῃ ἤπειρον. For χωρία = *regions*, *cf.* ii. 7. 16. ἐς is bracketed, with v. H., since τὰ ταύτῃ χωρία is closely connected with what goes before.

105. 5. ὅ ποτε Ἀκαρνᾶνες τειχισάμενοι κοινῷ δικαστηρίῳ ἐχρῶντο. The view of Kruse (*Hellas* ii. p. 333), that Thuc. refers to a court of justice common to the Acarnanians *and the Amphilochians*, is supported by Steph. Byz. Ὄλπαι φρούριον, κοινὸν Ἀκαρνάνων καὶ Ἀμφιλόχων δικαστήριον, Θουκυδίδης τρίτῃ, and has been adopted by Cl. and others. But to this view is opposed, Steup thinks, not only the fact that the Amphilochians, who are not mentioned, cannot be thus supplied in mind, but also that Thuc. modifies κοινῷ δικαστηρίῳ ἐχρῶντο by ποτε and τειχισάμενοι. If construed only with τειχισάμενοι, as Kr. suggests, ποτε is useless, and a reference by it to a later disuse of Olpae as κοινὸν δικαστήριον is intelligible only if the place had been simply a federal court of the Acarnanians. So the mention of the fortification of Olpae, esp. after τεῖχος ἐπὶ λόφον ἰσχυρόν, is appropriate only if Thuc. refers to a time when no agreement existed between the Acarnanians and the Amphilochians. Under these circumstances, no weight is to be attached to the fact that a federal court of the Acarnanians was hardly to be expected in Amphilochian territory, and the remark of Steph. Byz., from which Niese (*Hermes* xiv. p. 428) infers a lacuna in the text here, doubtless proves only that the misconception of the passage is very old.

106. 11. Ἀγραϊκόν. Müller's conjecture, which is justified geographically, is the more to be approved, since ἀγροῖκος, which is freq. applied in the sense of rusticus and agrestis to persons and manners, seems not to be used as horridus, incultus of a landscape. See Steph. *Thes. s.v.*

108. 9. οἱ Ἀμπρακιῶται ... τυγχάνουσιν ὄντες. Steup thinks the text corrupt, on the following grounds. Since not only τὸ κατ᾽ Εὐρύλοχον, but τὸ πλέον τοῦ στρατεύματος had turned to flight (*cf.* l. 13 ὡς ἑώρων τὸ πλέον νενικημένον), the words οἱ Ἀμπρακιῶται καὶ οἱ κατὰ τὸ δεξιὸν κέρας seem to mean, "the Ambraciots and the *rest* of those on the right wing" — which would imply that *all* the Ambraciots were on the right wing. But this hardly agrees with c. 107. 26 Πελοποννήσιοι δὲ καὶ Ἀμπρακιῶται ἀναμὶξ τεταγμένοι πλὴν Μαντινέων. The explanatory clause, καὶ γὰρ ... ὄντες, offers a difficulty, too, not only in syntax — in its reference, across καὶ οἱ κατὰ τὸ δεξιὸν κέρας, to οἱ Ἀμπρακιῶται — but in matter. For the victory of the right wing was doubtless due largely to the superior numbers of the Ambraciot-Peloponnesian army (c. 107. 16), and at all events to Demosthenes's efforts being directed first esp. against the left wing. In spite of their warlike character, the Ambraciots had been obliged repeatedly to invoke the aid of the Spartans against the Amphilochians and Acarnanians. Besides, granted that they were μαχιμώτατοι τῶν περὶ ἐκεῖνα τὰ χωρία, what could this avail when ὁ κράτιστον ἦν τοῦ στρατεύματος did not hold its ground?

108. 15. αὐτῶν. Steup, who refers αὐτῶν to the right wing only, argues that, even with Jowett's view, the words ἀτάκτως ... Μαντινέων lack proper connexion with the preceding, since προσπιπτόντων was to be expected, and the sense of προσπίπτοντες is not clear, as it is nowhere stated that there was a general retreat to Olpae. Besides, even if ταῖς Ὄλπαις be supplied with προσπίπτοντες, it seems strange that the difficult retreat of the right wing is not also mentioned as a cause of the great losses. Hence Steup assumes a lacuna after αὐτῶν, and suggests that something like the following words may have dropped out, κατέφυγε δ᾽ ἐς τὰς Ὄλπας καὶ τὸ ἄλλο στράτευμα αὐτῶν (sc. τῶν Πελοποννησίων καὶ Ἀμπρακιωτῶν).

111. 6. ὅσοι μὲν ἐτύγχανον οὕτως ἀθρόοι ξυνελθόντες. So reads the vulgate, against which objections have been raised from several sources and on various grounds, but without sure results. All explanations seem to assume the connexion of ἐτύγχανον with ξυνελθόντες, the latter referring, just as ξυνεξῇσαν in

c. 113. 5, to the retreat made by the Ambraciots along with the Peloponnesians. Accordingly, either ξυνελθόντες is replaced by ξυνεξελθόντες, with Ullrich (*Beitr.* i. p. 12), or is understood, with Bm.³, as equiv. to ξυνεξελθόντες. Objection has been made to μέν, without antithetical δέ clause, and οὕτως has been variously understood, e.g. Kr., Bl., and Arn., "for this purpose" (i.e. ἐπὶ λαχανισμὸν καὶ φρυγάνων ξυλλογήν); Bm.³, "just so, without further object"; Jow. '"on the instant, at once," or οὕτως may answer to ὡς before ἔγνωσαν, "who happened to have come together when they saw the others running away."' *Cf.* iv. 135. 4. P'p. conjectures ὄντως for οὕτως. But Cl. objects to the above const. of ξυνελθόντες (= ξυνεξελθόντες), on the ground that ὅτε . . . ξυνεξῆσαν in c. 113. 5 proves beyond doubt, that the Ambraciots only *attempted* (impf.) to escape with the Peloponnesians, when they were checked with great loss by the attack of the Acarnanians; and that a mere *attempt*, expressed at the outset by the impf. ξυνεξῆσαν, could not be represented as accomplished here with the aor. ξυνελθόντες or ξυνεξελθόντες. Besides, it is inconceivable that Thuc., after narrating so carefully and graphically in § 1 the at first secret, then open, retreat of the Mantineans and other Peloponnesians, should have added, as if a matter of course, in a rel. clause, that the Ambraciots had withdrawn *in a body* with them — a proceeding which would have frustrated the purpose of the Peloponnesians. With this view, too, not only οὕτως, but esp. ἁθρόοι, is difficult to understand. For how is it that these, who have had no such purpose, come together for a retreat of which they have no knowledge? Besides, as P'p. observed, Thuc. construes ἐτύγχανον (i.e. the expression of a state or condition which coincides with some other circumstance), never with the aor. partic., but only with that of the pres. or pf., which indicates a relation still existent or still continuing in its results.¹ In the not very numerous cases where a momentary occurrence is to be represented as coinciding with another event, the aor. partic. is construed with ἔτυχον: c. 112. 6; i. 70. 23; iv. 9. 9; 13. 17; 70. 14; 73. 14; iii. 6; 116. 7; v. 8. 17; 12. 6; vi. 61. 8; vii. 2. 17; 70. 27; 79. 9; viii. 41. 10. The const. of ἁθρόοι ξυνελθόντες with ἐτύγχανον being abandoned then, the former words appear as the natural introduction to what follows, "after they had come together in a body" (i.e. for consultation; *cf.* iv. 46. 8; 68. 25; vi. 91. 6). — As to the now isolated ἐτύγχανον, one of two explanations is obviously necessary: either to substitute for it a suitable independent verb, or to assume the loss before ἐτύγχανον of a pres. or pf. partic. What the context demands, οὕτως most clearly indicates; for since this refers to the conduct, as just narrated, of the Mantineans and other Peloponnesians, it follows that for the Ambraciots and their allies no other consequence can be

---

¹ For the first case, *cf.* c. 62. 8; 70. 20; 102. 10; i. 55. 10; 92. 4; ii. 13. 5; 49. 3; 51. 3; iv. 70. 3; 132. 6; v. 31. 5; 75. 8; vi. 89. 24; vii. 23. 13; 50. 28; 81. 17; viii. 12. 11; 54. 15; 66. 13; 91. 8; for the second, c. 98. 10; vi. 96. 15; viii. 5. 29; 105. 18.

named except that they saw themselves abandoned and deceived. Since now to express this by the substitution of an independent verb would require a violent change (perhaps κατελείφθησαν, ἐμεμόνωντο), nothing is left but to seek a suitable partic., — a remnant of which is prob. preserved in μεν — either μεμονωμένοι, or, as the occurrence is not yet at an end, the more unusual, and therefore more liable to be miscopied, pres. μονούμενοι. The verb μονοῦσθαι occurs in various forms in Thuc. *Cf.* c. 105. 20; ii. 81. 23; iv. 126. 2; v. 8. 16; 40. 5; 58. 8; vi. 101. 31. It seems then that all difficulty would be removed by reading, οἱ δ' Ἀμπρακιῶται καὶ οἱ ἄλλοι, ὅσοι μονούμενοι ἐτύγχανον οὕτως, ἀθρόοι ξυνελθόντες ὡς ἔγνωσαν ἀπιόντας, ὥρμησαν καὶ αὐτοὶ καὶ ἔθεον δρόμῳ ἐπικαταλαβεῖν βουλόμενοι, *but the Ambraciots and the rest who chanced to be left, came together in a body, and when they had ascertained that those were going away, set off also themselves and ran at full speed, wanting to overtake them.*

Widmann, in Bm.⁴, adopts Cl.'s view. Stahl also (*N. Jahrbb.* xcvii. p. 111) accepts it, except that for μονούμενοι he would substitute μένοντες, and, comparing i. 65. 6, would render, *all the rest who chanced in this way to remain in Olpae, or who were thus left behind;* v. H., who remarks (*Stud. Thuc.* p. 49), Merito in his haesit Classen, sed infelicissime coniecit μεμονωμένοι, conjectures ὅσοι μὲν ἐτύγχανον τούτοις (*i.e.* Mantineensibus et sociis) ἀθρόοι ξυν(εξ)ελθόντες ὡς ἔγνωσαν ἀπιόντας (Mantineenses) ὥρμησαν καὶ αὐτοί. Madvig (*Adv.* i. p. 318) remarks, Classenius, difficultate animadversa, frustra molitur, and conjectures, ὅσοι ἐνετύγχανον αὐτοῖς, ἀθρόοι ξυνελθόντες, ὡς ἔγνωσαν ἀπιόντας, ὥρμησαν καὶ αὐτοί. But Cl. believes that the considerations urged by him above make both of those conjectures inadmissible.

Steup thinks some points in Cl.'s argument open to attack. Since in what is said before of the Mantineans and their allies (l. 2 ff. πρόφασιν ἐπὶ λαχανισμὸν καὶ φρυγάνων ξυλλογὴν ἐξελθόντες ὑπαπῆσαν κατ' ὀλίγους, ἅμα ξυλλέγοντες ἐφ' ἃ ἐξῆλθον δῆθεν· προκεχωρηκότες δὲ ἤδη ἄπωθεν τῆς Ὄλπης θᾶσσον ἀπεχώρουν) ἐξελθεῖν is certainly used both times, not of the whole retreat agreed upon, but merely of coming out of the fortress, there is no reason why mention could not be made here of a ξυνεξελθεῖν of the Ambraciots and others not included in the agreement. For of course ξυνεξελθόντες, as opp. to the further retreat, would simply mean, *leaving Olpae with.* — With a correct conception of ξυνεξελθόντες, even ἀθρόοι is not objectionable. For why could not the Ambraciots and their allies have come out in a body with the others, either to cover their retreat in case of attack, or really to do what they pretended? In what follows there is hardly a doubt that the whole army really did march out together. Otherwise how could the Ambraciots have thought of overtaking the others, and how could they have actually accomplished this? That they did overtake them seems clearly implied in l. 15 καὶ ἦν πολλὴ ἔρις καὶ ἄγνοια εἴτε Ἀμπρακιώτης τίς ἐστιν εἴτε Πελοποννήσιος. In c. 113. 4, however, where it is said of the Ambraciots of Olpae, ὅτε μετὰ τῶν Μαντινέων καὶ τῶν ὑποσπόνδων ξυνεξῆσαν ἄσπονδοι, it is not strange, considering how far that passage is from the one under consideration, that ξυνεξῆσαν is there used in a somewhat different, i.e. more comprehensive sense, = ξυναπεχώρουν. Thus the reading of Laur. ἀθρόοι ξυνεξελθόντες seems to suit the context exactly, and a mention of the simultaneous withdrawal of the Ambraciots is not to be dispensed with; whereas Cl.'s view, based on the reading ἀθρόοι ξυνελθόντες, that for the moment the Ambraciots remained in Olpae, and, before marching out, came together in a body to deliberate, involves great difficulties. See Müller-Strübing, *Thuk. Forsch.* p. 83 f. — As to the const. of ἐτύγχανον, L. Herbst (*Philol.* xvi. p. 305) calls attention to the fact that in viii. 105. 18 the pf. ἐνδεδωκότες is followed by the aor. ὁρμήσαντες, both construed with ἐτύγχανον. On account of that passage and vii. 2. 16, where Vat. has ἐτύγχανε ... ἐλθών, together with instances of the aor. partic. with ἐτύγχανον occasionally found in other authors (see J. R. Wheeler, *The Partic. Const. with τυγχάνειν and κυρεῖν,* in *Harvard Stud. in Cl. Philol.* ii. p. 143 ff.), the possibility of construing ξυνεξελθόντες or ξυνελθόντες with ἐτύγχανον cannot be absolutely denied. Steup thinks, however, that the context decidedly favours Cl.'s assumption, that μέν is the remnant of a partic. belonging to ἐτύγχανον, and that μονούμενοι, though a bold conjecture, is decidedly preferable to Stahl's μένοντες and makes οὕτως intelligible. Müller-Strübing (p. 82 f.) wrongly objects that with Cl.'s conjecture ἐτύγχανον is almost purely periphrastic; for τυγχάνειν is freq. so used (e.g. c. 9. 7; i. 70. 23; iv. 124. 22; v. 36. 1). So then Steup approves Cl.'s conjecture μονούμενοι, but prefers the reading of Laur. ξυνεξελθόντες.

115. 3. μετὰ τῶν Σικελῶν ἄνωθεν ἐσβεβληκότων ἐς τὰ ἔσχατα τῆς Ἱμεραίας. Cl. defended the vulg. μετὰ τῶν Σικελιωτῶν. Steup, while agreeing that ἄνωθεν ... τῆς Ἱμεραίας refers to the Sicels, denies that it is sufficient simply to substitute Σικελῶν for Σικελιωτῶν, contending that iv. 25. 31 — where Kr. conjectured οἱ Σικελοί οἱ ὑπὲρ τῶν ἄκρων — is not adequate for the assumption that the Sicel allies of Athens could be designated here simply as οἱ Σικελοί. Besides, he thinks that μετά is out of place in the sent., whether as it stands in the vulg. or as emended by Bl., even though it be said in the same sent., that the Sicels from the interior had invaded Himera. He objects also, with Cl., that with Bl.'s emendation the Hellenic allies of Athens are left out of consideration. Holding then to the view formerly advanced by him (*Jen. Literaturzeitung,* 1877, p. 55), that the passage is corrupt, he conjectures that after Σικελιωτῶν the words ξυμμάχων καὶ τῶν Σικελῶν, or ξυμμάχων ἅμα τῶν Σικελῶν, have dropped out: "with the Siceliot allies and after (or "when moreover," cf. ii. 5. 4) the Sicel (allies) from the interior had invaded, etc." For the adj. use of Σικελιωτῶν and Σικελῶν, see on c. 103. 2.

GREEK INDEX.

[The references to the Greek text are by chapters and thirds of chapters; to the notes, by chapter and line of text annotated: e.g. 88 a refers to the Greek text at the first third of c. 88; and 49. 4 refers to the note on line 4 of c. 49.]

ἀ- : ἀναλγητότεροι, 40. 24;
ἀνέλπιστος, 30. 6 ; ἀνεξεύρετος, 87. 8 ; ἀνεπιεικέστερον, 66. 7 ; ἀνεύθυνος, 43. 15; ἀνήκεστος, 45. 19; ἄκυρος, 37. 15 ; ἀμαθία, 37. 16 ; ἁμαρτάνειν, pass., 67. 30; — ἐς, 59. 2 ; ἀξύμβατον, 46. 11 ; ἀπαιδευσία, 42. 6 ; 84. 7 ; ἀρρωστία, 15. 11; ἀστάθμητος, 59. 7 ; ἀσφάλεια, 82. 28 ; ἀτιμώρητος, 57. 19; ἀτοπία, 82. 23; ἄτοπος, 38. 23 ; ἄφρακτος, 82. 47.
ἀγαθὰ πράγματα, 82. 15.
ἀγών, 37. 27 ; 40. 11 ; 67. 28 ; 104. 17. 25, 26.
ἀγωνίζεσθαι, 38. 10; 82.59.
ἀγώνισμα, 82. 50.
ἀγωνιστής, 37. 25.
ἀγωνοθετεῖν, 38. 16.
αἰεί ποτε, 95. 7.
ἀκροβολίζεσθαι, 73. 1.
ἀλκή, 30. 7.
ἀλλ' ἤ, 71. 3.
ἀλλόκοτος, 49. 14.
ἅμα τῷ σίτῳ ἀκμάζοντι, 1. 2.
ἀμβλυτέρα, 38. 4.
ἀνὰ τὸ σκοτεινόν, 22. 6.

ἀνα- : ἀνάγειν, 104. 18 ; ἀναγαγεῖν, 16. 7 ; ἀναδιδάσκειν, 97. 2 ; ἀναδιδόναι, 58. 18 ; 88. 9 ; ἀνελέσθαι, 98. 24 ; ἀνήκειν ἐς, 45. 13 ; ἀναλαμβάνειν τιμωρίαν, 38. 6 ; ἀναλογισμός, 36. 16 ; ἀναμίξ, 107. 26 ; ἀναπείθειν, 94. 14 ; ἀναστῆσαι (levy troops), 7. 10 ; ἀναστέλλεσθαι, 98. 3 ; ἀνατιθέναι, 104. 11; ἀναφέρειν κίνδυνον, 38. 15.
ἀνδραγαθία, 57. 2 ; 64. 16.
ἀνὴρ μάντις, 20. 8.
ἀντι- : ἀνταγωνίζεσθαι, 38. 25; ἀντανάμένειν, 12. 10;
ἀνταπαιτῆσαι, 58. 4 ;
ἀντισοῦμαι, 11. 5 ; ἀντισχυρίζεσθαι, 44. 11 ;
ἀντίπαλος, 9. 8 ; 11. 7 ;
49. 2; ἀντιπαταγεῖν, 22. 7 ; ἀντιτιμωρεῖν, 82. 43 ;
ἀνθυποπτεύεσθαι, 43. 11.
ἀξιοῦν, 84. 16.
ἀξίωσις, 82. 23.
ἁπλῶς τε, 38. 31 ; 45. 29.
ἀπό : "on the part of," 36. 24 ; 82. 41 ; ἀπὸ βραχείας διανοίας, 36. 12 ; ἀπὸ ἑσπέρας, 112.

8 ; ἀπὸ τοῦ εὐθέος, 43. 5 ; ἀπὸ τῆς ἴσης, 40. 30; ἀπὸ τοῦ προφανοῦς, 82. 48.
ἀπο-: ἀφαιρεῖσθαι, 58. 28 ; ἀπαλλαξείειν, 84. 4; ἀπέβη, 93. 5; ἀπόγνοια, 85. 13 ; ἀπηλιώτης, 23. 24 ; (οἱ) ἀποθανόντες, 109. 9; 113. 23 ; ἀποκεκινδυνεύσεται, 39. 41; ἀπολιπεῖν ἐκ, 10. 8; ἀπομονοῦν, 28. 2 ; ἀποκνεῖν, 20. 10 ; 30. 12 ; 55. 10 ; ἀπόστασις, 13. 8; ἀποστῆναι πρός, 46. 21 ; ἀποτρέπειν, 63. 10 ; ἀποτροπή, 82. 29 ; ἀποχρῆσθαι, 81. 11 ; ἀποχωρεῖν, 42. 16.
ἄρα, 56. 15 ; 67. 4.
ἀργυρολόγος, 19. 4.
ἀρετή. 10. 1.
ἀριστοκρατία, 82. 57.
ἄρτι, 3. 2.
ἄρχοντες τῶν Λακεδαιμονίων, 93. 12.
αὐθέντης, 58. 25.
αὐτάγγελος, 33. 11.
αὐτερέτης, 18. 16.
αὐτοβοεί, 74. 6 ; 113. 27.
αὐτός, 18. 6 ; 27. 9 ; 57. 6 ; 58. 8 ; 61. 2.

αὐτοῦ, 81.15; 98.11; 112. 17.
βιάζεσθαι, 55. 3.
βοηθεῖν ἐπὶ τόπον, 97. 14.
βουλεύειν, 42. 24.
βούλησις, 68. 8.
βραχύς, 36. 12; 39. 38; 40. 12; 58. 7.
βραχύτης, 42. 6.

γενέσθαι ὑπό τινι, 59. 14.
γενναιότης, 82. 43.
γέρας, 58. 26.
γνούς, with inf., 48. 1.

δέ, in apod., 98. 2; =γάρ, 11. 7; 58. 21; transitional, 10. 7; 61. 9; omitted, 88. 1.
δεδρασμένων, 54. 3.
δεξιότης, 37. 16.
δέος, 11. 7; 45. 15.
δέχεσθαι, with inf., 53. 4.
δή, 10. 18; 104. 2; with sup., 39. 2; 113. 22.
δῆθεν, 68. 4; 111. 4.
δῆλον ποιεῖν, with partic., 64. 2.
διά: δι' ἐλαχίστου, 39. 23; δι' ὀλίγου, 43. 14; διὰ πάθους, 84. 5; διὰ παντός, 58. 14; διὰ πολλοῦ, 94. 21.
δια-: διαβάλλειν, 109. 17; διαγνώμη, 42. 1; διενεγκεῖν, 83. 4; διηγγυημένοι, 70. 4; διαλαθεῖν, 25. 5; διαλλάσσειν, 10. 5; 82. 13; (ὁ) διαλύσων, 83. 5; διαλυτής, 82.33; διαμάχεσθαι, 40. 5; 42. 7; διάνοια, 82.

22; διοκωχή, 87. 3; διαπολιορκεῖν, 17. 12; διασῴζεσθαι, 108. 14; διατείχισμα, 34. 9; διάφευξις, 23. 27; διαχρήσασθαι, 36. 15.
δικαιοῦσθαι, 40. 19.—δικαίωσις, 82. 24.
δόκησις, 43. 3; 45. 6.
δοξάζειν, 45. 29.
δούλωσις, 10. 14.
Δρυὸς Κεφαλαί, 24. 6.
δύναμις, 87. 5.
δύνασθαι, valere, 46. 10.
δυναστεία, 62. 11.
δυσεσβολώτατος, 101. 9.
Δωρὶς γλῶσσα, 112. 14.

ἐθελοπρόξενος, 70. 11.
ἔθνος, 92. 22.
εἰ, in indir. ques., 62. 20; =ὅτι, 9. 11; εἰ ἄρα, 56. 15; 66. 6; 84. 19.
εἶδος, 62. 6.
εἰκὸς ἦν, 40. 26.
εἰπεῖν, command, 3. 16; 8. 2.
εἴργειν, with inf., 6. 7; 86. 15; 92. 27.
ἐκ: =ὑπό, 69. 3; ἐξ ἀνάγκης, 40. 9; ἐκ καινῆς, 92. 24; ἐκ τοῦ ἀκινδύνου, 40. 23; (οἱ) ἐκ τῆς πόλεως, 29. 4; ἐκ τοὔμπαλιν ἤ, 22. 28; ἐκ τῶν παρόντων, 29. 11; ἐκ τοῦ προφανοῦς, 43. 10; 109. 10.
ἐκ-: ἐξάγειν, 45. 19; ἐξαιρεθῆναι, 114. 4; ἐξαλείφειν, 20. 15; 57. 12; ἐξαπιναίως, 3. 9; ἐκβοήθεια, 18. 9; ἐξηγεῖσθαι,

55.14; 93. 15; ἐκλιπεῖν, 87. 2; ἐξουσία, 45. 17; ἐκπιμπλάναι, 82. 64; ἐκπεπληγμένος, 82. 33; ἔκπυστος, 30. 3; ἐκστρατεύεσθαι, 105.2; ἐκτρυχοῦν, 93. 9; ἐξυβρίζειν, 39. 28; ἐκφροντίζειν, 45. 21.
ἑκατέρωθεν, 6. 5.
ἔλασσον ἔχειν, 5. 8.
ἐλευθεροῦν τὸν ἔσπλουν, 51. 13; ἐλευθεροῦν (τὴν Ἑλλάδα), 13. 26; 32. 5; 63. 16.
ἐλευθέρωσις, 10. 11.
Ἕλλην, adj., 103.2; Ἕλληνες, 109. 18.
Ἑλληνικόν, 82. 3.
ἐλπίς, with aor. inf., 3. 14; ἐλπίδα ἔχειν, with μή and inf., 32. 14.
ἐλπίζω, think, 30. 10.
ἐν: not local, 13. 24; ἐν δυνάμει εἶναι, 93. 6; ἐν καταλήψει, 33. 14; ἐν ὅσῳ, 28. 8; 52. 16; 81. 9; ἐν ποσίν, 97. 5; ἐν σπονδαῖς, 56. 4; 65. 4; (οἱ) ἐν τέλει, 36. 20; (οἱ) ἐν τοῖς πράγμασι, 28. 1; ἐν τοῖς πλείσται, 17. 1; 81. 2; ἐν τῷ τοιῷδε, 42. 19; 43. 12; ἐν ὑμῖν, 57. 14; ἐν χερσίν, 66. 10.
ἐν-: ἐνδιατρίβειν, 29. 3; ἔνεργος, 17. 2; ἐγκαταληφθῆναι, 33. 15; ἐγκατωκοδόμηται, 18. 18; ἐνορᾶν, 30. 14; ἐμπλεῖν, 77. 8; ἐμπλήκτως, 82. 27; ἐγχρονίζειν, 27. 2.
ἐναντία, 53. 11.

ἔξω, 61. 4, 13.
ἐπειγόμενος, 10. 15.
ἐπειδή, 68. 32 ; 70. 1.
ἔπη, 67. 31 ; 104. 20.
ἐπί : ἐπὶ πλέον τι, 45. 29;
ἐπὶ πολύ, 83. 4; ἐπί τινι,
against one. 13. 18 ; 63.
8; 92. 15; ἐπὶ τοῖσδε,
114. 15.
ἐπι- : ἐπαγγέλλειν, 16. 15;
ἐπάγεσθαι, 62. 14 ; 84.
5; ἐπαγαγόμενοι, 34. 8;
ἐπαγαγωγή, 82. 9; 100.
5; ἐπαίρεσθαι κέρδει, 38.
12; ἐπανελθεῖν, 89. 7 ;
ἐπαναχωρεῖν, 33. 14 ;
ἐπαναχώρησις, 89. 16 ;
ἐπαυλίσασθαι, 5. 8; ἐπιβοήθεια, 51. 15; ἐπιβοηθεῖν, 26. 6; ἐπιβουλεύειν,
with inf., 20. 5; ἐπιβουλεύσασθαι, 82. 29; ἐπιβοώμενοι, 59. 11; ἐπιγενέσθαι, 30. 6; 74. 11;
ἐπιγνῶναι, 57. 6 ; ἐπιδεικνύναι, 64. 17 ; ἐπιδιώκειν, 33. 14; 69. 3 ;
ἐπεξελθεῖν, 26. 15 ; 38.
5; 67. 21 ; ἐπιείκεια, 40.
7, 14 ; 48. 2 ; ἐπιεικής,
4. 9; 9. 10 ; ἐπελθεῖν,
52. 24 ; ἐπεσβαλεῖν, 13.
20 ; ἐπεσενέγκασθαι, 53.
17; ἐφίστασθαι, 82. 14;
ἐπικαλεσάμενοι, 52. 19 ;
ἐπικατάγεσθαι, 49. 18 ;
ἐπικαταλαβεῖν, 111. 8 ;
ἐπικλασθῆναι, 59. 5; 67.
5; ἐπικλύζειν, 89. 16 ;
ἐπίκλυσις, 89. 13, 21 ;
ἐπίκουρος, 18. 3 ; ἐπιλείπειν, 26. 16; 27. 3; ἐπιμένειν, with inf. or acc.,

2. 7; 26. 13; ἐφορμεῖν,
31. 8; ἐφόρμησις, 33. 17;
ἐπιπλεῖν, 16. 17 ; 76. 6;
ἐπιρρωσθῆναι, 6. 1; ἐπισκήπτειν, 59. 25; ἐπιστροφή. 71. 9 ; ἐπιτυχεῖν, 3. 23; ἐπιφέρειν,
46. 26 ; 58. 18 ; ἐπιφθόνως. 82. 66; ἐπίχαρτος,
67. 17.
ἐπίτηδες, 112. 3.
ἐρημοῦτε, 58. 29.
ἐς : ἐς ἀγῶνα τῆς δόξης,
49. 3; ἐς ἀλκὴν ὑπομεῖναι, 108. 5; ἐς ἔδαφος,
68. 19 ; ἐς λόγον χρημάτων. 46. 17; ἐς ὀψέ,
108. 18 ; ἐς πόλεμον
ἐπέρχεσθαι, 47. 6; ἐς τὸ
ἀληθές, 64. 19 ; ἐς τὸ
ἀνέλπιστον, 83. 6 ; ἐς
τὸ κοινόν, 37. 20; ἐς τὸ
λοιπόν, 44. 9; ἐς τὸ ξυμμαχικόν, 91. 6; ἐς τὰ
πρῶτα, 39. 9; 56. 22; ἐς
τοῦτο ξυμφορᾶς, 57. 12;
ἐς φυγὴν καταστῆσαι,
108. 8.
ἐσ- : ἐσβολή, 112. 8; ἐσηγεῖσθαι, 20. 7; ἐσφερόμενοι, 98. 14; ἐσφορά, 19. 2.
ἐσσαμένων, 58. 29.
εὐπρέπεια, 11. 10; 82. 65.
εὐπρεπές, 38. 12 ; 44. 12 ;
82. 26.
εὑρίσκειν, 47. 19.
ἐχέγγυος, 46. 1.
ἔχειν = παρέχειν, 53. 12 ;
ἔχειν τὰ πράγματα, 62.
11 ; 72. 3.

ἤ = εἰ δὲ μή, 40. 22.
ἤδη, 95. 8.

ἡγεμονεύεσθαι, 61. 13.
ἡλικία, 67. 11 ; 98. 21.
θανάτου ζημία, 45. 1 ; 46.
1 ; θανάτου κρίνεσθαι,
57. 17.
θεαταὶ τῶν λόγων, 38. 16 ;
θεαταὶ σοφιστῶν, 38. 32.
θεῖν δρόμῳ, 111. 5.
θεωρεῖν ἐς, 104. 16.
θήκη. 58. 15 ; 104. 5.

ἰδέα, 62. 5 ; 81. 22 ; 83. 1;
98. 15.
ἰέναι γλῶσσαν, 112. 14.
ἱερά, 58. 28.
ἱερομηνία, 56. 4 ; 65. 2.
ἴσα καί, 14. 2.
ἰσονομία, 82. 55.
ἰσοπλατής, 21. 8.
ἰσόψηφος, 11. 13; 79. 11.
ἴσχειν. 58. 26.
ἰσχύειν, 46. 13, 17.
ἰσχύς, 62. 13.

καί, = *atque*, 43. 12 ; *just*,
42. 14; καὶ ὥς, 33. 9.
κακοτροπία, 82. 1.
κάλλος. 17. 2.
καμφθῆναι, 58. 3.
κατά : κατὰ κράτος, 97. 9;
103. 3; κατὰ μέρος, 49.
12 ; κατὰ νώτου, 107.
21 ; κατὰ ξυλλόγους γίγνεσθαι, 27. 7 ; κατ'
ὀλίγους, 111. 4 ; κατὰ
πλοῦν, 32. 2; κατὰ πόδας, 98. 11 ; κατὰ στάσιν, 2. 10 ; κατὰ χώραν
γίγνεσθαι, 24. 14.
κατα- : καταγιγνώσκειν,
45. 4 ; κατάγνωσις, 16.
1 ; 82. 63; καταγώγιον,

GREEK INDEX.

68. 20; καταδούλωσις, 10. 10; κάθεξις, 47. 16; κατέχεσθαι, 12. 6; κάθημαι, 38. 22; καθίζειν, 107. 2; καθιστάναι, 36. 23; 53. 21; 56. 28; καταστῆσαι ἐς, 65. 8; καθεστώς, 9. 1; κατακλύζειν, 89. 9; καταλέγειν, 75. 13; καταλύειν, 46. 4; 81. 20; κάθοδος, 84. 9; κατοικεῖν, 34. 2; καθορᾶν, 20. 19; κατορθοῦν, 14. 5; 39. 29; καταπλεῖν, 26. 6; καταπροδοῦναι, 63. 14; 109. 18; κατατίθεσθαι, 28. 14; καταφρονεῖν, 83. 13.
κεῖσθαι, 45. 12; 47. 19.
κεφαλαιοῦν, 67. 32.
κοινὸν δικαστήριον, 105. 6.
κολασθέντων, 39. 21.
κομίζεσθαι, 58. 5.
κρατεῖν μάχῃ, 91. 16.
κρούεσθαι πρύμναν, 78. 12.
κυματωθεῖσα, 89. 8.

λαβέσθαι, with gen., 24. 10; 106. 10; λαβών, abs., 59. 6.
λανθάνειν, usual const. reversed, 51. 8; 74. 16.
λαχανισμός, 111. 2.
λῃστής, 51. 10.
λιμός, ὄλεθρος αἴσχιστος, 59. 21.
λοχίζειν, 107. 18.
λοχμώδης, 107. 18.

μάλιστα, 20. 11; 21. 4; 34. 4; 109. 9.
μέγα = δεινόν, 36. 17.
μέλλησις, 12. 9.

μέσον, 78. 5; 80. 6; τὰ μέσα τῶν πολιτῶν, 82. 67.
μετά τινων στῆναι, 39. 12.
μετα-: μεταγνῶναι, 40. 5; μεταπεμπόμενοι ἦσαν, 2. 8; μετέωρος, 33. 15; 72. 7; 89. 11.
μέχρι, 10. 12; μέχρι οὗ, 28. 15; μέχρι τοῦ δεῦρο, 64. 11.
μή, 32. 14; 39. 17; 41. 3; 57. 3; 62. 16; 75. 18; 84. 15.
μισθοφόρος ὄχλος, 109. 16.

ναύαρχος, 16. 6; 26. 3.
ναύσταθμος, 6. 10.
νέμειν μέρος, 3. 5; 48. 2.
νέμεσθαι, 68. 27; 88. 4.
νεοκατάστατος, 93. 9.
νεόκτιστος, 100. 9.
νεώριον, 74. 6.
νεωτερίζειν, 4. 15; 11. 2; 66. 9; 75. 23; 79. 3.
Νῆσοι, 104. 11.
νόμιμον, 9. 1.
νόμος, 58. 12.

ξύν: ξὺν ἀνάγκῃ, 40. 30; ξὺν ξιφιδίῳ, 22. 14; ξὺν κακῶς ποιεῖν, 13. 19.
ξυν-: ξυναποστῆναι, 39. 35; ξυμβαίνειν πρός, 25. 10; 27. 3; ξύμβουλος, 42. 19; 69. 7; ξυγγνώμην λαμβάνειν, 40. 2; ξυγγνώμων, 40. 4; ξυνεξαμαρτεῖν, 43. 19; ξυνελευθεροῦν, 62. 22; ξυνελθεῖν, 111. 7; ξυνέχεσθαι, 98. 5; ξυνίστασθαι, 70.

24; ξυμμαχικόν, 3. 19; 91. 7; ξυμμεῖξαι, 110. 4; ξυμμετρεῖν, 20. 13; ξύνοδος, 104. 15; ξυνοικία, 74. 8; ξυνοικίζειν, 2. 12; ξυνοίκισις, 3. 8; ξυντυχεῖν, 59. 24; ξυντυχία, 45. 18; 82. 14; 112. 26; ξυνωμοσία, 64. 7.

οἰκεῖν, 37. 18.
οἰκειοῦν, 65. 17.
οἰκιστής, 34. 22; 92. 22.
ὀλίγοι ἀπὸ πολλῶν, 112. 30.
ὅμαιχμος, 58. 19.
ὅμιλος, 1. 6.
ὁμοβώμιος, 59. 10.
ὅπερ, 59. 18.
ὅπλα, *watch-posts*, 1. 7.
ὀργή, 42. 4; 44. 15; 82. 19.
ὀρθοῦσθαι, 30. 15; 37. 26; 42. 20.
ὄρθρος, 112. 9.
ὁρμή, 36. 10.
ὅσον, *quatenus*, 11. 10; in indir. ques., 47. 1; with inf., 49. 16; ὅσῳ, 45. 24.
ὅστις, 45. 30; 64. 16.
ὅτι ἐν βραχυτάτῳ, 46. 4.
οὐ, 42. 11; 62. 3; 66. 7, 19; οὐδὲν ὅ τι οὐ, 81. 24; οὐχ ὅπως, 42. 27; οὐκ οὖν, 113. 11; οὐχί, 53. 19; 67. 21.

πανοικεσία, 57. 11.
παρά: παρὰ γνώμην, 12. 2; 42. 29; παρὰ δόξαν, 37. 28; παρὰ πολύ, 36. 27; παρὰ τοσοῦτον, 49. 18.

παρα- : παραγγέλλεσθαι, 55. 13; παράγειν, 38. 13; 68.10; παρανίσχειν, 22. 35; παραυτίκα, 56. 27; παραβαίνειν, 45. 12, 14; παραβαλεῖν, 32. 15; παραβάλλεσθαι, 14. 5; 65. 12; παραγίγνεσθαι, 75. 2; παράδειγμα. 10. 19; 39. 14; 57. 1; παράδειγμα καταστῆσαι (ποιῆσαι) with supplem. partic., 40. 37; 67. 28; παρεῖναι, 8. 2; παρελθεῖν, 60. 3; παρέχειν, 62. 23; παρέχεσθαι, 36. 3; 54. 1. παρακινδυνεύειν, 36. 11; παραλείπειν, 26. 11; παράλογος, 16. 9; πάροικοι, 113. 29; παραπλήσιος, 17. 3; παρασκευάζειν, 36. 20; παρασκευή. 39. 7; παραστήσασθαι, 34. 2; παρατενεῖσθαι,46. 9; παρατυχεῖν, 82. 47.
πειθώ, 53. 16.
πεντετηρίς, 104. 13.
περί τινος δεῖσαι, 102. 11.
περι- : περιαιρεῖν, 11. 16; περιέχειν, 107. 16; περικτίονες, 104. 15; περίνοια, 43. 9; περιοικίς, 16. 13; περιοικοδομεῖν. 81. 26; περιπόλιον, 99. 4; περιστῆναι, 54. 18; περιτέχνησις, 82. 22; περιφρουρεῖσθαι, 21. 14; περιωθεῖν, 57. 17.
πιθανός, 36. 27.
πιστός, 40. 1.
πλεῖν, 17. 1.
πλέον ἤ, 12. 6; 67. 20.
πληγῆναι, 18. 10.

πλῆθος, 70. 19.
πλῷ χρησάμενος, 3. 23.
πολιτείας μεταλαβεῖν, 55. 12.
πολιτεύειν κατὰ ὀλιγαρχίαν, 62. 8.
(τὸ) πολύτροπον, 83. 11.
πολυψηφία, 10. 16.
πρᾶξις, 114. 7.
πρέπον, 59. 9.
πρίν, 29. 5.
προ- : προάγειν, 45. 26 ; προαισθέσθαι, 38. 27 ; προαναβῆναι, 112. 6 ; προγεγενημένοι, 10. 20 ; προδεῖξαι, 47. 12 ; προδεδογμένα, 40. 5 ; πρόεδρος, 25. 6; προεπαινέσαι, 38. 27; προίσχεσθαι χεῖρας, 66. 12; προκαταγνῶναι, 53. 19; προλοχίζειν, 110.6; προνοεῖν, 58. 11 ; πρόξενος, 70. 4; προοίμιον, 104. 20; πρόπειραν, 86. 18 ; προτιθέναι, 36. 21 ; 38. 2; 39. 20; 40. 1; 42. 1; 44. 10; 82. 61; προτολμηθῆναι, 84. 1; προυργιαίτερον, 109. 19; πρόφασις, 111. 2.
πρός : πρὸς δέ, 58. 27 ; "as against," 43. 15 ; 56. 16; with gen., 38. 3; πρὸς νότον, 6. 4 ; πρὸς ὀργήν, 43. 17; πρὸς χάριν, 42. 29.
προσ- : προσαγαγών, 107. 13; προσάγεσθαι, 32. 9; 42.30; προσαναγκάζειν, 61. 14; προσμεῖξαι, 22. 4; προσνεῦσαι, 112.26; προσξυνεβάλετο, 36. 10;

προσποιεῖν, 70.5; προσποίησις, 82. 9; προσκέψασθαι, 57. 1.
πω, 45. 6.
ῥεῦμα, 116. 6.
ῥήτωρ, 40. 11.
ῥύαξ, 116. 1.
σοφιστής, 38. 31.
στατήρ, 70. 18.
στρατεύειν, 114. 16.
σῶν καὶ ὑγιᾶ, 34. 14.
σωφρονιστής, 65. 16.
ταλαιπώρως, 4. 19.
ταλαιπωρεῖσθαι, 3. 1; 78. 3.
ταξάμενος, 50. 10; 70. 19.
τάφος, 59. 13.
τε, "and so," 25. 11 ; in résumé, 40. 16; "besides," 45. 20 ; correl. to μέν, 46. 9; correl. to δέ, 52. 13.
τεκμηριοῦν, 104. 38.
τεκμήριον δέ, 66. 1.
τελευτᾶν ἐς, 78. 16 ; 104. 28; τελευτᾶν λόγον, 59. 19; 104. 28.
τέναγος, 51. 15.
τί ἄλλο ἤ, 39. 10.
τίνα ὅντινα οὔ, 39. 38.
τις, 111. 13; between art. and subst. of depend. gen., 5. 5 ; "about," 68. 16 ; τινες ὀλίγοι, 70. 27.
τὸ ἴσον φέρεσθαι, 53. 5 ; τὸ μή. with inf., 1. 7 ; τὸ ξύμπαν, 68. 27 ; τὸ ξυμφέρον, 56. 9, 25 ; τὸ παντάπασιν, 87. 2 ; τὸ

GREEK INDEX.

πλεῖστον τῆς γνώμης, 31. 11; τὸ τῆς ξυμφορᾶς, 59. 8.
τόδε, 45. 15.
τοιόνδε τι, 97. 1.
τοιοῦτος, 58. 23.
τοσαῦτα, 31. 1.
τότε, 57. 16; 69. 2.
τυχεῖν, 39. 42; 42. 18, 26; 43. 17; 82. 31.
τύχη, 45. 24.

ὑγιές, 75. 18.
ὑδατώδης, 23. 24.
υἱός, 26. 8.
ὑπερ- : ὑπέρβατον, 25. 4; ὑπερέχον, 107. 20; ὑπερενεγκεῖν, 81. 3; ὑπερόπτης, 38. 23; ὑπερφρονεῖν, 39. 30.
ὑπό- : ὑπ' ἀνάγκης, 32. 7; ὑπὸ σπουδῆς, 33. 12.
ὑπο- : ὑπαγωγή, 97. 19; ὑφαιρεῖν, 13. 32; 31. 8; 82. 17; ὑπαναλίσκειν, 17. 8; ὑποδεδέσθαι, 22.

11; ὑποδέχεσθαι, 12.
2; ὑπεξανάγεσθαι, 74.
15; ὑπεξελθεῖν, 34. 11;
ὑφέχειν, 53. 3; ὑποκεῖσθαι, 84. 17; ὑπονείφεσθαι, 23. 25; ὑπονοστεῖν, 89. 9; ὑποτιθέναι, 45. 22; ὑποτοπῆσαι, 24. 4.
ὑστερεῖν, 31. 11.
ὕστερον χρόνῳ, 85. 10.

φαυλότερος, 37. 17; 83. 8.
φθάνειν, with pres. partic., 83. 11; φθάσας θαρσῆσαι, 82. 47.
φθινόπωρον, 18. 14.
φιλεῖ, 42. 5.
φιλέταιρος, 82. 25.
φονεύειν, 81. 19.
φρόνημα, 45. 17.
φρουρεῖν, obsidere, 17. 10.
φρύγανα, 111. 3.
φρυκτοὶ πολέμιοι, 22. 34.
φρυκτωρία, 22. 38.
φρυκτωρεῖν, 80. 7.

φυλή, 90. 9.

χαράδρα, 98. 7.
χάραξ, 70. 16, 17.
χάρις, 58. 5.
χείρ, a military force, 96. 12; χειρί, = βίᾳ, 82. 63.
χρή, with inf. = delib. subjv., 11. 18; 53. 9.
χρῄζειν, 109. 18.
χρησθέν, 96. 3.
χωρὶς δέ, 17. 6.

ψιλῶσαι, 109. 15.

ὠμοφάγοι, 94. 26.
ὡς : ὡς εἰπεῖν, 38. 29; ὡς ἐπί τινι, 4. 6; ὡς ἐπὶ τὸ πλεῖον, 37. 18; ὡς τὰ πλείω, 83. 8; ὡς πρὸς τὸ μέγεθος, 113. 25; ὧς = οὕτως, 37. 26.
ὥστε, pleonastic, 31. 10; "on condition that," 28. 4; 75. 7.

Words once used (ἅπαξ εἰρημένα): ἀνάδοτος, 52. 9; ἀνεξεύρετος, 87. 8; ἀντανάμενειν, 12. 10; ἀντισοῦμαι, 11. 5; ἀντιμελλῆσαι, 12. 13; ἀντοικτίζειν, 40. 9; ἀντιπαταγεῖν, 22. 7; ἀπόγνοια, 85. 13; διαπολιορκεῖν, 17. 12; ἐκβοήθεια, 18. 9; παρανίσχειν, 22. 35; περιφρουρεῖσθαι, 21. 14; τὸ πολύτροπον, 83. 11; πολυψηφία, 10. 16; προεπαινέσαι, 38. 27; ὑπεξανάγεσθαι, 74. 15.

Words once used in Thucydides: ἀγωνιστής, 37. 25; ἀγωνοθετεῖν, 38. 16; ἀλλόκοτος, 49. 14; ἀναλγητότερος, 40. 24; ἀνεξεύρετος, 87. 8; ἀνεπιεικέστερον, 66. 7; ἀνεύθυνος, 43. 15; ἀναμίξ, 107. 26; ἀντισχυρίζεσθαι, 44. 11; ἀντιπόλεμοι, 90. 6; ἀντιτιμωρεῖν, 82. 43; ἀνθυποπτεύεσθαι, 43. 11; ἀξύμβατον, 46. 11; ἀργυρολόγος. 19. 4; αὐτάγγελος, 33. 11; αὐθέντης, 58. 25; γενναιότης, 82. 43; δεξιότης, 37. 16; δίδραχμος, 17. 9; διεγγυᾶσθαι, 70. 4; διαλυτής, 82. 33; διάφευξις, 23. 27; διοκωχή, 87. 3; δικαιοῦσθαι, 40. 19; δοῦπος, 22. 24; δυσεσβολώτατος, 101. 9; ἐθελοπρόξενος, 70. 11; ἐκπιμπλάναι, 82. 64; ἐκφροντίζειν, 45. 21; ἐμπλεῖν, 77. 8; ἐμπλήκτως, 82. 27; ἐνεργός, 17. 2; ἐγχρονίζειν, 27. 2; ἐπαναχώρησις, 89. 16; ἐπιβοήθεια, 51. 15; ἐπεσβαλεῖν, 13. 20; ἐπεσενέγκασθαι, 53. 17; ἐπικλύζειν, 89. 16; ἐπίκλυσις, 89. 13, 21; ἐπίτηδες, 112. 13; ἐπίχαρτος, 67. 17; ἔσθημα, 58. 17; ἐχέγγυος, 46. 1; ἰσοπλατής. 21. 8; κάθεξις, 47. 16; κακοτροπία, 82. 1; κάλλος, 17. 2; καμφθῆναι, 58. 3; κατακλύζειν, 89. 9; κεκμηῶτες, 59. 14; κυματωθεῖσα, 89. 8; λαχανισμός, 111. 2; λοχμώδης, 107. 18; νεοκατάστατος, 93. 9; νεόκτιστος, 100. 9; ξυνεξαμαρτεῖν, 43. 19; ξυνοίκισις, 3. 8; ὅμαιχμος, 58. 19; ὁμοβώμιος. 59. 10; πάροικοι, 113. 29; πειθώ, 53. 16; περικτίονες, 104. 15; περίνοια, 43. 9; περιοικοδομεῖν, 81. 26; περιτέχνησις, 82. 22; ποδώκης, 98. 12; προκαταγνῶναι, 53. 19; πρόπειραν, 86. 18; προτολμηθῆναι, 84. 1; προυργιαίτερον, 109. 19; προσνεῦσαι, 112. 26; σοφιστής, 38. 31; ταλαιπώρως, 4. 19; τέναγος, 51. 15; ὑδατώδης. 23. 24; ὑπαγωγή. 97. 19; ὑπαναλοῦν, 17. 8, 14; ὑπονοστεῖν, 89. 19; φιλέταιρος, 82. 25; φρύγανα, 111. 3; φρυκτωρεῖν, 80. 7; φρυκτωρία, 22. 38; χάραξ, 70. 16, 17; χρῇζειν, 109. 18; ψιλῶσαι, 109. 15.

Words, Ionic and poetic: ἀλκή, 30. 7; ἀνά, 22. 6; ἀνάγειν (χορούς), 104. 18; δικαιοῦσθαι, 40. 19; ἐξαπιναίως, 34. 17; 70. 25; ἐξαπίνης, 89. 20; ἐπιβοώμενοι, 59. 11; θήκη, 58. 15; 104. 5; κράτος (victory), 13. 36; ὅμιλος, i. 6; ὀργή, 82. 19; (οἱ) πέλας, 39. 15; τέρπειν, 40. 10; ὑπονοστεῖν, 89. 9; φιλεῖ, 42. 5; φονεύειν, 81. 19; χείρ (a troop), 96. 12; χρῇζειν, 109. 18; χρησθῆναι, 96. 3.

Words, poetic: ἀναλγητότερος. 40. 24; ἀναλοῦσθαι, 81. 16; δόκησις, 43. 3; 45. 6; δοῦπος, 22. 23; ἐπίχαρτος, 67. 17; ἔσθημα, 58. 17; εὐπραξία, 39. 23; ἐχέγγυος, 46. 1; (οἱ) κεκμηῶτες, 59. 14; κρατύνειν, 18. 7; 82. 40; πάροικοι, 113. 29; περικτίονες, 104. 15; ποδώκης, 98. 12; ὥς (= οὕτως). 37. 26.

INDEX OF SUBJECTS.

Acarnania, 102. 24; 106. 4, 10.
Acarnanians, 7. 5, 10; 94 a; 95 b; 102. 14; 105 a, c; 107; 109. 12; 111; 112; 113; 114. 16.
Accent, 109. 12.
Accusative, abs. 40. 20; 53. 10; 63. 6; 73. 1; cognate, 36. 25; 40. 12; 55. 9, 13.
Achaeans, 92. 21.
Achelous, 7. 11; 106. 4.
Adjective, articular neut. = abstract noun, 30. 4; 38. 12; 62. 10; 82. 26, 27, 36; 83. 2, 9; 84. 12; neut. pl., 16. 10; 88. 4; 92. 28; of two terminations in comp. or sup., 89. 21; 101. 9; force of pred., 113. 24.
Adverb, qualifying subst., 94. 12; 95. 11.
Aegina, 72 a.
Aeginetans, 64. 9.
Aegitium, 97. 9, 14.
Acimnestus, 52. 23.
Acolis, 102. 19.
Aeolus islands, 88. 3; 115. 5.
Aetna, 116. 1, 2, 5, 6.
Aetolia, 102. 10; 105 b; 114. 6.
Aetolians, 94. 23, 25; 95. 3; 96 a; 97 a; 98; 100. 1; 102. 26.

Agis, 89. 3.
Agraeans, 106. 10; 111 c; 113. 2; 114 b.
Agrais, 111. 18.
Alcidas, 16; 26; 31; 32; 33; 69. 1; 76 b; 79 c; 80. 9; 92. 23.
Alcinous, 70. 17.
Ambracia, 113. 25; 114. 22, 25; gulf of, 107. 4.
Ambraciots, 69 b; 102 c; 105 c; 106. 2, 14; 107. 9, 25; 108. 9; 109. 15; 110. 2; 111; 112; 113. 23; 114. 11.
Ammeas, 22 b.
Amphilochia, 105 b; mountains of, 112 a.
Amphilochians, 107. 8, 25; 110. 3; 112. 19. 29; 113 c; 114.
Amphissians, 101. 5.
Anacoluthon, 30. 10; 34. 15; 36. 8; 39. 14; 62. 18; 67. 24; 71. 2; 94. 17; 96. 11.
Anactorium, 114. 19.
Anaea, 32. 4.
Anaeitans, 19. 8.
Androcrates, 24. 3.
Antissa, 18. 5; 28. 16.
Aorist, 16. 16; 22. 14; 24. 4; 28. 5; 35. 2; 45. 29; 46. 7, 9; 52. 25; 53. 2; 81. 13; 82. 25; 83. 13;

95. 7; 103. 6; 104. 11; 105. 13; 107. 16; 112. 7; 115. 8.
Apodotians, 94. 23; 100 a.
Apollo, 3. 12; 94. 10; 104. 20.
Apposition, 7. 4; 21. 5; 63. 10; partitive, 13. 17; 23. 1, 15; 32. 3; 34. 6.
Archidamus, 1 a; 26. 7; 89. 3.
Argeia, Amphilochian, 105 a; 106 c.
Argives, Amphilochian, 105 a; 106 c; 107 a.
Argos, Amphilochian, 102. 23; 105. 3; 106 a; 107. 10; 108 b.
Aristoteles, 105. 16.
Article, with gentile names, 25. 2; omitted with name of a god, 14. 2; omitted with second noun, 2. 6; 10. 1; 56. 7; 61. 5; 82. 8.
Asopius, 7.
Assimilation, 62. 4.
Astymachus, 52 c.
Asyndeton, 37. 10; 63. 8; 58. 10; 59. 4; 63. 3, 9; 93. 6.
Atalante, 89. 12.
Athenians, *passim*; exhausted resources of, 17; ἐσφορά of, 19. 1.

INDEX OF SUBJECTS.

Attica, third invasion of, 1 a; fourth invasion of, 26; proposed invasion of, 89 a.
Attraction, 39. 38; 36. 8; —of prep., 5. 1; 22. 21; 24. 15; 35. 4; 102. 10.
Augment, 111. 14.

Boeotia, 61 b; 62 c; 67 b; 87. 10; 95. 8.
Boeotians, 2. 14; 13 a; 95. 4.
Bomians, 96. 14.
Boriades, 100. 3.
Brachylogy, 44. 2; 53. 19.
Brasidas, 69. 7; 76. 6; 79. 10.
Bribery, insinuation of, 38. 12; 40. 13; 42. 17.
Budorum, 51. 7.

Caecinus, 103. 13.
Callians, 96. 14.
Callias, 96. 14.
Calydon, 102. 20.
Camarina, 86. 10.
Caria, 19. 6.
Catanaeans, 116 a.
Cenaeum, 93. 4.
Cephallenians, 94 a; 95 b.
Chalaeans, 101 c.
Chalcidian cities, 86 b.
Charoeades, 86. 3; 90. 7.
Chians, 10 c.
Chiasmus, 40. 36; 56. 7, 20; 57. 20; 62. 21; 63. 15; 65. 16; 82. 52.
Chios, 104 c.
Chromon, 98 a.
Cithaeron, 24. 6.
Clarus, 33 a, b.
Cleippides, 3. 11.

Cleomenes, 26. 7.
Cleon, 36. 25; speech of, 37-40; 50. 3.
Cleruchs, 50. 9.
Cnidians, 88. 5.
Collective singular, 15. 11; 20. 21; 74. 4.
Comparative, double, 42. 16.
Concrete, for abstract, 62. 10.
Condition, minatory, 2. 15; mixed, 9. 6; 40. 19; unreal, 10. 20.
Construction, change of, 5. 10; 25. 8; 40. 24; 58. 17; 81. 19; 82. 7; 84. 2; 86. 18; 87. 3; elliptical, 43. 17; κατὰ ξύνεσιν, 39. 43; 54. 17; personal, 11. 1; 16. 12.
Co-ordination of different constructions, 4. 4; 25. 9; 34. 17; 35. 5; 39. 39; 45. 7; 55. 5; 67. 8; 69. 11; 77. 1; 82. 13; 84. 10; 94. 17.
Corcyra, civil conflicts of, 70. 85.
Corcyraeans, 70-85; 70. 3; 94 b; 95 c.
Corinthians, 70 a; 102. 8; 114. 21.
Coronaea, 62. 20; 67. 13.
Crenae, 105. 10; 106 c.
Crocyleum, 96. 5.
Cyllene, 69. 5; 76 a.
Cyme, 31 a.
Cytinium, 95. 5; 102. 2.

Damagon, 92 c.
Dative, of agent, 64. 15; 85. 10; causal, 97. 6;

98. 27; of purpose, 82. 8, 38; temporal, 54. 14; terminal, 5. 12; 39. 22; 70. 2; 113. 1; with νομίζειν, 82. 65.
Delos, 29. 5; 104; purification of, 104. 1.
Delphi, 57. 10; 92. 18; 101. 2.
Demonstrative, epanaleptic, 64. 4.
Demosthenes, 91. 2; 94. 12; 95. 3, 4; 97; 98; 102; 105. 13; 107. 5, 12; 108; 109; 110; 114. 5, 6, 7.
Didyme, 88. 7.
Diitrephes, 75. 1.
Diodotus, 41. 1; speech of, 42-48.
Dionysus, temple of, 81. 27.
Dioscuri, 75. 15.
Dorian cities, 86. 6.
Dorians, 92. 9.
Doriens, 8. 5.

Earthquakes, 87. 9; 89. 4, 19.
Ellipsis, 3. 15; 39. 10; 85. 13.
Ellomenus, 94. 4.
Embaton, 29. 8; 32 a.
Emphasis, 5. 10; 39. 13, 36; 42. 14; 53. 1, 14; 54. 5; 55. 13; 56. 10; 58. 1; 59. 13; 68. 2; 82. 7; 87. 5; 111. 14.
Epanaphora, 18. 8.
Ephesia, 104. 16.
Epibatae, 95. 14.
Epidamnus, 70 a.
Eresus, 18. 5; 35. 2.

INDEX OF SUBJECTS. 317

Erythrae, 24. 10; Erythraea, 29. 8; 33. 7.
Euboea, 17 a; 87. 10; 89. 6; 92. 15; 93 a.
Eupalium, 96 b; 102. 4.
Euphemism, 46. 2.
Eupompidas, 20. 9.
Eurylochus, 100 c; 101; 102 b, c; 105 a; 106 a; 108. 6; 109 a.
Eurymedon, 80. 10; 81. 17; 84; 85 a; 91. 13; 115. 17.
Eurytanians, 94 c; 100 a.

Fact, in hypothetical form, 32. 6; 43. 19; 47. 14; 55. 7.
Fear of punishment as a preventive of crime, 45. 1.
Formulae, concluding, 1. 9; 18. 19; 25. 11; 26. 17; 50. 15; 68. 31; 114. 25; 115. 7.
Future, inf. after δυνατοί ὄντες, 28. 1; inf. with μέλλειν, 11. 4; mid. for pass., 46. 9; perf., 53. 19.

Genitive, abs. with subj. or obj. same as in leading clause, 4. 14; 13. 30; 22. 6; 26. 14; 49. 13; 55. 5; 78. 17; 112. 21; chorographic, 106. 10; elliptical, 45. 30; between prep. and its noun, 14. 2; 70. 16; 81. 26; 96. 1; partitive in attrib. position, 22. 26; 36. 19; 65. 14; partitive in pred. position, 47. 10; with ὀνειδίσαι, 62. 16.
Geraestus, 3. 22.
Gorgias, 57. 4; 86. 12.
Graice, 91. 9.

Halex, 99. 4.
Helots, 54 c.
Hephaestus, 88 b.
Heraclea, 92. 1; 93. 24; 100. 8.
Heraeum, 62. 20; 75. 22, 25; 79 a; 81. 11.
Hesiod, 96. 2.
Hessians, 101 c.
Hiera, 88. 7.
Hiereans, 92. 4.
Hierophon, 105. 17.
Himeraea, 115. 2.
Hippias, 34. 19.
Hipponicus, 91. 12.
Homer, 104. 19.
Hyaeans, 101. 13.
Hyllaic harbour, 72. 8; 81. 8.
Hyperbole, 81. 24.
Hysiae, 24. 10.

Idomene, 112. 2; 113. 10.
Imbrians, 5. 4.
Imitations of Thucydides, 10. 5, 19; 12. 6; 20. 10; 22. 1; 30. 3; 36. 10; 37. 15; 38. 1, 25; 39. 10, 27; 40. 2; 42. 26; 45. 7, 16, 31; 51. 13; 52. 14; 57. 12; 67. 19; 82. 11, 23, 67; 83. 6; 84. 7, 11, 12; 107. 18.
Imperfect, 11. 23; 15. 5; 16. 15; 22. 15; 24. 18; 34. 5; 49. 5; 52. 25; 53. 18; 57. 14; 58. 22; 68. 15; 75. 4, 16; 81. 13; 82. 25; 85. 15; 92. 2; 105. 6, 9; 107. 15; 111. 5, 14; 112. 7, 14; 113. 5; 115. 12.
Infinitive, without art. as subj., 37. 5; pass. after adjs., 40. 8; after ἄριστος, 38. 21; of purpose, 40. 28; after subst., 58. 4; 66. 16; after σπένδεσθαι, 109. 14; impf., 89. 20.
Inessa, 103. 5.
Ionia, 31. 2; 32. 15; 33 b; 36 b.
Ionians, 86. 13; 92. 21; 104. 15.
Ionic forms, 13. 16.
Ipneans, 101. 9.
Irony, 29. 2; 31. 11; 53. 21; 61. 7; 81. 1.
Istone, 85. 14.
Itamanes, 34. 3.
Ithome, 54 c.

Lacedaemonians, 2. 13; 82. 5; 93. 11; boast of, as liberators of Hellas, 13. 35; 32. 5.
Laches, 86. 2; 90 b; 103 c; 115. 7, 19, 21.
Lacon, 52 c.
Lemnians, 5. 5.
Leontines, 86 a, 12.
Lesbos, 2. 2; 5 a; 13 b; 35; 50 b; 51. 2.
Leucadia, 94. 4.
Leucas, 7 c; 80. 8; 81. 3; 94. 5; 102 b.
Leucimme, 79. 11.
Limnaea, 106. 9.

Lipara, 88. 6; Liparaeans, 88 a.
Litotes, 57. 5.
Locrians, Amphissian, 101. 5; Epizephyrian, 86 b; 99; 103 c.; Opuntian, 89. 12; Ozolian, 95. 4, 17; 97. 7; 101 a.
Locris, Opuntian, 91. 21; 96 b.
Lysicles, 19. 4.

Macarius, 100 c; 109 a.
Malea, 4. 17; 6 c.
Malians, 92. 3; Malian gulf, 96. 13.
Maloeis, 3. 13, 25.
Mantineans, 107. 26; 108. 26; 109; 111; 113.
Medeon, 106. 8.
Megarians, 51 b.
Melians, 91. 5.
Melos, 91 a; 94 a.
Menedaius, 100. 11; 109. 1.
Messapians, 101. 10.
Messenians, 75 a; 81. 6; 88. 11; 90. 16; 94. 15; 95. 1; 97 a; 107. 5, 29; 108. 8; 112. 12.
Methymna, 2. 2; 18. 2; Methymnaeans, 2. 9; 50 b.
Metropolis, 107. 2.
Middle, 3. 3; 20. 15; direct, 77. 10; 'dynamic,' 53. 17.
Minoa, 51. 3.
Molycreum, 102. 7.
Mood, change of, 22. 38; 113. 8.
Myconus, 29. 6.
Mylae, 90. 9.
Myonians, 101. 8.

Myonnesus, 32. 1.
Mytilene, 2. 12; 18 c; 26 a; 29; 30 a; 35.
Mytileneans, 2. 10; 3-6; speech of, 8-14; 18; 27; 28; 35; 36; discussion as to punishment of, 37-48; fate of, 49; 50.
Myus, 19. 6.

Naupactus, 7 b; 75. 2; 78 b; 94 b; 96. 9; 98 c; 100 b; 101 a; 102 a, b; 114 a.
Nemea, 96 a.
Nericus, 7. 14.
Nicias, 51. 2; 91. 5.
Nicostratus, 75. 1, 20.
Nisaea, 51. 11.
Notium, 34.

Oeantheans, 101 c.
Oeneon, 95. 16; 98. 17; 102. 4.
Oeniadae, 7. 10; 94. 6; 114. 12.
Oetaeans, 92. 5.
Olpae, 105. 5, 18; 106. 2; 107. 7, 13; 108 c; 110; 111 a; 113 a; Olpaeans, 101. 12.
Olympic festival, 8. 5.
Ophioneans, 94 c; 96. 9; 100. 3.
Optative, 42. 22; 46. 6; 49. 10; 84. 4.
Oracles, 96. 3.
Orchomenus, 87. 11.
Order of words (see also s. v. position), 2. 4; 9. 3; 23. 27; 40. 6; 42. 4; 46. 18; 54. 14, 19; 56.

3, 5; 57. 3, 7, 15; 58. 1, 15; 60. 4; 61. 6; 63. 16; 67. 7, 11; 68. 9; 69. 11; 70. 16; 75. 5; 81. 27; 82. 52, 63; 88. 14; 91. 10; 95. 1; 105. 9; 116. 3.
Orobiae, 89. 7.
Oropus, 91. 9.

Paches, 18 c; 28; 33. 6; 34 b; 35 a; 36 b; 48 b; 49 c; 50. 2.
Paralians, 92 a.
Paralus, 33. 2, 12; 77. 12.
Parataxis, 5. 16; 10. 20; 20. 16; 36. 5; 39. 28; 52. 4; 57. 3, 9; 70. 11; 75. 8; 88. 6; 107. 16; 110. 1.
Parnassus, 95 a.
Paronomasia, 39. 10; 82. 31.
Part, joined to whole, 111. 2, 14; 113. 4.
Participle = adj., 34. 14; articular neut. = abstract noun, 10. 5; 38. 11, 19; 61. 2; 82. 47; 84. 13; attrib. in pred. position, 34. 4; 54. 19; 88. 3; collective neut. with pers. force, 39. 29; impf., 103. 3; 113. 13; pres. where fut. might have been expected, 52. 11; with subst. like verbal noun, 53. 14; 66. 15.
Passive, impers., 22. 1, 33; 61. 12; 107. 21; of deponent, 61. 4; with ὑπό, 36. 24; 82. 41; with ἐκ, 69. 3.

INDEX OF SUBJECTS. 319

Patmos, 33. 13.
Pausanias, 54. 15; 58 c; 68. 5.
Peisistratus, 104. 3.
Peloponnesus (περὶ Πελοπόννησον), 7. 1; 91. 2; 105. 15; 107. 3; 113. 2; 114. 8; Peloponnesians, *passim*, 1. 1.
Peparethus, 89. 6.
Perioeci, 92. 20.
Periphrasis, 2. 11; 9. 4; 20. 20; 22. 31; 23. 13; 30. 3; 33. 2, 13; 34. 15; 36. 5; 40. 2, 32; 46. 18; 54. 3; 59. 8; 67. 33; 68. 12; 74. 14; 75. 11; 82. 19; 97. 13; 115. 15.
Phocians, 95. 6; 101. 5;
Phormio, 7. 4; 17 c.
Phytia, 106. 8.
Pissuthnes, 31. 9; 34. 7.
Pithias, 70.
Plague, 87. 1, 5, 6.
Plataea, 21. 3; 36 a; 58. 24; 61. 10; 68 c.
Plataeans, 20–24; (speech of) 53–59; 68. 13, 15, 31.
Pleistoanax, 26 b.
Pleonasm, 5. 14; 39. 43; 40. 35; 49. 17; 53. 9; 86. 7; 89. 22; 100. 1; 111. 8; 112. 5, 13, 16; 113. 3; pleonastic neg., 36. 17; 46. 3.
Pleuron, 102. 20.
Plural, 82. 68; 97. 12; 109. 12; 110. 6; 113. 10.
Polycrates, 104. 9.
Pontus, 2 b.
Position (see also *s. v.* order), 4. 1; 5. 5; 12. 1;

15. 4; 42. 11; 44. 15; 46. 4, 26; 48. 7; 54. 18; 56. 8, 15, 27; 57. 3, 4; 61. 7; 62. 3; 63. 7, 8; 77. 6; 81. 11; 88. 8; 89. 6; 90. 16; 94. 3; 97. 2; 104. 5; 113. 21, 25; 115. 19.
Potidaea, 17. 9.
Potidania, 96. 5.
Preposition, repeated, 53. 3.
Prepositional phrase, as subj., 6. 12; 20. 11; 85. 5; as obj., 111. 17; 114. 22.
Present, with perf. force, 64. 6; 67. 30.
Procles, 91. 3; 98. 23.
Prolepsis, 5. 1; 51. 8; 53. 8; 59. 8; 105. 10; 106. 2.
Proschium, 102. 21; 106. 3.
Proxenus, 103 c.
Pyrrha, 18. 5; 25. 3; 35. 2.
Pythodorus, 115. 16.

Reflexive pron. after comp., 11. 6.
Relative, as emphatic connective, 39. 1; 43. 1; 46. 20; 54. 21; 56. 21; clause loosely connected, 66. 9; omitted in second clause, 51. 4; 55. 12.
Revision, lack of final, 32. 11; 40. 21; 80. 10; 109. 6; 116. 3.
Rhegium, 86. 19; 88. 13; 115. 5; Rhegians, 86 b; 88 a.
Rhenaea, 104. 8, 12.

Rhetorical exaggeration, 54. 12.

Salaethus, 25 a; 27 b; 35 a; 36 a.
Salaminia, 33. 2, 12; 77. 12.
Salamis, 17. 4; 51. 7.
Salynthius, 111. 18; 114. 10.
Samians, 32. 4; 104 a.
Sandius, 19. 7.
Sarcastic tone, 29. 2; 31. 11; 81. 1.
Siceliots, 90. 2; 103. 2.
Sicels, 88 c; 90. 1; 103. 3; 115. 3.
Sicily, 86. 2; 88; 90; 99. 1; 103; 115; 116. 4.
Singular, after preceding plural, 17. 10.
Sollium, 95. 10.
Sophocles, 115. 17.
Spartiate, 100. 9, 11.
Spurious chapters, 17; 84.
Stratians, 106. 6.
Strongyle, 88. 7.
Substantive, as adj., 20. 8.
Sybota, 76. 7.
Syracusans, 86 a; 88. 12; 103 b; 115. 10.

Tanagra, 91. 11, 15.
Teians, 32. 2.
Teichium, 96. 5.
Tepedians, 2. 9; 28 c.
Ten years' war, 3. 2; 113. 22.
Teutiaplus, 29 c; 30.
Text emended, 7. 2; 10. 19; 12. 5, 13; 16. 12; 22. 27; 26. 2, 3, 10; 30. 13; 31. 3, 7; 34. 8, 12;

36. 9; 38. 6; 40. 15, 20; 42. 14; 43. 13; 44. 8; 45. 7, 14, 18, 21, 29; 52. 13, 21; 55. 15; 56. 2, 24; 57. 1; 59. 11; 62. 14; 64. 1; 65. 2, 13; 66. 14; 67. 14; 68. 6, 16; 76. 4; 78. 3; 80. 5; 82. 1, 34, 38; 87. 10; 90. 6; 91. 6, 9; 92. 27; 97. 10; 98. 16; 101. 6; 102. 24; 103. 4; 104. 14; 109. 16; 114. 12; 115. 3.

Text, variation from Steup, 11. 4, 7, 10, 13, 15; 15. 4; 20. 19; 26. 6; 38. 25; 42. 4; 44. 6; 63. 4; 67. 19; 69. 4; 81. 6; 82. 51; 107. 7; 115. 3.

Text suspected, 6. 5; 11. 21, 23; 17. 2; 26. 9; 29. 3; 34. 24; 36. 25; 39. 43; 47. 19; 50. 4; 51. 4, 8, 17; 53. 20; 57. 17; 58. 29; 59. 12; 67. 3, 21; 68. 9; 81. 3; 82. 11, 37, 46, 53; 85. 1; 94. 4; 100. 1; 101. 5; 102. 5, 14, 19; 104. 21; 107. 23; 108. 9, 15; 111. 6; 113. 12; 114. 18; 115. 3.

Theaenetus, 20 b.
Thebans, speech of, 61–67; 68. 27; 91 c.
Thebes, 22 c; 24 a.
Thermopylae, 92. 27.
Thessalians, 93. 6.
Thrace, 92. 17.
Thucydides, 25 c; 88 c; 116 c; evidence of careful investigation, 113. 26; inference as to his death before 396 B.C., 116. 6.

Thyamus, 106. 11.
Tisamenus, 92. 8.
Tisander, 100. 4.
Tithes for the gods, 50. 8.
Tolophus, 100. 3; Tolophonians, 101 c.
Trachinians, 92. 2.
Trimeter, 40. 39.
Tripod, 57. 10.
Tritaeans, 101. 10.

Verbal nouns in -σις, 23. 27.

Xenocleidas, 114. 23.
Xerxes, 56 c.

Zacynthians, 94 a; 95 b.
Zeus, 14. 2; 70. 16; 96. 1.

www.ingramcontent.com/pod-product-compliance
Lightning Source LLC
Chambersburg PA
CBHW021159230426
43667CB00006B/470